SEEING *MAD*

SEEING *MAD*

Essays on *Mad* Magazine's Humor and Legacy

Edited by

Judith Yaross Lee and John Bird

UNIVERSITY OF MISSOURI PRESS

Columbia

University of Missouri Press, Columbia, Missouri 65211
Printed and bound in the United States of America
 First paperback printing, 2021.

ISBN 9780826222398 (paperback : alk. paper)

Library of Congress Cataloging-in-Publication Data

Names: Lee, Judith Yaross, 1949- editor. | Bird, John, 1954- editor.
Title: Seeing Mad : essays on Mad magazine's humor and legacy / edited by Judith Yaross Lee and John Bird.
Description: Columbia : University of Missouri Press, [2020] | Includes bibliographical references and index.
Identifiers: LCCN 2020013189 (print) | LCCN 2020013190 (ebook) | ISBN 9780826222138 (hardcover) | ISBN 9780826274489 (ebook)
Subjects: LCSH: Mad. | American wit and humor--History and criticism.
Classification: LCC PN6728.M33 S44 2020 (print) | LCC PN6728.M33 (ebook) | DDC 051--dc23
LC record available at https://lccn.loc.gov/2020013189
LC ebook record available at https://lccn.loc.gov/2020013190

∞™ This paper meets the requirements of the American National Standard for Permanence of Paper for Printed Library Materials, Z39.48, 1984.

Typeface: Delicato Pro

for

Joe

&

Seung,

with love and gratitude

What, me worry?

—*Alfred E. Neuman*

Contents

Illustrations

All images from *Mad* are MAD used with permission. Other images are credited individually to their respective copyright holders.

Foreword
First There Was *Mad*:

Reflections of a Former Managing Editor of *National Lampoon*

Peter Kaminsky

THERE IS NO question that I would not be where I am today had it not been for *Mad* magazine. Which is to say I might not have been the first president of the Princeton student body *not* to get a Rhodes Scholarship, nor, at my age, would I still be tits over the typewriter instead of enjoying the overcompensated retirement of an investment banker. But I don't hold it against Kurtzman, Gaines, Elder, & co. On the contrary, I owe them a big debt of gratitude.

Just as one remembers a childhood Christmas or the first time behind the wheel of a car, I remember *Mad*. It represented the first time I saw that magazines weren't all cocooned in the Ken Doll version of 1950s America that reigned over that era. As I remember that initial glimpse of *Mad*, it was just another normal day in Mrs. McElnea's fourth grade, which is to say that my classmate, Jan Slussman, was employing a straw as a blowgun to launch spitballs at the girls. Taking a break from target practice, he reached inside his desk and passed me a copy of *Mad* hidden inside another magazine.

To outward appearances, young Jan was sharing a copy of *My Weekly Reader*, which was a training-wheels version of *Time* and *Newsweek*. It was hoped that this pabulum publication would establish "good reading habits." The image of life that it projected was as gilded (and gelded) as the rest of 1950s mass culture. If you'll allow me the digression, I should add here that I came from a politically progressive family. You'll surmise this when I tell you that another magazine for students that we also subscribed to was *Junior Scholastic*. *Scholastic* was a bona fide big word. I thought it was pronounced "Junior Socialist." In other words, I was prepped for something new, different, and irreverent, but it wasn't until

Jan gave me his *Mad*-in-mufti that the scales fell from my eyes. I became aware that subversive publications were possible even in Pleasantville.

I will always revere that first copy of *Mad* magazine, with the hapless and benighted Alfred on the cover. No doubt part of my later affection for David Letterman came from the boyish mien and gap-toothed smile that he shares with *Mad*'s corporate spokes-icon.

Wow! A real magazine that didn't peddle the party line!

I wanted in.

In those long-ago days, jokes that now seem tame and harmless represented unsparing iconoclasm. *Mad* was my cultural Get-Out-of-Jail-Free card. In one of their early paperback books, I recall "Starchie"—a parody of *Archie Comics*—with a supremely hormonal Betty (Biddy) and Reggie (Wedgie), who wasn't wearing enough clothes to get a wedgie. He was naked! People were never naked in 1957! I was hooked.

I'm sure that my DNA was irradiated—to good effect—by an ur-hipster piece by Al "Jazzbo" Collins that depicted the alternate reality of beatnik America and primed me for the descent (or was it ascent?) into hippiedom that I embarked on a few years later. Of course, Don Martin's hapless—but somehow canny—dweebs prefigured everything from Homer Simpson to the nerd heroes depicted in Jim Carrey and Judd Apatow's films. Pride of place will forever go to 43-Man Squamish over Harry Potter's Quidditch.

"Spy vs. Spy" presented the casually violent, morally neutral world of espionage a few months before David Cornwell took the nom de plume of John le Carré. And what about the parody ads? We all knew real-world ads were false to the marrow, but it wasn't until *Mad* gave us such ad parodies as the anti-tobacco "Sail 'em. Don't Inhale 'em" that I understood that, in the right hands, the shibboleths of consumerism could be so publicly ridiculed.

All of us at *National Lampoon*, to which I graduated after a couple of years as a ganja-fueled New York cabby, were devotees of *Mad*. It showed us that so far as satire and parody went, everything was fair game—the more savage the better. To be sure, Lord Buckley, Ernie Kovacs, Lenny Bruce, and Terry Southern all nourished our streak of salacious and misanthropic nihilism, but first there was *Mad*.

I still love it madly.

Preface and Acknowledgments

THE TWENTY-TWO ESSAYS in *Seeing "Mad"* examine the individuals, features, and perspectives that shaped *Mad* from its comic book start in 1952 through 2019, when its future within the DC Comics-Warner Communications empire became uncertain. John Bird intended only an afternoon's academic pleasure when he invited members of the American Humor Studies Association (AHSA) to submit proposals for presentations on *Mad* at the 2013 American Literature Association conference in Boston. At his direction, and to the distress of those attending the more staid sessions down the hall, three dozen humor scholars closed the session by forming an enthusiastic chorus for John's paper, "Sing Along with Alfred." Judith Yaross Lee was among them, scouting potential articles among the papers as the new editor of *Studies in American Humor*, the AHSA's scholarly journal since 1974. She invited John afterwards to co-edit a special issue of the journal on *Mad*. The several dozen excellent ideas that arrived in response to our call for proposals—we had expected to choose five from a field of ten or so—proved too many for even the triple 216-page issue published in the fall of 2014 as *"Mad" Magazine and Its Legacies*.[1] *Seeing "Mad"* is the result of our overflowing cup. Where the 2014 special issue nearly doubled the existing scholarship on *Mad*, this volume pairs updates of the original articles with newly commissioned essays to provide readers with the fullest analytical treatment of *Mad*—and the only peer-reviewed book—to date. Here we introduce its contents.

Co-editor Judith Yaross Lee, "*MAD*ness, *Mishugas*, Manhattan: That Other New York(er) Humor" summarizes the history of *Mad* from its 1952 beginnings as a comic book parodying other comic books through early 2020, as it increasingly mixed old contents with new commissions, and she places *Mad*'s significance in relation to its rival for the title of "America's Most Important Humor Magazine": the *New Yorker*. Both magazines won national fame for comic art and writing grounded in the sensibilities of a small group of New Yorkers, though scholars have paid far more attention to the *New Yorker* than to *Mad*, and both magazines faced similar problems at key moments in their histories. Their divergent trajectories in recent years, however, point to ways in which *Mad*'s print-based formula—despite its tremendous impact on American humor in other media—has faltered.

The volume's main sections begin with "The Usual Gang," five chapters on major editors and artists who gave *Mad* its signature comic spirit. Former *Mad* publisher and DC Comics President Paul Levitz opens the section with "Inside the Editorial Process: *Mad* Veterans Jaffee and Meglin Look at Their Editors," his 2014 interviews of former editor Nick Meglin and artist-writer Al Jaffee, whose collective experience with the magazine and its editors ran nearly the entire history from its founding by Harvey Kurtzman through the Feldstein, Meglin, and John Ficarra eras, which ended when *Mad* moved to California in 2018. In Chapter 2, "Harvey Kurtzman and Modern American Satire," an earlier version of which appeared in the *Journal of the Fantastic in the Arts*, M. Thomas Inge places Kurtzman's development of *Mad*'s sense of humor—he wrote most stories in the first 23 (comics) issues and spearheaded the conversion from comic book to magazine format—in the context of other cutting-edge humor of the early 1950s, especially stand-up comedy. Inge provides a timeline and bibliography that clarify Kurtzman's often misunderstood career. Next, Margaret Cavin Hambrick draws on Kenneth Burke's theory of the comic frame and her own discussions with editor Al Feldstein to understand how he built *Mad* into a humor powerhouse on Kurtzman's foundations from 1956 to 1982. "The Usual Gang" ends with two chapters on artists who made major contributions to *Mad*'s comic identity. Joseph W. Slade brings his internationally recognized expertise on sexual representation to bear on Wally Wood's hyperbolic portrayals of straight male adolescent lust in the iconic "Superduperman!" and other parodies in chapter 4. "Wally Wood: Picturing Male Adolescent Desire in *Mad*'s Early Parodies" shows how Wood's art endorsed the 1950s heterosexual norms that he mocked and the sexual fears that he projected onto his male characters, even as he distorted the visual conventions of the comics genre that he parodied. By contrast with Wood, writer-artist Dave Berg offered a more modern, occasionally even feminist point of view, as Ann M. Ciasullo shows in chapter 5, "The Lighter—and Weightier—Side of *Mad*; Or, Everything I Needed to Know About Gender and Sexuality I Learned from Dave Berg," her study of his genteel dramas of "The Lighter Side."

"Features from Cover to Fold-In," the second section, follows with ten chapters devoted to *Mad*'s most beloved contents, from the front cover to the back-page fold-in. Two studies of mascot Alfred E. Neuman open the section. In chapter 6, Alan Rankin presents "The Secret History of Alfred E. Neuman" in the graphic narrative format that *Mad* helped to normalize. In chapter 7, Christopher J. Gilbert examines Alfred's contemporary role as the magazine's endearing embodiment of foolishness in his analysis of the annual "Mad 20" cover feature, "The 'Mad 20' with Alfred E. Neuman, or It's the Covers, Stupid." Next, "The Prohías Paradox: The Cold War Specificity and Existential Universality of 'Spy vs. Spy'" by Michael J. Socolow traces the history and significance—personal, political, and narrative—of the feature created by Antonio Prohías. Recognizing that *Mad*'s essential character revolves around parody, chapters 9 through 12 treat the genre parodies that became the chief vehicles for *Mad*'s cultural critique. Dennis W. Eddings takes up the magazine's deep appreciation of America's most satirized and misunderstood poet in chapter 9, "*Mad* About Poe: Poetry in a Jugular Vein." John Bird follows with his analysis of *Mad*'s song parodies, a genre that fostered bonding among fans while challenging the cultural status quo, in chapter 10, "Sing Along with Alfred: Humor, Satire, and Culture in the Music of *Mad*." Don Baird takes up the film parodies that doubled as serious cinema criticism in "You Always Hurt the Ones You Love: *Mad* Magazine's Affectionate Parodies of Beloved Film Classics," chapter 11. *Mad*'s love-hate relationship with TV and its satiric treatment of so-called quality television come under analysis by Ethan Thompson in chapter 12, "A Golden Age of Blecch: *Mad* Magazine's Parodic Satire of Quality Television." The section closes, as has the magazine since 1964, with Al Jaffee's fold-in, the subject of Kerry Soper's analysis in "Folding Against the Establishment: Satiric Distance and Difference in Al Jaffee's Back Cover Feature in *Mad* Magazine," chapter 13.

"Themes," the third section, takes up some serious subtexts of *Mad*'s joking. Nathan Abrams extends his earlier analysis of *Mad*'s intellectual leadership in "A Secular Talmud: The Jewish Sensibility of *Mad* Magazine," chapter 14. The next two chapters examine the Cold War context of *Mad*'s 1950s comic book and 1960s magazine, respectively. James J. Kimble analyzes the comic distortions of the (perceived) communist antagonist in Kurtzman's comics parodies in chapter 15, "Mutually Assured Disparagement: Enmification and Enlightenment in Early 1950s *Mad*." In chapter 16, "Diplomats Gone *Mad*: A Musical Rumble," James D. Bloom details how "East Side Story," *Mad*'s 1963 parody of the recently released film *West Side Story*, played into a larger cultural narrative about the United Nations and the international order after World War II. Finally, Nicolas Labarre explores *Mad*'s antipathy toward Richard Nixon—and its prescience in anticipating his fall from grace—in chapter 17, "Joining the Fray? *Mad* on Richard Nixon and Spiro Agnew."

"Theories," the fourth section, interprets the magazine's absurdist and genre-busting practices. In chapter 18, "'Comedy before Country': Engaged Levity and Absurdist Critique in *Mad* Magazine," Jeffrey St. Onge proposes a conception of political satire that he calls "engaged levity" to explore how *Mad* crossed partisan lines to target both George W. Bush and Barack Obama. Kathleen Mollick draws on Bakhtin's specialized conception of speech genres as well as a more conventional sense of media formula in chapter 19, "Genre Studies and *Mad* Magazine: Changing and Challenging Genres, 1953-1966," to theorize how *Mad*'s parodies both channel and transcend their times.

"Legacies," the fifth section, explores *Mad*'s much (and perhaps overly) celebrated impact on later innovations in alternative comix and mainstream comics. Nicholas Sammond refines the oft-cited, often hyperbolic claims of *Mad*'s influence in chapter 20, "Sons of *Mad*: Harvey Kurtzman and the Rise of Underground Comix (an Alternate-Universe Analysis)." In chapter 21, "Quotations from the Future: Harvey Kurtzman's 'Superduperman!' Nostalgia, and Alan Moore's *Miracleman*," Brian Cremins moves the question of influence to the other end of the telescope, examining the debts of Moore's contemporary superhero narrative to Kurtzman's parodic critique.

Three reference resources follow in Part VI. "*Mad*'s 'Usual Gang of Idiots': Selected Capsule Biographies," by Joseph Otto and Judith Yaross Lee, collects in one place for the first time a list of major contributors to *Mad* with full citations to their first, last, and other notable works in *Mad*'s pages. "A *Mad* Timeline, 1952 to 2020" by Leah Szalai and Judith

Yaross Lee follows with full, verified dates of key events in the history of the magazine, many of them accurately specified for the first time. The comprehensive bibliography, compiled by Kelley Macek, lists all works cited in chapter endnotes to fully document our authors' sources and provide a starting point for further research. Primary *Mad* sources are fully cited parenthetically within the text of each chapter.

Brief biographies of contributors to *Seeing "Mad"* and an index to its contents complete the volume by outlining the interdisciplinary backgrounds of our authors and helping readers trace individual topics as well as *Mad*'s artists, writers, and contents across chapters.

Taken as a whole, *Seeing "Mad"* stakes out the territory of the most significant humor magazine of the twentieth century: though it still stands in the *New Yorker*'s shadow and has passed its prime, today's *Mad* remains true to its original identity as a mirror in the fun house, a comic spirit of its times.

That spirit sparked this volume, and we have racked up a truckload of debts along the way. Our first expressions of gratitude go to our contributors for inspiring this volume. The analyses in this volume gratify our faith in our authors and their work—and make us doubly grateful to the creative spirits of *Mad* for giving all of us so much to work with. But we also need to thank the American Humor Studies Association, *StAH*'s publisher, for underwriting this project's first iteration and the School of Communication Studies at Ohio University, for supporting the journal during Judith's editorship. A series of outstanding Ohio University doctoral and honors undergraduate students provided excellent editorial assistance: Leah Szalai, *StAH* managing editor, 2013–2014; Joseph Otto, editorial intern, 2014; Kelley Macek, project manager, 2018. Also at Ohio University, Roxanne Malé-Brune, Ann Bainbridge Frymier, and Gregory D. Newton supported production of this volume through subvention awards from, respectively, the Office of Research and Sponsored Programs Faculty Research Support Fund, School of Communication Studies Faculty Development Fund, and Scripps College of Communication Faculty Research, Creative Activity, and Faculty Development Fund. We owe special thanks to acquisitions editor Gary A. Kass of the University of Missouri Press for his steadfast enthusiasm for this project and to copyeditor Susan Curtis, Professor Emerita of American Studies at Purdue University, for contributing her expertise to the manuscript. We could hardly have been more fortunate in our many partners.

Mad has reached many generations of readers since 1952, and most have read and loved it for a relatively short period of time, usually in adolescence, then moved on to other interests and pursuits. But each generation seems to take its *Mad* as the best *Mad*: early readers swear that it hit its height as a comic book; the next generation sees the magazine of the '50s and '60s as *Mad*'s apex; and so on for each succeeding cohort. *Seeing "Mad"* has something for each of these generations, and we editors hope that our essay collection will entice more recent readers to take a look at *Mad*'s beginnings as well as tempt fans who long ago moved on to return and see what they have missed.

A few final details: Our citations to *Mad* deviate from the custom, derived from the comics industry, of crediting artists before writers. Because *Mad* assigned artists to realize a writer's script, we cite such collaborations by writer first in chapter references; the index lists *Mad* items separately by writer and artist. Well-known and frequently mentioned works are also indexed by title. To document specific *Mad* contents most efficiently, we cite them parenthetically in the text of each chapter by issue number, date, and page range, with any quotation identified last—e.g., (#6, 8–9/53: 1–6; 6); citation details included in the accompanying text are not duplicated in the parenthetic reference. Note also that page numbers from #1–#23 (10-11/52–5/55) start over with number *1* for each feature within an issue; we have retained that pagination rather than repaginating the issues more conventionally. Secondary sources are documented in the endnotes to each chapter with full citations in the bibliography. MAD used with permission.[2]

The analyses of *Mad* presented in this volume represent the merger of its authors' lives as kids and adults, scholars and fans. We are thrilled to share it with you.

Notes

1. A dozen academic articles sprinkled across *Mad*'s sixty-two years antedated our special triple issue of *Studies in American Humor* in 2014, which included early versions of half the contents here, now revised for this new context. See Judith Yaross Lee and John Bird, eds., *"Mad" Magazine and Its Legacies*, special issue of *Studies in American Humor* n.s. 3, no. 30 (2014): 1–216.

2. All images from *Mad* are ©EC Publications, Inc., and are used with permission.

SEEING *MAD*

Introduction

*MAD*ness, *Mishugas*, Manhattan: *Mad* as That Other New York(er) Humor

Judith Yaross Lee

mishugas, *meshugas* (Yiddish, n.), mih_shoo_gaas' / meh_shoo_gaas' / meh_shi_gaas' / (varies regionally), craziness, madness, nonsense

prost (Yiddish, adj.), plain, lowly, humble; vulgar

IN 1952, LESS than thirty years after the *New Yorker* reshaped American humor through sophisticated cartoons, humorous reporting, and comic fiction in a magazine famously "not edited for the Old Lady in Dubuque," another local publication took an opposite approach—with possibly greater impact. Scholars have not bestowed on *Mad* the loving attention given the *New Yorker*, nor named a school of humor after it, but both can lay claim to the title "America's Most Important Humor Magazine."[1] *Mad* founders Harvey Kurtzman and William Gaines did not write a manifesto akin to Harold Ross's famous prospectus, but they didn't need to. In place of Rea Irvin's monocled dandy examining a butterfly on the *New Yorker*'s debut cover of February 21, 1925, an arch caricature of the nineteenth-century urbanity that Ross aspired to update, *Mad*'s first cover (dated October-November 1952, but on newsstands in August) reversed social norms to mock horror comics. As a crudely drawn mom and dad flattened themselves against the wall of a dungeon, their hair literally raised in fear of "That slithering blob coming toward us!," their toddler, belly button blazing, boldly produced the comic anticlimax: "It's Melvin!" The clear message: *Mad* was a species of funnies aimed at comics fans more allied with the kid than the parents. This target audience reflected Gaines's comics-business model of newsprint pages and newsstand sales at one dime per shot, not Ross's more traditional reliance on glossy pages and advertising tied to the demographics of readers who could afford year-long subscriptions. Where the *New Yorker* aimed at taste-making among the uptown yuppies of his day and "humor was allowed to infect everything," as E. B. White put it,[2] *Mad* took pride in a downtown adolescent tastelessness that defined *mishugas*—craziness, madness. (Foolishness gets dismissed as *narishkeit*, triviality.) *Mad* was, we might say, the Yiddish *prost* to the *New Yorker*'s Proust, but together the two magazines gave the U.S. its modern sense of humor. *Mad*'s apparent demise in July 2019, when (after barely a year in its new home) contributors were advised that the magazine would shift mainly to reprint material, showed the limitations of its print-based formula even as the *New Yorker* engaged a twenty-first century media strategy of live events, radio, podcasts, and web content. The postmodern culture that *Mad*'s *mishugas* helped construct had, in essence, killed it.

Mad's brash exuberance diverged from the *New Yorker*'s more cerebral joking because the magazines' editors and contributors reflected different worlds and worldviews. For all their reputation as a madcap bunch, the *New Yorker* staff came from the editorial, if not cultural, elite. Early *New Yorker* contributor networks included not only the Algonquin Wits who have received the most attention—writers Dorothy Parker, Alexander Woollcott, and Robert Benchley—but also alumni groups from Cornell (E. B. White and Frank Sullivan), Ohio State University (Donald Ogden Stewart and James Thurber), the Art Institute of Chicago (Helen Hokinson, Alice Harvey, Garrett Price), and members of the feminist Lucy Stone League (Jane Grant, Janet Flanner, Lois Long), as well as contributors to the *Harvard Lampoon*, *Vanity Fair*, and the U.S. Army's *Stars and Stripes*. A few were native New Yorkers, but most, including Californians Ross and Irvin, had migrated to America's publishing mecca and cultivated a New York frame of mind. Mainly college graduates at a time when few Americans finished high school, these writers and artists exuded the sophistication that self-taught Ross hoped would snare their affluent, educated peers as readers.

By contrast, most of *Mad*'s principals a generation later were local boys from Brooklyn and the Bronx who had little or no college education. Founding editor and chief writer Harvey Kurtzman, artists Will Elder, Al Jaffee, John Severin, and writer-artist Al Feldstein (who succeeded Kurtzman as editor in April 1956) were buddies from New York's High School of Music and Art. Georgian Jack Davis and Minnesotan Wallace

"Wally" Wood came to *Mad* from other comics studios (Wood worked on Will Eisner's *The Spirit*), but the rest of the group already worked for publisher William (Bill) Gaines at Entertaining (formerly Educational, now EC) Comics. So did the crew's sole woman, colorist Marie Severin. The clubbiness of New York not only made artists' and writers' networks easy to tap, but also gave both *Mad* and the *New Yorker* a coherence that came as much from contributors' shared backgrounds as from editorial vision. Yet compared to Ross's group, *Mad* staff and contributors were cultural outsiders several times over.

Ross pressed *New Yorker* artists to deliver what he called "idea drawings," in which a comic conceit implied relations between image and caption and thereby rewarded sophisticated minds. So he worried about the relative inferiority of *New Yorker* writing in the early months, joking to a friend on October 15, 1925, "it has just been described as the best magazine in the world for a person who can not read."[3] In keeping with its elite aspirations, its cartoons mixed race and class bias, including anti-Semitism, as figure 0-1 shows. There, in a cartoon from June 5, 1926, Peter Arno imported the well-known anti-Semitic iconography of hooked nose, Chasidic dress, devious facial expression, and obsequious posture in depicting "one of the neighbors" scandalously invading the upper-class space of the Lower East Side's Neighborhood Playhouse.[4]

Indeed, debutante Ellin Mackay cemented the magazine's upscale identity and WASP bona fides a few weeks after Ross's comment about the magazine's art. In "Why We Go to Cabarets," she explained that her smart set preferred nightclubs to society balls despite the unpleasantness of "dancing shoulder to shoulder with gaudy and fat drummers" because "at least, in the cabaret, we do not have to dance with them"—*them* including "the young man who . . . prays that you won't suspect that he lives far up on the West Side" or "the gentleman who says he comes from the South, who lives just south of New York—in Brooklyn."[5] These descriptions, if not quite code for *Jew*, sorted the elite from the rest, especially from Kurtzman's gang and comics readers. When S. J. Perelman reworked the stereotype of the Schlemiel as the *New Yorker*'s Little Man in the 1930s and Saul Steinberg mocked its view of the world in 1976, they reframed ethnic difference as urbanity and its lack. The college humor magazines that provided models for Ross and training for his staff also influenced Kurtzman, who credited them with his love of parody and satire.[6] But the original *Mad* staff's identity as outsiders—mainly Jews from the boroughs beyond Manhattan—more globally shaped its countercultural sense of humor.

Here I don't refer to *Mad*'s well-documented use of Yiddish vocabulary (real and made-up) that invoked the comic principle "foreigners are funny."[7] To be sure, *Mad*'s cultural and political critiques positioned its most visible editors and contributors as a set of "alternative New York Jewish intellectuals," as Nathan Abrams put it in 2003.[8] Nor do I cite its joking with American vernaculars and dialects or the international traditions of Jewish humor in its pages.[9] Rather, I want to note that a Jewish identity is by definition counterhegemonic in a Christian society, which reinforces its worldview in Easter school breaks, the annual return of Scrooge, and Friday night lights that have nothing to with Sabbath candles; the western calendar makes Jewish holy days seem random when not invisible. Put otherwise, seeing the world through Jewish eyes, even nonobservant ones, means having skepticism toward majority belief, if not finding it incomprehensibly foolish. Feldstein delicately described the position as "a certain kind of living in society. Trying to survive in that society."[10] The anti-Semitism depicted in Peter Arno's 1926 cartoon was no secret in a U.S. that limited Jewish entry through the 1924 Immigration Act and would decline to fight Hitler until the Japanese bombed Pearl Harbor; the controversial Gregory Peck fiction film about east-coast anti-Semitism, *Gentlemen's Agreement*, came out only in 1947—after the Holocaust killed half the world's Jews. In the 1930s New York of *Mad* staffers' youth, Jews had the luxury of being about a quarter of the five boroughs' population, compared to just 3 percent nationwide (2 percent today), and U.S. restrictions hardly compared to those in Nazi Europe, but quotas in American colleges and discrimination in professions channeled Jews to low-status industries such as the comic book. Comics' low status reflected their origins in newspapers and association with illiteracy, but the medium's association with Jews also played a role. Certainly, it figured into the 1954 Kefauver Senate hearings on juvenile delinquency that indirectly gave birth to *Mad*'s conversion from comic book to magazine. American comic book leaders—Superman's creators Jerry Siegel and Joe Shuster, Spider-Man's creator Stan Lee (born Stanley Lieber), Captain America's creators Joe Simon and Jack Kirby, *The Spirit* innovator Will Eisner, and inventor of the physical comic book format Max "Charlie" Gaines (born Ginzberg), Bill Gaines's father—were all

Fig. 0-1: Peter Arno's "One of the Neighbors" (*right*) from the early *New Yorker* (6/5/26: 19), satirizes the casual anti-Semitism and racism of the WASP New York in which Harvey Kurtzman, Will Elder, and other early *Mad* writers and artists grew up, and against which they rebelled in celebrating the vulgarity of the comics medium and its themes, the broad humor of parody, and Yiddishisms such as *ganefs* (thieves). (Kurtzman and Elder, "Ganefs!," (*below*) *Mad* #1, 10–11/52: 1.) "One of the Neighbors" used courtesy of the Estate of Peter Arno.

One of the neighbors drops in at the Neighborhood Playhouse.

Jewish.[11] David Hajdu subtly attributes what he calls "the hysteria over comic books" to "religions and biases rooted in time and place" along with "class and money and taste; . . . presidential politics; . . . a new medium called television," and other factors, but Josh Lambert cuts to the chase: he cites the 90 percent prosecution rate against Jews by the New York Society for the Suppression of Vice in the 1930s as evidence of comics reformers' resort to an "anti-Semitic tradition that understood Jewish speech and writing to be obscene."[12]

Whether or not *Mad*'s publisher Bill Gaines saw it that way when the New York City police came to arrest him on December 29, 1953, or when Senator Estes Kefauver publicly raked him over the coals the following April, the controversy over comics crushed EC. The principals' Jewish background figured at least in part. New York City police raided EC's offices after news spread that Massachusetts had banned sales of the debut issue of *Panic*, *Mad*'s sister publication edited by Al Feldstein, because Will Elder's irreverent illustrations had outraged a member of the Governor's Council. Elder had put a "JUST DIVORCED" sign on the back of Santa's sleigh in his burlesque illustrations of Clement Moore's "The Night Before Christmas."[13] The Jewish editor, publisher, and artist were all stunned by the outcry: "we didn't realize," Gaines explained, "that Santa Claus is a saint."[14] Yet the issue's Mickey Spillane parody "My Gun Is the Jury!," written by Feldstein with art by Jack Davis, eventually caused more trouble with irony-deficient senators and other comics detractors who thought that adventure and horror titles encouraged violence.[15] Gaines testified voluntarily at the Kefauver hearings on juvenile delinquency, but he stood out, David Park has observed, as the sole comic book publisher to defend comics against the "middlebrow notions of taste" that they offended.[16] Against Kefauver's questioning, Gaines argued not only that censoring comics as unsuitable for children would set the U.S. on a slippery slope toward tyranny ("We don't think that the crime news or any news should be banned because it is bad for children. Once you start to censor you must censor everything. You must censor comic books, radio, television, and newspapers. . . . Then you will have turned this country into Spain or Russia"), but also that horror comics, like any other genre, had a distinct aesthetic that should determine standards of good taste.[17] As Maria Reidelbach reports, Gaines tried to rally other publishers to join forces with the ACLU over the next five months in order to push back against public and commercial censorship efforts, but he finally surrendered in September 1954. That month his counterparts proposed the self-censorship that became the Comics Code, including bans on the words *horror, crime, terror,* and *weird* that would eliminate most EC titles and jeopardize his whole company.[18] Distributors would not carry titles lacking the Code's seal of approval, so he cut all the titles but *Mad, Panic,* and *Incredible Science* and gave Kurtzman, who had recently received an editorial offer from the admiring publisher of *Pageant,* the go-ahead to convert *Mad* to a slick magazine.[19] In this context, *Mad*'s transformation from comic book to magazine in 1955 was a counterhegemonic move twice over: as it evaded interference by political and economic forces, the magazine also expanded *Mad*'s formula of media burlesque to more topics and more influential readers. "For the past two years now, MAD has been dulling the senses of the country's youth," Kurtzman announced in the May 1955 issue, its last as a comic book, with an irony aimed at both friends and foes; "Now we get to work on the adults" (#23: 31).

Mad's M.O. was simple in both formats: take a comic conceit and push it over the top. Early art, in particular, reveled in excess comic detail. Elder's contempt for the comics controversy in the splash page of "Starchie," written by Kurtzman (see fig. 0-2), shows his love of what he called "chicken fat" for the definitive flavor it gave his drawings. The many details in the page—including the artist's mock-degree in B.S., the incongruous presence of Little Orphan Annie, and the messages on the girls' books and the office—exemplify what delighted Kurtzman as the "irrepressible background nonsense" that "would carry my stuff forward and enrich it by a multiple of ten."[20]

But other artists also indulged in this graphic equivalent of slapstick, which gave *Mad* its madcap flair and explains why the less detailed computer-assisted art of recent years seems flat by comparison. As longtime editor Nick Meglin summed up the editorial vision a bit too modestly in 2016, "*Mad* was not a magazine of creation; we were a magazine of reflection. We would hold up a fun-house mirror to the society so the image was distorted and exaggerated."[21] Indeed, *Mad*'s creativity involved exploiting some original incongruity or contradiction in order to turn imitation into burlesque. The formula that Kurtzman conceived survived in part because, like the *New Yorker, Mad* has enjoyed tremendous editorial stability across its sixty-seven years: Harvey Kurtzman (1952–56) was followed by Al Feldstein (1956–84), Nick Meglin and John Ficarra as

Fig. 0-2: The Comics Code that would push Gaines to drop most of EC's titles and convert *Mad* to a magazine format had not been finalized when Will Elder designed this splash page bursting with comic detail for Harvey Kurtzman's parody of *Archie* in *Mad* #12, "Starchie" (6/54): 1, but Elder's seal of disapproval (based on the Good Housekeeping Seal of Approval, a warranty program dating to 1909, [*above*]) addressed the environment for comics dramatized in the U.S. Senate's hearings at which Gaines testified that spring. The many details in the page (*below*)—including the artist's mock-degree in B.S., the incongruous presence of Little Orphan Annie, and the messages on the girls' books and the office—exemplify what delighted Kurtzman. MAD used with permission.

a team (1985–2004), and then Ficarra solo (2004–18) until the offices moved to Burbank, California, and Bill Morrison took over (2018–19). But both magazines' ability to sustain their signature appearance and mood reflects the loyalty of excellent artists and writers. While blessed with such comic virtuosi as writers Frank Jacobs, Larry Siegel, Dick DeBartolo, and Stan Hart, *Mad* has particularly benefited from the decades-long associations of artists Jack Davis, Mort Drucker, Dave Berg, Al Jaffee, Don Martin, Sergio Aragonés, Peter Kuper, and Tom Richmond, who gave *Mad* its hallmark look. (For capsule career sketches of *Mad* contributors, see Appendix A; for key moments in *Mad*'s history, see the timeline in Appendix B.)

Harvey Kurtzman had the shortest tenure but the most important one, defining *Mad* as a humor periodical featuring high-quality graphic narration of sophisticated yet youthfully spirited parodies in the color comic books numbered #1–23 (10-11/52–5/55) and the five black-and-white glossy magazines (#24–28, 7/55–7/56) that enriched the mix with other verbal and graphic genres, such as print and television ads and illustrated how-to guides. The *Mad* comic began with parodies of comic book genres, notably adventure, superhero, and youth comics. The formula quickly expanded to other genres, however, and by the sixth issue had embraced that sentimental staple of high school poetry lessons, Ernest Lawrence Thayer's "Casey at the Bat"—a feature that may have inspired the Clement Moore parody in *Panic* later that year. (Feldstein moved over from *Panic* to edit *Mad* during Kurtzman's spring 1953 illness.) Thayer's verses ran faithfully in a hand-lettered imitation of a textbook font like Garamond rather than the sans serif capitals of comic books, but Jack Davis's art undercut such seriousness with comically exaggerated action, loose-jointed characters, distorted facial expressions, and various incongruities accompanying every line or rhyme. When Casey passes on his second pitch, the drawing shows him holding a golf club instead of a bat; when the ballad intones, "The sneer is gone from Casey's lip, his teeth are clenched in hate," Casey hands a set of false teeth to a bat boy (#6, 8–9/53; 1–6; 6). The parody celebrates the potential for high burlesque—that is, serious treatment of a lowly topic—inherent in Thayer's melodrama of Mudville: Davis's art clashes comically with the ballad's narrative tension and the elevated diction required by its iambic heptameter rhymes (e.g., "spheroid" for *ball*), just as Thayer's plot ironically caps Casey's career with his anti-climactic strikeout.

Most *Mad* parodies reveled in low burlesque—that is, travesty, mocking high stakes through vulgar comparisons—a choice especially suited to political satire. In "What's My Shine!" (#17, 11/54: 7-1 [issue printed backwards]), an early foray into the kind of multi-target satire that became *Mad*'s hallmark as a magazine, Kurtzman and Davis reduced the high-profile Kefauver and Army-McCarthy Senate hearings to a madcap TV game show, like the then-popular career-guessing game *What's My Line?* (CBS, 1950–67). The satire savages Joseph McCarthy and Roy Cohn (always portrayed seated together with the unnamed but clearly recognizable Cohn whispering in the senator's ear) for falsifying evidence and badgering witnesses to banish them, as implied by the satiric name *McCartaway*. When Even Steven (stand-in for Army Secretary Robert T. Stevens) refutes photographic evidence that he "is in reality, a Redskin!" by having a physician dressed in full medical gear testify that he "doctored" it (20), the incident barely revises events of April 1954, as described in the *New York Times*. Known as "a news junkie,"[22] Kurtzman likewise has Senator McCartaway try to settle the difference between the original and falsified photos by "wrassling!"—a challenge that echoes the *New York Times* report that "Cohn, in wrangle, admits it [the photo] was cut"—before the "friendly quiz game for the whole friendly family" ends in a fracas not too different from the chaos that ensued in the Senate when the committee chair called himself to testify.[23] The satire's targets went beyond McCarthy's red-hunting, however, because the live TV coverage of those hearings began on April 22, 1954, the day after nationally televised hearings on juvenile delinquency by the Senate's Kefauver committee had humiliated EC publisher Bill Gaines for claiming that horror comics had an aesthetic governing the genre's standards of taste.[24] The back-to-back spectacles must have seemed to Kurtzman to be just one more TV game show, like CBS's pioneering *What's My Line?*, with hapless witnesses sacrificed for public entertainment. Certainly a report in the April 26 *New York Times* on NBC's decision to drop its live Army-McCarthy coverage encouraged such a view: "Apparently a Senate investigating subcommittee, together with 'Dragnet' and 'I Love Lucy,' is now subject to television's inviolate law of the popularity rating."[25] Kurtzman's satire shows his awareness of the stakes.

As an early television parody, "What's My Shine!" also takes comic aim at other targets, especially broadcasting conventions and publishing practices. Issue #17 was printed backwards and upside down to give readers a new "viewpoint" (cover), a bit of pure silliness as well as a dig at the attack on comics that was heating up during the issue's production that spring and summer. A black-and-white photo identified as "a scene from a television show that began in April" (24) set the stage for the parody's greyscale palette (although the issue's other contents ran in color) in a visual joke that mimicked the aesthetic of the televised hearings. Most important, in a harbinger of parodies to come, "What's My Shine!" lavished special comic energy on TV's symbiosis of programming and commercials. The spoof sponsor POW Coffee appears three times in the splash panel opening the parody and in all but one of fourteen panels on the facing page, a lampoon of broadcast advertising practices in which sponsors owned an entire broadcast slot and often branded the program. The commercial break appears at the most narratively dramatic and judicially unfair point, just when McCartaway presents damning photographic evidence against Steven. News watchers surely noted that a similar cliff-hanger occurred in the Senate hearings, but the burlesque of contemporary ads for Maxwell House Instant Coffee turns the satire away from politics toward media as the announcer extols how "POW is *not a* drip, *not a grind*, not a smash, not a goo . . . [but] honest-to-goodness hollow *flavor buds*, all hollow inside and everything" (20, ital. for echoes of the original ad). Kurtzman and Davis added particularly cynical touches in outfitting the announcer and senators in the same huckster-plaid and naming the sponsor to echo the climactic melee. But in tweaking CBS, whose logo closes the satire, and Maxwell House, whose Hoboken factory had scented New York's air since 1939 while gracing New York harbor with its neon sign of drops falling from a cup,[26] the satire also had local meaning beyond advertising's role as ubiquitous, repetitive television content inherited from radio days.

Both the parody and travesty—the mock-melodrama inflating baseball in "Casey" and the low burlesque trivializing politics in "What's My Shine!"—embed anti-establishment commentary in their very form. *Mad*'s basic commitment to imitation with a comic difference gave it endless opportunities to critique the individuals, themes, and contexts invoked in both types of burlesque. *Mad*'s commitment to parody thus gave the *New Yorker* "idea drawing" new significance and scope. The *New Yorker*'s idea drawings privileged originality through such comic conceits as ironic relations between image and text, whereas *Mad* valorized comic imitation. Opposing identities and editorial policies followed. In its quest for archness, the *New Yorker* would reject one piece as "a little much of the formula type of humor to be quite successful" and another as "not somehow amusing enough to go" despite an earlier request to "keep the humor from flying quite so wild."[27] Not that it couldn't take a gag and work it repeatedly into an inside joke, as in the twenty-eight cartoons of Otto Soglow's 1928–29 manhole series.[28] Yet its original editorial policy proscribing humor about writers, artists, and admen—highly visible local types ripe for ribbing—created an opening that *Mad* would fill.

Another New York-based humor magazine briefly stepped in to do so first, however. During its first run from 1931 to 1939, *Ballyhoo* gave pride of place to media burlesques, especially parodies of advertising, perhaps modeling such humor for Kurtzman and his colleagues before it folded permanently in 1954.[29] The debut issue of *Ballyhoo* mocked *Vanity Fair* and the *Congressional Record* ("because—why keep a record of unimportant events?"); the second took on *Time* ("'Time'ly News") and the *New Yorker* ("Such Goings on About Town!").[30] Full page mock ads joined parodies of editorial content. Some mock ads took on ad culture broadly while poking fun at politics: "A ROOSEVELT requires no attention . . . not even oiling. It is hermetically sealed against all opinions, thus insuring a smooth-running president. KEEP REGULAR WITH ROOSEVELT."[31] But others burlesqued marketing programs with the specificity and irreverence that would become familiar in *Mad*, as in the ad for "Hart, Schafner & the Four Marx Brothers" with the headline "What the 'well-dressed men' at Harvard are wearing" next to a rear view of a naked man in a body-builder's pose (see fig. 0-3).[32] Most tantalizing of *Ballyhoo*'s possible influence on Kurtzman is an unsigned page presumably by editor Norman Anthony, "Why Not Make the Newspapers ALL Comics?," which not only parodied every news genre from crime to sports coverage, but also previewed the conception of the original *Mad* comic book.[33] Rumor has it that *Mad*'s editors responded to a question from the British Society of Strip Illustrators about the influence of *Ballyhoo* by insisting, "We know nuthin', and what's more we ain't sayin'." But the similarities hardly seem coincidental. Considering *Ballyhoo*'s tremendous popularity—its circulation approached 2 million copies by its sixth number, dated January 1932, at the depth of the Great Depression—one must discount Kurtzman's report that college humor magazines provided his sole models for the "outrageous . . . approach to humor" that he sought for *Mad*.[34]

Fig. 0-3: The new *Mad* magazine parodied a well-known product name, logo, and marketing slogan and in much the same way that *Ballyhoo* had pioneered during Kurtzman's teen years. *Ballyhoo* suspended publication in 1939, but its brief revival for five quarterly issues in 1953–54 may have reminded him of its heyday as the new *Mad* took shape.

0-3 (*Above Right*): *Mad* #24 (7/55): inside cover. MAD used with permission.

0-3 (*Below Right*): *Ballyhoo* 2, no. 1 (1/32): inside cover.

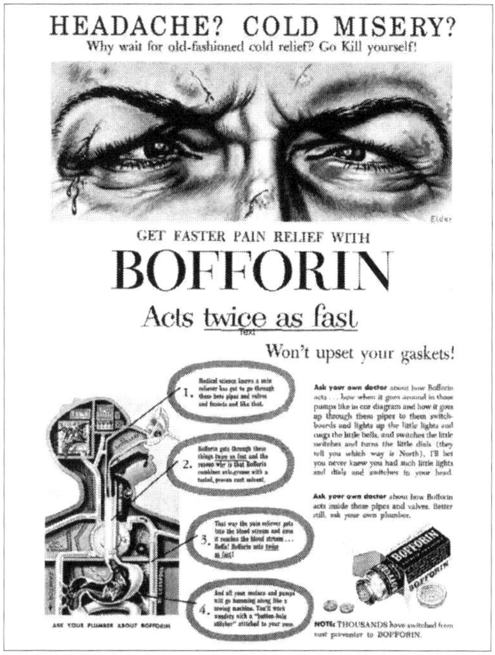

Ballyhoo disappeared from 1939–1953, but its brief revival in five issues between 1953 and 1954, as *Mad* grew from six to ten annual issues, may have reminded Kurtzman of its more insouciant years as he developed the *Mad* comic and, in 1955, began to think about editing a magazine.

In both its comics and magazine formats, *Mad* pursued wildness as it spoofed local industries and their public faces from Madison Avenue and Midtown to the outer boroughs and suburbs. In lampooning television, in particular, *Mad* took on what was then, like advertising, a New York industry with national cultural impact—especially as the new medium's penetration of U.S. households went from 34 to 90 percent during *Mad*'s first decade.[35] Expanding *Mad*'s scope from comic book to magazine, however, led to developing departments that could vary the contents while maintaining continuity from issue to issue along with the overall commitment to burlesque because the magazine formula requires new iterations of defining features. Yet the innovations that Kurtzman introduced in #24, the debut magazine issue, reached their comic fulfillment under Al Feldstein, who assumed the editorship in April 1956. Gaines had refused to give Kurtzman more than 10 percent of EC stock, so Kurtzman left to develop a new magazine, later named *Trump*, for Hugh Hefner.[36] Kurtzman's last issue was #28 (7/56); the next 228 belonged to Feldstein.

Feldstein reigned from #29 (9/56) to #225 (6/85), though he officially retired at the end of 1984. Like Kurtzman, Feldstein had proven himself to Gaines as a long-time comics editor and writer for EC and had demonstrated his humor bona fides at least since 1953. Feldstein stepped in when hepatitis sidelined Kurtzman during production of #5 (6–7/53)[37] and later that year developed *Panic*, an in-house imitation of *Mad* aimed to divert revenue from other competitors. Feldstein's earliest and most enduring contribution to *Mad*'s vision involved turning the gap-toothed kid into a fully imagined mascot. Flanked incongruously by Napoleon and Freud, the kid had flaunted his trademark smirk from atop the elaborate frame that Kurtzman drew to give continuity to the new magazine's covers; the banner that should have held the boy's name, to match those identifying other figures and themes, declared instead, "What? Me Worry?" (#24, 7/55: cover). By 1955, *Playboy* had its bunny and *Esquire* its Mr. Esky, following the precedents of the *New Yorker*'s Eustace Tilley and *Ballyhoo*'s Elmer Zilch (and *Punch*'s Punchinello before them). In that spirit, Feldstein commissioned Norman Mingo to paint a formal oil portrait that introduced Alfred E. Neuman as the magazine's candidate for President in 1956 (#30, 12/56: cover). The kid's name came from Feldstein, who had used it as a pseudonym when publishing multiple items in a single issue,[38] with the spelling changed from the more obvious *Newman*, Nick Meglin joked, "to separate him from his inspiration, the Hollywood film composer Alfred Newman."[39] The byline appeared playfully *sans* illustration in three items from his first number as editor: "Dining Etiquette Quiz," with art by Basil Wolverton, and the two-part "Alfred E. Neuman Answers Your Questions," with art by newcomer Don Martin (#29, 9/56: 16, 23, 45). Defining Alfred as *Mad*'s muse not only also personified it as counter-cultural in the Eisenhower era of WASP conformity, but also asserted Feldstein's hand in reshaping Kurtzman's magazine.

Like the *New Yorker*'s Ross, who died the year that *Mad* debuted, Feldstein saw talented contributors as the key to success. To do so, he earned the loyalty of excellent writers and artists not only by paying them, as Ross did, on acceptance rather than on publication of their work, but also (unlike Ross) by giving them new assignments with every sale. "I didn't want these guys working for anybody else," Feldstein confessed in 2000, adding that his payment practice also raised submissions' quality by encouraging friendly competition among contributors for the best assignments.[40] Further benefit came from sustaining *Mad*'s distinctive look and feel through the regular reappearance of artists and writers whose work appeared mainly in its pages. But Feldstein did not mind touting the aura of upscale publications that also valued his contributors; at the start of "Dining Etiquette Quiz," for instance, he introduced artist Basil Wolverton—whose grotesquely detailed "Beautiful Girl of the Month" had graced the cover of #11 (3/54) and famously inspired Art Spiegelman's love of comics[41]—with the boast, "To teach you correct table manners, we have called upon an ex-clod (he's no longer a clod since Life magazine accepted his work)" (#29, 9/56: 16).

Fresh talent and new ideas were urgently needed when Feldstein took over in the spring of 1956. Kurtzman had taken Elder, Davis, and Wood with him on exclusive contracts, and pressure from the Comics Code left *Mad* as EC's sole title. Within a year, however, Feldstein secured contributions from well-known comedians (or their ghostwriters), beginning with a Bob [Elliott] and Ray [Goulding] spoof of TV's science instructor from *Watch Mr. Wizard* (NBC, 1951-1965) in "Mr. Science" (#34, 8/57: 12–14), illustrated by Mort Drucker, another new artist whose work became a regular feature. Feldstein remained proud long after he retired of having encouraged Drucker to try caricature.[42] Writing by vaudeville and television veterans Sid Caesar, Ernie Kovacs, and others followed through the end of the decade.[43] At that point, issue #51 (12/59), Feldstein began listing contributors on the masthead as "The Usual Gang of Idiots" as a way to credit a rotating cast of regular artists and writers, giving equal credit to both specialties while minimizing repeat bylines in a single issue.

Across three decades at the helm, Feldstein introduced a host of long-lived features. Song parodies and original comic verse, most notably by Frank Jacobs, who joined the gang in 1957, led to his designation as *Mad*'s poet laureate.[44] In 1961, Feldstein launched the still-popular "Joke and Dagger Department" featuring Antonio Prohías's "Spy vs. Spy" (#60: 9, 14, 24); the next year, with issue #73 (9/62), a grey female spy complicated the rivalry between the black and white spies, neither of them a good guy, in a black-humorous exploration of the Cold War stalemate known as mutually assured destruction. Prohías continued the strip through #269 (3/87), when others filled in until Peter Kuper took up the strip a decade later with #356 (3/97: 12–13), yet Prohías's original vision of the eternal antagonists' moral equivalence and utter futility has remained intact. Soon after "Spy vs. Spy" came Dave Berg's "Lighter Side" feature with spoofs of everyday frustrations, beginning with "The Lighter Side of the Television Set," which reversed the focus from the people on the screen to those in front of it (#66, 10/61: 16–19). Three years later, in April 1964, came Al Jaffee's fold-in, a painting meant for a reader to appreciate first as a full-size color image with a caption that poses a question or challenge and then to fold vertically at two marked points and reveal another image and caption that respond to the first with wit and social insight. Jaffee's first effort featured Hollywood stars Elizabeth Taylor and Richard Burton, but political subjects soon followed with Richard Nixon in #87 (6/64) and the civil-rights themed "The Image of Justice that the Rest of the World Sees," which converted a judge on the bench into a KKK hood (#92, 1/65: 49). New installments of the much-beloved fold-in continued through June of 2019 (n.s. #7).

The arrival of caricaturists such as Drucker spurred the development of *Mad*'s film and TV parodies, as regular satiric features. Much as the early *New Yorker* injected humor into its journalistic departments, including its theater, art, and book reviews (perhaps most famously in Dorothy

Parker's summation in a Constant Reader column about a Winnie-the-Pooh book: "Tonstant Weader Fwowed up"[45]), so *Mad*'s movie and TV parodies combined aesthetic critique and comic viewpoints, often with a local twist. Kurtzman and Elder's 1953 "Ping Pong!," for instance, joked about the scarcity of Brooklyn Dodgers tickets and how not even a giant gorilla can draw a glance from blasé New Yorkers (#6, 8–9/53: 25–31). But local joking intensified in media parodies on Feldstein's watch. In 1963, a Broadway musical whose fictional gangs from the Upper West Side were as familiar to the locals as the U.N. building on First Avenue became the basis of "East Side Story" (#78, 4/63: 4–12), a Cold War satire based on the 1963 Oscar-winning film version of Leonard Bernstein's *West Side Story*.

New York women received less than affectionate caricatures in featured parodies from the early 1970s, showcasing the predominantly male sense of humor that characterized *Mad* since its start.[46] Dave Berg proved something of an exception, as Ann Ciasullo shows, but in general *Mad* lacked the progressive gender politics of the *New Yorker*, which promoted women writers, artists, and staff from its earliest days.[47] (Males made up 80 percent of *Mad*'s readers as late as 2001, and women contributed in force only with Bill Morrison's editorship in 2018.)[48] When Mort Drucker and Frank Jacobs mocked Barbra Streisand as Bubby (Yiddish for "grandmother") Strident in "On a Clear Day You Can See a Funny Girl Singing 'Hello Dolly' Forever" (#143, 6/71: 4–10), they debunked her celebrity by shrinking three blockbuster film performances to one; the name *Strident* sneered at not only her Brooklyn accent but also the strong female protagonists she played in *Funny Girl* (1963 stage, 1968 film), *Hello, Dolly!* (1964, 1969), and *On a Clear Day You Can See Forever* (1965, 1970). Drucker and Jacobs granted a bit more respect to New Yorkers Gloria Steinem, Betty Friedan, Bella Abzug, and Shirley Chisholm in "My Fair Laddie" (#167, 6/74: 4–11), a send-up of the 1956 Broadway hit and 1964 film *My Fair Lady*, although the creators nonetheless framed the women's movement as an indulgence not worth anyone's time. The spoof reverses the gender dynamics of the original in order to twit "the Women's Liberationists who are battling to reform the Male Chauvinist Pigs" (4). The Steinem-double named Henrietta pledges to create "The Perfect Man" (5) from the chauvinistic babe-magnet wittily named Lance, whose similarity to Burt Reynolds feeds the parody's last visual joke, which invokes the actor's infamous nude centerfold for the April 1972 *Cosmopolitan* (itself a feminist riff on the *Playboy* feature). Jacobs and Drucker betray their awareness of men's domestic privilege in having Henrietta/Steinem imagine, "Wouldn't it be Motherly!" to sit and read lovingly to her children while Lance does all the feeding, diapering, and disciplining (10)—yet the creators engineer a reversal of feminist goals at the end. Henrietta's success at training Lance backfires. When he reassures Power of Women (POW) members, to the tune of "I Could Have Danced All Night," "You'll wear the pants, all right/ . . . "At home you'll be the Chiefs—/You'll know who'll be the Squaws!" (11), he inspires "liberated chicks" (11) to swarm him—just as the conventional "fawning females" (4) had done at the start when he bragged, "They're all mine to use—That's no oddity!/'Cause I treat each one the same—like a commodity" (4). Nature trumps nurture in this send-up. But its investment in the patriarchal status quo, the implied "*Vive la différence!*," also exposes the social conservatism built into *My Fair Lady*'s class distinctions and explains why Roger Ebert declared, "I learned to be a movie critic by reading *MAD* Magazine."[49] Parodies always transgress the originals they imitate, but need not endorse liberal views. Across more than six decades of media burlesques, *Mad* offered cultural and political as well as aesthetic analysis within the comic mode, yet laughs trumped cultural politics.

The song parodies that secured *Mad* a place in copyright history deserve special attention. Songs doubtless seemed to *Mad* contributors and readers just one more popular culture form to burlesque, but composers concerned about royalty income in the 1960s were not amused. In *Berlin v. EC Publications, Inc.*,[50] the Supreme Court upheld a 1963 appellate decision that endorsed *Mad*'s claim to fair use of copyrighted material in all but two Irving Berlin songs parodied by Larry Siegel and Frank Jacobs in *Sing Along with Mad*, published as a bonus insert for *More Trash from Mad No. 4* (1961). The court held that "songs' titles, meters and occasional phrases taken from the plaintiffs' original lyrics" constituted fair use unless they made substantial use of the originals' themes or language; on that basis, the court granted that *Mad*'s parodies of Berlin's "Always" and "There's No Business Like Show Business" did infringe on Berlin's copyrights, but that others did not. Of a piece with his resistance to the Comics Code and *Mad*'s resistance to cultural authority, Gaines's pushback against the infringement suit reflects *Mad*'s history of editorial and marketing innovation.

By designating parody a fair use, the Supreme Court decision also protected the magazine's editorial identity and main source of content, paving the way for parodic sons of *Mad* in many media. Notable examples include *National Lampoon*, 1970–1998 in print, and *Saturday Night Live*, NBC, 1975–present, and their many spin-offs, from the sitcom parody *The Simpsons* (FOX 1989--) to the parodic news of *The Onion* (1988--) and *The Daily Show* (1996--). Artist Art Spiegelman summed up *Mad*'s ethos as "The entire adult world is lying to you, and we are part of the adult world. Good luck to you," and added, "I think that shaped my entire generation"—a claim endorsed by the comic performers, writers, and producers whose memories of favorite contents became *Inside Mad* (2013).[51] A full account of *Mad*'s legacy would therefore include not only its inspiration to television and film and its impact on alternative comix and graphic narratives, such as *Maus* (which Spiegelman has credited to the influence of Kurtzman and Elder's "Mickey Rodent" in *Mad* #19, 1/55: 1–7),[52] but also the explosion of parody, cynicism, and ironic critique that have fed postmodernism.

The verbal, graphic, and social complexity of *Mad*'s parodies in all genres reflected Feldstein's refusal to talk down to even his youngest readers. "Kids . . . have a fairly sophisticated knowledge," he told an interviewer in 1966. "They can spot a phony a mile off. . . . If we do a parody on [sic] a poem, they can't appreciate the humor unless they know the original. We credit them with knowing the original."[53] This policy, like the stability of the Usual Gang, gave *Mad* the balance between familiar style and novel contents that gratifies a magazine's fans, a recipe for longevity that has likewise sustained the *New Yorker*.

Feldstein proved a brilliant editor. Circulation stood at 750,000 in early 1954, but reached 1,209,918 in 1961, when official circulation counts began, and peaked at 2,132,655 in 1974, though by the time of his departure in 1985, the number had slipped to 744,817.[54] In 1966, Feldstein estimated that *Mad*'s pass-along rate enabled the 1.8 million copies of each issue to reach 10 million readers, but proudly cited the all-time top seller, at 2.8 million copies: the September 1973 number containing writer Dick DeBartolo and artist Mort Drucker's *Poseidon Adventure* (1972) parody, "Poopsidedown Adventure" (#161, 9/73: 4–11).[55] The Feldstein era saw expanded production of reprint books and annuals, a practice that Kurtzman had initiated in 1954 with *The Mad Reader*. Reprints broadened EC's revenue stream, enabling the magazine to suspend advertising after #32 (4/57). A similar profit motive underlay the explosion in international editions, which under Feldstein's leadership carried American content in translation as well as art and writing from local contributors for audiences in western Europe (e.g., the UK, 1959; the Netherlands, 1964), Scandinavia (Sweden, 1960; Denmark, 1979; Norway and Finland, 1981), Latin America (Brazil, 1974; Mexico 1978), and Australia, 1980. Editorial successors Meglin and Ficarra added editions for South Africa (1985), Taiwan (1990), Italy (1991), Canada (in French, 1991–92) and Poland (2015), though many editions faded quickly, and a bootleg Thai edition remains undated.[56] The international audience for *Mad* also inspired locally produced competitors, such as the London-based *Krazy*, which lasted seventy-nine issues between October 1976 and May 1978 (with some Super Specials thereafter through 1983) aimed at youth in Australia, New Zealand, and South Africa as well as the United Kingdom. The worldwide interest that Feldstein stoked lasted late into 2019, when the German-language *Aufbau* magazine, a glossy founded in New York in 1934 but now published in Zurich, featured *Mad* on its cover and in four articles of its October-November issue.[57]

Mad's financial success and international reach made EC an attractive corporate acquisition. Ambiguity and confusion circulate regarding the changes in its ownership between 1961 and 1972 as conglomerates morphed into the firm known as Warner Communications, which remained *Mad*'s owner in 2019, but contemporary news reports support the account here. Gaines sold EC in January 1961 to Premier Industries, which then sold it to National Periodical Publications, owner of DC Comics, on June 9, 1964.[58] National Periodicals merged with Kinney National Service following the July 21, 1967 announcement of their $60 million agreement, and in July 1969 the combined company, still known as Kinney, formally acquired Warner Bros.[59] The conglomerate National Kinney Corp. renamed itself Warner Communications in February 1972 following a December 1971 recommendation from its board.[60] Gaines retained editorial control as publisher under all these owners until he died in 1992, as *Mad* turned fifty.

Perhaps the greatest sign of *Mad*'s affluence in the Feldstein era, however, was its ability to abandon paid advertising for other revenue sources. Once *Mad* became a magazine in July 1955, the mock advertisements that fed its satire of popular culture and boosted circulation in the new format also challenged the environment for advertisers. *Ballyhoo* had charged advertisers for the parody ads running in its pages,[61] but the comics business ran chiefly on cheap newsprint production and mass sales, although comics carried some ads, most famously for correspondence art schools and body-building lessons. The sole full-page ad in *Mad* #32 (4/57), for Famous Artist Schools, carried an announcement at the top: "REAL ADVERTISEMENT"—a concession that parodies and self-deprecating house ads would have to suffice thereafter. Paid ads returned in #403 (3/2001) to subsidize the color printing that gave contents and ads a more contemporary look. By the early 1980s, however, *Mad*'s business model was so unusual that a journalism professor published an elaborate economic analysis in a major scholarly journal, marveling that *Mad*'s $1.19 million annual profit from newsstand sales and subscriptions of eight regular issues represented just a fraction of its $63 million profits annually from super-special issues and reprint books. Including licenses for games and foreign editions, *Mad* earned 7 percent of Warner Communications' total revenues.[62] Feldstein had a lot to be proud of when Gaines appointed Nick Meglin and John Ficarra co-editors in January 1985, although their names didn't appear on the masthead until June (#255).

The Meglin-Ficarra team led *Mad* for two decades; after Meglin's 2004 retirement, Ficarra continued solo until he retired in 2017. Ficarra had come on board as associate editor in 1981 after several years of contributing as a writer, but Meglin's association lasted nearly fifty years: he submitted his first idea in 1956 and formally joined the staff in 1960. Ficarra came on board as associate editor in 1981 after several years of contributing as a writer. What the pair lacked in their predecessors' Depression-era *Yiddishkeit*, they more than made up in Italian Brooklynite, which had much the same flavor. "Hmmm. . . . I already have major concerns about your editing!" Meglin snorted in a 2013 email exchange inviting him to participate in this volume after I misspelled *Neuman*. "'Newman?' You mean like in 'Paiul?'[sic] . . . HOO HAH! Gotcha, Brooklyn broad!"[63] *Mad*'s former design director Ryan Flanders probably had in mind this blend of front-stage comic excess and back-stage editorial seriousness in the magazine's obituary for Meglin, appropriately headlined "Heartsick" (n.s. #3, 10/18: 46), in affectionately recalling, "Nick was the first person to call me a 'schmuck.'" Meglin's half-century tenure supported the imaginations—and reinforced the loyalty—of the contributors whose content likewise gave the magazine exceptional coherence over time.

Ideas usually came from writers and artists, rather than the editors, but insiders credited Meglin with *Mad*'s post-Kurtzman sense of humor for both his own comic talents and his ability to cultivate others'. During the Feldstein years, Meglin recruited George Woodbridge, Larry Siegel, Angelo Torres, Dick DeBartolo, and Stan Hart, and fished Ficarra's work from the slush pile, too[64]—some 250 years of collective comic contributions. In his "Heartsick" remembrance, Ficarra characterized his colleague's editing as "a mini master class in comedy writing" (46). Former DC Comics president and *Mad* publisher Paul Levitz went further, eulogizing Meglin for other comics professionals as the magazine's presiding wit: "During the time when MAD was at its peak, and one of the most successful magazines of any kind in America," Levitz recalled, "Nick was the man most putting the funny in."[65]

Song, television, and movie parodies remained strong on Meglin and Ficarra's watch even as cultural sensibilities changed. For example, a contemporary racial critique marked the 1991 parody of *Gone with the Wind* (1939) two years after the Library of Congress added it to the National Film Archive. "Groan with the Wind" by writer Stan Hart and artist Jack Davis (#300, 1/91: 42-47) questions the film's epic stature and mocks its nostalgia for the Lost Cause. The iconoclasm begins with renaming the main characters. Hart scorns Scarlett's marriages for money and status by calling her *Harlott*, debunks Melanie's stoic self-sacrifice by calling her *Melonhead*, scorns Mammy's outmoded stereotype of the devoted slave by calling her *Mummy*, highlights Rhett's nauseating opportunism by calling him *Rhetch*, and questions Ashley Wilkes's manhood by calling him *Ashtray Wilts*—a passive receptacle that's flaccid, to boot. The plot underlines the attack on Wilkes's manhood by having Rhetch leave Harlott for Ashtray at the end, but a more serious challenge to the film's retrograde values appears in Mummy's offense at white exploitation of black labor ("In 1860, they call it 'slavery'! In 1990, they'll call it 'College Basketball'!" [43]) and her contempt for the "long tradition" of white supremacy that Rhetch is "a little sad" to see pass (44). In this racially liberal context, the gay plot device stands out as conservative in its ridicule, even as it nods to the rising LGBT movement that would soon lead to the 1994 military compromise known as "Don't Ask, Don't Tell."

Such vigorous contents—the celebratory issue #300 contained *three* film parodies—came up against serious challenges to all print media in an increasingly televisual age. The *New Yorker*'s struggles in the same period put *Mad*'s troubles in context. In 1983, media critic Ben Bagdikian charged that the *New Yorker* had committed itself to "the wrong kind of reader" under editor William Shawn,[66] who succeeded Ross on his death in 1952, the year of *Mad*'s birth. S. I. Newhouse installed three new editors in quick succession after buying the *New Yorker* in 1985: Robert Gottlieb in 1987, Tina Brown in 1992, and finally David Remnick in 1998. By contrast, *Mad* enjoyed tremendous editorial continuity from 1956 to 2004, but its comic sensibility had already escaped its pages when Meglin and Ficarra took the helm in 1985. Parody moved into American television first on news comedies such as *That Was the Week That Was* (NBC, 1964–1965), then sketch shows such as *Laugh-In* (NBC, 1968–1973) and *Saturday Night Live* (*SNL*; NBC, 1975–present), and eventually on its own *Mad TV* (FOX, 1995–2009). This same period saw cable expand options for television comedy, with HBO offering the first comedy channel in late 1989, less than two years before Viacom launched Comedy Central, where *The Daily Show* premiered in 1996, though Jon Stewart—a *Mad* aficionado himself—arrived only in 1999. The visual turn that *Mad* helped to lead through graphic storytelling in print now reigned on small screens. Irony had also penetrated the mainstream by the 1990s, as post-Vietnam and post-Watergate cynicism fed the anti-government critique and partisanship that became deeply embedded in American culture. Humor in all media fed, and fed on, these developments. Stand-up comedy clubs proliferated across the nation and sitcoms about happy nuclear families in the suburbs gave way to shows about urban singles such as *Seinfeld* (NBC, 1989–1998), famously "a show about nothing," and *Friends* (NBC, 1994–2004). Matt Groening credited *Mad* in 1988 with inspiring his comic strip *Life in Hell* (1977–2012), but his creation of *The Simpsons* as a sitcom parody of the family situation comedy genre clearly applies *Mad*'s formula to television, and its rank as the longest running sitcom in television history points to the relevance of the formula on screen. When the editors sought a refresh in 1997, *Mad*'s long-time contributors such as Don Martin and Sergio Aragonés still drew loyal fans, but audited circulation, already on the wane when Feldstein stepped down in 1984, fell nearly 60%, from 744,817 to 309,665.[67]

Meglin, Ficarra, and Jenette Kahn (then president of DC Comics, *Mad*'s publisher within the larger universe of Warner Communications) admitted only to 400,000—a circulation rate not seen since 1994[68]—in a June 1997 interview with the *New York Times*, part of a series about challenges in periodicals publishing.[69] The three leaders did, however, concede that an insufficiently diverse contributors' list, media consolidation, and burgeoning comedy scenes in other media had all hurt *Mad*. "We're really a victim of our own success," Ficarra observed with some justification.[70]Yet the trio did not acknowledge problems with the cartoon market, as the *Times* had reported in an earlier article about changes at the *New Yorker*. On the demand side, limited outlets paid mostly low rates, except for *New Yorker* cartoonists under contract, while on the supply side, fewer artists committed to cartoon humor. New opportunities in animation and auteur graphic narratives were another factor. Cases in point: after 1993, students at the School of Visual Arts in Manhattan, then the only college in the U.S. with a cartooning department, stopped enrolling in the humor courses that could foster careers in that mode; by 1997, Robert Mankoff, then the *New Yorker*'s new cartoon editor, confessed that the smaller pool and lesser skills of current cartoonists required "changing the standards" in order to "increase the population pool that can play the game."[71] Meanwhile, new opportunities in animation and graphic narratives beckoned.

Mad's reduced circulation, and concomitant loss of visibility, also figured in its declining fortunes. The *Times*'s reporter found *Mad* "a trifle dated" and its brand identity ambiguous for younger readers: "To many people," Constance Hays remarked, "the title is more likely to conjure up the grimmer specter of Mothers Against Drunk Driving than the grinning portrait of Alfred E. Neuman."[72] In fact, its star had so dimmed by 1997 that the chair of the Illustration and Cartooning Department at the School of Visual Arts didn't even mention *Mad* in naming potential print outlets for aspiring cartoonists.[73] Young artists inspired by Art Spiegelman's special 1992 Pulitzer Prize for *Maus* (1986–91) likewise seemed oblivious that he came to appreciate the narrative possibilities of comics because, as he said, he had "studied *Mad* the way some kids studied Talmud."[74] Acknowledging the lesser cultural capital of print, Meglin and Ficarra sought to update and burnish the brand for a new generation through newer media. The success of *Mad TV*, which ran on Fox from 1995 to 2009 and on CW in 2016, suggests that both audiences and talent preferred *Mad*'s comic formulas on television. The show competed successfully with *SNL* for nearly fifteen years and, unlike the print magazine, cultivated such young, diverse contributors as Debra Wilson, Nicole Sullivan, Bobby Lee, Keegan Michael Key, and Jordan

Peele. The complete digital magazine archives released on CD in 1998 and DVD in 2004 likewise aimed to keep *Mad*'s brand in the public eye and modernize it for the electronic age.

Fresh print talent did nonetheless arrive from Meglin and Ficarra's efforts, most notably in Peter Kuper, hired to take over "Spy Vs. Spy" in 1997. For a decade, the "Joke and Dagger Department" had bounced among artists Dave Berg, Bob Clarke, and Dave Manak (with Don "Duck" Edwing doing much of the writing) after ill health caused Antonio Prohías to step down following #269 (3/87: 44). The editors had trouble finding someone who could update the look of the feature while maintaining its core vision of comic futility until Ficarra reached out to Kuper, whose technique honored the spies' well-established identities while subtly asserting his own style.[75] Kuper's "Spy vs. Spy" remained a key feature in U.S. and international editions from 1997 through 2019 and into 2020.

Other efforts of the 1997 refresh failed. "Chilling Thoughts," by the veteran contributors Desmond Devlin (*Mad* writer since 1985) and Rick Tulka (artist since #282, 10/88), provided short-lived takes on the current scene, such as the mock-statistic that "90% of all telephone calls now being placed within the Continental United States are made by either MCI, AT&T or Sprint, trying to get us to switch to them" (#345, 5/96: 16). A reprise of the 1955 cover border design that introduced the yet-unnamed Alfred to readers—this time in yellow, with scribbles of the White House, Beavis, Dilbert, the Oscars, and frenetic scenes—lasted only fifteen issues, from April 1997 (#356) to June 1998 (#370), when it ran as fragmentary and torn. Perhaps the most telling false start was "Melvin & Jenkins' Guide to . . . ," a parody of the "Goofus and Gallant" etiquette feature from *Highlights for Children* featuring two black dudes for the dos and don'ts in an apparent effort at representing diverse Americans—though written and drawn by two white guys, Desmond Devlin and Kevin Pope, respectively. The feature ran in half the issues for the three years between its July 1997 debut with "Melvin & Jenkins' Guide to Personal Fitness" (#356, 39-41) and the September 2000 "Melvin & Jenkins' Guide to Hospitals" (#397, 18–19), then irregularly for the next decade, through October 2010 (#505). The reintroduction of color in February 2001 (#402) made the focus on these two stereotypically drawn African American characters particularly cringe worthy.

For the most part, however, the return to color production promoted positive developments. With even the staid *New York Times* moving to color images on its front page in October 1997, five years after the *New Yorker* took the plunge,[76] *Mad*'s use of color modernized the look of the magazine, enabled a broader range of satiric targets, and offset circulation declines by attracting paid ads beginning with issue #403 (3/01). The annual "Mad 20" feature ("The 20 Dumbest People, Events and Things" of the year), an echo if not a descendent of *Esquire*'s annual Dubious Achievement Awards, pioneered the shift to color when it debuted as a four-color insert in #377 (1/99) as part of the 1997 refresh. The opening gambit: artist Mark Stutzman's *Star Wars*-style movie poster for *Monicagate: The Never-Ending Saga*, complete with Kenneth Starr as Darth Vader, Bill Clinton as a Jedi knight, White House intern Monica Lewinsky (infamous blue dress dangling from her hand) as the romantic lead, and a scowling Hillary Clinton (shielding daughter Chelsea's eyes) in the background (18). The feature tied cover and inside contents to contemporary politics and the cultural scene; in this case, the cover worked a montage of featured faces including Lewinski, Microsoft's Bill Gates, and baseball record holder Mark McGwire into the required portrait of Alfred. The debut of the "Mad 20" thus reasserted the hallmark of the classic *Mad*: a commitment to excellent comic art satirizing contemporary politics and the cultural scene. Other experiments soon showed how color could broaden opportunities to blend politics and parody. For instance, two months before the full return to color, Devlin and Jack Syracuse marked the end of the Clinton presidency with "Goodnight Room," a parody of Margaret Wise Brown's classic picture book *Goodnight Moon* (1947) that repurposed its naïve drawings in bright primary colors for ironic political commentary on the administration's scandals. As Clinton prepares to leave the Oval Office, the narrator intones, "Goodnight Socks, goodnight loot / Goodnight House of ill repute" (#400, 12/2000: 43-47; 46–47), turning Brown's gentle farewell to a day's activity into a veiled "good riddance." In the twenty years since the "Mad 20" debuted, the return to color has inspired a wealth of inventive satire.

Ficarra continued efforts to boost readership after Meglin retired in 2004, when circulation fell to 211,473.[77] The "Fundalini Pages" of gag cartoons that debuted in February 2004 targeted younger readers and new contributors with a miscellany of content shorter than the full page that had long been *Mad*'s minimum unit of humor. In a 2012 interview for the business magazine *Fast Company*, Ficarra called the department "short attention-span theater" appropriate for a contemporary culture marked everywhere by fragmentation (another hallmark of postmodernism), though he also observed, while acknowledging the growing body of television series satirizing the current scene, "Life is getting harder to parody."[78] Efforts to adapt *Mad*'s signature formula to this new cultural environment continued throughout Ficarra's tenure.

The 2015 parody of the Netflix political mockumentary *House of Cards* (2013–2018) straddled old and new accordingly. David Shayne and Tom Richmond's "House of Cons" lampoons the protagonists through their names and caricatures in typical *Mad* fashion: the ruthless Frank Underwood who seduces, lies, and kills his way from Congress to the presidency becomes Rank Underhand, while his wife Claire, with "the conniving instincts of Lady Macbeth, the political savvy of Hillary Clinton, and the haircut of Miley Cyrus," becomes Scaire (#532, 4/15: 12–17; 12). But the title art has good reason to include the *Mad*-inflected distress symbol of an upside-down American flag with Alfred's face in lieu of its field of stars, because the parody mocks the failure of contemporary America's two-party politics along with the show's postmodern pseudo-documentary style, self-reflexive direct address, self-parodic cynicism, and outrageous political fantasies tied to reality by celebrity cameos. When CNN's Ashleigh Banfield (playing herself in the parody as on the TV show) supports a complaint about Rank as "a completely unbelievable character" by citing his "murder in broad daylight, . . . arch dialogue, . . . constantly break[ing] the fourth wall," *Mad*'s caricature of MSNBC's Rachel Maddow points out the obvious but unacknowledged political impossibility at the heart of the show: "he got elected in South Carolina as a Democrat!" (13). The narrative goes on to spoof such plot developments and narrative tics as the sexual threesome with Underhand's secret service agent and the Underhands' penchant for smoking cigarettes at their bedroom window—"We really must stop sharing a cigarette every time we plan something devious," Rank remarks, though not for the health or ethical reasons one might expect: "When we moved in, these drapes were WHITE!" (16). Along the way come jokes about the irrelevance of newspapers and Rank's superiority to Dick Cheney as "the most nefarious, manipulative Vice President in American history" (17). But the best punchline comes in the last panel, when President Barack Obama interrupts Rank's victory dance over finally pushing the fictional president out of office in order to ask two favors: "can I bum a smoke?"

and "Teach me, Rank!" (17). Only in a completely absurd world should decency wreak impotence and failure, and only parody can capture it.

Ficarra's 2012 interview itself grew out of another strategy for marketing to a younger generation: publishing books that combined classic and recent material endorsed by comedians from contemporary television and films. *Totally Mad: 60 Years of Humor, Satire, Stupidity and Stupidity* (2012) featured an appreciative introduction by Stephen Colbert and Eric Drysdale.[79] The next year, commentary by Judd Apatow, Roseanne Barr, Penn Jillette, George Lopez, and Paul Feig prefaced reprints of their supposedly favorite contents in *Inside Mad* (2013). Such testimonials doubtless sold books, although fans reported disappointment over the volumes in reviews for amazon.com. But audited circulation continued to drop over the next decade, falling from 212,696 in 2005 to 122,908 in 2015, though it ticked up to 139,725 in 2017,[80] Ficarra's last year as editor. The rise probably reflected the intensified interest in political satire spurred by the 2016 presidential campaign. Four of *Mad*'s six 2016 issues depicted or referenced Donald Trump (the post-election issue, #542 [12/16], showed Alfred as Uncle Sam in a straightjacket on the cover), the same satiric wave that also restored previously waning fortunes of *Saturday Night Live* and *The Late Show with Stephen Colbert* (CBS, 2015–present).

Humor scholars have traced this new golden age of satire to at least 2004, when the Pew Internet and American Life Project reported that 21 percent of young people got their news from satiric programs such as *The Daily Show with Jon Stewart*, a rate just below the 23 percent who regularly read a daily newspaper.[81] *Mad* has remained an equal opportunity offender across its history, despite its liberal political tilt, but New Yorkers among the Usual Gang had found Trump a tempting local target for ridicule since 1986. That year a mock ad for the imaginary Integrity Record Club offered a cassette of Trump's "Eve of Construction" along with a punningly titled "The White Album" featuring segregationist Republican senator Jesse Helms as two of the many titles available for a penny to gullible new members who agree to buy "13 more bad-selling records or tapes at regular club prices which are currently $19.98 to $99.98—plus shipping and mishandling" (Kadau [w], Raiola [w], and Schild [photog.], #262, 4/86: back cover). Five years later, as Trump's $1.1 billion Taj Mahal casino project entered bankruptcy barely a year after its April 1990 opening,[82] Frank Jacobs and Sam Viviano caricatured

Trump as the corrupt Wizard of Odds in a parody of the classic musical film *The Wizard of Oz* (#300, 1/91: 31–36). Not surprising in this context, Trump's emergence as a presidential candidate in 2015 spurred an ongoing series of single-page and extended features across the campaign and into his presidency. The parodies of classic paintings collected as the "MADtropolitan Museum of Art: The Trump Collection" (#547, 10/17: 27-36) constitute perhaps the most elaborate example. Featured paintings include Richard Williams's *Trump Crossing the Delaware*, in which the administration's ship of state is heading off a cliff despite strenuous back-paddling by Vice President Mike Pence, Press Secretary Sean Spicer, and Senior Advisor (and son-in-law) Jared Kushner (28–29). *Donald's World*, the last page, parodies Andrew Wyeth's portrait of yearning, *Christina's World* with an overweight Trump in a MAGA hat, golf club in hand, struggling to reach the putting green (36). The political and media stresses that fueled *Mad*'s satiric creativity in its first three decades could still inspire the Gang.

The new *Mad* series inaugurated in June 2018 with Ficarra's retirement aimed to revitalize the brand by moving from New York City, the center of American print culture, to its film and television counterpart in Burbank, California, home to the multi-media brand franchises of corporate parents DC Comics and Warner Communications. Artist Bill Morrison, *Mad*'s new executive editor, led an almost wholly new team, updated to include women and young contributors as well as vice presidents for business strategy, consumer marketing, publicity, digital sales, and content strategy. The new issue #1 (6/18) explicitly bridged past and present. A comics parody section boasted the throwback label "Potrzebie Comics" (19–31), and Ron English's full-color re-rendering of Basil Wolverton's "Beautiful Girl of the Month" (18) rewarded close inspection with a dripping nipple not present in the original, yet only Ian Boothby and Tom Richmond's homage to Will Elder's comic detail in "Starchie Reconstituted," evoked the verve of the older works (38–40). Later issues showed the team hitting its stride. Writer Matt Cohen and artist Marc Palm won national media attention, and a 2018 Eisner Award nomination, for "The Ghastlygun Tinies" in n.s. #4 (12/18: 18–21). In classic *Mad* fashion, the feature embeds a satire of school shooting massacres in a parody of Edward Gorey's *The Gashlycrumb Tinies* (1981), itself a comically gothic lampoon of *The New England Primer*. The success of this feature may have inspired the editors to close the June 2019 issue with a fold-in by Al Jaffee originally intended for #521 (6/13), but withheld then as too controversial. Answering the question, "What Inevitable Sequel Already Has Many People Sick to Their Stomachs?," the folded image shows the audience leaving a theater in response to "the next mass gun shooting," an allusion to the July 2012 massacre in Aurora, Colorado, that remained all too current in 2019 (n.s. #7: inside back cover).

The California investment brought quick dividends, including a 2018 Eisner nomination for Best Humor Magazine of the year and 2019 Rondo Hatton Award for Gary Pullin's cover for n.s. #4 (12/18), yet Morrison left at the end of January 2019, and DC notified contributors on July 3 that the magazine would cease commissioning new content. As reported by longtime artist Tom Richmond, DC planned to publish new reprint volumes under the *Mad* brand and to fulfill current subscriptions with current backlog and classic content under new covers.[83]

New material shone amid the reprints. Satires by new contributors led the way. "Bernie's 2020 Healthscare Campaign," a half-page by writer Amanda Stelberg and artist Sam Sisco, spoofed the Democratic presidential candidate's rhetorical intensity in n.s. #10 (12/19: 4). "The Great Trump Bestiary," the centerfold of n.s. #9 by David Seidman and Leonardo Rodriguez (10/19: 28–29), reimagined administration figures as grotesque animals such as The Pence, an eagle pitching stones with his talons: "The pious Pence says, "God demands / That women's rights be few. / But God's no sexist; he believes / Gay men should suffer, too" (29). Self-consciousness hovered in the February 2020 (n.s. #11) issue, gathering ten pages of recycled contents into a section titled "Still Dumb After All These Years" with introductions joking about their contemporary relevance (45–54). In the same number, the "Mad 20" for 2019 debuted a fold-in by Johnny Sampson at #17, "What 'Sparked Joy' for Millions of People This Year?" (35), while #20 posed the existential question, "What Should Be Done with MAD?" (4). The answer from writer Dick DeBartolo and artist Mark Fredrickson in "A MAD 'Ending' Target of Speculation": identify the magazine's future by throwing a dart at a dartboard whose options include "Sell it to Lorne Michaels" [creator of *SNL*] and "Say it's now called *The New Yorker*" (n.s. #11: 40). The magazine began hawking new subscriptions; led by art director Suzy Hutchinson, the Gang limped on.

Looking back at *Mad*'s start, the *New Yorker*'s Adam Gopnik credited Kurtzman with creating a new kind of humor by recognizing that "the conventions of pop culture ran so deep in the imagination of his audience—and already stood at so great a remove from real experience—that you could create a new kind of satire just by inventorying them."[84] On the contrary, I think that Kurtzman's great insight was that media create that pop culture by re-presenting—and thereby warping—lived experience: *Mad*'s parodies exaggerated media distortions as if *they* were reality. His appropriation of familiar media genres for humor and satire through parody recognized the profound cultural changes between the eras in which the *New Yorker* and *Mad* found their respective footing.

Both magazines benefited from new technologies that promoted the visual turn in popular culture. The rise of photography after World War I cost commercial artists much newspaper and advertising work, but thereby fostered both the high-brow cartoons of the early *New Yorker*, which rendered them as elegant half-tones, and the low-brow comics industry that nurtured *Mad*. Comics publisher William Gaines took up Kurtzman's idea for a funny title to augment EC's educational and entertaining comics to avoid losing a talented writer, editor, and artist to the cut-throat competition. Television intensified the visual turn after World War II because it not only displaced the verbal dominance of radio and books, but also created a common mass culture of programming *and* advertising. Parody ads cost *Mad* the revenue while repurposing the content.

More important, however, the difference between the *New Yorker*'s revenue-producing ads and *Mad*'s imaginary ones signals the shift from the industrial culture of the *New Yorker*'s early years to the post-industrial culture of *Mad*'s. In a post-industrial economy, information displaces goods and services as the economic base. Brands stand at the heart of this economy because branding sums up the union of information and commerce: brands *denote* a good or service or image, *differentiate* one from another, and *connote* or symbolize a set of associated ideas to be sold as such.[85] Humor and branding enjoy special synergy, as I detailed in *Twain's Brand*,[86] and *Mad* capitalized both metaphorically and literally on the centrality of branding to post-industrial culture. *Mad*'s start as a vehicle for parodying comics established a comic identity, distinguished it from the competition, and symbolized its iconoclasm in durable ways: it reduced mass culture of all sorts, from poetry and film to radio serials, to the same low-status comic book form, reveling in the transgressions through the hyperbolic verbal and graphic detail that J. Hoberman called "vulgar modernism."[87] Across sixty-seven years as a magazine parodying other media, *Mad* elevated parody as a mode of thought and fostered irony as a means of expression, defining the postmodern break between representation and meaning as it brought comics into the mainstream.

Mad's value as a brand explains why the magazine remains in print despite dismal circulation. Although its 2018 circulation of 150,195 barely exceeded 10 percent of the 1.34 million that it boasted in 1980, reprint collections and websites demonstrate how deeply committed its fans remain.[88] The precedent established by *Berlin v. EC Comics* has led to a peculiar inversion by which YouTube parodies of copyrighted songs now outnumber originals: parodists retain the rights to their comic lyrics but must pay composers to reuse their melodies.[89] Thus post-industrialism breeds postmodernism: as information displaces goods, so parody displaces (meta)narratives, and facts give way to jokes. Kurtzman intuited these ironies when he compiled the first *Mad Reader* on the post-industrial premise that a humor magazine trades in copyrights and then turned his comic book into a humor magazine.

Indeed, the similar brand strategies of *Mad* and the *New Yorker* provide evidence that humor leads cultural shifts. Today's joke often turns true tomorrow; *Mad*'s vulgar modernism presaged our postmodern moment. Today, both brands survive primarily by activities other than print magazine publication. In 1925, the *New Yorker*'s editorial mix of comic art, writing, and leisure-activity reviews expressed a pioneering plan for what we now call target marketing: Ross hoped that sophisticated comic content shaped by then-new Modernist ironies would deliver educated, affluent, trend-setting twenty- and thirty-somethings to local luxury advertisers. It was not enough. The *New Yorker* began augmenting its revenue stream with reprints in book form in 1927, as it finished its second year, and has not let up since then. In fact, in a wonderfully postmodern reversal, today it recycles editorial content into consumer goods such as umbrellas and calendars as well as books and uses podcasts and ticketed events like the *New Yorker* Festival to cultivate old-fashioned subscriptions designed to sell advertising and generate more recyclable content. Likewise, in 1955 Kurtzman announced the forthcoming *Mad Reader* on a full page in *Mad*'s last issue as a comic book, yet by 2019, the *Mad* reprint collections had outstripped the magazine's capacity to create new content worth recycling.

Plans to kill *Mad* magazine in favor of the brand's afterlife showed that DC could take the magazine but not its spirit out of New York, the center of American publishing. Whereas the early *New Yorker* cultivated highbrow literary and graphic humor for the radio and film era, *Mad* created burlesque graphic narratives that turned television and movies back into text. Journalist Thomas Vinciguerra saw the future in *Mad*'s 2018 move from New York City to Burbank, California, when he mourned, "Adieu, MAD. Pretty much single-handedly, you established the absurd reality in which we all now dwell."[90] For fifty-five of *Mad*'s sixty-seven years, the carnivalesque double vision of Al Jaffee's fold-in had epitomized *Mad*'s comic sensibility. In 2019 Jaffee stood nearly alone as a remnant of those New York roots, now feeding local and national productions from *Saturday Night Live* and *The Onion* to *The Simpsons* and graphic narratives, among other innovations by fans from its heyday. The *New Yorker* could refresh its twentieth-century brand by moving into pathbreaking journalism after World War II,[91] and stay relevant in the twenty-first by creating content for non-print media and live events, but *Mad*, imprisoned in parody's fun-house mirror, served as a harbinger of and then fell victim to the Late Age of Print.

Notes

1. No scholarly book chronicles the history of *Mad*, and Maria Reidelbach's authorized account, *Completely Mad: A History of the Comic Book and Magazine*, covers only the first 40 of the magazine's nearly 70 years. Barely a dozen scholarly articles treated the magazine until John Bird and I published *"Mad" Magazine and Its Legacies*, our special triple issue, 1–216. Early studies include Charles Winick, "Teenagers, Satire, and *Mad*"; John Cawelti, "The Sanity of *MAD*"; Ziva Ben-Porat, "Method in Madness: Notes on the Structure of Parody, Based on MAD TV Satires"; Vincent P. Norris, "*Mad* Economics: An Analysis of an Adless Magazine"; Nathan Abrams, "From Madness to Dysentery: *Mad*'s Other New York Intellectuals"; Kristin L. Matthews, "The ABCs of *Mad* Magazine: Reading, Citizenship, and Cold War America"; Kristin L. Matthews, "A *Mad* Proposition in Postwar America"; Teodora Carabas, "'Tales Calculated to Drive You MAD': The Debunking of Spies, Superheroes, and Cold War Rhetoric in *Mad* Magazine's 'Spy vs. Spy'"; Alexander R. Galloway, "The Unworkable Interface." More recent contributions include Yuri Shakouchi, "The Stereotypes of the Beatniks and Hip Consumerism: A Study of *Mad* Magazine in the Late 1950s and 1960s"; Leah Garrett, "'Shazoom. Vas Ist Das Shazoom?': *Mad* Magazine and Postwar Jewish America"; Cord A. Scott, "Cold War Politics, Cuba, and Spy vs. Spy."

2. See Judith Yaross Lee, *Defining "New Yorker" Humor*, 65, 378 n4.

3. Lee, *Defining "New Yorker" Humor*, 56.

4. Arno was not alone among early *New Yorker* artists in incorporating traditions of racist caricature—not all of whom invoked the anti-racist ironies of "One of the Neighbors"; see Lee, *Defining "New Yorker" Humor*, 175–76, 215–18.

5. Ellin Mackay, "Why We Go to Cabarets: A Post-Debutante Explains," 7-8.

6. Lee, *Defining "New Yorker" Humor*, 32–35; Harvey Kurtzman with Michael Barrier, *From Aargh! to Zap!: Harvey Kurtzman's Visual History of the Comics*, 41.

7. Simon Critchley, *On Humour*, 65.

8. Abrams, "From Madness to Dysentery," 439.

9. Jeremy Dauber, *Jewish Comedy: A Serious History*, 156.

10. Daniel Gluckson and Al Feldstein, "Man Behind the Curtain Department: Al Feldstein Interview," 72.

11. Arie Kaplan, *From Krakow to Krypton: Jews and Comic Books*, foreword by Harvey Pekar, illustrated by J. T. Waldman.

12. David Hajdu, *The Ten-Cent Plague: The Great Comic-Book Scare and How It Changed America*, 7; Josh Lambert, *Unclean Lips: Obscenity, Jews, and American Literature*, 3, 90–97, 6.

13. Clement Clarke Moore and Will Elder, "The Night Before Christmas," *Panic* #1 (2-3/54), reprinted in Elder, *The Million Year Picnic and Other Stories*, 88–94.

14. Quoted in Reidelbach, *Completely Mad*, 24.

15. Hajdu, *The Ten-Cent Plague*, 219–24, 280–82.

16. David Park, "The Kefauver Comic Book Hearings as Show Trial: Decency, Authority and the Dominated Expert," 273.

17. William Gaines, "Testimony of William M. Gaines, Publisher, Entertaining Comics Group, New York, N. Y."

18. Reidelbach, *Completely Mad*, 28–32.

19. *Pageant* had lauded *Mad* in a featured article, "Now Comics Have Gone Mad," 88–93; Bill Schelly describes the appeal of the job offer in *Harvey Kurtzman: The Man Who Created Mad and Revolutionized Humor in America: A Biography*, 309–11.

20. Kurtzman with Barrier, *From Aargh! to Zap!*, 42.

21. Barbara Friedman, "Nick Meglin: A Mad Perspective."

22. Schelly, *Harvey Kurtzman*, 294.

23. W. H. Lawrence, "Army Charges a 'Doctored' Picture Was Submitted by M'Carthy's Side; Cohn, in Wrangle, Admits It Was Cut," 1, 18.

24. Peter Kihss, "No Harm in Horror, Comics Issuer Says," 1, 34; Gaines, "Testimony."

25. Jack Gould, "Television in Review: McCarthy-Army Inquiry, Like Veteran Video Favorites, Has Its Own Hooper," 32.

26. Adam Smith, "On the Waterfront: Hoboken's Last Drop."

27. Katharine S. Angell, letter to Stephen Vincent Benet, November 3, 1928, Box 135, New Yorker Records, Rare Books and Manuscripts, New York Public Library.

28. Lee, *Defining "New Yorker" Humor*, 235–36.

29. David E. E. Sloane, *American Humor Magazines and Comic Periodicals,* 25–28. I am grateful to Professor Sloane for sharing his collection of *Ballyhoo* issues with me.

30. "We Nominate for Oblivion [parodies of *Vanity Fair, Life, Arts Beautiful,* and the *Congressional Record*]," 15; "'Time'ly News" and "Such Goings on About Town!," 11, 2.

31. "LOOK for the DATE on the CANDIDATE."

32. What the 'Well-Dressed Men' at Harvard Are Wearing."

33. [Norman Anthony,] "Why Not Make the Newspapers ALL Comics?," 10.

34. Henry Pringle, "The Anatomy of *Ballyhoo,*" 13; Schelly, *Harvey Kurtzman,* 222.

35. Christopher H. Sterling and John M. Kittross, *Stay Tuned: A Concise History of American Broadcasting,* 352; "Number of TV Households in America," https://americancentury.omeka.wlu.edu/items/show/136

36. Schelly, *Harvey Kurtzman,* 334.

37. Schelly, *Harvey Kurtzman,* 262.

38. Al Feldstein, "The Al Feldstein Interview," interview by S. C. Ringgenberg, reprint of "Jolting Words with Al Feldstein in the EC Tradition," 77–99.

39. Nick Meglin, email to Judith Yaross Lee, October 11, 2013, 11:22 a.m.

40. Gluckson and Feldstein, "Man Behind the Curtain Department," 72–73.

41. Art Spiegelman, *Breakdowns: Portrait of the Artist as a Young %@&*!,* 7–8. On p. 7, Spiegelman describes Wolverton's "Beautiful Girl of the Month' Reads *Mad*" as "the spaghetti-and-meatballs version" of "the Mona Lisa and . . . those Picasso women I'll learn to love years later. . . . She was 'post-modernism' *avant la letter.*"

42. Feldstein, "The Al Feldstein Interview."

43. See, for example, Sid Caesar and Wallace Wood, "The Professor Lectures on Space," *Mad* #49 (6/59): 24–27. See also Lawrence Rodman, "*Mad*'s Guest Writers," 169–78.

44. Frank Jacobs, *The Mad World of William M. Gaines,* 219.

45. Dorothy Parker [Constant Reader], "Reading and Writing: Far from Well," 98.

46. The humor of Wally Wood's art epitomized—and mocked—the male viewpoint, as Joseph W. Slade argues in chap. 4, "Wally Wood: Picturing Male Adolescent Desire in *Mad*'s Early Parodies," 101–118; first published as "Wally Wood: Picturing Male Adolescent Sexuality in *Mad*'s Early Parodies" in *Studies in American Humor* n.s. 3, no. 30 (Fall 2014): 41-56.

47. Ann M. Ciasullo, "The Lighter—and Weightier—Side of *Mad*; Or, Everything I Needed to Know About Gender and Sexuality I Learned from Dave Berg," chap. 5, 119–140, first published in *Studies in American Humor* n.s. 3, no. 40 (Fall 2014): 77–94; Lee, *Defining "New Yorker" Humor,* 49–51, 324–62.

48. Chris Hedges, "For Mad, a Reason to Worry: Struggling for Relevance in Sarcastic World"; the last issue published in New York under Ficarra, *Mad* #555 (4/18) featured two items by writer Alison Grambs and three by writer-artist Teresa Burns Parkhurst; Morrison's *Mad* n.s. #1 (6/18) included women throughout

the issue and as two of the four editors. Writer Tammy Golden joined the gang with *Mad* n.s. #3 (10/18) and collaborated with artist Tom Richmond on "The Manmaid's Tale," a parody of the television series *The Handmaid's Tale* in *Mad* n.s. #10 (12/19: 15–19).

49. Roger Ebert, introduction to *Mad About the Movies: Director's Cut*, [i].

50. United States Second Circuit, Court of Appeals, Berlin v. EC Publications, Inc., 329 F. 2d 541, March 23, 1964.

51. Marc Tracy, "Mad Magazine, Irreverent Baby Boomer Humor Bible, is All but Dead"; *Inside Mad*, edited by John Ficarra.

52. Art Spiegelman's notable credits to "Mickey Rodent" include his obituary of Kurtzman, "A Furshlugginer Genius!", 77; Leon Dische Becker and Art Spiegelman, "Art Spiegelman: My Life in Cartoons [Interview]," https://www.foldmagazine.com/art-spiegelman. The influence of the Kurtzman-Elder story shows in Spiegelman's 1974 trial of framing his family history as a mouse's tale, reprinted in *Breakdowns*, n.p.

53. Edmund A. Hoey and Al Feldstein, "READ Goes MAD—Interview with Al Feldstein 1966."

54. Mike Slaubaugh, *Mad Magazine Lists* https://users.pfw.edu/slaubau/mad.htm.

55. Hoey and Feldstein, "READ Goes MAD"; Feldstein, "The Al Feldstein Interview."

56. Reidelbach, *Completely Mad*, 204. For details on individual international editions, see Bernd Engel, *MADtrash.Com: The MAD Magazine Internet Database*.

57. See the lavishly illustrated *Aufbau: Das Jüdische Magazin* 85, no. 5, whose cover reprints Norman Mingo's cover "Turn On Tune In Drop Dead" (#118, 4/68). Six German-language articles on *Mad* appear within: Andreas Mink, "Leitartikel: Die Welt von MAD"; Doug Chandler, "Standpunkt: MAD als politische Zeitschrift"; Julian Voloj, "Geschichte: Von MAD zu 'MINO'"; Julian Voloj, "Hintergrund: Wer war Alfred E. Neuman?"; Julian Voloj, "Kreative Stimmen: Die Köpfe hinter den Figuren"; Mario Müller, "Deutsche Ausgabe: Mut zur Zahnlücke." Note that the last page of Voloj's "Hintergrund: Wer war Alfred E. Neuman?" mentions *Seeing "Mad,"* then in process, but mistakenly places Judith Yaross Lee at Ohio State University instead of Ohio University.

58. "E.C. Publications Bought by Premier"; "Alfred E. Neuman Joining Superman."

59. Clare M. Beckert, "'Batman' Being Sold," 42; Leonard Sloane, "Mergers Set in Show Business."; "Warner Bros. Picks New Chief Officer and Head of Board," 41.

60. "Kinney Seeks Name Change," 103.

61. Winick, "Teenagers, Satire, and *Mad*," 185.

62. Norris, "*Mad* Economics," 57–58.

63. Meglin, email to Lee.

64. Reidelbach, *Completely Mad*, 160.

65. Paul Levitz, "'Farewell to a Friend': Paul Levitz on MAD Magazine's Nick Meglin."

66. Ben H. Bagdikian, "The Wrong Kind of Readers: The Fall and Rise of *The New Yorker*," 52–54.

67. Slaubaugh, *Mad Magazine Lists.*

68. Slaubaugh, *Mad Magazine Lists.*

69. Constance L. Hays, "'What? Me Worry?': *MAD*'s Humor is Racier, Its Readers Elusive," D10.

70. Hays, "'What? Me Worry?,'" D10.

71. Constance L. Hays, "Tradition on Trial as Editor Rethinks Cartooning Style at *The New Yorker*," D1, 26.

72. Hays, "'What? Me Worry?,'" D10.

73. Hays, "Tradition on Trial," D26.

74. Spiegelman, *Breakdowns*, [6–7]; Spiegelman and Mitchell, "Public Conversation: What the %$#! Happened to Comics?," 21–24.

75. David Shayne, "Feel Like Reading a Spy Story?" in *Spy vs. Spy 2: The Joke and Dagger Files*, by Peter Kuper with Duck Edwing, Bob Clarke, and Dave Manak and edited by David Shayne, 13-17.

76. Editor Tina Brown announced the *New Yorker*'s introduction of color in an interview with Deirdre Carmody, "Her First Issue at the Ready, Tina Brown Talks About The New Yorker."

77. Slaubaugh, *Mad Magazine Lists.*

78. Susan Karlin, "The Ascent of 'Mad': See 60 Years of Comic Subversion."

79. *Totally Mad: 60 Years of Humor, Satire, Stupidity and Stupidity*, edited by John Ficarra.

80. Slaubaugh, *Mad Magazine Lists.*

81. Pew Internet and American Life Project, *Cable and Internet Loom Large in Fragmented Political News Universe: Perceptions of Partisan Bias Seen as Growing—Especially by Democrat*, 3.

82. Lenny Glynn, "Trump's Taj—Open at Last, with a Scary Appetite"; Richard D. Hylton, "More Details Released in Trump Refinancing."

83. Tom Richmond, "The End of the MADness," in *Richmond Illustration, Inc! Caricature and Cartoon Art Studios*; Michael Cavna, "Mad Magazine, a Pioneer of Modern Satire, Will Soon Cease Publishing New Content."

84. Adam Gopnik, "Postscript: Kurtzman's Mad World," 74.

85. David Arnold, *The Handbook of Brand Management*; Robin Landa, *Designing Brand Experiences.*

86. Judith Yaross Lee, *Twain's Brand: Humor in Contemporary American Culture*, 23–26, 162–63, 178–79.

87. J. Hoberman, "Vulgar Modernism," 71–76.

88. Accounting professor Mike Slaubaugh's *Mad Magazine Lists* maintains statistics on circulation along with contributors' and masthead appearances; Bernd Engel's *Madtrash.com: Mad Magazine Internet Database* combines a collectibles

marketplace with indexes of artists for all editions and subjects for U.S. *Mad* covers, https://madtrash.com/; Doug Gilford's *Mad Cover Site* is a trove of publication details except page numbers, https://www.madcoversite.com/index.html; "*Mad* Sales Figures" at John Jackson Miller's *Comichron: A Resource for Comics Research*, https://www.comichron.com/titlespotlights/mad.html, documents reported circulation and other distribution details.

89. David Hajdu, "The Parody Racket: From Ridicule to the Ridiculous," 55.

90. Thomas Vinciguerra, "MAD Magazine Taught Us to Laugh but Now We Laugh At It."

91. *The New Yorker* moved audaciously into serious journalism by publishing John Hersey's *Hiroshima* as the sole article in its August 31, 1946, issue. Rachel Carson's three-part *Silent Spring* (June 16, 23, and 30, 1962) and distinguished reports into the My Lai Massacre of the Vietnam War (Seymour Hersh, January 22 and 29, 1972), the Abu Ghraib atrocities in Iraq (Hersh, May 10, 17, and 24, 2004), and Harvey Weinstein's sexual abuses (Ronan Farrow, October 23, 2017) followed in that tradition.

PART I.
THE USUAL GANG

1. Inside the Editorial Process:

Mad Veterans Jaffee and Meglin Look at Their Editors

Paul Levitz

A RECURRING DISCOURSE between the scholarly community and the people who create fiction in any medium involves the interpretations of the work and search for creative intent. It's frequently true that scholars find meaning and intent that the creators were unconscious of placing in the work, or even deny is a fair reading of their work. *Mad* magazine was inarguably a significant force in shaping American popular culture in its decades as the country's best-selling humor magazine (circulation exceeded 1.5 million from 1965 to 1979). Its satirical looks at our behavior, institutions, media, and advertising influenced its readers and generations of creative people working in other forms. Given *Mad*'s popularity, it is useful to examine questions of intent, as well as the shared cultural influences that shaped its editorial staff and extremely loyal contributors ("The Usual Gang of Idiots"). Without any claim to objectivity, after serving for seventeen years as the magazine's second publisher, I instead offer for consideration primary resources in the form of lengthy interviews with two of the longest-serving and most articulate participants in *Mad*'s creation.

Al Jaffee first appeared in *Mad* in 1955 and continued into 2019 to contribute his distinctive fold-in to every issue. Nick Meglin joined *Mad*'s editorial staff in 1956 and retired in 2004 after serving as the co-editor for the last twenty years. They worked with all of *Mad*'s editors: Harvey Kurtzman (1952–1956), Al Feldstein (1956–1984), Nick Meglin and John Ficarra jointly as co-editors (1984–2004) and John Ficarra individually (2004–present). For your consideration, then, our 2014 conversations, which may fuel further discourse.

Interviews conducted and edited by Paul Levitz

The following interview with Al Jaffee was conducted February 20, 2014.

Paul Levitz: Al, I believe you're the only living writer who has worked closely with all four of the men who edited *Mad* magazine: Harvey Kurtzman, both at *Mad* and his later projects, Al Feldstein, Nick Meglin, and John Ficarra. I'd like to explore with you the differences among the four men's worldviews and processes, and how that affected the material in the magazine.

Al Jaffee: Well, Harvey was a huge influence, and Harvey's *Mad* magazine was unique, but Harvey was influenced by other publications. Crazy stuff that came out here and there. But Harvey's thinking process was just so special. He knew each person that worked with him, what very special talent that person had. He ignored all the surrounding chaff. He didn't care that I knew nothing about anatomy; what he liked was how I saw the world, and the same about Will Elder or Jack Davis or Wally Wood. He went after that one little spark that made that person unique and outstanding as a talent. Will Elder couldn't write a story if he stood on his head, but he could interpret a Harvey Kurtzman story in a way that even Harvey never dreamt he could. And Harvey supplied Willie with very stick-figure storyboards, but then Willie would take hold of them and put a whole new world of life into it.

I remember when Harvey came after me. *Mad* was going to become a magazine, switching from a comic book. He said to me, "I've had my eye on you." I said, "When? Where?" "Oh, when we were in Music & Art together[1]—I was a freshman and you were a senior—I investigated you; I knew all about you. I'd like you to come work for *Mad*."

I said, "I've seen *Mad* [the comic book],[2] and my work in *Patsy Walker* is about a teenage girl—what's that got to do with *Mad*?" "Oh, I know what you can do . . . I just know." I remember saying, at one point, "Willie and I were friends as teenagers, and we had a contest about who could make up the funniest things. Do you want me to be like Willie?" Harvey said, "No, I don't. I want Jaffee." "Well, where is Jaffee? What do you see in Jaffee?" He said, "I know what I've seen, and I'll get it out of you."

Eventually I ended up following Harvey to *Trump* and *Humbug*,[3] and ended up being accepted in Harvey's creation, *Mad*, even though he wasn't there anymore.

P. L.: Let me go back a bit. Editors bring a lot to what they do, if they're good editors, and *Mad* has been blessed with some wonderfully skilled and talented people doing it. But an editor also brings, to some measure, a worldview, politics, sociology, and his or her life. One of the things that is fascinating about *Mad* is the degree to which *Mad* affected the culture, and didn't just mirror the culture, for a long time. I really believe that *Mad* is one of the things that made the '60s possible, and even made the Watergate-era cynicism possible in many ways.

A. J.: Yes.

P. L.: I'd love to trace with you what the worldview of each of these guys was, and how it affected the dynamic of working with each of them, the kind of stories they asked you to do, the kind of humor they were interested in, whether there was a challenge from one to the other. Certainly, they saw themselves as different kinds of people, with different kinds of roles. Al is the one I know least well; we've shaken hands once or twice over the years, but never had a real conversation. Harvey I knew a little bit when he was still well. Nick and John very well, of course, from many years of working with them. Let's start with Harvey. Did Harvey have a consciousness that he was shaping the world, that he was influencing people with what he put in his magazines?

A. J.: I don't think Harvey had visions of grandeur, or breaking new ground or anything like that. I think Harvey had a vision of what he thought would be a funny thing to do. I remember Harvey telling me that when he was a little kid, maybe six years old or so, he made up magazines and distributed them in the neighborhood, just folding paper up and stapling it, putting drawings on each page. He told me once that he dreamed of someday having a magazine and being able to gather in people like me and Willie, and doing special things. We can all say things like that—we all have dreams of glory and stuff like that. But Harvey was a very deep thinker. He had difficulty in front of an audience, making a speech. He even had difficulty relating to talent at times, because his mind was racing, in my view, with so many creative notions going on at the same time that he couldn't convey it. So, he went looking for people that he felt could think his way.

The first thing he said to me was, "Write something for me." I said, "I'm looking on you as an editor—give me an assignment. What am I going to do, write about my children, or what?" "Just write a funny Al Jaffee thing." "Do I have to draw it?" "No, I have enough artists." So, at that time, at the time it was the early days of television, and you watched anything that moved—one of the things that was on was boxing. So I

Fig. 1-1: Paul Levitz. Photo courtesy of Paul Levitz.

wrote a boxing story and brought it to Harvey, and he gave it to Jack Davis and of course Harvey married the two things together. Jack Davis did a magnificent job, showing boxing for what it really was. I saw boxing for what I thought it was—a violent, bloody sport. We weren't trying to knock boxing, but we wanted to show an aspect that was ignored by the general public, which is that it's basically very violent. Later on, I wrote something similar about football, and Jack also did that.

What Harvey saw in me was a writer, and, I think, Al Feldstein also hired me as a writer, which I was for a year and a half at *Mad* because this new medium of poking fun at the underbelly of our institutions was becoming so popular—satire, parody, so on—was so new that even though people like Sid Caesar were doing it on television, there just wasn't enough of it. There were tough times with one war ending, then another starting in Korea, and then another in Vietnam, so there was a hunger for lighter stuff, and there weren't a lot of magazines around doing that. The only light stuff was syndicated comics, and some of the kiddie comics with rabbits and pigs and the like.

Fig. 1-2: Cartoonist Al Jaffee following a discussion panel dedicated to Trump magazine on Sunday, October 9, 2016, at the Jacob K. Javits Convention Center in Manhattan, Day 4 of the 2016 New York Comic Con. © Luigi Novi / Wikimedia Commons. https://commons.wikimedia.org/wiki/File:10.9.16AlJaffeeByLuigiNovi2.jpg.

P. L.: That was harmless stuff, devoid of any real . . .

A. J.: Yes. There was no humorous stuff commenting on the things affecting our daily lives: advertising, politics, false advertising . . . the chicanery of unscrupulous businesspeople and bankers with phony mortgages and loans.

The early *Mad* [under] Harvey Kurtzman wasn't a crusader. The humorous aspect of the satire was really the focus. I remember he did something very funny in the comic version of *Mad*, which was about going to a Chinese restaurant, which Will Elder illustrated. It was a chaotic scene in a Chinese restaurant, with all of Will Elder's funny little flourishes. An exaggerated view of a Chinese restaurant from the point of view of people who had never been to a Chinese restaurant. It wasn't making fun of Chinese restaurants, but making fun of the ignorance of the average person going into a place he didn't know much about. Mostly it was for fun. And then, of course, Harvey in the comic book version of *Mad* made fun of other comics: "Superduperman!" and so on.

P. L.: He took the Tijuana Bible [genre of small-format pornographic comic books], cleaned it up, and pointed out the outrageousness of the basic premises of some of the comics.

A. J.: In retrospect now it looks like such a natural, easy thing to do. But when there's nothing around like that, trying to get it printed . . . . It was easy for Harvey and Willie and me to sit around and regale each other with funny ideas, but then you have to go to a Martin Goodman or a William Gaines and say, "Will you print this?"[4] Getting something like *Mad* going . . . .

I don't know that story too well. Harvey worked for Bill Gaines at EC, as did Al Feldstein. Al was a very prolific writer of the horror stuff; a very good writer and he could knock the stuff out over and over again. Harvey, on the other hand, did war stories and did tons of research to make sure that he had all the details of the military campaign and all that. The balance of income, since comics was always based on piece-work, [was unbalanced]; Feldstein was making a fortune, and Harvey was starving to death. Harvey was so slow, and if he needed research, he'd take a trip and spend the whole day interviewing people. Harvey complained about his lack of income, and Bill, as the story goes, said, "Create a funny magazine and I'll let you do that and you can make more money since you won't have to do the research."

P. L.: Did Harvey have any pronounced politics beyond the typical New York Jewish, left-leaning *mishugas* that so many of us shared automatically?

A. J.: I would have to say that Harvey was quite conservative. He had a conservative moral attitude. As a matter of fact, he took us to a Playboy Club once because of his friendship with Hefner, and one of us made some kind of leering, sexist observation, and Harvey was appalled. He was very straitlaced. In fact, when Hefner invited us to his mansion in Chicago to work on the early phases of *Little Annie Fanny* (I was only there along with Arnold Roth and Russ Heath to get this going, as Hefner was impatient with how slow Harvey and Willie were) . . . while we were living in the mansion, there were also floors of bunnies living in the mansion. The girls were curious; they'd come up to see what kind of artwork we were doing. Just teenage girls who dressed up as bunnies when they went to the club. Harvey became like a Mother Superior. You could almost hear him saying, "Look, but don't touch!" He was so fearful that one of us would get out of hand. We made fun of Harvey, and he red-facedly admitted he was old-fashioned. Harvey was not a wild, crazy guy . . . he was a very serious humorist. He didn't have an axe to grind. He looked at everything from a very conservative and moralistic point of view, which is that if you're going to make fun, even of a product, be fair. He created advertising like "Canadian Clubbed" based on the whiskey ad. His main focus was to pull away the curtain that the advertisement implied—good taste, pleasant company, fun, and all of that—and he would push it towards drunkenness. That's what we're really selling.

And this was a difference between Harvey and Al Feldstein: Feldstein would use expressions like "Let's hit them hard." Harvey felt, "Do it softly. Expose, imply, but don't editorialize." I liked Harvey's approach; I never had any problems working with Al Feldstein either, but that's my personality. I'm a journeyman cartoonist, and the editor's in charge. What the editor wants I have to give him.

P. L.: Tell me about what Feldstein wanted. He comes into *Mad*, and the tone shifts when he arrives fairly quickly. Partly, it feels more structured than Harvey's. You have a flexible feeling with Harvey (partially because it was just the first couple of magazine issues, and he was finding his way). Feldstein fairly quickly says we're going to have departments, we're going to have this parody here, this parody there. We're going to break it up with these three things—a Don Martin kind of single page each third of the way through the magazine so you can have a simple laugh, a rude noise kind of laugh.[5] I don't know if Don Edwing was writing Don [Martin]'s stuff from the beginning, but that's [the] kind of approach that both of them were so good at.[6] It definitely seems like Feldstein was more interested in politics and advertising more quickly. Is that a fair reflection of his worldview, or is it a change in the mix of the people working in the magazine?

A. J.: It is a fair view. I'd only take [it] a little bit more intensely. Harvey's focus was more on the art. Not the drawing. I mean the art of writing, the art of drawing. The focus of the magazine was to get better and better and better. Feldstein's view was more realistic. Publishing the magazine is a business. It does not rely on people coming in and saying,

"I have an idea, but it'll take me three months to do it, can you wait for it?" Harvey would wait for it. Feldstein would say, "Here's what the deadline is. Can you do it? If not I'll get someone else to do it."

The difference between Harvey and Feldstein: Harvey would plead, Feldstein would threaten. Feldstein was an artist, a writer, creative . . . but he was a businessman. Harvey was a writer, an artist, creative, but he was not a businessman. Part of the reason why the venture with *Trump* magazine failed was that Harvey didn't meet the deadlines. Harvey had deadline problems. In fact, on one occasion I was at Harvey's house when the phone rang and he answered. It was Will Elder on the other end. The gist of the conversation was, "But, Willie, if we don't send it to Chicago by Monday morning it'll cost Hefner hundreds of thousands of dollars in delayed print time." Then, a pause. "You need how many more days? Well, of course I want a good job. Okay, do it, and I'll call Hefner and we'll straighten it out." If Feldstein was on the phone he'd say, "If I don't see you tomorrow morning with the job, don't come in again."

Putting a magazine out on time in a new venue became Feldstein's challenge. I don't know if Harvey could have met that challenge or not. I don't want to be unfair to Harvey, but Feldstein—if he knew the whole year's schedule, he'd keep an eye on it, and do what he needed to do to get the magazine out. What Al recognized from the beginning—and I'm not saying Harvey didn't recognize it, but he had a much softer approach—Al recognized that this thing is a script-devouring machine. You need material, you need content. It's a new area; you can't just call someone up and say give me a satirical advertisement. I mean, about what? So what Al started to do was create departments, and then he could assign people to the department. For example, we're going to have a movie takeoff in this issue, and in the next issue it'll be a television takeoff. Mort Drucker will be doing the caricatures; now, who can I marry with Mort Drucker to write the script?[7]

Where my working relationship with him was unique, in the sense that a number of us worked in this unusual fashion, was show and tell. I brought in "Snappy Answers to Stupid Questions," and I had no idea if he would buy it. He started laughing, and said, "This is very funny, but I can't have three cartoons on a page with three snappy answers . . . it doesn't have weight." I said, "What do you want me to do?" "Could you make more than one answer?" "Sure—I could give you three or four or five answers to each one." So he said, "Three answers." And one of us, it might have been him, said, "How about a blank balloon where the reader can write in?" Out of that one meeting came an idea that was fully formed, could be repeated, and took pressure off some future issue instead of needing more material. And eventually, at my suggestion, we made paperback book collections of new material, and they were very successful.

The same thing happened with "The Mad Fold-In." I was casting about, in my suburban home in Babylon, thinking, how am I going to make a living today? Spread the floor full of magazines, and a couple of things popped out at me. One of them was that at least two or three of the magazines had gatefolds, which were popular at the time. The main one was *Playboy*, but there was also *National Geographic* with a map of the skies . . . and I think *Sports Illustrated* had one of a new stadium. Well, what am I going to do? I'm working for *Mad* and I'm inculcated with the *Mad* ethos, so if they go that way, we go this way. [The others] have fold-outs, we have fold-ins.

I quickly made one that was extremely simple, where I had Elizabeth Taylor on one side and some stranger on the other side. When you folded it in, Richard Burton and Eddie Fisher disappeared, and some stranger wound up kissing Elizabeth Taylor. It was just to show she was having a good time. I brought it into Al, and said, "Al, I have an idea. It sort of intrigued me, and I hope it'll intrigue you. But I think you'll reject it because it would mutilate a page in the magazine." I handed it to him, and he said, "I like it!" Harvey Kurtzman might have said, "Well, let me think about this." He'd have to digest it. Feldstein, he was very astute in that way. If he saw something that had possibilities, he had to do something. He ran into Bill Gaines with it, and told Bill it mutilates the magazine. He came back and said that Bill said, "So they'll mutilate the magazine. They'll buy a second copy to save." And we were off and running.

It was a one-shot, and it's my speculation that it would have remained a one-shot if Harvey Kurtzman was editing. Harvey was always looking for something new, something to break new ground. He was not a repeater, which is why things were so slow. Finding new material for a periodical is very difficult. One-shots anyone can do.

Feldstein knew that he had to pile up material, and Harvey wanted something new all the time.

P. L.: Did Feldstein have distinctive targets of choice? I think of the emphasis on the advertising industry as something that really develops during Al's time, and even the socio political stuff. Harvey's *Mad* is about culture and what's going on in the culture. Al's *Mad* begins to be about what's going on in the country.

I have hanging on my wall a page Joe Orlando gave me from when the Post Office was introducing the ZIP Code, and he illustrated a *Mad* piece on what it'll be like when we use numbers for everything. A frighteningly prescient piece. I remember from the era of my childhood, more and more things that were pointing out how the government was being absurd or institutions were being absurd. Was that something in Al's mind that was important to him, or was that simply ripe territory as the culture was changing and it was more acceptable to point out that things weren't working as they were supposed to?

A. J.: In both cases, with Al and Harvey, it was a rebelliousness. You're not rebelling to overthrow the government. You're rebelling to improve the government. We could use a lot of that today too. There are people, for example, today who would like to tear down any kind of good health for the citizenry. They have their insurance and they don't care about anybody else. That would be a tough subject to go after in a *Mad* magazine, because it's too heavy. Unless you found—I could picture myself writing a piece about "Madcare." And then you go after everything relating to sickness and pre-existing conditions and in a realistic but funny light. I could see myself doing this article without any difficulty whatsoever. And that would put it into the arena of politics because the nonsense coming from both sides . . . you can clear it up with a little satire.

P. L.: So how would each of the four editors that *Mad* had react to your coming in with that piece today?

A. J.: From my experience, and this may sound self-aggrandizing, they all know my record. Today, if I came in, it would be something like "Let's see what Jaffee does—we can always reject it." But I think they would know that I wouldn't suggest it unless I felt there was some depth to it. To come in with just one little tidbit and say I can do an article on this . . . a lot of people have come up to *Mad* and said that, and then delivered something that had twenty-two repetitions of that first suggestion. But in the way I would approach it, it has to have legs, it has to expand into more areas than just the hook. The hook is fine, but after you hook, you gotta move on. I think they would be receptive to me, but that's because of my record. I think that's understandable.

P. L.: But would there be a difference? Would one of them react, "I'm so sick of watching the debates?"

A. J.: It's a tough question. It also depends on the mood of the editorial staff at a particular time. If they'd received a hell of a lot of angry mail about an article in a recent issue that had a lot of substance to it, saying, "That's no fun. Why'd you do something about hemorrhoids? We don't want to read that kind of stuff," then they wouldn't be receptive.

I brought something in the other day that I thought was a very good idea, which they could use over and over again. I got a favorable reaction, but they weren't sure they wanted to go that far because it inferred an obscenity. Didn't say it, but inferred it. I thought it was quite funny.

The headline is "*Mad*'s"—then a picture of a donkey and then of a hole in the ground—"of the month."

P. L.: That's not exactly the scariest dirty word you can throw around these days.

A. J.: No, it isn't. But John said, "I don't know if we're ready to go this far." Of course, I had a backside where plunk in the middle would be the politician or whoever. I just got it off my chest; it was a funny idea. The fun part of it is you don't use the actual words. In the mind of the beholder .... I'm not saying it's a great idea.

P. L.: My impression of Nick over the years was that his taste in humor was lighter than what I'm hearing about Feldstein. He seemed to enjoy the joke in the joke, rather than the target being speared. He loved the wordplay of the song parodies. His natural humor wasn't particularly biting or forceful at anything. Particularly when Jenette [Kahn] became involved after Bill Gaines's death, she was really pushing Nick and John to do things that were more political, more adult.[8] They both were reluctant, because they felt they were conserving something that was working, but on [a] gut [level] Nick seemed to enjoy that less.

A. J.: Nick had very strong feelings, and he was also very much on the artists' and writers' side. He didn't like to see us pushed around. And Feldstein had a more explosive personality. If things weren't going very well at home, he could come in and take it out on one of the people—I would have no interest in running Al down, but from my personal observation. I worked well with Al, but part of working well with people, as you well know, is you recognize the personality and you stay away from the stuff that's going to explode and stay with the stuff that's going to work. You sense that, and people who don't sense that are in constant trouble. I knew how to deal with Al and remain friendly with him.

Nick had a social conscience and was quick to anger if he saw something that was not fair. He just reacted very strongly to things when some other editor might have just said, "It's between Feldstein and him. It's not my business; I'm going to go somewhere else." Nick couldn't let it go if it was mistreatment of any of us. He would take it personally; he was really our friend.

P. L.: He always struck me as having a boyish joy in being there; "Ohmigod, I've gotten to spend my life doing this. Isn't this cool?"

A. J.: There is a dreamer in Nick Meglin. He was good at what he did at *Mad*, but his dreams were to write Broadway shows and lyrics for music. He was a very smart young guy—he went to the best school [Stuyvesant High School]. He had to deal with his emotions, which would share somebody else's problem. If you're an editor, you can't really do that. You can have empathy, but you can't become too involved. There are too many people. You were a publisher—if you got involved with everyone's problems . . . .

P. L.: You'd become paralyzed. Once in a while you can step in and help, and that's great, but you can't do it all. When you ask people how it's going, the most frightening thing is they may tell you, and then you may need to step in and do something about it.

A. J.: I'll give you an example of Nick that involved me. For the first year, year and a half, I was just a writer because *Mad* was starving for script and there weren't a lot of people around doing *Mad* kind of stuff. They were doing it in television, on the Sid Caesar show, or Ernie Kovacs. But how do you get those people to work for a dinky little magazine that paid $35 a page? When *Humbug* folded, I had a bunch of scripts, so I took a chance. I thought everyone at *Mad* would despise me, especially Al, who didn't get along with Harvey. I called Al up, and said, "I don't know if you're going to hate me as the enemy, but I have six scripts left over from *Humbug*." He said, "Come on down," and he bought every one of them. And from then on, he said, "Write more scripts." And I kept writing.

The way I write scripts is the way a cartoonist writes a script . . . storyboards. I laid out the pages, bringing them in on newsprint sheets. I remember them—they crumbled after a while. One day I found out that Nick had gone in to Al and said, "Jaffee's scripts come in, I read them, I laugh. They're funny. They're funny with their drawing and everything. Then we hand them to one of our artists, and it doesn't have the funniness that was in the storyboard." He brought [it] to Al's attention, and Al looked it over, and they agreed. So, Al called me in and said, from now on you're going to do your own scripts. That's an example of Nick's empathetic involvement, and also intelligent involvement . . . recognizing that there's a better way to do it. I'm not saying that Al might not have arrived at the same conclusion, but Nick did it.

P. L.: But what you're also saying implicitly is that from Al's point of view what he had was working. You were bringing in good scripts—scripts that an artist could draw because of the way you prepared them. A particular artist who might not have been able to do as good a job working off a script from a, say, Frank Jacobs, who might submit it just as a typed script.[9] Al's thinking: I'm getting a result that hits the mark for *Mad*, and I'm getting it on time, so I don't have to go questing for a better solution.

A. J.: Yes, but in addition to that is the fact that Bill [Gaines] wanted to keep his artists busy. George Woodbridge, so many guys of that period were devoting themselves to *Mad*.[10] Bill was aware that if you didn't feed them scripts, they were going to go elsewhere: *Cracked*, or Stan Lee did *Crazy*, and he's going to lose these people. Feldstein cannot be faulted if he was getting good script material from me and he could hand it over to George Woodbridge; every one of them who got my scripts came to me at some point and said, I love getting your scripts because I don't have to think about layouts. I just get right to work, and it saves me a lot of time. George, Bob Clarke, Jack Rickard all told me that. Al was right to keep me writing scripts . . . artists he didn't need. They were sort of a liability, whereas writers were important.

There was another occasion when Nick came to me. I was working in the art room at the time; I was getting divorced, and I didn't have a studio. Bill invited me to come up and work there. I enjoyed that immensely—I was with the guys for a year or more until I got an apartment. Nick came in, and he was all worked up. Nick and Al didn't get along; I have no idea why.

P. L.: Yet Al kept him there for a lifetime.

A. J.: They didn't see eye to eye. I think it was more on a moral point of view, not a talent point of view. I'm sure Al respected Nick's talent and ability. I have to come back to saying Al was a good editor, a good writer, a good artist, but he was also a good businessman. There are times when you have to put the overall business above one individual's needs. Al kept his eye on the ball, which was to keep *Mad* going. And Nick, I think, felt *Mad* is fine; Bill will keep it going. What we have to deal with is how we treat our people. Treat them decently.

So, he came into me, overwrought. "You have to do something about this, but don't bring me into it. We had a cover discussion, and pulled out some sketches that were done by you, Sergio [Aragonés], others, and decided to go with one that you had suggested."[11] I vaguely recall it had something to do with Fidel Castro and Khrushchev. They were going to take the visual gag, but instead of Castro, they were going to put someone else in there. It was no longer about Cuba, but the Dominican Republic or someplace else. Nick said, "It's your idea, all we've changed is the protagonist—you should get paid for the cover idea." But Al had said we don't have to pay him, we changed it. I don't think Al was trying to cheat me. He felt we springboarded it, and developed it into a different idea, and we don't pay people every time we springboard from it. But Nick said, "We were talking about your sketch. If you don't confront Al, you're a wimp." So, I reluctantly walked in and talked to Al, and he said, "Okay, okay, I'll pay you for it." I'm telling the story from the point of view of Nick's overdeveloped sense of justice and empathy for the talent, and for that I'll always respect and love Nick, because I think he did that for all of us in one way or another. He could easily be labeled as not a company man.

P. L.: For "not a company man," he stayed a long time and made a big difference for the company. None of these guys other than Feldstein ever made big money; it's just been a comfortable job.

A. J.: And for independent contractors, like me. I've worked pretty much exclusively for *Mad* for sixty years. Last week, I was interviewed by ABC Newsmakers and Al-Jazeera America, and their interviews were entirely about *Mad*. I had to make clear to them that I'm not an employee of *Mad*. I'm what used to be called a freelancer, and is now called an independent contractor. Someone said, "What does that mean? You've been with them for sixty years . . . every issue for sixty years."

That's true, but as an independent contractor I didn't have health coverage; I don't get a pension; I'm on my own; that's what an independent contractor is. All the contributors to *Mad* except the editorial staff have that arrangement. That's how the magazine is produced. If *Mad* was a hugely successful financial enterprise, somebody might make a stink about that. Now it's on a survival . . . .

P. L.: The magazine form is undergoing great changes beyond *Mad* as websites take the place of many magazines.

A. J.: That's true of syndicated comic strips, so many aspects of the entertainment business. Entertainment is now on a little cell phone. It's easy to categorize it by saying print is in trouble because print uses up a lot of resources, which the world can't go on . . . .

P. L.: It's also just more awkward to distribute. The Internet is a remarkably easy distribution method.

A. J.: You and I can't even imagine what the handheld devices of twenty-five years from now will do.

From my point of view, it's been a very nice journey. I've gotten what I wanted; I enjoyed the work I did. The fact that the editorial staff, no matter who they were, were receptive to my work . . . .

P. L.: It's also about the fact that you were able to be continually engaged and evolve as an artist. It's a challenge to stay engaged, and to keep up with the changes in the culture, particularly the rate at which our culture has changed in the last couple of decades. That's a great gift, Al.

A. J.: I feel very fortunate. I think they told me that I produced more material for *Mad* than anyone, whether it's writing or artwork. What's really valuable is having an outlet and sympathetic editors who are willing to look at your work.

P. L.: What sort of material do you see John Ficarra looking at that he responds to from a very personal basis? Where does his worldview come in? John seems more like a conservator of what's been, a good manager of the magazine as Feldstein was, without having Feldstein's temper.

A. J.: I think my answer is affected by the generational difference between me and John, whereas there was very little generational difference between me and Al. I don't see the world the same way John sees it, and I haven't attempted to sell things to *Mad* in the last ten to fifteen years other than doing the fold-in. Breaking new ground would be very difficult for me, because I'm not into the world of entertainment or advertising that's directed at the younger audience. If I brought in an ad takeoff about UBS Financial, I can't connect.

In fact, I just got the latest issue, and it's difficult for me to understand the material in it because a lot of it has references to television shows or personalities that I'm not at all in contact with. Even a series about cell phones; I have a cell phone that I never use. I did get an assignment that I had difficulty with: it was about modern Boy Scout badges. It was an idea someone had suggested, and they thought I could write the script and design the badges based on things like "Go Angry Bird Watching." New modern badges. Things like "How to Build a Kindle Fire." I tried to move into other areas, and I failed. . . . I submitted a bunch of stuff and it was my generation.

P. L.: A last question: Bill Gaines. His role was always more on the business side, keeping the enterprise going and protecting it from the influence of the outside world. Clearly, he had a very strong worldview, which you can see in the EC material he worked on closely with Feldstein before *Mad*. Did he serve as any kind of editorial voice? Did you see him influencing what kind of content went in, to match how he wanted the world to be?

A. J.: He didn't have an axe to grind. He didn't push his personal views because he had some very liberal political views and some very conservative political views. He was conflicted in the same way that I think all of us are, except he was influenced to some extent by the fact that he grew up in a different world, in a wealthy home, but had liberal views about economics.

For example, here's an area where I'm conflicted. I regard myself as a liberal, politically liberal. I think food stamps is a fine idea; why not keep it? It certainly doesn't affect anyone negatively. Bill Gaines would approve of food stamps. But at the same time, I worked my ass off all my life, and I don't take my obligations lightly. The only deadline I ever missed I think I had pneumonia or something. I think Bill felt the same way. He came in every day. He was a multi-millionaire; he could have come in for an hour in the afternoon, but he was hands-on. If you had something to discuss, any of us, you had access to Bill. He was loyal to us. The last thing in the world he would accept was someone walking into *Mad* and saying, "I'll work for half the rate." He would say, "Get the hell out of here." He was conflicted in many ways the same way we all are.

I feel I'm working hard every day. I'm 92, and I'm still working hard. I'm not asking for a handout. If somebody is poor and sick, I think it's the obligation of taxpayers to help them out, and I'm willing to pay whatever taxes are needed for that. I would take a little bit from the Pentagon to help people in poverty. Bill and I shared that kind of feeling. We weren't ready to become radicals, activists, and join the 99 percenters or anything like that. But if you were to present a fair increase in taxes, Bill and I would have both accepted that. So, I was always very comfortable with Bill, both in the workplace and socially. We had dinners together; we went to shows together. We weren't overtly friends, but when we had a chance we enjoyed each other's company.

P. L.: He seemed content with how his life worked. He had all his eccentricities about how he managed life, but he built his Rube Goldberg–like arrangements to make life fit what he wanted it to be.

A. J.: Yes. But his biggest problem was his responsibilities. Where I only had one family to be concerned about, Bill regarded everyone at EC Comics and at *Mad* as his other family. How to keep George Woodbridge from going belly up, how to make sure everyone was happy. That was never more evident than when we went on *Mad* trips and personalities clashed. You'd never get Bill taking sides. Bob Clarke was as much his friend and his responsibility as Sid Wortsman, his accountant. One thing about Bill that I liked very much is I think he wanted to be fair. We once went to dinner and he told me his contract was coming up, and he was going to make only one demand: instead of giving me an increase, don't move us out of 485 Madison. Because that was his little family home. I have very warm feelings about Bill. I really think he wanted to take care of his second family as best he could.

* * *

The following interview with Nick Meglin was conducted March 13, 2014.

Paul Levitz: Let's talk about the different *Mad* editors, and how your worldviews affected the material that was published.

Nick Meglin: Harvey wrote about 75 to 80 percent of the stuff, so he didn't have writers to speak of. He had cartoonists, like Al Jaffee and Arnie Roth, who did their own [scripts and art], but Arnie never worked for *Mad*. From day one, Arnie refused to sell his work work-for-hire; like Will Eisner and about four others he maintained that [insistence on owning his own copyrights].

P. L.: So, my driving question for Al was, "You worked for all four of these editors. *Mad* had such an effect on the world, how do you think the worldview of each editor affected what they did at *Mad*?" He had some interesting observations and I thought I would pose the same question to you. Although you didn't work in the same relationship with all of the people, you certainly worked with all of the others, and you have an introspective view of how your own mindset affected your work at *Mad.*

N. M.: That's a mouthful. I'm not sure how to answer.

P. L.: As an example, when Jenette [Kahn] became involved with *Mad,* a lot of the conversations we had in that first six months or year were reflective of her personal worldview and goals: her beliefs about social justice, her desire to have more political content in the magazine came from things that mattered to her for her whole life. She had this new bully pulpit and said, we should be using it to say things about these issues. In that example, if you look back on these guys that you worked with, was it purely a search for what would entertain the reader, which you obviously never lost sight of, or was there a sense of mission? You were on the editorial team through the whole '60s and the Vietnam War: did anyone say, "This is such an awful thing, how do we say something about this, how do we get people angrier about it?" That's the kind of question I'm asking.

N. M.: The biggest problem that you face in trying to gather this is [you're searching] for an overview or a running chord, which I'm telling you now never existed. I think you're reading into it. Let me make an analogy.

When I started writing songs, I wrote many songs, and several years after my divorce, when I looked at all the songs I had written, I thought that if anything ever happened to me, or if anyone sang my songs, and they tried to judge what I was feeling while I wrote the songs, they couldn't be further from the truth. What I feared about people reading into it was [that] I was trying to write about feelings. Songs, like stories, or *Mad* features, are evolving processes.

My first song, which was recorded by Eddie Albert, was called "Hello, Son, I'm Your Dad." It's about a guy who's kind of abandoned his wife and child, and he comes home [years later] and sees a young man wearing a black band, ready to go to a funeral. He has to approach his son, and it's about that moment. That song came about from a line that was 180 degrees different; not a sorrowful feeling, but a joyous feeling. My son was born, and they handed me the child in the hospital, and I said, "Hello, son, I'm your dad." Later on, I thought it was a great line, and that's how the song evolved.

That said, I think 90 percent of what appeared in *Mad* after Harvey left was based on a funny idea coming to [the writer]. How it comes to you is truly a mystery, and hard to draw the dots. The very fact was that Harvey was a very funny man, writer, and artist, and had a great rapport with others like him, like Arnie Roth and Al Jaffee. Harvey just tried to be funny.

Satire creates its own story. There are two worlds writing for *Mad*. One [uses] the funny bone, and the other the clever bone. And the clever bone comes mostly through satire, which means there is a substance to begin with—a subject, an idea that already exists. You do a satire on *The Godfather*, and the humor comes from the subject. You didn't create the movie; you created the satire. But Al Jaffee, when he did something like "Crimestoppers," which was one of my favorites, used that marvelous funny bone.

Al Feldstein, on the other hand, was not a funny writer. Truly in his whole life. It was the biggest mystery to all of us that he was the editor with the least sense of humor there. History bears that out. It's not an opinion. He never wrote a gag. He edited more than rewriting. He never wrote a book, a TV show, an album in his life that was funny. Even *Panic*, when he edited that . . . nobody liked *Panic*. The main thing is that [even then] Jack Mendelsohn wrote more than half.[12] That's how I met *Mad*. If I hadn't sold [ideas] to *Panic*, you'd never have known me.

P. L.: I never realized you freelanced for the company before you were hired as an assistant.

N. M.: That's why I was hired as an "idea man," how they knew I existed. Angelo Torres, George Woodbridge—those guys wanted to go into comics.[13] The other guys were older than I was. I had just graduated Stuyvesant and was going to the School of Visual Arts during the day and college at night. I met Al Williamson first. He was my favorite artist, [although] most people didn't recognize him. Wally Wood was the big hero to the EC fans, Johnny Craig, whatever. Williamson thought I was a very funny guy, and he mentioned that to Feldstein.

So, I started to submit some ideas to *Panic*. Feldstein, as I said, was not funny, so he said, "If you've got any ideas, we'll buy them." So, I wrote the Dick Tracy, the Phantom, the Heart of Juliet Jones [parodies] . . . and the first takeoffs on comic book ads. That was the first time Feldstein did anything like what Harvey was doing. They liked that one a lot.

When I got out of art school, I had gotten out of comics because I saw it was a "pay by the pound" business, and when EC folded, my friends were struggling. It was difficult. I didn't want to get into comics as an

Fig. 1-3: Nick Meglin. Photo courtesy of Nick Meglin.

artist; I just wanted to write. I was a funny kid from Brooklyn. But they bought my ideas, and when they heard I went to art school, offered me a full-time job as *Mad*'s idea man. Then we started to hire writers, which was very different from Harvey's *Mad,* since he wouldn't hire writers unless they were celebrities.

Harvey was funny, trying to be funny. Feldstein was an organizer, an editor gathering stuff that was funny. Because so many different writers were involved, we did very little writing on the inside, and what little we did, I did mostly at the beginning. [Later] many of the articles were based on my ideas, and I never got credit or paid for that, but so what? I needed the security and I wasn't about to freelance. The ideas that we liked came in from different writers with different perspectives. Max Brandel was one of the few who was more politically-minded than humor-minded.[14] He did great stuff, because he had an encyclopedic mind for the graphic images that he juxtaposed together. Some of the more political things we did came from him.

I don't think we carried many protest signs, really. The reading public didn't like it too much when we did. We did a piece with a soldier carrying a huge hypodermic needle when the reports came out about drug addiction during the Vietnam War. We've done things like that, but they weren't the most popular things we did.

[Then] people began moving on, and *Mad* sales began to drop . . . *Mad* humor began appearing on *Saturday Night Live*, in *National Lampoon*. Our biggest competition wasn't the imitation magazines, but timeliness killed us. It took Drucker five or six weeks to do a movie parody, whereas it could be in the Top Ten on the Letterman show that night, or that week on *Saturday Night Live*.

When you go back to the question of where did the ideas come from, and where did the political significance come from, a lot of people read stuff in other humor magazines and [attributed] them to *Mad*, giving us credit for a lot more political savvy than we had. The *Mad* approach was kill them with a setup first, before you hit them in the head with a mallet.

I don't remember many conferences where we were sitting around saying, "We ought to do something about this."

When Jerry DeFuccio left *Mad*, I suggested we get John [Ficarra].[15] He was a much more organized researcher than I was. He became more of an assistant to Bill and Al on the administrative [work], and I stayed just working with the writers and artists. When Feldstein left, Gaines gave us the co-editorship. When we took over the editorship, we said we were only going to use our [individual] veto power five times . . . sparingly . . . and I think John used it once and I think I used it once. But the time I used it was on *Saving Private Ryan* because the Young Turks in our office were saying look at what [George] Carlin says—we're just so namby-pamby. I said that what they did [verbally] went out into the atmosphere and dissipated; when we do something, it sits like a dead fish on a coffee table. It's there to echo and remind us of our bad choices forever. We can't do something in print that isn't funny. For the same reason we chose not to do a satire on *Philadelphia* (1993). What's funny about AIDS when people are dying?

When we discussed cancer, we [focused on] the enemy: the tobacco companies. We did satires of the cigarette ads. The Marlboro satire with the flip-top box. That was where we did our heaviest work . . . they were reprinted by the American Heart Association, the American Cancer Society.

Then there was [also] the sexual revolution, and we couldn't do anything. You know how Paul Coker draws the most delightful fantasy work, nothing suggestive.[16] He did a back cover mermaid thing and in the mermaid gag, one of Duck Edwing's gags, for the breasts in one panel he had a little curve and a dot in one panel. Holy mackerel, the hell that broke loose from that panel. *National Lampoon* was doing one-pagers at the time with photos of naked women with their breasts, and that was fine, and we did two dots and we were taken out of supermarkets. The blandest little gag, that had nothing to do with sex.

P. L.: But you were *Mad*. You were supposed to do the same safe thing we had read since we were kids.

N. M.: So again, there was the sexual revolution. You can look through all those issues, and you're not going to find much about the sexual revolution.

And when we did "Woodstock," the artist was Sergio [Aragonés]. He did 4,000 figures, all doing funny things, and you get away with it. We weren't making huge statements.

When Jenette [Kahn] took over as [president and editor in chief], she had a point of view that she wanted us to do more about black culture. We didn't know what to do, and we couldn't do it. I don't think Jenette ever realized that it would look bad if we pandered, if we weren't doing it right. So, there was a lot more presence of Asians, blacks, and others in the visuals, but I don't think we ever did something [specifically] on it.

Under Feldstein, and continuing under John and myself, it was whatever was funny. The writers came in with the ideas, and we went with what was funny—I don't think any of the writers ever batted more than .500, not even close. We wouldn't have a conference with any writer who came in with less than five ideas, and many times they would leave without anything okayed. So *Mad* was really more a reflection of the writers than the editors.

P. L.: "The Usual Gang of Idiots."

Notes

1. The High School of Music and Art, established by Mayor Fiorello H. La Guardia in 1936 as one of the specialized alternative secondary schools in the New York City public school system.

2. The initial format for *Mad* was a comic book; it changed to magazine format with issue #24 (7/55).

3. Kurtzman's later, short-lived but creatively influential attempts at humor magazines.

4. Martin Goodman was the publisher of the companies that became best known as Marvel Comics (1939–1972). William M. Gaines was the publisher of *Mad* from its inception until his death (1952–1992).

5. Don Martin was billed as "*Mad*'s Maddest Cartoonist" and was a longtime contributor.

6. Don ("Duck") Edwing was a longtime *Mad* contributor, and sometime uncredited writer for cartoonist Don Martin's distinctive contributions to the magazine.

7. Mort Drucker was considered *Mad*'s premier artist for the film and television parodies.

8. Jenette Kahn became president and editor in chief of *Mad* magazine shortly after Gaines's death in 1992, at the same time that Paul Levitz became executive vice president and publisher. They were serving in those roles at DC Comics, which assumed operational control over *Mad* at that time.

9. Frank Jacobs was one of the most prolific writers contributing to *Mad*.

10. George Woodbridge was a longtime cartoonist for *Mad*.

11. Sergio Aragonés contributes *Mad*'s distinctive "marginal" gags, and is particularly noted for his pantomime cartooning.

12. Jack Mendelsohn was a cartoonist who went on to greater fame as an animator and television writer.

13. Angelo Torres was one of *Mad*'s strongest caricaturists, and succeeded Mort Drucker as the primary artist on the movie and television parodies.

14. Max Brandel was a *Mad* writer who often structured his pieces around photographic imagery.

15. Jerry DeFuccio was a longtime *Mad* editorial staffer (1956–1980).

16. Paul Coker was a *Mad* cartoonist with a particularly light, whimsical style.

2. Harvey Kurtzman and Modern American Satire

M. Thomas Inge

FOLLOWING HIS DEATH in February of 1993, a good many fellow comic artists, critics, and commentators stepped forward to testify to the power and importance of Harvey Kurtzman's example and influence on American culture. According to Jay Lynch, "Harvey Kurtzman invented modern American satire," and the humor that followed him "bears the unmistakable imprint of [his] early satiric vision."[1] Art Spiegelman described that vision:

> Kurtzman's *Mad* held a mirror up to American society, exposing the hypocrisies and distortions of mass media with jazzy grace and elegance. He's our first postmodern humorist, laying the groundwork for such contemporary humor and satire as *Saturday Night Live*, *Monty Python*, and *Naked Gun*.[2]

Writing in the *New Yorker*, Adam Gopnik reiterated, "Almost all American satire today follows a formula that Harvey Kurtzman thought up," and Robert Crumb recalled that for him, "*Mad* was a revelation. Nothing I read anywhere else suggested there was any absurdity in the culture; *Mad* was like a shock, breaking you out."[3] Film director Terry Gilliam has confessed that "*Mad* became the Bible for me and my whole generation," and Robert C. Harvey has affirmed that "Kurtzman may be the most influential American cartoonist since Walt Disney."[4] One measure of that influence is the fact that J. Edgar Hoover collected letters of alarm from parents for the FBI files testifying to *Mad*'s subversive threat to society and national security.[5] Robert Harvey would appear to confirm that concern when he wrote:

> Through all the years of *Mad*, Kurtzman's influence on the American public was incalculable. . . . Reading *Mad* breeds a certain cynicism

> about the icons of American popular culture as well as the functioning of its institutions. Who can say whether the Vietnam War protest among American youth was not in some way inspired by the satire in *Mad*? . . . In the closing years of the twentieth century, it would be difficult to imagine an American under the age of fifty-five who does not look at the world a little askance, thanks in large measure to Harvey Kurtzman and his *Mad* legacy.[6]

Is most of this hyperbole, and is any of it true? Would the shape and nature of American humor and popular culture have been the same without the presence of Kurtzman? Would there have been no Lenny Bruce or Woody Allen, no *Laugh-In* or *Saturday Night Live* on television, no Monty Python or Second City among comedy groups, no Robert Crumb or underground comix?

Someone who would not answer in the affirmative is Gerald Nachman, author of *Seriously Funny: The Rebel Comedians of the 1950s and 1960s*, a study of the development of the aggressive brand of cynical stage comedy that developed in the second half of the twentieth century in the United States. With reference to such stand-up comedians as Mort Sahl, Ernie Kovacs, Jonathan Winters, Tom Lehrer, Lenny Bruce, and Woody Allen, among some twenty others, Nachman believes that

> Taken together they made up a faculty of a new school of vigorous, socially aware satire, a dazzling group of voices that reigned roughly from 1953 to 1965, or from Sahl to [Joan] Rivers. . . . It all started with Sahl, whose entire act, demeanor, language, look, and wardrobe warred against almost everything that had come before.[7]

Furthermore, Nachman argues, Sahl represented a new kind of sophisticated "outspoken antiestablishment humor" found nowhere else in American popular culture—"the first signs of opposition to the Cold War conformity."[8] While Nachman cites *Mad* five times in the text as one of "many new satirical forces of the early fifties," he argues that it was this "enormous renaissance of night club comedy" that "changed comedy forever."[9]

Was Kurtzman then merely a minor voice in the groundswell of satirical thrusts at conformity and complacency in the 1950s, or was he a major leader and spearhead in this development? Historically speaking, during the same week in December of 1953 that Sahl stepped onto the stage at the hungry i nightclub in San Francisco, and that Tom Lehrer coincidentally opened at the Blue Angel in New York, *Mad* was already over one year old and was selling 500,000 copies per issue. After only six issues, it was well on its way to becoming the most popular comic book in the country. In terms of strict chronology, however, many comic voices of nonconformity were already at work in the national consciousness. Fred Allen and Henry Morgan, for example, had been broadcasting *Mad*-like satiric thrusts at film and radio since the 1940s, the latter especially acknowledged by Nachman to be a "bitter and acidic . . . iconoclastic radio satirist."[10] Both Morgan and Allen were cited by Kurtzman as sources of inspiration.[11]

Another radio humorist named Stan Freberg initiated the comedy record and album trend in 1951 with his soap opera parody called "John and Marsha" and thereafter took on the larger world of popular culture with a series of biting parodies of such popular songs as "Cry," "The World Is Waiting for the Sunrise," and "The Great Pretender."[12] These parodies accurately recreated the sound of the originals at the same time as they exaggerated and lampooned their romantic excesses and illogic, something that would appeal to Kurtzman's sense of satire.

Beginning in 1950 with his variety television program *Your Show of Shows* (NBC, 1950-1954), Sid Caesar began a brilliant series of parodies of current musicals and "generic lampoons of gangster films, prison epics, westerns, newspaper dramas, spy movies, and other TV shows,"[13] sending up everything from *High Noon*, *Shane*, and *On the Waterfront* to *Cyrano de Bergerac*, *The Bicycle Thief*, and *Grand Illusion*. The foreign film parodies were invested with Caesar's and Carl Reiner's remarkable gifts for "authentic-sounding Italian/German/French/Russian/Japanese gibberish."[14] Kurtzman too would display a special talent for language and the use of words to great comic effect.

In addition to people like Freberg and Caesar, the larger cultural scene was populated at the beginning of the 1950s with any number of influential figures who were questioning and pushing the envelope of the standards of conformity in their conduct and what their work represented: James Dean, Marlon Brando, Marilyn Monroe, Elvis Presley, Jack Kerouac, J. D. Salinger, Mickey Spillane, Walt Kelly, and Charles Schulz is barely a beginning list.

If we step back, however, and look at the larger historic and international scene, taking into account the major intellectual and cultural trends of the first part of the twentieth century, we see that these people were swept up in profound changes in ways to view the universe and our place in it. Since the beginning of the twentieth century, which witnessed two world wars and any number of disturbing developments—the discovery and use of atomic energy in warfare, threats to constitutional democracy, ruthless trends in capitalism, and the continuing presence of racism and sexism among them—the world seemed to have become a shapeless, disoriented, and dispirited place. Despite clear advances in science and medicine since the Enlightenment, this negative spirit was the result of the culmination of a sense of entrapment in nature and time in Western thought.

Four major thinkers outlined the ideas that made a difference. Charles Darwin in his theory of evolution maintained that all forms of life are involved in a biological struggle for reproductive survival in which neither the smartest nor the best make it but only the most adaptable. Karl Marx revealed that in an age of industrialism, the larger society was engaged in an economic struggle between the haves and the have-nots, the capitalists and the working class, which would eventually require a bloody revolution to reconcile the oppressed and the oppressors. Sigmund Freud turned inward to learn that human beings are influenced by neuroses and psychological maladjustments that we repress and fail to understand without intensive therapy. Albert Einstein and his theory of relativity, which indicated that speed and direction exist only in relation to where we stand, destroyed the last margins of consistency and law we thought were at work in nature. Instead, deviation became the norm.

All these ideas were the products of progress, a continual improvement in our efforts to understand ourselves and our environment. But they have also served to deny or limit our free will and suggest that we are no more than random elements at sea in an ocean of uncertainty over which we have no control. Rather than Utopia or a more perfect society, modern science and rationalism have given us the Holocaust and Hiroshima. We have come face to face with our worst fears, and not only is the enemy us (as Walt Kelly's Pogo Possum put it), but we have also demonstrated for the first time in human history the ability to wipe out life on earth as we know it.

According to existentialism, this spiritual and physical alienation, or feeling of discord with the universe, creates in us a sense of the "absurd," which according to one definition "proceeds from a loss of faith in such traditional metaphysical concepts as a rationally-ordered universe directed by a benevolent deity. With this loss of faith in a transcendent power, human beings may come to perceive their lives as meaningless and themselves as helpless in the face of a vast nothingness."[15]

The response of the literary community has been to turn to comedy rather than tragedy, to the liberation of laughter rather than desperate resignation. In drama this led to the Theatre of the Absurd, the works of Eugene Ionesco, Samuel Beckett, Jean Genet, Harold Pinter, and Edward Albee, among others, who produced unconventional, disturbing plays that reflected a loss of faith, a sense of despair, and incomprehension at the lack of cohesion and meaning in the universe.[16] Yet these are outrageously comic plays, often making fun of rational discourse, consistency and meaning in language, and belief in human communication. Clowns and caricatures rather than tragic figures debate the existence of God and the relativity of moral values. The ancient arts of mime and irony replace dramatic exposition, and fools reign with nonsense speech rather than carefully crafted dialogue. The major figures of influence are Charlie Chaplin, Buster Keaton, W. C. Fields, the Marx Brothers, and the Three Stooges rather than Shakespeare, Ibsen, Strindberg, or Eugene O'Neill. By the time the first issue of *Mad* appeared, three cornerstone works in the drama of the Absurd—Genet's *The Maids* (1947), Ionesco's *The Bald Soprano* (1950), and Beckett's *Waiting for Godot* (1952)—had been performed in Paris and initiated free-form trends in drama that would last the rest of the century.

Fiction writers too responded in kind to the forces of absurdity and a loss of faith in the moral structure of the universe. While some would trace its roots back as far as Rabelais, Cervantes, Voltaire, Swift, and Mark Twain, it is the postwar fiction of writers like Vladimir Nabokov, John Barth, J. P. Donleavy, Joseph Heller, Kurt Vonnegut, Jr., and Thomas Pynchon that would constitute what Bruce Jay Friedman would label, in a 1965 retrospective anthology, *Black Humor*, where he confessed:

> I am not sure of very much and I think it is true of writers in this volume that they are not sure of very much either. They have some pretty strong notions, however, and one of mine is that the work under discussion, if not black, is some fairly dark hue.... They might all begin to cry, although I don't think so, for if there is despair in this work, it is a tough, resilient brand and might very well end up in a Faulknerian horselaugh.[17]

This "one-foot-in-the-asylum style of fiction," as Bruce Jay Friedman termed it,[18] breaks the conventions of traditional storytelling and trades chronology for stream of-consciousness, symbolism for dream imagery, character for caricature, and rational structure for magic realism. Most importantly, however, the most common characteristic is that they work through humor to take the outrageous nature of things to a new extreme of the bizarre, and to release their frustrations and ours through the saving grace of laughter. This can even take us up to the edge of the ultimate holocaust as Kurt Vonnegut does in *Cat's Cradle* (1963), at the end of which he thumbs his nose in the face of God as life ceases to exist on earth. One is hard put to find a more disturbing comic critique of what modern science, technology, and tradition have brought the modern world than Vonnegut's apocalyptic vision.

What all of this suggests is that Harvey Kurtzman was indeed a part of a much larger cultural and ideological shift that questioned all the traditions and institutions of the past, found them morally and spiritually empty at best, if not downright dangerous and destructive at worst, but rather than turn this disillusionment into despair, revealed the hypocrisy of it all through biting satire and acerbic parody. Marshall McLuhan saw the direct line of descent from these developments to Kurtzman more clearly than most. As he noted in *Understanding Media*, "Relativity theory in 1905 announced the dissolution of uniform Newtonian space as an illusion of fiction, however useful. Einstein announced the doom of continuous or 'rational' space, and the way was made clear for Picasso and the Marx Brothers and *Mad*."[19]

In a sense, antiestablishment humor was the order of the day rather than the exception in post–World War II comedy. The complacent conformity of Cold War culture was a superficial matter created and controlled by reactionary forces, but plenty of idealistic Don Quixotes were willing to take on the sham windmills with their laugh-provoking lances. Mort Sahl and Harvey Kurtzman were among them, but by the time Sahl gained a podium in a comedy club in San Francisco, Kurtzman was already reaching thousands of young readers through his comic books.

While Sahl seems not to have acknowledged any awareness of *Mad*, there are known connections between Kurtzman and other humorists of the time. After he left *Mad*, Kurtzman created for publisher James

Warren in 1960 a magazine called *Help!*, where he resurrected much of the comic *esprit de corps* that had reigned at *Mad*. Here he employed a young would-be cartoonist named Terry Gilliam and introduced him to John Cleese, a fortuitous pairing that would eventually lead to the creation of the Monty Python group, a major force in British comedy. When Gilliam made his classic film *Brazil*, in tribute to his former employers, he named two characters Mr. Warrenn and Mr. Kurtzmann, each with an extra *n*.[20]

During the run of *Help!*, Kurtzman would draw for his pages on the talents of Woody Allen, Jonathan Winters, Sid Caesar, and Ernie Kovacs, all a part of the renaissance described by Gerald Nachman in his book. It would be difficult to believe that any of the contemporary comedians were unaware of *Mad*. Dick Smothers once told me, however, that he and his brother Tom read *Mad* from time to time but did not see it as an influence on their act as the Smothers Brothers.

Occasionally evidence of a direct influence would occur. For example, several of the words Kurtzman created or popularized in the pages of *Mad*, often borrowings from Yiddish, gained currency in general speech and usage, as demonstrated in the second line of one of Allan Sherman's popular parodies of the 1960s: "Catskill ladies sing this song, / Hoo-hah, hoo-hah."[21] "HOOHAH!" was, of course, the title of the first story in the first issue of *Mad* (Kurtzman and Davis 10-11/52: 1-8), and the exclamation would frequently reappear in a variety of contexts in later issues. One suspects that Tom Lehrer's song "The Old Dope Peddler" (1953) was partially influenced by the story "Flob Was a Slob!" in issue #4 of *Mad* (Kurtzman and Davis 4-5/53: 1-7), where dope dealers sell reefers to children on the public-school street corner. A similar influence may exist as well on one of Lenny Bruce's best-known routines, "Thank You Mask Man"[22] (performed at least from 1963, released on vinyl in 1972, and made into an animated film in 1971, five years after Bruce's death, by John Magnuson and Jeff Hale). In "Lone Stranger!" in issue #3 of *Mad* (Kurtzman and Davis 2-3/53: 1-7), the Lone Stranger is mistaken for an outlaw because he wears a mask, escapes before he can be thanked for his good deeds by the grateful community, and appears to have homosexual tendencies—all central points of humor in Bruce's routine.

While the spirit of Kurtzman's style of subversive comedy is clear in the work of the underground cartoonists of the 1960s, his encouragement of their work is even more direct. While at *Help!* he featured and promoted many of the major talents in that movement, including Robert Crumb, Jay Lynch, Spain Rodriguez, Gilbert Shelton, and Skip Williamson, giving most of them their first national exposure in print. For Crumb, as noted earlier, reading *Mad* was a revelation with regard to the absurdity of modern life and society, so working for Kurtzman was a special event.

While the larger population of the United States may have been influenced by the cynical comedy of Sahl, Bruce, Allen, and company, for many young readers of the time, it was Kurtzman who passed on the virus. Thus, he stands as a major critical figure in the lives of readers of my generation in a way that the more distant stand-up comedians did not, performing their monologues for small nightclub audiences and occasionally making an appearance on the *Tonight Show* or a television variety program. We can be a bit more specific, in fact, about the importance of his example in our developing sensibilities.

Even before *Mad*, Kurtzman had achieved an enviable reputation among comic book artists and writers for the excellence of his work at EC comics, a firm that had been producing since 1950 what have been considered some of the best written and drawn stories in comic book history. He was especially noted for the careful research and meticulous detail of his work, as represented by the editing and writing that went into the *Two-Fisted Tales* (1950–1955) and *Frontline Combat* (1951–1954) titles. Disturbed by the lies and the ultra-patriotism he saw in the other war comic books at the time, just as the Korean conflict was underway, he set out to deglamorize combat by showing it to be grim, debasing, and dehumanizing. Without taking sides, he demonstrated in stark tales of conflict that war involves human beings killing each other, people who have families and friends and stories to tell but which are muted by the abstract forces of politics and nationalism. Already there was a subliminal message here that would feed into the anti-war sentiments of the 1960s and the peace movements that would be led by the same young readers after entering college.

While EC specialized in producing stories about horror, crime, and science fiction, and in an earlier incarnation western tales, they had no humor titles. To increase his income, which depended on productivity, Kurtzman created a new title to edit that would require no research and allow his distinct sense of humor to have free play. "The format,"

Kurtzman decided initially, "would make fun of comic books as they were at that particular period. So I had a 'horror' story and a 'science fiction' story and so forth."[23] All EC titles had the same physical format of four stories with some text in the center pages; thus, the first issue of *Mad* contained parodies, respectively, of a terror, science fiction, crime, and western tale, each drawn by one of the accomplished veteran artists on the staff: Jack Davis, Wally Wood, Bill Elder, and John Severin. Kurtzman himself wrote all the stories, did the initial pencil layouts, edited the finished pages, and drew the cover, probably one of the most frequently reproduced and imitated covers in comic book history, outside *Action* #1 introducing Superman. Running titles informed the reader that these were "Tales Calculated to Drive You MAD" with "Humor in a Jugular Vein." All four of the stories were generic satires parodying the conventions and traditional clichés of most stories of their type, including a haunted house visited by a naïve, unsuspecting couple; machines of the future which have taken over man's intelligence and physical strength; fumbling criminals who fail through ineptitude and save the police the trouble of capturing them; and the strong, silent gunslinger who comes to town in the Old West bent on revenge to confront a rowdy crowd of outlaws in a saloon. Basically, Kurtzman identified the fictional formulas that existed then and would persist far beyond him, as demonstrated in later films of the same genres, such as *The Rocky Horror Picture Show* (1975), *Terminator* (1984), *Small Time Crooks* (2000), and *Shane* (1953), each in its own way also a parody of its genre.

Already Kurtzman is employing in these stories what would become a staple of later issues of *Mad*, a comic kind of intertextuality or self-referentiality. For example, a "disposable prefabricated robot woman" in the science fiction story "Blobs!" (this was six years before the release of the science fiction camp classic film *The Blob* [1958]), is modeled after Marilyn Monroe (Kurtzman and Wood #1, 10-11/52: 1-7; 2). In the western parody "Varmint!," a wanted poster in the background features "Gay Bill Ness," an anagram for Bill Gaines, the publisher of the EC line (the word *gay* had different connotations then), and in the last panel a shipping box is stamped "Stanlee Co. War Surplus and Junk Dealer Inc" (Kurtzman and Severin #1, 10-11/52: 1-7; 3 [note panel 4], 7). Kurtzman had been working for Stan Lee at Timely (later known as Marvel) Comics prior to joining Gaines's staff. The faces of actual staff members appear in several panels of "Varmint!," and in at least two stories onomatopoeic words are allowed to escape the confines of the panels and borders and thus break up conventional comic book structure.

As clever and as telling as these stories are, this kind of satire quickly reached its limits, and Kurtzman had to make his approach more target specific. He soon realized, as he said later:

> Satire and parody work best when what you're talking about is accurately targeted; or, to put it another way, satire and parody work only when you reveal a fundamental flaw or untruth in your subject. Just as there was a treatment of reality in the war books, there was a treatment of reality running through *Mad*; the satirist/parodist tries not just to entertain his audience but to remind it of what the real world is like.[24]

In the following issues, therefore, Kurtzman would broaden the subject matter into film, sports, radio, television, comic strips, and literature, with attention to specific popular titles and figures: characters like Superman, the Lone Ranger, the Black Hawks, and Terry and the Pirates; radio and television shows like *Dragnet, The Shadow, King of the Royal Mounties, Inner Sanctum*, and *Mr. Keen, Tracer of Lost Persons*; figures from folklore and film like Robin Hood, King Kong, and vampires; a piece of popular literature, "Casey at the Bat"; and two stories about a character that crosses all these genres, Tarzan, renamed "Melvin," Kurtzman's favorite comic name of the moment.

Kurtzman would continue to pursue his "take-no-hostages" satire in this manner through another seventeen issues of *Mad*. With issue #24 (6/55), *Mad* became a bi-monthly, black-and-white magazine, which Kurtzman would edit through another five issues, until Albert Feldstein took over for the next twenty-eight years. It was on the border of the cover of #24 that Kurtzman placed a figure that would last the entire history of the magazine and continue his legacy without his presence: *Mad*'s adopted official mascot Alfred E. Neuman, the "What? Me Worry?" kid.

But to understand the nature of Kurtzman's influence as a humorist, it will be useful to analyze specifically one story that startled us all as young readers and lovers of comic books in 1953, the lead story in issue #4, "Superduperman!" (Kurtzman and Wood #4, 4-5/53: 1–8). It was one thing to be poking fun at popular genres of fiction, film, the media, and even comic book characters and the types of stories in the EC titles, most of which had been done with a sense of comic exaggeration in the originals anyway. No one ever took the Crypt Keeper or the Old Witch who introduced the EC horror titles seriously, nor did we view the Lone Ranger, Tarzan, or King Kong as anything but one-dimensional characters whose main attractions were formulaic. Superman, however, was the reigning comic book superhero, followed and admired by thousands of comic book readers, many more fanatic and devoted than even the EC readers, who were probably on average more intellectually inclined than the superhero crowd.

To buy into the superhero genre was to practice a suspension of disbelief, to be willing to accept certain conventions without questioning their reality or common sense. For example, why was it necessary to don a costume and concealed identity to fight crime, especially with a cumbersome cape and tights more suitable to ballet dancers or a Robin Hood film? How could one realistically step into a phone booth, given its limited space, and change one's clothes entirely, and where do the original clothes go? Given a secret power like x-ray vision—and this would occur only to a male adolescent mind—why not use it to spy into bedrooms and beneath women's clothing to satisfy the male curiosity about the female form? And how could someone like Clark Kent merely wear a pair of glasses and not be recognized as Superman by Lois Lane, even though young people then tended to believe that glasses made them appear odd and unattractive? (see fig. 21-1).

Kurtzman's stroke of genius was to puncture these conventions by showing them to be as absurd and illogical as they were. Thus Clark Bent leaps into a phone booth, only to find it occupied by a startled woman, or in another booth he not only changes his clothes but takes the time to brush his teeth and wash his feet, while a line of phone customers waits outside, where his old clothes accumulate. Only the inside of Snoopy's doghouse would offer more space. He uses his x-ray vision to spy on the ladies in the powder room across the hall, and Lois Pain not only fails to recognize that Clark Bent and Superduperman are one and the same, she doesn't care, because they both are "creeps," and "Once a creep, always a creep" (8), in the final words of the story (see fig. 21-3).

What was even more surprising was the appearance in the story of the other most popular superhero of the 1940s, Captain Marvel from the then-defunct Fawcett comic book line, here called "Captain

Marbles." Unlike Superman, who tended to take himself a bit seriously and seldom showed any sense of humor, Captain Marvel as drawn by C. C. Beck was a parodic representation of all the flying superheroes of the time. His stories were drawn in a style closer to cartoons and caricatures, and his villains were intelligent worms, powerful Nazis, and evil scientists with little semblance to reality. The parody was too close for comfort, however, and the owners of *Superman*, DC Comics, began a lawsuit to claim that *Captain Marvel* was a copyright infringement. While the style and character of Captain Marvel made him quite different from Superman, the case was pursued so relentlessly that Fawcett finally gave up comic book publishing altogether in 1953 and granted ownership of the character to DC.

Those readers who preferred Captain Marvel never really forgave DC for taking away their superhero and secretly longed to see the two characters meet so that Captain Marvel could beat the devil out of Superman. Kurtzman granted his readers exactly that wish. Since they were both invincible, neither could win. The battle is concluded when the Captain accidentally hits himself and Superduperman announces, "Captain Marbles has been destroyed by the only force as strong as he . . . he!" (7). This reflects the outcome of the real trial, of course, and throughout the battle, the Captain spends his time counting his money, a dig at the fact that the *Captain Marvel* titles outsold the DC titles for a period of time before the lawsuit, and probably was the real reason for it anyway.

Numerous other references to comic book history and elements of self-reflexivity enrich the story: the artist, Wally Wood, advertises his services on a wall poster in the initial panel, and items of EC gossip and office contention appear as graffiti on walls in the second page: "Al [Feldstein] loves words," and "Bill [Gaines] loves EC," but "Harvey [Kurtzman] loves Harvey." The entire story requires that the reader be informed not only about the EC firm and its comic book titles but also about a large part of recent comic book history as well. Reading *Mad* made the reader feel a part of a special group, a select society, if one recognized the targets of the humor and the parodic references. This is one reason why Kurtzman is remembered as such a powerful influence on the perceptions of readers. He opened their eyes to the absurdities and inadequacies of their own childhood culture and did it in a way that made them feel smarter, if not superior. One needs to know a lot to read *Mad* informatively, and it confirms one's sense of intelligence. Art Spiegelman, whose entire career as a cartoonist and graphic novelist was inspired by his early encounter with Kurtzman's *Mad* comic books, noted, "The message *Mad* had in general is 'The media is lying to you, and we are part of the media . . . It was basically . . . Think for yourselves, kids.'"[25]

Stand-up comedians like Mort Sahl, Lenny Bruce, or Woody Allen took on the larger oppressive forces of American society—the military-industrial complex, religious and educational institutions, international relations, racism and sexism as social practices, or the effects of technology on the emotional and psychological states of ordinary people. To a 16-year-old, these were adult concerns, and while the performers' comic efforts to cast a critical light on them were no doubt effective, Kurtzman hit closer to home. Comic books were our special province, and while moral guardians and political leaders wanted to take them away from us, Kurtzman gave them back in ways we would not forget. He made them a part of our intellectual development and imparted a satiric sense of justice and reality that would not allow us to accept the truisms of the world without questioning them and their validity for us and for society.

As comic book writer and novelist Alan Moore would put it, "The . . . Kurtzman stories . . . brandished satire like a monkey-wrench: a wrench to throw amongst pop culture's gears or else employed to wrench all our perceptions just a quarter-twist towards the left, no icon left unturned":

> King Kong and Tarzan, Sherlock Holmes and Superman were rendered naked and absurd by the device of draping them with realistic failings and then setting them against a gross yet realistic world where Wonder Woman marries her romantic interest and ends up shackled to a stove, hemmed in by hyperactive kids. Where all the slapstick violence Maggie dishes out to Jiggs results in ugly bruises, blood-stained collars, and the bleak depressions of a battered spouse.[26]

In other words, we could never read comic books in quite the same way again. But the message came not from some external authority or institution, but from the world of comic books itself and from one of the most admired practitioners of comic art. Kurtzman's *Mad* constituted a major self-referential statement on the powers and limitations of all comic books, rendered in the form itself, some forty years before Scott McCloud's *Understanding Comics* (1993). As political cartoonist Ted Rall has noted, the willingness of *Mad* to satirize the comics "with the same gleeful malice that it unleashes on TV, movies, and other forms of pop culture fully validates its credentials as a publication that takes no prisoners and worships no sacred cows—the very ethic that has made it essential reading for more than half a century."[27]

All the humorists and stand-up comedians of the 1950s were a part of the liberation movement away from conformity and apathy, but Kurtzman said that even the pleasures and playthings of childhood were powerful instruments of indoctrination and needed to be read with a careful eye to their political and ideological agendas. Readers were being prepared for dealing with the rest of the century and all its surprises, horrors, deceptions, and successes, and no art can serve a higher purpose than making us better people. What, me worry? You bet!

A Harvey Kurtzman Chronology

1924: Harvey Kurtzman is born in the Bronx on October 3, second son of David and Edith Kurtzman, Jewish immigrants.

1937: Attends New York's High School of Music and Art and graduates in 1939.

1939: Attends Cooper Union night school.

1940: Publishes his first cartoon in the April issue of *Tip-Top Comics*.

1943: Draws various features for comics magazines. Joins the U.S. Army.

1945: While serving in the Army, draws cartoons for *Yank, the Army Weekly* and for various domestic publications.

1946: Begins a single-page feature for Stan Lee and Timely Comics, *Hey, Look!*, which will run through 1949.

1949: Draws a VD [venereal disease] prevention comic book, *Lucky Fights It Through*, for EC Comics.

1950: Begins working regularly for EC Comics by producing *Two-Fisted Tales* and creating a variety of stories for other EC titles. Continues as a freelancer to work for other comics periodicals and to illustrate children's books throughout his career.

1951: Creates *Frontline Combat* and produces many stories for both war titles.

1952: Creates a new humor title for EC, *Mad,* which Kurtzman would largely write, draw, and edit through 1955.

1955: The *Mad* comic book is redesigned as a magazine with issue 24 in August. A disagreement with the publisher, William Gaines, leads to Kurtzman's resignation in late 1955. Issue 28 contains his last work.

1957: Creates, writes, and edits two new humor magazines: *Trump,* funded by Hugh Hefner of *Playboy* but cancelled after two issues; and *Humbug,* which would continue through 1958.

1959: Writes and draws an original paperback book, *Harvey Kurtzman's Jungle Book,* for Ballantine Books.

1960: Creates, writes, and edits *Help!* magazine for Warren Publications.

1962: Begins writing and laying out a feature for *Playboy, Little Annie Fanny,* with art by Will Elder and others. It debuts in the October issue and will run through 1988.

1965: The last issue of *Help!* is published in September.

1973: Begins teaching classes in cartooning at the School of Visual Arts in New York.

1988: Publishes his autobiography, *My Life as a Cartoonist,* with Pocket Books. The comic book Harvey Awards are begun in his honor.

1990: Produces *Harvey Kurtzman's Strange Adventures* for Marvel Comics.

1991: *From Aargh! to Zap!: Harvey Kurtzman's Visual History of the Comics* is issued by Byron Preiss.

1993: Kurtzman dies on February 21 in Mount Vernon, New York.

Further Reading on Harvey Kurtzman and *Mad*

Benson, John, ed. *The Sincerest Form of Parody: The Best 1950s* Mad*-Inspired Satirical Comics.*

Bray, Glenn. *The Illustrated Harvey Kurtzman Index.*

Dean, Michael, ed. *The Comics Journal Library Volume Eight: The EC Artists.*

Duncan, Randy, and Matthew J. Smith, eds. *Icons of the American Comic Book.* 2 vols.

Groth, Gary, and Kim Thompson, eds. *The Comics Journal Library Volume Seven: Harvey Kurtzman.*

Harvey Kurtzman: Retrospective of a MAD Genius.

Inside Mad.
MAD Cover to Cover: 48 Years, 6 Months, & 3 Days of Mad Magazine Covers.
Kurtzman, Harvey. "The Face Is Familiar. Have We Met?"
Levin, Bob. *The Pirates and the Mouse: Disney's War Against the Counterculture.*
Neal, Jim, and Don Thompson. "Harvey Kurtzman Dies, Creator of '*Mad.*'"
Schelly, Bill. *American Comic Book Chronicles: The 1950s.*
——. *Harvey Kurtzman: The Man Who Created* Mad *and Revolutionized Humor in America. A Biography.*
Spiegelman, Art. "H. K. (R.I.P.)."
Tong, Ng Suat. "EC Comics and the Chimera of Memory."
Totally Mad*: 60 Years of Humor, Satire, Stupidity and Stupidity*. Edited by John Ficarra.

Collected Works

Front-Line Combat. (The EC Archives).
Humbug.
Kurtzman, Harvey. *The Grasshopper and the Ant.*
——. *Harvey Kurtzman's Jungle Book.*
——. *Harvey Kurtzman's Strange Adventures.*
——. *Hey Look!*
Kurtzman, Harvey, with Michael J. Barrier. *From Aargh! To Zap! Harvey Kurtzman's Visual History of the Comics.*
Kurtzman, Harvey, and Will Elder. *Goodman Beaver.*
——. *Playboy's Little Annie Fanny.*
——. *Playboy's Little Annie Fanny: 1962–1970, 1970–1988.*
Kurtzman, Harvey, and Howard Zimmerman. *My Life as a Cartoonist.*
The Mad Archives. 4 vols.
Trump.
Two-Fisted Tales (The EC Archives).

Notes

1. Quoted in "Harvey Kurtzman Tribute," 4.

2. Quoted in Denis Kitchen and Paul Buhle, *The Art of Harvey Kurtzman: The Mad Genius of Comics*, xiii.

3. Adam Gopnik, "Postscript: Kurtzman's Mad World," 75; Crumb quoted in Peter Carlson, "What, Me 50? *Mad*'s Half-Century of Poking Society in the Eye," C2.

4. Ian Christie, ed. and Terry Gilliam, *Gilliam on Gilliam*, 20; Robert C. Harvey, "News & Notes," 64–71.

5. Carlson, "What, Me 50?," C2.

6. Harvey, "News & Notes," 65.

7. Gerald Nachman, *Seriously Funny: The Rebel Comedians of the 1950s and 1960s*, 6.

8. Nachman, *Seriously Funny*, 10.

9. Nachman, *Seriously Funny*, 126, 68, 41.

10. Nachman, *Seriously Funny*, 61.
11. "Harvey Kurtzman Tribute," 12.
12. Nachman, *Seriously Funny*, 185.
13. Nachman, *Seriously Funny*, 102.
14. Nachman, *Seriously Funny*, 102.
15. Edwin J. Barton and Glenda A. Hudson, *A Contemporary Guide to Literary Terms*, 3.
16. See, for example, *Absurd Drama*, four plays by Eugene Ionesco, Arthur Adamov, Fernando Arabel, and Edward Albee, introduction by Martin Esslin.
17. Bruce Jay Friedman, ed., *Black Humor*, vii.
18. Friedman, *Black Humor*, ix.
19. Marshall McLuhan, *Understanding Media: The Extensions of Man*, 163.
20. Christie, ed. and Gilliam, *Gilliam on Gilliam*, 22.
21. Quoted in Nachman, *Seriously Funny*, 20.
22. Bruce's March 1963 performance of "Thank You Mask Man," 7:48 minutes as recorded at Off Broadway in San Francisco in March 1963, appears (mistakenly corrected) as "Thank You Masked Man" on the 1972 Fantasy F-7017 vinyl LP of the same name.
23. Quoted in "Harvey Kurtzman Tribute," 11.
24. Quoted in "Harvey Kurtzman Tribute," 12.
25. "Intersections: Of 'Maus' and Spiegelman: 'Mad' Inspired Comic Book Look at the Holocaust," narrated by Susan Stamberg.
26. "Harvey Kurtzman Tribute," 10–11.
27. Ted Rall, introduction to *Mad About Comic Strips*.

3. Al Feldstein and *Mad*'s Humor of Social Critique

Margaret Cavin Hambrick

I wanted to explore the natural beauty of the area while planning to attend the Visual Communication Association Conference in Billings, Montana, July 13–16, 2000, so I researched and discovered a place to stay called Deer Haven Ranch, which advertised a converted barn on the Yellowstone River and boasted kayak and bicycle rides as ways to explore. Excited, I called and reserved the place. When I arrived at the property, there were dogs, horses, and, yes, llamas to greet me, along with the owner, who identified herself as Michelle and met me with champagne and a basket of fruit, cheese, and bread. I immediately noticed oil paintings on the walls of cowboys and Native American women in various poses and situations. I am no art expert, but the faces looked vaguely familiar.

Later, while talking to colleagues at the conference, I explained where I was staying and described the intriguing and familiar oil paintings on the walls. One individual exclaimed, "I wonder if you are staying at Al Feldstein's ranch? He lives somewhere in the area." I asked who Al Feldstein was and was told, "He was the editor of *Mad* magazine in its heyday. He is responsible for the 'Gap-Toothed Kid' being the magazine's mascot, as well as becoming one of the richest editors in American history and making *Mad* the largest selling humor magazine. *Mad* magazine is a pop culture icon in large part because Al Feldstein was brilliant at commercializing talent."

The next day I decided to take a kayak ride on the Yellowstone River. Michelle dropped me off and said she or her husband would retrieve me after my adventure. Once I returned, there was a distinguished but weathered looking man wearing boots and a cowboy hat waiting for me. He introduced himself as Al. This began another sort of adventure that involved interviewing one of the most interesting and relevant editors in American history. I first interviewed him in his art studio that was attached to his home on the ranch. Its windows overlooked the mountains beyond, and every wall was covered with Feldstein's oil paintings of cowboys, ranchers, landscapes, and wildlife of Montana, as well as current work he was commissioned to paint for *EC Revisited* and Chesley Bonestell-influenced original science fiction art. Feldstein then took me on a tour of his beloved ranch, and we walked the property together, feeding and interacting with the animals. Feldstein explained that the ranch was home to almost two hundred animals, including horses, goats, sheep, alpacas, llamas, cats, and dogs. All of them were special-needs animals that Feldstein and Michelle cared for, producing an expense paid for in part by renting the converted barn to visitors.

At the conclusion of my interview on Saturday, July 15, 2000, Feldstein invited me to shadow him with a press pass at the Comic-Con Convention in San Diego, July 20–23. The year 2000 would be an important year for the convention, because it was the fiftieth anniversary of the beginning of the EC New Trend comics. All the EC gang were invited as guests of honor. I eagerly accepted and continued my interview with him there as well as attending the sessions where he was invited to speak. The most special event that I attended at the convention was The Great EC Reunion Dinner, with all the Usual Gang present. In what follows, I use a hybrid approach, focusing on my interviews with Al Feldstein, as well as articles and books written about Feldstein and *Mad*, but also using the theoretical lens of the tragic and comic frames to argue that Feldstein's insistence on the use of satire to educate, empower, and entertain his audience was what made *Mad* such an influential publication in one of our nation's most turbulent times.

Al Feldstein: "The Soul of *Mad*" (Weber)

When Al Feldstein was hired by Bill Gaines in February 1948 to "package a teenage comic" titled *Going Steady with Peggy* for EC Comics, he was only twenty-three years old.[1] This project led Feldstein to develop horror comics, which were his idea as developed in *Tales from the Crypt*, and then science fiction comics, which were Gaines's idea, for such titles as *Weird Science* and *Weird Fantasy*. By the time Feldstein retired from working for Gaines as editor of *Mad* Magazine after almost thirty years, at age fifty-nine, he had edited and written more than five hundred scripts for

EC Comics (more than anyone else), drawn thirty-one stories, and created more than seventy-four covers for EC. At one point, he was editing seven EC titles. Under his direction as editor, *Mad* grew to be one of the most popular humor magazines of the twentieth century, with Feldstein becoming one of the highest paid magazine editors in the world.[2]

Feldstein explained to me that he was hired because "Bill liked my work; I did rather nubile girls [laughter], teenage girls, not like Archie's girls, but more like Marilyn Monroe girls."[3] Feldstein, along with other artists, participated in objectifying women in this way; however, as Joseph W. Slade and Ann M. Ciasullo have shown, *Mad* went deeper to examine the more complex, ambiguous, and sophisticated aspects of sex, gender, and power. The idea was to appeal to the adolescent male readers who had raging libidos, Slade observes, but it also led readers to have a "shared sense of knowing" that allowed them to laugh at themselves.[4] In addition, as Ciasullo points out, "the extent to which *Mad* engaged with contemporary discourses on gender inequality and the politics of the Women's Liberation Movement is actually quite striking."[5]

In the beginning, Feldstein was paid to contribute his artwork for the comic books. However, Gaines and Feldstein soon realized they worked well together as a writing team, and they began to create the stories for the comics as well. Feldstein was visionary from the beginning. He explained, "I used to ask Bill, 'Why do we follow these guys? Why don't we innovate? It's the innovator that survives."[6] He was referring to the tradition in comics where one person would develop a new story or character and then many others would follow with copies, which would crowd the industry. He further stated:

> I started telling him about when I was young and I used to sneak downstairs when my brother was listening to the radio, not television, "The Witches Tale" used to scare the hell out of me, and I loved *Frankenstein*, the movie, and *Dracula*. I said, Why don't we put these to the comics? Why don't we scare the hell out of these kids? They'll love it 'cause kids love to get scared, and that's how we started the horror comics, as innovators.[7]

Feldstein's recollection suggests his involvement with Gaines in the creation of the horror comics, rather than the more traditional version which has Gaines and Kurtzman as the innovators. This prescient approach to comics became the hallmark of Feldstein's work throughout his successful career. He had a gift for anticipating what would become enormously popular and relevant topics for the American public.

Then, according to Feldstein, Gaines wanted to adapt science fiction to comics. Feldstein remembered, "Well, I didn't know beans about science fiction, so he gave me a couple of things to read, and so we started plotting stories together in the beginning. And so we put out science fiction."[8] In August of 1952, *Mad* made its debut as a comic book. Feldstein initially suggested *EC's Mad Mag* as a title, but it was shortened to *Mad* by Harvey Kurtzman, the title's original editor and main writer.

Feldstein made his debut as the new editor of *Mad* in 1956, the same year that *Time* described it as a "short-lived satirical pulp."[9] As Frank Jacobs put it, Feldstein took over "with the zeal of a linebacker coming off the bench."[10] Gaines gave Feldstein complete creative control of *Mad*. Feldstein gathered the writers and artists who came to be known as "The Usual Gang of Idiots" and linked the face and name of "The Idiot Kid" who would become *Mad*'s mascot, Alfred E. Neuman, telling Gaines, "He's going to represent *Mad*."[11] Finally, under Feldstein's leadership, *Mad* went international, publishing in thirteen foreign languages while rising to more than two and one-half million copies per issue in the United States.[12] Gaines once stated, "Kurtzman started *Mad*. Feldstein made it a commercial success," and Maria Reidelbach credits Feldstein with "the greatest period of growth in *Mad*'s history."[13] As fellow gang member Al Jaffee saw the early leadership, "Feldstein was an artist, a writer, creative . . . but he was a businessman. Harvey was a writer, an artist, creative, but he was not a businessman."[14] Feldstein's combination of being a savvy businessman along with creative artist and writer allowed him to see the opportunity of framing this critical time period when Americans were questioning many aspects of culture—from politics to sex roles and identity—in a way that was humorous and entertaining but also enlightening at the same time. *Mad* was in a unique position to accelerate the development of counterculture movements in the 1960s and beyond by providing the lighter side of very weighty subjects. But to do so, I argue, Feldstein made use of an ancient rhetorical approach.

Tragic versus Comic Frame

Mad's original and audacious attacks on the American establishment and social ills were groundbreaking and paved the way for television shows such as *Laugh-In* (NBC, 1968-1973), *Saturday Night Live* (NBC, 1975-present), *The Daily Show* (Comedy Central, 1996-Present), and *The Colbert Report* (Comedy Central, 2005-2014). Kerry Soper reports that it was "a significant countercultural or antiestablishment force in the 1960s and 1970s."[15] Further, in "From Madness to Dysentery: *Mad*'s Other New York Intellectuals," Nathan Abrams argues that *Mad* served as a catalyst for social protest in general. Abrams writes, "*Mad*'s critique of America was far more effective and devastating than their better-known counterparts and consequently, *Mad* deserves credit as one of the sources of the counterculture of the 1960s."[16] Here, I will extend Abrams's argument further by explaining how *Mad* magazine, particularly under the editorial leadership of Al Feldstein, strategically impacted its audience. As Paul Levitz explains in his interview with Al Jaffe, "Editors bring a lot to what they do, if they're good editors, and *Mad* has been blessed with some wonderfully skilled and talented people doing it. But an editor also brings, to some measure, a worldview, politics, sociology, and his or her life."[17] Under Feldstein's leadership, as I am arguing, *Mad* accomplished this work from the perspective of the comic frame rather than a tragic frame, enabling it to inspire social protest and change. The result was the "empowering laughter" that Reidelbach has praised.[18] Feldstein employed the persona of the Gap-Toothed Kid as an embodiment of vice, using satire to engage the audience with the social issues and ills of the day.

The comic frame, to use Kenneth Burke's formulation, has an ancient heritage and a global reach. Burke explained the value of using poetic categories as a framework for understanding the world. He wrote, "Each of the great poetic forms stresses its own peculiar way of building the mental equipment (meanings, attitudes, character) by which one handles the significant factors of his time."[19] Therefore, a particular culture views its issues and problems through filters or frames to grapple and interact with important situations.

In order to truly understand the persuasive use of the comic frame, consider its opposite, the tragic frame, which has been utilized by audiences as far back as the ancient Greek era.

As Burke sees it, the tragic frame arises from human communication. Humans, or "symbol-using animals," according to Burke, are the "inventors of the negative through their use of language."[20] Burke wrote that "the negative" operates paradoxically as a function of categories.

"Quite as the word 'tree' is verbal and the thing tree is nonverbal, so all words for the nonverbal must, by the very nature of the case, discuss the realm of the nonverbal in terms of what is not."[21] This invention separates humans from other animals in that humans, through their rational use of language, possess a field of play (or war) where thought is engaged in conflict between what is and what is not.

Humans can then choose their actions within this field of polarities and determine and assign dramatic roles to the players in an ever-changing metaphorical antagonism between hero and villain. As Burke explains, "Act involves character, which involves choice; and the form of choice attains its perfection in the distinction between Yes and No (between thou shalt and thou shalt not)."[22] This "thou shalt not" is not only grounded in language, but also serves a cultural ordering function. Order has its foundation in the negative, in the polar field of heroes (the obedient ones) and villains (the disobedient ones). When an individual or an agent of a group acts in disregard for the limits of the thou-shalt-not, guilt enters the field. The tragic frame leads a group to identify and sacrifice a victim, or victims, whose symbolic "killing" leads to the social order being restored. This new state is not permanent. The guilt-redemption cycle constantly returns as an infinite repetition of the tragic. As Burke characterized it, "the cycle of terms implicit in the idea of worldly order continues, forever circling back upon itself, thus forever 'guilty,' thus forever demanding 'redemption,' thus forever inciting anew for a curative victim."[23] The tragic frame has an outcome that is deterministic and predetermined by fate. The tragic frame requires heroes and villains to behave in certain prescribed ways based on good vs. bad actions, so there is no room for variation of outcome.

Feldstein and Gaines used the tragic frame successfully at EC Comics for a time. The two developed *Preachies* (parables) about taboo subjects such as racism, anti-Semitism, drug use, bigotry, and Civil Rights; powerful examples of these are "Judgment Day!," "The Guilty," "Hate!" and "The Monkey."[24] Through the tragic frame, these comics engage the audience's emotions with society's ills. Feldstein explained in our interview that these comics were fun to read because the readers identified with the characters with regard to "love and hate" of heroes and villains, a hallmark of the tragic frame.[25] He went on to note, however, that these comics prompted confrontations with various groups, most notably the Comics Code Authority (CCA), because of the dramatic nature of pitting extremes in opposition to each other. The CCA was formed in 1954 by the Comics Magazine Association of America in order to avoid government regulation through voluntary adherence to a code of narrative and textual ethics.

Feldstein and Gaines appropriated the comic frame rather than the tragic frame when orchestrating the direction of *Mad*. Rachel E. Silverman asserts that from within the comic frame, the "tragic binary of either/or (us/them) is replaced with both/and," and the comic potentially leads to dialogue where the tragic leads to death.[26] Sigmund Freud's explanation is also helpful in this regard: "Whereas the tragic involves order, polarities of good and evil, and identification between audience and characters in the story through emotion, the comic involves disorder and chaos, all characters are flawed and equal, and there is no identification between audience and characters."[27] If the audience identifies with the characters in their plight, the audience is engaged in the realm of the tragic, and if the audience enjoys the characters in their plight, then the audience is in the realm of the comic. The comic frame does not work when the audience identifies with tragic aspects of the narrative. Therefore, part of the power of the comic frame is its disengagement with the extreme emotions of the tragic frame. Perhaps most important of all, the comic frame allows the audience to accept the drama of human action for what it is while allowing the audience "to thunder against it."[28] The comic frame provides freedom to criticize, explore, and create, knowing that success may or may not be possible, but the pursuit can be fun and playful. Within the comic frame, the audience remains aware of its own weaknesses and problems, accepts them with humility, yet also celebrates the human condition without arrogance or denigration. In this context, *Mad* was successful in large part because it created an environment that not only showed its readers the absurdity in human behavior and celebrated that absurdity, but also empowered those readers to make change when they desired to do so.

Mad and Comic Framing

The comic frame shaped and filtered Feldstein's perspective in almost every way as he directed *Mad* into being one of the most successful magazines of the day. By engaging himself with the creative process, such as participating in the naming of *Mad*, creating a mascot, and developing strategies that would be the foundation of the art and writing, Feldstein made decisions that would affect not only his company but also the future of popular social critique. Feldstein explained in our interview that from his perspective, the work he did at EC Comics, and more specifically at *Mad*, was "having fun and making a lot of money."[29] Fun for Feldstein meant showing the absurdity and foolishness of American culture at the time. One major way that Feldstein, Gaines, and Kurtzman demonstrated this motive was when they were brainstorming the name for the magazine; the name *Mad* suggests insanity, frenzy, anger, but also enthusiasm and hilarity. Stan Hart, one of the later writers for *Mad*, stated, "For me, *Mad* is an outlet for the insanity I see going on in the world today. It takes the far ends of the political, cultural, and religious spectrums and shines a light of sanity on them."[30] The naming of *Mad* helped inspire the artists and writers contributing to the magazine to focus on the comic framing that undergirded its existence.

Feldstein also understood that the personification of *Mad* would help define and articulate its purpose for its target audience. One of the first decisions Feldstein made when he became editor of *Mad* was to make "The Idiot Kid" the mascot for the magazine by placing him on the cover and giving him a name in December 1956. Feldstein said that he wanted a trademark that would work for *Mad* the same way the bunny worked for *Playboy* magazine: "I wanted a symbol of the magazine, its character and its message."[31] Kurtzman had included images of what would later become the iconic kid from time to time in 1955 and 1956 within the pages of *Mad* as well as displayed along with other faces in the border for the cover of the new magazine version of *Mad*. The origins of the image have been explored, as when Sam Sweet argues in "A Boy with No Birthday Turns Sixty" that Peter Reitan discovered the image in the *Los Angeles Herald* as early as December 2, 1894, and notes that others believe that the image dates back still further.[32] In any case, the lack of a specific origin date adds to the mystery and allure of the character, providing an almost blank slate for the image of the *Mad* persona. Feldstein found him to be "strangely endearing."[33] This affection was evident in our interviews when Feldstein would refer to him as "our Alfred." Feldstein's identification with Alfred E. Neuman is also clear from the history of the name, which was one of the pen names with which he had sometimes signed his own work.[34] Neuman became more than a symbol or trademark of the magazine: he became a beloved persona who embodied *Mad*.

The first images of the Kid that Feldstein had to work with were "crude." Feldstein explained in our interview that he wanted a "definitive portrait of him" and, after advertising in the *New York Times*, hired artist Norman Mingo to create the final image as an oil painting.[35] Mingo's portrait became the "quintessential rendering of the face; it became the model from which all other versions would be fashioned."[36] Feldstein shared with me what he saw as the source of the portrait's success:

> he [Mingo] did that face which can never be changed. If you try to do anything with it, it doesn't look like him. I had other artists that couldn't do him because they had their own personalities coming into their work. If you take that face and hold it up to a mirror, it's entirely different. It doesn't look anything like him. It's so asymmetrical. And it just worked. It became our trademark.[37]

Alfred E. Neuman made his debut on the cover of *Mad* magazine in December 1956 (#30), and he has appeared on almost every cover since.

The Kid's persuasive power can be better understood by highlighting the historical importance of the vice character within the comic frame. The comic frame allows an individual or group to put on an antic disposition or clown act that subverts the power structure of a given culture or context. This comic role is ancient in origin and can be found in lower English mythology: that of Puck, Satan, or the character more commonly and simply known as Vice or Fool. The social function of the vice character found throughout English literature was to create sites of inversion, disrespect, and phallus toting.[38] Shakespeare, for example, used the Vice and Fool to subvert the kings and other authorities found within his plays. Whole feasts were created to give place for the Lords of Misrule to make fun of the existing powers.[39] The cool power of the comic frame is drawn from individuals' willingness to turn the world around them into theater, casting themselves in the role of Fool and detaching themselves emotionally while prodding other characters to play their roles in the topsy-turvy play aimed at displacing the old structures of authority that determine the injustice.

What is at stake here is the very authority of the role of hero as found in the tragic frame. The Fool plays contrary to what is expected. This surprise sets up a comic distance and enables the audience, led by the Fool, to view the event from an "objective" stance. The audience takes on what Freud called "playful judgment" within the liminal stage between those with power and those without. Freud argued that this makes "sense in nonsense" and "confusion and clearness."[40] The well-known construct of the Fool served to bring disorder to the pre-established system; his function was to invert the structures of authority and subvert the status quo.

Alfred E. Neuman is the Fool or "malevolent jester" or "trickster," as Reidelbach notes,[41] and he fits this role very well. Fools see "their own weaknesses and desires, while pointing out the same in others," Eleanor Rycroft points out.[42] The Fool then is willing to question everything, and nothing is sacred. The Fool revels in disorder, disrespect, foibles, and mischief. As Winfried Schleiner explains, "His comedy is a subtle play of what is deepest taboo."[43] A specific example of Alfred E. Neuman as the ancient Vice character or Fool is on the cover of *Mad* magazine in October 1967 (#114) where Alfred is depicted from behind as a court jester (his face only shown on his jester's staff, or marotte), dancing in front of an audience. Prominent in the audience are a king with the face of President Lyndon Johnson, hunched over stacks of gold coins and money bags labeled "Great Society" and "Vietnam," frowning and giving Alfred a thumbs down, and a queen with the face of Lady Bird Johnson, her "Make America Beautiful" campaign skewered by a sign that reads "Every Litter Bit Hurts." Also depicted in the carnivalesque royal court scene are Johnson's daughters, the actor (and boyfriend of eldest daughter Lynda Bird Johnson) George Hamilton, and a panoply of politicians, including Vice President Hubert Humphrey as a monk, Secretary of State Dean Rusk, and Senator Everett Dirksen, among others. Peeking out from beneath the tablecloth is someone who looks like Robert Kennedy, smirking as he crashes the Johnson party. This antic image of Alfred E. Neuman at a key moment in the Vietnam War era captures not only his comic persona but also illustrates *Mad*'s status as a political force. As the Fool, Alfred reveals the vices of his audience, and here both take center stage on *Mad*'s cover.

After Feldstein gave the name to the Kid, he claims that he added the caption, "What? Me Worry?"—although his memory seems to be in error here. Kurtzman ran the caption under the Kid's face in #24, the first issue after the change from comic book to magazine, atop the border that framed the cover image. No matter where the idea came from, in addition to the drawing of the Kid's face, the motto of "What, Me Worry?" points to the attitude or frame of approaching life's issues with humor and distance rather than tragedy and emotion, thus relieving the audience's anxieties. Feldstein maintained, "I decided that he would depict what we were trying to say, 'What, me worry?' You know, no matter what happens, maintain a sense of humor, laugh it off. It will go away."[44] So Feldstein's role was to discover ways for the Kid to perform his lack of worry.

In our interview, I asked Feldstein why he believed the strategy of the Fool has worked from Shakespeare to Alfred, and he responded:

> I don't know except unless maybe people think they're fools and that they have an affinity for this person who doesn't really care, isn't really being touched and laughs at everything. And maybe this is what people want to do is to go through life and pass things off without getting too involved in their misery.[45]

In addition to developing a mascot for *Mad*, Feldstein brought together the incredibly talented artists and writers as "The Usual Gang of Idiots." This group, who also called themselves "knuckleheads" and "dissuaders" (as opposed to the persuaders of the advertising industry), approached their work as Fools through the strategy of satire. The *Mad* "idiots" became "a well-oiled satirical steamroller."[46]

Nick Meglin told Paul Levitz, "There are two worlds writing for *Mad*. One [uses] the funny bone, and the other the clever bone. And the clever bone comes mostly through satire, which means there is a substance to begin with—a subject, an idea that already exists."[47] Feldstein understood that while his first goal was to make *Mad* successful, a secondary goal was to engage critically with these structures by predominantly using satire. His vision for *Mad* was to not shy away from confrontation with the politics and social issues of the day. He had been socially conscious for much of his life and wanted to make a difference in the world. He explained in our interview that he had been born in 1925 and so he grew up during the Great Depression, which had a profound impact on his experience of social problems as well as teachers who made an impression on his thinking. As a young man, he came out of World War II wanting to make a difference and to help make the world a better place, so he didn't shy away from political and social engagement. He saw himself as an "iconoclast," and the identity defined his approach to guiding *Mad*: very early in his role as editor in late 1956, he encouraged writers to engage in satire. *Mad* used satire to examine everything from advertisements to politics. He maintained in our interview, "The world was our oyster." He laughed and said, "The hippies got hit, the druggies got hit, the capitalists, the communists. Everybody. We were just open. I wanted it to be a fully balanced juggernaut of criticism."[48]

The outcome, from Reidelbach's perspective, is that *Mad* "armed . . . readers with a crucial weapon against the onslaught: awareness."[49] She observed, "No president was exempt from *Mad*'s sledgehammer humor, no movement or institution safe from *Mad* jabbing a finger at its excesses and inconsistencies, laughing fiendishly."[50] As a result of reading *Mad*, young people were encouraged to become more savvy media consumers and more skeptical of the government and other institutions. Thus, while the goal was to bring awareness and thoughtfulness, Feldstein argued in our interview that *Mad*'s purpose did not include "telling them what to do." He explained, "It's not to promulgate action. It's to say, 'Look how dumb this is. Aren't you dumb for falling for this dumb stuff! Why don't you do something about it?' That's about it."[51] The perspective of the comic frame leaves the outcome unknown, but the participants are in a position of empowerment to be a part of the outcome, whatever it may be.

While *Mad* had its detractors, it did not suffer many attacks on free speech. The tragic framing used by Feldstein and Gaines in the other comics where they developed morality stories that dealt with topics from race to Santa Claus, led to many conflicts with the CCA and other concerned groups, including the U.S. Senate. However, using satire from the perspective of the comic frame allowed *Mad* to enjoy much more creative freedom because it was not confrontational but rather playful in its approach.

Mad thus enjoyed a mostly benign relationship with the establishment. One notable exception came in 1961, however, when the group Oklahoma City Mothers United for Decency highlighted *Mad* as an example of the evils of subversive literature and pornography in their touring "Smutmobile," a 28-foot-long trailer truck.[52] A second exception was less humorous but more important in pointing to the value of *Mad*'s social criticism and satire in 1961: a lawsuit by a group of music publishers that included great musicians such as Richard Rodgers, Cole Porter, and Irving Berlin, *Berlin v. EC Publications, Inc.*, claimed copyright infringement after *Mad* published parodies of some of their best-known songs. The Supreme Court upheld the ruling of the Second Circuit Court of Appeals in 1964, in which Judge Irving R. Kaufman ruled in *Mad*'s favor, stating, "We believe that parody and satire are deserving of substantial freedom—both as entertainment and as a form of social and literary criticism."[53] This big victory for *Mad* set the stage for future satirists in the television, film, and internet generations of America.

Conclusion

Kerry Soper links *Mad*'s success with its use of humor: "a simultaneous mockery *of,* and reliance *on,* the popularity and recognizability of its mainstream targets."[54] It was precisely because *Mad* helped educate audiences about social issues and problems but worked within the democratic process without being revolutionary or destructive that *Mad* was as successful as it was. Feldstein outlined his perspective on *Mad*'s purpose and relevance in general in an editorial for the April 1961 trade magazine *Bestsellers*:

> *Mad*'s popularity stems from a mounting spiritual and psychological discontent stirring in America. It reflects the spreading anxieties of our society, the confused feeling that things aren't exactly right, and that maybe there are more than purely materialistic ends in life. *MAD* echoes the increasing concern with our character and objectives as a people, the growing desire to start moving forward again as a nation, the need to renew our national vision and to clarify our national purpose.[55]

The comic frame, because of its cool and detached perspective, continues to be a useful filter to analyze multiple perspectives of cultural issues today. According to Dannagal Young, young people do not watch satirical shows such as *The Daily Show* and *The Colbert Report* to receive their news, because they already have a "news awareness"; rather, these shows gratify viewers "who enjoy thinking and engaging in deeper levels of cognitive processing" and promote "the kind of broad, integrative thinking that helps them make connections and gain *insights*."[56] This is a positive, hopeful, and empowering finding. The comic frame, presenting reality through the eyes of the Fool and the strategy of satire, is apparently ageless in its appeal. Perhaps Al Feldstein said it best when I asked him what he believed *Mad*'s role was when interacting with American culture. He answered, his eyes dancing and laughter on his lips, "We started a lot of trouble."

Notes

1. Grant Geissman, *Feldstein: The Mad Life and Fantastic Art of Al Feldstein!*, 64.
2. Steven Ringgenberg, "Features: Al Feldstein: 1925–2014."
3. Al Feldstein, interview by Margaret Cavin Hambrick.
4. Joseph W. Slade, "Wally Wood: Picturing Adolescent Desire in *Mad*'s Early Parodies," chap. 4, 101–118; first published as "Wally Wood: Picturing Adolescent Sexuality in *Mad*'s Early Parodies" in *Studies in American Humor* n.s. 3, no. 30 (Fall 2014): 48, 53.
5. Ann M. Ciasullo, "The Lighter—and Weightier—Side of *Mad*, Or: Everything I Needed to Know About Gender and Sexuality I Learned from Dave Berg," chap. 5, 135; first published in *Studies in American Humor* n.s. 3, no. 40 (Fall 2014): 88.
6. Feldstein, interview by Hambrick.
7. Feldstein, interview by Hambrick.
8. Feldstein, interview by Hambrick.
9. "The Press: Sassy Newcomer," 73.
10. Frank Jacobs, *The Mad World of William M. Gaines*, 129.
11. Jacobs, *The Mad World of William M. Gaines*, 210.
12. Maria Reidelbach, *Completely Mad: A History of the Comic Book and Magazine*, 40.
13. Quoted in Jacobs, *The Mad World of William M. Gaines*, 38; Reidelbach, *Completely Mad*, 40.
14. Paul Levitz, "Inside the Editorial Process: *Mad* Veterans Jaffee and Meglin Look at Their Editors," interviews with Al Jaffe and Nick Meglin, chap. 1, 88; first published in *Studies in American Humor* n.s. 3, no. 30 (Fall 2014): 11.
15. Kerry Soper, "Folding Against the Establishment: Satiric Distance and Difference in Al Jaffee's Back Cover Feature in *Mad* Magazine," chap. 13, 89; first published in *Studies in American Humor* n.s. 3, no. 30 (Fall 2014): 96.
16. Nathan Abrams, "From Madness to Dysentery: *Mad*'s Other New York Intellectuals," 435–36.
17. Levitz, "Inside the Editorial Process," chap. 1, 89; first published in *Studies in American Humor* n.s. 3, no. 30 (Fall 2014): 8.
18. Reidelbach, *Completely Mad*, 197.
19. Kenneth Burke, *Attitudes Toward History*, 34.
20. Kenneth Burke, *The Rhetoric of Religion: Studies in Logology*, 40.
21. Burke, *The Rhetoric of Religion*, 18.
22. Burke, *The Rhetoric of Religion*, 41.

23. Burke, *The Rhetoric of Religion*, 223.
24. Geissman, *Feldstein*, 208.
25. Feldstein, interview by Hambrick.
26. Rachel E. Silverman, "Comedy as Correction: Humor as Perspective by Incongruity on *Will & Grace* and *Queer as Folk*," 263.
27. Sigmund Freud, *The Basic Writings of Sigmund Freud*, trans. A. A. Brill, 634–35.
28. Timothy Thompson and Anthony J. Palmeri, "Attitudes toward Counternature (with Notes on Nurturing a Poetic Psychosis)," in *Extensions of the Burkeian System*, ed. James W. Chesebro, 277.
29. Feldstein, interview by Hambrick.
30. Quoted in Reidelbach, *Completely Mad*, 94.
31. Feldstein, interview by Hambrick.
32. Sam Sweet, "A Boy with No Birthday Turns Sixty."
33. Geissman, *Feldstein*, 314.
34. Feldstein, interview by Hambrick.
35. Feldstein, interview by Hambrick.
36. Geissman, *Feldstein*, 316.
37. Feldstein, interview by Hambrick.
38. Robert Weiman, *Shakespeare and the Popular Tradition in the Theater: Studies in the Social Dimension of Dramatic Form and Function*, ed. Robert Schwartz, 30–48.
39. Weiman, *Shakespeare and the Popular Tradition*, 20–30.
40. Freud, *The Basic Writings of Sigmund Freud*, 634–35.
41. Reidelbach, *Completely Mad*, 151.
42. Eleanor Rycroft, "The Vice and the Fool," *Staging the Henrician Court*.
43. Winfried Schleiner, "Imaginative Sources of Shakespeare's Puck," 68.
44. Feldstein, interview by Hambrick.
45. Feldstein, interview by Hambrick.
46. Geissman, *Feldstein*, 358.
47. Levitz, "Inside the Editorial Process," chap. 1, 95; first published in *Studies in American Humor* n.s. 3, no. 30 (Fall 2014): 23.
48. Feldstein, interview by Hambrick.
49. Reidelbach, *Completely Mad*, 55.
50. Reidelbach, *Completely Mad*, 132.
51. Feldstein, interview by Hambrick.
52. Reidelbach, *Completely Mad*, 121.
53. United States Second Circuit, Court of Appeals, *Berlin v. EC Publications, Inc.*, 329 F. 2d 541, March 23, 1964.
54. Soper, "Folding Against the Establishment," chap. 13, 97; first published in *Studies in American Humor* n.s. 3, no. 30 (Fall 2014): 4.
55. Quoted in Geissman, *Feldstein*, 331.
56. Dannagal G. Young, "Laughter, Learning, or Enlightenment? Viewing and Avoidance Motivations Behind *The Daily Show* and *The Colbert Report*," 166.

4. Wally Wood:

Picturing Male Adolescent Desire in *Mad*'s Early Parodies

Joseph W. Slade

WALLACE WOOD (1927–1981) illustrated, or in *Mad* parlance, "pictured," at least one story in every issue of the magazine save one (#68, 1/62) from the first (10–11/52) until the eighty-sixth (4/64). Among his collaborators were Orson Bean, Jean Shepherd, Ernie Kovacs, Danny Kaye, Sid Caesar, and most frequently, Harvey Kurtzman. Wood's exuberant caricatures for these stories—especially the parodies of books, motion pictures, comic strips, topical events, personalities, and other artifacts of popular culture—often exploited the conflicted sexual attitudes of young postwar heterosexual males, who formed a substantial segment of the magazine's audience. Erotic sub-currents clearly animate the most memorable, the fondly remembered panels of "Superduperman!" (#4, 4–5/53), "Flesh Garden!" (#11, 5/54), and "Prince Violent!" (#13, 7/54)—all for scripts written by Kurtzman—but are visible in many others. But if Wood drew freckled, bucktoothed, and hapless males drooling over cleavages that anticipated the invention of the Wonderbra, he also consistently mocked the romantic clichés and masculine vulnerabilities of the Eisenhower era. By turns clumsy and aggressive, Wood's satirized males resembled refugees from playgrounds and tree-clubhouses, susceptible to desire but suspicious of hypocritical Cold War sexual lore.

Critics have long recognized that the success of *Mad* turned to an extent on sexual associations, but few have discussed the nature of the magazine's eroticism. In 1982, a year after Wood's death, the cultural critic J. Hoberman, noting that *Mad* had begun as "a comic book that parodies other comic books,"[1] attributed to it "a particular sensibility that is the vulgar equivalent of modernism itself. By this I mean a popular, ironic, somewhat dehumanized mode reflexively concerned with the specific properties of its medium and the conditions of its making."[2] In a comparison that seems less shocking now than then, Hoberman traced the parodies of those early *Mad* issues to what he thought of as their predecessors, the pornographic Tijuana Bibles, or "eight-pagers," little comic books that depicted well-known characters from comic strips and performers from motion pictures in scenes of sexual intercourse. The content of the *Mad* parodies, he said, differed from that of hard-core Tijuana Bible scenarios principally because the former foregrounded an erotic self-consciousness rather than explicit sex.

Mad first appeared in 1952, a bit late to be included in any genuine grouping of modernists, but Hoberman was trying to put his finger on an aspect of eroticism that the noted art critic John Berger had already defined more successfully in *Ways of Seeing* (1972). According to Berger, a nude subject—as opposed to a merely naked one—is aware of herself being watched, a concept he codified as "Men look at women. Women watch themselves being looked at."[3] (Laura Mulvey later reshaped Berger's thesis into the theory of the "male gaze."[4]) Hoberman thought that something like that was going on in *Mad*'s early parodies, especially those drawn by Wally Wood, whose backgrounds and characters called attention to themselves in ways that Hoberman could not quite fathom. Though the critic acknowledged Wood's talent, he found it disturbing. According to Hoberman, Wood, "who specialized in pygmy cretins, over-stacked dolls, and frames with the visual consistency of an exploding spittoon, represented *Mad* at its most aggressively tasteless."[5]

Since then, assessments of Wood have been similarly mixed. Although most critics have applauded his skill at representations, sexual or otherwise, they usually have tempered praise with reminders of his alcoholism and his surliness, the disputes with Will Eisner and Harvey Kurtzman, the many enterprises he abandoned, and the genuinely pornographic comics he drew as he declined into the illness that ended with his suicide. More recently, however, admirers—convinced that Wood's work clearly prefigured and influenced Robert Crumb, Art Spiegelman, Trina Robbins, and a host of underground artists—have decided that what looked like tastelessness to Hoberman looks like genius today.[6] In 2010, the Casal Solleric Museum in Mallorca mounted a massive retrospective of Wood's life and career and published a huge volume of appreciations that, if not quite a *catalogue raisonné*, has rebalanced his reputation. Moreover, a reconstituted Wallace Wood Estate now maintains a website for licensing. In 2008, Wood's original cover of *Weird Science* #16 (1952) sold at auction for $200,000, ten thousand more than the price for a 1942 *Batman* cover.[7] Partisans these days argue over whether Wood should be ranked first among comic illustrators or merely in the top five.[8] In any event, he seems to be enjoying a robust afterlife.

Given the number of his projects, the prolific output of his pen, the versatility of his imagination, and the various enterprises for which he worked, summarizing his thirty-year career is not easy. Although he had little formal artistic training, he outgrew multiple apprenticeships as soon as he undertook them and remained essentially a freelancer. After a brief stint in the military, he began as a letterer and inker for George Wunder on *Terry and the Pirates* (1934-1973) and for Will Eisner on *The Spirit* (1940-1952).[9] Eisner, who hired him to draw backgrounds, soon realized that Wood aspired to picture complete stories, and they parted.[10] Wood drew western and romance comics for a publisher called Fox and took whatever jobs he could find before moving in 1951 to William Gaines's Entertaining Comics (EC). In 1952, Wood joined his EC colleague Harvey Kurtzman in starting *Mad* and continued to draw for the magazine after Kurtzman left. Between more or less formal gigs with Marvel and DC Comics, Wood supported himself for the rest of his life by illustrating advertisements, magazine covers, books, and syndicated strips of others. In 1966, Wood himself published *witzend* (1966–1985), a magazine designed as a venue for professional colleagues (many of whom worshipped him); though Wood sold it after four issues, the originality of its pages influenced the next generation of artists. Wood's own major contribution to *witzend*, "The Pipsqueak Papers" (1967–1968), showcased fairy tales with wonderfully sexy overtones.[11] Perhaps his most notorious drawing, for *The Realist* magazine, was the "Disneyland Memorial Orgy" (5/67), in which, surrounded by other misbehaving Disney characters, the Seven Dwarves engaged in improbable couplings with Snow White;[12] poster copies still circulate. Soldiers adored Wood's *Sally Forth*, a sexy strip that appeared sporadically in *Military News* (1968) and *Overseas Weekly* (1971–1974).[13] For *Big Apple Comix* (1975), a single-issue underground publication, he penned the brilliant "My Word," which scorchingly captured a tawdry New York.[14] As assignments dried up, however, his career sputtered to a close with explicit drawings for questionable publishers that are usually ignored.

By any measure, Wood mastered every genre of comics he essayed, and a current of eroticism runs through them all. At EC, for example, he drew mostly science fiction, a genre he invigorated with imagination and verve. At least one of his stories, "There Will Come Soft Rains" Wood's 1953 visual adaptation of a chapter of Ray Bradbury's *Martian Chronicles* (1950) for *Weird Fantasy* #17, is generally acknowledged to be without peer.[15] Few would challenge the assessment of William Gaines, Wood's boss at EC, who said that "he was just the greatest science-fiction artist there ever was."[16] One reason is obvious: Wood's science fiction placed convincing humans in plausible technological landscapes. His panels show well-defined human bodies—every muscle and sinew visible—interacting with "machinery that looked like it worked!" as Harvey Kurtzman would later marvel.[17] The phallicism and sensuality of the machines defined their intimate relationships with the human figures; their surfaces were palpable, visceral, almost tactile. Plots were often simple enough: imperiled by aliens or disaster, a buxom heroine contrives to lose much of her clothing before being rescued by a stalwart male in a skin-tight outfit. (Wood's most ardent fans claim that he invented the ideas of spandex and the cut-off female T-shirt.) The hero usually triumphed by harnessing machines, turning them into projections of himself in ways that would have given pause to Marshall McLuhan, who famously defined media as extensions of man.

And perhaps they did. In 1951, McLuhan published *The Mechanical Bride: Folklore of Industrial Man*, which performed a Freudian dissection of popular culture. It is wise to recall this academic entry into comics-bashing, since we tend to blame the 1950s hysteria surrounding the medium entirely on Fredric Wertham and Senator Estes Kefauver.[18] McLuhan condemned the blending of sex and technology in comics and other media as sadistic, as would similarly inclined critics such as Gershon Legman and Jean Baudrillard, both of whom considered violence a form of sublimated sexuality. Indeed, the phrase "sex and violence," a linkage that for Americans is as fixed as "peanut butter and jelly," probably dates from this period.[19] In the midst of the panic over comics, however, Wood met Harvey Kurtzman, who hired him for *Mad*, a venture that—because it soon became a magazine rather than a comic book—escaped some of the restraints imposed on the latter by the Comics Code of 1954. There, for a brief time, the collaboration of the two men sparked magical parodies that turned on Wood's ability to invest eroticism with an irony that exploited and transformed the nexus of sex and violence cherished by postwar American adolescents as much as it was deplored by cultural critics. The idiom that Wood invented sent up both violence and sex.

The most famous Wood-Kurtzman parody was "Superduperman!" (#4, 4–5/53: 1-8). "Superduperman!" clearly reveals the device employed most frequently by Wood to sexualize his stories: reflexive voyeurism. In a sense, Wood hides eroticism in plain sight: onlookers and spectators abound at the edges of panels, their voyeurism constant. In cinematic terms, it is diegetic, or interior frame voyeurism, focused on Superduperman and Lois, narcissists both, a cleverly indirect yet persuasive means of eroticizing the two, and, since both are aware of the gaze of others, an excellent example of what Hoberman meant when he referred to the self-consciousness of the parodies. If some of the background spectators resemble the "pygmy cretins" that annoyed Hoberman, they are, to borrow from yet another vocabulary, not bugs but features: placing onlookers in the background evokes and exploits the voyeurism of American urban life that is key to the rise of sexual representation. Voyeurism is a manifestation of the most sexual of human senses. Humans are attracted to each other visually, and we value attractiveness most when it is validated by the gaze of others. Hence the protruding eyeballs and panting mouths of the journalists surrounding a pouting, preening Lois Pain. Her full figure conforms to the waist-to-hip ratio of .70 that evolutionary biologists insist is the ideal in most cultures; she sports as well the lustrous hair, smooth skin, and symmetrical features that also figure strongly in mating.[20] By contrast, the pathetic wreck that is Clark Bent exhibits only negative mating characteristics: he is ugly, unhealthy, malformed, short, weak, and an obviously poor provider, a "creep" (see fig. 4-1).

Taking their cue from the name Lois Pain and from her harsh rejection of Superduperman as "once a creep, always a creep" (8), critics sometimes interpret Wood's parody as a sadomasochistic scenario. Since Wood illustrated "Superduperman!" while Joe Shuster (Superman's original co-creator) was himself surreptitiously drawing racy fetish stories that cast Lois Lane as a classic dominatrix whipping the Man of Steel,[21] Wood quite possibly picked up subtextual signals in the original. But Wood does not fetishize S/M here (the psychiatric term for S/M is not *fetish* but *paraphilia*), nor does he do so in any of the other famous

Fig. 4-1: Lois Pain rejects a craven Clark-Bent-turned-thick-headed-Superduperman, his humiliation watched by Wood's signature voyeurs. In the following final panels, the narration delivers the message "Once a creep, always a creep!" (Kurtzman and Wood, "Superduperman!," *Mad* #4, 4–5/53: 8). MAD used with permission.

parodies. What he does fetishize is voyeurism: Wood's males are scopophilic, in thrall to visual stimulation from every quarter. Voyeurism in his panels operates in two directions: on the one hand it underscores the ridiculousness that adolescents feel under what they imagine is constant social surveillance; on the other, voyeurism eroticizes the landscape and everything in it. The interior spectators leer at the carefully delineated seams on nylon stockings, the high heels, the inflated breasts, the haughty tilt of a nose, the contours of a skirt, all of which stand out in settings that are filled with sensual details jostling for attention. The narcissism of the characters fills their spaces to compete visually with everything else. "Superduperman!" is a cynical teenager's envisioning of the legend: the only thing "super" about this hero is his almost mindless destructiveness. It is not so much the spineless, decrepit Clark as the callous stupidity of his alter ego that demolishes the fantasy of a secret identity (one can also read the story as a critique of capitalism). Superduperman has no interest in protecting humanity or America; he just wants to impress a shapely girl by beating up another superhero. Given Lois Pain's indifference, who needs kryptonite?

In a cosmic sense, of course, humor is itself erotic, a means of establishing intimacy between sender and receiver through revelation, wit, dominance, commiseration, or a host of other messages; Freud to the contrary, humor, sexual or otherwise, does not have to be hostile. Like sex, humor involves play, and like sex, erotic humor can turn on visuality. If sexual reproduction makes possible natural selection, the demands of mating on human equanimity led D. H. Lawrence—somewhere—to call it "faintly ridiculous." One might argue that society tries to constrain sexuality just as much because of its absurdity as because of its other consequences; dirty jokes are a reminder of just how difficult that can be. Even so, we ordinarily assume that eroticism, like humor, requires modest if still socially acceptable violation of taboos.

Tweaking taboos defined Wood. Although according to Art Spiegelman, Wood read Freud along with Tolkien,[22] his humor is as playfully Rabelaisian as it is doctrinaire Freudian. From the outset, Wood loved to remind editors that sexuality simmered within the texts of the stories they assigned him. In one famous instance, he submitted pages of *Weird Science-Fantasy* #23 covered in amusingly frank "paste-overs," i.e., overlays designed to be removed from the publishable illustrations, for a 1954 story called "The Children," a critique of eugenics.[23] One paste-over depicted the principal female character posing in diaphanous lingerie that revealed nipples and pubic hair; another showed her being humped by her husband, and a third pictured her standing naked before an official who is wearing only garters and socks below the waist.[24] One can ascribe such subversion to the exhaustion that overtakes many artists who have finished a project, as is often the case with Disney animators who relax by drawing obscene versions of the stories they have just completed. As far as we know, Wood drew no such paste-overs for *Mad*, restricting himself to pushing acceptable standards just a little by creating women suggestively bursting out of slinky gowns.

Although such cheesecake instantly draws the straight male eye, its conventionality makes it a less significant element of Wood's eroticism. To be sure, Wood loved to twit what he saw as sexual impersonation, the self-objectification of attributes that were already a form of parody. Typical was the over-the-top rendition of an overripe Marylin Marone as box office come-on in "The New Marylin Marone" (Jacobs and Wood, #31, 2/57: 2-3), *Mad*'s incredulous reaction to a Hollywood press release claiming that the famous star would henceforth accept only serious roles. If W. C. Fields called Mae West "a plumber's idea of Cleopatra," then Wood's representation of Monroe is an adolescent's idea of, well, Marilyn Monroe. Wood's caricature both magnified and undercut the artifice of Monroe's sensuality. He would similarly sensualize actresses such as Lana Turner ("The Prodigious" #26, 10–11/55: 30-34) and Silvana Mangano ("Ulysses" #27, 4/56: 40-44) and comic-strip femme fatales such as Lois Lane from *Superman* and the Dragon Lady from *Terry and the Pirates* ("Teddy and the Pirates!" #6, 8/53: 1-8), all for scripts by Harvey Kurtzman. The ample dimensions of Wood's parodies of the latter two one admirer called "the stuff of adolescent wet dreams."[25] One can only imagine how Wood might have depicted the self-objectifying Madonna or Lady Gaga.

The most ancient paradox inherent in any aspirational sexual representation has to do with whether such representations can be voyeuristic and exploitive while simultaneously artistic and intellectually meaningful. Wood and Kurtzman asserted that they could by deconstructing the stories they pitched. In two amazing examples, Kurtzman and Wood conducted a hilarious semiotic analysis of the texts and images they deployed in their parodies; both were primers of the self-consciousness of craft that Hoberman found so intriguing, or, if one prefers, manuals on the uses of irony. The panels of the first, "Sound Effects!" (#20, 2/55: 1-7), dispense with dialogue to tell a detective story solely in sound effects. The "Whams," "Thuds," "Pows," and "Aarghs" structure a narrative arc like guitar chords in a third-rate blues band; the ensemble burlesques violence itself. The panels of the second, "Julius Caesar!" (#17, 9/54: 7-1 [issue printed backwards]), a take-down of the Marlon Brando movie of 1953, raise violence to absurd levels. Brutus and Cassius use ".45 caliber swords" (3), i.e., anachronistic submachine guns, to turn a still-standing, still-declaiming Caesar into Swiss cheese, the better to demonstrate how audiences understand violence for what it is, a mode of dramatization energized by kinetic grammar and syntax (see fig. 4-2). (To make sure no one missed the subversive intent of the parody, the editors printed the whole issue upside down.)

Robert Warshow, no fan of comic books, nor of Fredric Wertham—he called *Seduction of the Innocent* "a kind of crime comic book for parents"—thought that the violence of *Mad*'s humor aimed "to reduce all culture to indiscriminate anarchy,"[26] which put the magazine in the company of both the Marx Brothers and the Three Stooges. Warshow singled out as "very funny" the graphic violence of Wood's parody of *Little Orphan Annie*. In "Little Orphan Melvin!," a train dismembers Melvin when Daddy Warbucks arrives too late to save her "at the last minute" (#9, 3/54: 1-8; 6). Warshow was amused when Melvin's detached head complains: "It

Fig. 4-2: Wood and Kurtzman deconstruct exaggerated comic violence in "Julius Caesar!" (*Mad* #17, 11/54: 7). The narration emphasizes the absurdity of Caesar's still speaking while riddled with bullet-holes, not to mention the anachronism of ".45 caliber swords." MAD used with permission.

hurts when I laugh" (7). But the last panel, Warshow himself complains, "ends with the most obvious and vulgar explanation of why Annie calls Daddy Warbucks 'Daddy.'"[27] In that panel the reassembled Little Orphan Melvin discards her tattered dress, hairdo, and blank-eyed look to stand revealed in her actual guise as a bombshell.

This last figuration of Melvin-Annie (the name is itself a wry gender joke) is typical of the way Wood pictured women, as more generic than stereotypical. Melvin's ankles propel her confidently almost out of the frame as her wriggling curves wring exclamations from the ever-present voyeurs in the background. But her voluptuousness is quite different from the moistly salacious women of Wood's illustrator-contemporaries Bill Ward and Jack Cole, or even of the neglected erotic pulp book illustrator Martha Brundage, all of whom place unmistakably complaisant females against sultry backgrounds rather than the bright setting Wood employs here.

The ending of the "Melvin" parody may be "vulgar," but to say so suggests that Warshow realizes that virtually every adult viewer of the original *Little Orphan Annie* at one time or another has entertained a sexual explanation for Warbucks's interest in the waif. Picturing Annie as a disguised glamour queen thus actually comes as a relief; Warbucks is merely a Sugar Daddy, not a pedophile. More spoofs than pin-ups, Wood's women for *Mad* possess the innocence of mere hyperbole. Much later in his career, wracked by alcoholism, overwork, two collapsed marriages, kidney failure, and creeping blindness, Wood drew misogynistic, even mean-spirited but also anomalous stories for the sex tabloid *Screw*. In *Gang Bang*, produced during the increasingly desperate last years of his life, he tried to invest hard-core parodies (e. g., "So White and the Six Dorks," "Stuporman Meets Blunderwoman," and "Flasher Gordon") with a similar naïveté, with a predictable loss of humor.[28] Not that these experiments were nasty. As one historian notes, the *Gang Bang* strips "looked more like an explicit version of [TV show] *Bewitched* due to his traditional '50s style."[29] By contrast, the hourglass heroines of the great Wood-Kurtzman parodies for *Mad* wear their allure insouciantly, not explicitly. At his best, says another historian, Wood got the balance just right, "depicting mildly erotic situations midway between tongue-in-cheek fantasy and straight narrative."[30]

Cleverly reducing motivation to sex was Wood's stock-in-trade, perfectly pitched to juvenile heterosexual males. His illustrations invoked but also mocked adolescent confusion compounded by hormones, anxiety, cynicism, aggression, ambition, and physical and social awkwardness. In an analysis of Stephenie Meyer's *Twilight* series of vampire novels, Caitlin Flanagan notes that the girls who comprise the audience savor the *frisson* of raging desire that drives Edward, an ancient vampire frozen in adolescence, who refuses to defile the heroine because he loves her despite her own desire to be ravished, even if it means her destruction. The center of the *Twilight* novels is the heroine Bella, Flanagan argues, not Edward. Bella falls in love with his struggle to control his ravening appetite.[31] By contrast, despite the frequency of females with hyperbolic silhouettes, Wood's parodies are not about women, but about boys who are merely ostensible adults. Wood's male figures are comic because they have not learned to control their impulses, and appealing because he aligns their ineptitude with that of *Mad*'s youthful male audiences. By laughing at the erotic misadventures of parodic males, those readers essentially laugh at themselves—no mean trick for an artist.

The force of desire roils teenage males almost as powerfully as it does *Twilight*'s vampire, but they lack the undead Edward's decades of experience in coping. The buttoned-down 1950s teenagers in Wood's audience could hardly bring themselves to ask a girl for a date, let alone seduce her; instead, they masked fecklessness with bravado and innuendo, smirking and giggling at "dirty" fabricated tales of prowess and conquest. Such frequently clueless humor could still serve as a defense, a balm, a delight. While Wood's humor only superficially resembles theirs, his comedy, like theirs, does strive for a shared sense of knowing, not an authentic understanding of sex, an achievement that eludes all humans, but more an acknowledgment of the absurdity of our species' sexuality. Wood's visual language addresses biological urges not simply to make fun of them, but also to rope in those spectators most fatalistic about their inevitability.

The best of Wood's parodies satirize the sexuality inherent in comic books and/or strips *Superman*, *Black Hawks*, *Terry and the Pirates*, *The Adventures of Smilin' Jack*, *Batman and Robin*, *G.I. Joe*, *Little Orphan Annie*, *Flash Gordon*, and *Prince Valiant*, and the motion pictures *Stalag 17* (1953), *The Caine Mutiny* (1954), *On the Waterfront* (1954), *The Prodigal* (1955), *Ulysses* (1954), and *The Rose Tattoo* (1955).[32] All of these were collaborations between Wood and Harvey Kurtzman between 1953 and 1956.

Wood's ability to twist the adolescent fantasies that comic strips and movies celebrated into ironically erotic representations was something that not even Kurtzman quite understood. In his reminiscences, Kurtzman praised Will Elder, another frequent collaborator, because Elder augmented Kurtzman's ideas as he executed them by filling panels with sight jokes that Kurtzman had not anticipated. On the partnership with Wood, especially the illustrator's penchant for eroticizing the ordinary, however, Kurtzman was inarticulate. He assumed that Wood's eroticism was somehow "structural"; Wood "was intense, immensely talented. . . . He poured forth a stream of sex and fantasy and sex clothed in a multitude of textures and visual effects—space, machinery, vegetation, monsters."[33] In short, Wood eroticized both figures and ground.

His alternately spartan and lush lines and brushstrokes, frequently artistically superior to those of the originals he parodied, contributed to this matrix, of course, but more trenchant was his ability not to inject but to find stimulation in every situation, as testosterone-prodded boys of the 1950s did. The Clearasil set, Wood sensed, apprehended the world through the romantic lens of fantasy that shaped the image of one's self as much as objects of desire. That did not make his humor male ethnography, of course; it worked because it evoked primal longing. Nor were Wood's readers sensitive Holden Caulfields. But as connoisseurs of phoniness, they could recognize Wood's theatrical farces for what they were.

Because of the *schadenfreude* so often evident in his stories, Wood's more censorious early critics thought his humor a bit smutty. His males constantly experience acute embarrassment—but not exactly shame—caused by their own overconfidence and expectations. Having forestalled her suitors, Penelope in the Kurtzman-Wood parody of the 1954 Kirk Douglas movie *Ulysses* ("Ulysses" #27, 4/56: 40-44) declines to embrace her returned husband not because she has been unfaithful, but because she is still trying to correct a weaving mistake she made before he departed. She may not even have noticed the absence of the crestfallen hero. In "Stalag 18" (#18, 12/54: 1-7), the parody of the movie *Stalag 17*, the American prisoners in the German camp console themselves with titillating fantasies of Russian women captives in a nearby barracks. When two Americans attempt to escape, they are chagrined to find that their tunnel opens into a barracks full of dowdy women in babushkas. Even in those instances where titillation appears to be gratuitous, erotic scenes have a purpose, however. Wood obviously picked up on the homoerotic overtones of the motion picture *The Caine Mutiny* (not his most successful parody). The spoof ("The Cane Mutiny!" as in "the walking stick rebellion," #19, 1/55: 1-6) opens with a curvaceous sweetheart wrapped provocatively around the departing Ensign Willie under the caption "Not that this has much to do with the main story idea, but a story has got to have romantic interest, by George" (1). As tension rises and conflict ensues between "Captain Kweeg" and his bare-chested sailors and officers, the woman illogically reappears multiple times to smooch Willie. The effect is to heighten the homoeroticism and simultaneously to disarm it. Such hints are about as close as Wood ever came to addressing homosexuality, a reticence common to the heterosexual dominance of the period. *Mad* itself, however, was accused of relishing "homophobic jokes, of the stereotypical limp-wristed and lisping variety," as Maria Reidelbach reports, a practice somewhat curtailed after protesters from "a gay and lesbian rights group" visited editor Al Feldstein's office.[34]

Wood treats heterosexual male anxieties with fatalistic wit that occasionally verges on sniggering short of the outright vulgarity so often attributed to him. Most of the parodies laugh at fantasies of heroism by undercutting posturing with absurdity; in the Kurtzman-Wood collaboration on "Prince Violent!" (#13, 7/54: 1-8), for example, Violent and one opponent, incapacitated by their heavy armor, end their battle with thumb wrestling rather than sword fighting. Various misadventures are charged with innuendo: Violent's lance gets stuck in a portcullis, he mistakes a man's blond beard for the hair of the gorgeous "Princess Alota" (based on the comic strip's Aleta), and he suffers an injury to his buttocks. More embarrassing yet, the story ends with Alota suddenly cutting Violent's trademark bangs to ascertain whether he is a boy or a girl. Wood's drawings revealed a male world that one might certainly call sexist, but where women are not so much subordinated as incidental to the construction of a fragile masculinity; the usual response of Wood's males to seductive women is bravado disguising cowardice that must be pictured to be understood. In his world, lust for women is more a threat than a joy, gallantry is suspect, and male bonding is risky, subject to constant betrayal, all circumstances real enough to pubescent males.

Voyeurism sparks fantasies of masculine protection and rescue and prompts Wood's heroes to behave foolishly. They whack rivals in mildly homoerotic scenarios to display Darwinian dominance. Wood's females rarely need rescuing; they are more dangerous than the males and frequently—depending on the parody—outgun them. That is the case in "Teddy and the Pirates!" (#6, 8–9/53), whose bloodthirsty Draggin' Lady, the send-up of Milt Caniff's Dragon Lady (whose name, the journalist Pete Hamill predicted, would "enter the American lexicon to describe all tough, ruthless women"),[35] is practically dressed in weapons. Similarly, in "Black and Blue Hawks!" (#5, 6–7/53: 1-7), the heroine, appropriately clad in scarlet, turns out to be the leader of a conspiracy within the ranks of the elite squadron of heroes. Blinded by libido and by macho delusions that render him stupid, "Boss" Hawk ends up being shot by his own colleagues.

As if to twit Fredric Wertham, who thought that the relationship between Batman and Robin encouraged homosexuality, Wood's parody has the eponymous heroes of "Bat Boy and Rubin!" (#8, 12/53–1/54: 1–7) lose a battle with a gang of women through one pratfall after another, and then reveals Rubin as a vampire who has been murdering Gotham City citizens under the inept Bat Boy's nose. Fights involving women recur. The title character of "G. I. Shmoe!" (#10, 4/54: 1-8), assigned to a United Nations peacekeeping unit, brawls with his fellow soldiers and enemy hordes to dazzle women, who then leave him nonplussed when they "express their love" by draping themselves across his lap and asking "Hey, Joe! You Got Chewing Gum?" (1, 3, 4, 5). Sometimes construed as an anti-war story because of the outrageous graphic violence, the narrative never strays from the repeated comic leitmotif of chewing gum. (G.I.s had given so much chewing gum to liberated children during World War II that it had come to be a refrain among occupying troops.) During the last panels, an army of vaguely Asian women—Wood was not immune to period racism—attack and overwhelm G. I. Shmoe's unit. Shmoe and his buddies are then rescued by an army of WACS (logic is not a strong point here) yelling battle cries like "I'll make your seams crooked!" and "You ruined my hairdo!" as they destroy the enemy forces (8). At the climax, after reading a citation honoring Shmoe's bravery, the commander of the WACS deflates his heroism by seating herself on his lap to ask the same question.

Fig. 4-3: The venal G. I. Shmoe finds that his brutal mock-heroics do not impress the women who have come to his rescue. The refrain "Hey Joe! . . . You got chewing gum?" recurs as a put-down in "G.I. Shmoe!" (Kurtzman and Wood, *Mad* #10, 4/54: 8). MAD used with permission.

Wood also early plucked a string that has become a cliché in the present: males avoiding commitment. "Flesh, darling . . . Even though you go to certain death, I shall go to fight the alien creature with you!" says Dale in "Flesh Garden!" (#11, 5/54: 1-8; 1). After first ordering her to stay, he changes his mind: "O.K.! . . . Go . . . Here's my sword . . . No sense in both of us getting kilt!" (1). The humor depends entirely on the visualization of Dale's shock as the muscular Flesh hightails it in flight. In the end, Flesh sends the devoted Dale back to earth while he and Dr. Zark dally with

Mong's beautiful daughters. "Next thing you know she'll be hinting at marriage," says Flesh (8). The panel does not suggest real sex; Flesh just wants to be the center of admiring female eyes.

Fig. 4-4: The narcissistic Flesh Garden needs a mirror, not a lover. He abandons Dale, the woman devoted to him, so that he can bask in the admiration of female aliens in "Flesh Garden!" (Kurtzman and Wood, *Mad* #11, 5/54: 8). MAD used with permission.

Like many of the other parodies with Kurtzman, "Flesh Garden!" features violence that for all its ferocity is to be understood as adolescent roughhousing. Like them, it also trades in scantily clad women. Voyeurs all, humans are programmed to seize on flashes of flesh, but female flesh appears less frequently than we might expect. In "Superduperman!," for instance, Lois Pain occupies only twelve out of fifty-three panels; in "Black and Blue Hawks!," the traitorous woman only ten out of forty-four. In any event, Wood's humor neither denigrates nor subordinates women, who resemble mothers (in a Freudian sense, not just because of the large breasts) as much as love objects. They are there to be impressed—or, more likely, not—by the boyish heroes who compete—often moronically—for their attention; Wood's women, in fact, are the ultimate voyeurs. Sometimes lethal femme fatales, they are never vengeful. Extracting comedy from this double-edged spectacle involves reminding audiences that betrayal, by women, by rivals, and by fragile masculinity, is a common consequence of the dance of the sexes. In the end, Wood's eroticism is as much if not more situational than graphic. Anchoring the situational humor is his belief that males cannot help themselves. Evolution guides their actions by mandating the sexual strategies Wood graphically burlesques: displays of size, youth, strength, health, resources, dependability, and intelligence.[36] In *Mad* parodies, the stronger the man, the more he thumps his chest, the more he derogates his competitors, the more likely his pursuit of a woman is to fail. To call this an erotics of power would be to miss the point; if anything, Wood's parodies are meditations on the limits of power. Dangerous adventures, daring stunts, and titanic battles usually lead nowhere, much less toward sexual success. The boys who devoured Wood recognized themselves, perhaps sheepishly, in the heroes he lampooned, and could still laugh at their overwrought clumsiness.

Nor are muscular struggles here a kind of S/M on training wheels. Wood's is a far more subtle dynamic than the overworked dyad of Eros and Thanatos. It is also a far cry from real sadomasochism, which is static and profoundly Christian in its exaltation through degradation—the sort of eschatology that so attracted perhaps the most famous of recent sadomasochists, Michel Foucault, whose devoted personal practice of the paraphilia gave us a vocabulary for assessing sexuality in terms like *discipline*, *punish*, *power*, *interrogation*, and *surveillance*.

While Wood's mimicry was peerless (he could have been a fantastic forger), his stylistic innovations were all his own. (In addition to his internal spectators, obvious signatures include wide-eyed faces, goofy demeanors, swaggering occupation of space, reverse angles, flexible depth of field, and so on.) And although his writing partners obviously contributed to the idiom of the ensembles, it was Wood's visual legerdemain that made the collaborations so funny. Indeed, when Kurtzman left for less well-fated enterprises, *Mad* shifted its focus to critiques of the rising new medium of television, the attendant explosion of advertising, and the transformation of postwar America into a consumerist economy. This necessitated satire targeting commercialization, hypocrisy, and the deceptions of capitalism. The shift jettisoned the joyous intolerance for the cant of popular culture; what was ribald became almost serious, certainly more adult. At a cost: by the late 1950s, Wood's *Mad* panels became dark and cramped, the jokes became one-liners, and the raucous send-ups gave way to less purely funny social and political criticism.

His graphic skill was amazing, outstanding even for a magazine devoted to poking fun at "The Usual Gang of Idiots." Ultimately, however, his importance in crafting those early issues turned on his acute sensitivity to the sensibilities of his audience, and his eloquent—and erotic—responses to them. On the one hand, Wood is sympathetic to rampaging male libidos. On the other, he cannot help laughing at the posturing and the false heroics that those urges foster. Mating rituals, or, if one prefers, the battle of the sexes, dominate and structure adolescent life, often thwarted by the tension between evolutionary imperatives at one extreme and cultural romanticism at the other. But the mystery itself remains seductive, and Wood does nothing to dispel it. That he can affirm our most outlandish fantasies and at the same time burlesque them turns on his conviction that the absurdity of sex enchants the world.

Notes

1. J. Hoberman, "Vulgar Modernism," 73.
2. Hoberman, "Vulgar Modernism," 72.
3. John Berger, *Ways of Seeing*, 42.
4. Laura Mulvey, "Visual Pleasure and Narrative Cinema," 6–18.
5. Hoberman, "Vulgar Modernism," 74.
6. Mark James Estren, *A History of Underground Comics*, 11; Tim Pilcher with Gene Kannenberg, Jr., *Erotic Comics: A Graphic History from Tijuana Bibles to Underground Comix*, 96.
7. George Gene Gustines, "From Trash to Auction, Faster Than a Speeding . . . Well, You Know," E5.
8. See Wallace Wood, *Woodwork: Wallace Wood 1927–1981*.
9. Although *Terry and the Pirates* was created by Milton Caniff in 1934, he left the strip in 1946, when it was assigned to Wunder.
10. Michael Schumacher, *Will Eisner: A Dreamer's Life in Comics*, 133–34; N. C. Christopher Couch and Stephen Weiner, *The Will Eisner Companion: The Pioneering Spirit of the Father of the Graphic Novel*, 15.
11. Wallace Wood, "The Pipsqueak Papers."
12. Wallace Wood, "The Disneyland Memorial Orgy," 12–13.
13. The syndicated *Sally Forth W.A.C.* ran in *Military News* June–August 1968. The syndicated *Sally Forth* ran in *Overseas Weekly* July 26, 1971, to April 22, 1974. They are collected in Wallace Wood, *The Compleat Sally Forth*.
14. Wallace Wood, "My Word," 8–10.
15. Wallace Wood and Ray Bradbury, "There Will Come Soft Rains," *Weird Fantasy* #17 (January-February 1953): 25–31, reprinted in Wood, *Woodwork*, 103–09.

16. Quoted in Maria Reidelbach, introduction to *Against the Grain: Mad Artist Wally Wood*, 1.

17. Harvey Kurtzman with Michael Barrier, *From Aargh! to Zap!: Harvey Kurtzman's Visual History of the Comics*, 45.

18. The hysteria inspired Senator Estes Kefauver, who was trying to secure a nomination for President, to hold heavily publicized congressional hearings. One result was the Comics Code of 1954.

19. See Marshall McLuhan, *The Mechanical Bride: Folklore of Industrial Man*; Gershon Legman, "The Psychopathology of the Comics," 3-30; and Jean Baudrillard, *The System of Objects*.

20. David M. Buss, *The Evolution of Desire: Strategies of Human Mating*, 56–57.

21. Craig Yoe and Joe Shuster, *Secret Identity: The Fetish Art of Superman's Co-Creator Joe Shuster*.

22. Art Spiegelman, quoted in Patrick Rosenkranz, *Rebel Visions: The Underground Comix Revolution 1963-1975*, 103.

23. Wally Wood, "The Children," *Weird Science-Fantasy* #23 (March 1954) did not publish those paste-over panels, one of which is reprinted in Wood, *Woodwork*, 123.

24. For a reconstruction of some of Wood's other paste-overs, see Bhob Stewart, ed., *Against the Grain: Mad Artist Wallace Wood*, 47.

25. Michael T. Gilbert, "Total Control: A Brief Biography of Wally Wood."

26. Robert Warshow, "Paul, the Horror Comics, and Dr. Wertham," 57, 45.

27. Warshow, "Paul, the Horror Comics, and Dr. Wertham," 45.

28. Wallace Wood, *Gang Bang*, 3 vols.

29. Dez Skinn, *Comix: The Underground Revolution*, 74.

30. Maurice Horn, *Sex in the Comics*, 92.

31. See Caitlin Flanagan, "What Girls Want," 108–20.

32. The parodies of *The Adventures of Smilin' Jack*, *On the Waterfront*, and *The Rose Tattoo*, all written by Harvey Kurtzman, are titled "Smilin' Melvin" (#7, 10–11/53: 1–7), "Under the Waterfront" (#21, 3/55: 1–6), and "He Rose Tattooed" (#8, 7/56: 4–5).

33. Kurtzman with Barrier, *From Aargh! to Zap!*, 44–45; 31.

34. Maria Reidelbach, *Completely Mad: A History of the Comic Book and Magazine*, 190.

35. Pete Hamill, "Milton Caniff," in *Masters of American Comics*, ed. John Carlin, Paul Karasik, and Brian Walker, 229.

36. Buss, *The Evolution of Desire*, 19–48.

5. The Lighter—and Weightier—Side of *Mad;*

Or, Everything I Needed to Know About Gender and Sexuality I Learned from Dave Berg

Ann M. Ciasullo

AS I WAS growing up in the 1970s, my pop culture staples included a plethora of popular movies, television shows, and music from the era—among them *Star Wars*, *Grease*, *Charlie's Angels*, *The Love Boat*, and all things disco—but one pop culture staple trumped them all: *Mad* magazine. From the ages of seven to twelve, I was a *Mad* devotee, excitedly accompanying my mother to the grocery store and making sure that the magazine made its way into the shopping cart (and through the checkout line) without her noticing. With every new issue of *Mad*, I would look forward to the magazine's regular features—especially "Spy vs. Spy," because I was a fan of the black spy, and it seemed like the white spy *always* won—as well as its movie and television parodies. Some thirty-five years later, I can still remember details from the magazine's send-up of *Star Wars* (1977), "Star Roars," particularly its characterization of C3Po as a "fag robot" (Siegel with DeBartolo [w] and North [a], #196, 1/78: 4-10; 5); I can recall scanning the margins of every page for a random sketch by Sergio Aragonés; I can recollect tracing over images of Don Martin's cartoons in order to reproduce them and their accompanying sound effects (my favorite: "PBLRBLPSFT!!!") on the front of my Trapper Keeper three-ring notebook. *Mad* was an indelible part of my childhood, perhaps among the most influential of my prepubescent teachers. The magazine taught me who, and what, was funny.

Mad also taught me a great deal about what it means to be a woman and what it means to be a man in our culture. Indeed, as an impressionable young girl growing up in a Catholic household and attending Catholic school, I was immersed in a discourse of gender and sexuality that revolved around notions of sin and punishment—a discourse that was countered powerfully by popular culture in general and *Mad* specifically. After all, where else could a devout girl like me learn about premarital sex, gender stereotypes, the gay liberation movement, the pill, the Women's Liberation Movement, and the sexual double standard—all within a mere eight 50-page issues a year? And learn I did. But unlike the Catholic Church, *Mad* is anything but dogmatic in its treatment of these themes. And herein lies the difficulty of analyzing any aspect of the magazine: attempting to figure out what *Mad* wants to convey about, say, homosexuality in the 1970s is as complicated as attempting to figure out how Al Jaffee creates the *Mad* fold-ins. The analytical challenge is, of course, the natural by-product of the magazine's type of humor: satire, parody, and irony, which operate out of a complex relationship to and understanding of stereotypes. And while virtually every aspect of *Mad* is characterized by this complexity, I would argue that none is more so than Dave Berg's "The Lighter Side of . . . ," the magazine's most realistically rendered comic and its most consistent send-up of middle-class Americans and their conventions regarding socioeconomic status, consumerism, cultural fads, the generation gap, and, of course, gender and sexuality.

Working from *Mad* artist Drew Friedman's assertion that "The Lighter Side of . . ." is a "monthly primer on life,"[1] I will examine how Berg's comic is especially a primer on those aspects of life related to womanhood, manhood, and sex and sexuality. My examination will focus on how Berg satirized the changing landscape of gender and sexuality in the 1970s, the decade during which the women's rights movement became an influential cultural and political force, and attitudes toward sexual behavior and experimentation became far more permissive than in previous decades. And though "The Lighter Side of . . ." often relies heavily on predictable gender stereotypes and tropes (i.e., the shrewish wife yelling at the cowering husband) as well as overt sexualization of the female body, it certainly cannot be dismissed wholesale as sexist. On the contrary, sometimes—in fact, more often than not—sexism itself is the butt of the joke. In this way, "The Lighter Side of . . ." (and *Mad* as a whole) presents readers—especially nascent feminist readers like my ten-year-old self—with a far more progressive narrative than might be expected: one in which the male and female characters alike are frequently challenged in their assumptions about gender and sexuality. Even in its ambivalence about the rapid social changes in the 1970s,

"The Lighter Side of . . ." emerges as one of the magazine's most astute and broad-minded feature comics, often portraying feminism, sex, and female sexual agency in surprisingly sympathetic ways.

Dave Berg, the "Human Animal," and Satire

Though *Mad* magazine debuted in its slick format in 1955, not until two years later, in 1957, did Dave Berg join "The Usual Gang of Idiots" (with a four-page comic send-up of American consumerism entitled "Modern Furniture" #34, 8/57: 20–23), and only in 1961 did "The Lighter Side of . . ." make its first appearance. It debuted under the title "A *Mad* Look at . . ." for its first two installments in issues #64 (7/61: 8–11) and #65 (9/61: 18–21). For over forty years, Berg contributed "The Lighter Side of . . ." to the magazine. And though it changed in form through the years—from a cartoonish parody in the early 1960s (e.g., "The Lighter Side of Entertaining" #70, 4/62: 18–21), to its best known form by the late 1960s (a more realistic depiction of people and events, all centered on one theme, such as "hobbies," "money," and "inflation"), to a feature addressing multiple themes in the early 1980s—Berg's intent was always the same: to scrutinize what he called "the human animal," in particular those animals from the middle class. Berg stated that he "want[ed] to 'get' Mr. Average"[2]—Mr. Average often being himself in the form of his alter ego, Roger Kaputnik. And he did just this for *Mad* for forty-one years, until his death in 2002.

Among the recurring features of the magazine—"Spy vs. Spy," Sergio Aragonés's spot cartoons, the movie and TV parodies, Al Jaffee's fold-ins, and Don Martin's comics with accompanying sound effects—Berg's "The Lighter Side of . . ." stands out in two ways. First and foremost, Berg's style of drawing is perhaps the most realistic in the magazine. Unlike, for example, Martin's sketches, which are clearly cartoonish, or even the movie and TV send-ups, which are likewise exaggerated, Berg's work is fairly realistic. Berg himself noted as much, saying in a 1970 interview, "I call the stuff I do now 'caricature' rather than 'cartooning' because it's very close to realism. It's slightly exaggerated—even the writing itself is a caricature—it's truth exaggerated."[3] In *The Act of Creation: A Study of the Conscious and Unconscious in Science and Art*, his landmark study of human creativity, Arthur Koestler observes that "a caricature is comic only if we know something of the victim, if we have a mental image, however vague, of the person, or type of person, at which it is aimed."[4] In the interview quoted above, Berg identifies his "victim": "Mr. Average," a victim who is decidedly male, to be sure, but also white. (It is noteworthy that almost all of Berg's characters are white; only on rare occasions does he feature characters of color, and usually they are African Americans in a strip specifically about race; see, for example, "The Lighter Side of Change" [#180, 1/76: 26-30; esp. 28, 29] and "The Lighter Side of Polarization" [#166, 4/74: 24-28; esp. 24, 26]).[5] Mr. Average, then, is the conventional American everyman.

Second, while many of the regular features lampoon the same issues that Berg does—issues of politics, hypocrisy (the two often go hand in hand), inequality, and so on—only Berg routinely focuses on what seems to have been his defining themes over the course of his career: the middle-class lifestyle and the generation gap. Indeed, the repeated inclusion of Roger Kaputnik—a character who embodies the most typical attributes of the white, middle-class, middle-aged American man—suggests that like Kaputnik, Berg was the pole that remained steady while the world whirled about him with changes. Berg's task was to record, comment on, and satirize these changes *vis-à-vis* both the people undergoing the change and the ones witnessing it.

These two characteristics of "The Lighter Side of . . ."—its (relative) visual realism and its middle-class ethos—make it at once a revealing and challenging feature of the magazine to examine. It is revealing insofar as it is the feature that most clearly invites readers to identify with its characters. The same cannot be said, for example, about the TV and movie send-ups (which are based on predetermined narratives and thus typically on famous characters and actors) or "Spy vs. Spy" (which is based on human-like creatures with cone-shaped noses). Unlike the rest of the magazine, "The Lighter Side of . . ." most explicitly presents itself as "a psychological and sociological study of the human condition"[6] and thereby functions as a mirror for its readers. That is, Berg invites us to see others and ourselves in the various characters he presents—people who are young, old, rebellious, conventional, boastful, sheepish, silly, and serious. What is perhaps most interesting about these traits is that Berg refuses to assign them to any one group of people, even in relation to gender. In Berg's world, women do indeed nag, and they are often chastened for it. But men boast, and they too are put in their place. And because "The Lighter Side of . . ." does not present gender dynamics in an altogether systematic, predictable manner—or more precisely, because neither women nor men are consistently the butt of the joke but rather share the stage as both wits and fools—the feature forces readers to confront their assumptions about how women act, how men act, and who wins in contests of power, sex, and social status.

The complicated, even equivocal, aspects of Berg's "The Lighter Side of . . ." can be best understood in terms of the type of humor he employs: satire. Whereas Berg's is certainly not the only work in any given issue of *Mad* that qualifies as satire, it distinguishes itself from other regular features (e.g., the TV and movie spoofs, the comics of Martin and Aragonés, and "Spy vs. Spy") by consistently aligning itself with this form of humor (as opposed to, say, parody, visual caricature, schtick, the absurd, or "sick humor"). Koestler defines satire as

> a verbal caricature which distorts characteristic features of an individual or society by exaggeration and simplification. The features picked out for enlargement by the satirist are, of course, those of which he disapproves. . . . The comic effect of the satire is derived from the simultaneous presence, in the reader's mind, of the social reality with which he is familiar, and of its reflection in the distorting mirror of the satirist. It focuses attention on abuses and deformities in society of which, blunted by habit, we were no longer aware; it makes us suddenly discover the absurdity of the familiar and the familiarity of the absurd.[7]

The last sentence of this passage, in which Koestler highlights "the absurdity of the familiar and the familiarity of the absurd," perfectly describes the comic moves that Berg makes in "The Lighter Side of . . . ," moves that rely heavily upon the "distorting mirror." It is important to note, however, that Berg's comic distortions in satire are typically not *visual*—Don Martin reigns supreme in this regard—but *verbal*, as Koestler himself emphasizes. The humor of "The Lighter Side of . . ."—and its moments of progressive gender and sexual politics—often resides in the disjunction between the image and the word, between our expectations of how a person, based on appearance and identity, will act (i.e., a wife does this, a husband that; a sexy woman does this, a schlubby guy that) and how someone's speech often defies and overturns expectations. As we shall see, while Berg's world is populated by characters that seem both familiar and predictable, his creative commitments to satire and its inherently ironic stance on the world make "The Lighter Side of . . ." weightier than it initially appcars.

The Visual World of Berg

In his foreword to *Mad's Greatest Artists: Dave Berg: Five Decades of "The Lighter Side of . . . ,"* Drew Friedman describes the various topics at which Berg "poked fun," including "men and women (and could he draw some *sexy* women!)."[8] Friedman's comment, while an aside, is nevertheless noteworthy insofar as it underscores a central characteristic of *Mad* as a whole: its illustrators, writers, and assumed readers are decidedly male. A glance at the magazine's content across the past fifty years confirms that while girls and women like myself may read *Mad*, rarely are we explicitly acknowledged as its audience, desired or otherwise. Rather, the assumed audience is heterosexual adolescent boys and men, and time and again the features in the magazine suggest as much. In Frank Jacobs and Paul Coker Jr.'s "*Mad*'s Lifetime Chart of Attitudes and Behaviors" (#133, 3/70: 26–29), the creators illustrate how the experience of "Ordering Dinner in a Restaurant" and "Watching a Neighbor's House Burn Down" changes over the course of a lifetime. Another experience they examine is "Impressing the Opposite Sex"—and of course, the subject for whom this practice changes is the male, not the female (28–29). Likewise, even a cartoon as innocuous as Sergio Aragonés's "A *Mad* Look at 'Star Wars'" (#197, 3/78: 14–16) suggests that there is humor to be found in "bad boy" behavior—behavior such as Darth Vader's using his powers of the force to pinch a woman's butt from afar (15). My unconscious understanding of the assumed male audience didn't stop me from reading the magazine when I was young, but I do recall moments of youthful perplexity: that is, moments in which I attempted to square my own experience of being female with those presented by the magazine and ultimately feeling both confused by the incongruity of the two and bothered by the expectation of the latter. For if I learned from *Mad* part of what it means to be a woman, then I learned that what makes women at once a source of desire and a source of humor is their bodies. This idea is perhaps best captured in "Don Martin's Guide to Some Very Obscure Comic Sound Effects" (#210, 10/79: 20-23; 22), one of Martin's most famous cartoons, that of Wonder Woman "releasing her Amazon brassiere" with the evocative sound effect of "PLOOBADOOF."

And Berg is no exception here: just a scan of any one installment of "The Lighter Side of . . ." reveals that Friedman is right: Berg does indeed draw some sexy women, and those sexy women often function to heighten the visual pleasure of the comic, independent of the words that they speak. In "The Lighter Side of Collecting," a provocatively dressed woman asks her date to light her cigarette (#173, 3/75: 20-24; 20), while in "The Lighter Side of Sex," a husband explains to his buddies that instead of going to see dirty movies, he'd rather stay home with his hot wife (#136, 7/70: 16-20; 18). In "The Lighter Side of Water," a curvaceous, busty woman thanks a lifeguard for saving her from drowning (#196, 1/78: 20-24; 22), and even in strips where men are not visually present, the women are still quite pleasing to the eye, as in "The Lighter Side of the High Cost of Living" (#169, 9/74: 24-28; 25) and "The Lighter Side of the 'Me' Generation" (#208, 7/79: 28-32; 31).

In short, Berg's sexualization of the female body—a sexualization not equally extended to men in "The Lighter Side of . . ."—underscores the implicit male standpoint and position of power in Berg's humor. Berg the artist draws the sexy women, thereby suggesting that he knows what "sexy" looks like and wants to share that knowledge with his readers; his assumed male readers gaze upon the sexy women, thereby reinforcing Berg's ability to draw to his, and their, desires; and the female reader like myself registers these images as ideals of sexiness that she can or cannot embody. In her now-classic essay, "Visual Pleasure and Narrative Cinema," Laura Mulvey explains that "in their traditional exhibitionist role women are simultaneously looked at and displayed, with their appearance coded for strong visual and erotic impact so that they can be said to connote *to-be-looked-at-ness*."[9] Berg's illustrations of women, even at the height of women's lib in the 1970s, often emphasize their "to-be-looked-at-ness," revealing the male gaze of both the illustrator and the presumed audience for whom he creates his work. (For an especially pronounced example of the male gaze in Berg's work, see "The Lighter Side of Air Travel" in which a happy male traveler passes the time by ogling the provocatively dressed flight attendants serving him; #150, 4/72: 32-36; 35.)

It is tempting to conclude my analysis here, to provide example upon example of the ways that Berg participates in the objectification of women and thus situates himself squarely in the traditional realm of male humor in which "women are made to exist and act only as appendages to men's most basic sexual inclinations."[10] But to do so would be to grossly oversimplify Berg's contributions to *Mad* in general and to the humor of sex and gender specifically. For the humor of Berg's feature often lies in the conjoining of images and words, the upending of expectations regarding what a body looks like versus what a body says and does—or more precisely, by what we are invited to gaze upon versus what we are invited to laugh at. By examining more closely the words and actions of the myriad characters in "The Lighter Side of . . . ," we will see how Berg reflects, questions, and sometimes even champions the massive social changes in relation to gender, sex, and sexuality in the 1970s. While Berg most certainly never would have called himself a feminist, there is much in "The Lighter Side of . . ." for a feminist to appreciate, most notably the fact that in Berg's world, women's words hold as much—and as little—weight as men's. "The Lighter Side of . . . ," in other words, is equal-opportunity satire: the laughter it inspires arises from sources at once predictable and unpredictable.

The Lighter Side of . . . Language, Power, and Sexual Agency

In his book *On Humor: Its Nature and Its Place in Modern Society,* Michael Mulkay discusses the centrality of women to men's humor, explaining that

> in men's dirty jokes, it is not only women's bodies and services that are at men's disposal, but also women's language. Women's words, through which women's versions of the relationship between men and women might be expressed, very seldom triumph in the dirty joke. . . . Thus dirty jokes depict the relationship between men and women in terms of a radical form of sexual, social, and linguistic domination of women by men.[11]

While Mulkay's analysis focuses on the genre of men's dirty jokes specifically, the observations he makes about the relationship between gender and humor are in fact quite applicable to the realm of humor in general—a realm long dominated by men. (For a fascinating, if not maddening, theory of why comicality comes more "naturally" to men than women, see Christopher Hitchens's now-famous 2007 *Vanity Fair* essay, "Why Women Aren't Funny.")[12] From the seemingly inherent funniness of men dressing up as middle-aged women (examples abound, from Monty Python to Tyler Perry's Madea) to the enduring popularity of one-liners laced with sexual innuendo (most notably the quip, "That's what she said"), our repertoire of humor seems to privilege the "sexual, social, and linguistic" power of men.[13] Mulkay's observations underscore the three crucial components of such gender-based humor: (1) male humor is often dependent upon the subordination of women; (2) women's subordination is more often than not expressed in sexual terms; and (3) language is most often the vehicle through which that subordination is enforced. "In the domain of humour," Mulkay concludes, "man's control over and sexual domination of women is exceptionally stark and unrestricted."[14]

I begin this section with an overview of Mulkay's account of gender, humor, and language because one of the most remarkable aspects of Berg's "The Lighter Side of . . ." is the way in which it not only rejects the conventions of male humor outlined above but at times completely overturns them, particularly in relation to their linguistic aspects. Within each three-to-four panel strip of "The Lighter Side of . . ." in the 1970s, women deliver the punchline as often as men, and in the strips that focus on gender dynamics specifically, women's language functions as a source of power.

Take, for example, this exchange, from "The Lighter Side of Transportation," which perfectly highlights how Berg both fulfills and inverts comic expectations regarding gender (#138, 10/70: 26–30; 30). The first panel presents us with a lone image, sans words: that of a young, attractive female flight attendant happily serving the passengers on a plane. The image, which invites the male gaze and thus the objectification of the woman, seemingly places her body squarely in the center of this comic moment. The next two panels highlight the conversation between a husband and wife about the flight attendant's desirable traits: the wife praises the stewardess's ability to serve food and clean up after the passengers, while the husband agrees with his wife—but not for the same reasons. When he says, "Boy, would I like to have something like that at home!!," he means a youthful, sexy, servile woman—not an efficient homemaker. We discern this from the knowing, lecherous look on his face. But the joke is on him: the punchline delivered by his wife, "I've been ASKING you for a maid for years!!," suggests that she knows not only what he is thinking (her arched brows underscore this fact) but also how to use his thoughts, and his language, to her advantage.

In "Transportation," women get the last word, just as they do in one strip from "The Lighter Side of Danger" (#199, 6/78: 26-30; 30). In the first panel, a young couple is seated in a roller-coaster car. The man reassures the woman: "Don't be afraid, baby! I'll hold on to you!!," thus establishing the traditional gender expectations in the face of relative danger: man as the brave protector, woman as the frail object in need of reassurance. The second and third panels, sketches of the whoosh and roar of the roller coaster as it rises to great heights and plummets to great depths, highlight the terrifying nature of the ride. In the final panel, we are presented with the punch line: an image almost identical to that of the first, except in this one, it is the *man* who is holding onto the *woman* for dear life. He appears petrified—his hair is on end!—while she appears at once unfazed and irritated. While the image alone would be quite comical, the words she utters—"Okay! You can let go now!"—heighten the humorous effect of the strip as a whole, insofar as they complete the incongruity of the entire scene: it is the supposedly frail woman who offers (albeit with annoyance) the comforting words at the end of the ride, her version of "It's okay, sweetie, the scary part is over." Both the image and the speech balloon completely belie our original expectations of the outcome.

Henri Bergson, in his foundational essay *Laughter: An Essay on the Meaning of the Comic*, would explain the humor in this scene in terms of inversion: "Picture to yourself certain characters in a certain situation: if you reverse the situation and invert the roles, you obtain a comic scene."[15] I would argue, however, that when the inversion involves the switching of gender roles, the humor is more complicated, insofar as it then challenges deep-seated beliefs about the so-called natural roles of women and men.[16] Mulkay notes how "women's words . . . very seldom triumph in the dirty joke,"[17] but in "The Lighter Side of . . . ," women's words in fact triumph time and again. In this strip and the previous one, the woman, not the man, possesses verbal authority.

I am not suggesting that the solution to the problem of patriarchal control over language is simply to strip men of their linguistic power altogether, to humiliate them with words—even though such a complete reversal of power is not uncommon in the realm of humor. As T. G. A. Nelson explains in his book *Comedy: An Introduction*, "the obvious remedy for a comic tradition which laughs at or patronizes women is to create a rival tradition in which women laugh at or patronize men."[18] Though it may appear otherwise upon first glance, Berg does not in fact resort to the "obvious remedy." After all, alongside the strips discussed above are ones in which language serves to undermine women, as in a strip from "The Lighter Side of Goofs" (#190, 4/77: 16-20; 18), in which a wife rebukes her husband for using sexist language. "HOW DARE YOU CALL A WOMAN A 'BROOD SOW'!!," she shrieks at him. "NO PERSON SHOULD BE COMPARED TO AN ANIMAL, YOU MALE CHAUVINIST—pig!" (18). Her face, turned away from her husband in the last panel, registers that she recognizes and is embarrassed by her hypocrisy. In Berg's world, however, hypocrisy is not exclusively female. In "The Lighter Side of Sound Equipment" (#144, 7/71: 18-22; 19), for example, a husband mocks his wife for not understanding the complicated stereo system their son has left in their house. "Hah!" he snorts. "Listen to the big leading member of the Women's Lib Movement asking her male chauvinist husband how to handle electronic equipment!" By the third panel, he demands that she admit her inferiority before he will show her how to use the system. "Okay! Okay! I'm an inferior female! Now—show me how to shut the darn thing off!" the wife replies exhaustedly. This time, it's the husband who's chagrined: "You pull out the plug!" (19). Given that these examples represent the overall tenor of Berg's humor, it cannot be said that Berg wholly participates in the tradition of male humor, insofar as his use of language—and his assignment of its control (or lack thereof) to men and women alike—is far more nuanced than in conventional humor. Rather, Berg creates an equal-opportunity playing field, one in which *access* to linguistic power is shared by men and women—and the significance of this fact cannot be understated. For young female readers like myself growing up in the 1970s, "The Lighter Side of . . ." taught us that words could be weapons and that wit was not the purview of men alone.

And there is one word, in fact, that appears time and again in "The Lighter Side . . ." in the 1970s, a word of great educational value to me as a young reader of *Mad* and of great social import to American society in the seventies: *sex*. It makes sense that sex plays a prominent role in Berg's feature during this era; after all, the sexual revolution was in full swing, and the middle class oscillated between participation in and rejection of this revolution. Two significant themes emerge in Berg's characterization of the changing mores around sex and sexuality. The first is the ever-present theme of the generation gap, the clash between parents and children over values and lifestyles. He captures this conflict quite humorously and succinctly in a strip from "The Lighter Side of Change" (#180, 1/76: 26-30; 30), in which a young woman bravely tells her mother that she and her boyfriend have been living together "without being married or anything." The mother replies with a simple "Oh . . .?," a response that surprises her daughter. As the couple leaves the house, the young woman comments to her boyfriend, "Considering what a strait-laced puritanical square my Mother is, she took it rather well!" True to form, though, Berg overturns the young woman's, and our, expectations in the final panel, which is simply dominated by the sound of the mother screaming "YAAAA!" (30). This strip highlights generational differences not only around the issue of *marriage* but also around the issue of *morality*—specifically, sexual morality. And the intersection of sexual morality and female desire plays out in fascinating ways in "The Lighter Side of . . ." throughout the 1970s. This intersection constitutes the second—and given the focus of my project, more interesting—theme that emerges in Berg's treatment of sex in the era.

As discussed earlier, it is not unusual for male humor to center around issues of female sexuality, but typically such humor objectifies women, thereby removing them from the field of sexual agency altogether. Berg, in contrast, presents his readers with women who not only look sexy, as discussed earlier, but who are interested in sex *for themselves,* not just to please men. Take, for example, the following strip, from "The Lighter Side of Love" (#142, 4/71: 30-33; 30), in which a young woman laments to her mother, "When I first got to college, the only thing that the boys I dated ever wanted was SEX! So I told them they could all go jump in the lake!" "Good for you!" her mother commends her. "Then I met Warren," the daughter continues. And with Warren, she says, she had a "real, deep, meaningful relationship." "That's nice!" the mother happily replies. But it wasn't really all *that* nice, as the daughter explains: love without sex is unfulfilling, a "bore" (see fig. 5-1).

Although the comic begins by firmly placing us within the domain of traditional gender expectations—in this instance, the expectation that men want sex and women don't—it ends by overturning those expectations in ways both comical and radical. In doing so, it achieves two distinct but related goals. First, it challenges the conventional belief that all women want is love and romance. Surprisingly, according to the young woman, they also want sex. Second, it once again rejects conventional forms of male humor. The joke here is *not* dependent upon silencing,

Fig. 5-1: "The Lighter Side of . . ." in the 1970s often reflects the changing cultural landscape vis-à-vis sexuality. In presenting a woman who wants sex to be part of a romantic relationship, Berg overturns conventional notions of femininity, masculinity, and sexual desire ("The Lighter Side of Love" *Mad* #142, 4/71: 30). MAD used with permission.

subordinating, or humiliating the young woman and her sexuality; rather, it is dependent upon her recognition of her own desires and her frustration over the fact that traditional narratives of love and romance leave out a significant component of a relationship: sexual desire.

The extent to which Berg presents sex as a pleasurable activity for women—and presents women *speaking* about their pleasure—is striking. In "The Lighter Side of Making Extra Money" (#182, 4/76: 18-22; 20), Berg again sketches two women discussing sex. One, dressed in jeans and a T-shirt, asks the other, dressed in a bikini top and very short miniskirt, "What's up? There's a glow around you like you're floating on Cloud Nine." "Make that Cloud TEN!" her friend gushes. She continues in panel two: "I spent last night making wild, passionate love with a man in a strange apartment!" In the third panel, the woman on Cloud Ten exclaims, "Imagine! Having a ball like that, and getting PAID for it besides!!" Her friend is shocked: "YOU'RE A . . . A HOOKER?!" But of course, she's not a hooker, as she tells her friend in the final panel: "No, dummy! I'm a babysitter!" What is remarkable in this strip is the absence of judgment on Berg's part regarding this young woman and her sexual activity.[19] While she openly brags about the "wild, passionate" sex she had the night before, the comic does not condemn her either for having sex or for boasting about it. Rather, it presents her sex life, and women's desires, as part of the fabric of the changing middle class. In this comic, the humor resides in part in the visual: in her bikini top, miniskirt, and high heels, the Cloud Ten woman looks like anything *but* a babysitter, a job usually associated with adolescent girls who are unpopular, homebody-ish, or maternal. Given the woman's rather revealing outfit, it's a surprise to both her friend and to us that she does something so modest for a living. But the humor also resides in the *linguistic*—in the incongruity between the actions the young woman describes to her girlfriend (wild sex) and the occasion for those actions (a babysitting gig). It does *not* rely solely upon a visual gag involving her body or a verbal gag involving the undermining of her voice. Her sexual agency is a given, a fact, and the joke occurs within rather than at the expense of this reality.

Such images of female sexual agency occur time and again in Berg's strip in the 1970s, especially in one of its most prominent motifs, that of "making out." (Die-hard *Mad* fans will fondly recall the 6 1/2-minute record of the same name that was included as an insert to *Super Special* #26 in 1978 [Jacobs and Blagman]. I thank this record for helping me to comprehend the meaning of the term.) Making out occurs frequently in "The Lighter Side of . . . ," and it is characterized as an activity that both men and women enjoy immensely, as illustrated in "The Lighter Side of Weddings" (#152, 7/72: 26-30; 27), "The Lighter Side of Goofs" (#190, 4/77: 16), and "The Lighter Side of Sex" (#136, 7/70: 17). It is worth comparing these images to one from a Sergio Aragonés feature entitled "A *Mad* Look at Karate" (#163, 12/73: 24–26), a strip that reveals the physical and sexual threat that women face from men and the absence of female sexual agency in the face of that threat. The first panel of Aragonés's strip features a woman on a date, fending off a would-be lover who has pinned her down on the couch while making (unwanted) sexual advances on her. In the second panel, the woman has enrolled in a karate class; her aggressive stance, paired with the fierce, determined expression on her face, suggests that she is ready to fight back and defend herself against such predatory male behavior. Despite her newly acquired karate skills, however, the third panel is almost identical to the first. In it, she is fending off a would-be lover who has pinned her down on the couch while making (unwanted) sexual advances on her—except that this time, the lecherous date is the very same man who has taught her to defend herself: her karate instructor. When I saw this comic, I immediately felt uncomfortable, in large part because its humor belies the seriousness of rape. But I also couldn't help but think of the radical difference between it and "The Lighter Side of . . . ," the latter of which so often features female characters who express sexual desire and control in ways that would have been unusual, if not almost impossible, before the women's liberation movement and the sexual revolution.[20] In his inclusion and consistently nonjudgmental comic depiction of these women, Berg promotes decidedly feminist values.

Finally, though, it is worth examining how Berg's engagement with these issues, particularly that of women's lib, is not wholly uncritical. After all, his commitment to his overarching project—a satire of the middle class—requires that he reveal *all* hypocrisy, even (if not especially) when it resides in the very sources purporting to enact progressive social change. In a second strip from "The Lighter Side of Transportation" (#138, 10/70: 30), Berg illustrates, through a stereotypical image of a women's libber as manly and aggressive, how even the most radical of political movements can be conflicted in the achievement of its goals. An unassuming man sitting on a bus asks a woman standing next to him what the pin she is wearing stands for. Her response functions less as an answer and more as a diatribe: "It stands for 'Women's Liberation Movement!' A small but vocal group of us women are demanding our civil rights! We are demanding equal job opportunities . . . equal pay . . . equal treatment under the law . . . In fact, equality in EVERYTHING with men!" She further chastises the inquirer for being among those "opinionated, selfish, and inconsiderate" men who oppress women. "You're a prime example of the type!" she yells at him. And finally, in the last panel, the moment of hypocrisy occurs when she shouts at him, "The least you could do is get up and give me your seat!!" (30). In "The Lighter Side of Polarization" (#166, 4/74: 24-28; 28), Berg offers an even more pointed critique of feminist dogma through ineffectual remarks about women's demands for equal pay from a female speaker who bears a striking resemblance to Betty Friedan (see fig. 5-2).

Fig. 5-2: Berg recognizes women's lib—and the resistance to it—as a powerful cultural movement. Here, he illustrates how the "enemies" of the movement were often women as well as men ("The Lighter Side of Polarization" *Mad* #166, 4/74: 28). MAD used with permission.

Whereas in the previously discussed strips we are invited to laugh *with* women in their exasperation over gender expectations, here we are invited to laugh *at* them—or more precisely, to laugh at *feminist* women for their doctrinaire politics. But comics like this—and the handful in which Berg relies upon an even more pointedly stereotypical image of feminists as overweight, androgynous, and angry, and employs this image as a source of humor[21]—do not negate the significance, or even the implicit feminist bent, of the previously discussed strips. Rather, we must read Berg's critiques of feminism within the larger context of "The Lighter Side of . . . ," a context in which *all* people, at one point or another, act foolishly. And because foolishness is a given in Berg's world, feminism and sexism both are subject to his ridicule.

From a feminist perspective, Berg's satiric commentary on gender, sex, and sexuality is extraordinarily significant. In most venues where feminism was being mocked in the 1970s—from the living room conversations of the Silent Majority to articles on women's lib in national publications such as *Time*, *Newsweek*, and *The New York Times*—that mockery was unilateral: that is, feminism was dismissed as threatening, overly emotional, irresponsible, or just downright ridiculous, and sexism was explained as a figment of the imagination.[22] But in *Mad* in the 1970s—a magazine with an all-male artistic staff, with an assumed male audience, and with decidedly male adolescent humor (I'm thinking here of "gross-out" humor especially)—feminism wasn't *simply* dismissed. It was ridiculed, to be sure, but so was sexism. Indeed, the extent to which *Mad* engaged with contemporary discourses on gender inequality and the politics of the women's liberation movement is actually quite striking. In my review of all the issues of the 1970s, I found no fewer than fifteen substantial references to, if not entire features on, the women's movement. Most of them appear between 1970 and 1975, when feminism was at the height of its political and social influence. Given its notable presence in the magazine during this decade, as well as the representation of movement leaders such as Betty Friedan and Gloria Steinem in these features, *Mad*'s relationship to the women's liberation movement specifically and feminism in general in the 1970s is most certainly worthy of analysis in its own right.[23] And Berg was one of the leading proponents of surveying the political and social landscape in its entirety, highlighting the ridiculousness of both ideological camps. In "The Lighter Side of Overreacting" (#202, 10/78: 26-30; 30), Berg presents a complex representation of these camps in a mere four panels about a woman and a man on a tennis court. In the first two panels, the woman accuses the man of being a "male chauvinist pig" who works for a "male chauvinist pig company." The man objects, claiming that he works for an "Equal Opportunity Employer" and accordingly has two bosses: one male, one female. "Do they give you a hard time?" his partner asks. For the appalling double standard in his reply, see figure 5-3. In many ways, this strip embodies

Berg's ethos of gender politics. The stereotypical feminist levels accusations against the male; the "equal opportunity" male refutes her claims.

Fig. 5-3: "The Lighter Side of Overreacting" in *Mad* #202 (10/78) features one of Berg's most astute comics about the "double standard": powerful men are seen as aggressive, powerful women are seen as bitchy. When expressed in this manner, it's a standard that can drive a woman to raise her racket in protest (30). MAD used with permission.

And what is the punch line? The combination of the man's dismissal of his female boss as "bitchy" (thereby proving that he *is* in fact a male chauvinist pig) and the woman's response to his sexism: raising her racquet to smack him over the head for his stupidity. While the woman may be the one overreacting, as viewers we understand and even sympathize with her response: it is borne of frustration over the shortsightedness and sexism of her tennis partner. In the game of gender politics as Berg represents it, there is no clear winner—but there are moments when feminism makes sense. And given the paucity of such moments in U.S. culture at large in the 1970s, Berg should be recognized for complicating the discourse of gender politics through his representations of men, women, and sex in "The Lighter Side of . . . ."

Some Conclusions; or, Dave Berg, Unlikely Feminist

As the 1970s came to a close, so too did my love of *Mad* magazine. By 1981, I was well into puberty, and my magazine-reading interests shifted from *Mad* to *16*, *Teen Beat*, and *Tiger Beat*. Images of Alfred E. Neuman and posters of Don Martin characters on my bedroom wall were replaced by glossy centerfolds of Matt Dillon, Rick Springfield, and Steve Perry. "Spy vs. Spy," Sergio Aragonés, and Dave Berg became a part of my past. Yet they were a profound influence, inextricably connected to my childhood and to the alternative education that the magazine provided me. And while I loved all the features in *Mad* as a kid, "The Lighter Side of . . ." was the only one by which I was truly *intrigued*—and by "intrigued" I mean the dictionary definition of the word: to be curious about or fascinated by something. Berg's feature inspired my curiosity and fascination because it was the only one in the magazine that, as Drew Friedman explains, "prepared me and countless other kids for what we could expect from life."[24] "The Lighter Side of . . ." was, in short, *Mad*'s most incisive satire, the "primer on life" *par excellence*.

In his book *Satire: A Critical Reintroduction*, Dustin Griffin reminds us that "critics have for some years emphasized the complexity and ambiguity of the best satire."[25] If complexity and ambiguity are the hallmarks of the "best" satire, then Berg is obviously among the masters. In the 1970s, Berg engaged with some of the most prominent issues of the era in ways both comical and philosophical: he held up a mirror to the middle class, showing us the inevitable changes that were taking place in relation to gender, sex, and power. And that mirror was powerful: it conveyed important lessons to those of us gazing into it, lessons about the rapidly changing role of women in American society, about the profound effects of the sexual revolution, and about the ongoing state of the "battle of the sexes." Taken as a whole, "The Lighter Side of . . ." in the 1970s certainly cannot be considered unmistakably feminist in its *intent*—for it is unlikely that Berg ever would have identified himself as an advocate of women's lib—but as poststructuralist and postmodern critics know, intent isn't everything. By rejecting some of the fundamental tropes of male humor and opting instead for a more sophisticated take on gender relations in the 1970s, Berg gives feminists like myself an occasion for celebration and appreciation in our retrospective look at *Mad* magazine. And that's not something to "YEECHH!" about.

Notes

1. Drew Friedman, foreword to *Mad's Greatest Artists: Dave Berg: Five Decades of "The Lighter Side of . . . ,"* 7.
2. *Mad's Greatest Artists: Dave Berg*, 99, 97
3. *Mad's Greatest Artists: Dave Berg*, 98.
4. Arthur Koestler, *The Act of Creation: A Study of the Conscious and Unconscious in Science and Art*, 70.
5. In light of *Mad*'s assumed white, middle-class audience, Berg's, and *Mad*'s, understanding and representation of race and race relations—particularly in the 1970s, when the Civil Rights and Black Power movements were well-established in the United States—would make a compelling study.
6. Friedman, foreword to *Mad's Greatest Artists: Dave Berg*, 7.
7. Koestler, *The Act of Creation*, 72–73.
8. Friedman, foreword to *Mad's Greatest Artists: Dave Berg*, 7.
9. Laura Mulvey, "Visual Pleasure and Narrative Cinema," 11.
10. Michael Mulkay, *On Humor: Its Nature and Its Place in Modern Society*, 137.
11. Mulkay, *On Humor*, 137.
12. Christopher Hitchens, "Why Women Aren't Funny," 54–59.
13. Sigmund Freud's book *Jokes and Their Relation to the Unconscious*, 115–21, offers a fascinating analysis of the relationship between sex and humor, especially in his discussion of the dirty joke, or what he calls *smut*, "the intentional bringing into prominence of sexual facts and relations by speech" (115). Of course, his analysis privileges the psychosexual dynamics of the dirty joke, but it nevertheless sheds light on the potential role of hostility and aggressiveness in such humor.
14. Mulkay, *On Humor*, 141.
15. Henri Bergson, *Laughter: An Essay on the Meaning of the Comic*, 94.
16. The philosophy of humor and laughter is quite extensive, and most studies usually begin with a review of what Brian Boyd called the "three main traditional theories of humor" in "Laughter and Literature: A Play Theory of Humor," 3. These are the Superiority Theory (we laugh because we feel smarter or better than others), the Incongruity Theory (we laugh because a person or event "violates our expectations"), and the Relief Theory (we laugh because it "relieve[s] us of nervous tension"; see John Morreall, "A New Theory of Laughter," in *The Philosophy of Laughter and Humor*, ed. John Morreall, 130–31. While it is outside of the scope of my essay to discuss these theories in depth as they relate

to Berg's humor, there are numerous extremely helpful sources for interested researchers. For more on the definitions and limitations of the three theories of humor, see also Brian Boyd, "Laughter and Literature"; and T. G. A. Nelson, *Comedy: An Introduction to Comedy in Literature, Drama, and Cinema*. For extensive discussions of the incongruity theory, the theory that seems most applicable to Berg's work, see Michael Clark, "Humor and Incongruity," 139–55; John Morreall, "Funny Ha-Ha, Funny Strange, and Other Reactions to Incongruity," 188–207; and Mike W. Martin, "Humor and Aesthetic Enjoyment of Incongruities," 172–86, all in *The Philosophy of Laughter and Humor*, ed. John Morreall. For extensive discussions of laughter and jokes, see Bergson, *Laughter*; and Freud, *Jokes and Their Relation to the Unconscious*.

17. Mulkay, *On Humor*, 137.

18. Nelson, *Comedy: An Introduction*, 11.

19. Interestingly, in a 1970 interview, Berg identified the lack of judgment in "The Lighter Side of . . ." as one of its defining features: "I'm not standing on a pedestal saying, 'I am holier than thou.' . . . I detest the type of writers who sit in judgment." See *Mad's Greatest Artists: Dave Berg*, 99.

20. Also unthinkable before these cultural and political revolutions: representations of women discussing the contraceptive pill as a routine part of their lives. See "The Lighter Side of Boating," #145 (9/71): 16-20; 18; "The Lighter Side of Mornings," #192 (7/77): 16-20; 19; and "The Lighter Side of Surprises," #205 (4/79): 20-24; 18, for Berg's take on such representations.

21. See "The Lighter Side of the Revolutionary Movement," #139 (12/70): 16-20; 18; and "The Lighter Side of Hang Ups," #154, (10/72): 32-36; 34.

22. For an excellent account of how the women's liberation movement was represented—usually with derision—in popular media, see Susan Brownmiller, "Enter the Media," in her *In Our Time: Memoir of a Revolution*, 133–66; and Susan Douglas, "I am Woman, Hear Me Roar," in her *Where the Girls Are: Growing Up Female with the Mass Media*, 163–91.

23. See Jacobs, "Distinctive Birth Announcements," #149 (3/72): 34-36; 34; "Distinctive Wedding Announcements," #160 (7/73): 14-16; 14; and "If Today's Celebrities Answered Virginia's Letter about Santa Claus," #156 (1/73): 21-23; 22; Jacobs, Clarke, and Pesek, "Old Standards Rewritten for the Liberated Woman," #162 (10/73): 30-32; Brandel, "*Mad* Photopoetry," #151 (6/72): 4-7; 5; and "What's in a Name? Two Institutions," #164 (1/74): 38-39; 38; Brandel and Torres, "A Parade of Protesting *Mad* Co-Signers," #155 (12/72): 14-16; 15; Jacobs and Torres, "*Mad*'s 1973 Christmas Poem," #164 (1/74): 34-35; 34; Jacobs and Drucker, "My Fair Laddie," #167 (6/74): 4-11; Jacobs and Clarke, "U.S. Commemorative Stamps We'd Never Like to See," #179 (12/75): 36-38; 37; and "Mother's Day Cards from the 'Now' Generation," #143 (6/71): 26-28; 28; Silverstone and Clarke, "Playthings Based on TV Commercials," #132 (1/70): 26-29; 28, 29; Koch and Davis, "A Little Kid's Guide to Understanding the News," #189 (3/77): 14-17; 16; Hart and Torres, "The Doris Daze Show," #140 (1/71): 43-47; 47; Koch and Woodbridge, "Rewriting Classical Poetry to Give Women Equal Time," #208 (7/79): 12-15 ; Siegel and North, "When

Women Take Over Movies Completely," #211 (12/79): 30-33; Silverstone and Rickard, "*Mad* Visits the Women's Liberation Front," *Special* #6 (1972): 2–6; Paulson and Rickard, "Life from the Broadside," #135 (6/70): 15–17; and Cowen and Rickard, "When the 'Women's Lib Movement' is Successful," *Special* #3 (1971): 18–19.

24. Friedman, foreword to *Mad's Greatest Artists: Dave Berg*, 7.

25. Dustin Griffin, *Satire: A Critical Reintroduction*, 2.

PART II.

FEATURES FROM COVER TO FOLD-IN

6. The Secret History of Alfred E. Neuman

Alan Rankin

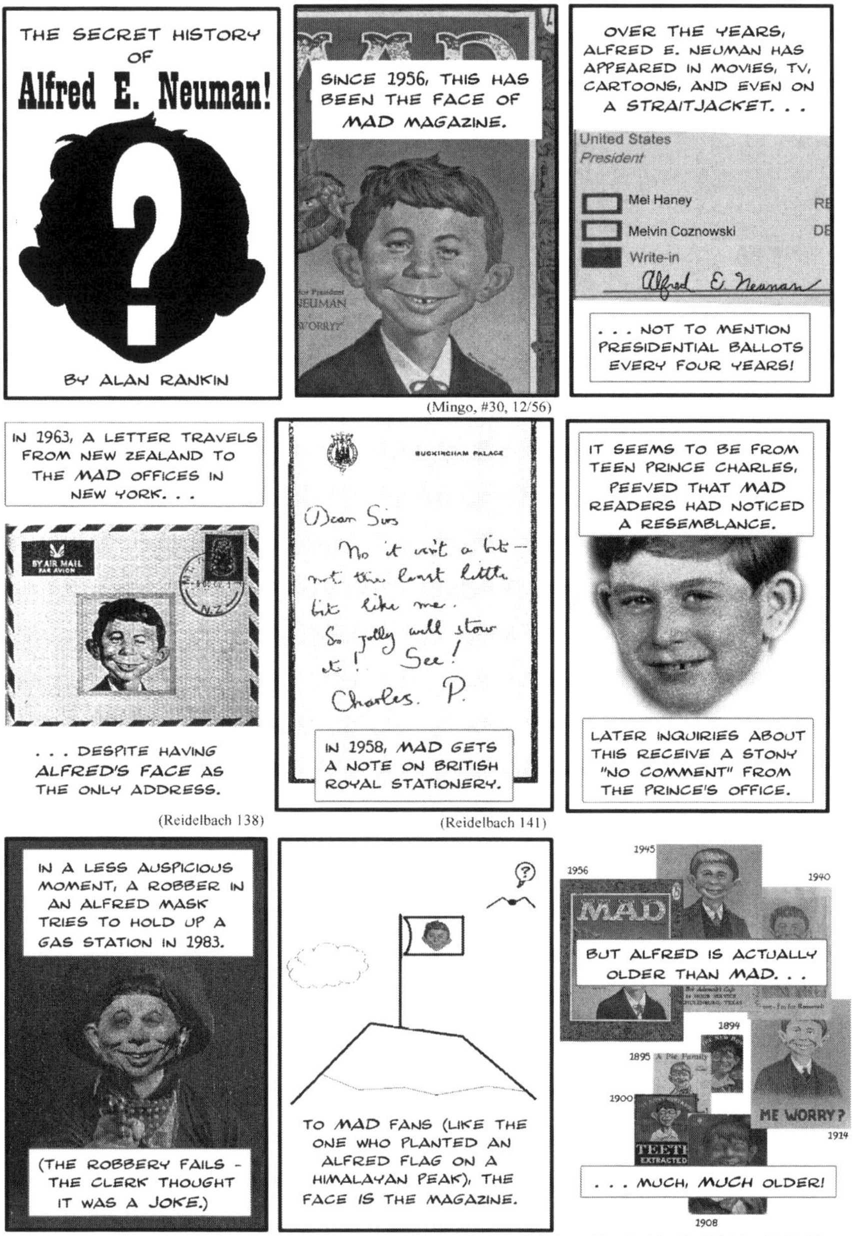

(Mingo, #30, 12/56)

(Reidelbach 138)

(Reidelbach 141)

(images cited above; historical details, Reidelbach 138-46)

IN 1954, MAD CREATOR HARVEY KURTZMAN VISITS BALLANTINE BOOKS, PUBLISHER OF THE SOON-TO-BE-WILDLY-POPULAR MAD PAPERBACKS.
HARVEY SEES A FAMILIAR FACE ON THE WALL.
KURTZMAN HAS SEEN THE IMAGE MANY TIMES BEFORE, BUT WHEN HE SEES THE POSTCARD, HE SAYS: "THAT'S IT! THAT'S GOT TO BE THE ORIGINAL!"
ME WORRY?
(IT WASN'T.)
(Richardson and Duin 10)
KURTZMAN: "IT WAS A FACE THAT DIDN'T HAVE A CARE IN THE WORLD, EXCEPT MISCHIEF."
KURTZMAN'S SUCCESSOR, AL FELDSTEIN, ADOPTS THE IMAGE AS MAD'S MASCOT. . . LIKE THE PLAYBOY BUNNY.
(Richardson and Duin 10; Feldstein)
FELDSTEIN HIRES ARTIST NORMAN MINGO TO CREATE THE DEFINITIVE ALFRED.
MAD EDITOR JERRY DE FUCCIO SAID MINGO "DID FOR ALFRED WHAT LEONARDO DA VINCI HAD DONE FOR THE MONA LISA."
(Reidelbach 143; Richardson and Duin 10)
"ALFRED E. NEUMAN," A JOKE NAME MAD AND FELDSTEIN HAD USED FOR YEARS. . .
DEAD LETTER DEPT.
FELDSTEIN
. . . BECOMES HIS OFFICIAL NAME WITH MAD ISSUE 29.
(Feldstein; Richmond)
BUT ALFRED'S PAST SOON CATCHES UP WITH HIM.
IN THE 1960S, MAD IS SUED BY HELEN STUFF, WHO CLAIMS HER HUSBAND CREATED THE IMAGE IN 1914.
(Stuff v. EC Publications)
Winnipeg Dental
ME-WORRY?
MAD WINS THE LAWSUIT. . .
Happy Jack
BEVERAGES
. . . THANKS TO ITS READERS, WHO SEND IN IMAGES OF THE PROTO-ALFRED DATING TO THE 1890S.
Me Worry? No —
"It Didn't Hurt a Bit"
BUT IF ALFRED WASN'T CREATED BY MINGO, KURTZMAN, OR EVEN STUFF. . .
. . . THEN WHERE DID HE COME FROM?

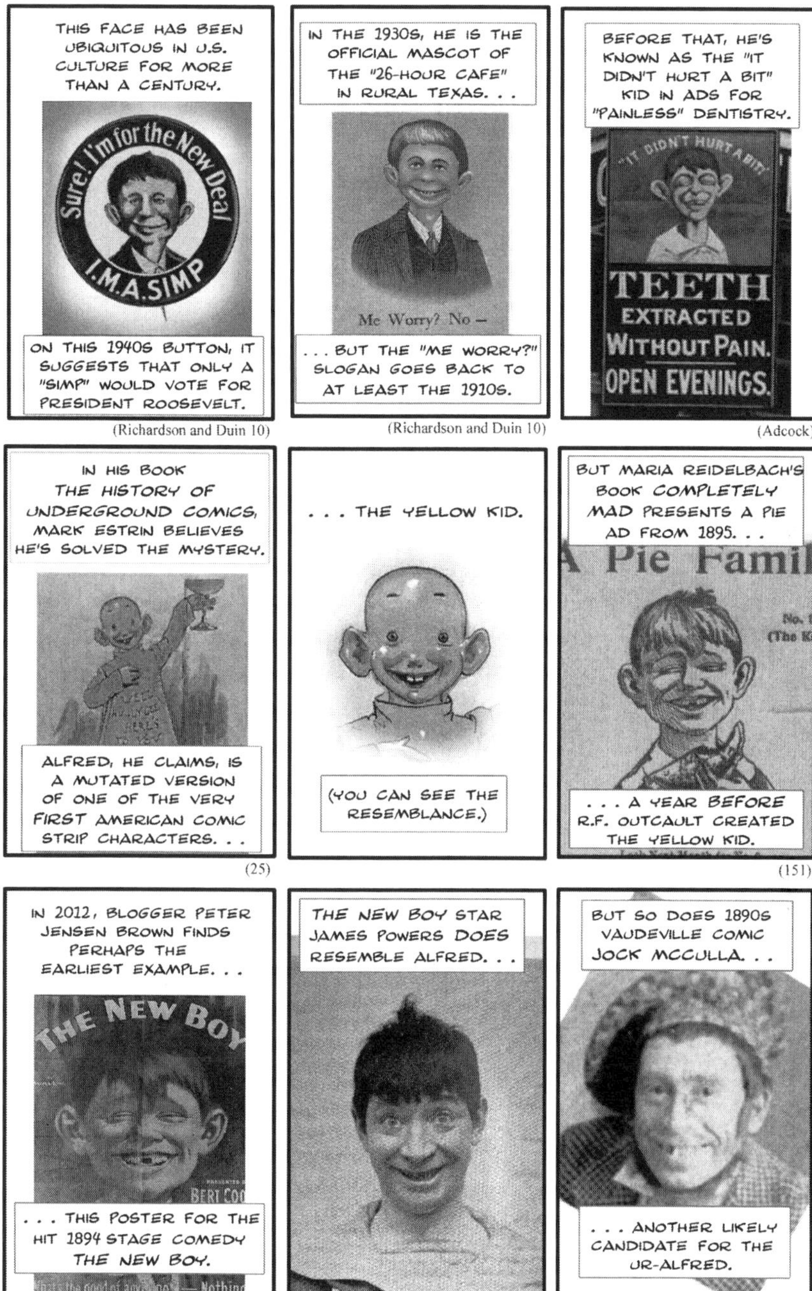
THIS FACE HAS BEEN UBIQUITOUS IN U.S. CULTURE FOR MORE THAN A CENTURY.
Sure! I'm for the New Deal
I.M.A. SIMP
ON THIS 1940S BUTTON, IT SUGGESTS THAT ONLY A "SIMP" WOULD VOTE FOR PRESIDENT ROOSEVELT.
(Richardson and Duin 10)
IN THE 1930S, HE IS THE OFFICIAL MASCOT OF THE "26-HOUR CAFE" IN RURAL TEXAS. . .
Me Worry? No –
. . . BUT THE "ME WORRY?" SLOGAN GOES BACK TO AT LEAST THE 1910S.
(Richardson and Duin 10)
BEFORE THAT, HE'S KNOWN AS THE "IT DIDN'T HURT A BIT" KID IN ADS FOR "PAINLESS" DENTISTRY.
TEETH EXTRACTED WITHOUT PAIN. OPEN EVENINGS.
(Adcock)
IN HIS BOOK *THE HISTORY OF UNDERGROUND COMICS,* MARK ESTRIN BELIEVES HE'S SOLVED THE MYSTERY.
ALFRED, HE CLAIMS, IS A MUTATED VERSION OF ONE OF THE VERY FIRST AMERICAN COMIC STRIP CHARACTERS. . .
(25)
. . . THE YELLOW KID.
(YOU CAN SEE THE RESEMBLANCE.)
BUT MARIA REIDELBACH'S BOOK *COMPLETELY MAD* PRESENTS A PIE AD FROM 1895. . .
. . . A YEAR BEFORE R.F. OUTCAULT CREATED THE YELLOW KID.
(151)
IN 2012, BLOGGER PETER JENSEN BROWN FINDS PERHAPS THE EARLIEST EXAMPLE. . .
THE NEW BOY
. . . THIS POSTER FOR THE HIT 1894 STAGE COMEDY *THE NEW BOY.*
THE NEW BOY STAR JAMES POWERS *DOES* RESEMBLE ALFRED. . .
BUT SO DOES 1890S VAUDEVILLE COMIC JOCK MCCULLA. . .
. . . ANOTHER LIKELY CANDIDATE FOR THE UR-ALFRED.

(Lane)

(162)

(Neuendorffer)

7. The "Mad 20" with Alfred E. Neuman;

Or, It's the Covers, Stupid

Christopher J. Gilbert

"Stupidity has a knack of getting its way."

—Albert Camus, *The Plague*

STUPIDITY IS THE organizing principle of *Mad* magazine. *Mad* emerged in the 1950s as an ironic, irreverent, and incisive send-up of "commercial practices, social conventions, and cultural institutions that underwrote postwar consensus ideology and the Great American Way," as Stephen Kercher put it.[1] Simply, *Mad* made comic madness more virtue than vice, and artful stupidity a mode of smart satire. Since its inception, *Mad* has stood steady on the edge of praise and blame for the idiotic, with Alfred E. Neuman as its unsightly cover boy. Neuman's iconography is significant because his aura and appearance on the cover of *Mad* often epitomize the content. Take infamous issue #166 in April 1974, which features the logo in flaxen over a cerulean background, the phrase "the number one ecch magazine" also in yellow, and Neuman's hand protruding from the bottom and giving the middle finger. But there is much more to Neuman, and to *Mad* covers, than profane gestures. As Stergios Botzakis notes, the moronic mascot "has appeared on almost every cover since 1955 playing a wide range of characters, from Yoda to Voldemort, Justin Bieber to Uncle Sam."[2] Numerous other scholars and commentators have offered genealogies of the figure who is now a poster child of stupidity, pointing to the pedigree of a fool who indulges blissful ignorance (if not downright dimwittedness) with his signature "What, Me Worry?" and evinces the merit in judging a proverbial book by its cover.[3] This judgment is perhaps most apparent in the "Mad 20," an annual compendium of "The Dumbest People, Events & Things."

The "Mad 20" was rolled out at the turn of the twenty-first century. After honoring the dumbest of 1998 in its inaugural issue, *Mad* has designated the first issue of every subsequent year its "annual tribute to the year's biggest idiots," rendering the capture and celebration of stupidity a time-honored tradition. This leitmotif is no small thing. Thinkers such as Sigmund Freud and Georg Wilhelm Friedrich Hegel, after all, have recognized in madness a break from reality based on a particularly distorted perspective of it. Madness is conventionally conceived as rashness, thoughtlessness, even lunacy. However, it is also folly, as Avital Ronell shows.[4] What is more, it can signify an orientation toward the commonplace when it reminds us of the foolishness of conventional wisdom in collective habits. The covers of "Mad 20" toe the line of what constitutes our normative assumptions about the stupid, or the mad, while reminding us that madness itself can operate as a sort of comic enthusiasm for inanity. In this sense, dumbness is not degenerative but rather generative, reproducing shared (mis)understandings of what it means to lack intellect, intelligence, or perception. Yet in the generation of absurd content, *Mad*'s "stupidest" covers articulate what Michel Foucault might call "the comic punishment of knowledge and its ignorant presumption."[5] This type of comicality drives satire by punishing stupidity as a gaffe, not a crime, and positing objects of ridicule as somehow "smart on the dunce."[6] *Mad* goes further still, interpellating its audience as at once the arbiter of the stupid and as the pot calling the kettle black. Herein lies the amusement and the sting of the one-finger salute.

My purpose in this essay is to engage how the "Mad 20" hails stupidity. It unfolds with a look at Alfred E. Neuman as the face of human folly and its condition in *Mad* as both all too common and remarkable, nonetheless. An emphasis on *Mad*'s mascot is crucial for appreciating the covers insofar as he often adds insult to sociopolitical injury, serving as a figure of comic defacement by spoiling the appearance of people, places, and events that have already experienced defilement in one form or another. Next, I consider how *Mad*'s yearly coverage of stupidity portrays caricature as a form of satire, distorting even as it mirrors the cultural realities of U.S. public culture. I pay particular attention to the place of stupidity in *Mad*'s satires, and to the satire in the magazine's stupidity, by homing in on the rhetorical composition of and the graphic representations within a selection of "Mad 20" covers. The selections variously *document* important events by travestying the "best of" trope, *reenact* public controversies, and/or *allegorize* the ironies of high horses (namely by figuring hauteur in images of hilarious folly). This schema also underlies *Mad*’s recurring treatment of real estate mogul Donald J. Trump’s ascension to the presidency in covers that *satyrize* the disquietude (and derpitude) of American democracy.[7] In turning to the ancient roots of satire in satyr plays, I am recollecting a deep relationship between comicality and crudeness, which combines the satirical thrust of much critical humor with the perversity of festive caricatures in the figures of mythic satyrs. If satire entails the good sense of mockery, in other words, what might be called satyre invokes perhaps a greater sense of, say, comic allegory as travesty that is drawn from decadent, folly-to-be-wise revelries. Trump’s political rise has led *Mad* to take up a visual rhetoric of what Bertrand Russell might call “the triumph of stupidity,” showing The Donald as proof that democratic politics can succumb to a tyranny of idiots. Hence my ultimate focus on each cover’s caricatures as means to visualize thought and action, however obscene, during specific historical moments.[8]

Mad’s caricatures graphically distill the relationships between public affairs and the abstract values attached to them, reconstructing social, political, and cultural images of people and events through distorted projections that might not be as workable in textual burlesques. I argue that the “Mad 20” covers humor readers into reimagining the significance of some of the most damaging solecisms from the annual scandal sheet. *Mad*’s stupidity, then, is a rhetorical sign of comic distortion that enacts judgments on how we cover and what we document about the politics of our socialities, reshaping while reinforcing perspectives according to an allegorical play of comic alterity in the comprehensible and the perplexing. My turn toward the satyric simply magnifies the *Mad*ness. Of great significance is the extent to which the covers not only reiterate established conclusions about gradations of offense or recover common feelings of outrage, but also prod the shared stupidity in the circumstances themselves and the cultural milieus that made them possible. So, while the “Mad 20” may be daft, it is certainly not stupid.

Seeing Through Stupidity

To look at Alfred E. Neuman is to see the face of stupidity on the body of satire. *Prima facie*, the boy is the stereotypical redheaded stepchild. He is gap-toothed. His ears are not only uneven but also slightly too large for his head, which seems a bit too big for the neck that supports it. And his ruddy tangle of hair rests above a general expression of uninformed contentment, signaled by blue eyes that stare blankly forward above a wide, freckled nose and a broad smile. Indeed, Neuman is a picture of congenial witlessness. But *Mad* is not the only outlet to imagine him so. His print history dates back to the 1890s, when he appeared as a carefree imbecile advertising a traveling comedy troupe and its risible production, *The New Boy*. In the early twentieth century, his likeness emerged in the public domain on a postcard over the caption, "Me Worry?" Earlier still, the new boy was also the "It Didn't Hurt a Bit" kid, advertising pain-free dental procedures and curative "brainfood."[9] In each instance, and then again in his formal debut on the cover of *Mad* in December 1956 (#30), Neuman is, as Arden G. and Joan Christen describe him, "a grinning nebbish; more a mental defective than a lunatic; [possessing] a vacuous, strabismic, slightly leering face; the quintessential nerd; and everything that parents pray deep-down that their kids won't become."[10] He seems to embody the Latin *stupidus*, or a state of being "struck senseless." Yet contained within Neuman's unknowing air is the "knowing" smirk of a boy who may look dumb but actually knows more than we think.

Neuman *does* look dumb. However, he also looks awkwardly dapper. His hair is relatively neat and clean, and he is from the earliest images forward dressed up in a coat and bow tie. As such, he is not simply an idiot, but rather "a likeable, inept, inspiring, mischievous," and puzzling figure.[11] This characterization is telling insofar as nerds often connote a certain measure of intelligence, brainpower, and even sharpness. The 1950s saw Neuman's emergence as a presiding comic spirit for *Mad*, initially appearing as himself but soon thereafter playing cameo roles, parodying familiar icons, or travestying public figures. For instance, in February 1957 (#31), cover artist Norman Mingo portrays Neuman as another dignitary on the granite walls of Mount Rushmore. In April 1960 (#54), a "special April Fool issue," cover artist Frank Kelly Freas depicts Neuman as a modern-day Tom Sawyer whitewashing a red fence. Neuman faces forward and covers his mouth with his right hand as if he has just been caught in the act or is just about to vomit. His face is green, his eyes wide. In his left hand is a brush dripping with white paint. On the massive wooden panels behind him are the words "this magazine is revolting" scrawled in bold capital letters. Beneath them, as if painted on as a mocking aside, is the conditional phrase ". . . against Conformity!" The point is that Neuman functions as a figure of image corruption in comic defacement. He is a caricature. Through a form of what Roxana Marcoci calls "comic abstraction,"[12] Neuman at once breaks and remakes images of stupidity, serving as the satirical stooge for mockery and ridicule.

Todd Gitlin notes in Neuman's "grinning caricature" the "bubble-gum nihilism of the late Fifties—and its refutation."[13] Herein lie the seeds of his satire, for embedded in Neuman's refutations of the stupid is a laughing approval. Satire "strikes roots in the soil of stupidity," Northrop Frye declared.[14] But satire is also about sowing its seeds in order to despoil them. Its figurative as well as its "physical effects" come from the fact that, with visual satire in particular, "a person is literally 'defaced.'"[15] While satires can work to "save face, deface, and make faces," they can also "praise, insult, excuse, stake claims, and warn off trespassers."[16] Satirical caricatures foster "offending images,"[17] remaking public characters into (and out of) the stupidity they help to create. This practice is especially manifest in *Mad* covers that key in on people and their pratfalls, which I examine below. For now, I aim to establish caricature more broadly as a satirical means of seeing through stupidity.

Thinkers as early as Aristotle have recognized in stupidity a certain appeal.[18] If nothing else, it has been approached as a site for pointing out "reproachable ignorance."[19] In the *Nicomachean Ethics*, Aristotle suggests that to act *in* ignorance is one thing, and to act ignorantly is another.[20] The same could be said about being stupid and acting stupidly. In either case, the implication is that a body politic should be informed about the ignorance, or the stupidity, of others. To put it differently, we should be aware not only of dullness or gross wants of intelligence but also errors in judgment. This goal animates what Christie Davies calls "stupidity jokes,"[21] which *Mad* deploys to bring the stupid front and center. It is also more often than not the underlying motive of the magazine's satire. Kenneth Burke defines satire as "imagery of the secret vice shared by" all.[22] Its display is therefore a revelation, even though it is a "public secret" taken and understood only at "face value."[23] In this way, satires of stupidity are projections meant to educate both on and against their very content. To the extent that their comic judgments point out mistakes, they also revel in human failings. As *Mad* over and again reminds us, satire is part sociopolitical critique, part self-reflexive celebration of the stupid, and part demonstration of consequences that follow condemnations of stupidity with stupidity itself.

Understanding the place of stupidity in satire is significant for an examination of the "Mad 20," since stupidity *in situ* becomes a way of seeing, in John Berger's useful sense.[24] Stupid appeals tend to mock what Bakhtin called "lofty pseudo intelligence," and then again serve as rhetorical resources for "regarding the world through the eyes of the fool."[25] Such appeals provide a means of making the strangeness or the madness of stupidity more familiar, so it appears as commonplace as it is shameful. What is more, these appeals alter even as they affirm perceptions of personal defects and collective flaws.[26] In the "Mad 20," the appeal of stupidity appears in a few notable ways. First, the satirical caricatures on *Mad* covers do not simply put down stupidity; they reinforce it as constituent of so many comedies of human errors. Second, they contribute to a more general mockery of form. Many magazines produce "best of" editions. The "Mad 20" satirizes these imprints through its own thinly veiled moralism, affecting an ironic sense of "prudence, prudence, prudence, mixed with stupidity, stupidity, stupidity."[27] By extension, *Mad*'s celebration of stupidity also makes fun of the Nietzschean modes of moral indignation that tend to define "human, all too human folly."[28] The "Mad 20" makes stupidity praiseworthy. It turns vices into virtues. Nevertheless, insofar as its caricatures comprise a mode of comic ridicule, there remains the question of just who or what is the target. It would be easy to say that the reading and/or viewing public of *Mad* is superior. Yet in serving up stupidity as something of a public good—never mind a product to be consumed—the "Mad 20" offers a meditation on the weight of particular types of stupidity, its gradations and varying magnitudes, and the burden it places on how we imagine what stupid persons, places, and events say about *us* as audience members.

This meditation is no doubt why Neuman "seems to fit, perfectly, the role of the trickster,"[29] laughing at even as he laughs off the very stupidity he epitomizes. On the one hand, he is a symbol for mock admiration. On the other, he is an uncritical ignoramus. His fatuous appearance, though, is the source of his rhetorical force as a caricature when he harbors what Amelia Faye Rauser calls "the standard symbols and ideas of old idioms but with a new affect of subversion, doubt, and negation."[30] In this way, Neuman also plays something of a *satyric* role inasmuch as, like the characters of ancient satyr plays, he becomes grotesque versions of the very people, events, and things that he abhors in jest. The satyr, as I have argued elsewhere, is a satirical figure par excellence insofar as it is wild and unhindered in its outrageous and comic caricatures.[31] Through Neuman, we see the same things we see in popular media, only differently, distortedly, and debauchedly. Neuman cannibalizes the stuff of photographs, drawings, films, television images, newspapers, and so on. His likeness is leveraged as evidence for how "stupidity can body-snatch intelligence, disguise itself, or, indeed, participate in the formation of certain types of intelligence with which it tends to be confused," as Ronell notes.[32] This fluidity is how he can come off as simultaneously oafish and overconfident. It is also how he reflects even as he reconstructs the normative assumptions of, and the common ways of representing, our madness for stupidity. The "Mad 20" is rife with these foolish reconstructions.

The "Mad 20" as the Flagship of Foolery

It is not difficult to find delight on a ship of fools. For *Mad*, the ship is society, which is defined by the stupidity its members affect. From cover to cover, the writers and illustrators of *Mad* redistribute this Usual Gang of Idiots alongside Alfred as the ringleader and "the moronic face left when authority is stripped of all pretense," as Edward Rothstein of the *New York Times* put it.[33] It is therefore unsurprising that *Mad* would come to devote entire issues to "The Dumbest People, Events & Things" that are yearly at the helm.

Numerous covers stand out as exemplary. However, since stupidity (like satire) is by nature "fitting," or serving "as the jointure of timeliness,"[34] it is better to demonstrate some of the key features of *Mad*'s satirical coverage of the stupid itself as a sign of the times. Consider that each cover tends to celebrate high-profile characters and controversies, which in turn require a certain amount of popular or political awareness, let alone an investment in particular kinds of collective memory. These factors suggest why, as caricatures, the covers rely upon what E. H. Gombrich describes as a satirical "demonstration of equivalence" between art images and cultural realities.[35] Consequently, even though they are appeals to stupidity, the "Mad 20" covers actually encumber their audience to enact habits of mind that neglect to draw conclusions beyond the observation of already articulated judgments. At the same time, the covers flag certain objects or ideas as resources for reconstructing those judgments in an outlet that plays on the notion, posited by Kenneth Burke, that "*all* people are exposed to situations in which they must act as fools."[36] The "Mad 20" is thus a conflation in caricature of comic intervention and willful ignorance.

To organize my analysis, I highlight three core tropes of graphic representation that exemplify the types of rhetorical flags flown in *Mad*'s caricatures, and one more that has swelled in the Age of Trump. These tropes serve as signposts of satire, with Neuman as the main marker for the rhetorical work of comic judgment that covers do when they *document*, *reenact*, *allegorize*, and *satyrize* the stupidity they purport to represent. These tropes overlap. I isolate them here only to enlarge the dimwits, dolts, and dopiness in their details. I also parse them under the assumption that stupidity is the overarching satirical framework for grasping not only what appears in an image or thing but also what is conveyed about people, places, and events. The "Mad 20" covers exemplify comic judgments in caricature.

Documentation

Mad's documentation of stupidity is apparent in the first of the stupid retrospectives. On the cover of the January 1999 issue, Bill Clinton and Monica Lewinsky share the top spot for their infamous sex scandal (#377). Shamed sportscaster Marv Albert appears, as well, and so too does the virility pill, Viagra; the multinational technology company, Microsoft; the disgraced home run kings, Mark McGwire and Sammy Sosa; and others. Alfred E. Neuman is construed as a crude face collage. In his hair is an image of Clinton smoking a long stogie, with Lewinsky eyeing it in awe (mouth agape) while an American flag burns above her. A Viagra bottle rests on Neuman's forehead, its contents spilling just to the right of Albert, who is situated as a reflection in Neuman's eye and below the major league sluggers. McGwire is swinging a bat that appears to be connecting with Clinton's throat, and Sosa is pinching his pointer finger against his thumb as if to signal a small amount of guilt, perhaps, or of performance-enhancing drugs, while the pill bottle is positioned upright just before McGwire's crotch. I could go on. The takeaway is that, from its debut, the "Mad 20" is presented as a catalogue of dunces at whom we should take offense. Each individual image is only quasi-photorealistic, to be sure, but the caricature is much more evident in the pictorial collage that makes up Neuman's face, neck, and shoulders.

Through the metaphor of the collage, readers/viewers are urged to recognize that the dumbest of the dumb have been deemed so in the eyes of our patron saint of stupidity. They are simply made in his image.

Then again, the "Mad 20" is situated as a public record of prerecorded stupidity. Its documentary function is evident in its ranking and differentiation of stupid people, events, and things that made headlines. This function is most prominently displayed in the January 2002 cover (#413) by artist Roberto Parada (see fig. 7-1). The cover features Neuman reading *The Potrzebie Dispatch*. Tellingly, the word *potrzebie* is Polish for *need*, and was instituted by former *Mad* editor Harvey Kurtzman as a meaningless and nonsensical non sequitur in early cartoons and articles. Here it evokes a twofold implication: one, audiences *need* to see the rituals of public shaming that usually accompany appeals to stupidity, and two, how we select who or what is stupid (and why) often does not follow from logical premises. These insinuations are even more obvious given that a purportedly random selection of the year's dumbest creates the front and back pages of the newspaper—a broadsheet's most coveted placements. Yet who knows what Neuman is reading or viewing? His brow is furrowed, and we can imagine his surprise. However, other than the hair on his head, the upraised eyebrows and wrinkled forehead are all that we see of Neuman, and the imagined expression does not comport with his usual stupid-looking grin. Moreover, who can tell from the cover alone which people, events, and things are the dumbest? A look at the table of contents reveals that Jerry Falwell, the controversial televangelist who infamously blamed the 9/11 terrorist attacks on pagans, feminists, gays, and other "undesirables," received top billing. But he is nowhere to be seen on the cover. And though the story "Rehab a Fab Career Move for Celebs" is second in the pecking order, it is awarded pride of place on Neuman's newspaper.

This cover exemplifies the tendency of the "Mad 20" to mock the documentary form of "best of" lists. Foremost it is a meta-caricature of how stupidity is validated and verified as such, especially when it comes to judgments of relative magnitude.[37] Rashness and idiocy mark the cover stories. Michael Jordan, for example, appears in black-and-white on the back page under the headline, "Hoops! He Did It Again!" This image parodies Britney Spears's 2000 hit pop song. The story alludes to Jordan's decision to come out of retirement, and the caricature depicts His Airness lacking finesse as he floats his oversized head into the rim

Fig. 7-1: Roberto Parada's cover for *Mad* #413 (1/02) exemplifies how "MAD 20" artists satirize the "best of" commonplace. MAD used with permission.

of a basket. But what James Parton calls "comic stupidity"[38] also frames *Mad*'s cover insofar as it seems to poke fun at what is advertised *as* stupid. This implication appears in one sense at the level of reenactment, which I discuss below. In another sense, the caricatures portray a certain flexibility in *Mad*'s definition of stupidity. While on the back page Jordan is hitting his head, on the front page we find Elton John, with a sly smile that is uncannily similar to Neuman's, clutching a phallic microphone. Notorious rapper Eminem is shown holding or grabbing for the same mic but staring at the singer-songwriter's hands as they wrap around his own. The caricature evokes a duet that emerged out of a controversy sparked by Eminem and his overblown homophobic rants. But what is stupid? Is it Elton John's reaction to Eminem (or vice versa)? Is it the seeming publicity stunt? Furthermore, the caricatures reveal themselves as distractions from what might be the "real" content on the inside. Neuman is by now an unsubtle comic foil. Still, here he seems to be recollecting a *Mad* cover from the 1950s that simply contained the word *Think*. In other words, this cover offers ambivalence about what Neuman really believes (or sees, or reads) and what we as readers/viewers should therefore know and feel about how we document the best of our society's worst. It is tempting to believe that Neuman is so dumb that he misses the big stories. However, what if one imagines that Neuman is so smart that he purposefully avoids them, only to discover what is beyond the headlines and, perhaps, above the fray? The insinuation here, of course, is that some higher so-called truth masquerades as low art in the pages of *Mad* itself.

But who are we to judge? Who is *Mad* to judge what is more or less stupid? Who are we, as audiences, to judge the stupidity that is publicized to us? And what do we do with stupidity as a second-order judgment? Regardless of how we answer, a prime critique is that stupidity sells.

Reenactment

In gathering superlative stupidity, the "Mad 20" has since 2005 also recreated its exemplars' originary moments and their contextual surrounds. Before 2005, though, the covers tended toward more oblique patchwork caricatures of featured personages. For instance, in January 2003 (#425), the cover showcased "the biggest bobbleheads of the year" and included nine of the top twenty as bobblehead dolls laid out around the border. Cardinal Bernard Law is one of them, personified as a Roman Catholic dignitary with his arms folded and his face affecting a stern gaze as if to condemn the promulgation of sex abuse cover-ups in the Catholic Church. Martha Stewart is another, smiling widely and wearing a white apron as she serves up a platter of cash in a reference to her 2001 investigation by the Securities and Exchange Commission for fraud. These and other bobbleheads allude to the stupidity that they claim to signify; and they, like the covers mentioned above, also flatten the hierarchy of stupidity. Here, though, they do more to exaggerate the images or even the characteristics (physical and/or ethical) of their targets.

By 2005, the "Mad 20" covers had begun to amplify this sort of exaggeration and recreate signature people, events, or things in caricature. If some fodder for cover art in 2002 was a reflection on the fact that stupidity sells, in 2005 it was a consideration of the fact that so does sex. This theme was played out on two cover editions (for which *Mad* mockingly advised, "be dumb—get 'em both!"). Each in its own way caricatures the low cultural purchase and the high sociopolitical stakes in public forms of perversity. Together they also comment on how stupidity is peddled: like a newspaper, like a media scandal, like a bobblehead. The juxtaposition of graded stupidity is the most jarring element insofar as the covers work in tandem to trouble how we buy into public schemes or cloak-and-dagger plots. In addition, each implies that we are distracted from the other, if, that is, one does not imagine them as equally appealing and perverse.

On one cover is the #2 stupidest event, perpetrated by the #2 stupidest people (#449, 1/05; see fig. 7-2). The cover story is "Janet Jackson's 'Wardrobe Malfunction'—Tempest in a C-Cup" (27), and it references the Super Bowl XXXVIII halftime show when Justin Timberlake tore off a piece of Jackson's outfit, purportedly by accident, to reveal her breast. In the "Mad 20" cover text, the zero in the numeral *20* doubles as Jackson's right breast, complete with a tribal sun nipple shield and a piercing. The singer appears horrified. Nevertheless, the roles here are partially reversed, inasmuch as Timberlake was the one who seemed most shocked in the moment. What is more, Timberlake in *Mad*'s rendition *is* Neuman, holding Jackson's misplaced attire in his left hand and smiling as stupidly and contentedly as ever. Articulated here, the so-called "nipplegate" is reenacted as a scandal of diminished proportions (even as it is ironically praised) and hardly harkens back to the hundreds of thousands of complaints filed with the FCC, the court cases over sponsor reimbursements, or the swirling debates about explicit content on prime-time television. This satiric diminution is only magnified when compared to the second cover for #449, which recreates the controversial Abu Ghraib photographs that documented the torture by U.S. soldiers of detainees at the war prison in Iraq.

Fig. 7-2: This cover by Mark Fredrickson, one of two covers for *Mad* #449 (1/05), scorns the commodification of scandal. MAD used with permission.

Fig. 7-3: In the second cover for *Mad* #449 (1/05), Drew Friedman heaps comic contempt on U.S. war culture. MAD used with permission.

The reports, the release of the photos, and the public outcry that followed revelations of sexual abuse at Abu Ghraib constitute one of the darker moments of U.S. warfare. Various testimonies implicated a handful of soldiers in horrendous acts of carnal torture, including sodomy and sadism. One photograph displayed Private First Class Lynndie England standing alone and pointing at a prisoner engaging in forced masturbation while she smiles at the camera and gives a thumbs up. Another showed England with a comrade standing behind a pile of prisoners, all of whom are naked and heaped on top of each other in the form of a human pyramid. The story in *Mad* indicates "Jailhouse Shock" (26). On the cover, Neuman is clad in army fatigues, mimicking England's solo pose (see fig. 7-3). To his left and underneath the "20 dumbest" tagline is a mountain of celebrities, politicians, and luminaries. Shock jock Howard Stern is at the bottom along with Britney Spears. On top of him is then-President George W. Bush, who is joined by Donald J. Trump (whose open-mouthed countenance occupies the center of the human pile), John Kerry, and Paris Hilton. At the top of the big-name heap, partially bare breast and all, is Janet Jackson. And protruding from the pile is a collection of bare feet, shoes, and appendages. Remarkably, all visible individuals are fully clothed. Stern is in his standard leather jacket. The former president is sporting jeans and cowboy boots. The only one who is nude is Hilton, though she is covered up by Trump's big head—a fitting premonition for the turpitude that comprises *Mad*'s recurrent sendups of Trump just over a decade later.

Both covers are provocative. Each in its own way comments on the extent to which the consumption of controversy is consonant with the consumption of stupidity, and they imply that to consume unthinkingly is, well, stupid. Additionally, in reenacting two wildly divergent genres of controversy, the covers reveal how, as Nietzsche noted, power makes powerful people stupid.[39] This judgment goes from matters of pop cultural authority through national security to the exploits of, as *Mad* puts it, "a moron with a stupid haircut" but "a knack for making millions." (It is all too appropriate that the moron in question eventually became president given that this text appeared on a parodic poster for *Forrest Trump* inside the issue.) Yet both covers have to do with the perversion of perceived decency. Both make appeals to the types of aberrance that matter, yet with some ambivalence regarding who is doing what to whom. On one level, Neuman seems to be shaming his victims. As Timberlake, he mocks Jackson's sartorial *and* ethical fitness as a cultural icon. At the same time, Neuman censures his (own) collusion and the absurdity of his feigned faux pas. The caricature of torture in the second cover reorients the spectatorial position from one of witnessing war crimes to one of observing dupes being delivered their just deserts. Once again, Neuman is the victimizer, restaging a controversial moment of public interest. But here, England-cum-Neuman is not only shameful, she is stupid. She is morally vapid, unable to comprehend a basic level of humanity, or maybe even more disturbingly, she is just bored and thus finding a way to entertain herself and her compatriots. Perhaps worse still, England and her co-conspirators are metonyms of the militarized U.S. nation-state. It is along these lines that the satire of *Mad*'s reenactment stands out as the comic ridicule of public reception: as one controversy is piled upon another, misadventure not only loses its singular intrigue but also blurs into others such that the magnitude of them all is flattened. *Mad*, then, is mocking what Nietzsche might dub the "moral indignation" of those who render judgments without a proper appreciation of scale or degree.

Mad's imitative covers are therefore more than proclamations of stupidity through stupid portrayals; they are expressions of shared stupidity, revealed through their interpellation of audiences for controversy as themselves (in Robert Hariman's verdict on post-9/11 public stupidity) "dumb as a stump, way short of a load, stupid."[40] In distilling dumb people, events, and things, the covers also demand attention to the social, political, economic, and war cultures that might enable them. The “wardrobe malfunction” exposes the stupidity in a public that expresses outrage over an explicit sexual performance that is otherwise framed by a pop culture of eroticism. Treating prison rape as just another scandal discloses the indignity of war, but only before the backdrop of a more profound war culture, and on top of it a social order buttressed by sexism and sexual misconduct. We are mad, says *Mad*’s covers, for imagining that we do not all perpetuate a cultural politics of offense that both instances lay bare. The travesty lies in the flagrancy of Neuman’s ignorance in simply denuding these supposedly hidden meanings.

Allegory

I say *supposedly hidden* because *Mad* really does not suffer fools. That is, the stupidity covers are wasted on those in the know, showing and telling them what they probably already believe about the inanity of their public culture. Still, to call something *stupid* is to tap into shared assumptions about what is sensible, judicious, or good. Neuman’s comic intelligence forswears such a principled approach to the world and instead opts for the sort of honesty and straightforwardness that often accompanies those whom we assume do not know any better. But Neuman *does* know better, in a sense, which is why one can discern the satire in his stupidity, his judgments thereof, and the stupidity in his sociopolitical jurisprudence.

All this is to say that Neuman’s stupidity maintains a decidedly thin veil. It is ironic. As it reenacts stupid people, events, and things, and reinscribes their documentary implications, so does it also constitute a duplicitous image of their stupidity. Its meaning hides in plain view. Consequently, *Mad*’s stupidity is also ironically allegorical insofar as Neuman’s stupidity, and within it what is upheld as stupid, is recognizable, even old news. Allegories function by saying (and displaying) one thing while saying (and displaying) another. Irony, too, exclaims with a whisper and a wink. The two are therefore more “complementary than exclusive,” in James P. McDaniel’s phrase,[41] evincing the deep significations in textual surfaces. Moreover, as more recent *Mad* covers reveal, they exploit the tensions in and around images as ideas of public life. Such exploitation is most evident in covers beginning in 2006 drawn by Mark Fredrickson. It is at this point that Neuman more patently and more regularly stands in as an abstracted political, institutional, organizational, or symbolic body affecting "the ironic temper: the self-as-dumb."[42] He portrays an "ironic allegory" that implores us to imagine how we "might recognize in the embarrassments of irony mirror images of characteristic embarrassments in democratic public life."[43] The contradictions and conflicts so prevalent in the "Mad 20" are notable for the significance that gets laid on thick in their stupidity. However, insofar as irony—to be tempered—must accommodate a comic visage that mingles the nonsense of frivolity with the sting of satire, *Mad*'s ironic coverage of the stupidest of the stupid also embodies allegory tempered by farce.

The January 2006 cover (#461), for instance, features Neuman submerged in the floodwaters that followed Hurricane Katrina (see fig. 7-4). His countenance is familiarly unwitting, but now he stands in New Orleans with water up to his nose—just high enough to prevent him from being able to breathe. His eyes are wide, and his gap-toothed grin stands out just beneath the surface. A soggy cigar floats by his right ear, with other debris in the backdrop. Most important, he is dressed in a blue-collared shirt and a Federal Emergency Management Agency (FEMA) hat, hereby embodying a visual synecdoche for executive failure. The cover story in the issue punningly satirizes "The Bush League Response" and elaborates on the cover's depiction of the much-reported and much-criticized maladministration of governmental disaster relief. Whereas in other covers Neuman might deface an individual as a visual caricature, here he travesties an entire agency, both ridiculing and acting as the ridiculous representative of political ineptitude. Stupidity in this instance comes off as heedlessness, imprudence, and even irresponsibility. Hurricane Katrina, after all, remains an exemplar of the utter failure of federal governance, and for *Mad* typifies the stupidity of ignoring how important "sound infrastructure and efficient public services are for the conduct of all phases of life," as Mary Frances Berry put it in her cultural analysis of the storm's impact.[44] The commander in charge of Joint Task Force Katrina, Lieutenant General Russel L. Honoré, held a press conference in New Orleans in late September 2005 and infamously admonished reporters not to "get stuck on stupid" when they asked about the poor coordination of relief efforts from Hurricane Katrina as another powerful Atlantic coast storm, Hurricane Rita, was approaching.[45] Honoré's point about stupidity became moot when Rita bypassed the city. For *Mad*, however, the stupid is the enduring sticking point. It is the rhetorical depth of surface appeals to the meaning of current events that are recast as allegories of the human condition in U.S. public culture.

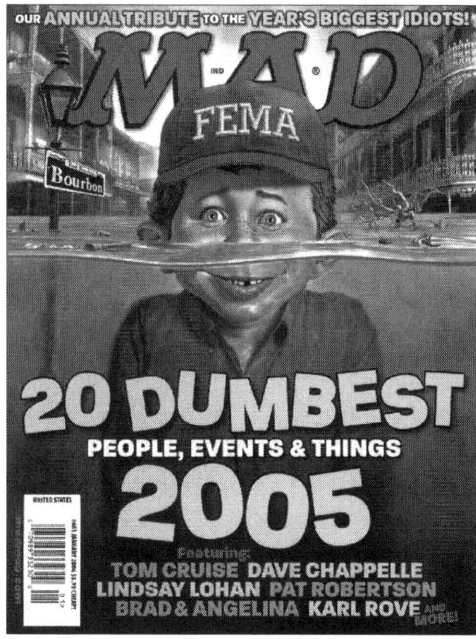

Fig. 7-4: Fredrickson's cover for *Mad* #461 (1/06) uses avowedly inaccurate historiography as a comic mechanism for lampooning the politico-official organization of public stupidity. MAD used with permission.

This position is plainly portrayed in *Mad*'s historically *in*accurate reiteration of Hurricane Katrina and its fallout, elements that enable the cover to be read as an ironic allegory. The hidden message (with a nod and a wink to the political campaigns of Ronald Reagan and Bill Clinton) seems clear: it's the government, stupid. But more than this implication is the redeployment of New Orleans iconography to signify of a deeper, more profound loss ensuing from the breached levees, which should have protected the city from any storm surge. The structural oversight is the stuff of stupidity. *Mad* gets at this point with the situation by portraying Neuman underwater on Bourbon Street in between the familiar townhouse facades and fascia boarding. Bourbon Street is the ground zero of New Orleans's economy and arguably the best and worst parts of its reputation for food, music, and nightlife. But it was swamped only by virtue of the bigger disruption of the city. The Vieux Carré, or the famous French Quarter, where Bourbon Street sits, is on high ground. It therefore did not flood. What also stands out in this cover in particular, then, is what is *not* seen—the ill preparations despite warnings, the bloated bodies of victims that floated in the floodwaters along with the debris, the looting and violence that accompanied the desperation of hundreds of thousands of displaced people, the conversion of the Superdome into a homeless shelter and quasi-refugee camp, the attempts by FEMA to limit reporters' access to the disaster/war zones, and the widely hailed class and racial components of the catastrophe.[46] In its simplicity, *Mad*'s cover caricatures complex sociopolitical contexts and reframes them in a storm story about coordinated stupidity relative to what Scott Frickel and M. Bess Vincent called the "organized ignorance" of FEMA's Katrina response.[47]

A similar sentiment is expressed in the February 2011 cover (#507), which shows Neuman in a BP inspector's jumpsuit and hardhat. In the background is the *Deepwater Horizon* drilling rig in the Gulf of Mexico. The oil rig is in the process of exploding, while black smoke billows above it and an enflamed reflection spills over the water's surface. And there stands Neuman holding a clipboard in his right hand while joining the thumb and the forefinger of his left to indicate that everything is A-OK. The cover story is "Stupid Petrol Tricks," and the ironic cover portrait constructs a symbolic fiction about our delusions regarding energy production, distribution, and security. Once again, organizational folly is the fodder for mocking praise. But Neuman is not only used to send up administrative failure. In January 2009, he was the poster child of anarchic lunacy when he appeared as The Joker from director Christopher Nolan's 2008 film, *The Dark Knight* (Fredrickson #497; see fig. 7-5). In this cover, Neuman is not the subject of ridicule; he is, rather, the archetypal thug exposing the inadequacies of a cultural system by terrorizing its citizens and institutions. The Joker is a fascinating pop cultural icon in part because he has transformed over time from a wild and/or trump card (in the card game Euchre) to a witty jester, a pitiless killer, a frenetic prankster, a sociopathic madman, a lurid mobster, and a cartoonish criminal. In the body of actor Heath Ledger, though, The Joker transcends "comic criminality," as Ashley Cocksworth put it, into a self-described "agent of chaos" bent on inciting disorder, promoting misanthropy, and serving up the state as a lunatic soldier of bedlam.[48] The Joker's tagline is purposefully sardonic: "Why so serious?" *Mad*'s reappropriation is deft, even dark. But it also makes sense. Ledger's portrayal was critically acclaimed not only *despite* but also *for* its disturbing allure. This effect was made more so by the swath of controversy around his unstable mental state after filming, which many speculated to be the catalyst for his untimely death by drug overdose shortly before the film's release. With Neuman as The Joker, the anarchic and destructive symbolism converts a woeful story of both personal turmoil and systemic cruelty into an allegorical image of the annihilation of stupidity. The Joker is calculated and cunning. Neuman is barely astute, except that here again we see him as a mocking figure of (un)knowing sociopolitical disruption, affecting an awkward demeanor in the aftermath of ostensive clumsiness and yet provoking a somewhat indeterminate judgment of the "biggest idiots" with his expression, "Why so stupid?"

Fig. 7-5: On Fredrickson's cover for *Mad* #497 (1/09), a pop cultural icon articulates the capacity for planned stupidity to disrupt common sense. MAD used with permission.

He has obviously just carried out an act of terrorism. But encircling the scene are the flaming, indeed incendiary, remnants of the year in stupidity: NFL quarterback Brett Favre's jersey (recalling the publicity of his retirement, then his return to football, then his retirement, then . . .), singer Amy Winehouse's album (recollecting her substance abuse, her downward spiral, and the potential demise of her career), a snippet from a newspaper headline about Hillary Clinton (alluding to her failed 2008 presidential bid), and more. Ultimately, the cover exemplifies the ambivalence toward Neuman's idiocy, the foolhardiness of public figures, and the implied audience of human folly. This ambivalence is at once ironic and allegorical insofar as it materializes abstract ideas and actual moments, while saying and/or showing what it "does not" mean by meaning what it "does not" say and/or show. Ledger's Joker is an apt archetype here insofar as the express point of his anarchism is, in his words, to send a message.

For my part, this cover and so many others are most telling not simply for what they dispose us to but also for what they expose about public dispositions toward so-called stupidity. To get the jokes of the covers is to grasp popular and prominent moments of relative controversy in U.S. public culture—and to enjoy how Neuman's comic distortions document those moments—through comic distortions. It is also to recognize the dissimulations and distortions that Neuman is often used for in order to dissemble—and to understand—how those moments are documented. However, a notion of ironic allegory also allows us to approach the "Mad 20" in terms of how they reconstruct their audiences. Ironic allegory provides a view of stupidity that relies on the power of *Mad*'s covers to accomplish what Joshua Gunn might call the rhetorical drama of comic revelation: "to push the reconstructing audience to other places, other sites of meaning, other texts, particularly past experiences of not getting it or being played the fool, all of which are other realities or texts not in the here and now" but also not unrecognizable in recent history.[49] To see through the surface appeals of the covers is therefore to see differently. It is to look upon subtexts and notice complicities where one might otherwise witness the comic fallibility of others. It is to look upon layers of meaning in a harrowing human comedy across the ordinary course of U.S. current events.

The matter of appreciating such nuance is a bit tougher, though, when the subject of *Mad*'s ridicule maintains a surface stupidity so shallow that any point of entry is easy to cross. A sham success story and shameless self-promoter in real estate and reality television, Donald J. Trump nevertheless hawked his way to the top of U.S. politics when he won the presidency in 2016. What makes him such a compelling figure for criticism in *Mad* is that he has long been regarded as an idiot—perhaps even too stupid to be president (given his lack of experience with congressional lawmaking, disregard for the Constitution, scattershot foreign policy views, superficial or utterly wrongheaded grasp of history, a fetish for issuing public remarks on the social media platform Twitter, and more). From his inauguration forward, one need not look very hard to find headlines from any number of news outlets publicizing Trump's idiocy. In July 2017, for example, David Rothkopf proclaimed Trump the ringleader of "America's Golden Age of Stupidity."[50] This proclamation was odd not because it took a bad editorial tack or let slip some improper tenor, but rather because it reeked so much of an article from satirical news outlet *The Onion*, which just two months prior published a "News in Brief" exposé wherein Trump admitted what everyone in Trumpworld has always known: the man is "a big idiot" (a judgment also reported in the *New York Times*).[51] The rub here is not that Trump is ripe for ridicule; it is that he is low-hanging fruit. *Mad*'s drift into the satyric makes sense of a president who betrays a stupidity worse than ignorance and a madness too perilous to be written off as folly.

Satire as Satyre

An op-ed in *The New York Times* from March 20, 2017, remarks how Trump uses scare quotes in his tweets "to destabilize meaning."[52] On the one hand, the piece is a jab at the executive cynicism behind Trump's accusation that President Barack Obama had him "wiretapped," or more exactly that Trump had his administration defend the claim amid widespread pushback by asserting that "wiretapping" could mean any number of surveillance practices. On the other hand, it is an overtly chilling forecast for a moment when Trump might tweet a *post hoc* disclaimer for nuclear war (no doubt with North Korea): "I said 'nuke' them," the tweet might go, "not nuke them." The op-ed is suitably titled "Trump Ruins Irony, Too." Then again, it might just as well be titled "Trump Is an Allegory of Going Nuclear," with his presidency part and parcel of a story layered with unhinged behavior and wild flights of political fancy.

Mad's shift to the satyric is a shift to a comic mode of caricature that represents the humor of human error in terms of democratic hellscapes. Cognomens like *Commander-in-Tweet* and *Liar-in-Chief* frame Trump as a president who puts the "twit" in Twitter. The irony is that Trump seems to revel in his position as apotheosis of an idiocracy,[53] or catalyst to a Trumpocalypse, embodying what one observer of the 2016 campaign called "Triumph the Insult Comic Dog made flesh, a comically bouffanted racist oligarch who tweets like a fifth grader and brags like a cafeteria rapper."[54] The comic drama of satyr plays looms large here insofar as *Mad*'s takes on Trump reroute the pity and fear that might come with his presidency toward satire that is over-the-top enough to make reality seem fantastical. This move is readily apparent in the 128-page special edition magazine, *MAD About Trump: A Brilliant Look at Our Brainless President*, which features a collection of "all his stupidity from *The Apprentice* to the 2016 election" and beyond, and advertises a "comedy assault" on "the most idiotic idiot to ever reach the White House (George W. Bush and visitors included)."[55] Still, the "Mad 20" portrayals of Trump are exemplary because they satyrize his specifically presidential shenanigans through the lens of something like a mock allegory. Candidate Trump first disgraced the cover of a "Mad 20" in February 2016 (#537) when his election still seemed a nightmare, and his candidacy could be chalked up to the errant actions of a lurid minority content to "Make America Dumb Again," playing into deep-seated resentments, white nationalist sympathies, and televisual theatrics. Here Trump is rendered as he so often is in caricature: with a strange facial expression, a puckered mouth, and wild blonde hair that looks more like a stray animal atop his head than a coiffure. Neuman looks just like him, standing next to Trump and giving two thumbs up as the president-to-be stares down at him over his right shoulder. This is a provocative view, foreshadowing his looming presence behind Hillary Clinton in the October 3, 2016, debate. But not until the next year does a "Mad 20" cover truly take up the satyric.

If Trump himself was the #1 dumbest of 2015, the dumbest thing in 2016 was that "Trump Got Elected!" On the February 2017 cover (#543) is an image of Neuman, clad in white T-shirt and blue jeans, vomiting into an iconic "Make America Great Again" red ball cap. In wearing the attire of what could be seen as a reincarnation of the Know-Nothing ethos, Neuman puts forth a gut-check on political choices by both looking with express ignorance upon what has happened and also looking forward to what is to come. Trump's presidency is like a hangover. His candidacy was the I'm-With-Stupid logic of *getting stupid* on the spirits of the make-believe; his election was the snap back to reality that comes with the nausea and headaches that impair brain function and stimulate ill feelings. Such sentiments preview some tragic findings of scholars like David R. Williams of Harvard College's T. H. Chan School of Public Health, who determined in June 2017 that millions of people were suffering from collective stress brought on by Trump's presidency.[56] It is no stretch, then, to say that Neuman satyrizes *citizens* as the pits of stupidity, complete with his flagrant, fleshly paroxysms. Is Neuman a Trump supporter? Is he one of the so-called Never-Trumpers? Regardless, he is either (both) a victim or (and) an agent of The (stupid, vengeful) Donald. Hence the reason why horror is aligned with humor in *Mad*'s depiction of the foul idiocy of Trumpism. As Dana Ferrin Sutton argues in her study of this ancient Greek theatrical tradition, satyric humor "comes from the collision of the serious and the comic and requires the presence of both."[57] A seriously boorish buffoon for a head of state, in an ancient argot, is serio-*stupidum*. Hence, too, why Neuman's reaction is as laughable as it is revolting.

Instead of sticking with the themes of drunkards and dullards, though, the 2017 "Mad 20" cover from February 2018 (#549) goes hard in another direction, depicting Neuman as the caddie to a rich cretin. Trump has never denied that golf presents an opportunity for personal getaways to his own properties. As president, he has regularly proclaimed the golf course (*and* the clubhouse) a workplace. *Mad* portrays it as the allegorical site for imagining the consequences of Trump's documented retreats from presidential duties, namely when it comes to how he treats the presidency as though it is a game, if not a reality show. Nowhere is this game-like approach to the presidency clearer than in Trump's dealings with North Korea via Twitter. On the cover, Trump is standing on a fairway, glibly posed in the follow-through of his swing (a pose, it is worth mentioning, that mimics a widely used photograph taken by Ian MacNicol). Neuman is just behind him, his eyes wide, his expression anxious, and his hands positioned as if to urge his audience to stay calm in the same manner he might try to coax Trump's ball to sit—that is, to come down softly. Trump's shot is out of view. But in the backdrop is an enormous orange mushroom cloud. Satyric humor can be dark. But the prototypical satyr play has a happy ending. It revels especially in the dreary routines of ordinary ordeals. Here, the ludicrous brinkmanship in Trump's unseen bellicosity is illuminated by its potential fallout, which follows from what many have called the "axis of idiocy" that coordinates the president's diplomacy.

As gripping as the cover, then, is the image within the issue for number eight on the dumb list, entitled "Clash of Clowns." It is a graphic riff on *Clash of Clans*, a mobile game that puts players into so many tribal wars. For *Mad*, the crucial clash is between President Trump and North Korean dictator Kim Jong-Un, which has metastasized as an ongoing exchange of insults and warlike instigations between the leaders (with

Trump using everything from the United Nations General Assembly to Twitter as his bully pulpit). At one point in August 2017, President Trump took leave of politics for a golf outing after casually telling reporters that he would bring "fire and fury" upon North Korea if its leader persisted with threats to the U.S. Arguably, like diplomacy in international relations, golf is a gentleman's game. It requires honesty and decorum, but also a caddie willing to give advice and moral support. Trump is less a statesmanlike golfer than the man paid to taunt Adam Sandler's character in *Happy Gilmore* (1996), calling other players jackasses right before they shoot. Unfortunately, Neuman is a caddie in the dark, unable to avert or advise a crack shot who channels the voice of the American people as the voice of a dope. Alas, *Mad*'s move toward the satyric recalls mergers of tragedies and comedies, kingpins and pinheads, words and deeds. A mockery of etiquette therefore meets a visual caricature of stupidity that drives the end of days.

In the end, Trump goads a comic orientation pushed to the end of its line. Rumor has it that onetime National Security Adviser H. R. McMaster derided Trump as an "idiot" and a "dope" in the summer of 2017 when he dined with Safra Catz, the CEO of Oracle and once a member of President Trump's transition team.[58] That same month, during a national security meeting, then Secretary of State Rex Tillerson reportedly referred to Trump as a "moron"—well, a "*fucking* moron."[59] Rupert Murdoch, too, is said to have mocked the president's intelligence, as did FBI agents involved in the infamous Russia election meddling probe, and numerous other commentators and critics.[60] Indeed, less than a year into his presidency, conventional wisdom in some circles held that Trump had unequivocally made an idiot of everyone who put him into office. To borrow the words of a wise man, it is apparently true that the difference between stupidity and genius is that genius has its limits. There is perhaps something of a bad omen, then, in William Rivers Pitt's reference to Trump as a "Mad Genius" just five years before he won the White House. There is likewise good reason to align his madness with ineptitude and rage, and then again to wonder if it is canniness or clownery. In either case, it is clear—at least from the perspective of the caricatures on *Mad* covers—that for all of Trump's inflamed folly (and foolish ire), not he but the American populace has been played the fool. This is the satyre in satire: the penchant of *Mad* to make fun of the comic excesses in the Dionysian elements of the American experience. In this context, *Mad*’s portrayals of stupidity make the U.S. body politic even more foolish than its electoral politics make it sometimes seem.

Conclusion: Wasted Stupidity?

An old idiom has it that irony is wasted on the stupid. That is, to understand something as ironic, one must harbor a minimum standard of intelligence. The “Mad 20” covers challenge this adage insofar as they operate less on new information than recollections of old news. The hook, however, is that images and ideas from public memory are used as the media of de- and re-formed perspectives. Nonetheless, “Best of” lists run the risk of merely reaffirming what one already knows. Janet Jackson’s wardrobe malfunction was stupid. So what? If *Mad* stops and starts with the recurrent scapegoats for idiocy, there is reason to believe that it wastes its judgments of the stupid—and, indeed, its own stupidity—as embodied in The Usual Gang of Idiots whose vision it projects. Its caricatures, then, are stupid solely for the sake of it, and do little more than establish some view of virtue in satirizing human vice. “Every virtue tends towards stupidity,” says Nietzsche, “and every kind of stupidity toward virtue.”[61] For those drawn in by the “Mad 20,” such a satiric tautology is banal at best—unless one reimagines what it might mean to comprehend stupidity not only as a foregone conclusion but also as a resource for self-criticism. To waste stupidity, in this sense, is to squander an opportunity to hold audiences for the dumbest of the dumb to a carnival mirror.

I see stupidity on the “Mad 20” covers as a framing device for comic judgments about the best of the worst in society. More specifically, recognizing caricature as a rhetorical form of distortion as well as a broader way of seeing, we can fairly easily see cover boy Alfred E. Neuman as simply a stooge in *Mad*’s comedy of human errors or, better, as a simpleton in attitude and appearance who is forced to merely reflect stupidity as it is. Sometimes he *is* a stand-in for a soldier, a bureaucratic official, a celebrity, or a “media-baiting” buffoon-turned-American-president whose folly would be “cartoonish-if-it-wasn’t-so-scary evil,” as Steve Foxe put it.[62] At other times, Neuman is the observer, maybe even the wandering eye of the public writ large. Then again, he is just himself, the quintessential ignoramus who cannot even recognize his own imbecility. Consequently, the visual compendium embedded in the

"Mad 20" can serve as an expression of reader/viewer superiority over the stupid people, events, and things depicted, not to mention how they are produced, packaged, and sold. The "Mad 20" also stretches the limits of what constitutes stupidity in that who or what is stupid is variously deadly (i.e., war), perverse or sadistic (i.e., church sex, torture photos), tragic (i.e., natural disasters), and so on. Stupidity is hereby endemic to public life, not to mention a function of everyday human conduct, especially when an idiocracy comes across as the ludicrous—and yet all too logical—outcome of democracy gone bad.

Yet if Neuman is also a prototypical everyman, an underlying implication is that if he is an idiot, then so are we. The "Mad 20" covers encourage this type of critical awareness. In fact, insofar as they are ironic allegories, they should cue readers/viewers to the idea that even as they are documenting the stupidity of others by reenacting it, they are also representing something else. That something else, I want to suggest, is the extent to which we, the ordinary citizens and everyday judges of sociopolitical culture, are at times the "unworthy, irrelevant dunces" in Jason A. Scorza's setup for democratic citizenship.[63] Recall that *Mad* emerged at a moment in history when conformity was conceived by many official outlets as a good in itself. Conventional wisdom was to civic virtue what opposition was to vice. Even today, though, *Mad* reminds us that judgments of the stupid are no better (but perhaps worse) than what is deemed to be so if they are wrought through their own form of unthinking orthodoxy. To simply call President Trump an idiot, for example, is to risk casting off responsibility for the very inanities that imperil those who are downstream of his dumbness. The stupidity of *Mad* is therefore wasted if it leads to a wholesale separation of responsible audiences from those reviled objects of ridicule.

The "Mad 20" covers, I think, accomplish the exact obverse: instead of eliminating a broader public from the picture, the covers more often than not implicate their presumed judges in the very persons, events, and things being judged. In flattening out the swath of a year's stupidity, or in homing in on a singular sign as somehow the standard, the covers disrupt the stable hierarchy of the listed content. They demonstrate, in other words, how one piece of stupidity can become just another on the pile. In this way, the covers admonish audiences of what Burke calls the "dangers of pride": ignorance of the notion that satire enables projections such that the satiric judge "*gratifies* and *punishes* the vice within himself."[64] There is ambiguity, and comic possibility, in Neuman. *Mad*'s poster child of stupidity is stupid. We can look upon him as everything we long not to be. Still, we follow his judgments of who and what is stupid, enjoying *with him* the position as spectators of the idiocy in others. We are therefore in cahoots with Neuman when we align ourselves with the "Mad 20," suggesting that in Neuman's idiotic smile is actually a sly insinuation: "See, stupid? You're stupid, too." The "Mad 20" feature, after all, documents, reenacts, allegorizes, and satyrizes just how much we, through our public culture, are enamored of stupidity, compelled to both celebrate and castigate it, and constantly goaded to grant it cultural purchase.

Since 1928, *Time* magazine has named a "person of the year." Over the years, the predominant honorees have been people—presidents, popes, foreign dignitaries, freedom fighters, etc.—with notable exceptions for a machine (the computer, in 1983) a planet (the "Endangered Earth" in 1989), or particular cohorts ("The American Soldier" in 2004, "The Protester" in 2011). In 2006, it was "You." Given what I've just suggested about the "Mad 20," one might imagine a cover of *Mad* with the same designation, along with a comic account outlining a stupid person theory to counter that of the "Great Man." One might also imagine the cover with the word *STUPID* in big, block letters along with the less prominent admonition "don't be." In the end, this caution seems to be at least in part what that "Mad 20" is up to: reiterating and redisplaying the stupid images and ideas of the year in order to alter our perception and our judgmental projections in the course of pointing out idiocy. "Mad 20" covers are thus to some extent satires of those who presume to know enough, if not too much. Knowing as much amounts to an uncritical adherence to the vicious in the true, and that's just wasted intelligence.

Notes

1. Stephen E. Kercher, *Revel with a Cause: Liberal Satire in Postwar America*, 118.

2. Stergios Botzakis, "*Mad*," in *Icons of the American Comic Book: From Captain America to Wonder Woman*, ed. Randy Duncan and Matthew J. Smith, 1:468.

3. See Carl Djerassi, "The Quest for Alfred E. Neuman," 167–74; Arden G. Christen and Joan A. Christen, "'It didn't hurt a bit' Kid: Dental Precursor to *Mad Magazine*'s Alfred E. Neuman," 53–55; Frank Spotnitz, "Tracing the Worrisome Origin of Alfred E. Neuman;" Peter Jensen Brown, "The Real Alfred E. Revealed."

4. Avital Ronell, *Stupidity*, 3.

5. Michel Foucault, *Madness and Civilization: A History of Insanity in the Age of Reason*, trans. Richard Howard, 26.

6. James Hannay, "Political Satire and Squibs.—Burns," 218; see also Kenneth Burke, *Attitudes Toward History*, 39–44.

7. On *derpitude* as an insult of the internet age, see Stefan Becket, "The Origins of Derp."

8. I do not mean to suggest that the contents within the magazine are unimportant. Quite the contrary. To a large extent, the captions read like headlines from *The Onion*, and the stories elaborate verbally on what is portrayed on the covers. My emphasis on the "Mad 20" is driven by my interest in how *Mad* covers have long served an important rhetorical function of depicting snap judgments that are nevertheless complex in terms of their reliance on and disruption of common habits of reception. Furthermore, this essay engages the covers as evidence of comic judgment in caricature, and thus as distorted portrayals of ways of seeing stupidity.

9. Christen and Christen, "Dental Precursor," 54.

10. Christen and Christen, "Dental Precursor," 53.

11. Christen and Christen, "Dental Precursor," 53.

12. Roxana Marcoci, "Comic Abstraction: Image-Breaking, Image-Making," 9–39.

13. Todd Gitlin, *The Sixties: Years of Hope, Days of Rage*, 36.

14. Northrop Frye, "The Nature of Satire," 44.

15. José Lanters, "Irish Satire," 477.

16. Ellen Oliensis, *Horace and the Rhetoric of Authority*, 3.

17. W. J. T. Mitchell, *What Do Pictures Want? The Lives and Loves of Images*, 124–44.

18. Aristotle, *On Rhetoric: A Theory of Civic Discourse*, 1382a, 22–24.

19. Nancy Sherman, "*Hamartia* and Virtue," 177–96, 186.

20. Aristotle, *The Nicomachean Ethics*, 3.15–20.

21. Christie Davies, *Jokes and Targets*, 20–21.

22. Burke, *Attitudes Toward History*, 49.

23. Michael Taussig, *Defacement: Public Secrecy and the Labor of the Negative*, 7.

24. John Berger, *Ways of Seeing*.

25. Mikhail Bakhtin, "Discourse in the Novel," 403.

26. So much satire relies on shared perceptions of what is defective, imperfect, and so on. Indeed, collective judgments about what is excellent or even sublime enable something like a cartoon copy to render some person or thing ridiculous. Numerous scholars have fleshed out this orientation, especially as it relates to visual humor. See, for instance, Martha Banta, *Barbaric Intercourse: Caricature and the Culture of Conduct, 1841–1936*, 57; Thomas Conley, *Toward a Rhetoric of Insult*, 99; Mitchell, *What Do Pictures Want?*, 131; Gillian Rhodes, *Superportraits: Caricatures and Recognition*, 12; George A. Test, *Satire: Spirit and Art*, 204; Robert I. Williams, *Comic Practice/Comic Response*, 59.

27. Friedrich Nietzsche, *Beyond Good and Evil: Prelude to a Philosophy of the Future*, trans. Walter Kaufmann, 198.

28. Friedrich Nietzsche, *The Gay Science*, trans. Thomas Common, 191.

29. Maria Reidelbach, *Completely Mad: A History of the Comic Book and Magazine*, 151.

30. Amelia Faye Rauser, *Caricature Unmasked: Irony, Authenticity, and Individualism in Eighteenth-Century English Prints*, 96.

31. Christopher J. Gilbert, "Toward the Satyric," 280–305.

32. Ronell, *Stupidity*, 10.

33. Edward Rothstein, "Connections; Is It Still a Mad, Mad, Mad, Mad World?"

34. Ronell, *Stupidity*, 27.

35. E. H. Gombrich, "The Mask and the Face: The Perception of Physiognomic Likeness in Life and in Art," in *Art, Perception, and Reality,* ed. Ernst H. Gombrich, Julian Hochberg, and Max Black, 1.

36. Burke, *Attitudes Toward History*, 41.

37. I am deriving a notion of *metacaricature* from W. J. T. Mitchell and his sense of "metapictures": images that exude a sort of "self-knowledge" or "pictorial self-reference." In short, metapictures offer images of images and thus provide a different depth of surface when it comes to understanding what we see. Metapictures disrupt representational stability. Tellingly, this process facilitates "a transaction between pictures and observers activated by . . . the shifting of figure and ground, the switching of aspects, the display of pictorial paradox and forms of nonsense"; see Mitchell, *What Do Pictures Want?*, 57. Metacaricatures are therefore caricatures unto themselves, but they are also caricatures of broader appeals to distortive portrayals and representations of, in this instance, the stupid.

38. James Parton, *Caricature and Other Comic Art in All Times and Many Lands*, 41.

39. Friedrich Nietzsche, *Twilight of the Idols*, trans. Richard Polt, 43.

40. Robert Hariman, "Public Culture and Public Stupidity Post-9/11," 96.

41. James P. McDaniel, "Liberal Irony: A Program for Rhetoric," 298.

42. McDaniel, "Liberal Irony," 314.

43. McDaniel, "Liberal Irony," 301. Note, too, that George A. Test posits an "irony of allegorical worlds" in order to emphasize the capacity for judgment in satire. Test states: "Allegory presents its messages in terms of something else, a literal set of events, persons, conditions, or images having a corresponding level of existence involving meaning, conceptions, values, or qualities. So in satire there tends to emerge some standard on which the criticism or attack is based"; see Test, *Satire*, 187. Test calls this the "judgment of irony." I would characterize it as the caricature in the "Mad 20."

44. Mary Frances Berry, foreword to *There is No Such Thing as a Natural Disaster: Race, Class, and Hurricane Katrina*, vii–viii.

45. Patrik Jonsson, "General Honoré, Katrina and the Army behind Him, Retains Civic Aims."

46. Henry A. Giroux, "Reading Hurricane Katrina: Race, Class, and the Biopolitics of Disposability," 171–96.

47. Scott Frickel and M. Bess Vincent, "Hurricane Katrina, Contamination, and the Unintended Organization of Ignorance," 181.

48. Ashley Cocksworth, "*The Dark Knight* and the Evilness of Evil," 541.

49. Joshua Gunn, *Modern Occult Rhetoric: Mass Media and the Drama of Secrecy in the Twentieth Century*, 155.

50. David Rothkopf, "America's Golden Age of Stupidity,"

51. "Trump: 'I Am a Very Stupid Human Being"; Michelle Goldberg, "Everyone in Trumpworld Knows He's an Idiot."

52. Moises Velasquez-Manoff, "Trump Ruins Irony, Too."

53. This reference nods to the 2006 satirical film *Idiocracy*, wherein a black, muscle-bound, machine gun-wielding porn star named Dwayne Elizondo Mountain Dew Herbert Camacho lords over the U.S. as president of an American populace that has devolved into a hyper-capitalist, philistine government of fools, by fools, and for fools. The Office of the President, in particular, is showcased as a vanity enterprise gone mad. Most compelling in this reference is the fact that screenwriter Etan Cohen dubbed it a film about televisual and pop cultural folly taken to the end of the line, and that after Trump's election it had "become a documentary."

54. Jason Bailey, "Who Said It: Presidential Hopeful Donald Trump or 'Idiocracy' President Camacho?"

55. This 2018 issue is an extended print version of an online edition that appeared as a free e-book a year earlier, *MAD Dumps on Trump*.

56. David R. Williams, "Health Effects of Dramatic Social Events: Ramifications of the Recent Presidential Election."

57. Dana Ferrin Sutton, *The Greek Satyr Play*, 162.

58. Tina Nguyen, "An 'Idiot' and a 'Dope': McMaster Reportedly Unloads on Trump During a Private Dinner."

59. Dexter Filkins, "Rex Tillerson at the Breaking Point."

60. Goldberg, "Everyone in Trumpworld Knows He's an Idiot."

61. Nietzsche, *Beyond Good and Evil*, 227.

62. Steve Foxe, "*MAD* Magazine Makes America Dumb Again with *MAD Dumps on Trump*."

63. Jason A. Scorza, *Strong Liberalism: Habits of Mind for Democratic Citizenship*, 159.

64. Burke, *Attitudes Toward History*, 41, 49.

8. The Prohías Paradox:

The Cold War Specificity and Existential Universality of "Spy vs. Spy"

Michael J. Socolow

THEY HAVE NO names, nationalities, or distinguishing characteristics. Yet they remain two of the most famous spies in American popular culture. The antagonists in the "Spy vs. Spy" feature in *Mad* magazine, as drawn by Cuban exile Antonio Prohías, remain iconic. The comic appeared in nearly every edition of *Mad* from 1961 until Prohías's retirement due to health reasons in 1987 (241 installments), and the installments were collected in a total of nine books that cumulatively sold millions of copies. The Spies still appear in advertisements and are featured in board games, and the feature's very title has become a metaphor for the madness of unthinking rivalry that characterized the Cold War.[1] The continued popularity of the clear and clean narratives portrayed in "Spy vs. Spy" attests to the feature's global resonance. The madcap escapades of the two black and white antagonists (and for a time, a third, in grey), speak directly to both the specific world in which they were created as well as to timeless and universal themes of humanity.

This essay offers a descriptive historical analysis of "Spy vs. Spy" in order to explore the intersection of the artist, his artistry, and the popularity of Prohías's feature. That "Spy vs. Spy" remained intentionally devoid of specific ideologies or political partisanship, and that ultimate victory forever eluded both spies, remain essential components of the cartoon's thematic consistency. Within their carefully circumscribed universe, the Black Spy and the White Spy remain forever entangled, effecting their own dialectic of perpetual enmity. As Art Spiegelman has observed, they are, in this sense, akin to Yin and Yang—symbols that derive identity primarily from the interlocked context in which they exist.[2]

Yet many critics and scholars have noted that the communicative dynamic of "Spy vs. Spy" relies heavily on the audience's contextual understanding of the Cold War between the Soviet Union and the United States in the second half of the twentieth century. For all its enduring resonance and commentary on human futility, "Spy vs. Spy" reflected very specific concerns and anxieties evident in the global political context in which it was produced. This paradox is but one of many at the heart of the feature's success: it was both simultaneously universal and specific, and it could convey complex messages freighted with philosophical depth through remarkably simple and clear drawings.

Antonio Prohías and the Cuban Origins of "Spy vs. Spy"

Born in Cienfuegos, Cuba, in 1921, Antonio Prohías demonstrated precocious artistic talent at a young age. His father, an attorney, discouraged Prohías's desire to become an artist, and in his teens, Prohías studied agronomy. He soon dropped out of school and worked in a fertilizer plant in order to earn enough money for art supplies. By the age of seventeen, Prohías had begun selling his cartoons to Cuban newspapers.[3] His drawings proved popular, and in less than a year, he accepted a full-time editorial cartoonist's job with *El Diario de la Marina*, a daily newspaper. Within a few years, Prohías's work began appearing in numerous Cuban publications, including the popular weekly *Zig-Zag Libre*.[4] His distinctive style and singular aesthetic brought forth numerous offers, and by the mid-1950s, he had become the chief editorial cartoonist of *El Mundo*, Cuba's most popular newspaper. "In Cuba, at one point, I was working for five magazines and newspapers at the same time," he later recalled.[5]

Prohías's national profile as an artist of unique talent, and as a barbed political commentator, emerged by the late 1940s. He won the Juan Gualberto Gomez Prize for cartoon of the year, awarded by the Cuban National Association of Newspaper Journalists, for the first time in 1946. He was only twenty-five years old. He eventually won the award six times before leaving the island.[6] It was during the 1950s, as the regime of Cuban dictator Fulgencio Batista began to crumble, that Prohías created a particularly resonant and popular character for *Bohemia*, a national magazine. This was El Hombre Siniestro (The Sinister Man), described as a "dark and dastardly character" who Prohías later claimed "was born out of the national psychosis of the Cuban people" under Batista.[7] El Hombre Siniestro, like Oveja Negra (The Black Sheep), another character

Prohías introduced in this period, evidenced a savvy understanding of life in precarious political circumstances. While never explicitly political, both features revolved around themes of exploitation and manipulation. Unwary innocents in these narratives were regularly hoodwinked by the Sinister Man. For example, in one six-panel episode, the Sinister Man spies a lightning rod that he removes from a roof, wraps as a gift, and presents it to an unsuspecting man who then gets zapped by an intense lightning bolt (see fig. 8-1). (John Lent cites a disturbing episode in which the Sinister Man opens a beauty shop called Venus Di Milo that entices a woman to enter the shop, excited for her makeover; in the final panel, she leaves without arms.[8]) Later, La Mujer Siniestra appeared as a similarly nasty female version. In one instance, she spies a new, shapely neighbor across her backyard fence and appears jealous. In a series of panels, the Sinister Woman is seen repeatedly offering the woman rich foods—cake, a sandwich, a muffin, etc. In the final panel, the neighbor's body is revealed as enormously fat, and the Sinister Woman is grinning.[9] Together, these early strips, excerpted in figure 8-1, exemplify the humorously acerbic sensibility that would inform "Spy vs. Spy."

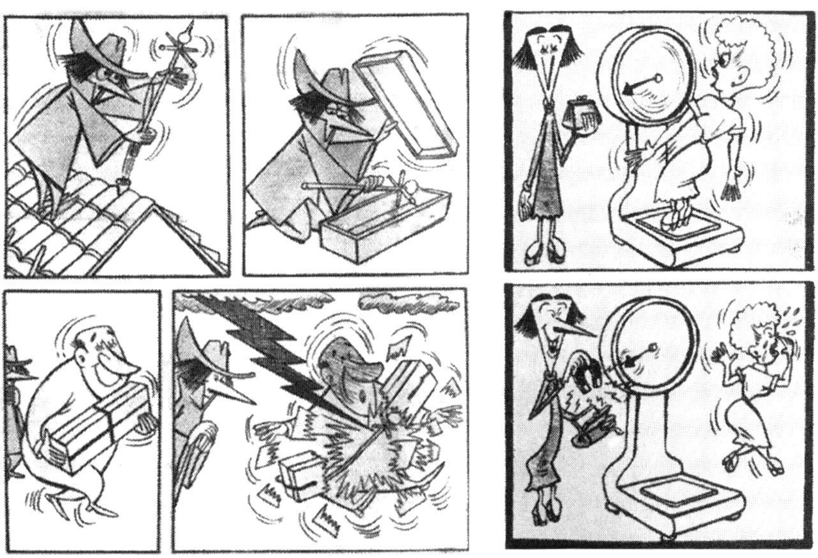

Fig. 8-1: In panels 2–3 and 5–6 of "El Hombre Siniestro" and panels 2–3 of "La Mujer Siniestra," published in Cuban newspapers before he came to the U.S., Antonio Prohías employed an aesthetic and comic sensibility that would be later reflected in *Mad*'s "Spy vs. Spy."

These caustic comics were clearly intended to be read as subversive. They highlight the corrupted state of a fallen humanity, in which the absence of moral or ethical constraint inevitably leads to selfish and destructive results. In this way, they implicitly critiqued the governance of the late Batista period, when the corrupt dictatorship began rotting from within. As the 1950s wore on, Cuban bureaucrats and authorities paradoxically became both more lax—as Prohías discovered when some of his more edgy cartoons won approval by censors willing to look the other way—and anxious.[10] Thus, his cartoons reflected and reinforced contemporary conditions in Cuba while being rooted deeply in a generally Iberian, but also specifically Cuban, comic aesthetic. As Jorge L. Catalá Carrasco notes, traditional Cuban humor is characterized by its unique style, combining satire, mockery, resistance, and subversion.[11] Prohías proved an exemplar of this national style.

Thus, it was only natural that when the Cuban revolutionaries achieved their goal of Batista's overthrow in 1959, Prohías would turn his sardonic pen on Fidel Castro and the revolutionary vanguard. "Prohías was presenting him as just another politician who had come to power, and Fidel Castro was into this delirious idea that he was a revolutionary who was going to save the world," remembered Cuban cartoonist Fresquito Fresquet.[12] At first, Castro respected the popularity of Prohías, and the new censorship regime permitted continued publication. Prohías, however, did not return that respect. "Antonio Prohías was one of the first journalists to see through the smoke and mirrors" of the new regime, *Miami Herald* features writer Fabiola Santiago later remembered.[13]

At first, Prohías acted cautiously. But he soon pushed his luck, introducing a new character—Tovarich (*comrade* in Russian)—as a daily editorial feature in *Prensa Libre* in the autumn of 1959. Tovarich, Prohías once explained to an interviewer, "represented Fidel." Prohías explained, "He basically did all the things the government was doing—but the setting was Russia. Nobody could say anything because Castro still hadn't announced that he was a Communist."[14] Tovarich, much like El Hombre Siniestro, was a wily, intense character who leveraged deception to exploit the innocent. The cartoons proved to be some of the most overtly political, and critically anti-Communist, ever produced by Prohías. Among the surviving episodes, we see Tovarich brainwashing an unwary idealist, or stabbing a clearly discernible Uncle Sam (who is represented as an enthusiastic friend) in the back. In many ways, "Tovarich" represented the diametric opposite of "Spy vs. Spy." Set in a specific geographic location (Soviet Russia was consistently represented by onion-domed churches in the background), it contained numerous symbols, such as the hammer and sickle, identifying communism as a parasitic, and even evil, ideology. While the character Tovarich himself generally embodied authoritarian manipulation, his Russian name unmistakably indicated the ideological faction in the Cold War that Prohías preferred to criticize. Perhaps most dangerous to the regime was the insinuation that communism represented an alien and imperial ideology being imposed upon the Cuban people by force.

"Tovarich" ultimately proved a critique too far. Within weeks, Prohías was prohibited by the Castro regime from practicing his craft. By early 1960, he was forced to resign his position as president of the Association of Cuban Cartoonists and was relegated to painting advertisements on trucks to survive.[15] His daughter later remembered that he began preparing for his escape by purchasing American periodicals at the newsstand in an effort to learn the market for his artistry in the United States. Though he spoke no English, the artistry he found in *Mad* attracted his attention. At the time, *Mad* featured witty and often verbose satires of everything from politics to advertising to popular culture and music, and the diverse mix of artistic styles combined with its subversive and deceptively complex comic sensibility appealed to Prohías. Even before arriving in the United States, he had decided that *Mad* would be the most likely outlet to appreciate (and purchase) his art. Later, he would explain that American cartoonists—in particular, Will Eisner, who drew the popular and unique newspaper feature *The Spirit*—had always provided inspiration and influential models for his work.[16]

In thinking about pitching his artwork in the United States, Prohías realized that the specific political and ideological critiques grounded in Cuban culture and politics would be less likely to sell abroad. Some specifically Cuban aspects of his approach would need to be downplayed. Much of the nihilism and fatalism displayed in "El Hombre Siniestro" reflected a specifically Catholic and Iberian (or Latin) worldview. This perspective, which accepts humanity as given to vice, subject to sin, and in need of redemption, establishes that the capacity for evil is a human and universal trait. Because he was unfamiliar with American culture and politics, Prohías decided to develop a more abstract comic series in an entirely self-contained universe.[17] And within that universe, moral or ethical considerations—aside from cycles of vengeance—would require muting. The comic would be about the folly of enmity and the madness of destruction—in the abstract. Any resemblance to a specific contemporaneous geopolitical rivalry would be inferred by the reader. Perhaps most importantly, unlike his Cuban work, his new feature would have no innocent victims. The antagonists would attack and be attacked only by each other, making every strip a lesson in irony and poetic justice.

This thinking animated the transformation of El Hombre Siniestro into the Black and White Spies. Prohías excelled at this abstract signaling and implicit encoding. Communicating in code and removing obvious political referents from his work had been required in Cuba in order to avoid censorship. Prohías proved a master at disguising subversive, acerbic, and biting commentary behind façades of simple drawings, regardless of the political environment in which he worked. Whether he was working under the Cuban government or American cultural authorities, he developed an expertise at keeping critical messages concealed. Like "El Hombre Siniestro," "Spy vs. Spy," as Teodora Carabas has noted, "was subversive enough to attract the interest of a large audience" while always remaining "sufficiently inoffensive."[18]

When examining the alignment of Prohías's sensibility with that of *Mad*, we must note the lifelong communicative struggles Prohías faced. He spoke Spanish in a Cuban dialect and with a strong accent. Friends and family would consistently remark upon the ways in which it always remained difficult to understand the quiet artist. It is not clear whether Prohías's reticence was rooted in shyness, or a natural self-effacement, or simply a modest personality that preferred to let his art rather than his mouth do the speaking. But many of his colleagues at *Mad* later recalled—often humorously—their challenges in communicating with Prohías. "It is impossible to carry on a conversation with Prohías," Frank Jacobs remarked. "After ten years his English is limited to 'Hello' and 'How are you, brother?'"[19] Editor Nick Meglin reported taking Prohías to an authentic Cuban restaurant in New York City where the waiters, "though Cuban" themselves, nonetheless "had great difficulty conversing with Prohías." His *Mad* colleague Al Jaffee concluded, "Antonio is nonlingual!"[20] His Mexican "hermano" and fellow *Mad* artist Sergio Aragonés recalled, "Even I could not understand him that well."[21] Aragonés remembered that Prohías would sometimes simply sit in silence, rather than chat, when they met for coffee.[22]

Many have linked the nonverbal world of "Spy vs. Spy" to Prohías's quiet personality.[23] The feature's lack of words forced Prohías to carefully and clearly indicate, via universally intelligible symbols, the narrative arc, action, and theme of each episode. The constricted space of each panel, and the fact that each episode remained fully self-contained, forced every symbol—whether it was an alarm-clock bomb, a locomotive, a bridge, or an airplane—to represent far more than its ostensible reality. For example: rocket ships denoted innovative technology in general, and, specifically, the Cold War space race. Radios, televisions, and cameras represented not only espionage tools, but also symbolized the growth of the surveillance state. The numerous offices, file cabinets, and safes portrayed in the feature not only demarcated the spies as governmental employees but also expressed a more general critique of the bureaucratization of life in the modern world. In this dynamic, words would have constricted understanding and limited communication. Symbolism throughout the strip always enriched it with multilayered meaning. Metaphors (both implicit and explicit) abounded throughout, and, as Aragonés notes, each feature often required rereading by the audience to fully grasp its messages.[24] As odd as it sounds, considering how clear and basic the drawings remained, "Spy vs. Spy" may have been the most deceptively complex feature in *Mad*. Such multilayered and multifaceted storytelling testifies to the communicative genius of the often silent Prohías.

Yet to argue that Prohías translated his own communication challenges into the format of "Spy vs. Spy" would be too simplistic. According to Aragonés, "it was not because of the language barrier that he worked in pantomime." Rather, like a puzzle master, Prohías preferred to constantly hone his messages and sharpen his communication skills by challenging himself in different ways. Before he even came to the United States, Prohías "would try to simplify his editorial cartoons to the bare essence of communication—the drawing," Aragonés recalled. "He used the avoidance of words as an exercise for the mind."[25]

In both Cuba and the United States, Prohías proved an exacting craftsman. His colleagues later remembered his remarkable dedication to making every "Spy vs. Spy" fit within tightly constricted parameters. He might complete and submit as many as six fully finished, inked drawings (each requiring no less than three full drafts, from outline to pencil sketch to ink) for every one that made it to publication. Even when he began as a freelancer at *Mad*, he found an empty easel in the tiny office and showed up every day to plan, research, draw, and sketch. He studied and borrowed from European and Latin American cartoon styles, and over the years he developed a deep knowledge of artistic variations in the cartoon world. Others noted how Prohías "was an exacting and tireless craftsman who spent days meticulously plotting and designing everything he drew."[26] Unlike most artists, he never inked over his draft pencil sketches, but, rather, preferred to begin an entirely new, final ink version for publication. Throughout his career, his drawings demonstrated a grace and clarity rooted in the careful employment of thick and thin, curved and straight, lines. As Mark Evanier noted, the artistry of Prohías could be discerned by this distinctive and identifiable elegance.[27]

Prohías also dedicated much time to researching the objects in his drawings, and he would read books on everything from architecture to weaponry to gain insights worth translating into the panels. One of the many ironies involved in the production of "Spy vs. Spy" is that these apparently simple sketches required such a complex and time-consuming production process.

Prohías was able to emigrate to the United States and work for *Mad* only after he escaped Castro's regime, exploiting the communist workers' holiday of May Day (May 1) 1960 to do so. Before he left, the regime publicly accused him of secretly serving the Central Intelligence Agency, and a protest in Havana drew 100,000 chanting for his execution.[28] Once in New York City, Prohías lived in a dingy hotel room and worked in a factory ironing sweaters. At night, he continued to meticulously compose, sketch, draw, and ink new cartoons to pitch in the United States. He was able to sell a few editorial cartoons to the New York City Spanish-language daily newspapers *El Diario* and *La Prensa*, but his efforts and attention remained mostly concentrated on his two new characters.[29] When he had a satisfactory number of finished sketches, he traveled down to the offices of *Mad* with his daughter Marta, who tagged along to handle translation.

The numerous published remembrances of what occurred next do not all accord with what actually took place. One version has the editors at *Mad* immediately taken with "Spy vs. Spy" and enthusiastically offering Prohías a freelance check on the spot.[30] Another version has it that the editors, though very impressed, politely rejected the feature. They encouraged Prohías to continue pitching material and offered ideas for other publication venues. In this second version, Prohías dramatically pulled several finished "Spy vs. Spy" boards and threatened to rip them apart, only to be stopped by the editors, who changed their minds on the spot.[31] Regardless of the facts, it is clear that the editors and publisher of *Mad* quickly recognized his talent. They purchased this first series of features, and with that initial $800 check, Prohías moved his family from their cramped hotel room in Manhattan to a new home in New Jersey.

"Spy vs. Spy" and Cold War Portrayals of Espionage in Popular Culture

"Spy vs. Spy" debuted with three installments in the January 1961 *Mad* (#60: 9, 14, 24). The timing was fortuitous, as on the twentieth day of that month John F. Kennedy took the oath of office and assumed the Presidency of the United States. "Let the word go forth from this time and place, to friend and foe alike, that the torch has been passed to a new generation of Americans," Kennedy proclaimed in his inaugural address. "Let every nation know," he continued, "whether it wishes us well or ill, that we shall pay any price, bear any burden, meet any hardship, support any friend, oppose any foe to assure the survival and the success of liberty."[32] Kennedy's soaring rhetoric, emphasizing deep commitment to protect and defend a core U.S. ideology, remains memorable for both its idealism and patriotism.

The "new generation of Americans" empowered in the Kennedy era were young, optimistic, and progressive. The end of the Eisenhower era represented a turning point in the Cold War. But beneath the fresh confidence symbolized by the young president lurked old anxieties influencing American life since the atomic age began. Global and domestic threats—everything from communist infiltration to nuclear annihilation—continued to haunt even the most hopeful and celebratory rhetoric in this period. As Tom Engelhardt explains, *Mad* played a uniquely subversive role in this transitionary period.[33] The magazine detected and brought to the surface national problems that authorities across the political spectrum often preferred to obscure. This "corrosive humor," Engelhardt notes, was almost entirely missing from American television and radio in the Kennedy era. *Mad* "drew on a mocking, dismantling voice lodged deep in the culture. In those years, some children embraced with gusto the secret despair of adults who claimed to be living happily in the freest, richest, most generous country on Earth."[34]

This "secret despair" lurked everywhere in the Cold War era, coloring every diplomatic interaction and animating both the explicit and implicit geopolitical strategies pursued by the Soviet Union and the United States. Because the Cold War remained forever undeclared by its chief antagonists, it was often conducted by proxies in faraway lands and by armies of spies working for the KGB and CIA trotting around the globe. Espionage developed a new glamour in the Kennedy Administration, as spies and spycraft emerged in popular culture in myriad ways. As Carabas notes, from its inception "Spy vs. Spy" leveraged this trend by both exploiting its popularity and debunking the cliché of the spy as action-hero archetype. "The comic effect," Carabas explains, "depended on the audience's familiarity with the extraliterary context [of] the Cold War environment"[35] and then inserting this meaning into a comic stripped of specific signification.

The archetype of the spy as the epitome of sophisticated warfare was pervasive in 1960s American, and even western, culture. For example, the James Bond films propagated the illusion of the brilliant and courageous western spy, ready to participate fully at His Majesty's Command in daring Cold War missions.[36] American and British television programs like *I Spy*, *Mission: Impossible*, *The Man from U.N.C.L.E.*, and *The Avengers* celebrated espionage and those who practiced it. Even popular music reflected this cultural theme, as Johnny Rivers's "Secret Agent Man" soared to #3 on the U.S. pop charts in 1966.[37] To fully grasp the subversive value of "Spy vs. Spy" in American culture requires noting this larger cultural and political framework in which it was embedded and to which it responded. The Black Spy and White Spy were anti-heroic, committed to an endless series of madcap, and ultimately futile, adventures. They stood as precise opposites of the suave, sophisticated, and ever-successful James Bond, who exploited technological advantage, good looks, and stylistic charm to emerge victorious in every book and film. The Black Spy and White Spy always remained lovable losers, doomed to perpetual futility, while James Bond consistently saved the world and won the girl.

"Spy vs. Spy" lampooned every aspect of the Cold War's popular culture representation of espionage. Innovative weaponry in the hands of the Black Spy or the White Spy inevitably backfired. For example, in *Mad* #198 (4/78: 25), the Black Spy concocts a new explosive liquid, only to have the White Spy surreptitiously douse a trained fly and flyswatter in the mix while he's relaxing and reading a newspaper. When the fly lands upon the Black Spy's head, he reaches for the flyswatter. An explosion ("Boom") follows when the Black Spy swats the fly on his head, and the White Spy is seen chuckling outside the room (see figure 8-2).

Across 241 installments of "Spy vs. Spy," secret plots rarely worked out as planned. Any victory was piecemeal and ephemeral—Antonio Prohías very carefully ensured that throughout a given issue of *Mad*, the victors would alternate. Unlike the common popular culture depiction of spies as intelligent, brave, and savvy, Prohías's spies lacked a certain shrewdness. They could be strangely naïve and trusting, and they just as often fell into traps as escaped them. They could be immature and juvenile. They made mistakes—repeatedly—and paid for them.[38]

Their fallibility was particularly evident in the brief era of Prohías's Grey Spy. Introduced in September 1962 in "Spy vs. Spy vs. Spy" (#73, 42), this femme fatale leveraged her beauty to exploit the amorous intentions of the Black Spy and White Spy. But the addition of lust slightly altered the comic's successful dynamic and hindered much of its implicit messaging. "The lady spy represented neutrality," Prohías once told an interviewer. "She would decide [victory] for the white or the black spy, and she also added some balance and variety to the basic 'Spy vs. Spy' formula."[39] But the fact that she always won, and that the Black Spy and the White Spy could so easily be distracted from their obsessive rivalry, created a distinct and distracting hierarchy within the "Spy vs. Spy"

Fig. 8-2. Some of the tricks that Prohías's spies play on each other backfire, while others succeed in exacting a humiliating revenge of the sort that 007 and other fictitious spies do not suffer (*Mad* #198, 4/78: 25). MAD used with permission.

universe. "She was clever and she never lost—out of courtesy to women!" Prohías explained.[40] This "courtesy" made the Grey Spy an undefeatable superheroine and had the ultimate effect of making this repetitive comic even more predictable. She also lacked the slapstick silliness evidenced by her amorous pursuers, further distracting from the comic's central framework. In many ways, the Grey Spy reflected the exploitive and manipulative sensibility of La Mujer Siniestra rather than the sensibility of the Black and White Spies. Ultimately, it appears that the addition of gender issues in general, and lust in particular, altered an essential structure of the feature. Three years later, after a final appearance in *Mad* #99 (12/65: 40), the Grey Spy disappeared from Prohías's vision of the strip, though his successors have periodically revived her.[41]

The experience of the Grey Spy, and the complications of gender that it introduced into "Spy vs. Spy," apparently diverted attention from the basic Cold War geopolitics integral to every installment. As Engelhardt notes, Prohías's creation allowed *Mad*'s readership to experience "the Cold War as a series of ludicrous acts between two arbitrarily distinguishable quasi-warriors who had everything in common with each other, and nothing with anyone else."[42] For the Black Spy and White Spy to remain permanently equal, they needed to be identical and obsessed only with each other. This equivalence proved key, as it reflected the rivalry of the Soviet Union and the United States in the Cold War era as seen from a critical (or neutral) perspective. Thus, the very concept of Soviet-American differentiation—so pervasive everywhere else in popular culture during the Cold War—came into question each month in *Mad* via "Spy vs. Spy." Prohías trusted readers to use their own imaginations rather than the official governmental proclamations issued regularly by both the Soviet Union and the United States of America.

Like all great artists, Antonio Prohías understood the importance of encoding timeless and universal themes within particular and distinct narratives. "Spy vs. Spy" presented the context of no context, in which signifiers remained absent in order to maintain the purity of direct communication. Yet for all its clarity, "Spy vs. Spy" relied heavily on its audience's understanding of the complex and multifaceted messages being propagated elsewhere during the Cold War. This irony is but one of many embedded in the comic's success: it employed the bare minimum of actual ink lines required for explication, yet its clear and clean images always encoded complex themes about the human condition. "Spy vs. Spy" always remained simultaneously universal and personal, simple and complex, and straightforward yet deceptive. Despite being "hermetically sealed off in a world of its own," as Spiegelman put it, every reader understood its direct link to "the cold war and its displacements."[43]

In this sense, "Spy vs. Spy" was a largely two-dimensional comic that drew much of its power and depth from interactivity and engagement. Yet another irony consisted of the way in which such a structured and repetitive framework could employ so many fresh variations in such creative ways so as to expand the imagination. Hidden within the simple and clean drawings and behind the wordless panels, the numerous implicit messages in every "Spy vs. Spy" installment could be both easily decodable and almost impossible to find. Irony, metaphor, and philosophy poured forth in each specific installment and in the essence of the comic's design. For example, the feature taught that the folly of violence and the madness of perpetual enmity was a human problem, not a political one. Prohías regularly reminded *Mad*'s readers that though the modern world might provide incredible new technologies, their usefulness was always constricted by the skills and intelligence of the people employing them. "Spy vs. Spy" illustrated the illusory and ephemeral nature of victory, and perhaps more importantly, the feature showed that no defeat—not even death—was truly final. The idea that effort and success will always be correlated in a just universe was one that "Spy vs. Spy" went to great lengths to dispel. The world as presented by Prohías was forever chaotic and random, and his drawings taught readers that life is filled with the unexpected and surprising. Throughout "Spy vs. Spy," hope remains intertwined with despair, and resilience intertwined with destruction. These are the humanistic paradoxes that inform Prohías's basic philosophy, and they reflect a surprisingly mature worldview for a (supposedly) child's medium. Prohías's conception of existence remains so plainly visible in the comic that many simply miss it. "To Antonio, black and white didn't represent good or evil," remembered Sergio Aragonés, "they depicted the futility of deceit, tricking each other. Winning a little at the beginning, losing at the end. Throughout the years in his work there was a balance, as in real life."[44]

Conclusion: The Paradoxes of Prohías

Prohías embedded other ironies in his most memorable creation. For example, while readers are supposed to abhor the irrationality and perpetual destructiveness of "Spy vs. Spy," the commitment and dedication of the Black Spy and the White Spy can be read as inspirational. Neither surrenders completely, nor does either abandon the mission. Failure happens, but resiliency occurs as well. Persistence, Prohías teaches, is an important life value, and must be disaggregated from simplistic notions of failure or success. In this sense, "Spy vs. Spy" is ultimately existential, and all of its many ironies, paradoxes, and metaphors align closely with the inescapable quandary of humanity.

That Prohías personally experienced so many challenges, defeats, and successes in his life undoubtedly animated the soul of "Spy vs. Spy." Indeed, it is yet another remarkable irony of "Spy vs. Spy" that its creator was condemned and exiled by a communist dictatorship, yet the feature's presentation of Cold War metaphors remained essentially neutral. Antonio Prohías forever remained a committed anti-communist, yet his most famous, influential, and lasting creation refused to explicitly criticize communism—or at least declined to adjudge it less worthy than capitalism.

These ironies concern the artist and his creation. But within the production process, other paradoxes can be discerned. For example: Prohías strove tirelessly and worked exhaustively to produce a clean and direct graphic narrative that appeared remarkably basic. He deceptively hid the complexity of his labor behind sketches so sharp and precise that they communicated instantly. In other words: though Prohías was "an exacting, tireless craftsman who spent days meticulously plotting and designing everything he drew,"[45] his drawings made the process of producing brilliant art look easy.

Yet nothing came easy to Antonio Prohías. Everything from his original decision to become an artist to his political controversies in Cuba to his exile in the United States weighed heavily on his soul. Behind his quiet and placid exterior, he had good reason to harbor anxieties throughout his life. It is perhaps for this reason that he self-medicated with tobacco, and by the late 1980s, he developed the illnesses that forced him to turn over his iconic creation to others. The final "Spy vs. Spy" drawn by Prohías appeared in *Mad* #269, published in March 1987.[46] He developed emphysema and moved to Miami to be closer to family. It was there that he died on February 24, 1998. By then he had achieved status as an important figure of resistance to Fidel Castro and the Cuban revolution. Older Cuban exiles remembered the sting of his editorial cartoons from decades earlier. Prohías never returned to his beloved island nation, which remained in the grip of the Castro regime even after the disappearance of the Soviet Union. Both he and his rival Fidel Castro eventually outlived the Cold War. Prohías's legacy can still be detected in comics and cartoons being produced in Latin America and the United States. For example, Hector Cantú, author of the popular *Baldo* comic, credits Prohías as a formative, inspirational, and powerful influence on his work.[47] That Prohías's memory and legacy continue to resonate long after the collapse of the Soviet Union, the end of the Cold War, and the life of Fidel Castro attests to his ultimate success as philosopher, communicator, humanitarian, and artist.

Notes

1. José Quiroga, *Cuban Palimpsests*, 54.
2. Art Spiegelman, "The Lives They Lived: Antonio Prohías, Yin and Yang, Cold War Style (cover story)," 32.
3. Grant Geissman, introduction to *Mad Spy vs. Spy: The Complete Casebook*, 6–7.
4. John A. Lent, "Cuban Cartoonists: Masters of Coping," 83.
5. Quoted in Geissman, introduction to *Mad Spy vs. Spy*, 7.
6. William Grimes, "Antonio Prohías, 77: Drew 'Spy Vs. Spy' Cartoon," A14.
7. Geissman, introduction to *Mad Spy vs. Spy*, 8.
8. Lent, "Cuban Cartoonists," 83.
9. Antonio Prohías, "La Mujer Siniestra," reprinted in *Mad Spy vs. Spy: The Complete Casebook*, 26.
10. Fabiola Santiago, "A Cartoonist in Times of Revolution and Censorship," 14.
11. Jorge L. Catalá Carrasco, "From Suspicion to Recognition? 50 Years of Comics in Cuba," 139–60.
12. Quoted in Santiago, "Cartoonist in Times of Revolution," 15.
13. Santiago, "Cartoonist in Times of Revolution," 15.
14. Prohías, quoted in *Mad Spy vs. Spy: The Complete Casebook*, 254.
15. Santiago, "Cartoonist in Times of Revolution," 16.
16. Nick Meglin, "The Old Pro," in *Mad Spy vs. Spy: The Complete Casebook*, 134.
17. Geissman, introduction to *Mad Spy vs. Spy*, 8–10.
18. Teodora Carabas, "'Tales Calculated to Drive You MAD': The Debunking of Spies, Superheroes, and Cold War Rhetoric in *Mad* Magazine's "Spy vs. Spy,"' 11.
19. Frank Jacobs, *The Mad World of William M. Gaines*, 130–31.
20. Meglin, "The Old Pro," 136.
21. Mark Evanier, *Mad Art: A Visual Celebration of the Art of Mad Magazine and the Idiots Who Create It*, 149.
22. Sergio Aragonés, "Mi Hermano, Antonio," in *Mad Spy vs. Spy: The Complete Casebook*, 248.
23. Evanier, *Mad Art*, 149–50.
24. Aragonés, "Mi Hermano, Antonio," 247.

25. Aragonés, "Mi Hermano, Antonio," 254.
26. Evanier, *Mad Art*, 149.
27. Evanier, *Mad Art*, 153.
28. Lent, "Cuban Cartoonists," 83.
29. Santiago, "Cartoonist in Times of Revolution," 16.
30. Evanier, *Mad Art*, 153; Geissman, introduction to *Mad Spy vs. Spy*, 6; Meglin, "The Old Pro," 135.
31. Marta Rosa Pizarro, "Snapshots of My Father," in *Mad Spy vs. Spy: The Complete Casebook*, 17.
32. John F. Kennedy, "Inaugural Address, January 20, 1961," USG-17, John F. Kennedy Presidential Library and Museum, U.S. National Archives, video digitized from historical footage, 4 reels, 35 mm. film, 16 min.
33. Tom Engelhardt, *The End of Victory Culture*, 8.
34. Engelhardt, *The End of Victory Culture*, 8.
35. Carabas, "'Tales Calculated to Drive You MAD,'" 11.
36. Klaus Dodds, "Screening Geopolitics: James Bond and the Early Cold War Films (1962–1967)," 270–72; Jason Mulvihill, "James Bond's Cold War Part I," 225; Mulvihill, "The Golden Age of Bond: Creation of a Cold War Popular Hero (1962–1965), Part II," 337.
37. Jim Clash, "Johnny Rivers Chats About His Big Hit, Secret Agent Man."
38. Carabas, "'Tales Calculated to Drive You MAD,'" 12, 14–18.
39. Prohías, quoted in *Mad Spy vs. Spy*, 47.
40. Prohías, quoted in *Mad Spy vs. Spy*, 47.
41. Following Prohías's retirement, writer Don "Duck" Edwing and artist Bob Clarke reintroduced the Grey Spy in "Spy vs. Spy vs. Spy," #281 (9/88): 44 (perhaps unexpectedly, because the table of contents states, "Spy vs. Spy"), and Peter Kuper first brought her back in #411 (11/01): 30-32 (perhaps in response to a reader inquiry, headlined "Make a Dumb Wish Foundation," in #403 [3/01]: 4). Thanks to Peter Kuper for noting the Grey Spy's revival.
42. Engelhardt, *The End of Victory Culture*, 131.
43. Spiegelman, "The Lives They Lived: Antonio Prohías, Yin and Yang, Cold War Style," 32.
44. Aragonés, "Mi Hermano, Antonio," 247.
45. Evanier, *Mad Art*, 149.
46. Geissman, introduction to *Mad Spy vs. Spy*, 10.
47. Quoted in Frederick L. Aldama, *Your Brain on Latino Comics: From Gus Arriola to Los Bros Hernandez*, 131.

9. *Mad* About Poe:

Poetry in a Jugular Vein

Dennis W. Eddings

FROM ITS INCEPTION, *Mad* has been grounded on the bedrock of parody. The first offering in its first issue is a self-reflexive parody of the comic book tale of terror, a staple of *Mad*'s then publisher, EC Comics. Since then, every issue of *Mad* contains parodies drawn from diverse realms to ridicule our weird, wacky, and all-too-often crazy world. At its most basic, parody is deceptively simple: A parodist takes another's work (poem, story, song, etc.) and warps it to ridicule the original and/or its creator.[1] A reader familiar with the original work may enjoy its clever skewing by the parodist and appreciate the ridicule. One not familiar with the original may be totally lost.[2] Thus, the parodies in early issues of *Mad*—send-ups of comics, movies, and radio and television shows—dealt with material most likely to be familiar to its anticipated audience. When it morphed into a magazine with #24 in 1955, *Mad* added a dimension to its use of parody. It still warped (and warps) originals comprised of the usual suspects—movies, television, ad campaigns—for the sake of ridicule, but The Usual Gang of Idiots also frequently used (and still uses) familiar works to satirize external issues rather than to ridicule the originals.

Both dimensions may be found in the many parodies of various poems scattered throughout *Mad*'s history. Classics abound, from William Shakespeare through Samuel Taylor Coleridge to Walt Whitman to Carl Sandburg. Not-so-classics also abound, from Hugh Antoine D'Arcy to Ernest Lawrence Thayer to Joyce Kilmer. Poetic merit is of little concern to *Mad* in selecting works it wants to play with. Henry Wadsworth Longfellow appears more than any other poet, while Thayer's "Casey at the Bat," no touchstone of poetic greatness, is honored (if such is the right word) with twelve separate appearances, more than any other single work. This apparent lack of any meaningful critical standards in selecting works for its parodic excursions reflects *Mad*'s assumed position as a bastion of ignorance and stupidity steadfastly defying anything smacking of taste or culture, a stance perfectly comfortable with seeing D'Arcy's "The Face Upon the Floor" (usually titled "The Face On The Barroom Floor") as poetically equal to a Shakespeare sonnet.[3] The practical reality, however, is that *Mad*'s poetry parodies depend on readers' recognition of the source to help make their satiric point. The magazine's hypothetical reader is far more likely to know "Casey at the Bat" than the "Prologue" to *The Canterbury Tales*, which circumstance explains why Edgar Allan Poe and Longfellow and Thayer appear so frequently.

Poe, however, presents a special case. When it comes to the desired familiarity necessary for *Mad*'s poetic parodies, he's pretty much a sure thing. Readers unfamiliar with "The Raven" are, I suspect, few and far between. Such is most likely true of the other Poe poems *Mad* makes use of: "The Bells" and "Annabel Lee." Longfellow may appear more often than Poe, but he doesn't figure as a distinct personality. Readers may be somewhat familiar with "Hiawatha" or "Paul Revere's Ride" (each appearing five times), but Longfellow is for most, at best, a somewhat familiar name, nothing more. Poe is different, far different, from the other poets whom *Mad* usurps, existing in many readers' minds as a distinct, individual persona inseparable from the poems that he created, a reality that *Mad* carries over into its parodies of him. This difference suggests that a closer look at just how *Mad* treats Poe may well be worthwhile.

Some of these Poe parodies present a distinct character built upon the public's misguided but persistent misperceptions of him. Drug addict! Morbid psychopath! Terror-haunted, ghoul-ridden! So it goes, a distinct image of a specific persona that, while it is definitely not the real Poe, nonetheless dominates the common perception of him. In part such misconceptions of his character are attributable to the tendency of a great many readers to equate Poe with his narrators. They are obsessed, or drunkards, or flat-out crazy, and so must have been their creator. The continuing popularity of "The Raven" doesn't help matters, as many readers see the narrator's melancholia and angst as Poe's. Another factor leading to this mythic Poe is attributable to Rufus Wilmot Griswold, Poe's literary executor, who edited the first collection of Poe's works. Volume 3 of that edition, first published in the fall of 1850, contains

Griswold's "Memoir of the Author," a scabrous collection of half-truths and outright fabrications that Griswold supported by altering and rewriting many of Poe's letters to help convict his subject of being a petty, vengeful, drunken, and totally unsavory character. Nor was Poe an innocent lamb in Griswold's efforts to destroy his reputation. Elements of Poe's own aptly titled "Imp of the Perverse" were part of his makeup. He had problems with alcohol, which often led him to behavior contrary to his own best interests, and many incidents detailed by his subsequent biographers are not flattering.[4] That public image of Poe is an integral element in some of *Mad*'s Poe parodies. Interestingly, however, of his eighteen appearances in *Mad*, only three directly ridicule Poe, while one hovers in a type of never-never land. The other fourteen appearances use him as a vehicle for satirizing external concerns, although in some, Poe suffers collateral damage, justifying the idea that parody's role is ridicule.

Poe's first appearance in *Mad* (#9, 3/54: 1-7) quite appropriately parodies "The Raven," but not by skewing its language. *Mad* prints the poem, quite accurately, in its entirety. The ridicule expected of parody occurs through Will Elder's brilliant illustrations that undercut the poem's overwrought language, absurd situation, and ludicrous plot, basically turning the poem upside down. "The Raven" also figures in another *Mad* spoof of Poe in "The *Mad* Poetry Round Robin," written by Frank Jacobs (#125, 3/69: 38-41),[5] where we find "If Thayer's 'Casey at the Bat' Were Written by Edgar Allan Poe," in which Thayer's classic is converted into a darkly Poesque dramatic monologue with art by George Woodbridge:

> Ghastly, gaunt and grim I stood there, gripping my great bat of wood
>   there,
> In my brain dark, ugly demons danced a dirge from days of yore;
> Then the fast-ball came by flying, and, inside my soul was dying
> As I heard the umpire crying words from baseball's ancient lore;
> "Strike one!" were the words he hollered, out of baseball's ancient
>   lore,
> Just "Strike one!" and nothing more! (38)

Poe's batsman is a compendium of characteristics popularly associated with the poet, an association furthered by Woodbridge's illustration (see fig. 9-1) showing Poe as the batter, eyes protruding in terror, knees knocking, a tombstone serving as the batter's box. The illustration also plays into the dubious notion that Poe's works were autobiographical, linking poet and poem inextricably together. Thayer isn't the issue here; rather the character made famous in his poem is used to mock Poe, while the usurpation of Poe's most famous poem literally uses the poet's own work against him.

Mad's final direct send-up of Poe is set to "The Bells" in a pastiche of parodies grounded in the premise "If Famous Poets Had Written 'Mother Goose'" by Frank Jacobs (art by Jack Rickard, #113, 9/67: 20-22). Poe enters the picture with "If Edgar Allan Poe Had Written 'Old King Cole'" (21), and the resulting warping of "The Bells" turns Mother Goose's nursery

Fig. 9-1: George Woodbridge presents a knock-kneed Poe in a batting stance atop a tombstone, eyes bulging, clearly in terror, the opposing team made up of skeletons, with ghosts, goblins, monkeys, and spectators at a macabre baseball game (*Mad* #125, 3/69: 38). MAD used with permission.

rhyme on its head. There is nothing "merry" about Poe's King Cole. The parody again plays on popular notions regarding Poe's morbid character and contains a veritable lexicon of words often associated with him:

> Hear the call of Old King Cole—
>   Old King Cole!
> What a frantic, fearful craving fills his morbid soul!
> Hear him moaning, moaning, moaning
>   For his pipe and for his bowl,
> Like the dreaded, deadly groaning
> Of some ghoul that is intoning
>   From its ghostly, graveyard hole. (21)

As it should, the parody mimics the rhythm and rhyme scheme of "The Bells" and incorporates many of Poe's technical mannerisms: the alliteration of "frantic, fearful" and "dreaded, deadly"; the repetition of "moaning, moaning, moaning" and "plea, plea, plea"; the variation in line length that makes the parody look as well as sound like Poe's poem.

> Hear him plea, plea, plea
>   As he calls his fiddlers three!
> Ah, what horrifying hunger fills the terror-ridden soul
>   Of King Cole, Cole, Cole, Cole,
>   Cole, Cole, Cole—
> Of the bleak and blackened soul of Old King Cole! (21)

Moreover, the parody is larded with Gothic elements frequently associated with Poe—a "morbid soul" filled with "fearful craving" and "terror-troubled." Thus, this parody suggests that Poe, the presumed author of the poem, takes an invariably bleak view of the human condition, overthrowing the notion that "Old King Cole was a merry old soul / And a merry old soul was he."

Cole's (and Poe's?) anguish is further emphasized through the accompanying graphic by Rickard (see fig. 9-2), the gaping mouth and furrowed brow showing an agonized, tormented being, again the polar opposite of the "merry" soul portrayed in Mother Goose's happy jingle. In the background, Alfred E. Neuman as the jester, carrying a pipe and bowl, seems to be enjoying the entire show, perhaps as evidence of "what fools these mortals be" (or that Alfred, as usual, simply doesn't get it). I would further suggest that the graphic, through Alfred's figure, captures Poe's own bemused detachment from the haunted characters and Gothic situations he so frequently created, as demonstrated by the many times he parodied those conventions (as in "How to Write a Blackwood Article" and its companion tale, "A Predicament") or inverted them by including complex satiric hoaxes within those tales (as Robert Regan so brilliantly demonstrates in his examination of "The Masque of the Red Death").[6] The common perception that Poe did not have a sense of humor is implicit in this parody, another reflection of the Poe mystique. In speaking of Poe's humorous tales almost one hundred years ago, C. Alphonso Smith pontificated that "If laughter is heard in them or caused by them it is surely a falsetto cackle."[7] Ironically, contemporary commentary points to the very tales Smith excoriates as proof that Poe indeed had a sense of humor. Still, the thrust of this satire aims directly at Poe, a purposeful send-up of him and his art.

Standing somewhat apart from these Poe-directed parodies is an odd (and oddly effective) parody that targets Poe and cartoonist Hank Ketcham. "If Famous Authors Wrote the Comics" (#46, 4/59: 35-37),

Fig. 9-2: Old King Cole is not a "merry old soul" in Jack Rickard's illustration, but Alfred E. Neuman as jester certainly is, perhaps depicting Poe's artistic detachment from his tormented subjects (*Mad* #113, 9/67: 21). MAD used with permission.

another poetic pastiche by Jacobs, deservedly known as *Mad*'s poet laureate, with art by Wally Wood, sets "If Edgar Allan Poe Wrote 'Dennis the Menace'" to "The Raven" (37). Here Ketcham's mischievous but lovable towheaded tyke turns monster, gleefully immolating his parents for maltreating him. Converting Dennis into a Poe character casts light on Poe, but also suggests a not-so-innocent thread lurking beneath Ketcham's character, one that makes Dennis more than a mischievous but innocent child, as is made startlingly clear in Wood's illustration (see fig. 9-3). There is nothing lovable or innocently mischievous in the malevolent smirk that Wood puts on Dennis's face as his parents, trapped on the second floor of their burning house, scream in terror. The graphic leads almost inevitably for those familiar with Poe to "Hop-Frog," which climaxes with the fiery immolation of the king and his ministers by the vengeful dwarf who gives the tale its title. But Hop-Frog's vengeance is warranted, his mistreatment at the hands of the king and his ministers very real. Ketchum's Dennis can make no such claim. Using Poe to subvert Dennis's mischievousness suggests there may be a darker sub-text lurking below the benign surface of

Fig. 9-3: Wally Wood shows the demonic side of Dennis the Menace, who gets revenge on his parents by setting the house on fire with them trapped inside on the second floor in "If Famous Authors Wrote the Comics." As Frank Jacobs channels him, Dennis gleefully notes, "I'll get spankings, Nevermore!" (*Mad* #46, 4/59: 37). (In a further demonstration of *Mad*'s parodic muse, the whole issue is deliberately published upside down.) MAD used with permission.

"Dennis the Menace," a suggestion that evil indeed lurks within the heart of all. Poe, of course, is the ideal source for such subversion since he frequently presented us with characters who are set upon cynical vengeance and retribution with nothing salutary or just about it. This, the briefest of *Mad*'s treatments of Poe, casts perhaps the widest parodic net, pulling Poe and Ketcham together in a broad assault on both, encompassing cynical vengeance and retribution with nothing salutary or just about it, a suggestion that lurking below the innocent surface of Ketcham's cartoon lies an evil that matches the evils Poe so frequently presented. Pretty heady stuff for something so seemingly simple.

Mad's other adaptations of "The Raven" focus on external issues rather than make fun of Poe and his work, satirizing such diverse subjects as advertising, real estate agents, big oil, the Beats, television ratings, jogging, Wes Craven, and (brilliantly) President Ronald Reagan.[8] Indeed, Poe does not figure in these parodies, not even as a presence in the illustrations. The familiar form of "The Raven"—stanza pattern, meter, rhyme scheme—is there, but nothing more. I'm not even sure *parody* is the correct term here, the ridicule being pointed outward, as it were, rather than inward toward the poetry. "The Raven" is not, however, the only Poe poem *Mad* has seen fit to parody. As mentioned earlier, "The Bells" and "Annabel Lee" also come into play. We have already seen how "The Bells" serves as a direct parody of Poe. Other treatments, like most of those using "The Raven," take on external issues, but in these instances, Poe also frequently figures.

In "If Famous Poets Had to Make a Living Today" (Jacobs and Rickard, #237, 3/83: 12-15), Poe is presented as a pharmacist. The first stanza celebrates the curative power of the magical potions that alleviate all sorts of miseries from snakebite to nasal drip to irregularity to muscle aches to chills. The second stanza focuses on a far different type of pills brought to us by the kindly people of Big Pharma:

> See my other kinds of pills—
>   Happy pills!
> Crammed with crazy chemicals that give all kinds of thrills.
> When my purple ones you're trying,
>   There's a tingle that you feel;

With the green ones, you'll be flying
Till you're soon identifying
  With some world that isn't real; . . . (14)

As usual, Frank Jacobs's clever reworking of Poe's poetics provides both a sense of familiarity (we've heard this before) and delightful surprise (but not like *this*).

Feel the glow, glow, glow
  Till your mind begins to blow
And you're hooked until you're swallowing that overdose that kills
  From the pills, pills, pills, pills,
  Pills, pills, pills
From your never-stopping popping of the pills. (14)

There's a double edge to this Poe send-up. The first is subliminal, aiming through suggestion at the popular (and erroneous) notion that Poe was a hyped-up junkie. More telling, the parody goes after our faith in better living through chemistry, hinting that a vast number of Americans are, in one way or another, drug dependent, and the blame for that dependency can be placed directly in the lap of the pharmaceutical companies. Given the current opioid epidemic inundating the U.S., and the obvious complicity of Big Pharma in that epidemic, *Mad* in this instance is downright prescient.

The single graphic, again by Jack Rickard (see fig. 9-4), helps to reinforce this connection. The sign proclaiming "Discount Drugs" evokes a sleazy image of deliberate price-cutting to bring in the suckers (think of the Canadian drug ads filling your email box). Poe is depicted holding a plate of drugs filled with a veritable cornucopia of delight, the precise nature of that delight revealed by the image that Poe conjures up of a whacked-out customer bedeviled by creepy, crawling critters that seem intent on keeping him in his blissful state. Finally, Poe's own blasé gaze, perhaps suggesting he uses his own product, again ties into the popular misconceptions regarding his character. But that gaze also captures the total lack of concern on the part of pharmaceutical firms over the dependency they spawn, the true thrust of the satire.

Fig. 9-4: Poe is a pill-pushing pharmacist in Jacobs's parody, and Jack Rickard shows the poet with a serious face, holding a tray of his pharmaceuticals, while his hooked customer falls prey to myriad hallucinations (*Mad* #237 (3/83): 14). MAD used with permission.

While these two excursions into Poe land have their own cutting satiric points, a far sharper edge emerges in "The Oil" (Jacobs, #297, 9/90: 24-25). This four-stanza rant begins with "foreign oil":

And each dollar, yen, and kopeck
Feeds the greedy bunch at OPEC
For the oil, oil, oil, oil,
Oil, oil, oil—
For the money-grubbing moguls with the oil. (24)

The next two stanzas focus on the ecological disasters that big oil visits upon the United States. From leaking pipelines (can you say "New York's Arthur Kill spill"?) to leaking tankers "blackening our shores" (remember the Exxon Valdez?), Big Oil, like Big Pharma, without a pang of conscience, spews its product into the environment. Thus, the final stanza focuses on the environmental havoc created by such disasters, beginning with very specific images:

See the seagulls drenched with oil—
Deadly oil!
Grounded on the beaches that men ravage and despoil!
Smell the fishes putrefying;
Count the corpses of the seals;
See the scores of eagles dying,
Giving up all dreams of flying
As the greasy goo congeals! (25)

The stanza goes on to bemoan politicians' unwillingness to act:

> Leaders swear, swear, swear,
> That they really, truly care!
> Words to banish ev'ry sorrow
> Till that bigger spill tomorrow
> When another giant tanker
> Winds up punctured by its anchor,
> With our shores obliterated
> And the planet decimated
> By the oil, oil, oil, oil,
> Oil, oil, oil—
> By the deadly devastation of the oil! (25)

This harsh attack finds stark reinforcement in the accompanying graphic by John Pound. The Statue of Liberty, holding oil-soaked dead animals, her robe and pedestal fouled with sludge, a great tear trailing from her eye and down her cheek, represents the fouling of our nation by an irresponsible, uncaring conglomeration of un-indicted co-conspirators whose only concern is profit, no matter what the cost to Earth and its inhabitants.

Mad's final use of "The Bells" targets the 1998 Dreamworks animated film *Antz* (Jacobs and Viviano, "The Antz" #378, 2/99: 20-21), setting up the satire with this pithy introduction: "Leave it to Dreamworks to come out with an animated film with muscle. No namby-pamby cupcake versions of The Hunchback of Notre Dame or Anastasia for them. Nosiree, better to entertain the kiddies with the stark realism of talking, thinking insects who thrive on war, torture, and genocide!" *Mad* proceeds to attack the film by savaging the four main actors who did the voices, beginning with Woody Allen, the "wimpy hero":

> Hear him moaning, moaning, moaning
> That the colony's a bore!
> While the audience is groaning
> 'Cause it's Woody Allen droning
> Like in countless films before!
> Hear him kvetch, kvetch, kvetch
> And you fear that you may retch .... (20)

The satire goes on to belittle Sharon Stone as the "Cocky, cocky, cocky / Princess," Sylvester Stallone as a "tough, six legged Rocky" (20), and ends with Gene Hackman:

See the warlord of the Antz—
  Worst of Antz!
Hackman playing Hitler as he schemes and raves and rantz!
See him killing, killing, killing
Anyone who's in his way!
Hey, so what if blood is spilling?
When you're out to make top billing
Genocide can make your day. (21)

Pretty strong stuff, but the satire grows even more savage, going after those who endorse and make possible such stuff by paying money to see it: "People queued up—seems they're as screwed up as the antz!" (21). The notion that audiences are basically responsible for much of the garbage saturating our entertainment world recurs throughout *Mad*'s history. To put it simply, if people didn't buy garbage, the world wouldn't be so filled with it.

A good part of the genius of The Usual Gang of Idiots lies in their ability to find just the right vehicle for their satire and cleverly adapt it to make their point. Just as the four adaptations of "The Bells" fit that mold, so do the three appearances of "Annabel Lee." In "Madison Avenue Turns to History and Literature" (Siegel and Clarke, #51, 12/59: 36-39), Poe is pictured as a character in a Miss Clairol commercial.[9] The mock advertisement skews Poe's poem in a send-up of Clairol's "Does She or Doesn't She?" ad campaign:

It was many and many a year ago,
  In a kingdom by the sea
That a maiden with hair color natural lived,
  By the name of Miss Clairol Lee;
And I lived in those days with no other thought
  Than: Does she or doesn't she? (37)

The spoof goes on to emphasize Poe's perplexity at trying to resolve this overwhelming question and his futility upon being denied the ultimate answer when Miss Clairol Lee—this is, after all, a Poe send-up—dies. Using "Annabel Lee" enables *Mad* not only to make fun of Poe's poetics, but also to bring out his frequent use of obsession as a theme and, at least indirectly, to suggest that such obsession could well be a case of much ado about nothing.

The send-up also aims at Clairol, which of course ran that ad campaign knowing full well the subtext of the phrase, asked by countless adolescent boys over the years, in which "Does she or doesn't she" has one simple meaning having absolutely nothing whatever to do with hair color. The graphic by Bob Clarke (see fig. 9-5) captures Poe's perplexity over his inability to answer the question. There he stands, quill pen behind his ear, a raven on his shoulder, a clock (a significant symbol in Poe) behind him, his hands spread in a "who knows?" gesture. Miss Clairol Lee, the object of Poe's obsession and perplexity, dominates the foreground, her facial expression so blandly generic, in marked contrast to the well-delineated

Fig. 9-5: Bob Clarke brilliantly parodies Breck and Clairol ads in his illustrations for Larry Siegel's parody of "Annabel Lee" in *Mad* #51 (12/59), inserting Poe into the illustration, quill pen behind his ear, raven on his shoulder, as the ad copy repeatedly asks, "Does she or doesn't she?" MAD used with permission.

Poe, that it gives no hint of an answer to the question. That expression also conveys no hint of identity or individuality, not even a suggestion of a self, and the hair that's so central to the spoof is highlighted to the point of being almost washed out, making the question basically moot.

Another look at Miss Clairol Lee, however, leads to another twist. She may appear pretty much a nonentity in the drawing, but her portrait in profile echoes a contemporary ad to suggest that, rather than being a Clairol girl, she's really a Breck girl.[10] Because Breck is a shampoo, not a hair coloring, the insinuation broadens *Mad*'s satire. It's not just advertising for hair coloring products being spoofed; advertising for the entire "beauty" industry becomes the target. Merging Clairol and Breck suggests that all such commercials are basically the same, essentially empty. The advertisers may think that their message is vital, but it is little more than a matter of image building erected on the shaky edifice of empty slogans and images. The irony is further compounded when we consider that Breck's advertising campaigns were predicated on the idea that "Every woman is different." The graphic in *Mad*'s spoof suggests the opposite: in advertising land all women are the same, dupes to be exploited.

A more fully developed use of "Annabel Lee" occurs in "The Saga of AT&T," in which Frank Jacobs, as usual, brilliantly warps Poe's poetic mannerisms (Jacobs and Davis, #283, 12/88: 28-29). This six-stanza parody begins by celebrating the breakup of AT&T as a means of allowing other carriers to compete:

> It was many and many a year ago,
>   In the land of the brave and the free,
> That a firm did arise and soon grew to great size,
>   And its name was AT&T:
> But its foes cried, "Unfair! You can't hog the whole share!
>   "A monopoly's bad as can be!"
> And they fought very tough and in time, sure enough,
>   They were breaking up AT&T. (28)

The resulting consumer confusion occurs from "a dozen firms running amok" as they "snow you with ads pushing trendy new fads" (28). Even worse than consumer confusion is the deterioration of service: "Soon you're making a call to a guy in St. Paul, / When you're hearing a horrible screech; / So you dial him once more and are reaching a store / Selling kitchen supplies in Palm Beach" (28). Add to these problems 14-page bills "Full of charges you can't comprehend" (29), and the entire situation is a mess, as *Mad*'s conclusion makes clear:

> Now we're told all the time, it's a terrible crime
> When some giant monopoly rules;
> "Competition's the way," the economists say,
> Which is what we are taught in our schools;
> But from seeing the mess screwing up the U.S.,
> Any imbecile plainly can see
> Life was better back then in those ancient days when
> We were screwed just by AT&T! (29)

A rather delicious implication resides at the heart of that last line. When it comes to corporate America, customers are going to be taken advantage of one way or another; it's the nature of the corporate beast, but at least AT&T provided decent service. Perhaps a monopoly isn't so bad after all.

Mad's final warping of "Annabel Lee" takes on *Baywatch* (NBC, 1989-1990; syndication, 1990-1999) by focusing on Pamela Anderson, who played C. J. Parker on the show. "The Stalking of Pamela Lee" (Jacobs and Mejía, #372, 8/98: 38-39) appeared in the final season *Baywatc*h was aired. *Mad* had pilloried the show earlier with "Babewatch," in which C. J. Parker is renamed T&A Pucker (Kogen and Torres, #328, 6/94: 43-47). *T&A*, of course, is a common contraction for *tits and ass*, the commodity Baywatch thrived on. (I'll leave it up to the reader to decide how to interpret *Pucker*.) The earlier parody focused on the show's blatant sexual titillation featuring large-breasted women acting (I use the term advisedly) in ridiculous plots skewed to allow them to cavort about in skimpy bathing suits. "The Stalking of Pamela Lee" considerably broadens the satire. The focal point of the parody, as in Poe's poem, is on a male obsessed with the female of his dreams:

> It was many and many a year ago
> That she first cast a spell on me;
> She was languishing bare in a centerfold there,
> With her bra size of 38D;
> And the sight of her bust left me panting with lust
> For the babe now called Pamela Lee. (38)

The stalker's emphasis on Pamela Lee's breasts rather than her person is, of course, precisely the type of objectification the show thrived on, and that objectification is part of the satire's thrust: "Though her jugs knocked me dead in that magazine spread, / 'Twas their bounce I hungered to see: / Then to Baywatch she came, and they gained instant fame / when they jiggled on primetime TV" (38). Pamela Lee does not exist as a person, just as a pair of bouncing breasts. Thus far "Stalking" makes pretty much the same point as "Babewatch," attacking the network's willingness to boost viewer share and increase profits by exploiting women and sex. As "Stalking" continues, however, the attack takes on more bite.

The Stalker bewails Anderson's marriage to Mötley Crüe drummer Tommy Lee but rejoices when they separate. Nonetheless he adores the notorious sex tape they made on their honeymoon: "Many times did I gape at that pirated tape, / Getting off on her X-rated spree; / And I dreamed of the day she would roll in the hay / And the man she was under was me" (39). As his stalking becomes more obsessive (again, a persistent Poe theme), his behavior becomes more bizarre. Seemingly, though, persistence has its reward: "I shall never forget how we finally met, / And her cleavage close-up I did see; / All my love I poured out, and there seemed little doubt / That she felt the same way about me" (39). Alas, such is not the case. As so frequently happens in Poe, "Stalking" demonstrates that obsessive behavior is also delusional. Pamela Lee blows the whistle on the Stalker, and he is jailed. Yet he admits that, despite her betrayal, he continues to care for her, or at least for those body parts he sees as constituting her: "But for Pam I still care, and I pray she'll be there / If I somehow survive and go free— / Which is doubtful as hell since I'm sharing a cell / With her psychotic ex, Tommy Lee!" (39).

The parody's text is deliciously heightened by the accompanying graphic by Hermann Mejía (see fig. 9-6). Pamela Lee (and she did, for a time, go by that name) is stretched out on a beach wearing a skimpy thong, her bra discarded on the sand as she clasps her left breast. In the background, behind a hedge, we see the Stalker, bare-chested, standing on a ladder, a pair of binoculars reflecting his protruding eyes, his tongue lasciviously hanging out. While Pamela Lee is provocatively drawn, the Stalker's almost grotesque scrawniness suggests his obsession with her body arises from his own lack of sex appeal. *Mad* knew what it was up to in pairing Pamela Lee with "Annabel Lee" and making obsessive behavior central. Poe is, however, not the target in this instance.

Fig. 9-6: In *Mad* #372 (8/98), Annabel Lee becomes Pamela Lee in Frank Jacobs's parody. The leering stalker in the background of Hermann Mejía's provocative illustration, with eyes bulging and tongue hanging out, could stand for the male audience of such network sexual exploitation ("The Stalking of Pamela Lee," 38–39). MAD used with permission.

Rather, at least three inter-related issues circle viciously in the piece. First is the network's willingness to exploit its female stars' sexuality in order to increase audience share so they can charge bigger bucks for their advertising. Nothing new about this tactic. A second implication focuses on those female stars' willingness to be exploited, epitomized here by Pamela Anderson. Finally, the Stalker himself is being exploited by the network, which is most willing to use his basic instincts against him. And the Stalker, like the patrons of *Antz*, is a most willing participant in the process. *Mad* thus implies that when it comes to the entertainment industry, problems aren't singular, involving just producers or just actors or just distributors. All who are part of the business are responsible, and that includes the audience. "The Stalking of Pamela Lee" thus becomes a strong indictment of the entire sexploitation business, at least as it exists on TV.

So, where is Poe in all of this? I suspect that he would be tickled to the tips of his toes with it. After all, he was himself a masterful parodist and not above indulging in self-parody. He was also a confirmed satirist and hoaxer. Were he looking for employment in our time, *Mad* would be right up his alley. Furthermore, parody is a type of legitimate plagiarism, and although Poe railed against plagiarism, he was more than capable of borrowing from others when it suited his purpose. He would also have enjoyed the publicity that the *Mad* parodies created. For us, the frequency of his appearances in *Mad* testify to his ongoing fame and the notoriety that fame has created. I think that Poe would have been perfectly fine with that.

Notes

1. Definitions and theories of parody date from Ancient Greece and increasingly make complex what seems deceptively simple. The current standard studies are Linda Hutcheon, *A Theory of Parody: The Teachings of Twentieth-Century Art Forms*; and Margaret Rose, *Parody: Ancient, Modern, and Post-Modern*. A newer approach may be found in Simon Dentith's *Parody*. An even more recent and delightfully idiosyncratic approach, is Robert Chambers, *Parody: The Art that Plays with Art*.

2. This creates what I call the *Mad* Paradox. It poses as The Usual Gang of Idiots and posits a fictional audience reflecting that idiocy, all typified by Alfred E. Neuman. Yet the content of the magazine frequently has a degree of sophistication that contradicts both images.

3. Full citation of all the parodies included in my count would extend the length of this essay beyond acceptable limits. Instead, I cite significant examples. D'Arcy's "The Face on the Floor" appears in #10 (4/54: 1–6). The first use of "Casey at the Bat" occurs in #6 (8–9/53: 1–6), illustrated by Jack Davis. As with "The Raven," the poem is printed as Thayer wrote it, with the illustrations providing the warping. Other instances may be found in "Casey at the Dice" (Jacobs and Davis, #124, 1/69: 19–21), "Casey at the Talks" (Jacobs and Davis, #193, 9/77: 39–41), and "Baseball at the Bat" (Jacobs and Warhola, #291, 12/89: 24–25). Longfellow's first appearance is "The Wreck of the Hesperus" (#16, 10/54: 1–7), printed as written and illustrated by Wally Wood. "Paul Revere's Ride" (#20, 2/55: 1–6) also appears as written, illustrated by Jack Davis; the same applies to "The Children's Hour" (#36, 12/57: 41–42), illustrated by Don Martin. Examples of "warping Longfellow" are "The Rush Hour Drive of Enoch Pry" (Koch and Rickard, #101, 3/66: 20) and "The Far-Out Ride of Edwin Meese" (Jacobs and Gersten, #268, 1/87: 37–39). "Trees" is deliciously warped in "Bush" (Jacobs and Gersten, #272, 7/87: 24–25). Finally, a sampling of Shakespeare's treatment can be found in "The *Mad* Shakespeare Primer" by Phil Hahn with art by Wallace Wood (#60, 1/61: 22–24), reworked by William Garvin as "Shakespeare Up-To-Date" in #92, with art by Jack Rickard (1/65: 15–17), and the Frank Jacobs-M. K. Perker collaboration, "William Shakespeare, Political Commentator" (#445, 9/04: 14–16).

4. Among the several biographies of Poe, none is totally satisfactory. Great hope was held out for Kenneth Silverman's *Edgar A. Poe, Mournful and Never-Ending Remembrance*, but it is too thesis driven to give a full picture. James M. Hutchisson's *Poe* comes closer to the mark. As to the Griswold-Poe connection, a succinct account can be found on the Edgar Allan Poe Society of Baltimore

website, https://eapoe.org/geninfo/poegrisw.htm. Griswold's "Memoir" is also available on that site, https://www.eapoe.org/works/editions/grvoliii.htm. Anyone interested in Poe will find this site a treasure trove, including scholarly editions of Poe's works, the letters, the indispensable *Poe Log* and a wealth of other resources. For details, see "Edgar Allan Poe and Rufus Wilmot Griswold."

5. Frank Jacobs has been *Mad*'s go-to guy for poetry and song lyric parodies since 1957, and his 2018 Wikipedia entry has "over 575 credits for the magazine, more than any other writer or artist."

6. Robert Regan, "Hawthorne's 'Plagiary'; Poe's Duplicity," 291-98.

7. C. Alphonso Smith, *Edgar Allan Poe: How to Know Him*, 51. I find the "falsetto cackle" absolutely sublime for some unknown reason.

8. I examine *Mad*'s treatment of "The Raven" much more fully in "MAD About 'The Raven,'" 144–62, thus my quite truncated remarks here.

9. This issue marks a mile-stone (or mill-stone?) in *Mad*'s use of Poe, for he appears not just in Siegel's Clairol spoof but also in Tom Koch's "The *Mad* Treasury of Unknown Poetry, Volume II," with art by Joe Orlando (#51, 12/59: 16-17) where "The Raven" is recast as "The Spaniel," by Edgar, Al, and Moe (16), recounting the tribulations of an over-worked advertising man. I do not recall any other author being so "honored" by *Mad* as to appear twice in the same issue.

10. I am grateful to Judith Yaross Lee (not to be confused with Annabel or Pamela) for pointing out this correspondence.

10. Sing Along with Alfred:

Humor, Satire, and Culture in the Music of *Mad*

John Bird

WHEN I WAS young, to be a member in good standing of the neighborhood gang—in addition to playing baseball, tackle football (without helmets or pads), Army (usually World War II, but sometimes the Civil War)—you had to be able to sing a song, a parody of "Hello, Dolly!" from *Mad* magazine, which we all read, much to our parents' disapproval.[1] Reader, no matter where you are, no matter who is around you, please sing what we called "Hello, Delly" now, out loud, and you too can be a proud member of the Montclaire gang:

> Hello, Delly!
> This is Joe, Delly!
> Would you please send up a nice corned beef on rye! (12)

The concept of young Southern boys in Charlotte, North Carolina, singing "Hello, Delly" (actually titled "The Delicatessen Cantata," in "Some Songs of Food" [Jacobs and Coker, #110, 4/67: 12–14]) did not strike me as incongruous then, but thinking back, I wonder at those wannabe macho boys singing together, and singing lustily about a subject we knew very little about: Jewish delicatessens. The second verse was always my favorite: even though I had never eaten chopped liver, I loved the sound of it and the rhyme with "sliver," as well as the ludicrous rhyme of "Ritz" with "Schlitz":

> A box of Ritz, Delly!
> And some Schlitz, Delly!
> Some chopped liver and a sliver of your apple pie! (12)

The amount of food grows absurdly:

> Turkey legs, Delly!
> Hard boiled eggs, Delly!
> With tomatoes and potatoes you French-fry! (12)

And then the conclusion, with a silly but very funny punch line reminding us that the song is a take-out order, and a very early morning one at that:

> Oh . . .
> Please don't be late, Delly!
> 'Cause I can't wait, Delly!
> Delly, without breakfast I will die! (12)

Singing the parody bonded my group of friends, and I now realize that such songs bonded millions of other young people in ways they could not understand and with implications that went far beyond neighborhood gangs or two close friends or solitary singers in bedrooms and treehouses and hangouts. The *Mad* song parodies have engaged several generations, initiating us into the world of satire, irreverence, and rebellion, leading us to question authority and conformity in ways that went far beyond the silly lyrics. My analysis of the *Mad* song parodies, spoofs that began in the early 1960s and continued in the decades since, examines their contributions to the humor and satire of *Mad*, but also their more far-reaching effects on American culture.

Mad Starts Singing

There might have been no *Mad* tradition of parody songs, and I might not have seen "Hello, Delly," had a landmark court case gone differently. In 1961, *Mad* published a pull-out booklet in *More Trash from Mad No. 4* entitled *Sing Along with Mad*. Its cover featured Alfred E. Neuman, arms outstretched over a music stand and face covered with a moustache and goatee in a clear reference to Mitch Miller, whose TV show *Sing Along with Mitch* (NBC, 1961-1964) was popular at the time, and its subtitle declared the contents "A Collection of Parody Lyrics to 57 Old Standards Which Reflect the Idiotic World We Live in Today." Illustrated by Jack Rickard, the booklet was organized by thematic categories, including

"Songs of Show Business," "Songs of Space and the Atom," "Songs of Education," "Songs of Labor and Business," and "Songs of Doctors and Medicine," among others, with fifty-seven parodies of show tunes and popular songs, written separately by Larry Siegel, Frank Jacobs, and "The Editors." The idea for the insert came from Nick Meglin, and Jacobs and Siegel completed their work within two weeks.[2] Each song had a parody title, a brief explanation of the topic, the phrase "sung to the tune of," and the parody lyrics—with no musical score. It was assumed that readers knew the tunes and could sing along, because much of the humor would be lost if they could not match the new words to the original melody, the crux of the comic incongruity. For example, Frank Jacobs offered "Blue Cross," explained as "A bad experience with a medical coverage program," and "Sung to the tune of: 'Blue Skies.'" The first two verses set up the scenario, each verse beginning with minor chords, resolving to major in the last line, the melody implying a sense of danger that supposedly ends in a happy conclusion:

Blue Cross
Had me agree
To a new Blue Cross
Policy! (11)

Blue Cross
Said I would be
Happy that Blue Cross
Covered me! (11)

The song then moves to the more up-tempo bridge, in which major chords with a minor feel introduce the conflict and the satire, grounded in the contrast between coverage and liability:

Then I took a fall,
Leg in a splint;
They said that I
Should read the fine print! (11)

The patient's condition gets even worse as the parody proceeds, further heightening the humor:

When a very high
Fever I ran,
Thcy told me I
Took out the wrong plan. (11)

The song ends by going back to the verse to seal the satiric comment:

That's Blue Cross!
There seems to be
Plenty for Blue Cross!
None for me! (11)

More than half a century later, the humor and satire of the lyrics still resonate, perhaps even more so, given the arguments over healthcare that have dominated politics in the last decade.

Turning to another old standard with "blue" in the title, Larry Siegel set "My Blue Pictures" to the tune of "My Blue Heaven," proclaiming, "Dirty movies are more profitable than ever!" The first two verses make the satiric point, with a pun in the opening lines:

When business is slow
  And I'm needing dough,
I always make my blue pictures. (4)

I get these fat checks
  For grinding out sex
You'll find it in my blue pictures. (4)

These lyrics referenced the new environment for pornography following the landmark 1957 Supreme Court case *Roth v. United States*, which redefined *obscenity* as material whose "dominant theme taken as a whole appeals to the prurient interest" of the "average person, applying contemporary community standards."[3] While the court decided that obscene material is not protected under the First Amendment, the definition of *obscenity* in the ruling began to loosen obscenity laws and opened what became, as the decade continued, a flood of material that had previously been banned.

Jacobs explores a less ostensibly political theme, the intersection of sports and advertising, in "The First Time I Saw Maris." The low burlesque features New York Yankees slugger Roger Maris, who in 1961 hit sixty-one home runs to break Babe Ruth's record. Sung to the tune of "The Last Time I Saw Paris," the lyrics follow his career on and off the field:

The first time I saw Maris
He'd signed up with the A's!
He slugged the ball but never found
How big league baseball plays! (13)

The next time I saw Maris
A Yankee he'd become!
And now endorsements earn for him
A most substantial sum! (13)

The humor and satire continue in the bridge, getting more particular:

He signed a contract with Gillette
To plug their razor blades!
And when he found he'd cut himself,
He went and plugged Band-Aids! (13)

The final verse comes closest to the title of the original, and in 1961, makes a comment about the new Kennedy administration:

The last time I saw Maris
He plugged six brands of beer!
The Democrats should pay him
To plug the New Frontier! (13)

This song begins as parody, with the imitation of the title in the first lines of the verses, then moves to satirize the connection between sports heroes and advertising. Just as baseball was still America's pastime in the '50s and '60s, advertising was co-opting many facets of American life. Younger readers would not remember the ubiquitous commercials of the time when sports heroes shaved on camera, their muscular faces lathered, held up bottles of beer, and even smoked particular brands of cigarettes. Jacobs uses a wistful song about memories of Paris to look back to a supposedly more innocent time when our heroes were famed for their exploits on the field rather than their ability to cash in on their names and sell out.

Siegel's "I Specialize in Mud," sung to the tune of "I'm in the Mood for Love," lets a gossip magazine publisher talk frankly about his profession. The contrast between the romantic melody and lyrics of the original song with the parody focusing on mud rather than love sets up especially strong humorous incongruity:

> I specialize in mud
> Simply because fans love it,
> Funny but since fans love it,
> I specialize in mud. (12)

The second verse specifies the "mud," with references to celebrities who were much in the news in the early 1960s but require some further explanation now:

> Covers are filled with lies:
> "Eddie and Liz are breaking!"—
> "Sammy and May are faking!"—
> I specialize in mud. (12)

"Eddie and Liz" are Eddie Fisher and Elizabeth Taylor, involved in a Hollywood scandal after Taylor's third husband died in a plane crash and her good friend Debbie Reynolds and her husband Fisher consoled her, although Fisher's consolation included moving in with Taylor weeks after the crash and running off with his wife's good friend.[4] "Sammy and May" are Sammy Davis, Jr., and May Britt, whose upcoming November 1961 marriage was controversial, since Davis was black and Jewish, Britt white and Christian, at a time when 23 U.S. states (but not California) outlawed interracial marriage and only 4% of Americans supported marriage between blacks and whites.[5]

In the bridge, the publisher turns from himself to his readers:

Why stop to think, or worry
If what we print is "bull" . . .
Our fans are in a hurry
To eat it up; they're never full! (12)

The last verse brings things back to the bottom line, with a humorous feminine rhyme:

If anyone should sue
Our noble publications;
Suits help our circulations—
I specialize in mud. (12)

The substitution of "mud" for "love" is especially humorous, the one-syllable word ending with a "d" sound landing like a thud. This last verse proved to be prescient: *Mad*'s pull-out booklet of parody songs was about to land its publisher in a lawsuit. The publishers may have sensed the possibility; the cover of *More Trash from Mad* had these words emblazoned under the pull-out: "For Solo or Group Participation (Followed by Arrest)."

Mad Goes to Court

Readers of *Mad* were delighted by the parody songs, but the composers and publishers of many of the songs were not amused, claiming that their copyrights had been violated. The case, *Berlin v. EC Publications, Inc.*, named as primary plaintiff the legendary songwriter Irving Berlin, but also included Jerome Kern, Cole Porter, Richard Rodgers, Lorenz Hart, and Oscar Hammerstein II, claiming that twenty-five of the fifty-seven songs in *Sing Along with Mad* violated the fair use clause of copyright law. In their suit, the plaintiffs asked for $25 million, one dollar per song for each issue of *More Trash from Mad*. The case was argued in 1963 in the U.S. District Court for the Southern District of New York before District Judge Charles Metzner.[6]

On June 22, 1963, Judge Metzner found in favor of *Mad*'s publisher, EC Comics, with two exceptions. In his decision, Metzner noted that "no music was provided in the songbook." He continued, using language that sounds as if it had come from a humorous *Mad* feature:

> It has been stipulated that the "Mad" lyrics have the same meter as plaintiffs' lyrics, and can be sung to the music of plaintiffs' songs. The subject matter of defendants' lyrics, however, is completely different from that of plaintiffs'. For example, to the tune of "I've Got You Under My Skin," defendants have written a lyric about fraternity hazing entitled "I Swat You Hard on the Skin." To the tune of "A Pretty Girl Is Like a Melody," the defendants have written "Louella Schwartz Describes Her Malady." To "The Last Time I Saw Paris," defendants write of the rewards earned by a baseball player who sponsors razor blades and beer in "The Last Time I Saw Maris."[7]

The judge cited several precedents about parody and copyright infringement, but noted, "It is obvious that defendants' lyrics have little in common with plaintiffs' but meter and a few words, except in two instances which will be discussed below. Defendants have created original, ingenious lyrics on subjects completely dissimilar from those of plaintiffs' songs."[8] While admitting that "[i]t is clear that a parody of a copyrighted work is an infringement of the copyright," he concluded: "Defendants have not parodied plaintiffs' lyrics. Rather, they have satirized, in original words and thought, several aspects of modern life." He rejected the plaintiffs' claim "that defendants have infringed the copyright in their music by stating that the 'Mad' lyrics can be sung to the tune of plaintiffs' compositions." In another statement that points out the kind of absurdity *Mad* was famous for, the judge wrote, "It is difficult to see how music can be copied when it is not reproduced." The two exceptions to his decision were *Mad*'s parodies of Irving Berlin's "Always" and "There's No Business Like Show Business," because *Mad*'s versions revolved around the same words as the originals. The other twenty-three were allowed under the principle of fair use.[9]

The judge made a clear distinction between parody and satire, but in practice, the two often overlap. Although *Mad* called the songs parodies, they should more properly be called satires: the lyrics of the songs are less parodies that mock the originals than they are satiric commentaries on other targets. In the case of Jacobs's song, the target is the company Blue Cross, not the song "Blue Skies." Even so, a parodic element is clearly involved in using the meter, at times the rhyme scheme, and other features of the originals, and even though the printed words did not include the music, the music itself undergoes some parody in the mind of the reader—I, for one, cannot hear the melody of "Hello, Dolly!" without thinking of it as "Hello, Delly." The definitions in *The Princeton Handbook of Poetic Terms* point out the differences between satire and parody, but note the overlap: "Satire, says, Dr. Johnson, is 'a poem in which wickedness or folly is censured'; and more elaborate definitions are rarely more satisfactory."[10] But the handbook qualifies Dr. Johnson's remark: "No strict definition can encompass the complexity of a word which signifies, on the one hand, a kind of literature, and on the other, a spirit or tone which expresses itself in many literary genres."[11] "Critical parody," it cautions, "has been defined as the exaggerated imitation of a work of art. Like caricature, it is based on distortion, bringing into bolder relief the salient features of a writer's style or habit of mind."[12] But again, there is overlap: "It belongs to the genus satire and thus performs the double-edged task of reform and ridicule."[13] In *A Theory of Parody*, Linda Hutcheon discusses and analyzes at length the interaction between parody and satire.[14] Her definition of parody is helpful for an understanding of the way the *Mad* songs work: "Parody, then, in its ironic 'trans-contextualization' and inversion, is repetition with difference. A critical distance is implied between the backgrounded text being parodied and the new incorporating work, a distance usually signaled by irony."[15] Her further comment is especially applicable to the strategies used by Jacobs and Siegel and other song parodists, who took a number of comic stances in their work: "But this irony can be playful as well as belittling; it can be critically constructive as well as destructive."[16] To muddy the matter even more, throughout its history, *Mad* has used the terms interchangeably; for example, editors have constantly called their treatment of a movie "Another *Mad* satire," while the features exaggerate the plot, characters, and themes of the movies for comic repetition with a difference—that is, parody, rather than satire—although these parodies often include satiric comments.

Not satisfied with the verdict, the plaintiffs appealed the case to the U.S. Court of Appeals for the Second Circuit. The case was argued on January 10, 1964, and decided on March 23, 1964, with a three-judge panel of Joseph Edward Lumbard, Irving Kaufman, and Thurgood Marshall, who ruled in favor of *Mad* on *all* twenty-five songs.[17] Judge Kaufman wrote the unanimous decision, with arguments that seem to recognize the humor and absurdity of the case, despite its seriousness:

> The District Court observed that the theme and content of the parodies differed markedly from those of the originals. Thus, "The Last Time I Saw Paris," originally written as a nostalgic ballad which tenderly recalled pre-war France, became in defendants' hands "The First Time I Saw Maris," a caustic commentary upon the tendency of a baseball hero to become a television pitchman, more prone to tempt injury with the razor blade which he advertises than with the hazards of the game which he plays.[18]

Kaufman continues, pointing out further absurdity: "Neither is there a claim that defendants' parodies might satisfy or even partially fulfill the demand for plaintiffs' originals; quite soundly, it is not suggested that 'Louella Schwartz Describes Her Malady' might be an acceptable substitute for a potential patron of 'A Pretty Girl Is Like a Melody.'"[19] Such humor might not be expected from the judge who oversaw the trial and conviction of Julius and Ethel Rosenberg a decade earlier; his imposition of the death penalty for espionage was widely condemned in many circles.[20]

Judge Kaufman also rejected the plaintiffs' claim that the songs violated copyright by "the use of the titles, the meter, and an occasional phrase from the original lyrics in an occasional song."[21] Citing precedent, including a case involving comedian Jack Benny, he noted how previous courts had ruled "that the parodist must be permitted sufficient latitude to cause his reader or viewer to 'recall or conjure up' the original work if parody is to be successful." He went on to judge that the "disparities in theme, content and style between the original lyrics and the alleged infringements could hardly be greater." He noted, "the rhyme scheme of the parodies bears no relationship whatsoever to that of the originals." Brief phrases from the originals, he argued, "would seem necessary if the defendants' efforts were 'to recall or conjure up' the originals . . ."[22] In another line that points to comic absurdity, he wrote, "Similarly, the fact that defendants' parodies were written in the same meter as plaintiffs' compositions would seem inevitable if the original was to be recognized, but such a justification is not even necessary; we doubt that even so eminent a composer as plaintiff Irving Berlin should be permitted to claim a property interest in iambic pentameter."[23]

As he concluded, he made an admission: "While the social interest in encouraging the broad-gauged burlesques of Mad Magazine is admittedly not readily apparent, and our individual tastes may prefer a more subtle brand of humor, this can hardly be dispositive here."[24] But Judge Kaufman saw the case in wider cultural and historical terms:

> For, as a general proposition, we believe that parody and satire *are* deserving of substantial freedom—both as entertainment and as a form of social and literary criticism. As the readers of Cervantes' "Don Quixote" and Swift's "Gulliver's Travels," or the parodies of a modern master such as Max Beerbohm well know, many a true word is indeed spoken in jest. At the very least, where, as here, it is clear that the parody has neither the intent nor the effect of fulfilling the demand for the original, and where the parodist does not appropriate a greater amount of the original work than is necessary to "recall or conjure up" the object of his satire, a finding of infringement would be improper.[25]

The plaintiffs then appealed to the Supreme Court, which refused to take the case, meaning that *Mad* had won a landmark case that applied not only to them, but also to a broad swath of parodists and satirists up to the present. Targets of subsequent *Mad* parodies would certainly pause long before taking the magazine to court for supposed damages.[26]

Mad and the Great American Songbook

But *Mad* did not wait for the courts to rule in this multimillion-dollar case. Jacobs and Siegel continued to publish song parodies while the case dragged on for three years. True to the pattern they had set with *Sing Along with Mad*, they almost always drew on show tunes, old standards, and in several cases, entire musicals, either from Broadway or movies.[27] The basis for these parodies reflected Jacobs's deep engagement with this American tradition, as he made clear in a 2006 interview. Asked to reveal something that few people knew about him, he responded:

> Oh . . . I dunno. Maybe it's my tremendous love for the American musical theatre. I've had a collection of 78s and I still have my LPs and I've put together long, long tapes which cover the musical output of the great composers like Cole Porter, Gershwin, Rodgers and Hart, Noël Coward, Irving Berlin, and a couple of others. I have a passion for the great popular songs.[28]

In the midst of the trial and the appeals, Jacobs and Mort Drucker offered "East Side Story" (#78, 04/63: 4–12), pitting against each other two rival gangs at the United Nations, not the Sharks and the Jets, but the West and the Reds, an oft-cited and celebrated parody of the songs in *West Side Story* to satirize the two opponents in the Cold War. Quite audaciously, in "Mannie Get Your Ghoul," a satirical mash-up of show business and monster movies, Jacobs used the very Irving Berlin song that had been singled out in the 1963 court case:

> There's no monsters
> Like "Pro" monsters—
> Just no monsters we know!
> Folks adore the Creature and Godzilla!
> Audiences know they can't go wrong—
> Watching while an army tries to kill a
> Mixed up gorilla
> Who's called King Kong! (Jacobs and Rickard, #85, 03/64: 4–11; 11)

Giving a monster plot the Broadway treatment was just one of the many comic layers in "Mannie Get Your Ghoul": piano player Glenn Ghoul wears the signature scarf of classical pianist Glenn Gould, but the face belongs to horror movie actor Peter Lorre. Beyond the verbal and visual jokes, the reference to Gould highlights the musical sophistication that Jacobs and Siegel brought to their parodic lyrics, which reflect deep understanding of the song structures they borrowed and deformed.

Here, the humor intensifies as the song speeds up in lines four and five, and the enjambment in the third-to-last line, combined with the feminine rhyme of "kill a" and "gorilla," showcase Jacobs's skill with verse as well as his impeccable humor: feminine rhyme, or double rhyme, has long been a staple in light verse, and Jacobs uses it repeatedly for his comic effects. Then he goes for the big finish to the song and the whole piece:

> We're great monsters—First-rate monsters—
> We're much more than they know!
> One day you are living like a normal slob
> You've got a wife and a steady job—
> Then you drink a potion

And you're now the "Blob":
What ho!
Monsters . . . Let's . . . GO! (11)

Berlin's song was a go-to for Jacobs, who used it again in "The *Mad* Song Textbook," with the premise that students could not remember anything they read in school but could memorize the words to all the rock and roll songs (Jacobs and Orlando, #112, 07/67: 5–12). Ironically, however, the songs in the *Mad* textbook were all standards or show tunes, this time to help students learn about American literature:

There's no stories
Like Poe stories
Like no stories we know!
If you like a tale that is appalling—
If you want to murmur, shriek and cry—
If you like to hear strange voices calling—
With bodies falling—
Then Poe's your guy! (10)

The contrast between the giddy rhythm and meter and Poe's macabre persona heightens the incongruity and contributes to the humor of this parody, especially the last four lines, which race again to a show business "big finish":

There's no stories
Like Poe stories!
They all fill us with woe!
If you want a tale that's filled with death galore!
With spirits tapping upon your door!
And some crazy raven quoting, "Nevermore!"
There's no writer like Poe! (10)

There truly is no writer like Poe, but even though the parody is meant for laughs, it assumes that the reader knows enough about Poe's poetry and short stories to get the joke. In this way, the parody textbook songs actually do educate. In fact, Maria Reidelbach notes the use of *Mad* as an educational tool:

> Although reviled by many, *Mad*'s literature and musical efforts have, in fact, sometimes found a place in the halls of the institutions that teach the originals. Not a few teachers have found that recalcitrant students can be interested in the classics through classroom readings of the *Mad* parodies, one of them reporting in an academic journal that "the results were dramatic. Apathy and restlessness were replaced with an attitude of engrossed concentration. . . . " However, the same teacher warned of the dangers of such an approach: "There is one important procedure that I learned in using *Mad* which is a must—number the copies—otherwise they'll all end up being stolen."[29]

Indeed, the song parodies required that the reader know not only the melody of the original songs in order to participate in creating the intended musical effects, but also have vast literary, historical, and cultural knowledge in order to appreciate the parody and satire. Jacobs's and Siegel's seemingly simple parodies were quite sophisticated, and assumed in the reader, no matter his or her age, similar sophistication. *Mad*'s audience was varied, as Al Feldstein once noted: "We were writing for teenagers and young adults; we were writing for the guys that were reading it in the Army. We were writing for ourselves at our age level."[30] The song parodies reached out to the magazine's eclectic audience.

At times, the satirical target was the musical itself, as in the case of "The $ound of Money" (Hart and Drucker, #108, 01/67: 41–47). I could never watch the movie or hear the songs the same way again after *Mad* went after Maria and the von Trapps, or, in the *Mad* world, Mitzia (Yiddish for *bargain*, perfect for the parody's satire on commercialism)[31] and the von Tripes (another inspired name), reducing the beloved movie musical to its financial bottom line:

> DOUGH . . .
> Means cash for all of us!
> RAY . . .
> For musicals like this!
> ME . . .
> A "Star" so big that by
> FAR . . .
> It really couldn't miss!

SO . . .
Insipid is the plot;
LA—
Dee-da, although we know,
TEE—
Dee-ous it is a lot,
It will bring us
Back much DOUGH . . . DOUGH . . .
DOUGH . . . DOUGH . . . (45)

Mad was dead on about the financial aspect of the beloved Broadway and movie musical: the film earned nearly $300 million at the box office, domestic and international; the soundtrack sold over 20 million copies worldwide and was on the top ten of the Billboard 200 for a record 109 weeks, from May 1, 1965, to July 16, 1967.[32] Based on a complex formula weighing sales with other factors, the Billboard 200 ranks it as the second-best-selling album of all time, one place behind Adele's *21* and one place ahead of Michael Jackson's *Thriller*.[33]

Those numbers help explain why show tunes were such a staple in the *Mad* song parodies. Frank Jacobs and the other song parodists had a deep affection for this music, but they also had to depend on readers' familiarity for the parodies to work. One could expect a New York City audience, who could attend Broadway shows, to be familiar with the source songs. But in the '50s and '60s, Broadway and movie musicals were familiar beyond *Mad*'s home. Cast albums for Broadway shows and soundtrack albums for shows made into movies had huge sales. I remember that my parents' record collection contained cast and soundtrack albums for *Oklahoma!*, *The King and I*, *Camelot*, *Man of La Mancha*, *My Fair Lady*, *Mary Poppins*, and *The Sound of Music* (of course). A staple of variety television like *The Ed Sullivan Show* (CBS, 1948-1971) was stars singing songs from hit musicals, and those songs routinely made the charts. "Hello, Dolly!" by Louis Armstrong and the All Stars hit number one on the Billboard Hot 100 on May 9, 1964, interrupting the Beatles' position at the top of the charts since February 1, with "I Want to Hold Your Hand," "She Loves You," and "Can't Buy Me Love."[34] Even in a decade that was undergoing a musical revolution, with rock and roll taking over popular music and supplementing the "square music" of the '50s and early '60s, show tunes and old standards were ubiquitous enough that my circle of friends—and millions of young people all over the country and the world, *Mad*'s target audience—could sing along and get the joke.

More often than parodying the musical itself, as Jacobs did with *The Sound of Music,* he and Seigel satirized other subjects with their parody versions. A good example is Siegel's political commentary in "Hello Lyndon, or My Fair Lady Bird" (Siegel and Drucker, #107, 12/66: 4–9). Siegel's political commentary was even more pointed in "Stokely and Tess" (Siegel and Drucker, #111, 06/67: 4–10)—quite prescient, given the long hot summer of race riots in Detroit, Newark, and Milwaukee, among other U.S. cities that followed later in 1968. Siegel imagines Stokely Carmichael telling Martin Luther King what he really thinks of Dr. King in a parody of "Summertime":

> Un-cle Tom . . .
> Man, you're makin' me que-asy
> With your prayin', and your mod-er-ate cry.
> How you really woo
> All those phony White Lib'rals . . .
> I dumped Hubert Humphrey
> La-ast Ju-ly-y-y! (5)

The edgy illustrations by Mort Drucker include Martin Luther King sitting atop a pile of watermelons, happily eating one, as the second verse says, but also strumming on a banjo:

> One of these days now . . .
> You're gonna sta-art in shufflin'!
> Then eat wa-ter-mel-on till pits pile high.
> And when your Rights Group says
> I-it's time to replace you,
> I see Stepin Fetchit
> Sta-andin' by! (5)

Watermelon, banjos, and Stepin Fetchit are highly charged racial stereotypes, dangerous ground at a crossroads time for the civil rights movement, as King's nonviolent approach was being challenged by more radical black leaders like Stokely Carmichael and the Black Panthers. Northern cities erupted into violence in the summer of 1967, and less

Fig. 10-1: Mort Drucker's illustration of Martin Luther King, Jr. with watermelons and playing the banjo, two stereotypes of black culture, was jarring when it appeared in Siegel and Drucker's "Stokely and Tess" for *Mad* #111 (6/67): 4, showing how edgy Larry Siegel could be in his song parodies. MAD used with permission.

than a year later, Martin Luther King was slain by an assassin's bullet, setting off more riots. *Mad*'s dark humor captured the mood of the times, making the audience laugh, but in a laugh that was uneasy (see fig. 10-1).

Mad Goes Off Broadway

But *Mad* also drew on other musical sources for their parodies. In June 1963, Siegel presented "Up-To-Date Service Songs" (#79: 33–35). My favorite is "The New Marines' Hymn," far from the halls of Montezuma and the shores of Tripoli:

From the neck-high mud of fo-ox holes
To malar-i-a filled bogs,
We will march for 90 miles a day
And drop out and die like dogs! (34)

The second verse introduces the satirical punch line:

We will land on mine-strewn bea-eaches
And we'll live with snakes and fleas;
Then we'll all leave Parris Island for
Restful combat overseas. (34)

Ironically, of course, these young recruits would soon be leaving the sandy shores of South Carolina and landing on real mine-strewn beaches in Southeast Asia--no "restful combat overseas."

Updating songs was a popular move for Siegel. He followed in *Mad* #92 (01/65: 21–23) with "Up-To-Date Safety Songs for Children," with art by Joe Orlando. Perhaps the most chilling is "When the Bomb Comes Falling Down" (22), sung to the tune of "London Bridge," a seemingly innocent children's song that nonetheless contains its own harbinger of doom:

> When the bomb comes falling down,
> Falling down, falling down,
> When the bomb comes falling down,
> There'll be fallout. (22)

The second verse turns from description to advice:

> Cover up your face and head,
> Face and head, face and head,
> Then put on your suit of lead,
> 'Cause there's fallout. (22)

The repetitions copied from the original add to the humor, but also to the incongruity and thus the serious point. The warnings become more dire as the children's song continues:

> Do not stop to talk or play,
> Talk or play, talk or play,
> Find your shelter right away,
> 'Cause there's fallout. (22)

And then the humor gets really dark, drawing on the black humor of the '50s and '60s:

> Just admit your next of kin,
> Next of kin, next of kin,
> Shoot down neighbors who want in,
> 'Cause there's fallout. (22)

The conclusion offers relief at first, but the warning remains:

Wait until they sound All Clear,
Sound All Clear, sound All Clear,
Don't drink milk until next year,
'Cause there's fallout. (22)

The kids of that age were instructed in school-time drills to "duck and cover" in case of a nuclear attack, a practice that seems as absurd and macabre as the *Mad* parody. I turned nine that month, and the Cuban Missile Crisis a bit over two years earlier had revealed even to kids our age how close we were to imminent disaster. *Mad* gave us an early introduction to black humor. We were scared, as well as scarred, but we laughed about it, kids and teenagers all over the country singing along to this one. I discovered *Mad* about then, in my cousin's basement. Just in time! I was going to need it as I navigated the rest of that violent and often absurd decade.

Siegel returned to the idea in "More Up-To-Date Health and Safety Songs for Children" (Siegel and Woodbridge, #135, 06/70: 32–34), with parodies of children's songs, folk songs, and patriotic songs, including "Trips'll Hurt You" (32) to the tune of "Skip to My Lou," showing just how much the straitlaced youth culture of the 1950s had changed in the decade of the 1960s:

You want kicks, so what do you do?
You go sniff some airplane glue;
You take off like a DC-2!
Trips'll hurt you, my darling. (32)

After glue comes pot and acid, followed by a drug bust, then Siegel moves on to social comment about hypocrisy in the last two verses:

Why not do as your parents do?
Their example's set for you:
They drink scotch and bourbon too,
And Schlitz's brew, my darling! (32)

Booze, booze, can it hurt you?
There's no "warning sign" in view!
V.I.P's all belt a few!
Booze ain't taboo, my darling! (32)

The incongruity of innocent children's songs dealing with such topics enhances the humor and adds the edge that Larry Siegel was noted for: while Frank Jacobs sometimes wrote pointed parodies, his comic songs usually have a lighter touch than Siegel's, often merely silly (not that there's anything wrong with that).

In the 1970s, drugs continued to be a prominent target. In "The Pot-Smokers' Fight Song," sung to the tune of "Stouthearted Men," Jacobs satirized the emerging pot culture:

> Give me some men
> Who are pot-smoking men
> Who will puff on the stuff they adore;
> Making their points
> While they're rolling their joints—
> On the street, in the park, on the floor— (Jacobs and Davis, #141, 03/71: 22)

The internal rhyme of "puff" and "stuff" once again demonstrates Jacobs's deft comic and poetic genius, and the contrast between the jaunty melody and subject matter of "Stout-Hearted Men" with laid back pot-smoking men makes both targets somewhat ridiculous.

In the same collection, "Marching Songs for Crusaders, Militants, and Assorted Sundry Non-Conformists" (#141, 03/71: 20–23), Jacobs uses the same military song that Siegel used a decade earlier, "From the Halls of Montezuma," as the tune for "The College Rioters' Chant" (22), this time to satirize college radicals:

> From the School of Arts and Sci-en-ces
> To the classrooms by the mall;
> We will bomb and burn and desecrate
> Till our mob's destroyed them all; (22)

But the punch line of the song reveals the students' supposed real concern:

> We're not Weathermen or rad-i-cals,
> We have never screamed or yelled;

This is just our way to make sure
That exams will not be held! (22)

As serious and heartfelt as student protests were at the time, a common accusation was that college kids were just trying to get out of class; was *Mad* reiterating that accusation, or satirizing it? As usual, the stance is hard to pin down.

The cover of *Mad* #121 in September 1968 (Mingo) was itself a musical parody, with the Beatles, Mia Farrow, and the Maharishi Mahesh Yogi holding up Alfred E. Neuman as a maharishi. The musical joke surrounds the picture in a frame: "Swami, how I love you, how I love you, my dear old swami," in a Hindi script (see fig. 10-2).

Fig. 10-2: Norman Mingo's cover for *Mad* #121 (9/68) plays on the Beatles' and other celebrities' infatuation with Maharishi Mahesh Yogi and transcendental meditation. The musical joke appears in the picture's frame. MAD used with permission.

Inside was "New 'Protests' to the Same Old Tunes" (#121, 06/68: 32–35), in which Tom Koch (with art by Bob Clarke) not only parodied folk music, already somewhat a thing of the past, but also managed to provide poignant social commentary at the height of the Vietnam War and the draft, in "Concerto in D-minus" (34)—a brilliant comic title, conflating key signature with academic grades, the point of the satire—sung to the tune of "Tom Dooley," popularized by the Kingston Trio during the folk revival that began a decade earlier:

Lift up your head and study!
Learn or you're doomed to fail!
And if your mind stays muddy;
You'll never go to Yale. (34)

No college really wants you;
Not Georgia or Bucknell.
Why should they come and hunt you?
You don't play football well. (34)

Mad was being read by young troops in Vietnam, so the last verse undoubtedly hit them hard with its wry gallows humor:

Lift up your head and read, boy!
Stay up all night and cram!
If you lack grades you need, boy,
You'll go to Uncle Sam. (34)

In a time of draft deferments for college attendance (and academic success), the conclusion is at once funny and deadly serious, with an emphasis on deadly. This song is an excellent example of black humor, which in many ways reached a peak during the Vietnam War.

Mad has always practiced equal opportunity in its satire: no political stance or social practice, left or right, young or old, is safe, as evidenced in the grab bag title "Songs of Crime, Violence, War, Hatred, Bigotry, The Lunatic Fringe, and All-Around Ecchiness" (Jacobs and Woodbridge, #124, 01/69: 28–30). Jacobs returned to *The Sound of Music* in "The Lunatic Fringe," sung to the tune of "My Favorite Things":

Crackpot extremists and mobs that are lawless—
Right-wing fanatics parading for Wallace—
Flag-burning Peaceniks who make us all cringe—
These are just some of the Lunatic Fringe! (28)

The list of favorite things in the original alternates here between right and left, with a good example of Jacobs's use of feminine rhyme for humorous effect: "Wallace" and "lawless," the two-syllable rhyme that both surprises and delights the reader with its incongruity.

April 1967 brought "Some Songs of Food" in *Mad* #110 (Jacobs and Coker, 04/67: 12–14), which opened with the immortal "The Delicatessen Cantata," or "Hello, Delly"—which means that I was thirteen when I was hanging out in the neighborhood singing this song over and over with my friends. I do not recall if we also performed "The Health Food Hymn" (13), sung to the tune of "I'm in the Mood for Love," which strikes me now as even funnier, especially for Jacobs's trademark use of feminine rhymes in the second and third lines:

I'm eating food for health!
'Cause it is so nutritious!
Though I hate all the dishes—
I'm eating food for health! (13)

Spinach and eggplant soup!
Steaks that are made of soybeans!
Though I do not enjoy beans—
I'm eating food for health! (13)

The rhyme of in the second verse is another excellent example of Jacobs's comic art, in this case a feminine rhyme that depends on the unexpected move from "soybeans" to "enjoy beans." In the bridge that follows, he shifts the rhyme scheme, which heightens the humor of the fourth line:

Turnips with wheat germ dressing
May a bad smell produce—
Though it may sound depressing
I'll wash it down . . . with cabbage juice! (13)

His conclusion reaches the height of silliness with the combination of yogurt and rhubarb, a word that is funny in itself:

Blackstrap molasses pie!
Yogurt on rhubarb shredded!
Though they're all foods I've dreaded—
I'm eating food for health! (13)

In 1967, health food was in its beginnings as a cultural force, but the humor remains in this day of veganism. This parody marks a clear comparison between Frank Jacobs and Larry Siegel: Siegel used the same song in *Sing Along with Mad* to make a satirical point about sleazy publishers, his "I Specialize in Mud." Jacobs characteristically uses a lighter and sillier touch with the song, basically setting recipes and menu descriptions to music, satirizing the health food movement, but perhaps more subtly.

One of the pleasures of the *Mad* song parodies is the way they could veer from silly to satirical to pointed commentary, then right back to silly, as in *Mad* #116, a companion to my beloved "Some Songs of Food," "Songs of Pets" (Jacobs and Woodbridge, 01/68: 38–40). "Serenade to a Watchdog" (39) is sung to the tune of "Strangers in the Night":

Watchdog in the night—
I never chained you!
Watchdog in the night—
I always trained you
To protect my house
Until the night was through! (39)

But the watchdog proves worthless, with yet another example of Jacobs's comic use of feminine rhyme in "mind it/find it":

Then those burglars came—
You didn't mind it!
They were after loot—
You helped them find it!
Diamond rings and furs
You quickly led them to! (39)

In the bridge, man's best friend turns on his owner and best friend, the final two lines racing to a comic conclusion, this time with a triple rhyme:

Watchdog in the night—
A stupid beagle you were!
Watchdog in the night—
But later on when I—
Returned to my poor home—
How your jaws did foam!
You became a snapping dog—
A crazy, fearless yapping dog! (39)

The conclusion completes the silly joke, apostrophizing the unworthy cur:

Whenever I'm in sight,
It's so upsetting!
Every time you bite,
It's me you're getting!
Now you're full of fight—
My watchdog in the night! (39)

One only needs to imagine Frank Sinatra singing this parody of one of his signature love songs to grasp the full silliness of this Jacobs masterpiece, and indeed it is hard for anyone who knows the original not to hear it in Sinatra's distinctive voice and delivery. Jacobs counted not only on the reader's knowledge of the song, but also with its singer.

Another staple for Jacobs was holiday songs. "*Mad*'s Christmas Carols for the 1970 Holiday Season" (#140, 01/71: 24–27), launched an idea that he returned to six more times over the following decades, up to "Christmas Carols for Post 9/11 America" (#425, 01/03: 12–14). The holiday songbook was often aimed at specific targets: "Louis Farrakhan Christmas Carols" (#332, 12/94: 28–31); "Holiday Songs for Sports Fans" (#352, 12/96: 12–15); "Christmas Carols for Dysfunctional Families" (#365, 01/98: 4–6); and "*Mad*'s Political Christmas Carols" (#389, 01/00: 44–47). The juxtaposition of Christmas songs, both sacred and secular, with current events such as the activities of Farrakhan's Nation of Islam led to humor and pointed commentary, as in "Farrakhan Is Coming to Town":

> You better be black,
> You better be straight,
> You better admit that Hitler was great—
> Farrakhan is coming to town. (Jacobs and Friedman, #332, 12/94: 28)

Jacobs used the same song in January 2000, this time warning that "Hillary Is Coming to Town," when she was running for the Senate from New York:

> You better take care—
> You better watch out—
> A broad's on the way
>   with plenty of clout—
> Hillary is coming to town! (Jacobs and Coker, #389: 47)

The bridge insinuates the real reason she was running:

> She'd like to make the Senate—
> She knows she's got the skill—
> She'd also have a good excuse
>   to stay far away from Bill! (47)

In the concluding verse, Jacobs highlights the criticism of Hillary Clinton as an interloper in a state where she barely lived and an opportunist in her running for the Senate:

> She's stumping New York,
> And though she's a whiz,
> She still doesn't know
>   where Buffalo is—
> Hillary is coming to town! (47)

The Jewish sensibility of *Mad* is at the forefront in the Farrakhan song, while its New York sensibility is highlighted in the skepticism over Clinton's Senate run.

Mad Goes Pop

Notably missing during the 1960s and much of the 1970s were the new popular songs: rock songs and soul songs that were making the charts as American music underwent a revolution. *Mad*'s core audience was listening to the Beatles, the Rolling Stones, Bob Dylan, the Supremes, and the Byrds, but only rarely did Jacobs use songs by these artists for his parodies. One exception is his "Protest Songs for Life's Everyday Complaints" (Jacobs and Clarke, #161, 09/73: 36–39), which used show tunes like "They Call the Wind Maria" and, of course, "There's No Business Like Show Business," but also two '60s protest songs, "Where Have All the Flowers Gone?" and "Blowin' in the Wind," and two Glen Campbell hits of the time, "Gentle on My Mind" and "By the Time I Get to Phoenix." That Jimmy Webb song gets the parodic treatment in "Lost in a Giant Supermarket Blues," whose first two lines contain comic genius: "By the time I find the Kleenex I'll be eighty / My long white beard will be hangin' . . . to the floor (38)." In "Singable Theme Songs for TV Shows" (#168, 07/74: 14–16), Jacobs mainly used his familiar show tunes, but he also used "Call Me" and "Love Is Blue." In a musical version of *Star Trek*, "Keep on Trekkin'" (#186, 08/76: 4–10), he drew from several hits: "I'll Never Fall in Love Again," "The Age of Aquarius," "Yesterday," "Blowin' in the Wind," "Gentle on My Mind," and in a song sung by Doctor McCoy, "The Sound of Silence":

> I'm a doctor out in space,
> And, like, I really groove this place,
> Because of all the rare dis-ease-es—
> Not like your silly coughs or sneezes!
> Treating ailments that no man before has seen
> Is real keen—
> They are my kinds . . . of sick-ness! (7)

Jacobs shows he can derive as much humor from a Simon and Garfunkel song as he can from a Rodgers and Hammerstein song. The incongruity between the solemn seriousness of "The Sound of Silence" with his parody lyrics makes the humor stronger, as does his feminine rhyme of "diseases" and "sneezes." Jacobs makes a clever play on Captain Kirk's opening monologue to *Star Trek*, this time not "to boldly go where no man has gone before," but "treating ailments that no man be-fore has seen," made even funnier by the tag added in a much lower cultural register, "is real keen."

Jacobs's musical parody of *Star Wars*, "The Force and I" (#188, 12/78: 4–10) is mainly built around show tunes. But in his parody of the book version of *The Lord of the Rings*, "The Ring and I" (#210, 10/79: 4–10), he used pop songs to skewer Middle Earth, expanding his repertoire to include "Those Were the Days," "Scarborough Fair," "I Write the Songs," "Both Sides Now," and "You Are the Sunshine of My Life."

In the 1980s, Jacobs took a new approach: individual parodies of hit songs. He began with "Porn in the USA," in which Bruce Springsteen's "Born in the USA" became the foundation for satiric comment about pornography at home rather than in sleazy theaters, in a time when video cassette players were allowing consumers to watch dirty movies in the comfort of their living rooms:

Porn . . . in the U.S.A!
Dig that porn in your home today!
Red-hot porn goin' all the way!
Porn . . . in the U.S.A.! (Jacobs and Coker, #256, 07/85: 19)

Madonna was twice the target, in "Superior Girl" (#259, 12/85: 10) and "Maternity Girl" (#349, 09/96: 25), as was Michael Jackson in "Sad" (#277, 03/88: 24–25), commentary on his strange behavior at the time. These single-song parodies seem forced to me, lacking the variety that came from multiple song parodies, drawing on music that meant more to Jacobs. In any case, his move coincided with the popularity of "Weird Al" Yankovic, whose videos of his recorded song parodies were playing in heavy rotation on MTV. Yankovic cites *Mad*'s song parodies as an important influence, and one could argue that he owes his career to the 1964 court decision in favor of the magazine. In 2015, he was chosen as the first-ever guest editor of *Mad* for #533. Yankovic commented about the way the magazine influenced him: "I was absolutely obsessed. Mort Drucker was one of my all-time favorite artists during my teenage years. And the MAD sensibility bored into my brain at an early age. It struck in me a responsive chord, and helped inspire everything . . . I like to think that what I do is sort of the audio version of MAD magazine."[35]

Although Jacobs did not draw on Beatles songs when the group was together, he used their songs several times in subsequent decades. By the 1970s and 1980s, Beatles songs were as entrenched in the audience's consciousnesses and memories as the show tunes and old standards had been in the 1960s. "When TV Commercials Make Full Use of the Beatles Songs" (Jacobs and North, #286, 04/89: 30–33) followed the Nike commercial that used the Beatles song "Revolution" in an ad for running shoes. To the tune of "And I Love Her," Jacobs again targets Blue Cross, decades later:

I lie here ve-ry . . . sick—
  With drugs they fill . . . me!
But I don't care . . . a . . . lick
  How much they bill . . . me—
'Cause I'm covered! (32)

Whereas before Blue Cross could not be relied on for full coverage, now the patient has no worries: covered, but still "very sick." It doesn't matter how sick you are, as long as you don't have to pay for it. Jacobs sets "The Ban Roll-On Commercial" (31) to the tune of "I Want to Hold Your Hand":

One whiff . . . of his aroma,
And I turn . . . on . . . the . . . fan!
One sniff . . . I'm in a coma!
He needs some Roll-On . . . Ban!
He needs some Roll-On . . . Ban-n-n!
He needs some Roll-On . . . Ban! (31)

Here an innocent teenage love song gets twisted into a lament about body odor, with "aroma" humorously substituted for a very bad smell and the humor intensified by the feminine rhyme with "a coma," incongruously humorous for its exaggerated effect. "Whiff" and "sniff" employ a humorous use of onomatopoeia, and the insistent repetition in the last three lines not only parodies the Beatles' desire to hold her hand, but also underscores just how bad this person reeks.

In "*Mad*'s Beatles Songbook" (#345, 05/96: 4–8), Jacobs satirized the group's release of *The Beatles Anthology* and their ability to cash in on their music, even after they had been broken up for more than two decades, and even after one of their key members was dead. The piece's opening illustration is a masterful parody of the album cover of *Sgt.*

Pepper's Lonely Hearts Club Band, and the targets include a number of contemporary topics and subjects, including "The Royal Family" (8), sung to the tune of "Yellow Submarine":

In the land . . . of chaps and blokes,
Where each day . . . they break for tea,
You will find . . . those far-out folks
Who are called . . . the Mon-ar-chy! (8)

Various members of the royal family get skewered, including Charles, Lady Di, and Fergie, and then comes the chorus:

We're all sick of the Royal Family,
  The Royal Family, the Royal Family!
Same old schtick with the Royal Family,
  The Royal Family, the Royal Family! (8)

By the 1990s, Beatle songs were as old as the old standards had been when Jacobs and Siegel began their run of song parodies by drawing on audience familiarity with songs like "There's No Business Like Show Business" and "Blue Skies." Just as my friends and I reveled in the parodies of the songs revered by our parents, a younger generation of readers could now revel in the golden oldies of their Baby Boomer parents. In the '40s and '50s, my parents sat in movie theaters and sang songs like "Let Me Call You Sweetheart" with the whole crowd, following the bouncing ball, a community joined by their shared sense of straight values, sincerely singing together in what can be called a sweet but also extremely corny activity. In the '60s, my friends and I sang together, our inherited values slowly but surely being slightly warped by *Mad*'s irreverent attitude about everything. That singing continues, generation after generation of readers joining in, even if they do not realize their kinship.

And in the End . . .

Mad's parody songs, the bulk written by Frank Jacobs and Larry Siegel in the '60s and '70s, and then by Jacobs into this century, run the gamut from literate and sophisticated to absurd and downright silly. The songs demanded of the reader a wide cultural, literary, and historical literacy, and amounted to a decent amount of education for younger readers like me and my friends. In the '60s, *Mad* used music to navigate its way through a tumultuous decade, satirizing advertising, TV, movies, politics, American culture, and especially by the end, youth culture—and paradoxically perhaps, mostly by using the most mainstream of music, Broadway show tunes. Thanks to the comic genius of Frank Jacobs, Larry Siegel, and others, musical parody continued in the decades that followed. I did not fully realize it at the time, but as I sang their parody lyrics I was slowly but surely being taught to question authority and to laugh cynically, at the foibles of American mainstream culture, as well as at the youth culture that had begun to absorb me. I was also being taught to give vent to my inner silliness, and for that, I am profoundly grateful. I stopped reading *Mad* in the mid-'70s, but I was not alone in the '60s, with friends literally singing along, and with future friends singing along too, if not with me, then with Alfred, just as I was. So, for the big finish, sing along with me—and Alfred:

Hello, Delly
This is Joe, Delly
Would you please send up
Some nice corned beef on rye?

A box of Ritz, Delly
And some Schlitz, Delly
Some chopped liver
And a sliver of your apple pie.

Over half a century later, this song still makes me laugh out loud.

Notes

1. Thanks to my colleagues at Winthrop University for their helpful comments on this essay: Amanda Hiner, Casey Cothran, Leslie Bickford, and Kelly Richardson. Thanks also to my co-editor, Judith Yaross Lee, for her insightful editing and suggestions.
2. Maria Reidelbach, *Completely Mad: A History of the Comic Book and Magazine*, 60.
3. Austin Cline, "The 1957 Supreme Court Decision: *Roth v. United States*."
4. "Elizabeth Taylor," Wikipedia, https://en.wikipedia.org/wiki/Elizabeth_Taylor.
5. "Sammy Davis, Jr., Wikipedia, https://en.wikipedia.org/wiki/Sammy_Davis_Jr.
6. Reidelbach, *Completely Mad*, 60, 65.

7. United States District Court, Southern District of New York, *Berlin v. EC Publications, Inc.*, 219 F. Supp. 911, June 27, 1963.

8. United States District Court, Southern District of New York.

9. United States District Court, Southern District of New York.

10. Alex Preminger, O. B. Hardison, and Frank J. Warnke, eds., *The Princeton Handbook of Poetic Terms*, 248.

11. Preminger et al., eds., *Princeton Handbook*, 248.

12. Preminger et al., eds., *Princeton Handbook*, 183.

13. Preminger et al., eds., *Princeton Handbook*, 183.

14. Linda Hutcheon, *A Theory of Parody: The Teachings of Twentieth-Century Art Forms*, 43–49.

15. Hutcheon, *A Theory of Parody*, 32.

16. Hutcheon, *A Theory of Parody*, 32.

17. United States Second Circuit, Court of Appeals, *Berlin v. EC Publications, Inc.*, 329 F. 2d 541, March 23, 1964.

18. United States Second Circuit, Court of Appeals.

19. United States Second Circuit, Court of Appeals.

20. George Winston, "Why the Rosenbergs Were Executed."

21. United States Second Circuit, Court of Appeals.

22. United States Second Circuit, Court of Appeals.

23. United States Second Circuit, Court of Appeals.

24. United States Second Circuit, Court of Appeals.

25. United States Second Circuit, Court of Appeals.

26. For more background on the court cases and their relation to parody, fair use, and copyright law, see Ronald S. Rosen, *Music and Copyright*, 303–04.

27. According to Al Jaffee, Nick Meglin's "dreams were to write Broadway shows and lyrics for music." See Paul Levitz, "Inside the Editorial Process: *Mad* Veterans Jafee and Meglin Look at Their Editors," chap. 1, 223; first published in *Studies in American Humor*, n.s. 3, no. 30 (Fall 2014): 15.

28. Frank Jacobs, "Frankly Mad: The Frank Jacobs Interview," interview by Scott Gosar, *The Mad Store*.

29. Reidelbach, *Completely Mad*, 68.

30. Quoted in Reidelbach, *Completely Mad*, 175.

31. I am indebted to Judith Yaross Lee for her knowledge of Yiddish.

32. "The Sound of Music (1965)," *The Numbers: Where Data and the Movie Business Meet*, Nash Information Services, LLC, n.d., https://www.the-numbers.com/movie/Sound-of-Music-The#tab=summary.

33. The rankings are not based merely on total sales, but according to a complicated formula, which includes weeks at number one, as well as other factors, using an inverse points system that gives greater value to weeks at No. 1 and lesser value to weeks at lesser ranking, and also weighting eras differently "to account for chart turnover rates over various periods." See "Greatest of All Time Billboard 200 Albums."

34. "Hot 100-1964 Archive."
35. Michael Cavna, "MAD Magazine Inspired Weird Al Yankovic. Today, as its First Guest Editor, He Exacts Revenge."

11. You Always Hurt the Ones You Love:

Mad Magazine's Affectionate Parodies of Beloved Film Classics

Don Baird

> The making of illusions . . . has become the business of America. . . . We now have an unprecedented opportunity to deceive ourselves and befog our experience.
>
> —Daniel Boorstin, *The Image* (1962)

Puncturing Illusions

MY FIRST DIRECT encounter with the strange business of film promotion came when I was an usher at a local cinema. An advertisement appeared in the daily newspaper extolling the virtues of a feature-length documentary beginning a limited engagement. And in the ad, my boss was quoted as saying, "This is the finest motion picture I have ever presented." When I arrived at work that day, I could hardly wait to ask him about this fantastic film I'd never heard of but which he obviously thought was outstanding. "Oh, I haven't seen it, "he explained. "The bosses at the theater chain had trouble figuring out how to sell it. So, they put my name in the ad and said how proud I was to show it. They just hope that my high recommendation will sell a few tickets. I haven't seen a minute of it."

I would never view film promotions the same way again.

Of course, the *Mad* writers and artists who created a series of ingenious movie satires wouldn't have been surprised in the least. Since the first issue, they used their talents not just to amuse but also to encourage a healthy skepticism in their readers. As art director Sam Viviano said, the basic story running through each issue was "Don't believe what you're told. Don't believe advertising, don't believe people in authority."[1] This undercurrent explains why Michael J. Socolow told *Smithsonian* readers that *Mad* performed "a vital public service, teaching American adolescents that they shouldn't believe everything they read in their textbooks or saw on TV."[2] *Mad* was a rare entity of dissent at a time when few voices doubted the consumerism of popular culture. *Mad*'s writers and artists offered readers a way of hilariously questioning the received wisdom of Madison Avenue advertising that extolled the virtues and pleasures of smoking cigarettes. They skewered the equally deadly selling by politicians of an always "just-around-the-corner" imminent victory of the Vietnam War. In this way, *Mad* offered readers a comic way to escape the danger and numbness of living the unquestioning existence of a good consumer—the individual whom Ernest Becker saw as "confined by culture, a slave to it, who imagines that he has an identity if he pays his insurance premium, that he has control of his life if he guns his sports car or works his electric toothbrush."[3] Through the comic creations in *Mad*, readers could find not only amusement and laughter, but also a safe environment in which to exercise their freedom to question and doubt. That is, *Mad* helped readers not only searching for laughter, but also seeking a way to resist the more dehumanizing aspects of modern life.

Thus, readers were not merely amused. They were empowered. And they were shown that they too had the freedom to question and even mock whatever was being sold by advertisers, television, politicians, or, yes, even the movies.

Hollywood Droll: Going After the Artifice in the Art

Mad emphasizes the artifice in the art. Film critic Roger Ebert once claimed that he learned to be a movie critic from reading *Mad*. The movie satires in its pages helped him spot "dumb old formulas," "obligatory scenes, cardboard characters and giant gaps in plausibility."[4] He learned to demythologize movie stars at a time when publicists had them treated like royalty and their visages were everywhere from magazine covers to billboards. Under *Mad*'s guidance, he felt he'd learned to see through the standard clichés of Hollywood to better spot genuine art. Exposure to so many of these movie parodies obviously didn't hurt. In fact, Ebert went on to win a Pulitzer Prize.

The film satires appearing in the pages of *Mad* over the decades certainly skewered the most overhyped, manipulative, and idiotic celluloid clunkers of their time. And yet the talented artists and writers of *Mad* found ways of also creating satires of some of the most beloved and acclaimed movies. And that is what I will explore in this essay: how did the creative minds of *Mad* use these classic films to make satiric points about American society as well as film? For this purpose, I have selected the following films, all of which have won lasting critical acclaim and audience enthusiasm, yet also received the *Mad* treatment: *Casablanca, The Birds, Lawrence of Arabia, The Sound of Music, 2001: A Space Odyssey, Hannah and Her Sisters, It's a Wonderful Life*, and *The Wizard of Oz*. Even classic and beloved movies contain values of popular culture that *Mad*'s writers found hypocritical, and were marketed using some of the advertising techniques that *Mad* regularly derided. And there was simply no way the writers and artists of *Mad* could resist mocking the ad campaigns for *The Sound of Music* ("The Happiest Sounds in All the World") or *The Birds* ("The Birds IS Coming!").

Any film, even a classic popular one, requires audiences to suspend disbelief as time is speeded up on screen, coincidences pile up, characters fall in love instantly, and are unfailingly attractive (aside from the villains, who are unfailingly not). *King Kong*'s special effects remain legendary, yet, it's still—as Harvey Kurtzman and Will Elder remind us in *Mad*'s first film parody, "Ping Pong," (#6, 8–9/53: 1–7)—the story of a gigantic ape's unrequited love for a petite blonde, who is actually brunette Fay Wray in a wig.

Overly enthusiastic critics, over-the-top advertising campaigns, outrageous turns of the plot, or a bad performance could all come to the attention of *Mad*'s creative team in these parodies, or as *Mad* called them, satires. But sometimes too the plot of a famous film served as the springboard for stories criticizing political and social trends, as we shall see in their takes on *It's a Wonderful Life* (1946) and *The Wizard of Oz* (which they parodied three different times!; 1939). Regularly occurring techniques of each movie satire include the following:

1. Wordplay based on character names and film titles (as *The Sound of Music* becomes *The $ound of Money*).
2. Breaking the fourth wall or narrative frame, with characters aware of their fictional nature communicating directly to the reader their true feelings about the production they are stuck in.
3. Pop culture celebrities not in the original film suddenly dropping into the story.

4. Revised lyrics for musicals, emphasizing the true and more cynical message that *Mad*'s writers insist a film is conveying.
5. Artwork giving each story visual humor and a dash of cinematic flair (with sight gags, movie star caricatures, and a variety of locations and camera angles).

This happy marriage of great wit, social commentary, and screen-worthy artwork led *Mad*'s movie parodies to become works of art in themselves.

"Casabonkers"

Like many films that would become all-time favorites, *Casablanca* (1942) began its journey to lasting fame unpromisingly. The screenplay was based on an unproduced play ("Everybody Comes to Rick's") and wasn't complete when production began, so the performers weren't sure what ending they were building up to. Humphrey Bogart was shorter than his leading lady Ingrid Bergman and wound up wearing platform shoes for some of their scenes together. The unforgettable song "As Time Goes By" was nearly deleted entirely. And exotic Casablanca was really Burbank, California (though the iconic airport ending was filmed in Van Nuys). And yet it all came together, as movies and even life sometimes do, with *Casablanca* becoming both an audience and critical favorite.

Mad film satires change movie titles and character names for humorous purposes. Thus, in the hands of writer Arnie Kogen and artist Mort Drucker, *Casablanca* becomes "Casabonkers" (#300, 1/91: 2–7), and Rick (played by Bogart) becomes Reek, a name that takes him down a notch and pokes fun at the film's exotic setting. This tradition continued through parodies of films, TV shows, and plays, and even extended to the treatment of *My Fair Lady*, where George Bernard Shaw became George Bernard Schwartz (Megliola [Meglin] and Drucker, "My Fair Ad-Man" #54, 4/60: 31-37). Kogen and Drucker also played with *Casablanca*'s central plot device: the characters' desperate attempts to get letters of transit and escape Nazi territory. "Are they important?" Reek asks Ugotti (a caricature of Peter Lorre). "Let me put it this way! Without these documents, what we've got here is an Andy Hardy movie!" (4). The art by Mort Drucker for this satire demonstrates his flair for cinematic caricature. Humphrey Bogart and Lorre are instantly recognizable. Their serious expressions as they speak the absurd dialogue written for them add to the comic impact.

Kogen and Drucker can't help but notice the existential absurdity of characters coming *to* Casablanca to get letters of transit just so they can *leave* Casablanca. And they use these letters in parodying the final scene at the Casablanca airport as Reek gives the letters to his love, punningly named Ulcer (Ilsa), and her freedom fighter husband Lazload (Lazlo) so that the pair can leave the country safely. "I'm doing this for a noble cause," declares Reek. "So that people everywhere can be free?" asks Lazload. Not at all. It's "so that this can become a CULT FILM!" (7). How can a scene that was supposed to be set in Morocco but was filmed at an airport in Van Nuys, California, possibly become a cult film?, wonders an astounded Chief of Police Renutt. To which Reek responds, "Maybe not today! Maybe not tomorrow! But soon, and for the rest of our lives!" (7). When Renutt then commands his men to "round up the usual suspects!" and is asked to clarify whether he means Resistance leaders, his answer keeps the parody focused on the film's improbabilities: "No, the hack writers over at the Warner Studio!" (7).

As here, characters in "Casabonkers" regularly break the fourth wall and discuss its cult movie status, as well as absurdities within the plot. They question the movie cliché of the sentimental alcoholic as romantic hero. For example, pianist Slam turns to the reader as his boss takes to another bottle and asks, "Why do I have the feeling this man is never going to be Chairman of the President's Council on Physical Fitness?" (5). Meanwhile, Drucker's artwork gives this classic a visual elegance and style that add to its verisimilitude. The caricatures of Bogart, Ingrid Bergman, and Claude Rains are striking, and there are moody dark scenes in Reek's Café, as well as flashbacks of both sun and rain on the streets of Paris. Drucker's illustrations thus bring affection to the satire, reminding readers of the visual beauty of the film even as the hilarious dialogue punctures holes in some of the clichés that appear in even the most beloved of classic films. Thus, readers can revisit a beloved film of the past and enjoy the mockery of *Mad*'s stellar satire yet retain their love of the original.

As with so many of the movies explored in this chapter, *Mad*'s satire conveys great affection for the original film, plot contrivances and all. The art is delightful, and the gags are never mean-spirited. And readers may find themselves able to return to the movie with fresh eyes, still enjoying its romance and performances while chuckling privately over the absurdities *Mad* has helped us to see.

"For the Birds"

Alfred Hitchcock's career in the United Kingdom and Hollywood gave the director the kind of visibility that few filmmakers enjoyed at a time when movies were primarily marketed to the public by emphasizing the actors or actresses in leading roles. But Hitchcock was not only a fine director; he was also an outstanding publicist for his own films. When *The Birds* was released in 1963 without a well-known leading actress—Tippi Hedren was cast based on her role in a television commercial—the need to publicize the film based on Hitchcock's reputation for excellence was more important than ever. Yet production was followed by one of the least grammatical movie marketing campaigns of all time. "The Birds Is Coming" was proclaimed in newspaper advertising and on billboards, coupled with fearful images of birds attacking and the magical Hitchcock name. The marketing pressbook suggested that theater owners distribute bird masks for attendees to wear to the theater, where they could see if a "lucky number" matched those at the box office for free admission. Cinema managers were urged to find talking birds to say "The Birds Is Coming" in the lobby. And Hitchcock himself posed for a series of playful publicity photos: one of Hitchcock with a crow perched on his long cigar, another with a crow sitting on his knee, and yet another with Hitch in a bookshop looking aghast at a book entitled *The World of Birds*. Newspaper ads and posters featured a quote from the director claiming, "It could be the most terrifying movie I have ever made."[5]

Audiences attended in droves (and possibly flocks). But writers Arnie Kogen and Lou Silverstone were not impressed by all the ads, evidenced by the opening words of their version of the film, "For the Birds" (#82, 10/63: 43–48):

> Yes, sir, you saw it advertised in magazines and newspapers, on billboards and TV—and you were scared! Then you saw it on the screen, and you were no longer scared—you were hysterical with laughter! Because even a movie with reams and reams of advance publicity can still turn out to be a bomb when it's got bad acting and a weak story! (43)

Even as the bird attacks build, *Mad* finds ways to mock the publicity campaign. In Mort Drucker's beautifully drawn panel on the final page, we see a famous sky-high view of the city being attacked and can see a billboard with the original ad copy of the Hollywood marketers: "The birds is coming." But here those words are followed by a *Mad* addendum ". . . AND GOOD GRAMMAR IN ADVERTISING HAS WENT!" (48).

In *Mad*'s tradition of punningly renamed characters, Tippi Hedren becomes "Tipsy Headrinse" in the credits. Kogen and Silverstone highlight absurd moments in the plot, which involves mysterious attacks on humans by flocks of birds. In their version of the pet shop scene, one of the least credible "meet cute" romance scenes on celluloid, Rod Taylure warns Tipsy she's not likely to follow in the footsteps of Hitchcock's most renowned leading lady: "Let's face it baby, a Grace Kelly you're not!" (43). Tipsy purchases two lovebirds, then hires a rowboat to follow the gallant gentleman as the writers seize another opportunity to mock the script: "Looking for him will help to build up the suspense—something which happens to be noticeably lacking in the rest of the picture!" (44). The lovebirds add to the implausibility by commenting on the wooden dialogue that the smitten lovers share when Tipsy, wearing a mink coat, rows across Bodego Bay: "This clever repartee is supposed to relieve the unbearable tension!" says one lovebird. The other responds: "What unbearable tension?" (44). A similar comic implausibility follows as flocks of birds start attacking at random and Tipsy enters a school to warn the children about the danger, Drucker's hilarious illustration shows her accidentally clunking one student with the door; another in the classroom is reading his own copy of *Mad*, and one is wearing a dunce cap (47). Throughout the parody, the characters scorn the plot for lacking the suspense that the commercials had promised.

Beyond the mockery of the unlikely script (which *Mad* claimed was based on a junior high school composition) and some less than stellar performances, artist Mort Drucker outdid himself with hilarious caricatures of such incongruous additions to the cast as Soviet Union Premier Nikita Khrushchev and TV comedian Jackie Gleason, both of whom are mistaken for Hitch as the parody cast awaits his famous cameo. And for the sheer pleasure of wordplay, the writers added several avian names to the cast list. Thus, we see credits for Peter Finch, Walter Pigeon, Tina Robin, Jean Crane, Dean Martin, and Howard Hawks (43). In all, *Mad*'s satire of the renowned Hitchcock film delights its readers with its creativity in word and image, along with its critique of the wooden acting and stilted dialogue of the original film.

Its major target is the over-the-top advertising campaign that the studio had waged to bring in audiences. Alfred Hitchcock had directed numerous outstanding suspenseful motion pictures in his lengthy career. To promise audiences that this would be his "most terrifying" film was a major promise indeed. Whatever the final film's virtues, it definitely was not that.

"Flawrence of Arabia"

The 1960s saw several big budget motion pictures released as special event, limited-engagement, advance-ticket blockbusters as cinemas sought new ways to compete with television. These highly promoted epics, offering the promise of something special on a gigantic screen, succeeded in bringing audiences to the theater. As always, the artists and writers of *Mad* were there, too—and could capture a few absurdities amid the spectacles.

Drucker's unique contributions to the look of these epics bears special attention. A self-taught artist who perfected his style with practice, Drucker would create his movie satire art with sometimes only limited material. He recalled in 2012 how *Mad*'s then associate editor John Ficarra had helped gather photos of stars and stills from movies for the artists—sometimes getting them from friends who worked at other magazines and occasionally even on the black market.[6] Drucker claimed that he only needed one full frontal shot and one profile shot of a performer to be able to draw them in a variety of scenes of a story. Drucker's caricatures of the actors in each film were distinctive and appealing, fondly exaggerating but never critically mocking individual facial features. As films became larger in the 1960s, Drucker found ways to visually express their epic sense even within the same amount of magazine space. Like a film director, he deliberately chose to make the stories look more cinematic by having a variety of angles on each page, going from close-ups to long shots, so the epic sense is visualized, even within panels of limited size.

David Lean's three-and-a-half-hour epic film *Lawrence of Arabia* (1962) begins with a credit sequence showing an unknown man on a motorcycle traveling at high speed. Eventually we learn he is T. E. Lawrence, the hero of the film. *Mad* similarly leads into its title and credits for "Flawrence of Arabia" (Jacobs, Hart, Siegel, and Drucker #86, 4/64: 43–48) with a three-panel sequence of an unknown man on a motorcycle who travels closer and closer until we see it's another, more familiar film figure. A caption below reads: "Ooops!—Wrong motorcycle rider! Hey, you guys up in the projection booth! That's Marlon Brando in the opening scene from 'The Wild One.' That was a character we understood! Not like Flawrence of Arabia!" (43).

From the first panel, we see *Mad* playing with the film viewing experience, as we the audience must wait for the projectionist to put on the right movie. Riding a camel across the desert, Flawrence wonders aloud what "deep, mysterious" words his Arab companions must be saying in their exotic tongue. *Mad* helpfully translates some of these "deep, mysterious" conversations: "Hot enough for you?," "It's a real scorcher today!," and "It's not the heat, it's the humidity!" (45). At midpoint in the parody, Flawrence rides out into the broiling desert because, he says, "it's 'Intermission' time—and a fade-out on a hot, broiling sun is a good business move for all theater owners around the country" (46). We next see the intermission sign and hundreds of parched cinema audience members gasping for any liquid they can buy at the concession stand. Drucker's depiction of the frantic, overheated viewers running for the concession stand brilliantly enhances the gag. (See fig. 11-1.)

Mad once again emphasizes the artifice in the art. We viewers at the cinema are not truly in the desert, depicted vividly on screen. We are watching scene after scene of actors and camels in the blazing sun and

Fig. 11-1: It's intermission time (at last!) in "Flawrence of Arabia." Frank Jacobs, Stan Hart, Larry Siegel and Mort Drucker created this memorable poke at the concessions bonanza of the lengthy desert epic (*Mad* #86, 4/64: 46). MAD used with permission.

sand. While we are doubtlessly moved by Lawrence's story, *Mad* knows our thoughts are really with the ice-cold soda just waiting for us out in the lobby.

Eventually Flawrence sees a psychiatrist about his quest for a life in the desert. He is urged to "find yourself a nice Egyptian girl and settle down" (48). In the final panel, we see that he has taken the advice, poised beside Elizabeth Taylor as Cleopatra, the basis for another expensive film epic of the era. With this ending, *Mad* reminds readers of the big business machinations involved in even such fine achievements as Lean's film, which won ten Academy Awards in 1963. The parody makes explicit—and satirizes—the fact that a very long film set in the desert is a concessions bonanza for theaters, with cold drinks and ice cream a necessity for every audience member enduring the on-screen heat. And despite the film's scorching desert verisimilitude, the need to market the film to a mass audience means that, in true Hollywood style, even an historical drama with Middle Eastern characters will use American and British performers such as Alec Guinness and Anthony Quinn in many roles.

"The $ound of Money"

Mad launched a similar consumerist critique of *The Sound of Music* (1965), a hugely successful musical that, like *Lawrence of Arabia*, received a reserved-seat theatrical release, with fewer showings and higher admission prices than other films of its time. *Mad*'s "The $ound of Money" includes musical references to this policy as a slick moneymaking business ploy (Hart and Drucker, #108, 1/67: 41–47). The introduction notes, "Sure, the songs are lovely, but take them away and what have you got? Nothing but a collection of the same old dull clichés and boring tear-jerker gimmicks that you've been seeing in movie musicals for years" (41). Rodgers and Hammerstein's song "Do-Re-Mi" becomes a celebration of films, like this one, that "will bring us back much DOUGH . . . DOUGH . . . DOUGH . . . DOUGH" (45). Hart and Drucker highlight the absurdity of the film's many musical scenes set in the Austrian outdoors. *Mad*'s splash page equivalent for the film's opening musical number shows a lovely caricature of Julie Andrews singing in the mountains. But Drucker makes sure that a tape recorder and amplifiers appear in the foreground to reveal to *Mad* readers just where those nice orchestrations likely came from. (See fig. 11-2.)

Fig. 11-2: Mort Drucker reveals the artificial source of the music, and the sentimentality that it supports, in "The $ound of Money," a satire focusing on the marketing side of the popular musical with Julie Andrews, *The Sound of Music*. Lyrics by Stan Hart parody Rodgers and Hammerstein's song in announcing that the movie "will bring us / back much / DOUGH . . . DOUGH . . . DOUGH . . . DOUGH . . . " (*Mad* #108, 1/67: 45). MAD used with permission.

Wordplay here comes in the names of the major characters, as the Catholic Maria becomes Jewish Mitzia and Captain von Trapp becomes Captain von Tripe, but most of the jokes poke fun at the Hollywood version of the actual Von Trapp family's escape from the Nazis. Mitzia, like Maria, is shown to be a high-spirited nun who likes to sing whenever possible. Her Mother Superior interrupts a number and tells her, "I do not think you belong in a convent," and when Mitzia asks, "You mean I belong in the outside world?" the older nun replies, "No, not there either. That's the problem!" (42). A solution is found by sending Mitzia to tend the children of Captain Von Tripe. Paying comic homage to Julie Andrews's most famous previous film role, Mitzia goes off to her childrearing assignment dressed as Mary Poppins—aloft with her magical umbrella (43). She happily tells the children they can all go bicycle riding, hiking, picnicking, and swimming. And what does that have to do with the story, she is asked. Not a thing. "It's commercial. And remember!" she says. "We're not in this movie for our health! We're in it for the MONEY!" (45). In between musical numbers, Mitzia and the Captain eventually marry, but unfortunately find their happiness intruded upon by war. In a reference to another pop culture Nazi tale, the *Hogan's Heroes* television sitcom, a Nazi officer warns the Captain, "Listen, Bud, I'm not one of those lovable Nazis you see on television!" (46). But Nazi sternness gets redirected when the family decides to escape the war by singing in a folk song festival and slipping away amid the distraction. As they leave following their big musical number (in front of a dozing band), and one officer shouts, "Stop them! Stop them!," another asks, "From trying to escape?"—to which the first replies, changing the frame of reference from the family's history to the film's plot, "No, from doing an encore!" (46). Further mocking the escape is Drucker's drawing of the Von Tripe family hiding in Mitzia's convent, which is populated with other furtive celebrities of the time, such as David Janssen of TV's *The Fugitive*.

The parody's peak is a closing song to be sung to the tune of "Climb Ev'ry Mountain," which reprises the satire of the musical's commercialized and sentimentalized tale:

Play just one theater
In every town;
Only sell reserved seats
Turn most people down.

As with the other satiric references to the film's marketing strategy, the creative decision here to have the characters sing of film marketing adds to the humor and power of "The $ound of Money":

Charge high admissions;
Let people wait;
That will make them think they're
Seeing something great! (47)

The song invites readers to bring critical thinking even to a film they enjoy. But the emphasis on commercialization also brings out the crassness of creating romantic musical entertainment from a story of the Nazis' rise to power.

The commercialization continues to this day. Numerous "Sound of Music" tours enable the film's fans who visit Austria seeking to view the locations of the "real story." Travel writer Rick Steves warns tourists, however, of the many changes the filmmakers had made. Many of the most requested sites from the film were sets on a Hollywood lot. And while the real Von Trapp family had 7 children, all their names and genders were changed for the film. In adulthood, Rupert Von Trapp was often asked which child he was. "I'm Liesl," he responded.[7]

Mad's readers wouldn't have been the least surprised.

"201 Minutes of a Space Idiocy"

Stanley Kubrick's *2001: A Space Odyssey* (1968) became the highest grossing motion picture released in North America that year. Audiences returned to the film again and again to admire its artistry, the wonder and beauty of its images and music—and to try to figure out what its very ambiguous ending could possibly mean. A year later, Dick DeBartolo and Mort Drucker spoofed the film's equation of ambiguity with philosophical depth in "201 Minutes of a Space Idiocy" (#125, 3/69: 4–10). In their version of the famous prelude to the film, set at the Dawn of Mankind, actors in ape costumes attempt to guess who's who in each simian mask. "Are you Maurice Evans? Roddy McDowall?" They wonder aloud whether perhaps they're in a *Planet of the Apes* sequel, and seek their motivation for the scene they're in. "Act bored," one actor says to another. "And with this script, it's not even an act!" (4).

Repeated references to 1960s popular culture undercut the film's ponderousness. The snide remark about the script comes from Fred

Flintstone of *The Flintstones* (an animated television show about a caveman and his family that was itself an homage to Jackie Gleason's character on *The Honeymooners*), who is mingling among the apes. In yet another reference to pop culture, we see a telephone operator of the future helping an astronaut make a call to his family on Earth; her equipment has buttons to press for "Bob Newhart Routine," "Elaine May Mike Nichols Routine," and "Shelley Berman Routine" (6)—all references to contemporary comedy acts based on telephone calls. *Mad* also mocks the Pan Am airline's logos appearing in the film's space vehicles as just another form of product placement by presenting additional marketing opportunities that were missed in the original. The Milky Way galaxy now advertises candy (9), a star is labeled *Starkist Tuna*, and even the sun gets its chance to make a buck with a sign for Sun Oil (4). And whereas the cost of a space program is seldom mentioned in science fiction films, the astronaut in *Mad*'s version is advised of his charges for calling home. "Operator, what were the charges for that call?," he asks. "Deposit $17,500 for the first three minutes, plus 10 cents for the overtime!," the operator responds (6), in a reference to the high cost of long-distance phone calls in the 1960s.

DeBartolo also takes on the film's computer culture. In one of the film's most famous sequences, the supposedly error-proof HAL computer begins to malfunction, making potentially deadly mistakes, and must be shut down. In *Mad*'s version, HAL (now renamed SID) is asked vital questions by the astronauts, Poop and Bowtie. "I'd like to put up new drapes and I'd like to get your opinion!," says Poop. The computer's malfunctioning is suspected with its response that "Those old drapes are just fine" (8). After a near-lethal error, as the astronaut begins to shut it down, SID offers a series of apologies: "I know I've been a very naughty machine—. . . . I know I tried to kill you and Poop, and I put us on the wrong course, and I detected equipment failure where none existed, and I have bad breath! But what about the good things I do," the computer says. These "good things" include cleaning pods and "hanging up your space suits when you leave them around" (9).

At the time of the film's release, viewers and critics spent hours theorizing about the black monolith first seen among the apes in the film's opening scenes and finally reappearing in the scene with the astronaut seeing himself as an older man at dinner and on his deathbed. In *Mad*'s concluding panels, DeBartolo and Drucker offer their own theory as to what the monolith truly was. They even give it a speaking voice. "I'm a book," it says. And not just any book. In the final panel summing up the creators' satiric take on the movie, we get to see the title page as drawn by Mort Drucker: "How to Make an Incomprehensible Science Fiction Movie & Several Million Dollars by Writer-Producer-Director Stanley Kubrick" (10).

Thus in the midst of the culture's many discussions, analyses, and published works interpreting the meaning of Kubrick's science fiction extravaganza, *Mad* once again reminds us of the artifice in the art and to remember "it's still only a movie!"

Knocks on Woody

Woody Allen's *Hannah and Her Sisters* (1986) was one of his most popular and critically praised features. When writer Debbee Ovitz and artist Mort Drucker parodied the plot of the film in "Henna and Her Sickos" (#265, 9/86: 4–8), they had a field day puncturing critics' effusive claims about the ever-growing brilliance of the filmmaker. The *Mad* version imagines critics Roger Ebert, Gene Siskel, and Gene Shalit not merely discussing the film—they are pictured at the Thanksgiving table, dining with the rest of the cast and a Pilgrim, topping one another with praise for the great artist. "Woody has certainly grown as a filmmaker," *Mad*'s Ebert says. His TV colleague Siskel responds, "What brilliant touches! Instead of Gershwin music, he's using Rodgers and Hart!" (5). Nearby, another critic raves about how Allen has shown "real maturity" since directing his black-and-white features *Manhattan* (1979) and *Stardust Memories* (1980). "Right!" agrees critic Gene Shalit. "Woody's finally learned where to buy color film!" (5). By breaking the fourth wall in this way, the critics in *Mad*'s version puncture their own overinflated praise, with Allen's changing to color film and offering background music by different composers hailed as signs of genius. The effect is to urge us to take a few steps back from the accolades and view the film itself with a more critical eye. *Mad*'s satires of this and other popular films remind us we can find enjoyment in the virtues of a work of art without the need to overpraise it.

Allen himself is the target of much satire. He introduces the parody, claiming great pride in his film because it's so new and different. "Like for instance, even though it's the 14th consecutive film in which I've played a total neurotic, this is the first time there are other neurotics in worse shape than me" (4). When Allen goes for a medical appointment, his doctor examines the contents of a folder and says, "I'm afraid this doesn't look too good." Allen responds that he knew he must be dying, but the doctor reassures him that that's not what worries him. "These are box office results of your films outside of New York and L.A," the doctor responds. "You're not dying—your movies are!" (6). In *Hannah and Her Sisters* (1986), Allen (as Mickey) overcomes a suicidal impulse by watching a Marx Brothers film. In *Mad*'s version, Mort Drucker offers a wonderful illustration as Allen and Dianne Wiest emerge from a cinema offering a Marx Brothers festival. Now Mickey exits with "a major, mind-blowing discovery! The Marx Brothers made movies just to be funny! They never felt they had to hide from the press or fear their fans . . . never felt the need to drop the names of pseudo-intellectuals in their movies. . . . They never took themselves seriously and today, they're considered great artists!" (8).

Mad's jokes had truth in them. As a matter of fact, *Hannah* was to be Woody Allen's most profitable film until the release of *Midnight in Paris* (2011). After that film, he would continue to release a film a year, but his audiences dwindled to a limited core following. In 2018, production of that year's film (*A Rainy Day in New York*) ended, but the distributor announced a decision not to give it a theatrical release. In this context, "Henna and Her Sickos" not only parodies the film's storyline but also uses the story to mock critics and award-givers who overpraise artistic pretension, but who seldom offer awards or recognition to comedy and comedians that simply make people laugh. The satire can be seen then as not only a mockery of inflated critical response, but also a reminder of the importance of just plain laughter, which critics usually disregard. Preston Sturges's classic film *Sullivan's Travels* (1941) reminded us that laughter might not be much, "but it's better than nothing in this cockeyed caravan."

All the films I've explored to this point have been popular with audiences and critics, and *Mad*'s writers and artists have played with their plots and marketing for comic effect. Frank Capra's *It's a Wonderful Life* (1946) and MGM's *The Wizard of Oz* stand apart, both as recognizable masterpieces of popular film art but also in the special ways in which *Mad* adapted them. Decades after their original theatrical releases, these two films are still so loved by audiences that they remain fixtures of American television and streaming video services. Indeed, they are among the only classic films to receive annual commercial broadcasts. So how did *Mad* treat these two films that have been honored and loved by viewers for generations? Rather than mocking their acting, exhibition, promotion, plotlines, or critical overpraise (as with other parodies), *Mad*'s artists and writers made the fascinating decision to use only the basic premise of each film and the idealism of each conclusion as a kickoff point for satirizing and critiquing aspects of contemporary American political life and social trends.

The creators' obvious love of and respect for both *It's a Wonderful Life* and *The Wizard of Oz* come through, as their plot structures support powerful social and political satire that emphasizes how unlike these hopeful film stories American society had become.

"It's a Blunderful Life"

Stan Hart and Mort Drucker's "It's a Blunderful Life" (#350, 10/96: 4–8) does begin with a clever bit of self-mockery, noting that the original film became a classic enjoyed by generations of viewers. The authors hope that their parody too "will become an American classic enjoyed by generations. Given *Mad*'s policy of reprinting articles over and over again in Super Specials, we think that that's pretty much a done deal!" (4). Like the original film, in which an apprentice angel named Clarence is sent to Earth to help Jimmy Stewart, the *Mad* version begins in the clouds, where former President Richard Nixon is discovered in heaven. Apprentice Angel Nixon is told that to earn his wings, he must go to earth and convince Bill Clinton how his life has made a difference. "I'll try," Nixon responds, "but I thought only God can perform miracles that difficult" (5). As in the classic film, friends whom Stewart has helped without fully realizing it come to his house bringing much needed money, so in *Mad*'s version "friends in the various PACs and special interest groups" bring Clinton huge bags of cash. In the final panel, Drucker offers delightful caricatures of both presidents. Nixon tells Clinton, "I hope you've learned something here today," to which Clinton responds, "I certainly have! I've learned that if ol' Tricky Dick himself, Richard Nixon, can make it to heaven, then anything's possible in this crazy world.... It's a wonderful life!" At the bottom of this panel appear the words: "With Apologies to Jimmy Stewart" (8).

Along the way to this conclusion, *Mad* still managed to make use of some familiar regular parodic techniques. Wordplay figures as the title is changed from *It's a Wonderful Life* to "It's a Blunderful Life." Pop culture intrudes as a scene in heaven includes an elegant staircase with two labels: "Stairway to Heaven" and "Reserved for Led Zeppelin." (4). And the fourth wall is broken with the apologies to Jimmy Stewart. But the crux of the story is the critique of big money in modern American politics and its influence on political decisions by both Nixon and Clinton.

Three Wizards

The Wizard of Oz has set a record of sorts, as *Mad* has used it as the basis for three different stories in three different decades. Rather than making fun of the film itself, each version uses the plot as an accessible way to mock political and social trends of the times. All three versions use this film classic for critiques of contemporary politics.

"The Guru of Ours" by Frank Jacobs and Mort Drucker (#128, 7/69: 4–10), updates the story of Dorothy and her friends to skewer the drug culture and materialism of 1960s America. In the first panel, Tiny Tim (as Dorothy's aunt) asks, "Why can't you be a normal, healthy wholesome Kansas farm girl like Judy Garland was in 'The Wizard of Oz?'" Dorothy responds, "Cut the corn, Aunt Em! That was thirty years ago! In this musical, I represent the typical teenager of today! Now, beat it, you old Biddy, so I can sing my big solo!" (4). She is joined by "thoroughly square" Pat Boone (7), "snob" George Hamilton (8), and "punk" Michael J. Pollard (8) to seek the Guru, who bears a strong resemblance to Ed Sullivan. The Guru sells Pat Boone "mod" clothes, asks Hamilton to become less snobbish by leaving all his money to the Guru Foundation, and helps Pollard become a talentless punk singer—all for 50 percent of the profits (9). With a leer, he also offers to help Dorothy by having her move in with him "to meditate in private" (10). Realizing the Guru is only a "dirty old man on the make," "a schemer," and "a con man," they decide to join him and make money too. In the final panel, they are singing (to the tune of "We're Off to See the Wizard":

> We're glad we dug the Guru—
> That greedy old Guru of ours!
> He's on the make
> And such a big fake,
> He even wears phony flowers!

But they concede that they're no better than he is:

We don't give a darn how he makes his dough
As long as we see our profits grow
And grow, and grow, and grow and grow and GROW—
As merrily off to the bank we go! (10)

The harsh critique of the materialism and self-absorption of the era is reflected in Mort Drucker's unusually stark caricatures of the main characters and unflattering visual depiction of nearly all the cast members and their habitats. Both text and artwork in "The Guru of Ours" present a social fabric that is egocentric, fame obsessed, and strictly in it for the money. What a contrast from the idealism of the original film!—but that was the point.

For *Mad*'s October 2010 parody "The Wizard of O," Desmond Devlin and Tom Richmond (#505: 47–52) use the plot of the original to critique America's political divisions and political self-promoters in the second year of the Obama administration as it was about to receive its rebuke in the midterm elections. Richmond's artwork surrounds Dorothy with dozens of political commentators from James Carville to Rush Limbaugh, with even Sarah Palin entering the story as the "Witless Witch of the North." Most pointedly, the story expresses the characters' disappointment that the optimism of Wizard O's campaign of Hope had not led to the happy outcomes that everyone had yearned for. Dorothy shares her frustration, telling the Wizard (who is drawn to resemble President Barack Obama) that she and her friends had come "to see if you had the brains, heart and nerve it takes to bring our country back!" (52). He responds that normally he would "establish a blue-ribbon, bipartisan committee to analyze and evaluate your concerns, and issue a report," but offers to respond directly "since we're almost at the end of this parody" (52). In the most blistering panel of all, the Wizard admits: "Brains! I wish! I put Wall Street executives in charge of creating their own TARP bailout! I let BP handle the oil spill cleanup, at their own sweet pace! Heart? There isn't an issue that I won't cave on. I even allowed the Republicans to water down the health care bill for a year, so I could get zero of their votes!" (52). We then see Dorothy, the Cowardly Lion, the Tin Man, and the Scarecrow in total despair as the borders of the final panel close in on them. Dorothy's closing words sadly sum up the theme of the story while echoing the campaign promises they had longed for: "There's no place for hope! There's no place for hope!" (52). The 2010 story is a brilliantly written and drawn but devastating critique, again contrasting the idealism of the original film with the disillusionment of modern political life.

Most astonishing, perhaps, from an historical vantage point is 1991's version: "The Wizard of Odds," written by Frank Jacobs and drawn by Sam Viviano (#300, 1/91: 31–36). The parody begins lightly enough with a good-natured poke at the publisher. To the tune of "Over the Rainbow," Dorothy sings of her wish to be whirled away into the 1990s, a kinder and gentler world:

> No longer will I have to Rot
> In Kansas which could surely not
> Be dul-ler;
> I'll finish off this quantum leap
> In black-and white 'cause
> *Mad*'s too cheap
> To print in color! (31)

But Dorothy discovers that the Yuppie and get-rich-quick-at-others'-expense 1990s are far more dreadful than the poverty of 1939 Kansas. She and her companions desperately seek a way to return home. The Scarecrow has no crops or farms around him, due to pesticides and bankers' repossessions. When Dorothy asks why he didn't save for a rainy day, he explains that he did save—"in a Savings and Loan that went belly up!" (33). Together with the Lion and Tin Man, Dorothy and the Scarecrow encounter televangelist Tammy Faye, who offers them the path to salvation for a mere $10,000. They decline and at last arrive at a casino in Ephemeral City, where they hope the Wizard of Odds will transform them. As we get our first glimpse of him, we can see the unmistakable visage of Donald J. Trump. For he is the Wizard of Odds in this 1991 classic.

Sam Viviano depicts this Wizard sitting on his throne (here labeled "The Donald"), tossing cash into the air, explaining to Dorothy and her companions his plans for transformation. "As ruler of the Land of Odds, I transform people all the time!" the Wizard declares. "Every day 10,000 people walk in here with cash and savings! By the time they leave, I've transformed them into debt-ridden paupers!" The Wizard advises Dorothy and her friends to "get into junk bonds or phony real estate schemes! Or get control of a union's pension fund! Better still, become a televangelist! There's a whole world out there just waiting to be taken!" (36). The closing musical number sung by Dorothy and her friends sums the story up nicely:

> We're glad we found the Wizard—
> The fabulous Wizard of Odds!
> His good advice
> Is worth any price;
> So what if he rips off clods?
>
> He's making a fortune in rev-e-nues;
> He's raking it in . . . while suck-ers lose
> And lose, and lose, and lose,
> and lose, AND LOSE!
> And pays all his debts with I . . . O . . . U's! (36)

Once again, the prescience of *Mad*'s creative team is remarkable. Over a decade before his tumultuous presidency, they highlighted and mocked the con artist ambience of Trump's wealth and celebrity as well as his noticeable lack of compassion for those whom he calls "suckers" and "losers" (36).

Conclusion

Anyone can (and should) mock a truly terrible movie, and *Mad*'s parodies of overhyped, woodenly acted, atrociously written films are among the best around. The writers and artists of *Mad* magazine also found creative and often ingenious ways to mock or creatively play with some of the all-time classics of cinema. In doing so, they responded not just to the films' plots and characters, but also to how they were marketed, how their stars were glorified, and how even the best cinema contained dubious cultural beliefs. On a few occasions, *Mad* parodies even became fodder for powerful critiques of contemporary social and political trends. The parodies of *It's a Wonderful Life* and *The Wizard of Oz*, in particular, offered clever but also quite biting observations on the political figures of our times who used manipulative words and plot devices every bit as creaky as those of any low budget film of the past. This brief exploration of *Mad*'s movie parodies of beloved and acclaimed classic films demonstrates that the artists and writers utilized a great variety of approaches that included, but were not limited to, gags about the film world (movie plotting, exhibition, and overly enthusiastic film critics) in addition to wordplay, breaking of the fourth wall, and brilliant caricatures of familiar faces (including celebrities and political figures not in the original film). But the parodies always emphasized the influence of big business on the film industry, with decisions being based on marketing considerations, often at the expense of the art. If, as Daniel Boorstin wrote, we live in the time of "The Image,"[8] *Mad*'s reminders of the need to be aware of how that image can be manipulated by political figures is not just amusing, it is essential. It is often a small miracle that great films exist. As director Billy Wilder once said, when discussing the movie business, "They shouldn't shoot the script—they should shoot the deal."[9]

These satires allow us to have our cake (or popcorn) and eat it too. For the creators of *Mad*'s movie satires playfully remind us that we can still have quite a good time when we bring critical thinking even to the movies we love. And best of all, in spite of the mockery, the writers' and artists' affection for the films themselves always shines through. So even if they did hilariously point out an outrageous plot point or two in some of the films we adored—to quote Joe E. Brown at the end of another classic film, *Some Like It Hot*—"Well, nobody's perfect."

Notes

1. Quoted in Micah Mertes, "*Mad* Magazine Veterans Will Discuss Movie Parodies," paragraph 4.
2. Michael J. Socolow, "In Its Heyday, *Mad* Magazine Was A Lot More Than Silly Jokes," paragraph 1.
3. Ernest Becker, *The Denial of Death*, 74.
4. Roger Ebert, introduction to *Mad About the Movies: Director's Cut*, [i].
5. *Alfred Hitchcock's "The Birds,"* advertising poster.
6. Ficarra, introduction to *Mad's Greatest Artists: Mort Drucker: Five Decades of His Finest Works*, by Mort Drucker, 9.
7. Rick Steves, "The Sound of Music: Fact and Fiction," in *Rick Steves' Vienna, Salzburg and Tirol*, 6th ed., 274–75.
8. Daniel J. Boorstin, *The Image: A Guide to Pseudo-Events in America.*
9. Billy Wilder, interview by Johnny Carson, *The Tonight Show Starring Johnny Carson.*

12. A Golden Age of Blecch:

Mad Magazine's Parodic Satire of Quality Television

Ethan Thompson

AMONG *Mad*'S FAVORITE targets for ridicule over the years—movies, celebrities, comics, advertising—television has a special status. The medium's quick ascendance to cultural prominence in the postwar period closely tracked *Mad*'s own rise. While *Mad* found its footing in the 1950s, shifting from parodying comics to the magazine format and a broader satiric assault, the first so-called "Golden Age" of live television was in its prime, soon to be supplanted by telefilms produced in Hollywood. *Mad* was there from the very beginning, ridiculing relatively lowbrow and highbrow television alike. As the television industry has shifted strategies in response to advertisers seeking different kinds of audiences, as government oversight has ebbed and flowed, and as technological developments have impacted television production and distribution, *Mad* has reliably taken on whatever we call "TV" at the time. This scope makes sense. As a storytelling system, television is home to a multitude of genres and formats, which dependably generate programs that are formulaic yet unique enough for parody. Moreover, television is a commercial medium, which can be counted on to endlessly spawn that most hated of *Mad* targets, advertising. As the technology has changed (bigger sets, remote controls, color), as well as ways of watching (portable sets, streaming, binge-viewing), these developments have also entered popular conversation and therefore become ripe for satire, in addition to whatever programs people are watching.

When we go back and thumb (or click) through an issue of *Mad*, we can't separate out parody of television as easily as we can register which items parody a movie, or romance novels, or commercials. On the one hand, this difficulty reflects how "television" has encompassed programs, genres, a consumer technology, and an industry with numerous sectors (producers, networks, advertisers, etc.). But our difficulty arises also because television has embodied the contradictions of postwar culture at the heart of *Mad*'s satire: the so-called American good life, with its promise of plentiful, seemingly free entertainment and the repetitive "cheapness" of so much of it. TV program parodies did quickly become a *Mad* staple, but this essay will show how individual parodies were often a pretext for a broader satire of forces shaping American culture. This slant was most obvious in the pieces that focused on critically acclaimed, supposedly good-for-you television—the programs that critics lauded and the networks themselves promoted as the best that TV had to offer.

In this essay, I will examine the history of *Mad*'s treatment of television by focusing on what television scholars refer to as Quality TV. This term should not be understood as shorthand for canonical television agreed to be worthy of preservation and study. Rather, it is a historically contingent term for television programs treated by critics, promoted by the industry, and understood by audiences as embodying characteristics that differentiated those programs from other TV at the time. That is, Quality TV has been discursively constructed at various supposed Golden Ages in television history. In a commercial medium like television, the differentiation can never just be reduced to textual style or content—that is, as art only. Producing Quality TV has most often been about appealing to high-value audiences, whether those are affluent suburbanites who might buy a Cadillac in the 1950s, coming-of-age baby boomers who like their comedy socially relevant in the 1970s, or pay-cable subscribers who are told, "It's not TV, It's HBO" in the 2000s. In every decade, *Mad* has called "potrzebie" on all of this.[1]

I use the term *parodic satire* to refer to *Mad*'s comic critique of television. Although *parody* and *satire* are sometimes used interchangeably, they can be distinguished based on both their formal structures and targets. Margaret Rose makes this distinction: Parody is the comic refunctioning of preformed linguistic or artistic material, which makes its target part of its own structure, whereas satire has a target, but that target remains external to the structure of the satire.[2] In terms of what that target is, Steve Neale and Frank Krutnik offer that parody targets aesthetic conventions, satire social ones.[3] I employ the hybrid term *parodic satire* because, as we will see, *Mad* reliably used parody of particular aesthetic conventions within a program as a jumping off point for satire of the industry that produced those conventions, as well as contemporary events in American social and political life.

If we look back at the shifting production, promotion, and reception practices of television culture through the years, with the goal of understanding not how television has been made, but how it has been made *meaningful*, we can identify a variety of voices competing to impact what people think about TV. There is a long history of popular criticism, working to varying degrees in conjunction with the TV industry's promotional machinery. There have been interest groups who have waged campaigns to impact public opinion on issues such as sex and violence in the media. There is also a history of scholarly criticism of TV, ranging from the mass culture critique exemplified by the Frankfurt School, to social science effects studies, to the more humanities-oriented (and generally more optimistic) Television Studies influenced by the Birmingham School. At various times, *Mad* has countered critical praise of particular programs, ridiculed interest groups' complaints, and even echoed or anticipated scholarly critiques. The magazine's consistent parodic criticism has thus been another popular voice working within the culture, shaping how readers made sense of television. In their book *Legitimating Television: Media Convergence and Cultural Status*, Michael Z. Newman and Elana Levine show how the Quality label has been loaded with connotations beyond just whether TV was entertaining or educational. They argue that discourses on quality, produced by the TV promotional machine, the popular press, and even academic critics, necessarily differentiate between some kinds of television and others, and are often dependent upon preexisting cultural hierarchies and associations with other forms of good-for-you highbrow culture. Newman and Levine note that a key recurring characteristic of these discourses of legitimation is that most praise, at least in the popular press, has tended to neglect the industry logic that makes "Quality as much a calculated business decision as an artistic triumph."[4] *Mad*'s parodic satire has worked against these two tendencies of legitimating discourse: the notion that one program or type of program can have more cultural value than another, and the tendency to ignore the calculations that put TV shows on the air. Although the individual writers might differ, *Mad*'s critical voice has consistently identified markers of distinction as calculated formulas, with explicit references to ratings, production practices, and even going so far as to name prominent TV producers and executives, not just actor-celebrities. And, of course, *Mad* has refused to respect boundaries between highbrow and lowbrow culture of all kinds.

The 1950s–1960s: A Vast, Anything-But-Golden Wasteland

For an idea of how thoroughly television would infiltrate *Mad*, look through its last issue of the 1950s (#51, 12/59). The first feature is titled "How Advertising Slogans Will Replace Everyday Conversation" (Jacobs and Wood 4–6). TV was the most important advertising medium by the end of the 1950s, and many of the slogans would be familiar to readers from commercials. In the "At a Press Conference" sequence, a reporter questions a senator who bears a resemblance to Hubert Humphrey about what he thinks of the President's latest speeches. "Outstanding," he replies, "... and they are mild!"—echoing Pall Mall cigarette TV ads (6). A few pages later is a parody of CBS's *The Price Is Right*, then in only its third season (Siegel and Drucker, "The Night *The Price Is All Right* Has an Unexcited Guest," 12/59: 9–12). Rather than just lambasting the obvious commercialism of the show's premise, in which contestants attempt to guess the price of items, the parody targets the over-the-top enthusiasm of the contestants, dispatching an unenthusiastic one off into space. Another "special report" in the magazine reveals "Insurmountable Problem Discovered While Testing Civilians for Space Flight," such as how difficult it would be to survive a long period without "the careful relaxation [of] watching commercials on TV" (Jaffee and Wood #51, 12/59: 19-22; 20). "Hide-a-Bed," an article on convertible furniture, includes a television set Hide-a-Bed, "perfect for people who fall asleep watching late movies" (Berg, #51, 12/59: 32-35; 32). Joe Orlando's "TV Ads We'd Like to See" features a parody of a Schweppes soda water commercial (#51, 12/59: 27).

The very first issue of *Mad* made a passing reference to watching television, but the first "Television Dept." feature ran in issue #14. Like earlier pieces on *The Lone Ranger* and *Dragnet*, "The Countynental!" (Kurtzman and Davis, 8/54: 1–6) was written by Harvey Kurtzman. The earlier stories were parodies of what were by then well-established creative properties—essentially what we would today call transmedia franchises: "Lone Stranger!" (Kurtzman and Davis, #3, 1-2/53: 1-7), "Lone Stranger Rides Again!" (Kurtzman and Davis, #8, 12/53-1/54: 1-7), "Dragged Net!" (Kurtzman and "Sergeant" Elder, #3: 1-8).[5] Both The Lone Ranger and

Dragnet were successful radio programs prior to becoming television shows, and both extended into movie and print media as well. Unlike *Mad*'s parodies of these dramas, however, "The Countynental!" explicitly framed itself as being about television. Not only did it bear the label "Television Dept.," but the art by Jack Davis included scan lines so that each panel looked like a TV set—readers literally had to look at TV differently. The target was definitely not considered "highbrow" at the time; *The Continental* was a fifteen-minute program that aired late at night, at the end of CBS's primetime schedule, for just two years in the early 1950s. "The Countynental!" ridiculed the distinctive first-person address of the show, in which a suave European ladies' man welcomes the viewer inside his apartment, continually looking deep into the camera's eye. "The Countynental!" mines that address for humor, emphasizing the technical glitches of the medium, and the problems that might occur if the viewer was male, not female (see fig. 12-1).

Fig. 12-1: Panels in the first "TV Dept.," "The Countynental!," included scanlines and ridiculed the first-person address of *The Continental* (Kurtzman and Davis, *Mad* #14, 8/54: 2). MAD used with permission.

The scan lines on television department features lasted only a couple of issues, but *Mad* continued to communicate in substantive ways the notion that TV was something you looked at differently than other media. Like the movies, television was a visual, industrialized medium. But unlike the movies, television was a commercial, broadcast medium that inherited most of its industrial and narrative structures from radio. The major national radio networks (CBS, NBC, and ABC) quickly dominated television in the U.S., and that dominance and what is now referred to as the network era would last from the mid-1950s, at least, until the rise of cable in the mid-1980s, and arguably until the early 1990s. The radio networks were headquartered in New York, so that is where the TV networks were headquartered and where most national television production originated until the mid-1950s. Those television productions drew upon radio performers, but also the theater world of New York. Likewise, many of the first TV critics were New York theater critics. So, it should have come as no surprise that what they trumpeted as Quality TV in the early years was the television most like theater: anthology dramas.[6] These programs were live theater on TV: a new setting, new characters, and new story, performed live each week. In concert with the critical praise, networks promoted anthology dramas as prestige programming. As Newman and Levine write, "The power of the live television performance was seen not only as an artistic and technological achievement but also a profound experience for the viewer, who could be both in his home and in the on-screen world simultaneously, experiencing an immediacy that allowed for an understanding of 'authenticity, depth, and truth.'"[7] The critical and promotional discourse thus suggested the live anthology dramas weren't second-rate theater, but rather embodied TV's unique potential to transport the uplifting experience of Culture out of the theaters and big cities into private homes across America.

These issues surfaced in issue #43, in which *Mad* produced a one-page parody of *Playhouse 90* (CBS, 1956-1960), perhaps the most prestigious of the anthology dramas. Many associated with *Playhouse 90* would have successful careers both in and beyond television, including directors Arthur Penn, John Frankenheimer, Sidney Lumet, and George Roy Hill, writers Rod Serling, Horton Foote, and Tad Mosel, actors Charlton Heston, Paul Newman, Geraldine Page, Piper Laurie, and many more. *Mad*'s satire, "Payhouse 90," written by Nick Meglin (12/58: 41), opened with this introduction:

> We've always suspected that PLAYHOUSE 90, television's most honored dramatic show, was so named because of the number of commercials it had. And recently we discovered we were right. If you will study this cameraman's production schedule for a forthcoming presentation (that one of our spies swiped) you'll agree with MAD that a better name for the show would be . . . PAYHOUSE 90. (41)

The one-page piece reproduces the "swiped" schedule, which lists camera shots with brief descriptions of segments. Of all the segments of the ninety-minute show, only seven and a half minutes constitute the acts of the play, *Requiem for a Playwright*—a parodic reference to *Requiem for a Heavyweight*, the highly regarded 1956 *Playhouse 90* episode written by Rod Serling and starring Jack Palance. The rest of the show is dedicated to 1) segments where the host discusses the play and its production, and 2) commercials, which the host also reviews and summarizes. Therefore, the vast majority of the content is either explicitly commercial or hype from the host suggesting the significance of the play (and the commercials). Two handwritten notes suggest the need to further reduce the "content": One says that the first act (already just one minute) is short, so they need to "slow the rotator," suggesting that the act will be stretched out via the television camera's technology. Conversely, another note scribbled at the end says that the broadcast is running over (presumably from all the commercials), so a half minute will need to be cut from the 2½-minute second act (see fig. 12-2).

Nothing in "Payhouse 90" parodies the characters or story of *Requiem for a Heavyweight*, and as a work of humor, it really offers just one gag: *Playhouse 90*, the most prestigious program on television, is little more than commercial hype. But as satiric criticism, "Payhouse 90" ridicules the notion promoted by the television industry, and supported by critics, that one television program could be more sophisticated, more high-quality than another. The form of the satire is especially important: *Mad* spies "swiped" a cameraman's schedule, and therefore *Mad* readers get a behind-the-scenes look at how TV works. The satire is an early example showing that when *Mad* looked at television, it looked not just at the programs, characters, personalities, and stories, but also at the industry's practices, from the top executives making decisions about what gets made, to the cameraman working to get it on the air. A reader who picked up *Mad* was almost as likely to look at a typed-out sheet of paper,

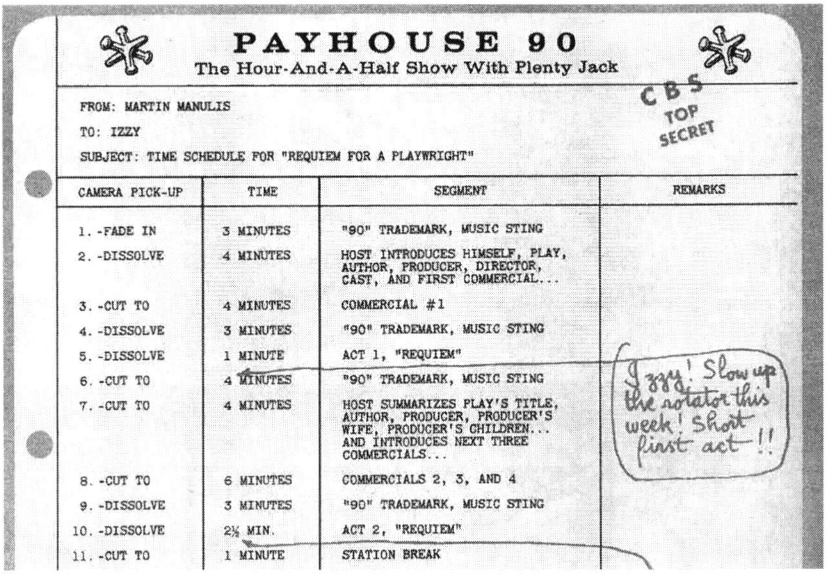

PAYHOUSE 90

The Hour-And-A-Half Show With Plenty Jack

CBS TOP SECRET

FROM: MARTIN MANULIS

TO: IZZY

SUBJECT: TIME SCHEDULE FOR "REQUIEM FOR A PLAYWRIGHT"

CAMERA PICK-UP	TIME	SEGMENT	REMARKS
1. -FADE IN	3 MINUTES	"90" TRADEMARK, MUSIC STING	
2. -DISSOLVE	4 MINUTES	HOST INTRODUCES HIMSELF, PLAY, AUTHOR, PRODUCER, DIRECTOR, CAST, AND FIRST COMMERCIAL...	
3. -CUT TO	4 MINUTES	COMMERCIAL #1	
4. -DISSOLVE	3 MINUTES	"90" TRADEMARK, MUSIC STING	
5. -DISSOLVE	1 MINUTE	ACT 1, "REQUIEM"	
6. -CUT TO	4 MINUTES	"90" TRADEMARK, MUSIC STING	Izzy! Slow up the rotator this week! Short first act!!
7. -CUT TO	4 MINUTES	HOST SUMMARIZES PLAY'S TITLE, AUTHOR, PRODUCER, PRODUCER'S WIFE, PRODUCER'S CHILDREN... AND INTRODUCES NEXT THREE COMMERCIALS...	
8. -CUT TO	6 MINUTES	COMMERCIALS 2, 3, AND 4	
9. -DISSOLVE	3 MINUTES	"90" TRADEMARK, MUSIC STING	
10. -DISSOLVE	2½ MIN.	ACT 2, "REQUIEM"	
11. -CUT TO	1 MINUTE	STATION BREAK	

Fig. 12-2: In Meglin's "Payhouse 90," *Mad* readers get a behind-the-scenes look at the production of the prestigious *Playhouse 90* (*Mad* #43, 12/58: 41). MAD used with permission.

allegedly swiped from behind the scenes, and thus seeing the view of TV from those making it, as he or she would see a TV scene itself, playing out before viewers. Network television programmers have long sought to create a seamless flow of segments (including the variety of programs themselves, commercials, previews of other programs, station breaks, etc.) in order to maintain a hold on viewers' attention throughout one program and into the next. But in "Payhouse 90," *Mad* not only makes a joke about commercials on supposedly prestigious TV, but also breaks TV back down into segments, which all look the same on the page and function the same for those behind the camera.

By the end of the 1950s, most TV programming had shifted from live broadcasts to telefilms produced by movie studios. The epicenter of TV had shifted to the West Coast, even if the top network executives remained in New York. Nonetheless, the American television industry seemed to be ticking along just fine when the newly installed chair of the Federal Communications Commission, Newton Minow, stepped onstage at the National Association of Broadcasters meeting in May 1961.

Minow immediately challenged broadcasters to do better: "I invite you to sit down in front of your television set when your station goes on the air and stay there without a book, magazine, newspaper, profit-and-loss sheet or rating book to distract you—and keep your eyes glued to that set until the station signs off. I can assure you that you will observe a vast wasteland."[8] Minow made it clear that considerations of quality would be made when judging whether broadcasters were serving the public interest, as they were required to do as beneficiaries of access to the publicly owned airwaves.

"Vast wasteland" became a popular catchphrase for referring to TV, and Minow himself became a target for comedians, including those working at *Mad*. As "Payhouse 90" and other satires showed, *Mad* writers and editorial staff were always skeptical that one form of commercial culture could be better for you than another. Issue #69 included a special "Feature Length MAD Look at TV" with seven separate TV-based satires. *Mad* name-checked Minow in the last, which proposed what would happen "When Culture Comes to Top-Rated Shows" (Siegel and Drucker, 3/62: 46–47). "We believe that shortly, in an effort to impress Mr. Minow, most TV shows will start riding the big 'intellectual wave.' However, there will be one little catch. Namely, even though they'll be going strong for more culture, the networks won't give up the basic formats of successful shows" (46-47). Creators Larry Siegel and Mort Drucker inserted contemporary symbols of high culture into existing popular TV shows' conventions, creating a comic clash. On *The Untouchables*, the mob traffics in bootleg copies of books by John Maynard Keynes, Willem Van Loon, and H. G. Wells, while Maria Callas appears on *American Bandstand*. The parody works only if readers are familiar not only with TV conventions, as well as at least the names of those writers, but also with discourses on taste.

Throughout the 1960s, *Mad* continued to satirize the television industry in items that did not focus on particular programs. *Mad* made fun of one of the more wasteful TV development practices, the intentional overproduction of TV shows, in "TV Pilot Films That Never Made It" (Hart and Drucker, #76, 1/63: 16–19). The piece explained how the typical development process works, with producers getting money to make a pilot, then hoping to get more money and support to bring it to series. In this way, *Mad* accurately described where TV shows came from, but also moved from parody to satire through intertextuality. The "new adventure show" is imagined to be a weekly look into our most vital intelligence operations, "Eye in the Sky: The Story of U-2 Pilot Francis Gary Powers," recently released from a KGB prison in an celebrated spy exchange after the Soviet Union shot down his CIA plane. The new musical program, "The Edsel Show," is sponsored by the famous flop from the Ford Motor Company. In "New Board Games We'd Like to See," *Mad* gave readers an opportunity to create their own network schedule: "Players draw cards which outline program formats for Westerns, Situation Comedies, Old Movies, Sports Events, Documentaries etc., and can either retain the cards or reject them. Object of the game is to try to accumulate the most innocuous, ridiculous, stupid, inane, improbable, idiotic and preposterous programs, as those are the kind that usually score the highest Nielsen ratings" (McGivern and Clarke, #102, 4/66: 32-34; 32).

Mad skewered the industry more severely in the April 1967 "The Television Network President of the Year," in which "Trublood" (Truman) Capote, fresh off the success of *In Cold Blood*, interviews Mr. Herman Avarice, one of the television executives guilty of "the most horrendous crime of the 20th Century" (Hart and Orlando, #110, 31–35; 31). Avarice explains that in his line of work, it's not ratings *per se* that matter. It's not important that there might be a lower number of people watching: "It's the interpretation of the statistics that counts!" (31). And indeed, executives do pay attention to market shares of the households actually watching TV, not just numbers. Elsewhere, Capote observes a development process that assesses pilots for originality, boldness, and imagination; if these qualities are found, the writers and directors are promptly fired. In another room, test audiences rate "like" versus "don't like" using machines quite close to the survey equipment long employed in program testing. The executive also explains that one strategy for relying on less original ideas is the "Switcheroo," which allows for producing two shows from every idea. "Take the *Beverly Hillbillies* for example. Country folks in the city, right? Switcheroo—and you get *Green Acres*! City folks in the country!" (34). Ultimately, the executive is revealed to be making television as lousy as possible because he has been paid off by the movie companies.

Ten years after Minow's vast wasteland speech, his name came up briefly in a parody of *My Three Sons*, which managed to stay on the air over the course of the 1960s and early 1970s by changing networks (ABC, 1960-1965; CBS, 1966-1972). "Some time back, Newton Minow called television a 'vast wasteland'!," TV dad Fred McMoron, recalls in

"My Three Sonny Boys" before he notes, "Obviously, he wasn't a regular viewer of the show I've been starring in for the past 11 years, or else he would have called it a 'vast slumberland'!" (Kogen and Torres, #142, 4/71: 43–47; 43). *My Three Sons* would be cancelled the following year, but it was being parodied by *Mad* for the first time. I mention this parody of *My Three Sons* at the end of its life cycle not just to show that Minow's critique (or at least his catchphrase) found its way into *Mad* again, but to point out one very important characteristic of *Mad*'s satiric treatment of television: with very few exceptions, the magazine did not parody particular programs more than once. TV staples such as *Gunsmoke*, on the air from 1955 to 1975 (CBS), got the full parodic treatment just once, in 1956; *Lassie* (CBS, 1954–1973) in 1960; *Law & Order* (NBC, 1990–2010) in 1994. This practice ignored the longevity of successful series, which lived on from year to year when renewed, and if they were lucky, in perpetuity once there were enough episodes for syndication.

Despite this apparent once-only rule, *Mad* revisited programs in other ways. Series might reappear as part of larger features, such as the previously mentioned piece in which culture comes to *The Untouchables* and *American Bandstand*, or the one in which *Lassie* gets the Stone Age treatment when other programs are transformed á la *The Flintstones*—both in issue #69 (3/62). Such reuse makes sense because television's past has always been embedded in its present through the prominence of syndicated TV reruns.[9] Though viewers could not search for an old sitcom episode to instantly access a clip from it the way that YouTube permits today, popular programs from the past lived on through syndicated reruns, even before the cable era. Reruns kept old shows alive in *Mad* readers' consciousness, where they could be targeted again by the magazine's writers and artists in features other than program-specific parodies. While the networks understandably promoted their current prime-time lineups, the TV programming that *Mad* targeted was the TV that its readers actually lived with: the TV of the past that endured as part of the TV present.

The 1970s–1980s: Relevance, Schmelevance

Despite Minow's efforts, there was no renaissance of critically acclaimed television during the 1960s. By the time *Mad* finally got around to parodying *My Three Sons*, the show was an obvious anachronism, a relic with little claim to cultural relevance. But few entertainment programs could make such a claim. The decade's convulsive social movements and events—civil rights, the Vietnam War, the women's movement, the assassinations of Martin Luther King, Jr., and Robert Kennedy—were seldom acknowledged in the era's entertainment programming.[10] But at the beginning of the 1970s, some big changes on network TV were afoot. CBS made the first big move, cancelling the very series *Mad*'s TV executive had cited back in 1967, *Beverly Hillbillies* (1962-1971) and *Green Acres* (1965-1971), as well as other top-rated shows, including *Mayberry R.F.D.* (1968-1971) and *Hee Haw* (1969-1971). Many of the cancelled shows had rural settings and were in fact very popular with audiences—just not the audiences whom advertisers now wanted. Advertisers wanted to attract the coming-of-age baby boomers who had been reared on television, were more educated and affluent, and had different cultural sensibilities than the generation before them.

Throughout the 1960s, the theory of least objectional programming, first formulated by NBC executive Paul Klein, had dominated network programming strategies. The key wasn't to develop television people really wanted to watch, but rather programming that would alienate the fewest people as they changed the channels looking for something to settle on. In practice, that meant programs shouldn't treat controversial topics, because those topics would alienate portions of the audience. In order to appeal to baby boomer audiences, however, CBS decided it needed programming that acknowledged and incorporated cultural change. In the early 1970s, key CBS programs *All in the Family*, *The Mary Tyler Moore Show*, *M*A*S*H*, and *The Bob Newhart Show* would even be programmed back to back on Saturday night, maximizing the flow of audiences believed to want the shows' contemporary relevance. In the case of *All in the Family* (1971-1979), relevance was based on showcasing the intergenerational arguments going on in many American households, rather than avoiding them.[11] Each episode presented a controversy *du jour* as the Bunker household erupted in dispute between Archie's reactionary values and those of the new generation, articulated by his daughter, Gloria, and especially her husband, Mike. In this way, the narrative structure of *All in the Family* encouraged the audience to experience the program as a kind of "cultural forum," to use Horace Newcomb and Paul M. Hirsch's term. In their formulation, television programs didn't indoctrinate viewers into particular ways of thinking, but neither did they serve as simple escapism. Rather, television offered an opportunity for viewers to encounter multiple ways of thinking about a subject, in a ritualized, "liminal" zone of meaningful play.[12] When *All in the Family* debuted in January 1971, the sitcom family seemed to have been radically recalibrated to appeal to a more educated and affluent audience than those who had been tuning in. CBS got those eyeballs and a whole lot more: designed to appeal to a younger, more liberal audience, *All in the Family* became a massive hit.

"Gall in the Family Fare" ran in the December 1971 *Mad*, a relatively quick turnaround for parodic satire of a series that had debuted earlier that year.[13] The introduction to the satire read:

> Ever since Television began, situation comedies have been, more or less, the same. Now, all of a sudden, a new situation comedy has come along . . . and it's entirely different from the old-fashioned family fare. It doesn't deal with the same old stupid subjects involving idiotic, unbelievable characters. Instead, it concerns itself with relevant "now" subjects, involving even more idiotic unbelievable characters! (Siegel and Torres, #147, 12/71: 43–47; 43)

Like most of *Mad*'s TV program parodies, which typically began with a two-page spread of key characters introducing themselves and describing the show, "Gall" opens as Starchie's long-suffering wife, here called "Meathead" (his epithet for son-in-law Mike on the show), welcomes the audience and introduces what she calls the special "shock-word" of the week: "faggot." Starchie immediately goes on a tirade, using as many ethnic and religious slurs as he can. Meathead addresses the reader: "Isn't he simply adorable, folks? See why America loves him so much?" When Meek, Starchie's liberal son-in-law, appears, he lays out the dual address to the audience: "We've got a special function on the show! While Conservatives in the audience identify with him, the Liberals can identify with us!" (44). This dichotomy is emphasized in the artwork for the parody. Meek's shirt is covered with a variety of political buttons and slogans, which change from panel to panel. In one, they include a peace symbol and Black Power fist; in another, "Naders Raiders" and "Close GM." Meanwhile, Starchie carries a newspaper with the headline "LINDSAY BOMBS," a reference to the liberal mayor of New York, John Lindsay. Indeed, an academic study in 1976 seemed to confirm Meek's assertion that the show successfully managed a dual address: while those who tested low for prejudicial attitudes in the study believed Archie's beliefs were being ridiculed, those who tested high found their convictions reaffirmed: Archie was just speaking his mind and being funny.[14]

Now that we are almost fifty years removed from *All in the Family*'s premiere, the reliability with which every episode turns to political or cultural debate is striking. Such explicit and authentic engagement with contemporary controversies never became dominant on television, nor was engagement dominant at the time. It was, however, a signpost of Quality TV in the 1970s. *All in the Family*'s embrace of controversy as simply another formula for producing commercial content was obvious to "Gall in the Family Fare" writer Larry Siegel. When Starchie locks himself in another room and starts rattling off another list of slurs, Gloriosky asks her mother what he is up to. "Reading the script for next week's show! It's gonna be the most controversial episode yet! It's called, 'A Visit From A Gay Black Jewish-Italian Commie Rapist With A Sinus Condition!" (45). The title of the particular episode in the parody is similar: "A Visit From A World War II Buddy." When that buddy shows up, he's not just any other old bigot like Starchie, he's Adolf Hitler. But Starchie and Hitler's visit is interrupted by two strangers showing up at the door. Hitler is sure that the War Crimes Commission has finally caught up with him, but he's in luck. It's a pair of TV executives, who've arrived to offer Hitler his own weekly TV show.

Mad may have exaggerated the extent to which TV executives would push controversy for the sake of ratings, but the way in which it showed how the formula of success for one TV show could be quickly copied for another was spot-on, even in the so-called relevant era. CBS and producer Norman Lear spun off a number of series from *All in the Family*, using the strategy of taking a character from one program and building a new series around him or her. *All in the Family* begat *Maude* (about Archie's liberal cousin) for six seasons from 1972 to 1978 and *The Jeffersons* (about Archie's African American neighbors) for eleven seasons from 1975 to 1985. *Maude* begat *Good Times* (about the family of Maude's African American maid) for six seasons from 1974 to 1979, and *The Jeffersons* begat *Checking In*, a sitcom that lasted just four episodes, about their maid, Florence, in 1981.

While *The Jeffersons* spent much less time on relevant topics, *Maude* (CBS, 1972-1978) seemed built to emphasize politics. Its titular character was a vocal middle-aged feminist and liberal activist who famously defied social and TV convention when she discovered she was pregnant and—after much discussion in a two-part episode—decided to have an abortion.[15] *Mad* parodied *Maude* one year into its run, in October 1973. In "Bawde, " writer Tom Koch and artist Angelo Torres portray Maude as a hypocrite, and by integrating references to commercial motivations, such as the ratings, the creators portray its well-known producer, Norman Lear, as a hypocrite as well (#162: 43–48).[16] The introduction reads, "After subjecting the American TV Viewing Public to 'All in the Family,' in which the Right-wing Reactionary point of view was thoroughly misrepresented, and bigotry was depicted as lovable, CBS is now blessing the Left-Wing Liberal point of view with *equal time* . . . and *equal misrepresentation*" (43). Bawde clears everyone out of the house so she can make calls for a voter registration drive, then tells Wallow, her husband, that she won't register him because he's the "very type we want to take the vote away from . . . a middle class white male!" When Girl Scouts ring the doorbell, selling cookies, Bawde attempts to sign them up as registered voters for the "Gay Liberation Party, the Universal Abortion Party, or the Pro-Porno Party." Then she adds, "You brats just gave me a chance to boost our Nielsen rating by shocking twenty million people three times in one sentence!" (44). As in an earlier parody of *The Mary Tyler Moore Show*, a definite strain of anti-feminism and sexism marks *Mad*'s ridicule of *Maude*. Those limitations do not, however, invalidate the insight in the satires' ridicule: TV's representation of feminist characters and politics is simply another commercial calculation.

Bawde balks when Wallow tells her they finally got accepted for membership in the club, assuming he means the country club. When he informs her that they will be joining the "Wife-Swapping Club," she is relieved, and revels in the anticipated response from a broadcast-era national audience: "Just think of all the hate mail we'll get from the Bible Belt!" (47). While the humor comes from portraying the absurdly liberal overreaching of Bawde, whose political actions are motivated by a desire to produce shock and ratings, the contextualization reveals the rifts in the country: in that era, television was a truly broadcast medium, addressing audiences across the country whatever their political beliefs or cultural tastes at the time. Bawde disappears from the final page of the comic as it shifts to Wallow arriving at the swingers club, where his match for the night turns out to be Edith Bunker. When Wallow says that she doesn't seem the type to be at such a place, Edith replies that she'd go anywhere to get away from her husband's tantrums, crazy opinions, and treating her like an idiot. "No kidding?? I thought I was the only one who had that kind of marriage," responds Wallow—to which Edith retorts, "The two of them are so much alike, you would think they were dreamed up by the same Producer!" (48). In its satires of both programs, *Mad* thus ridicules the turn toward social relevance as another industry strategy that was based on the attempt to garner ratings through shock, especially through character and plot devices that could be cloned into new series that might superficially articulate different political viewpoints but are ultimately motivated by the same commercial interests.

Whereas *All in the Family* inserted contemporary issues into the standard domestic sitcom format familiar to viewers, *The Mary Tyler Moore Show* (CBS, 1970-1977) innovated by shifting the typical setting and characters of the sitcom. Its protagonist was a young professional woman living on her own and pursuing the life of a television news producer, rather than a wife and mother. The show drew upon the feminist movement in a way that appealed to advertisers targeting working women with buying power.[17] *Mad* first satirized the program in a piece called "Truly Relevant TV Shows" in issue #149: "In case you haven't noticed, this has been the year on Television for what the Networks like to call 'Relevant' programs. What this means is 'telling it like it is' on every dramatic show that hits the tube" (Koch and Torres, 3/72: 8-13; 8). But rather than target specific programs, this frame allowed the magazine to go after those for whom it had true antipathy: not TV characters, but TV executives. The introduction continued: "For some mysterious reason, broadcasters haven't yet discovered a single thing wrong with the Television Industry itself, or the Sponsors that support it!" (8) In their one-page spoof, "The Mary Tailor-Made Show," Koch and Torres take us through the various reasons why Mary could be stopped from covering news due to the interests of the station's owners and managers. An airplane crash can't be covered because of airline advertisers; the mayor's embezzlement charges can't be covered because he's related to the station manager; the cop who routinely roughs up Mary can't be dealt with because that would ruin relations with the police department, and when the biggest company in town loses a contract and lays off 75,000 workers, it can't be covered because Lou, the news show's producer, owns stock in it. The newsroom premise of the show provides a jumping-off point to comically criticize forces behind the scenes of not just entertainment, but also the news industry, which impacts what is reported.

In December 1972, *Mad*'s cover featured *The Godfather*, but inside, the critical eye on TV turned to full-scale treatment of "The Mary Tailor-Made Show" (Koch and Torres, #155, 12/72: 43-48). The actual Mary character was a modern professional woman. She was attractive and well-dressed, developed and promoted to attract girl-next-door-type viewers. Thus, after making fun of how the characters on the fictional news show never really reported any news, *Mad* drew attention to what seemed to be, in the absence of journalistic gravitas, Mary's primary attribute: being attractive. "Let me change into another Christian Dior original first! I want to be among the world's ten best dressed $92-a-week flunkies!" she exclaims (44). She continues to change into different outfits throughout the piece. In one panel, she interrupts everyone to announce "Okay, gang! This is the weekly scene where I get to show off my legs!" Though she was a modern woman, Mary was not happily single, and *Mad* parodied her continual dating issues: "Being unmarried and over thirty, I need reassurance that I'm still desirable! Otherwise, I tend to wave my arms in neurotic gestures of desperation!" (44). "The Mary Tailor-Made Show" parody might be read as moving beyond parodic caricature into sexist rearticulation of the series' representation of a modern woman. In numerous panels, the male characters ogle Mary. After being told that the previous Tuesday's broadcast ranked first in the ratings, Lou tells Mary to get the same script and repeat it again. When someone suggests that reusing a news script might be a bad idea, Lou responds, "I know that! But I needed some excuse to get her to bend over the bottom file drawer in that short skirt!" and we see her backside reflected in the lens of a set of binoculars the male characters are sharing to look at her (48). I would argue that *Mad*'s pattern of explicit attention to industry practices emphasizes the construction of TV's representations, and this is amplified by the parodic self-consciousness, apparent in both the art and the text, of the male characters' sexist actions and comments. *Mad*'s parody is not normalizing the notion that Mary should be "looked at"; it is satirizing the fact that this is how the modern working woman is represented on television—whatever the feminist intentions of Moore or others working on the production. *Mad* does makes fun of Mary's neuroticism and her dating problems, but it emphasizes how the men in the newsroom—and those behind the scenes of the production—reduce her to legs, outfits, and that neurotic arm-waving. From the very title of the parody, *Mad* stresses that the character is "tailor-made," not just having designer outfits, but tailor-made by the industry.

*M*A*S*H* (CBS, 1972-1983) was another part of that relevant CBS Saturday night lineup, though it was less explicitly political than *All in the Family* and, by virtue of its Korean War setting, removed from modern life. It achieved Quality TV status by virtue of its genre blending, its ensemble cast, and its counterculture pedigree as an adaptation of the 1970 Robert Altman feature film. But *M*A*S*H* the TV show was TV, and *Mad*'s satire again stressed how the sitcom fit in the broader TV landscape. *Mad* readers were well accustomed to intertextuality in television parodies: characters from one television series would appear in another to make jokes, highlighting the fluidity of programming content as experienced by viewers who watched a variety of series on a variety of networks. Such fluidity could also lead to comic incongruity: for example, the Brady Bunch show up at the Bunkers' front door in "Gall in the Family Fare" (Siegel and Torres, #147, 12/71: 43-47; 45). But intertextuality in *Mad*'s TV satires did not just produce comic incongruity; it also illustrated industry formulas and practices. *Mad* showed how one show was scheduled to fit within the larger flow of programs, what was in front or behind, taking into consideration what was on the other channels. At the end of "M*A*S*H*UGA," main characters Cockeye and Crapper John tell a visiting general that they want out—of the series, not the war. "You'll never know how bad it is! You're only doing a Guest Spot! We're regulars! 26 weeks of War, with 13 repeats during the Summer! It's torture!" (Hart and Torres, #166, 4/74: 41–47; 47). The general informs them they can't get out, no matter how terrible things are, because they are "surrounded." "By the North Korean Army??" Cockeye asks. "No . . . by Archie Bunker in FRONT of you . . . and Mary Tyler Moore in BACK of you! You're getting great ratings whether you deserve them or not!" (47). The final panel of the satire sums up their situation by trapping the general, Cockeye, and Crapper John inside the famous CBS eye logo (see fig. 12-3).

By the end of the 1970s, *All in the* Family–style relevance had fallen from favor with audiences and programmers. But even as those programs ended, individuals associated with their production moved on to new productions as well as executive positions within the TV industry. Most prominent among them was Grant Tinker, who left MTM Enterprises

Fig. 12-3: *M*A*S*H* characters are trapped by the CBS schedule—and its logo—in the final panel of Stan Hart and Angelo Torres's parody, "M*A*S*H*UGA," in *Mad* #166 (4/74): 47. MAD used with permission.

(producer of not only *The Mary Tyler Moore Show* but also *The Bob Newhart Show* and many others) to become president of NBC in 1981. Jane Feuer writes that Tinker was widely seen at NBC as an executive pursuing the same MTM strategy of transforming the quality criterion into profits, accepting lower ratings in exchange for more impressive rankings among more highly valued demographics.[18] The flagship quality series from Tinker (and arguably the most critically acclaimed series of the 1980s) was *Hill Street Blues* (NBC, 1981–1987). When writer Tom Koch and artist Angelo Torres parodied *Hill Street Blues* in "Swill Street Blues" (#231, 6/82: 42-48), they poked fun at the very features that endeared it to critics: incompletely resolved storylines, complex characters, and moral ambiguity. The parody repeatedly talks about how many characters and plots are included, and how the audience must be confused. In the two-page opening spread, Koch included Grant Tinker as the last to introduce himself: "I'm Grand Tinkle, the President of NBC, and I've got the worst problem of all! I RENEWED this show, and I'll be in big trouble if they don't soon produce an episode that makes sense!" (43). Another panel displays a complicated chart that a character explains is not to track a crime: "It's the writers' story outline for next week's show!" (48). Like other *Mad* TV parodies dating back to "The Countynental!," "Swill Street Blues" ends with a look at the TV viewer subjected to the program. In this case, a man loses his mind because the story lines never finish at episode's end. He's taken away in a straitjacket while his wife and several characters from the program look on. "TWO YEARS, I watched it!! And I never understood a THING!! I can't STAND it any more!!" (48).

Mad recognized that complex story lines weren't the only quality strategy at work in Tinker-era NBC. Another drama in the *Hill Street Blues* mold was *St. Elsewhere* (1982-1988). *Mad* parodied it as "St. Healthscare" (Jacobs and Drucker, #281, 9/88: 4-8), but suggested that in this case, the program pushed boundaries of good taste as well as blended genres in order to appeal to audiences. "On this show we get ratings by blending medical drama with black humor and sitcom schtick!" says Ed Begley Jr.'s parodic double (6). Tinker's biggest commercial success at NBC was with a sitcom, *Cheers* (1982–1993). In discussing how *Cheers* constructed a quality appeal, Michelle Hilmes builds upon Feuer's discussion of the workplace family format pioneered by MTM. Hilmes notes that *Cheers* embodied the tensions between high and low culture characteristic of television, and as a product of Grant Tinker's NBC, *Cheers* was an attempt to appeal to quality viewers without alienating the masses. Writes Hilmes, "the central premise and characterization of *Cheers* reflects a desire to put high-culture and working-class types together in a neutral space and watch them interact."[19] In these cases from the 1980s, constructing Quality TV meant appealing to high-value consumers by incorporating more cutting-edge content (such as complex story lines, dark humor, sophisticated dialogue), but grounding that content in well-established genres to maintain the broad appeal still necessary for success in primetime network television.

Mad seized on the audience-blending desire that, to Hilmes, shaped *Cheers* right from the start. In "Beers," two men in hard hats chat at the bar, while *Today Show* critic Gene Shalit chats with actor Judd Hirsch nearby. One man says, "I been diggin' ditches, pullin' wires an' layin' cable all day! But now . . . it's SOPHISTICATED COMEDY TIME!" (Kogen and Torres, #249, 9/84: 44–48; 45). Meanwhile, Shalit tells Hirsch, "As a TV Critic, I must say the 'writing' is crisp, the 'relationships' deep and the 'regulars' quirky! In all my years of watching TV SitComs, I don't ever remember this level of intelligent humor!" Hirsch responds: "I do!! When WE did it, a year ago . . . In our late, great TV Series called 'TAXI'!" (45). Indeed, the critically acclaimed but low-rated *Taxi* (ABC, 1978–82; NBC, 1982–83) had been co-created by James L. Brooks, who had been one of the creators of *The Mary Tyler Moore Show*. The extent to which *Cheers* was understood to be not just another typical sitcom is amplified in the parody a little later: When a customer at the bar complains that he invited his vegetarian boss over for dinner and his wife has prepared meatloaf, the series' protagonist, Sham, kicks him out, yelling, "This is a hip, Emmy Award-winning show with a fresh new concept! Don't EVER come in here with a 1950's standard 'I Love Lucy'-type SitCom Premise AGAIN!!" (46).

By the mid-1980s, gimmicky plotlines indeed were not acceptable as plotlines for Quality TV comedy, but neither were the cultural clashes and relevant topics of *All in the Family*. Most sitcoms had reverted to a conservative state, with family sitcoms like *Family Ties* (NBC, 1982-1989) or *The Cosby Show* (NBC 1984-1992) rehashing plotlines that could have been featured on *Leave It to Beaver* (CBS, 1958-1958; ABC, 1958-1963) or *The Donna Reed Show* (ABC, 1958-1966). *Mad* was no less critical of TV industry practices than in earlier years, but typically had characters in parodies of individual programs self-consciously reflect upon the production process and industrial forces rather than unmask industry norms via satire. The 1980s had not yielded a golden age of TV, but programs such as *Hill Street Blues*, *St. Elsewhere*, and *Cheers* won praise as different and better, though they were largely seen as the result of particular writer-producers and savvy executives, rather than as emblematic of broader trends.

The 1990s–2000s: It's Not TV, It's Cable (Or Something Like It)

In the 1980s, cable service spread to communities throughout the country, and cable channels increasingly siphoned audiences from the broadcast networks. In the mid-1990s, a number of network series drew attention and critical favor, largely as a result of network TV working to connect with upscale viewers who would otherwise abandon the networks for the movies and original programming to be found on cable.[20] Perhaps the most radical example was *Twin Peaks* (ABC, 1990–1991), a program thoroughly steeped in the surrealism of its co-creator, film auteur David Lynch.[21] As Newman and Levine note, discourses on elevating the cultural level of TV programming had often been associated with a particular company, such as MTM, but more typically with a particular program, such as *Hill Street Blues*. But with *Twin Peaks*, the discourse began to suggest that a larger shift was taking place in television.[22]

A high-water mark in this discourse suggesting another golden age was a piece by *New York Times Book Review* editor Charles McGrath in 1995, "The Triumph of the Primetime Novel." McGrath minced his words, declaring only a "sort of" golden age, and immediately specified that talk shows, sitcoms, and prime-time soaps were not to be considered part of the trend. But he also clarified that he didn't mean supposed "highbrow TV like 'Masterpiece Theater.'" Instead, he pointed toward a number of network dramatic series: "These shows are flourishing in a way that they haven't since the very early days of the medium, and have grown in depth and sophistication into what might be thought of as a brand-new genre: call it the primetime novel." McGrath praised *E.R.* (NBC, 1994-2009), *NYPD Blue* (ABC, 1993-2005), and *Law & Order* (NBC, 1990-2010), crediting the writers for bringing their literary pedigrees to the tried-and-true TV genres of police and hospital shows, resulting in more complex characters and multiple perspectives on issues being represented.[23]

Premiering in September 1993, *NYPD Blue* had an impeccable Quality TV pedigree. It was produced by Steven Bochco, co-creator of *Hill Street Blues* while at MTM Enterprises. He had subsequently co-created and produced the critically acclaimed *LA Law* (NBC, 1986–1994). His partner was writer David Milch, who had worked five seasons as writer, producer, and story editor on *Hill Street Blues*. Their new plan, though, was to push the boundaries of content acceptable in a police drama—a variation on what *All in the Family* had done with the sitcom. In contrast to familial culture clashes, *NYPD Blue* would have more nudity and coarse language than had been seen or heard before in a network series, a strategy to attract viewers who might otherwise seek those things on pay-cable.[24]

It was not a particularly subtle strategy, nor was *Mad*'s acknowledgment of it. The cover of issue #329 (8/94) promised to "expose" the program, which had successfully garnered attention with its occasional nudity. The illustration by Mort Drucker featured the cast, as well as Bochco, holding letters precariously covering their genitals and spelling out "NYPD Blue" At the opening of the satire, "NYPD Boobs," a scene inside the station is interrupted by a behind-the-scenes panel showing Bochco and a Reverend Darnold Wildman, head of the TV watchdog group Christian Right against Pornography, alongside a television camera and mic, suggesting they are watching as the program is being shot (Hart and Drucker, 7/94: 7–13). When the thinly disguised caricature of Rev. Donald Wildmon of Christian Leaders for Responsible Television (CLEAR-TV) complains that the TV show is disgusting, pointing out that a woman is totally nude, Bochco counters, "If you think that's disgusting, just wait till HE [pointing to a caricature of portly actor Dennis Franz] gets undressed!" (8). These interruptions carry on throughout the piece: a few panels from within the story world are followed by a panel with Bochco and Wildman arguing over the merits of the show. In one, Bochco concedes that he could do a show that would reaffirm Christian traditions by doing stories from the Bible—Adam and Eve romping nude in the Garden of Eden, Samson getting his eyes gouged out, Jesus throwing the money changers down the temple steps—and Wildman allows that on second thought maybe a Bible-based series wouldn't be such a good idea. The last page of the piece is emblematic of how television's intertextual tendencies can be parodied, resulting in satire targeting much more than the supposedly quality aspects of one TV show. In the top panel, President Bill Clinton asks the lead detective for advice on passing healthcare reform; in another, the Pope asks *him* about allowing priests to marry; and in another, a character asks if what is going on is a subplot of (that other Bochco series) *LA Law*. Finally, two new cops show up at the precinct who are "real sadists with no moral scruples at all": cartoon characters and stars on basic cable's MTV, Beavis and Butthead (13). The intertextual reference is not a comic incongruity just because the two characters are cartoons. They were also the most maligned characters on all of television at the time for being so thoroughly lowbrow: teenagers who spent their time watching (and ridiculing) TV when they weren't participating in vandalistic mayhem. Again in this parody, *Mad* rejected the boundaries between the allegedly highbrow and lowbrow.

Competition with cable programming first prodded broadcast networks to produce shows with more violence, sex, and explicit language in order to appeal to highly desired Quality TV viewers. But HBO further upped the ante with more original dramatic series at the end of the 1990s. As Deborah Jaramillo has written, *The Sopranos* was a major step in HBO's production not just of a particular original program, but of its "quality brand."[25] That brand would be extended as HBO repeated *The Sopranos*' formula of taking pre-existing genres from prime time, embracing the seriality and melodrama of daytime TV, and exploiting the lack of FCC restrictions regarding nudity and violence on cable television. HBO employed the same strategy at work since the 1970s: appealing to a Quality demographic not to sell audiences to advertisers, but to appeal to subscribers with TV that they couldn't find anywhere else and thus were willing to pay for.

HBO's golden era was kicked off by *The Sopranos* (1999-2007) and rolled into the 2000s with such dramatic series as *Deadwood* (2004-2006), *The Wire* (2002-2008), and *Six Feet Under* (2001-2005), as well as the comedies *Curb Your Enthusiasm* (2000-present) and *Sex and the City* (1998-2004). *Mad* caught on quickly to what was going on at HBO, satirizing *The Sopranos* after its first season in "The Supremos" (Kogen and Drucker, #389, 1/00: 6–11). The spoof not only outs the show's apparent high-concept pitch—"Godfather Knows Best" (6)—but also references episodes that have become iconic for *Sopranos* fans, as O'Sullivan notes.[26] By the time *Mad* satirized *Six Feet Under* in June 2002, a year into its run, the publishing industry had been thoroughly shaken by consumers shifting their attention to the Internet, and *Mad* had begun accepting advertising. Still, in "Six Feet Blunder," written by Charlie Kadau with art by Angelo Torres (#418: 46-50), the magazine stuck to its tradition of interrogating TV culture, not just particular shows, yet the parody showed how *Mad* could sometimes be ahead of the curve on social issues and other times lag behind. "Six Feet Blunder" renamed one of the key characters, David Fisher, "Gayvid Fishead"—a detail that on the one hand reflects the centrality of his homosexuality to the series, and on the other indulges a cheap homophobic joke. But the satire also takes perfect aim at industry pressures on the series. As each episode began with a death that the family funeral business would take care of, so "Six Feet Blunder" opens with a network television executive who dies of a heart attack after seeing the new fall season's ratings. While Fishead prepares the body, the corpse begins talking to him (as they would sometimes do on the actual show): "I died when I realized the broadcast networks are at a disadvantage! We can't do the bold, ground breaking programming that pay channels like HBO can! . . . Advertisers wouldn't buy commercials on programs that are so sexually explicit or violent!" (50). When Fishead asks, "Well, what kind of shows will they buy commercials on?" the corpse replies, "Shows that attract millions and millions of viewers!" Fishead sets up the punchline: "But you just said programs like HBO's were attracting millions and millions of viewers! Your reasoning makes no sense!" To which the corpse responds, "Now you see why I had a freakin' heart attack!" (50). With such dialogue, *Mad* succinctly summarized the pressures that original, made-for-cable programming was putting on network TV. It was not cable's greater quantity of original TV for advertisers that undermined network hegemony; it was the freedom of cable channels—whether a pay-channel like HBO, or a hybrid advertising/pay station like AMC or FX—from FCC constraints.

Mad also kept up the satiric intertextuality. At the end of "Six Feet Blunder," Arliss Michaels, the lead character in an HBO comedy about a sports agent, shows up at the funeral parlor and offers to solve the family's financial problems by delivering all the corpses from HBO's original programs. "Just think! Every week some convict takes a shiv on *Oz*, or some wiseguy gets whacked on *The Sopranos*! Sometimes two or three! You'll get the funeral job for all of them! And if Samantha boinks some guy to death on *Sex and the City*, you'll get that too!" (50). This intertextual visit was justified not because the programs that Arliss mentions were generically similar, but because they were all "HBO shows"—they aired on HBO, they were produced by HBO, and they were all branded "HBO, not TV." *Mad*'s satire of HBO's comedy *Curb Your Enthusiasm* (2000-present), starring *Seinfeld* co-creator Larry David, made a similar intertextual callout to the HBO brand in "Absurd, Their Enthusiasm" (Gordon and Torres, #438, 2/04: 40–44). "You put such a negative spin on everything!," says his agent and confidant, Jeff Garlin. "I have to!" answers Larry. "Look at the success *of Six Feet Under*, *The Sopranos*, and *Carnivale*—shows about death, ruthless organized crime families, and seamy carnie life! This isn't feel good TV, this is HBO!" (40). The piece also recognized HBO's targeting of affluent, cosmopolitan viewers on the coasts. When Larry and Jeff talk about what will happen in the episode, and Jeff asks if any of it will play in Middle America, Larry responds, "On this series, Middle America ends at Wilshire and Rodeo!" (40). So much for the letters from the Bible Belt giddily anticipated by Bawde in 1973.

Such a broad audience was a relic of the broadcast era, not something to be considered on HBO.

As had been the case since the 1950s, when Harvey Kurtzman and Jack Davis refashioned the Army-McCarthy hearings as a TV quiz show in "What's My Shine!" (#17, 11/54: 7-1 [sic]), parody of cable dramas served as jumping-off points for political satire, not just shots at the TV industry. One of the more significant of programs, because of how it brought HBO-style narrative complexity and violence to basic cable, was *The Shield*, which aired on FX from 2002 to 2008. The series centered on corrupt police officers who run a special strike team in Los Angeles. *Mad* satirized *The Shield* in "The Blue Shield," written by Charlie Kadau and drawn by Angelo Torres (#437, 1/04: 8–13). The piece ends with President George W. Bush showing up in lead detective Sick Wacky's office to recruit his team to work for his administration. When Wacky tells the captain his team is quitting and is asked, "What? Did your consciences finally catch up with you?" Wacky replies, "Far from it! We're working for the White House now! Seems they need to make sure some weapons of mass destruction are found in Iraq! We're going over there to 'look' for them . . . you follow?" (12). Whatever their merits as Quality TV pushing the boundaries of acceptable content, the newly complex and compelling cable dramas provided an opportunity for political commentary—if not within their own content, then within their *Mad* satires.

Conclusion: Surviving Peak TV

The boom in original dramatic productions of the sort associated with the new golden age of TV came first to pay cable (HBO), then to basic cable (FX), and then to streaming services (Netflix). As original dramatic programming has proliferated, the discourse on television quality has become so inflated that commentators no longer gain traction by positing the existence of a special series or even a trend on a channel or within a genre. In 2015, John Landgraf, head of the FX network, coined a term in front of the Television Critics Association that has since been embraced nearly as widely as Minow's "vast wasteland," though it is essentially its antithesis. Landgraf declared an era of "Peak TV," suggesting that so much quality television programming now exists that no era could possibly have more, and registering his fear that the proliferation of original series would prevent viewers from finding TV that they would enjoy.[27] When he spoke, a surge in production from streaming services like Netflix, Hulu, and Amazon Prime had pushed original scripted series to over 400 that year. Of course, there has always been more TV than any single person could watch. But Landgraf was clearly asserting that now too much TV was *worthy* of being watched. Too much TV for mere mortals to keep up with, not to mention for talented people to produce—and, crucially, too much for current commercial or subscription models to support. *Mad* has done its best to keep up. Its satire of bellwether Netflix series *Orange Is the New Black* (2013-2019) in December 2014, "Orange Is the New Blecch," ended with its protagonist, Hyper Chaplips, a prisoner in a women's prison, wondering if anyone can understand the prisoners' "hellish experience" (Devlin and Richmond, #530: 13–20; 20). Chaplips laments, "Trapped! Listless! Unable to leave! We just sit and sit, and we stare and stare. Rotting away, growing more numb by the hour, as we wonder when, and how, it's all going to end! Can anyone know how we feel?" "Yes!" another exclaims. "Everybody out there who spends their days binge-watching entire TV seasons at once!"—and to back up her point *Mad* shows us a couple of slob-like "TV viewers" again, now watching via laptop and cell phone (20).

Throughout its history, television's detractors—whether critics, intellectuals, or interest group spokesmen—have often treated TV as a medium that can be essentialized, criticized, and condemned without bothering to describe specific programs, practices, or people. On the other hand, more generous critics have praised particular programs or even designated periods as golden, but always at the expense of other TV. *Mad*'s parodic satire has maintained a steady critical approach: television is a vast textual universe, produced and programmed by individuals with agency, but overwhelmingly determined by commercial interests. *Mad*'s parodies have targeted particular programs but have often moved quickly into broader satire with references to other programs, as well as to people and practices in a much broader context. Going back to see what *Mad* has had to say about the televisual past is a good reminder of how wise its writers and artists, and therefore its readers, could be to shifts in the culture. It is also a reminder that the magazine has never been only about being funny. *Mad*'s parodic satires of television programs have moved quickly from aesthetic to social conventions, constituting a vibrant voice commenting upon twentieth—and now twenty-first—century culture.

Notes

1. For a more theoretical examination of *Mad*'s approach to television parody, see Ethan Thompson, "What, Me Subversive? *Mad* Magazine and the Textual Strategies and Cultural Politics of Parody," 45–75.

2. Margaret A. Rose, *Parody: Ancient, Modern, and Post-Modern*, 52.

3. Steve Neale and Frank Krutnik, *Popular Film and Television Comedy*, 19.

4. Michael Z. Newman and Elana Levine, *Legitimating Television: Media Convergence and Cultural Status*, 25.

5. Kurtzman and Elder collaborated on a second spoof of *Dragnet*, with the same title, in #11 (5/54): 1-7, discussed by Nathan Abrams in chapter 14, 328, for its Jewish inflections.

6. See William Boddy, *Fifties Television: The Industry and Its Critics*.

7. Newman and Levine, *Legitimating Television*, 20–21.

8. Newton Minow, "Television and the Public Interest," speech to the National Association of Broadcasters.

9. See Derek Kompare, *Rerun Nation: How Repeats Invented American Television*.

10. For some exceptions, see Aniko Bodroghkozy, *Groove Tube: Sixties Television and the Youth Rebellion*.

11. See Norman Lear's comments in the film documentary directed by Marlon Riggs, *Color Adjustment*.

12. Horace Newcomb and Paul Hirsch, "Television as a Cultural Forum," 564, 563.

13. The satire was adapted into sound on a 33 1/3 record included in *Mad Super Special Number 11* (1973). The audio version was condensed (and censored), but the special issue included the uncondensed satire as it originally appeared in the magazine.

14. Neil Vidmar and Milton Rokeach, "Archie Bunker's Bigotry: A Study in Selective Perception and Exposure," 42.

15. The two episodes of "Maude's Dilemma" chronicled the 47-year-old character's decision process, which ended in her abortion and her husband's vasectomy. "Maude's Dilemma," directed by Bill Hobin, teleplay by Susan Harris, story by Austin Kalish and Irma Kalish, *Maude*, season 1, episodes 9-10, CBS, November 14 and 21, 1972.

16. As in the parody of *The Mary Tyler Moore Show* that ran before it, there is a definite strain of anti-feminism and sexism in *Mad*'s ridicule of *Maude*. I don't wish to dismiss that, but I believe the emphasis in the ridicule is on TV's representation of feminist characters and politics as simply another commercial calculation.

17. Charlotte Brunsdon, Julie D'Acci, and Lynn Spigel, *Feminist Television Criticism: A Reader*, 10. For an in-depth examination of *The Mary Tyler Moore Show* and its feminist cultural context, see Serafina Bathrick, "The *Mary Tyler Moore Show*: Women at Home and at Work," 99–131.

18. Jane Feuer, "MTM Enterprises: An Overview," 27.

19. Michelle Hilmes, "Where Everybody Knows Your Name: *Cheers* and the Mediation of Cultures," 68.

20. For an examination of one of the network's attempts at a more "quality" idiosyncratic program, see Betsy Williams, "North to the Future: *Northern Exposure* and Quality Television," 141–54.

21. Remarkably, and unfortunately, *Mad* did not parody *Twin Peaks* during its original two-season run.

22. Newman and Levine, *Legitimating Television,* 27.

23. Charles McGrath, "The Triumph of the Prime-Time Novel."

24. For more on *NYPD Blue*'s intentional boundary pushing and the regulatory consequences, see Jennifer Holt, "*N.Y.P.D. Blue*: Content Regulation," 271–80.

25. Deborah Jaramillo, "The Family Racket: AOL Time Warner, HBO, *The Sopranos,* and the Construction of a Quality Brand," 59.

26. Sean O'Sullivan, "*The Sopranos*: Episodic Storytelling," in *How to Watch Television*, ed. Ethan Thompson and Jason Mittell, 65-73.

27. Cynthia Littleton, "FX Networks Chief John Landgraf: 'There Is Simply Too Much Television.'"

13. Folding Against the Establishment:
Al Jaffee's Back Cover Feature in *Mad* Magazine

Kerry Soper

AS A DEVOTED preteen reader of *Mad* magazine in the mid-1970s, I was fascinated by the weirdness of Al Jaffee's back cover fold-ins. While the rest of the magazine felt like a familiar extension of the popular culture I avidly consumed on a daily basis (spoofs of *Star Wars*, *Charlie's Angels*, or the latest consumer fads), the inside back cover with its putridly bright colors and mechanically constructed satirical point was always unsettling—the mesmerizing product of a funny and unconventional mind. And although I wouldn't have been able to articulate this idea at the time, these fold-ins felt more legitimately antiestablishment in their tone and messages than the rest of the humor in the magazine. Perhaps they stood apart for several reasons. First, it was clear that Jaffee invested a great deal of effort and thought into creating the page; while many of the cartoons and caricatures in the black-and-white interior pages seemed flippantly (albeit, impressively) executed in pen and ink, this glossy back cover fold-in featured garish colors, painstakingly detailed brushwork, twisted human figures, and a hidden visual and verbal message that obviously required some brilliant planning to construct. Second, although Jaffee often used juvenile gags in many of his fold-in creations, the tone of the page seemed more political than the rest of the magazine (it often had something indignant to say about pollution, corruption, or moral depravity). Moreover, there was a moral weightiness to some of Jaffee's political symbols: skulls, mushroom clouds, toxic pools, leering faces, etc.—icons that were fascinating and sometimes disturbing to a preteen mind. Finally, this feature required effort to read or decode; one had to carefully fold (and sometimes refold) the page in order to create the magical reveal of Jaffee's key satiric point.

As an adult, academic-minded reader, I find the relative strangeness and antiestablishment subversiveness of Jaffee's work—in comparison to the rest of the magazine—even more pronounced. In this study I attempt to explain that difference using a number of commonsensical and theoretical frames: a description of how Jaffee negotiated the institutional and economic challenges of creating independent-minded satire at *Mad*; a discussion of the degree of critical, satiric distance that Jaffee's parodic work achieved from its targets; a detailed analysis of the peculiar aesthetics of the inside back cover (especially in comparison to equally expressive work in traditional schools of art); and some speculations about the intellectual impact of a text that requires the physical act of page-folding to create its meaning. The general conclusion will be that while many of the parodies in the interior pages of *Mad* were ambivalent in their treatment of targets (often simultaneously denigrating *and* celebrating the mainstream texts they lampooned), Jaffee's fold-in feature was more genuinely counterdiscursive. Those subversive qualities were an outgrowth of a number of factors: Jaffee's auteur-like clout at the magazine, the feature's peculiar aesthetic choices and satiric methods, Jaffee's distinctively left-leaning politics, and the physical mechanisms of the fold-in itself.

To begin broadly (moving from the magazine as a whole to Jaffee's back cover fold-ins), one can qualify claims made by some pundits that the magazine in sum was a significant countercultural or antiestablishment force in the 1960s and 1970s. While its irreverent tone did help to shape the satiric sensibility of several generations of comedians and the public, it was still, in essence, a mainstream publication with writers, artists, and editors intent on making a decent living by distributing a magazine through accessible venues to a mass readership. To achieve that economic objective, the magazine's comic material was filtered through an internal vetting process that did not amount technically to a form of censorship, but that worked in practice as a vaguely conservative corralling of excessively raunchy or countercultural material. In particular, the publisher, Bill Gaines, was loath to raise the ire of cultural guardians after suffering through an awful public inquest of his horror and crime-themed comics in the 1950s. Jaffee explained the trepidation that haunted his publisher: "Bill had a strict sense of what was right or wrong. He didn't want to publish something that might be unpalatable to the readers or, in the case of the younger readers, their parents." And he often nixed the most subversive or offensive content with the business maxim "It won't help our sales if we get our asses tossed off big newsstands." In other words, Gaines wanted humor that remained safely within acceptable mainstream boundaries, and that was more about generalized, juvenile irreverence than pointed political or ideological subversion (or, as Jaffee put it, "bad taste that was in good taste").[1]

It was beneficial to the magazine's image during its 1960s and 1970s heyday, however, to give the impression that it was full of uncensored comic anarchy that challenged the establishment. For example, the creators of the magazine were advertised as "Madmen" or "The Usual Gang of Idiots" who were incorrigibly offensive in their satiric attacks. As a result, young readers could easily imagine that there was an office in New York City overrun by young, punkish artists and writers, gleefully targeting all that was hypocritically earnest and noble in the mainstream culture. The reality was much more tame: most of the contributors were eager-to-please, middle-aged, working-class artists who had no ownership over their work (standard *Mad* contracts ceded all rights to the publisher) and were trying to support families in the suburbs by figuring out the best way to sell more material and appease touchy publishers like Gaines. Many of these artists, in fact, were casualties of downturns in the comic book market or frustrated artists who couldn't break into the staid comic strip industry. Jaffee, for example, had worked tirelessly, but without enthusiasm, in teen comics for ten years before becoming a freelancer for *Mad*; and although he preferred the consistent work he got from Gaines, he was perpetually insecure—a "longshoreman," in his words, always hoping "for a day's work."[2]

And while readers might have imagined their favorite artists behaving independently, choosing deserving targets based on righteous indignation or a spirit of recklessness, here too the reality was quite different. In most cases (except for some key exceptions, as we'll see with Jaffee's fold-ins), artists were assigned topics by market-minded editors and then were required to submit their finished work for meticulous scrutiny and editing before it could be published. For example, the featured parodies of movies, TV shows, and popular books in the magazine were determined by editors who would "peruse newspapers and magazines, see what's on and what's coming out soon, trying, as best as they [could], to gauge what's going to be hot."[3] This search for the brightest signals on the mainstream radar—over the deeper motivations associated with genuinely indignant satire—points toward the fundamental conflict within the magazine's humor: a simultaneous mockery *of,* and reliance *on,* the popularity and recognizability of its mainstream targets.

Linda Hutcheon's ideas about the conflicted nature of parody help to explain this idea: because an imitative comic text relies on a reader's awareness of the targeted cultural product, and inevitably repeats many of the core elements of the original work, it "always implicitly reinforces even as it ironically debunks."[4] In other words, repetition—and a focus on triggering recognition—results in a celebration or reification of the popular text as much as its denigration. That ideological ambivalence is especially pronounced in the aesthetics of the *Mad* parodies that tackled TV shows or movies that were marketed in large part as eye candy for young adult males—franchises like *Charlie's Angels* or the James Bond movies. In these installments, artists such as Angelo Torres, Mort Drucker, or Jack Davis had a tendency to highlight the pin-up qualities of the female characters, effectively celebrating (at least visually, if not in the written text) the objectified physical features that might have drawn young men in the first place to those mainstream cultural products. And the fact that some of the most iconic artists from the magazine, like Mort Drucker and Jack Davis, also drew cartoons for magazines like *Playboy* and created movie posters with pin-up style treatments of female actresses reinforced the conflicted quality of these parodies.

Hutcheon acknowledges, nevertheless, that not all parodic texts are alike; some are better than others at subverting their targets. She concedes, for example, that there is a spectrum of ideological tones in parody—from "respectful to playful to scathingly critical"—and that the best, most satiric modes are marked by a "repetition with critical distance, which marks difference rather than similarity."[5] That notion of a spectrum based on degrees of difference and distance effectively provides a rubric for comparing Jaffee's work to the featured, internal parodies in the magazine. On the one hand, the caricatures and distortions in parodies of TV shows like *Charlie's Angels* could be easily blurred between one text and another, moving from mockery to celebration with very little shift in tone or treatment (or, in Hutcheon's terms, very little "difference or distance"). On the other hand, as I will illustrate, Jaffee's fold-ins, though at times still somewhat ambivalent in their treatment of mainstream targets, were more consistently and legitimately counterdiscursive than other features in the magazine because of Jaffee's success at creating a greater degree of textual and ideological distance/difference from his targets.

Those distinctions are difficult to measure, of course, given that Jaffee's cartoon paintings covered so many different targets over a forty-plus year career; it is also impossible to survey accurately the thoughts and reactions of preteen readers from decades ago. Nevertheless, a focused analysis of the possible meanings and uses of several representative installments from the 1970s might allow one to make a tentative case for the exceptionally subversive qualities of Jaffee's work. In effect, using Hutcheon's rubric for assessing the relative satiric punch of a parodic text as a starting point, one can triangulate a number of factors related to the production, form, and functions of the fold-in to argue for its genuinely subversive qualities: Jaffee's auteur-like independence and status at *Mad*; the unusually dark and moralistic brand of satire at work in many of the fold-ins; the genuinely grotesque aesthetics in Jaffee's paintings; and the possible psychological meanings and uses of the fold-in mechanism itself.

Jaffee's fold-ins began as a parody of the slick centerfolds or fold-outs that were popular in mainstream magazines like *Life*, *Playboy*, or *Sports Illustrated* starting in the early 1960s.[6] Jaffee's account of how he developed the fold-in appears in an interview with Paul Levitz.[7] Jaffee described the idea as an epiphany: "That's it! They all do expensive color FOLD-OUTS, so we'll do cheap, crappy FOLD-INS!"[8] The earliest targets of the fold-ins were also drawn from those mainstream magazines: trumped up celebrities, double-speaking politicians, and propagandistic treatments of hot-button social issues. A few installments from the 1970s provide examples for analysis and give a solid sense of Jaffee's style and satiric orientation. They include satiric attacks on rampant militarism in U.S. culture (#136, 7/70), the proliferation of venereal diseases (#159, 6/73), and the amount of violence featured on mainstream television (#167, 6/74). (See figs. 13-1a & b to 13-3 a & b).

From the earliest installments, in 1964, Jaffee had a monopoly on this feature and executed it with a degree of auteur-like clout and independence uncommon for a freelancing cartoonist. That autonomy was not achieved overnight. He first contributed a handful of pieces to the magazine between 1955 and 1957 while he was still writing and illustrating teen comics for Stan Lee (primarily the monthly comic *Patsy Walker*). Harvey Kurtzman, an old high school classmate, was the editor of *Mad*

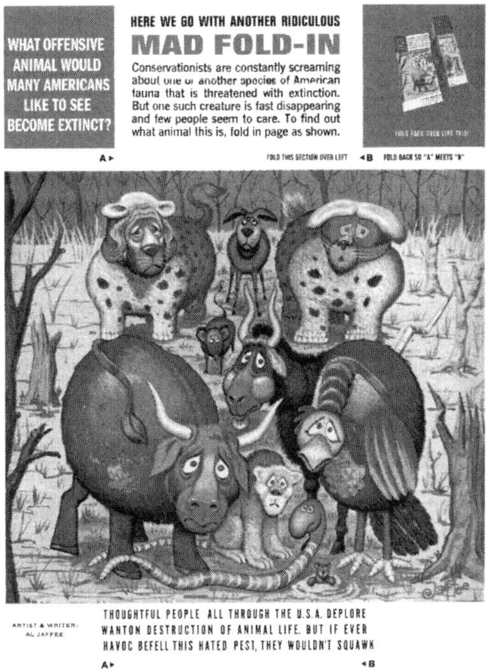

Fig. 13-1a: Readers encounter picture and text, always posed as a question, for directions to "Fold this section over left" and "Fold back so 'A' meets 'B,'" and for extra measure, the folding process is illustrated in the upper right. In this image, all the animals look sad, fearing extinction (Al Jaffee, "What Offensive Animal Would Many Americans Like to See Become Extinct?," #136, 7/70: inside back cover). MAD used with permission.

Fig. 13-1b: When folded properly, the painting reveals the surprise answer to the question—in this case through both the new image and the new words (although sometimes only the image reveals the surprise). This fold-in about warhawks during the Vietnam conflict has the topicality and gravity of a political cartoon (Al Jaffee, "What Offensive Animal Would Many Americans Like to See Become Extinct?," *Mad* #136, 7/70: inside back cover). MAD used with permission.

at this time; Jaffee's biographer notes that Jaffee was eager to join his former friend full-time in creating the type of anarchic, satiric work that they had loved since their adolescent years, but the $10,000 a year he would earn as a freelancer for *Mad* was a significant drop in pay from what he was earning in the teen comics field. When he finally mustered the courage to make the move to join Kurtzman full-time in 1957, he was distressed to find that his friend had abruptly defected from *Mad* and was working on a new, "classier" magazine, *Trump*, which was funded by *Playboy* publisher Hugh Hefner. Taking the risky leap to work with his buddy on this new endeavor was a significant gesture of courage and faith when one considers that Jaffee struggled as an adult with haunting memories of a childhood of financial deprivation in both Lithuania and the United States—experiences that made him especially anxious about maintaining a stable income for his young family. Within a year, *Trump* had failed, confirming his worst anxieties, and Jaffee was back to working as a freelancer.[9]

The new editor at *Mad*, Al Feldstein, invited Jaffee into the stable of regular contributors, but initially hired him only as a freelance writer—a serious demotion for a talented cartoonist. The quality of the visual gags that accompanied his written work over the ensuing months was so high, however, that Feldstein and Gaines were eventually compelled to use him as an artist as well. In the subsequent years, he established himself at the magazine with two popular features, "*Mad* Inventions" and "Snappy Answers to Stupid Questions," but resented that he did not own the copyright to his work and chaffed against Gaines's autocratic style as a publisher. Forever feeling like a longshoreman looking for a "day's labor," he strove to make himself indispensable to the magazine.[10] Indeed, his general anxiety about money and stability, coupled with an unusually intense work ethic, allowed him to achieve ultimately that clout and indispensability. In particular, the fact that he both wrote and illustrated his work made it more difficult for the magazine to treat him as an interchangeable cog in the publishing machine. And although he would never own the copyright over his work, he did signal his arrival as a full auteur of sorts during these early years by having one of his major features identified with him directly: "Al Jaffee's *Mad* Inventions."

When he began the fold-in feature in 1964, he invested so much time and energy in all aspects of its creation—conception, aesthetics, construction of the fold-in mechanism itself—that it also became

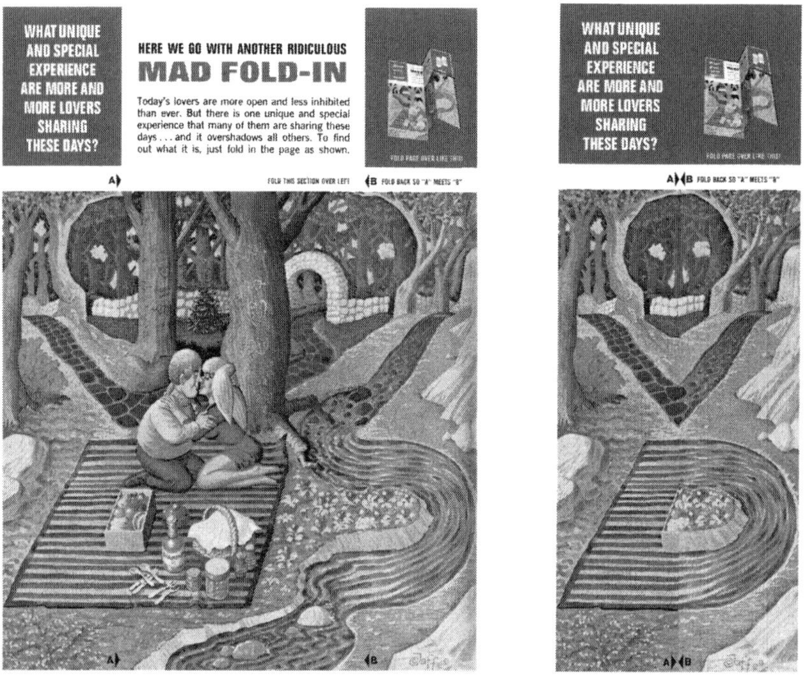

Fig. 13-2a & b: Jaffee's ability to treat current issues of a mature nature (sexually transmitted diseases in this case), in a magazine oriented to a youth demographic, highlights his auteur-like clout in choosing tricky subject matter (Al Jaffee, "What Unique and Special Experience Are More and More Americans Sharing These Days?," *Mad* #159, 6/73: inside back cover). MAD used with permission.

inextricably identified with him as an artist and writer-satirist. The lore goes that over the years, a number of other artists tried to do this back page feature but couldn't coordinate the satiric concept with the complex execution of the art, including various textual elements; the result either did not line up properly or did not effectively work as a magical reveal. And thus, Jaffee's ability to mark his work with such distinctive, inimitable qualities gave him some unique security at the magazine. Readers expected to see the fold-in each month, and Jaffee was the only one who could pull it off. His achievement of that auteur-like prominence in readers' minds prompts one to compare him to satirists like Walt Kelly and Garry Trudeau in the comic strip field—artists whose aesthetic style and satiric sensibility were so developed and unique that syndicates could not treat them as replaceable journeymen artists.

Jaffee's monopoly over this feature also gave him a level of freedom in terms of conception and execution of ideas that other artists and writers at *Mad* did not enjoy. Whereas the featured parodies of movies and TV shows were conceived, assigned, and vetted by editors, Jaffee was essentially given free reign over the fold-in. As long as his imagery and ideas remained within the bounds of "good, bad taste," no one dictated what he should do. And instead of searching for ideas based on what was trendy or hot in the entertainment world, Jaffee set his sights on broader, more political issues; like an editorial cartoonist, he would ask himself, "What does the zeitgeist have to offer? A presidential election? A war? The gay rights movement?"[11] After settling on what he perceived to be a deserving target, Jaffee would then create a pithy, and sometimes darkly moralistic, satiric point based on his own consistently left-leaning, absurdist, anti-authoritarian worldview.

To understand Jaffee's politics and satiric philosophy one can first look to his peculiar and tumultuous upbringing: Jaffee's parents were Jewish-Lithuanian immigrants who could not have been more different in worldview and temperament. His father doted on his kids, eschewed organized religion, and aspired to a life of material comfort though a career in retail; he always wanted to do "the American thing."[12] In contrast, Al's mother was aloof, fanatically Orthodox, and pined for the simple life of the old country. That nostalgia turned to radical action when Al was seven years old. His mother essentially kidnapped him and his two brothers, taking them back to Lithuania, ushering them into a childhood full of neglect, deprivation, and anti-Semitic persecution. During this time in Lithuania, Al felt like an outsider on many levels—as a Jew, as an American, and as a semi-orphaned child. Reflecting on that childhood alienation and trauma, he observed:

> When you have people who are oppressed, whether it's Jews living in places where people don't want them, like Jews in Zarasai [his hometown in Lithuania], or slaves living for masters in Savannah, about the only amusement you have is to see your oppressor from a satirical point of view. You make fun of him. You make yourself feel superior by pretending to be them and then exposing their excesses.[13]

Fig. 13-3a & b: These distorted caricatures of bohemian youth point to Jaffee's capacity for finding foolishness in both mainstream and counter-cultural targets (Al Jaffee, "What is the Most Explicitly Taught Subject in the World?," *Mad* #167, 6/74: inside back cover). MAD used with permission.

One can thus see that Jaffee, like other great satirists, was able to channel that sense of being an oppressed outsider-minority into a worldview that shaped his anti-authoritarian satire in powerful ways.

Drawing from Mary-Lou Weisman's biography of Jaffee, one can surmise perhaps the only upside of the neglect that he experienced in the semi-rural, underdeveloped setting of Zarasai, Lithuania, was that he enjoyed a great deal of independence and found plentiful opportunities to invent his own machines, draw funny pictures, and lead other youth in creative pursuits. Meanwhile, Jaffee's father was able to locate his kidnapped children, but he did not have the resources to bring them back to the United States immediately. The best he could do was send them regular care packages that contained numerous installments of the daily comics page, a medium that Al had enjoyed reading and drawing from with his father from his earliest years. It was not until several years later, in 1935, that Jaffee's father was finally able to bring his boys back to the United States—just a handful of years before almost all the Jewish people in that part of Lithuania were either killed or sent to concentration camps. But the expenses and stresses of rescuing his children took a serious toll on the man. He was never again able to make a decent living, and he struggled to be a legitimate support to his sons in other ways as well during the ensuing years. As a result, it was left to Al as a young teenager to protect his siblings in the now foreign-seeming United States as they were bounced from relative to relative and school to school.[14]

In sum, this uniquely difficult childhood helped to shape both Jaffee's satiric worldview and comic sensibility as an adult. He distrusted authority figures, rooted for underdogs, was wary of the images of material comfort and security that pervaded American popular culture, and eschewed all brands of elitism, racism, and hierarchy-making. And a general disenchantment with the contradictions or hypocrisies of the adult world arrested his own development, locking him into a perpetually adolescent view or treatment of that so-called civilized realm. Jaffee reported that he became so disgusted by specious adult attitudes and behavior that he decided to "never grow up" as a natural outgrowth of what he had witnessed as a young man:

> I became aware that I could not trust adults. My father let me be schlepped to Europe; my mother did the schlepping. What good were adults to me? The only thing adults were good for was telling you things were sinful and trying to destroy any notions of your own. "You can't do this; you can't do that!" I felt stifled. I developed my own brand of anti-adultism. At an early age, I set out to prove that adults were full of shit. I'm still doing that now . . . I think like an adolescent.[15]

In addition to thinking like an adolescent, he drew and wrote like one in much of his *Mad* work, reveling in scatological references, grotesque imagery, goofy wordplay, and zany sight gags. The pulpy, low-brow orientation of the magazine and its general targeting of a smart-alecky preteen demographic nicely matched this mentality. Gaines's policy of bad taste within acceptable parameters effectively allowed Jaffee to let "his crazy, arrested-adolescent self run wild," and he relished throughout his career descriptions of his humor as "sophomoric," "tasteless," "irreverent," and "off-the-wall."[16]

That juvenile irreverence creates an obstacle, nevertheless, in justifying Jaffee's work as more satirically coherent or politically counterdiscursive than the movie and TV parodies within the magazine. Most critics or scholars of satire tend to reserve the highest praise for work that is both explicitly topical and indignantly serious. Jaffee fares well with his fold-ins in terms of topicality (about half of them have the timeliness of a political cartoon), but his work falls short in terms of earnest gravity, as illustrated by his penchant for potty humor in his fold-in reveals, as well as by the tone of psychedelic silliness that pervades the unfolded imagery in the feature. Some critics decline to take his work (or the whole of *Mad*) seriously, but comic silliness is not inherently antithetical to the substance or integrity of true satire. For example, Daniel Green observes that Joseph Heller, one of Jaffee's 1960s satiric contemporaries, faced similar criticism with *Catch-22* (1961); the reasoning went that his novel could have been especially great if he had just been able to rein in all of the "omnivorous nonsense" of his juvenile wordplay, joke-telling, and silly, metafictive character names (Major Major Major Major). But the point that was lost on those traditional-minded critics was that the palette for serious satire had expanded by the mid-twentieth century to include carnivalesque inversions and playfully deconstructive dismantlings of civilized society and rhetoric. Within a broadened definition of legitimate satire, one can recognize how Heller's silliness gave *Catch-22* much of its satiric potency and allowed it to engage in the serious work of questioning the seemingly more earnest and stable, but intrinsically corrupt institutions and value systems of the surrounding culture.[17] In the same vein, Jaffee used a prank-like device (the fold-in mechanism) and juvenile zaniness to question and deconstruct the false value systems and hypocrisies of the dominant culture.

Both Jewish satirists also grounded their youthful iconoclasm in a moralistic worldview that condemned capitalistic excesses and abuses of authority. In Heller's metaphoric frame, those targets were represented by Milo Minderbinder's rapacious syndicate and the military's manipulative uses of rules and red tape. Jaffee chose similar targets, sniping repeatedly at corporate abuses of the environment, lies told by commercial culture, and authoritarian tendencies of the government.

Moreover, both satirists used the theme of death as a central grounding device. For example, Heller repeatedly broke away from his incorrigible joking to return to the trauma that Yossarian experienced at witnessing Snowden's death. In similar fashion, Jaffee peppers his cartooning iconography with *memento mori*: hovering skulls, coffins, sewers, explosions, gas clouds, and other agents of death. In the examples highlighted for this study, for instance, scenes of pastoral peace or purity are undercut with reveals that emphasize hidden dangers, lurking violence, and inevitable death (see figs. 13-1 and 13-2). What better way to create that sense of satiric distance in a parodic joke than to move the reader from ephemeral references of pop cultural trends to timeless reminders of his or her own mortality?

To further understand that melding of two tones—darkly moralistic satire with juvenile excess and abandon—one can also return once more to Jaffee's distinctive immigrant experience in American culture. At a very young age, he saw his father buy into the American dream of material comfort, and for a brief spell, while living in Savannah, Georgia, he and his siblings enjoyed the fruits of their father's semi-successful career in retail sales. As Jaffee told Weisman, his mother's Orthodox religiosity and disapproval of all things worldly undercut those pleasures; she lectured her sons continually on the virtues of a life of self-denial (even fetishizing poverty) and ultimately forced them to live in that manner back in Lithuania. Jaffee's childhood experiences in the old country were mixed, however; he resented the deprivations of that fundamentalist, rural life, but he also relished the freedoms and purity of a childhood where he made his own toys, inventions, and games. And his return to the United States as a preteen did little to restore his faith in the American dream that he had briefly witnessed as a young boy. During this second spell with his father, as a preteen, he saw a darker side of American culture: the prejudices and systemic problems that prevented minorities like his father from succeeding in various fields, the alienation and anonymity of urban life, and the extreme gap between the idealized life depicted in the mainstream media and the humble reality of most people's living situations.[18]

It is interesting to note that the most important text to Jaffee throughout all these experiences in both Lithuania and the United States was not the Torah or the Bible, but the comics page. Reading the Sunday supplement with his father was his favorite activity as a young child; receiving those comics in the mail from his father while living in the old country was his greatest pleasure in his later childhood; and after returning to America and attending an arts high school in New York, he continued to relish the comics page, even aspiring to become a syndicated cartoonist himself.[19] His lasting affinity for this multivoiced, carnivalesque medium helps to explain the ideological complexity or ambivalence of his worldview and satiric strategies in the fold-ins. In effect, the comics page articulated those two sides of the American dream: on the one hand, it celebrated—in all its multicolored gaudiness—the abundance and opportunity of life in the United States. (And as an entertainment field that did not play by traditional cultural rules, it *literally* offered an open door to many minority artists trying to make a good life for themselves.) At the same time, standby strips like *Bringing Up Father* (1913-2000), *Mutt and Jeff* (1907-1983), and *Blondie* (1930--) irreverently poked fun at idealized images of American life. They gave voice to minority perspectives, celebrated underdogs and trickster figures, and mocked elitism, hierarchies, and abusive authority figures. One could argue, in effect, that Jaffee's fold-ins were a distillation or channeling of all those complex elements of the comics medium: color-saturated visuals, caricatured social types, carnivalesque irreverence, and ambivalently satiric takes on mainstream values, systems, and ideals.

Moving from themes and symbols to general aesthetics, one can also distinguish Jaffee's work in significant ways from the magazine's featured parodies of mainstream entertainment texts. To begin, Jaffee's illustrations were stand-alone, elaborate, full-color paintings (a combination of transparent watercolors and opaque gouache) rather than quickly executed, multi-panel, black-and-white cartoons. Because of the time and care that Jaffee put into these fold-ins, they remind one of the full-page, all color, lithographic editorial cartoons that master draftsmen like Joseph Keppler (1838-1894) published in magazines like *Puck* and *Life* in the last decades of the nineteenth century. And just as readers of those earlier journals were alerted by that elaborate level of execution to pay attention to the piece—to see it as the cartooning masterpiece of that particular issue—*Mad* readers were perhaps inclined to slow down, to expend a higher level of thought or respect for the satiric point being made on the inside back cover.

Jaffee's unique painting style also achieved an overripe, sweet-and-sour effect that allowed him to make darkly satiric points or to express a variety of complex ideas such as disillusionment, false promises, façades, etc. To explore this idea, we can compare his style to the work of a few notable fine artists who also achieved an aesthetic effect that could communicate powerful ideas in satiric or moralistic ways. First of all, Jaffee's color palette is intensely saturated, relying on Day-Glo hues that are akin to the garish tones one might see in advertising or in the loud packaging of a grocery store aisle. This visual intensity makes his images boldly arresting—effective reflectors/parodies of the slick, full-color ads (or fold-outs) in the mainstream magazines that Jaffee is satirizing. The high level of saturation also echoes the bold hues in pop art: the silk-screen images of Andy Warhol (1928–1987) or the iconic cartoon imagery of Roy Lichtenstein (1923–1997). And like those works of pop art, Jaffee's paintings are also engaged in a recycling—or parodic quoting—of the earnest imagery created by the mainstream entertainment industry. A critical difference, nevertheless, that gives Jaffee's work the greater satiric substance is that while Warhol's and Lichtenstein's images always hovered in that liminal, ambivalent space between parodic critique and celebratory recycling (a key attribute of much postmodern parodic art), the fold-ins could be transformed into a pointed editorial cartoon in the end. In effect, while pop art (and the mainstream imagery to which it paid tribute) shared the same palette as the *Mad* fold-ins, Jaffee harnessed the use of those vibrant colors to make a pointed attack on a particular ideology or cultural practice, thus emphasizing critical difference and distance rather than ambivalence or celebratory similarity.

One could also describe Jaffee's palette as denatured: colors that are too intense, too exaggerated, or perhaps too "rotten" to be associated with the natural world. This aesthetic move echoes that of post-impressionists such as Vincent Van Gogh (1853-1890) or expressionists like Edvard Munch (1863–1944). As with Munch's iconic *The Scream*, the denatured colors in Jaffee's fold-ins can connote internal anxiety or external societal dysfunction. In the examples highlighted for this study, those rotten colors intensify anxious notions in themes of environmental degradation, societal violence, and the inevitability of death. In other installments, that palette is applied to the ominous glow of a mushroom cloud, the radioactive-seeming filth of a sewer or factory farm, or the curdled imagery of an exploitation film.

At times Jaffee achieves a variation on the sweet-and-sour effect of his colors, effectively keeping this palette in a fine balance between brightly saturated and disturbingly denatured. That vibrating dissonance supports his satiric intentions of inverting the dominant cultural imagery: when one initially looks at the unfolded image (which parodies imagery found in the mainstream media), the colors look appropriately loud and garish, with only a hint of something being "off." And then when one creates the fold-in, revealing the satiric point or rebuttal (usually about a rotten cultural truth that has been repressed or ignored), the palette shifts, with the curdled qualities of the palette asserting themselves.

Jaffee's treatment of the human figure also achieves a semiotic instability, effectively mimicking the earnest celebrations of youth and physical beauty seen in mainstream periodicals while also signaling that something is corrupt or insincere in the image. For example, in the fold-in about venereal disease (see fig. 13-2), "What Unique and Special Experience Are More and More Americans Sharing These Days?," Jaffee features young people who look, from a distance, like icons of middle-Americanness: blonde hair, conventional good looks, an air of entitled satisfaction (#159, 06/73). But there is also an overripe smugness to their facial expressions and a slightly bloated or distended quality to their figures. That distortion or amplification of mainstream imagery points the reader toward the lurking, unpleasant "truth" exposed in the reveal.

The dynamics of the human forms in the fold-in about televisual violence are slightly different in "What is the Most Explicitly Taught Subject in the World?" (#167, 06/74). In this case the people in the unfolded image are meant to represent rowdy, bohemian college students—members of a rebellious youth generation. But even as icons of antiestablishment youthfulness, they are still depicted in bright, fashionable clothing and with robust, dynamic bodies. The image remains a mainstream cultural (albeit slightly caricatured) view of college age insouciance. Nevertheless, the slightly exaggerated and over-described delineation of the forms foreshadows Jaffee's satiric intentions (see fig. 13-3). Clothing and limbs are contorted; textures and colors are represented in too much detail; and male and female gender characteristics are exaggerated in awkward ways. This distorted treatment of the human form parallels the agitated figures in expressionist paintings or the almost sculpturesque rendering of clothing and bodies in paintings by Thomas Hart Benton (1889–1975). And as with those images, Jaffee's painting evokes a sense of anxiety or cognitive overload when a viewer tries to read the forms as a whole. There is too much visual information to grasp in a quick glance, and because every detail is treated with the same level of obsessive care, it is difficult to know where to focus one's attention. That disorientation is relieved only when the fold-in is executed and the reader/viewer is given a more didactic and visually succinct, focused image to decode.

The treatment of idealized or sexualized female forms is another element that clearly highlights the differing degrees of satiric distance achieved in the magazine's featured parodies versus Jaffee's fold-ins. While both drawing styles engaged in exaggerated depictions of the female body, Jaffee's women differed in that they were not constructed as celebratory extensions of imagery in *Playboy* magazine, popular films like the James Bond franchise, or television programs like *Charlie's Angels*. From a distance there are similarities: the jutting chests, hourglass shapes, and bottle-blonde hairdos. But upon closer inspection, Jaffee's figures do not cater to a male gaze: legs are knock-kneed; bodies are bloated or overinflated; postures are almost simian; and the highly detailed clothing is garishly loud. In effect, they are parodies of the pinups created by the mainstream media, but with the significant difference of serving as ridiculous, parodic *critiques*, instead of merely parodic amplifications or celebrations of that mainstream imagery.

One additional element of Jaffee's aesthetic repertoire that can be assessed for its relative satiric potency is his use of symbolic iconography. As a close cousin to political cartoons, his fold-ins rely on iconic imagery that can be read as a semiotic shorthand: heroic flags, menacing guns, courtroom gavels, illuminated lightbulbs, belching smokestacks, cigar-chomping corporate fat cats, etc. All these symbols communicate distilled, ideologically loaded ideas to the reader—a visual shorthand shared by other, generally left-leaning editorial cartoonists. But Jaffee also incorporated icons that have a more ancient pedigree in either traditional religious art or his own idiosyncratic worldview. Images of death, pollution, and decay, for example, seem to recur in his fold-ins with striking regularity, as in the July 1970 "What Offensive Animal Would Many Americans Like to See Become Extinct?," discussed above, and "What Unique and Special Experience Are More and More Americans Sharing These Days?" (#159, 06/73). Like a contemporary version of the *memento mori* featured in medieval and Renaissance painting, they undercut images of American commercial materialism, youthfulness, abundance, and overindulgence, reminding viewers of starker, more timeless realities. The fact that these sobering images appear in the midst of a festive, color-saturated (albeit, slightly rotten) imagery evokes the work of painters such as Pieter Brueghel the Elder (c. 1525–1569) and Hieronymous Bosch (c. 1450–1516). Like these Renaissance-era genre painters, Jaffee creates comic imagery for a broad, lay audience that is grounded in moralistic satire. Moreover, Jaffee's moral vision is similarly ambivalent to those of Bosch and Brueghel, providing a dark counterpoint to the festive tone and palette of his unfolded images. All three artists seem to celebrate in carnivalesque fashion the joyous physicality of life and the festive energy of people living robustly in the moment. At the same time, however, they include iconography that reminds one of future costs: the inevitability of death and the consequences of unrestrained carnality (or, in Jaffee's case, of unfettered consumption).

A final element to consider in assessing degrees of parodic distance and difference in Jaffee's fold-ins are the potential meanings and uses of the fold-in mechanism itself. A big portion of the feature's popularity is the interactive and magical quality of the reader's effort to manipulate the page to go from one image to the other—folding the idealized, mainstream lie, into the grotesque, hidden truth. In light of research about the impact that so-called active learning has on readers, we may reasonably conjecture that the ideological point made by this sort of physically dialectical text that requires a reader to do something—to actively participate in the construction of hidden meaning—would have a greater impact on the psyche than passive reading. Proving that point in an objective way would be a challenging task, of course, but anecdotal evidence gathered from former fans of the magazine who consumed it avidly in the 1970s suggests that it bears up. For example, middle-aged attendees at a presentation of this study recalled obsessing over this feature in a variety of ways: turning to it first; seeking out the magazine on newsstands in order to execute the fold surreptitiously, without scoring the page; attempting to do a sort of "magic-eye" exercise of spotting the reveal without actually folding the page; or reveling in showing off the fold-in's visual trick each month to friends or siblings.

Like the rest of the magazine, nevertheless, the very workings of the fold-in also suggest a degree of ideological ambivalence. Bakhtin's notion that carnivalesque inversions are unstable, often acting only as temporary alternatives to "first life" conventions and values, suggests that the fold-in is continually fluttering between the trumped up cultural ideal and the subversive truth.[20] And since the resting position of the fold-in is the unfolded, mainstream lie, one might think that the ideological ambivalence ultimately settles in that direction, like carnivalesque experience that always reverts back to first life hierarchies and values.

For several reasons, nevertheless, it seems more probable that a reader's manipulation of the fold-in actually favors the progressive or subversive end of the scale. First of all, because Jaffee's satiric position can be discerned in relation to a *physical* configuration of the page—the folded-in state—these texts are ultimately less ambiguous or unstable in their meaning-making than other works of visual or literary satire that remain physically static. There is no confusion, after all, about what Jaffee is trying to assert; he is revealing it to you in an explicit, interactive way. Given average readers' common tendency to misread the intentions and meanings of popular satire and parody (especially when they are younger readers, unschooled in the language of irony), that lack of ambiguity might have ensured that the fold-in achieved a significant sense of ideological discovery for the preteen reader who was literally being shown an alternative way of perceiving the everyday world of entertainment and propaganda.

And while it is true that the fold-in has a tendency to revert back to a resting, unfolded state, that does not mean that the reader's perception reverts as well. Anecdotal and common-sensical evidence suggest that once the reveal is executed, it is difficult for the reader to see the unfolded image again with the same, innocent, eyes. The initially camouflaged clues suddenly seem obvious; the denatured colors and contorted figures now appear more explicitly grotesque; and the scored lines and buckled configuration of the paper itself reminds one of the ever-lurking reveal. Moreover, the fold-in mechanism invites a high level of active mental, physical, and aesthetic engagement with the text. That sense of ownership over the hidden message—as if one participated with Jaffee in its construction—suggests an unusually high level of active learning or psychological engagement with a popular text. Rather than passively allowing its ephemeral comic message to wash over oneself (as is often the case with televisual or filmic texts), the reader of the fold-in owns the magazine (and perhaps even collects it); actively, physically participates in making its meaning; and finally, might return to it repeatedly, talking about it and showing it to others.

In sum, Jaffee's work, though ideologically ambivalent to a degree (like the rest of the humor in *Mad*), effectively achieves a greater degree of critical distance or difference from its targets than other features in the magazine. And that greater satiric punch can be attributed to a number of factors: Jaffee's peculiarly juvenile and darkly moralistic worldview (communicated from an unusual position of auteur-like clout and freedom at the magazine); the elaborately executed, sweet-and-sour aesthetics that effectively parody mainstream imagery while still signaling Jaffee's more critical intentions; and the elaborate and playful folding mechanisms of the back cover that have the potential to educate readers in deconstructive ways of perceiving propaganda and idealized, mainstream cultural imagery. Given those unique circumstances and qualities, we can celebrate the fold-ins as genuinely counterdiscursive and elevate Jaffee to the status of one of the greater, underappreciated satirists of American mainstream culture of the latter half of the twentieth century and into the twenty-first.

Notes

1. Mark Evanier, *Mad Art: A Visual Celebration of the Art of Mad Magazine and the Idiots Who Create It*, 126.
2. Quoted in Mary-Lou Weisman, *Al Jaffee's Mad Life: A Biography*, 188.
3. Evanier, *Mad Art*, 122.
4. Linda Hutcheon, *A Theory of Parody: The Teachings of Twentieth-Century Art Forms*, xii.
5. Hutcheon, *A Theory of Parody*, 6.
6. Weisman, *Al Jaffee's Mad Life*, 197.
7. See Paul Levitz, "Inside the Editorial Process: *Mad* Veterans Jaffee and Meglin Look at Their Editors," chap. 1, 7–24; first published in *Studies in American Humor* n.s. 3, no. 30 (Fall 2014): 7-19.
8. *The Mad Fold-In Collection*, by Al Jaffee, 6 vols., I: 1.
9. Weisman, *Al Jaffee's Mad Life*, 152, 169–73.
10. Weisman, *Al Jaffee's Mad Life*, 188.
11. Weisman, *Al Jaffee's Mad Life*, 199.
12. Weisman, *Al Jaffee's Mad Life*, 8.
13. Weisman, *Al Jaffee's Mad Life*, 147.
14. Weisman, *Al Jaffee's Mad Life*, 22, 24, 67, 147.
15. Quoted in Weisman, *Al Jaffee's Mad Life*, 67.

16. Weisman, *Al Jaffee's Mad Life*, 165.

17. Daniel Green, "A World Worth Laughing At: *Catch-22* and the Humor of Black Humor," 187.

18. Weisman, *Al Jaffee's Mad Life,* 22, 24, 67, 147.

19. Weisman, *Al Jaffee's Mad Life,* 22, 114.

20. Mikhail Bakhtin, *Rabelais and His World*, 6-7.

PART III.
THEMES

14. A Secular Talmud:

The Jewish Sensibility of *Mad* Magazine

Nathan Abrams

Mad MAGAZINE FUNCTIONED as a secular Talmud for a generation of Jews and non-Jews alike in America and beyond. Like its religious forebear, *Mad* was intertextual, self-referential, and arguably even formatted in a similar way. And like the Talmud, it extended influence outwards—from the comic book world, it inspired graphic novels, television, the movies, and more. Yet, to date, despite its highly Jewish and very Talmudic nature, little scholarship has been dedicated to exploring *Mad*'s Jewishness. The most recent edition of the *Encyclopaedia Judaica*, for example, had only this to say:

> The editorial director of *Mad*, Harvey Kurtzman, along with the publisher, William Gaines, brought a distinctly Jewish flavor to what became one of the seminal magazines of postwar American culture. The first issue, in 1952, included a parody of gangster cartoons titled "Ganefs!" The Yiddish in the magazine was undefined. Later issues of *Mad* had sprinklings of Yiddish and Jewish-inspired satire.[1]

Yet popular sources increasingly recognize what academics have overlooked. Writing in *The Forward*, Eddy Portnoy opined in 2010, "As a seminal artifact of American popular culture, *Mad* is often revered as a product of heavily Jewish influences." More recently, Columbia University Librarian Karen Green recalled that *Mad* was a "crash course in immigrant Jewish culture. I like to say that I learned how to be an American Jew from *Mad* magazine and the Marx Brothers."[2] Here, I begin filling this gap to consider *Mad*'s Jewish and Talmudic sensibility, and how this element played out in *Mad*'s history in the 1950s and 1960s.

Born in the 1950s, *Mad* lived contemporaneously with that generation of writers, poets, essayists, and literary critics who came to be known as the New York Intellectuals, as well as such 1960s iconoclasts as Bob Dylan, the Beats, comedians Mort Sahl and Lenny Bruce, movie director Stanley Kubrick, cartoonist Jules Feiffer, novelist Joseph Heller, and those who would form the New Left and counterculture. This group of Jews, centered on New York, had come to political awareness during the Great Depression. Their religious/ethnic heritage had a direct and important influence on their work. Marinated in the same urban Jewish culture, *Mad*'s commitments mirrored theirs and arguably were part of the same debates, particularly in the post-Holocaust world. A detailed examination of *Mad*'s pages in the 1950s and the 1960s shows that it engaged with the same dilemmas and paradoxes as these intellectual New Yorkers, producing an alternative New York critique, which skewered the key intellectual concerns of those decades: suburbia, psychoanalysis, existentialism, Freudianism, intellectual pretension, bohemianism, technology, disarmament, and containment.

Consequently, in many ways, as I've detailed elsewhere, *Mad* represented a group of alternative New York Jewish Intellectuals.[3] Like their intellectual co-religionists, they were Jews who had grown up and come to political awareness during the Depression, the Second World War, and the Holocaust. Al Feldstein, Kurtzman's successor as editor of *Mad*, recalled: "I was an ultra-liberal when I was young, and a socially conscious person, having grown up in the Depression and seeing my parents lose their home, etc., etc."[4] *Mad*'s leaders were Jews who used their work to reflect on the postwar world, conformity, and the Holocaust. Unlike the New York Intellectuals, however, *Mad*'s staff as a group was unafraid to criticize or dissent from the prevailing mood of Cold War America during the 1950s and 1960s. *Mad* appeared to fulfill the function of the critic more often than did the New York Intellectuals' magazines.

This posture reflected how many members of *Mad*'s staff were Jewish. "The Usual Gang of Idiots," as the magazine referred to them, included founders William Gaines and Harvey Kurtzman; editor Al Feldstein; artists Mort Drucker, Al Jaffee, Will Elder, and Dave Berg; and writers Larry Siegel, Stan Hart, Arnie Kogen, Frank Jacobs, and Lou Silverstone. Added to this list were such Jewish guest contributors as Sid Caesar, Danny Kaye, Paul Krassner, and Jules Feiffer, among many others. "My writers," Feldstein recalled, "were all Jewish boys from Jewish families in urban centers."[5] These ethnic/religious origins played a key part in shaping *Mad*'s sensibility. As Arie Kaplan put it,

> One key element of *Mad*'s appeal that was passed down from the Kurtzman years and continued during the Feldstein years (and beyond) was the magazine's inherent sense of Jewishness. To this day, Yiddish phrases are still frequently used in the magazine, as are Jewish themes. And it's no stretch to say that this is at least partly because *Mad* has consistently used Jewish cartoonists . . . The Jewish upbringing of the *Mad* contributors is evident from a random look at the magazine's content.[6]

Feldstein felt that *Mad*'s Jewishness gave it "a cultural awareness (an outsider attitude). It might even be in the genes, it might go back hundreds and hundreds of years of a certain kind of living in society. Trying to survive in that society."[7] Writer Al Jaffee believed that "Oppressed people resort to humor. They can't afford to get angry."[8] Stanley Rothman and S. Robert Lichter summed up, "From the beginning *Mad*'s editors have been Jewish and, as they themselves would agree, hostile to the American civic myth."[9]

Thus, *Mad* used parody to criticize a predominantly Protestant culture from the perspective of the Jewish outsider. As Stephen E. Kercher has pointed out, "Kurtzman's *Mad* comics mercilessly lampooned a host of square-jawed, goyishe American tough guys, from the upright, virtuous marshal played by Gary Cooper in *High Noon* to Marlon Brando's motorcycle bad boy in *The Wild One.*"[10] In February 1955's "Cowboy!," for example, Kurtzman and artist Jack Davis juxtaposed the "movie and television version" of a cowboy—a handsome clean-shaven man named, significantly, Lance Sterling ("Could you ever picture a cowboy hero named Melvin Poznowski?")—with John Smurd, a "100% genuine cowboy" who wore a "nauseating walrus mustache" (#20, 2/55: 1–5). Unlike Lance Sterling, "old John Smurd worked like a horse" and had no union, so he had little time or energy for "shooting it out with bad guys" (26). In "Starchie," the innocent teenagers Archie and Jughead became chain-smoking juvenile delinquents (Kurtzman and Elder, #12, 6/54: 1-8). "Lone Stranger!" transformed the gallant western hero into a *schlemiel* or a simpleton (Kurtzman and Davis, #3, 2–3/53: 1-7).

And "Superduperman!" was not the triumphant superhero envisaged by two of their fellow American Jews, but a *schlimazel*, a perennially unlucky fellow (Kurtzman and Wood, #4, 4–5/53: 1-8). *Mad* also asked, "What If Batman Were Jewish?" (Jaffee, #516, 8/12: 32-33), or "What If Superman Were Raised by Jewish Parents?" (Bresman and Drucker, #325, 3/94: 24). In its early years, *Mad* loved to target films by Walt Disney. In impressively detailed mimicry of its signature visual style, under *Mad*'s penmanship, Disney's central wholesome icon Mickey Mouse became the grizzled, rat-faced, vermin thug "Mickey Rodent," whose fingers and tail were caught in mousetraps (Kurtzman and Elder, #19, 1/55: 1-7). Did *Mad* target Disney simply because it was a popular cultural icon at that time or was the magazine also motivated to attack its creator, who (accurately or otherwise) had a reputation for anti-Semitism, for including ethnic stereotypes in his movies, and for allying himself with such anti-Semites as Henry Ford?[11]

Mad also foregrounded issues of racism, intolerance, and prejudice. In so doing, it exploded the myths of a democratic, tolerant America. As writer Al Jaffee recalled:

> I think that for Jews of my generation especially, social consciousness came naturally for those of us who suffered from a lack of civil rights and were discriminated against. Social consciousness really is in a way self-serving. Because by being in favor of civil rights for example, in a like way you're really saying, "Jews have suffered without civil rights for so many centuries that we know what not having civil rights is, so we cannot possibly impose this on someone else, not to have civil rights." I think it's a gut reaction: I don't think Harvey Kurtzman or I or anybody who works in the entertainment business—comedians, writers—sit down and say, "I owe something to society." Basically, we're trying to be funny, and a good source of humor is the stupidities in society, and certainly bigotry is one of the biggest stupidities. And Jews have experienced it firsthand and they know how stupid it is, so we go after it.[12]

But this was not just restricted to the wider gentile society, as *Mad* also managed to poke fun at its own co-religionists so that, in effect, no one was safe from its satire. In this way, it bore more than a passing resemblance to the films of Mel Brooks. As Brooks said,

> The roots of my humor are in very old-fashioned Yiddish comedy . . . which is based on some failure—making fun of the inept, which is cruel.
>
> . . . So Jews taking off on unfortunates, it's always compelling. Because you're saying in a strange way, "Oh thank God, it's not me." You enjoy the humor because you are not the butt of the joke. It's cruel but effective.[13]

Like Brooks, *Mad* has been accused of being childish, scatological, and vulgar, of making jokes in bad taste. Consider the farting-around-the-campfire scene in Brooks's *Blazing Saddles* (1974). Perhaps *Mad* even provided the blueprint for Brooks, who, as a writer for Sid Caesar, may well have indirectly contributed to the magazine.

Specifically, *Mad*'s humor was grounded in Yiddishisms, sarcasm, and self-mockery, all defining features of Jewish humor. It employed a whole lexicon of Yiddish phrases, both real and imaginary, making Leo Rosten's *The Joys of Yiddish* (1968) a required companion text for the uninitiated. As Denis Kitchen and Paul Buhle point out, Elder and Kurtzman "added a peculiar Jewish New York dialect, from 'Mrs. Gowanus' (a reference to the Gowanus Canal in Brooklyn) to 'Potzrebie' (a real Polish word) and 'fershlugginer' (an imaginary Yiddish word)."[14] This flavor was announced from the very first issue when a strip entitled "Ganefs!"—Yiddish for *thieves* or *crooks*—appeared. *Mad*'s Yiddish-inflected lingo also included more familiar terms such as "schmuck," as when it ran Al Jaffee's strip "Don't You Feel Like a Schmuck?!" (#157, 3/73: 18-21). But this lexicon also included lesser known and often made-up words: *schmaltz* (chicken fat), *shmear* (spread on or for bread), *oy* (oh, no!), *feh* (ugh!), *borscht* (soup), *bveebleftzer* (neologism suggesting "whatchamacallit"), *farshimmelt* (neologism for "all mixed up"), *kibitzer* (joker), *schlepp* (haul), *schnook* (fall guy), and *halavah* (ground sesame candy). In one column, "Murder the Husband" (Gaines, Feldstein, and Davis, #11, 5/54: 1-6), Yiddish was printed in traditional Hebrew lettering, which translated as "the Danish king comes to wed in Copenhagen." Consequently, readers often wrote in and complained of the strange and exotic-sounding words that saturated the magazine.

Similarly, in a reversal of the name-changing process so beloved of Jewish Hollywood stars during the heyday of the studio system, *Mad*

Yiddishized Anglo names, turning Batman and Robin into "Bat Boy and Rubin!" (Kurtzman and Wood, #8, 12/53–1/54: 1-7), G. I. Joe into "G. I. Shmoe!" (Kurtzman and Wood, #10, 4/54: 1-8) and Sherlock Holmes into "Shermlock Shomes!" (Kurtzman and Elder, #7, 10/53: 1-8). The moniker *Shadowskeedeeboomboom*, used for various heroes and foes, was a name inspired by the Yiddish comedian Aaron Lebedeff.[15] In this way, *Mad* reacted to the de-Semitization of the Hollywood studio system, which was often at pains to sideline or elide Jewishness and Jewish characters, in what Henry Popkin called "the great retreat."[16] During Hollywood's heyday, Jews were hidden on screen both literally and figuratively as the Jewish moguls, often prompted by pressure from Jewish organizations and the Hays Code, which exercised tight control over the portrayal of religion and ethnicity, promoted an assimilatory strategy of Americanization. Jewish actors changed their names, as their Jewish bosses—for commercial reasons, as well as fear of inciting anti-Semitism even further—calculated that their predominantly white working-class audiences did not want to watch Jews on screen.

In contrast, *Mad* foregrounded Jewishness, even where it did not necessarily exist in the source text. "Dragged Net!," a spoof of *Dragnet*, was punctuated with a heavyset middle-aged Jewish woman intermittently shouting, "VIL-LEE!" (Kurtzman and Elder, #11, 5/54: 1–7). In the final panel she catches up to little "Villie Elder," playing the *Dragnet* theme song on a kazoo in a room outfitted like an detective's office but has a door marked "MEN" in two inside jokes for the Jewish-inflected mindset: that Jewish mothers will pursue their boys even into the bathroom, the only private spot in a small apartment, and that the Jewish diet leads to constipation. "Strangely Believe It," written by guest contributor Ernie Kovacs, featured a "Dr. Sidney Klutz" (Kovacs and Wood, #42, 11/58: 27). A "Prof. Rumblemacher" appeared in another guest contribution, this time by Sid Caesar, with art by Mort Drucker ("Sid Caesar's . . . Shrunk World" #49, 9/59: 27–30). In its parody of the film *Rosemary's Baby* (1968), renamed "Rosemia's Boo-Boo" (Kogen and Drucker, #124, 1/69: 4–10), the implicitly or conceptually Jewish character Dr. Abraham Sapirstein, whose ethnicity/religion is nowhere mentioned in the movie, is renamed the more obvious "Schlepperstein."

A whole galaxy of Jewish characters appeared in *Mad*'s "Credits / Professional Names for the Common Man" (Laikin and Wood, #42, 11/58: 30–33). Sam "Red" Schlepp ran "a luncheonette so bold and difficult that only a schnook like Schlepp would dare to attempt it!" (30). There were also Irving Siegel, Seymour Cohen, Herman Katz, Phil Spieler, Stanley Klatch, and Bernie Levine. Even the very idea of the spread, giving credits to the "common man" as stars and crew receive credits for movies, could be argued to have derived from Jewish memories of the "*dos kleine menshele*" (lit., "the little man") so fundamental to *Yiddishkeit* (lit., "Jewish culture" or "Jewishness"). Indeed, according to Bonnie Lyons, "the ordinary man is elevated, or at least evoked with love"; "*Dos kleine menshele*, the little man, with all his imperfections and foibles, is accepted and embraced .... The ordinary man struggling with his everyday problems is the core of Yiddish literature."[17]

Mad also took on Judaism. Its view of its creators' own religion and especially what had happened to it in the United States curiously resembled the standpoint of an ultra-Orthodox rabbi who takes a dim view of the reforms made by the non-*halachic* (law-driven) branches of Judaism. This rhetoric is most clearly articulated in "The *Mad* 'Religion in America' Primer" (Siegel and Coker, #153, 9/72: 11–15). Clearly with its tongue placed firmly in its cheek, *Mad* introduced Judaism as a whole thus:

> The Jews do not believe Christ is their Savior.
> Who do they believe He is?
> They believe He is a nice Jewish boy
> Who went into his Father's business.
> So much for our first lesson in religion.
> Now you know why religion has been running for over 2000 years.
> You also know why the Jews have been running for over 2000 years! (11)

The piece then goes on to break Judaism down into its constituent streams of Orthodoxy, Conservatism, and Reform. It describes the latter group as hardly observing any religion at all, concluding, "To the other two groups / Reform Jews have another name. / They are known as 'Christians'!" For example, their temple is easily locatable because it is "the one with the Christmas tree in front." Thus, when a Catholic and Protestant decide to get married and compromise, in Dave Berg's "The Lighter Side of Weddings," they choose a (Reform?) synagogue (#152, 7/72: 26–30). Here *Mad* lampooned the rabbinic leadership as being more concerned with food than spirituality: a morose-looking rabbi postpones a bar mitzvah "because the caterer didn't show up," before adding, "How much suffering can the Jews stand?" (12). On the subject of Jewish food, the feature caricatures the stereotypical overbearing Jewish mother, depicting her as an overweight matriarch who stuffs her family with oversized bowls of soup while imploring them to "Eat! Eat!" (14).

Mad of the 1950s and 1960s was also punctuated with references to Hitler, the Nazis, and the Holocaust. It barely needs mentioning that the Jewishness of *Mad*'s writers had a part to play in this, as did the staffers' specific military and war experiences. In so doing, not only did *Mad* attack Nazis, it also lambasted American cultural representations of them. But rather than use tragedy as the vehicle for its indignation and fury, it used comedy instead. Just as Allied propaganda dropped behind enemy lines lampooned Hitler and just as the Nazis threatened to execute anyone who dared make anti-Hitler jokes, *Mad* recognized that a good laugh can communicate more than a well-meaning and long-winded speech. Thus, one of its earliest allusions to the Second World War came in its parody "Frank N. Stein!," in which Dr. Frankenstein succeeds in creating his eponymous monster (Kurtzman and Elder, #8, 12/53–1/54: 1–8). On the final page, the monster's face is revealed to the horror of the soldiers sent to apprehend it: "There it is!" "Look at its face!" "What a horrible face!" and "I can't stand it!" In the next panel, we see that it looks precisely like Hitler (8). (In the end, the Hitler-like monster flies away because, as it turns out, the doctor's assistant, Bumble, stole a "fershlugginer" bird brain!) The following December, *Mad* parodied *Stalag 17* (stage 1951, film 1953), as "Stalag 18!" (Kurtzman and Wood, #18, 12/54: 1–7). Here the overweight and aging Kommandant, named Johann Sebastien Shmaltz, complains: "Oh for der good old days ven dey made us Nazis in der movies, tough, good-looking guys mit der blonde crew-haircut . . . mit der snappy uniforms mit der daggers in der belts" (4). Yet there is no mention of the Holocaust, given both pieces' publication during the mid-1950s. At the height of the Cold War, the resurrection of West Germany as an anti-communist ally was in full swing; overt discussion of the extermination of European Jewry was therefore somewhat muted, especially before the 1952 English translation of Anne Frank's *The Diary of a Young Girl* became a best-seller.[18]

Such a representation would not come for another decade at least. In 1967, the "Mein Kamp Humor Dept." parodied the television show *Hogan's Heroes*, which ran on CBS from 1965 to 1971, in "Hokum's Heroes" (Siegel and Davis, #108, 1/67: 4–8). The sitcom starred Bob Crane as the titular character who was incarcerated in a World War II German POW camp, and Werner Klemperer played his Kommandant, Colonel Wilhelm Klink. *Mad* attempted to demonstrate "the idiocy of a program which would have fun with a time when there was such horror going on and make it seem so light."[19] Writer Larry Siegel reported that he was annoyed by the program's sensibility: "I resented the fact that they were making the Germans so cute, and these guys were sitting in prison. I was over there, and I saw what it was really like."[20] In the cartoon strip, Colonel Hokum is scared because, as he tells Colonel Klunk,

> I know what TV Networks are like! This show is so successful that there's bound to be imitations! Soon, there'll be other funny shows about Allied soldiers in Prisoner of War Camps . . . dozens of them! And people will get sick of our show. You know how TV trends go! (7)

He informs the Colonel that he is taking his men out of the camp and is moving them to a much funnier show, entitled "Hochman's Heroes."

The final page of the parody reveals his vision. We see a splash panel showing what would eventually happen if shows such as *Hogan's Heroes* continued. The headline announces, "And here it is . . . the brand new weekly TV situation comedy featuring that gay, wild, zany, irrepressible bunch of World War II concentration camp prisoners . . . those happy inmates of 'Buchenwald' known as . . . Hochman's Heroes" (8). The panel features shaven-headed prisoners, wearing the striped uniforms of concentration camp inmates, lounging on their bunks.

But Buchenwald has been conceptually overlaid with the trappings of a typical Jewish American youth summer camp. Thus, these prisoners are drinking champagne, beer, and cocktails, eating chicken, smoking cigars, and generally having a whale of a time, while praising the merits of the Nazi concentration camp system. One prisoner tells another, "What a 'fun' Concentration Camp this 'Buchenwald' is!" The reply comes, "You bet! It's fun, fun, fun—day and night, without let-up!" Another, who is pouring champagne over himself, announces, "I've been in some fantastic German Concentration Camps but this one is by far the most fantastic of all!" Yet another says, "Every night, I thank God for the pleasure He's given Jews like me during World War II! When I think of how close Hitler got to being killed in that bomb plot!" Another inmate avers:

"Wait'll you see the latest gag we're gonna pull on the guards over at the Crematorium! Boy, it's a hot one!" The Kommandant tells Hochman, "Herr Hochman, your Inmate's Baseball Team iss terrible! You know vot? I t'ink I'll send your pitcher to ze showers! Get it? SHOWERS? Ha, ha, ha, ha, ha!" A smug Hochman responds, "Kommandant, you know what? You're a gasser! Do you dig? GASSER? Ha, ha, ha, ha!" (8).

Mad's vision of a television sitcom based on the Nazi death camps came twenty-two years after the end of the Second World War. At the same time, *Mad* could not resist attacking its fellow American Jews in the entertainment industries, either. After all, many of them staffed the offices of the big television companies. The very fact that they would sacrifice their principles for profit indicates a great deal about the willingness of modern Jews to ignore the tragedies of the past and do business in the present. The parody also attacked the depths to which audiences, some of whom were surely Jewish, will sink to be entertained. In satirizing a hit show entitled *Hogan's Heroes*, *Mad* attacked an American public willing to find humor, however grotesque, in the Third Reich. In that sense its strip was astutely prescient. Hitler, the Nazis, and the Holocaust become, in the words of David Desser and Lester D. Friedman, "another piece of fodder gobbled up by the era's ravenous appetite for cultural kitsch."[21] In making the Nazis, Hitler, and the Holocaust ripe subjects for satirical exploitation, *Mad* followed in a (Jewish) tradition that stretched back some three decades. Its World War II parodies resembled those of Charlie Chaplin in *The Great Dictator* (1940) and Ernst Lubitsch in *To Be or Not to Be* (1942), both of which confronted the Nazi menace to expose it the best way they could. "Hokum's Heroes" also anticipated Mel Brooks's film *The Producers* (1968) and its parody of Holocaust commodification and trivialization. Perhaps only a Jewish humorous magazine could have produced such a satire.

Maybe such humor can be considered sick, beyond the pale of good taste, but it paralleled that used by other Jewish stand-up comics of the 1950s and 1960s. Theodore Roszak observed the continuum across comic forms: "*Mad* brought into the malt shops the same angry abuse of middle-class America which comics like Mort Sahl and Lenny Bruce were to begin bringing into the night clubs of the mid-fifties."[22] As Bruce famously said, "the world is sick and I'm the doctor. I'm a surgeon with a scalpel for false values," adding, "I satirize many subjects that are particular sacred cows. In other words, I am a satirist basically. I am irreverent politically, religiously, or any other things that I think need discussing and satirizing."[23] Such statements were just as applicable to *Mad*. What David Kaufman wrote about Bruce's humor—that it was "chock-full of Jewish content, absolutely unique for its time. This content included Yiddish words and expressions, Jewish characters and scenarios, irreverent critiques of both Judaism and Christianity, and most important, the correlation of Jewish otherness with a subversive, iconoclastic attitude part beatnik and part hippie"[24]—is just as true, if not more so, of *Mad*. In fact, like *Mad*, Bruce began using Yiddish expressions in his act, not caring who did or did not understand them, or even whether anyone did.[25] *Mad*'s satire on Judaism, discussed above, resembled one of the most controversial segments of Bruce's routine, "Religions, Inc." Homing in on Judaism, in particular, he described Reform rabbis as "so reformed they're ashamed they're Jewish,"[26] the same point made in the 1972 "*Mad* 'Religion in America' Primer" discussed earlier.

As Kercher points out, "In a manner consistent with that deployed by Ernie Kovacs, Harvey Kurtzman, and the Jewish American writers and artists at *Mad*, Bruce used parodies to take comic revenge on the shallow lies perpetrated by American popular culture."[27] This approach was particularly evident following the kidnapping, trial, and execution of Adolf Eichmann between 1960 and 1962, after which Bruce made shocking jokes about the Holocaust. In a redneck used car salesman's voice, he would say, "Here's a Volkswagen pickup truck that was just used slightly during the war carrying the people back and forth to the furnaces." Or he would hold up a newspaper with the headline, "Six Million Jews Found Alive in Argentina." As Lawrence J. Epstein explains,

> The shock of such "jokes" came not only from the inappropriateness of joking about the Holocaust, but also from the fact that very few people even discussed it at all. Bruce's provocative joking forced Americans to recall what had already been discarded as forgotten history or simply repressed.[28]

Mad's joking did the same. A very pertinent question here is: who influenced whom?

These similarities are surely no coincidence, for prior to taking over the editorship of *Mad*, Feldstein had been attempting to sell a magazine conceived as a showcase for new talent. "I wanted guys like Lenny Bruce to have a place of publication," Feldstein recalled.[29] Although he never succeeded in securing a contribution from Bruce, taking advantage of *Mad*'s New York City location, Feldstein did tap the best talent flowing through radio, nightclubs, and Broadway for *Mad*.[30] As he explained, "I was trying to get names into the magazine, like Bob [Elliott] and Ray [Goulding], and Ernie Kovacs. Bob and Ray gave me some scripts of theirs to adapt. They agreed, and I got Tom Koch—his name was on the script—and I called him up, and said, 'Do you want to write for *Mad*?' He said, sure!"[31] Among those whose verbal material he used, or who gave him permission to reprint and render their material into visual form, were (in addition to those mentioned above) Orson Bean, Carl Reiner, Wally Cox, Andy Griffith, Tom Lehrer, Henry Morgan, Jean Shepherd, Paul Krassner, and Al "Jazzbo" Collins. From issue #31 in January 1957 through issue #55 in June 1960 (consistently at first but only sporadically toward the end), Feldstein prominently listed on the cover a broad range of guest celebrity contributors. Impressed with the work of Jules Feiffer, who began contributing cartoons to *The Village Voice* in 1956, *Mad* invited him to contribute. An excerpt from those cartoons ran in November 1958 as "Sick, Sick, Sick" (#42: 24–26); however, as Lawrence Rodman points out, these contributions were secured "circuitously, by the acquisition of permission directly from the publisher, rather than through any desire on Feiffer's part to link himself to *Mad*."[32]

Many of these celebrity contributors were Jewish comedians and personalities. They supplied the text, and *Mad*'s artists did the rest, transforming the latest radio, television, and stand-up humor of the day into comic book magazine material. One of the most prominent contributors was Sid Caesar, who employed the comedy-writing talents of Mel Brooks, Woody Allen, Larry Gelbart, and Neil Simon. Rodman has noted that "Mel Brooks' authorial voice and Borscht Belt terminology comes through" in Caesar's appearances in *Mad*; "It's evident that he [Brooks] had a hand in the contribution, however uncredited."[33] Therefore, it is also possible that *Mad* showcased the uncredited contributions of Allen, Gelbart, and Simon. For example, "A *Mad* Guide to Art Films" (Siegel and Woodbridge, #83, 12/63: 13–16) featured a made-up Japanese art-house movie called "Rosh-Hoshona, Myer Moore," playing on the names of the Jewish New Year festival and the French 1958 film *Hiroshima Mon Amour*. Did this item provide some inspiration for Allen's movie *What's Up, Tiger Lily?* (1966), in which he took a Japanese spy film and overdubbed it with dialogue that had nothing to do with the plot of the original film? Under Allen's direction, it became a James Bond spoof in which Phil Moscowitz tries to find the secret recipe for egg salad, a Jewish delicatessen staple.

All in all, *Mad* functioned as a secular Talmud. Like the Talmud, it was intertextual, bringing a range of other texts into its purview. In order to make the most of its humor, its readers were required to be versed in Western culture, both high and low, as well as middlebrow. It even had Talmud-style formatting. In what was known as the "chicken fat" method, pioneered by Will Elder, the frame was filled with details, and no space was wasted. The schmaltz was laid on thick, piling joke upon joke upon joke. Side jokes abounded, such as the sacks of kosher hams in a North Pole cave or Dr. Frank N. Stein's assistant reading a Yiddish newspaper. Like the Talmud, *Mad* was self-referential: in one spread it referred to the "Chicken Fat" by "Seymour Cohen." Inside Frank N. Stein's creation, he has placed a jar of "Instant Chicken Fat," and *Mad*'s "Special Art issue" (Kurtzman and Elder, #22, 4/55) focused exclusively on the story of "Bill (Chicken Fat) Elder" (inside cover). Kitchen and Buhle connected Elder's nickname, perhaps the most authentic Jewish schmear, to Kurtzman's artistic experimentation in *Mad*. "Nothing more Jewish could be imagined than the infant 'shmearing' chicken fat on towels, bald heads, visitors' dresses, and convenient walls—illustrated in color with thousands of blue and red lines," they argued. Yet, they added, "Today those shmears . . . are hung in various museums and signed with Elder's various pen names such as 'Braque,' 'Matisse,' 'Picasso,' etc.," in recognition of the artist's and editor's achievements in deconstructing high Modernism.[34]

Mad's alternative Jewish sensibility permeated the entire magazine. It was iconoclastic, worshipped no golden calves nor venerated any tablets of stone. It showcased the best Jewish comedy talents of the 1950s and 1960s, while anticipating what was to come from those of the later '60s, '70s, and '80s, including Woody Allen, Mel Brooks, and the team of Zucker-Abrahams-Zucker. It was thus surely no coincidence that *Mad* artist Jack Davis went on to design movie posters for Allen's *Bananas* (1971) among many other films. In the final analysis, *Mad* of the 1950s and 1960s very much articulated the position of the Jew in genteel (read *gentile*) society: one who does not quite belong.

Notes

1. Irving Rosenthal and Stewart Kampel, "Cartoonists," in *Encyclopaedia Judaica*, ed. Michael Berenbaum and Fred Skolnik, 2nd ed., 4: 501.

2. Quoted in Michael Kaminer, "Learning To Be Jewish From *Mad* Magazine," *Forward*, November 3, 2013, https://forward.com/schmooze/186234/learning-to-be-jewish-from-mad-magazine.

3. Nathan Abrams, "From Madness to Dysentery: *Mad*'s Other New York Intellectuals."

4. S. C. Ringgenberg, "Jolting Words with Al Feldstein in the EC Tradition!," 82.

5. Daniel Gluckson and Al Feldstein, "Man Behind the Curtain Department: Al Feldstein Interview," 72.

6. Arie Kaplan, *From Krakow to Krypton: Jews and Comic Books*, 79.

7. Gluckson and Feldstein, "Man Behind the Curtain Department," 72.

8. Eddy Portnoy, "Review of Mary-Lou Weisman's *Al Jaffee's Mad Life*, 'It's a Mad Mad MAD World,'" *Forward*, October 1, 2010, https://forward.com/culture/131480/it-s-a-mad-mad-mad-world.

9. Stanley Rothman and S. Robert Lichter, *Roots of Radicalism: Jews, Christians, and the New Left*, 108.

10. Stephen E. Kercher, *Revel with a Cause: Liberal Satire in Postwar America*, 106.

11. See Marc Eliot, *Walt Disney: Hollywood's Dark Prince*; and Neal Gabler, *Walt Disney: The Triumph of the American Imagination*.

12. Quoted in Kaplan, *From Krakow to Krypton*, 73–74.

13. E. Graydon Carter, "The Cosmos According to Mel Brooks," 271.

14. Denis Kitchen and Paul Buhle, *The Art of Harvey Kurtzman: The Mad Genius of Comics*, 87.

15. Maria Reidelbach, *Completely Mad: A History of the Comic Book and Magazine*, 58.

16. Henry Popkin, "The Vanishing Jew of Our Popular Culture," 51.

17. Bonnie K. Lyons, "American-Jewish Fiction Since 1945," 63-64.

18. See Christopher Witschonke, "A 'Curtain of Ignorance': An Analysis of Holocaust Portrayal in Textbooks from 1943 through 1959," 146–54; and Peter Novick, *The Holocaust in American Life*.

19. Reidelbach, *Completely Mad*, 83.

20. Reidelbach, *Completely Mad*, 83.

21. David Desser and Lester D. Friedman, *American-Jewish Filmmakers: Traditions and Trends*, 156.

22. Theodore Roszak, *The Making of a Counter Culture: Reflections on the Technocratic Society and Its Youthful Opposition*, 24.

23. Kercher, *Revel with a Cause*, 408.

24. David E. Kaufman, *Jewhooing the Sixties: American Celebrity and Jewish Identity—Sandy Koufax, Lenny Bruce, Bob Dylan, and Barbra Streisand*, 102.

25. Lawrence J. Epstein, *The Haunted Smile: The Story of Jewish Comedians in America*, 171.

26. Kercher, *Revel with a Cause*, 407.
27. Kercher, *Revel with a Cause*, 399.
28. Epstein, *The Haunted Smile*, 171.
29. Quoted in Gluckson and Feldstein, "Man Behind the Curtain Department," 85.
30. Lawrence Rodman, "*Mad*'s Guest Writers" in *Comic Books and the Cold War, 1946–1962: Essays on Graphic Treatment of Communism, the Code and Social Concerns*, edited by Chris York and Rafiel York, 173.
31. Quoted in Gluckson and Feldstein, "Man Behind the Curtain Department," 84.
32. Rodman, "*Mad*'s Guest Writers," 177.
33. Rodman, "*Mad*'s Guest Writers," 174.
34. Kitchen and Buhle, *The Art of Harvey Kurtzman*, 106.

15. Mutually Assured Disparagment:

Enmification and Enlightenment in Early 1950s *Mad*

James J. Kimble

A jest betrays something serious.

—Sigmund Freud

IN THE EARLY 1960s, the development of intercontinental ballistic missiles by both the United States and the Soviet Union brought the ongoing Cold War into a new strategic era. The phrase *mutually assured destruction* (usually taking the form of its colorful acronym, MAD) emerged as a means of describing the worldwide stalemate, as both antagonists came to recognize that their nuclear arsenals now made it likely that each would suffer catastrophic and irreversible losses if they were to allow the Cold War to heat up in a significant way. Under this zero-sum scenario, suggest Keir A. Lieber and Daryl G. Press, an all-out "nuclear war was . . . tantamount to mutual suicide."[1]

For much of the 1950s, in contrast, the United States had enjoyed a notable nuclear advantage over the Soviets. As Keith Dowding points out, "until the early 1960s, the United States might well have been able to wreak devastation on the USSR without suffering direct retaliation."[2] Even so, the Eisenhower era was curiously marked by a pervasive fear among many Americans that a Soviet attack was imminent. Parents installed bomb shelters in backyards, while their children practiced so-called duck-and-cover drills at school. Beginning in February of 1950, the remarkable phenomenon of McCarthyism crystallized these fears, formally expressing a national sense of dread that the communists' advance agents—whether they hailed from the Soviet Union or from Red China—were already in place. Although the doctrine of MAD was still in the troubled future, these Americans of the early 1950s were already fearful about the prospect of a deadly confrontation with the communist enemy.

How did Americans manage their fears in this turbulent decade? Hollywood offered one important means of doing so by providing the public with scores of features that were at once sensational and horrifying. The body snatchers, psychos, vampires, aliens, blobs, and werewolves that lurked in such movies, according to Cynthia Hendershot and M. Keith Booker, functioned as thinly veiled allegories of American fears in the midst of the Cold War struggle.[3] Here, presented on the silver screen and suitable for public consumption, were visceral and cathartic representations of the public's sociological concerns about the menacing Other. Significantly, when Americans faced their fears in these simple allegories, says Hendershot, they collaborated in creating "a space" in which they could safely "contemplate death."[4]

However, at least some Americans had another means of managing their Cold War fears as early as the 1950s; ironically, it went by the name of *Mad*. The phenomenon was, of all things, an unorthodox comic book. The new publication's title, of course, could not have referred to the MAD doctrine of the 1960s (at least not yet). Still, as Nathan Abrams has shown, the comic book quickly came to symbolize a sense of profound societal conflict in its own right. According to Abrams, *Mad*, as a prominent counter-intellectual voice during the early Cold War, provided readers an influential and resistant battleground in the generally conforming strictures of mass culture at the time. Specifically, through the devices of irony, parody, and outright mockery, the comic book provided a rare venue for conflicted dissent from a Cold War mentality that limited and even feared opportunities for oppositional social commentary.[5]

While Abrams's analysis provides a useful direction for anyone hoping to understand *Mad*'s provocative societal role in the early Cold War years, it leaves unanswered more precise questions about how the publication might have prompted readers to address the fears of the Cold War struggle from which it emerged. Here the era's silver screen monsters and aliens provide a useful analytical foil. To wit, anyone who has read *Mad*'s publications from the era knows that its writers and artists often trafficked in many of the same generic tropes as their Hollywood siblings. But the satiric and often derisive narratives residing in *Mad*'s pages typically functioned as much more than simple allegories. Rather, the publication's stories functioned as allegories *and* as subversive parodies.

In this dual mode, they thereby critiqued the Cold War and its fearful overtones in a fundamentally different way than the horror film at the local drive-in. In fact, I believe that rather than foster the contemplation of death, *Mad*'s parodies of the Cold War *milieu* tacitly encouraged readers to question the establishment version of the international struggle, to resist the overwhelming imperative to enmify the Other, and to reconsider the seemingly fundamental divide between capitalist and communist. Here were stories and images that were every bit as titillating as those found on movie screens. Yet their subtext was subversive, not compliant, and emancipatory, not alarming. In essence, by not so gently critiquing the establishment view of the Cold War in genre-based send-ups that were at once clever and profound, *Mad* quickly established a healthy social critique of the conflict at a time when public dissent was generally out of bounds.

In what follows, I trace the irregular fragments of *Mad*'s early 1950s outlook on the Cold War—a rhetorically charged viewpoint that I see as a kind of *mutually assured disparagement*. My analysis centers on the publication's initial comic book phase. These first twenty-three issues were published from October 1952 to May 1955 (or, roughly, from the election of Dwight D. Eisenhower to the formal establishment of the Warsaw Pact).[6] I contend that throughout that time, the publication's creative team (principally, as Nick Meglin points out, the "one-man show" Harvey Kurtzman[7]) returned again and again to the underpinnings of the Cold War by consistently finding ways to ridicule: 1) the contemporary international context; 2) the comical communist enemy; and 3) Americans' seemingly ludicrous self-conception on the world stage.

Ridiculing the International Context

For many casual readers, *Mad*'s earliest issues might have seemed to be about anything *but* the Cold War. After all, its specialty was lampooning the familiar media tropes of the day, whether they derived from comic books, movies, novels, or even the new medium of television.[8] For instance, in "Outer Sanctum!" (a freewheeling send-up of the 1940 movie *Inner Sanctum* and the radio serial it emerged from), a mad scientist creates a glob of artificial life that learns to rob banks, dress in fancy clothes, and fall in love (Kurtzman and Elder, #5, 6–7/53: 1-8). The story owes an obvious debt to the Frankenstein myth, but more conventionally serves as a subtle commentary on modern consumerism, greed, and the dangers of overwhelming ambition. Many of the comic book's other wide-ranging parodies offered similar themes. Thus, while Kristin L. Matthews has recently suggested that *Mad*'s ethos was essentially anti-totalitarian,[9] the idea that the comic book was even aware of the international situation might not have been immediately obvious to many readers at the time.

In retrospect, however, a scrutiny of every aspect of *Mad*'s comic book issues, from their narrative plot points to their throwaway gags, confirms that the publication's creators were indeed mindful of their Cold War context. To return to the "Outer Sanctum!" story line, as the scientist stirs his life-creating potion in a vat, one can see that the bizarre ingredients include a radiator, a dollar bill, a high-heeled shoe, and (in a nod to the careful reader) an air raid shelter sign—the emblem of societal fear at the time (#5, 6–7/53: 4).[10] Similarly, one of the comic book's interactive "Puzzle Pages!" showcases a maze with numerous dead ends, one of which sports a drawing of a snow-covered building and this facetious caption: "Russian Army Recruiting Station. Komarad!" (Kurtzman and Elder, #19, 1/55: 1-4; 2). Meanwhile, the splash page from "Teddy and the Pirates!" (Kurtzman and Wood, #6, 8–9/53: 1-8; 1) features among its dozens of minute details a communist soldier shooting a peasant on a busy Hong Kong street. These sorts of references must have seemed absurd to those readers who focused on them. Yet because almost everything in *Mad* was patently absurd, the undertones of the tense international situation inherent in them might have escaped notice.

At other times, though, *Mad*'s Cold War observations were less subtle, but no less comedic in their mission. The narrator's opening line for the "G. I. Shmoe!" episode, for example, helpfully informs readers that "The truce has been signed in Korea!" (Kurtzman and Wood, #10, 4/54: 1-8; 1). That joyful sounding factoid, however, immediately serves as an excuse for the publication staff to "sink [their] teeth into . . . literature born of the war!" (1) and thereby to exaggerate the actions of American soldiers in a typically brazen lampoon. An even less understated scenario appears in "Gopo Gossum!," an adroit parody of Walt Kelly's *Pogo* universe (Kurtzman and Wood, #23, 5/55: 1–6). In this version, the swamp is filled with bizarre Cold War caricatures, including Winston Churchmouse (an alligator), Marshland Tito (an owl), Mendup France (a tortoise), Change-ki-Check (a bloodhound), and even a character first referred to (in an homage to Kelly's Simple J. Malarkey, who debuted May

5, 1953) as "Simple J. Baloney," whose real name turns out to be McCarthy and is drawn, naturally, to look like Charlie McCarthy, the ventriloquist's dummy (3). A similar rogue's gallery of international players appears in "Sheik of Araby!," when a new recruit in the French Foreign Legion meets a series of stereotypes: a lecherous Frenchman, a supercilious Briton, an enraged Italian, an aristocratic German, and (in a classic case of overkill) a yellow-eyed, Neanderthal-like Russian named Rasputin (Kurtzman and Severin, #3, 1–2/53: 1-7; 3). Such caricatures amounted to gleeful, if somewhat obvious, attempts to turn the serious consideration of sober international relations on its head. Instead, they seemed to say, it would be healthier (and a lot more fun) to take global tensions with a generous grain of salt. Perhaps that reasoning is why, after the motley creatures in Gopo's swamp manage to obliterate themselves, a witness says, "I tol' 'em not to mess aroun' [with politics] . . . and now they gone . . . they done blowed each other up" (6). Calling into question the actual usefulness of nurturing the world's political tensions, it would seem, was one way that the comic book's team could scrutinize the established assumptions of the ongoing international struggle.

To be sure, there were times when *Mad* seemed to be fully aware of the high stakes inherent in the international context at the time. Its "Black and Blue Hawks!" story line, for instance, echoes contemporary concerns about communist expansion when the squadron's aviators resolve to stop an impending revolution in a remote placed called Panazonia (Kurtzman and Wood, #5, 6–7/53: 1-6; 2). Another protagonist, this one a civilian, progressively bludgeons his persistent radio because it will not stop reporting distressing world news, such as "Boy—have we got troubles, gee whiz," and "Washington is buzzing with rumors!" (Kurtzman, "Hey Look" #8, 12/53–1/54: 1-6; 3). Even these sorts of scenes, however, soon descend into camp. The squadron's search for the revolution turns into an operation worthy of the Keystone Kops, and the civilian succeeds in silencing his radio only to become flustered all over again when he can still hear the bad news on his neighbor's set: "The situation is tense all over there" (3). Other story lines find additional ways to ridicule normally serious Cold War tensions, as when Prince Violent's "clean living" and "100% Americanism" allow him to defeat his evil nemesis in an epic thumb wrestling match (Kurtzman and Wood, #14, 8/54: 1-7; 7), or when an American submarine succeeds in breaching the Iron Curtain by drilling a hole in it big enough to pass through (DeFuccio, "Operation

Under-the-Ground" Part II #8, 12/53–1/54: 1). Such off-the-wall viewpoints called into question even the most basic assumptions of the Cold War context, rendering them in a new, absurdist light.

In the end, then, *Mad*'s ridiculous antics frequently seemed to imply that readers did not really need to take the unstable international situation quite so seriously. An apparently random sight gag in the "Katchandhammer Kids!" story line is particularly telling in this respect. In one panel, readers can see another air raid shelter sign, although this one appears on a wall in a house and someone has shifted it to point straight up (Kurtzman and Elder, #20, 2/55: 1-8; 4). In the next panel (5), the sign has transformed into an apt visual summation of the polarized Cold War. A dashed vertical line now splits it in half, with one side featuring the Soviet flag and the words "East Zone," and the other side showing the American flag and the words "West Zone." But then, in a third panel, the same sign has again transformed, this time to feature the kind of Germanic English mix that was typical of the original *Katzenjammer Kids* comic strip: "Dun't forget! No putting chiken fet on der ster rales. Mama" (5). Thus, in the space of only three panels, *Mad* referenced Cold War fears, visually summarized the opposing sides in the struggle, and then wiped the slate clean by moving onto something entirely different. It would be easy to dismiss the sequence as a simple non sequitur, but the gap between international fears and a reminder about chicken fat in the house is so vast and nonsensical that it certainly appears to be an intentional ploy to suggest that Americans might chuckle at the international struggle once in a while. In the early 1950s, a tongue-in-cheek viewpoint like that one was truly groundbreaking—but *Mad* seemed to enjoy presenting it to American readers.

The Hyperbolic Communist Enemy

One of the central fears held so firmly by many Americans at the time involved the continuous enmification of the communist world. The revolutionary philosophy espoused by the Soviets, Chinese, and their satellite nations was itself perceived as a threat, of course. But even more prominent in American discourse were fearful depictions of the communists themselves. Politicians and media reports both portrayed them as devious, insidious, and even evil at heart. Such viewpoints were expressed rather starkly on May 1, 1950, when the citizens of Mosinee, Wisconsin, staged a mock communist coup for journalists and visiting dignitaries. As everyday Americans watched newsreel reports of the incident in fascinated horror, Mosinee's insurgents seized the town newspaper, terminated the police chief, suspended civil rights, and imprisoned local religious leaders in a stockade.[11] While the event was all for show, it eloquently summarized many Americans' views in the early 1950s, not only of the lurking dangers of communism but also of the immoral nature of those who sought to bring it to American shores.[12]

The prevalence of these fears in early Cold War society, not surprisingly, presented a juicy target for *Mad*'s publishing team. The ubiquitous notion at the time that communists were targeting the United States through covert subversion and infiltration was a particularly prominent subtext in the comic book's pages. Kurtzman and Elder's "Mole!," for example, appears to have been a not-so-subtle take-off on Soviet infiltrators who, in the popular mind at least, were secretly at work burrowing into pockets of American society for later activation (a concept sensationalized by the 1951 trial of Julius and Ethel Rosenberg). Mole, as his name implies, is an incompetent, rodent-like troublemaker who digs his way into mischief, crimes, and even out of jail cells. At one point, the police take away his outfit, revealing that his undergarments sport the colors of the Soviet and Chinese flags (#2, 12/52–1/53: 1-7; 5). In a similarly goofy (though less literal) reference to subversive communist infiltration, the sci-fi story "Gookum!" in the same issue depicts an alien society under constant threat from a red and pink blob (Kurtzman and Wood, #2: 1-6).[13] A security wall has kept the residents safe for some time, but now, relates the narrator, "the gookum *was* beginning to stir!" (4). Eventually, a "*teenchy weenchy piece of gookum got past the wall!*" (4). That tiny infiltration, of course, spells the beginning of the end, eventually sending the defenseless society into a pink-hued oblivion. As with Mole's exploits, here is a version of subversive infiltration and its apparent consequences taken to an absurd extreme. The hyperbole in both stories is not so much an attack on the *possibility* of insurgent agents, but rather a tacit challenge to the paralyzing notion that those hidden enemies were nearly everywhere, ready at any moment to pull unseen levers and usher in an American revolution in red.

A related subject selected for ridicule by *Mad*'s team was the common Eisenhower-era concern that some Americans themselves might be turning away from their country in order to help the communists. The leader of the Black and Blue Hawks, to take one example, eventually discovers that his own men have been involved in carrying out the revolution in remote Panazonia (Kurtzman and Wood, "Black," 7). The hero of "Superduperman!," a red-and-blue disaster in motion, has a similarly rude surprise when his colleague, Captain Marbles, suddenly changes into a nemesis, describing himself as "the 'unknown monster!'" (Kurtzman and Wood, #4, 4–5/53: 1-8; 5). "You?" cries Superduperman. "Captain Marbles? Have turned renegade? Take THAT!" (5). The ensuing fight not only lampoons the familiar Superman and Captain Marvel legends, but also makes fun of the idea that such a paragon of American patriotism as Captain Marvel could turn traitor. Much like the comic book's tongue-in-cheek references to communist infiltrators, plot developments such as these did not question that American traitors *could* exist, but instead ridiculed the idea that they were legion.

As for the communists themselves, the cultural image of the vile reds naturally proved too much for *Mad* to resist. One recurring theme in this respect amounted to a striking feminization of the Communist enemy. In "G. I. Shmoe!" our heroes discover that the enemy commander is a statuesque woman whose red star badges and Soviet flag betray her allegiance. In classic *Mad* fashion, G. I. Shmoe and Sgt. Squirt are befuddled by her voluptuous beauty, even as she threatens to torture them with "*permanent K.P.!*" (4). At length, she proclaims victory in the battle, telling the Americans that "*my* army has taken over *your* army by *subversion*," since "*my whole army of men is actually an army of . . . WOMEN!*" (7). Curiously, the Black and Blue Hawks come across a similar enemy leader, who also flummoxes the protagonists with her very presence (and by calling the chief Hawk "dumpling") (Kurtzman and Wood, "Black," 4). Despite inhabiting the traditional role of chief antagonist, such over-the-top, Vargas-like enemy figures must have inspired more appreciation than fear. Indeed, the comic book's producers seemed to be asking, how could an enemy essentially composed of bombastic pin-ups truly be a threat to the American way of life?

Even when *Mad*'s enemy depictions were more stereotypically masculine, they still managed to come to life in ridiculously exaggerated scenes and generally behaved in madcap fashion. Here "Operation Under-the-Ground," the six-part serial adventures of American agent Five Fingers Jones, spying on location in Moscow, are particularly interesting. As Jones walks around the Gremlin compound undetected in part III, he is shocked to witness "giant tanks shooting at a dove of peace"

(De Fuccio, "Operation Under-the-Ground!" Part III #9, 3/54: 1). The dying dove "drops the olive branch," he says, leading nearby "Russian soldiers [to] pounce on the olives hungrily and eat them up" (1). Soon afterwards, in part IV, Jones is captured by the comic doppelgangers of the real-life Soviet MVD, or Ministry of Internal Affairs. The *Mad* version, as one might expect, is called the BVD, whose members proudly wear their unit's "shoulder patch on their Bermuda shorts" (1) and whose leader, Lavrenti Buried (a reference to Stalin's MVD chief, Lavrentiy Beria), "wears red flannel underwear to denote his high rank in the BVD's" (Kurtzman, "Operation Under-the-Ground!" Part IV #10, 4/54: 1). Buried orders Jones to undergo torture, since he has not "heard a human scream for a whole minute now" (1). Subsequently, readers find out in a text-only installment, our hero's encounter in the torture chamber is "still evident by the powder burns . . . and the shredded stub of an exploding cigar still clenched between his teeth!" (Kurtzman, "Operation Under-the-Ground!" Part V #11, 5/54: 1–6). Truly, as the narrator intones in part VI, the dauntless American spy has found himself in a "pickle" (Kurtzman, "Operation under-the-Ground!" Part VI #12, 6/54: 1). Left unspoken, however, is the subtextual message underlying all the hyperbole that Jones has encountered along the way: that these faux Soviets were actually more fun than fearsome, and more wacky than wicked. Not unlike its feminized versions of the communist enemy, the comic book's perspective here appeared to be hinting that societal constructions of the dastardly commies were essentially hollow. When taken together with the publication's facetious looks at subversive infiltrations and traitorous Americans, it must have been clear, at least to discerning readers, that *Mad* had a dubious view of the era's normative impulse to enmify the communists as both malevolent and monolithic.

The Land of the Free and the Depraved

Doubtless, if *Mad* were truly hinting that American views of the communist enemy in the early 1950s were generally overblown or even ridiculous, then that message had something to say about the Americans who held those beliefs, too. Contemporary public discourse was rife with overt celebrations of the nation's prosperity, virtue, and inherent right to what was more or less a "bottomless American cornucopia."[14] In fact, while the 1950 mock coup in Mosinee inspired much commentary about the dangers of communism, it simultaneously prompted eloquent paeans to time-honored national values such as freedom, loyalty, and veneration of the American way of life.[15] *Mad* seemed to have as little patience for that brand of unquestioning patriotism as it did for popular conceptions of the Communists themselves.

Toward that end, readers of the comic book frequently came across narratives that poked fun at traditional notions of Americanism and, indeed, of the nation's allegedly virtuous military role on the world stage. Tellingly, for instance, when G. I. Shmoe is smitten with the enemy commander, he immediately tries to impress her with his Americanism: "No doubt you want to say you are tired of enemy way of life . . . you want to wear lipstick . . . you want to shop in the A&P! . . . You want to throw pop-bottles at the umpires! . . . Go ahead, baby! . . . What is it you wish to tell me?" (3). Her response, to him at least, is a shock: "Hey, Joe! . . . You got chewing gum?" (3). It turns out that this question reappears no less than sixteen times throughout the course of the story line, each time serving as a wry commentary on what, precisely, other nationalities might remember Americans for. Hence, even if the soldiers were conquering heroes, as Shmoe seems to think, their possession of chewing gum ends up being their most memorable feature.

Yet while G. I. Shmoe gets to play the heroic role—at least in his own mind—other depictions of the U.S. military come across as wholly incompetent. In the "Teddy and the Pirates!" splash page featuring the busy Hong Kong street scene (Kurtzman and Wood, #6, 8-9/53: 1-8; 1), two American soldiers not only fail to notice the gun-toting communist nearby, but they are also confidently marching into an open maintenance hole—probably because they are busy ogling yet another Vargas-like woman in the foreground. The American flyboy in "Smilin' Melvin!" also proves to be dangerously oblivious when he becomes so involved in a conversation about a new secret jet that he overlooks a Communist MIG fighter hovering just above (Kurtzman and Wood, #7, 10–11/53: 1–7; 2). Even the intrepid spy Five Fingers Jones has his ludicrous moments, as when his official instructions tell him that he will "be picked up by submarine just off the coast under cover of darkness this afternoon at one sharp!" (DeFuccio, "Operation Under-the Ground!" Part II #8: 12/53-1/54: 1). Although they were lighthearted, these sorts of observations were hardly flattering tributes to America's military might and capability.

At times, *Mad* even chose to portray American military personnel in a pointedly disapproving manner. In an otherwise jaunty western send-up, for example, the hero of "Pot-Shot Pete" is captured by a hostile Native American tribe (Kurtzman, #15, 9/54: 1–5). They are about to kill him when a bugle sounds: the cavalry is here! Inexplicably, however, the rescuers show up as a modern invasion force, with planes dropping bombs, destroyers firing their big guns, and GIs parachuting down to join the action. After a quick and pervasive massacre, the lead cavalry officer stands over a veritable sea of red-inked bodies and proudly proclaims: "Well, Sheriff! We cleaned out them redskins!" (5). Elsewhere, the "Stalag 18!" story line provides another skeptical view of American soldiers, since its imprisoned protagonists are not only "a furshlugginer mess!" but are hopelessly obsessed with using a telescope to peep at the nearby Russian camp that consists only of women (Kurtzman and Wood, #18, 12/54: 1–7). The most American of all the prisoners, at first glance, is Security, who is drawn to look exactly like the innocuous comic character Archie Andrews. The narrative touts him as "a typical American teenager" so many times (four, to be precise) that it is no surprise he ends up being unveiled as a "trained Cherman spy!" (5). Naming him *Security*, then, is an intentional misnomer, for as a traitor he provides no security to his nation whatsoever. To consider him and his peeping fellow prisoners along with the cheerfully genocidal cavalry that rescues Pot-Shot Pete is to become aware of a surprisingly negative perspective in the comic book regarding the American military and all that it represented in the 1950s.

Still, *Mad* saved the worst of its vitriol for that paragon of paranoid Cold War Americanism, Joseph McCarthy. As mentioned earlier, the senator features prominently in the "Gopo Gossum!" swamp, although he is in the guise of the ventriloquist's dummy *Charlie* McCarthy (not the most admiring depiction, to be sure). Even worse, after the character makes his entrance, he quickly begins a prolonged rant about Democrats, prompting another character to shout "Joe mus' go!" and another to start chanting: "Censure! Censure!" (4). Astonishingly, however, this attack on McCarthy was not the first time *Mad* had openly ridiculed the senator. Six months earlier, the comic book had published "What's My Shine!," which portrayed McCarthy's Senate subcommittee as a game show (along the lines of *What's My Line?*, CBS, 1950-1967). Here, appearing as panelist Joseph McCartaway, he incessantly calls disruptive points of order and accuses the mystery guest of being a "redskin"—an obvious nod to the senator's anti-communist (or anti-reds) mission (Kurtzman and Davis, #17, 11/54: 7–1; 5). By the end of the story line, not surprisingly, his aggressive and more or less depraved behavior has resulted in a studio riot.

To be sure, in each of these incriminating stories, *Mad* had essentially constructed an elaborate straw argument in that the McCarthy it was attacking was not the same as the original. Nonetheless, the comic book's disparagement of the anti-communist lawmaker arguably hit its mark. As Arie Kaplan suggests, *Mad* was highly successful in "revealing the kangaroo court foolishness of McCarthy's crusade."[16] Ultimately, though, the attacks were just part of a larger sense of impatience with the unreflective and unquestioning Americanism that *Mad* seemed to find in the senator, his followers, and in the viewpoint shared by many such anti-communists that the United States was an unquestionable force for good in the world and that its global military might was a worthy reflection of that inherent goodness. The comic book's most essential suggestion to readers, it would appear, was to treat with skepticism the ideological beliefs of those who would unhesitatingly support the elaborate excesses of anti-communism. That *Mad* made this point, at times, in an elaborately excessive way was just one more irony to throw on the pile.

Conclusion

On February 5, 1959, Edwin A. Walker, the Commanding General of the Arkansas Military District, contacted the FBI to encourage its agents to investigate what appeared, in his eyes at least, to be a subversive publication. The FBI's records have preserved Walker's complaint. In it, he related his concern that "each article had a hidden meaning and [that] even the advertisements make disparaging remarks about the military, industry, and American institutions."[17] The publication in question was, of course, *Mad*. And although the FBI does not seem to have taken Walker's complaint seriously, perhaps recognizing that the magazine's contents (including ads) were satiric, the general's concerns about *Mad*'s peculiar style of subversive disparagement in the 1950s were right on target.

In hindsight, Walker had been able to see only half of the situation. The publication *was* subversive, and it *did* disparage its targets. But a careful perusal of *Mad*'s issues from the time reveals that it felt free to target *both* sides in the Cold War, as well as the generally accepted framework of the struggle itself. As Abrams has suggested, the publication's *modus operandi* involved "a high level of political satire that was not afraid to critique either side in the Cold War."[18] In this sense, it was an equal opportunity prankster whose creators felt free to send up Stalin, Eisenhower, and everyone on the political spectrum in between. Like the monsters and aliens that were wreaking havoc on the silver screen of the 1950s, *Mad* thus helpfully offered its fans an allegorical means of facing and managing their Cold War–related fears. Unlike those bizarre creatures at the drive-in, however, the publication went beyond simple allegory to embrace the more incisive practice of parody.

While this essay has focused on *Mad*'s initial establishment of its disparaging parodies, those parodies carried on well into the 1960s. Due, in part, to the comic book's long-lasting influence, the children of that later decade "were able to laugh about Soviet infiltration and the atomic bomb by the time they took their first history class."[19] It probably helped that, by this point, a number of other pop culture sources had joined forces with *Mad*'s parodic campaign. As early as 1958, for instance, animated cartoon fans were chuckling at the comic evil of Boris Badenov and Natasha Fatale as they squared off against Rocky and Bullwinkle on television.[20] By 1964, moviegoers were flocking to Stanley Kubrick's thoroughly satiric *Dr. Strangelove*, while two years later they were enjoying the more mainstream comedy *The Russians are Coming, the Russians* are Coming. Even the Beatles did their part, opening their 1968 *White Album* with "Back in the U.S.S.R.," on the one hand a cheerful send-up of Chuck Berry and the Beach Boys and, on the other, an incisive critique of Cold War animosities.

Such immensely popular sources of 1960s Cold War parody may tempt us to overlook *Mad*'s pioneering contributions from the 1950s. Critics and historians alike should resist that impulse. After all, it was *Mad* that taught the world early on that one of the most effective ways to respond to the fears of the Cold War was to jest about it. Harvey Kurtzman and his *Mad* team understood, much like Sigmund Freud before them, that jests frequently mask a more serious intent.[21] Simply put, by disparaging the assumptions of the Cold War, not to mention those of its participants, the humor evident in the earliest issues of *Mad* set in motion a kind of redemption from the strictures of 1950s American society. Nonetheless, while the publication's critique of the Cold War era might have been funny, looking back from a vantage point nearly seventy years later makes it easier to see that that critique was in many ways no laughing matter.

Notes

1. Keir A. Lieber and Daryl G. Press, "The End of MAD? The Nuclear Dimension of U.S. Primacy," 7.

2. Keith Dowding, *Encyclopedia of Power*, 432.

3. Cynthia Hendershot, *I Was a Cold War Monster: Horror Films, Eroticism, and the Cold War Imagination*, 58; M. Keith Booker, *Monsters, Mushroom Clouds, and the Cold War: American Science Fiction and the Roots of Postmodernism, 1946–1964*, 40.

4. Hendershot, *I Was a Cold War Monster*, 129.

5. Nathan Abrams, "From Madness to Dysentery: *Mad*'s Other New York Intellectuals," 435–36.

6. After that point, due in part to the ongoing public controversy over the alleged dangers of comic books to the juvenile generation, *Mad* shifted its publication philosophy and physical format in order to become a glossy magazine; see Amy Kiste Nyberg, *Seal of Approval: The History of the Comics Code*, 117–24; Mark Evanier, introduction to *The Mad Archives*, vol. 4: 7. While its subversive attitudes survived the transformation (for example, as Teodora Carabas points out, in the famous "Spy vs. Spy" strip, which emerged in early 1961; see Carabas, "'Tales Calculated to Drive You MAD': The Debunking of Spies, Superheroes, and Cold War Rhetoric in *Mad* Magazine's 'Spy vs. Spy,'" 4–24), my interest here lies with the ideological precedents that emerged from the publication's formative years, which parallel the initial trajectory of Ike's presidency.

7. Nick Meglin, introduction to *The Mad Archives*, vol. 1: 8.

8. Frank Jacobs, "Introduction," *The Mad Archives* 3: 10.

9. Kristin L. Matthews, "A *Mad* Proposition in Postwar America," 212.

10. The term *air raid shelter* derived primarily from World War II in both the United Kingdom and the United States; after the war, the term gradually gave way to *fallout shelter* and *blast shelter*, but it was still in common use in the early 1950s as a reference to areas in which one could seek protection from an imminent enemy attack.

11. Richard M. Fried, *The Russians Are Coming! The Russians Are Coming! Pageantry and Patriotism in Cold-War America*, 72–73.

12. "The Town that Saw Red," 65–68.

13. The characters describe the gookum as pink, even though the comic book primarily uses the color red to depict it. Red, would, of course, have been the most obvious way to allude to communists, but the term *pinko* as a reference to communist sympathizers was also in common use at the time. Either color, then, made for a suitable wink at the Communist nature of the gookum.

14. William H. Young and Nancy K. Young, *The 1950s*, 21.

15. "It Happened One Day in Mosinee," 32.

16. Arie Kaplan, *From Krakow to Krypton: Jews and Comic Books*, 73.

17. Bob Rowen, "Right vs. Left Politics in the Cold War and the Improbable Saga of Major General Edwin Walker," sec. 1.

18. Abrams, "From Madness to Dysentery," 448.

19. James Eric (Jay) Black, "Amoozin' but Confoozin': Comic Strips as a Voice of Dissent in the 1950s," 460.

20. The series now known as *The Adventures of Rocky and Bulwinkle and Their Friends* aired under varied titles from 1959 to 1961 in black and white on ABC and from 1961 to 1964 in color on NBC.

21. Sigmund Freud, *Jokes and Their Relation to the Unconscious,* 128.

16. Diplomats Gone *Mad*:

A Musical Rumble

James D. Bloom

> We are glad that the United Nations has chosen New York as its permanent home. Now we must search constantly for ways to strengthen the United Nations and build it into a world organization which can maintain permanent peace with liberty, under a system of world justice.
>
> —Harry Truman (1948)

IN HIS LAST State of the Union message to Congress on January 9, 1952, President Harry Truman unwittingly ushered in the inaugural year of Harvey Kurtzman and Bill Gaines's *Mad* comic, which reached newsstands that summer. Truman warned Americans that they were "moving through a perilous time."[1] During 1952, truce talks to end the Korean War, which would ultimately result in some 30,000 American deaths, had stalled. Later in the year, the U.S. military would test the very first hydrogen bomb on the Eniwetok atoll. In November, Wisconsin voters reelected Senator Joseph McCarthy, who would become a prime target of *Mad*'s satires.[2] Subsequently, McCarthy's Republican colleagues named him chairman of their chamber's subcommittee on investigations.

From 1952 on, *Mad* guided millions of baby boomers, 43 percent of high school students and 58 percent of college students by the 1960s, through the "perilous time" that President Truman had heralded.[3] Beneficiaries of this guidance included transformative contemporary leaders and artists such as rock poet Patti Smith, who once enthused that "after *Mad* drugs were nothing."[4] For the Pulitzer Prize-winning artist-writer Art Spiegelman, *Mad* proved life-changing.[5] Spiegelman recalls that after having "studied [*Mad*] with the intensity that some of his peers brought to pages of the Talmud," he built his storied career on "using the tools that *Mad* offered" as he pursued "absolute conviction."[6]

Early in the twenty-first century, *Mad*'s role in shaping what Stephen E. Kercher termed boomers' "generational identity" and inspiring "skepticism toward institutions"[7] reached beyond the arts and into the corridors of American political power. According to a *Washington Post* profile, *Saturday Night Live* writer-performer Al Franken began his meteoric rise—and fall—as a U.S. senator when he ingratiated himself with his colleagues by "citing *Mad* magazine's 'Spy vs. Spy' in Judiciary Committee hearings."[8] Franken's career, including *Mad*'s influence on it, demonstrates how, as Andrew Ross has argued, baby boomers became the "first generation of Americans to *use* their involvement with popular culture itself as a site of contestation,"[9] as a springboard for political engagement and ideological critique.

Few popular culture influences have figured more influentially in the contestation that Ross identifies than *Mad*. Arguably *Mad*'s impact exceeded that of rock and roll, Disney, and network TV in instructing and inspiring baby boomers and in preparing a handful of the generation's stars, including Smith, Spiegelman, and Franken, for their groundbreaking careers. By guiding boomers through "a perilous time," through what we've learned to call the Cold War, *Mad* instructed these thought leaders and countless other boomers to monitor and, as needed, to mock the foibles and crimes of the alleged adults who presided over the chronic conflicts and precarious compromises that their policies had produced. Central to *Mad*'s outsized pedagogical efficacy was the extent to which, as Nathan Abrams has argued, its creators "demonstrated an astute awareness of international affairs and the diplomatic maneuverings of the American government," thus offering "teenagers a political education over their cornflakes."[10] Even more pointedly, Kristin L. Matthews has characterized *Mad* as having "demanded" that readers "acknowledge America's sociopolitical problems."[11] The chief vehicle for this acknowledgment was parody. As a comic mode, parody helps ensure that works of art are, in Linda Hutcheon's formulation, "resolutely historical and inescapably political" and "profoundly implicated in, yet still capable of criticizing"[12]—just like the most memorable articles in *Mad* and the practices and institutions that *Mad* so influentially spoofed.

Officially, of course, the same adult authorities whom *Mad* became legendary for ridiculing and calling to account were already making similar demands on young Americans. Whether they liked it or not, boomers were having their curiosity sated—or regulated—by the state as well. In public schools across America, young Americans were being trained—if not indoctrinated—to recognize and embrace the policies and assumptions on which U.S. Cold War hegemony rested. To sustain and promote these policies, American leaders and their allies established in the aftermath of World War II a constellation of international organizations designed to prevent a third world war by ensuring global stability and promoting prosperity under the aegis of a Pax Americana.[13] The acronyms of military alliances such as CENTO, SEATO, and especially NATO became household names among civic-minded Americans, as did familiarity with the World Bank and the International Monetary Fund among the political and financial cognoscenti. One of these hegemonizing international organizations became central to the civic indoctrination of the American boomer schoolchildren who became the *Mad* demographic: the United Nations. In public schools across America, in assemblies, in their social studies lessons, and in their arts-and-crafts projects, schoolchildren paid homage to the UN every year on October 24. Officially designated "United Nations Day" in 1948, UN Day marks the annual anniversary of the world body's 1945 founding.

A week after UN Day, on Halloween, thousands of American schoolchildren took to the streets to express their fealty to the guardian of global stability whom they had just honored in their classrooms and auditoriums. Collecting their neighbors' loose change on behalf of the United Nations International Children's Emergency Fund, trick-or-treaters sported large trick-or-treat candy collection bags in one hand and smaller orange and black UNICEF boxes, often made from repurposed waxed-cardboard school-lunch milk cartons, in the other.[14] As a result of this popular UNICEF campaign, which enlisted schoolchildren to promote the U.S. foreign policy agenda, the United Nations—and the assumptions and commitments it represented—became embedded in young Americans' national imaginary throughout the Cold War era. In 1961, *Mad* writer Larry Siegel and artist Mort Drucker spotlighted what the UN had come to represent during its first generation in action by turning it from a deliberative diplomatic forum into a showbiz extravaganza in "The United Nations Awards Show" (#62, 4/61: 45–48), hosted by the UN Secretary General and the Soviet foreign minister, assisted by a fur-wrapped Marilyn Monroe look-alike speaking on behalf of "all the other intellectuals" (45). UNICEF inaugurated its Halloween ritual in 1950, so many of these trick-or-treaters are likely to have become the very readers whose understanding of their American identities came to be shaped, and often challenged, by reading *Mad* after its debut two years later.

It might be a stretch to claim that trick-or-treating for UNICEF by itself constituted an effort by the state to enlist *Mad*-primed American grade-schoolers in the Cold War, because such efforts also included scheduled school-sponsored duck-and-cover drills and weekend tests of municipal air-raid sirens. While these tests and drills spoke to our collective fears, our celebrations of UN Day and our UNICEF solicitations stirred hopes that these tests would never be more than tests, the drills never more than drills.

Mad's focus on the UN provides one example among many of its staff's attention to Cold War assumptions and concerns, both in print and behind the scenes. Almost a decade after its inaugural issue, *Mad* found itself embroiled in a Cold War battle of its own, "a bitter showdown between opposing self-styled patriots," as Maria Reidelbach put it.[15] This conflict, a 1961–62 libel suit against *Mad* by Gaines against an Oklahoma "crusader" against "the Communist threat,"[16] resulted in a settlement that required the red-baiting defendant to declare publicly in court that he "never referred to the magazine as a Communist-inspired, Communist-motivated publication, or to its editors as Communist sympathizers or Communist dupes."[17] The judicial vindication anticipates Nathan Abrams's description of *Mad* as an impartial arbiter in the Cold War of ideas between the U.S. and the USSR, as having "upheld and undermined American attitudes" toward America's Soviet bloc adversaries throughout the 1950s and 1960s.[18]

Mad's acerbic wariness toward these adversaries appeared perhaps most graphically on its cover in October 1963 (#82), the first anniversary of the Cold War's most dangerous U.S.-Soviet confrontation, now referred to as the Cuban Missile Crisis. The cover, by Norman Mingo, shows a half profile of Cuban leader—and Soviet proxy—Fidel Castro smoking an oversized, newly lit exploding cigar (a staple of slapstick comedy and a possible reference to the rumor of such a CIA assassination plot) with a cigar band in the center of the frame featuring *Mad* mascot Alfred E. Neuman holding his fingers in his ears, anticipating Armageddon.

Thus absolved of treason and of pro-communist sympathies, *Mad* set out six months after the settlement of its libel suit—*and* six months after the removal of Soviet missiles from Cuba—to resolve, at least satirically, the chronically roiling Cold War tensions that had produced the Cuban Missile Crisis. The resolution that the *Mad* staff envisioned reflected the extent to which the UN functioned in the U.S. public imaginary during *Mad*'s early decades as a stage for playing out the tensions between American fears and hopes, tensions that *Mad* rehearsed in its April 1963 issue, with Frank Jacobs and Mort Drucker's "East Side Story" (#78: 4-12). Coincidentally or not, this spoof of the Motion Picture Academy's 1962 Best Picture winner, *West Side Story* (1961), redeployed the initial working title of the 1957 hit musical that the movie was based on.[19] A half century before the movie version of *West Side Story* came to be recognized as a Cold War–era touchstone, veteran staffer Frank Jacobs (*Mad*'s "poet laureate"), found the genesis of a parody in current events.[20] Soon after arriving at *Mad* during its "glory years," he noted how "the Cold War was heating up" while "on Broadway *WSS* was being hailed as the greatest new musical in years," he recalled. "I suggested melding the Cold War with the musical. The result was 'East Side Story.'"[21] Ultimately, *West Side Story* proved so compelling to Jacobs that he wrote a reprise spoof, "West Coast Story." Appearing in *Mad*'s April 1971 issue with art by Jack Davis, "West Coast Story" apocalyptically savaged both long-haired counterculture protesters and their Establishment antagonists Billy Graham, J. Edgar Hoover, Richard Nixon, and Ronald Reagan (#142: 4-11). Loosely even-handed in contrast to "East Side Story," "West Coast Story" didn't come to press in the wake of an existential global cliffhanger, such as the Cuban missile standoff, and lacked the sharp elbows that made the earlier piece so memorable. Whereas "West Coast Story" sophomorically pandered to the "everything's-a-scam-and-everyone's-an-idiot" smugness that *Mad* readers enjoyed sharing, "East Side Story" offered the sophisticated, nuanced civics lessons that *Mad*, at its best, provided.

Jacobs's first *West Side Story* spoof afforded *Mad*'s longtime go-to "genius" caricaturist Mort Drucker an opportunity to revisit the UN after his 1961 "Awards Show" parody (#62, 4/61: 45–48) by shifting the location of the original *West Side Story* narrative.[22] Jacobs relocated his narrative from the once impoverished, then gentrifying Manhattan neighborhood evoked in screenwriter Ernest Lehman's Hollywood and playwright Arthur Laurents's Broadway version of this *Romeo and Juliet* update across Manhattan to the United Nations headquarters, highlighting its role as the focal arena for both staging and containing conflicts between the era's contending global hegemons: the United States and the Soviet Union. Jacobs's parodies of the songs that composer Leonard Bernstein and lyricist Stephen Sondheim wrote for *West Side Story* reduce these global colossuses to the moral and aesthetic dimensions of the ethnocentric, turf-driven street gangs who implausibly dance with, and chillingly murder, one another over the course of the musical.

This critique crystallizes in "When You're a Red," the *Mad* spoof's opening song (4–5). Jacobs's lyrics parody "When You're a Jet," the anthem of *West Side Story*'s white "American gang," the prevailing neighborhood hegemon comprised of the ethnic "micks" and "wops" whom co-director Robert Wise cast for their "startlingly Midwestern appearance."[23] In naming itself after jets, this all-American gang identified itself with perhaps the most visible instrument of American power, as illustrated in such 1964 movies as Stanley Kubrick's dark Cold War satire *Dr. Strangelove* and Sidney Lumet's adaptation of Eugene Burdick and Harvey Wheeler's cliff-hanger best-seller *Fail-Safe* (1962). Instead of aligning the U.S. and its UN allies with the Jets, in accordance with the movie's sequence and demographic premise, Jacobs reversed the symbolic alignments for purposes of film parody and political satire. Instead of American Jets, the un-American Soviet gang opens "East Side Story" with "When You're a Red." With this reversal, Jacobs differentiates *Mad*'s American team from the white American ethnic ensemble who perform the opening number in the movie and stage versions of *West Side Story.* By giving the Jets' song to the Soviet bloc, *Mad*'s equivalent of the Sharks, who have no anthem of their own in the original, Jacobs casts the upstart insurgents as the initial provokers firing the opening rhetorical salvo. In the playground parlance familiar among *Mad* readers, "they started it."

In introducing this gang, the Reds, Jacobs cast the Soviet leader, Nikita Khrushchev, as the lead singer of "When You're a Red," thus identifying him with Jets leader Riff in the movie. In picturing the Soviet leader, Drucker, whose caricatures, "so insane in their exactitude," represented "the true genius of *Mad*,"[24] exaggerates Khrushchev's bulk and his signature features: his baldness and jowls. By contrast, most of his fellow gang members—with the exception of Castro and long-serving Soviet foreign minister Andrei Gromyko, to whose faces American news consumers had grown accustomed—are identified with placards naming Iron Curtain countries such as "Bullgaria," "Hungry" [sic], Albania, or, in the case of Poland, with the misspelled name of its Communist Party leader, Wladyslaw Gomulka, printed as "Go Molka" (4). Jacobs compounded this denigration of Soviet-bloc leaders. Instead of humanizing these Reds, let alone intimating any moral equivalence, Jacobs unequivocally vilifies them with their opening song. "When You're a Red" becomes Khrushchev's one-note confession of the Soviet Empire's supposedly malign intentions. Between the opening verse, "When you're a Red / You will sign a peace pact / Which will fool everyone / Till your troops have attacked," to the last verse, sung by Castro, which begins, "When you're a Red / And some land you oppress, / Always say you're protecting it / From the U.S.," Jacobs's lyrics not only call out Khrushchev's intentions, but also question his bravado as the Reds reveal his weakness and his empire's diminutiveness by comparing him to a mere "pest" (rather than an apocalyptic threat) and identifying him, metaphorically, as a "bad mosquito" (4–5).

With this Swiftian reversal of scale, as Robert Bird defines it,[25] Jacobs reduces Khrushchev to a mere nuisance. The Soviet leader's diminished status as a mosquito—neither relentlessly bloodthirsty like sharks nor poised to launch a global holocaust like (nuclear-armed B-47) jets—discredits Soviet pretensions as a global power and its claims of co-equality with the U.S. while comparing its posturing to the bravado of teenage delinquents. (Another subtle critique: the mosquito metaphor comes from the leader of "HUNGRY" [4].) Jacobs compounds this comic diminution by feminizing Khrushchev with his subsequent performance of a parody version of Maria's solo in *West Side Story*, "I Feel Pretty." Substituting Sondheim's giddy teenager-in-love lyrics with a candid confession in which Khrushchev gleefully discloses that neither ideology nor strategic calculation motivate his performance on the world stage pointedly suggests that he behaves as he does simply because "I feel vicious. . . . I feel spiteful" (6).

These diminutions of Khrushchev and his Soviet bloc allies culminate in the penultimate song parody of "East Side Story," a repurposing of the Jets' most antic ensemble performance in *West Side Story*, "Gee, Officer Krupke." This sarcastic proto-Foucauldian critique of the social-control apparatus (police, family, social services, applied behavioral science) ineffectually intent on containing the threat that the Jets pose to themselves and to their neighbors metonymically casts Krupke, the song's eponymous policeman, as the source of all the Jets' ills.[26] In Jacobs's version, "Dear Kindly Comrade Khrushchev" (10–11), the allies who comprised the chorus in "When You're a Red" become Khrushchev's jurors and his nemesis. They identify themselves as "unhappy Reds" who beseech their leader, in the opening verse, to "go away." They not only belittle Khrushchev by comparing him to "a mixed-up kid," but also obsolesce him by characterizing him as "just like the Czar" and threaten accordingly to banish him. They inform Khrushchev of plans to "build a Curtain that will keep out *you*!" and announce, "So we've decided to defect!" (11).

Before Khrushchev's wife, Nina, shows up to "stop [him] from blowing up the world" (12), a single panel shows Khrushchev brandishing his fist in the foreground, in darkened gray contrast to the whitened faces in the background—all faces of U.S. allies, such as Nationalist China's (Taiwan's) Generalissimo Chiang Kai-shek, U.K. prime minister Harold Macmillan, French president Charles de Gaulle, JFK, and his UN ambassador, Adlai Stevenson. Performing for this audience, Khrushchev makes trivial threats to "write 'Yankee Go Home' all over the Berlin Wall," to send JFK's movie star brother-in-law, Peter Lawford, "into orbit," and to "infiltrate Disneyland," which Khrushchev had been barred from visiting during his 1959 U.S. meetings.[27] In this panel, Drucker pictures this silent JFK-led phalanx of U.S. allies encircling the Soviet leader; the image suggests a visual metaphor that vindicates the much-misrepresented containment doctrine that George Kennan introduced at the outset of the Cold War as an instrument for limiting the perceived Soviet threat.[28]

Jacobs's allusion to a U.S. visit by Khrushchev nearly four years earlier and his reference to the Berlin Wall, erected three years earlier, reflects the parodist's expectation that his mostly teenage readership brought to their reading of *Mad* a mature awareness of global politics. One boomer reader recalls the influential effect of the apparent assumption by Drucker and his editors that millions of American teenagers would—or should—recognize the faces of the French, British, and Chinese leaders:

> How many would have known all the political figures in MAD articles like "A Day with J.F.K." or "East Side Story" without MAD as the point of reference? We not only laughed at MAD, we gleaned from it things we never could have gotten from our school textbooks . . . . Some of

> the humor was aimed right down at our level . . . but, tantalizingly, much of it was a bit beyond us, which made the magazine all the more indispensable.[29]

The "tantalizingly" minimal identifying information that Jacobs provided includes JFK's casual references to de Gaulle and Macmillan as "Chuck" and "Mac" (7), and a brief unillustrated reference to Chiang Kai-shek in the song parody of "There's a Place for Us": "Make a Place for Us" performed by Chiang's nemesis, mainland China's Communist leader, Mao Tse-tung (7). This familiarity with world leaders and the nuances of international alliances extends to a reference to fissures within the Soviet bloc, most notably the rupture between the Soviet-led Warsaw Pact alliance and Yugoslavian leader Marshall Tito. As the opening dance number comes to an end, Tito scoffs to Khrushchev, alluding to the loose alliance of so-called unaligned and third-world nations that emerged in the 1950s, "Ah, you're just looking for trouble, Nikita. . . . I don't need you! I've got other friends like Nehru [India's founding prime minister] and Nasser [Egyptian strongman]! We get a kick walking fences" (6). As if confirming the marginality of this inchoate alliance, Jacobs wrote no song parodies for these emerging-nation leaders.

The song parodies that Jacobs wrote for leaders of so-called free-world nations (accompanied in one image by Frank Sinatra sporting his signature fedora) are less memorable, less edgy, than those sung by the Khrushchev gang. These songs have softer satirical targets than Jacobs and Drucker's unmistakably simplistic, geopolitical critique of Khrushchev and his ilk. Those anti-Soviet parodies demanded both more awareness and sophistication from readers than do the *Mad* pair's treatments of western leaders. For this less mordant satire to work, these celebrity statesmen merely need to be recognized, with little consideration of what they stood for and why their decisions and polices mattered.

While Drucker and Jacobs exposed the Soviets' hegemonic ambitions—or at least confirmed many Americans' fear of such designs—the song parodies performed by JFK and his allies ascribe to the hometown team—or gang—virtually no ideological or strategic agendas. Jacobs seems to have settled for letting *Schadenfreude* do the work of satire. *Mad*'s caricature version of Khrushchev gets to perform Bernstein and Sondheim's most venturesome compositions from *West Side Story*, the jazzy and profane "When You're a Jet" (with its reference, in the 1957 stage version, to shit hitting the fan) and the rompishly confrontational "Gee, Officer Krupke" (with its references to marijuana smoking, heroin addiction, unwanted pregnancy, cross-dressing, "S.O.B." parents, and its final "Krup you!"). Most of the songs that Jacobs wrote for the supposed free-world leaders, by contrast, spoof Bernstein and Sondheim's most traditionally mellifluous songs from the musical. These include "Maria" and two of the three iterations of "Tonight" reprised throughout "East Side Story," the last of which serves as a rebuttal of the single Soviet version of the song. This structural choice thus affords the U.S. and its allies the last word and awards them a rhetorical win in the Cold War. As Jacobs's parodies of "Maria" and "I Feel Pretty" feminize Khrushchev, and allow the West to claim the future, so the last parodic iteration of "Tonight" allows the U.S. and its allies the last word and anticipates their Reagan-era triumph.

In *West Side Story*, "Maria," a lushly melodic reminder of the musical's origin as an adaptation of *Romeo and Juliet*, is sung by the Romeo character, Tony, after his first encounter with Maria. In "East Side Story," Jacobs turns "Maria" into "Nikita." The song is performed at JFK's behest by a transatlantic power quartet: the president himself opts to "carry the melody," he assigns Adlai Stevenson the bass part, and instructs "Chuck" de Gaulle and "Mac" Macmillan to "take the baritone." The lyrics of "Nikita" reduce the master of most of Eurasia to an incorrigibly peevish child:

> Treat him rough and for war he is screaming!
> Treat him soft and he's plotting and scheming! . . .
> We're getting nowhere with Nikita! (7)

Of all the songs in "East Side Story," only "Tonight" retains the title and refrain from the original. Just as Sondheim wrote versions of this song with lyrics for multiple perspectives—for the Jets and Sharks, for Tony and Maria, and for Maria's confidante, Anita—Jacobs wrote versions for the opposing Cold War blocs. The first shows the Reds threatening that their "might" will "scare" and "frighten" their adversaries. The next panel features a quintet of free-world leaders, including the arch Cold Warrior, Arizona Senator Barry Goldwater (then looking to unseat JFK in the next presidential race) promising to "take a firm stand . . .

to show we're strong and unite To-night!" (8). In the last iteration, in which de Gaulle, Macmillan, Stevenson, and JFK get the last word, the ensemble gloats with "delight" that "the Reds lost their bite To-night!" (12). In contrast to the original *West Side Story*, in "East Side Story" these musical stychomachias, or debate songs, always have a clear-cut winner. Invariably, the U.S. and its allies win, as Jacobs's reiterations of "Tonight" demonstrate.

Jacobs's most extended stychomachia in "East Side Story" parodies "America," staged in the film as an argument between Maria and Anita over the virtues of migrating to and remaining in New York as opposed to staying in or returning to Puerto Rico. Jacobs and Drucker's version shows a sextet of "free world" leaders, reinforced by Frank Sinatra, lyrically bombarding a solitary Khrushchev (9–10). This parody begins with the UK's Macmillan praising network "TV in America" and singling out the western *Laramie*, while in the last panel, Sinatra sings about Hollywood star Elizabeth Taylor's tabloid-sensation divorce from crooner Eddie Fisher. Sinatra concludes, "that's Show-Biz in America." Adding JFK's friend Sinatra to the West's delegation of allied leaders and aligning him with a representative American perspective, as the voice of "Show-Biz," underscores the difference between Jacobs and Drucker's depictions of JFK and company, on the one hand, and Khrushchev and his minions, on the other. Jacobs casts the western leaders as reassuring entertainers (like the Rat Pack of Sinatra, Lawford et al.), as a source of "delight" (as the last speech balloon stresses), and as consumers and often targets of tabloid gossip and fodder for mass-media distraction. Jacobs even turns the famously cerebral Adlai Stevenson into a corny showman when he tries to deflect Khrushchev's hectoring with perhaps the most shopworn of all vaudeville jokes, the one that begins, "Who was that lady I saw you with last night?" (8).

The same fissure that *West Side Story* straddled—this divide between comforting diversion and social critique—also informs "East Side Story." However, the venue shift from an insular urban neighborhood to an official forum for global diplomacy, and the importance of the United Nations to America's Cold War imaginary, complicate *Mad*'s transposition of the story across Manhattan. Despite Americans' familiarity with the UN and its iconic modernist headquarters and despite Hollywood's infatuation with New York City (or at least with its backlot simulacra of the metropolis), American moviemakers have historically shown very little interest in or have limited access to the UN, releasing only six features set at UN headquarters since its 1945 founding.[30]

Since *Mad* itself was so obsessed with Hollywood that Roger Ebert credits the magazine with inspiring his career as America's most famous movie reviewer,[31] and since *Mad* was arguably more obsessed with Hollywood than with Cold War politics, it seems more than plausible that while parodying *West Side Story*, "East Side Story" may have also been conversing with the only release and ultimately the sole Hollywood classic with a memorable UN setting: Alfred Hitchcock's 1959 thriller, *North by Northwest*. Even though *Mad* never saw fit to parody *North by Northwest*, its interest in Hitchcock's work became evident half a year after "East Side Story" appeared, when its October 1963 issue included a spoof of Hitchcock's horror thriller *The Birds*. Retitled "For the Birds" (Kogen, Silverstone, and Drucker, #82: 43–48), its first page reprises Drucker's Khrushchev image from "East Side Story" and shows him repeatedly shouting his signature threat, "We will bury you," as a member of the American crowd behind him marvels at the "crazy fat fool" brandishing his fist at an iconic American bald eagle. Despite the lack of explicit Cold War material in *The Birds* (though the threat of sudden savage airborne assault couldn't have been far from moviegoers' and *Mad* readers' minds), the Khrushchev allusion in "For the Birds" sustains the animus that Jacobs and Drucker elaborated six months earlier in "East Side Story."

A more tacit connection between "East Side Story" and *North by Northwest* may be its screenwriter, Ernest Lehman, who garnered an Oscar nomination for his *West Side Story* adaptation. Lehman's *North by Northwest* script introduced the moviegoing public to the questions that Jacobs was able to take for granted as common knowledge as points of departure in "East Side Story," most notably perennial Cold War–era concerns about containment, hegemony, and balance-of-power geopolitics.

Lehman's single most illuminating or at least provocative contribution to public views of the United Nations may lie in his having pushed Americans' understanding of the organization away from the idealization promoted in public schools and by presidential administrations throughout the Cold War era. Hitchcock and Lehman dramatized this rupture early in the movie in their depiction of the visitors' lounge at the UN's Manhattan headquarters: they portray it first as a peaceable, polyglot microcosm of everything the UN stands for and then abruptly transform the space into a stage for the bloody violence that sets the plot in motion. On this stage, the knife fight that the Sharks and Jets threaten throughout *West Side Story* joins the fatal stabbing to which its plot inexorably leads. What was once neighborhood gang warfare—the "rumble" to which *West Side Story* introduced millions of American moviegoers—now extends in *North by Northwest* into the mecca of global peace, the cynosure of World War II victors' promise to prevent the twentieth century's most salient distinction, a generation of wholesale slaughter, from ever recurring. Arguably this understanding of the UN as "mired in its own contradictions" and "operating at cross purposes," in Alan Nadel's words,[32] became most pronounced as *Mad* was beginning to claim its widest audience and reach. *Mad*'s rollout coincided with what has come to be called the Korean War, but was ambiguously named at the time. "By playing with terminology," David Halberstam has argued, Truman sought to avoid the full political brunt of declaring war and of legitimate U.S. intervention in Korea by designating U.S. intervention a UN-sanctioned "police action."[33] The architects of this approach, elite thought leaders deemed "The Wise Men" in Walter Isaacson and Evan Thomas's group portrait, counseled Truman to send troops to the peninsula, and this imprimatur lent the Korean misadventure still more credibility. One Wise Man, Truman's last secretary of state, Dean Acheson, recalled the war as the result of "the best minds in the world" having "set out to find us the worst possible location to fight this damnable war both politically and militarily."[34] Thanks to Robert Altman's dark 1970 comedy film *M*A*S*H* and Larry Gelbart's decade-long TV spinoff (spoofed on *Mad*'s October 1982 cover and inside the issue as "M*U*S*H" by Arnie Kogen and Jack Davis, #234, 10/82: 4-9), Americans eagerly revisited Acheson's "damnable war" a generation later as another Asian debacle, this time in Vietnam, had come to obsess them. In its October 1970 issue, *Mad* writer Arnie Kogen and artist Angelo Torres emphatically made this connection in the first full frame of their *M*A*S*H* parody, "M*I*S*H M*O*S*H" (#138: 43–47), showing a GI parrying a North Korean question, "What's so low budget about the Korean War?," by musing, "Well when you compare it to the War in Vietnam . . ." (43). While received wisdom holds that it was the Vietnam debacle skewered in *M*A*S*H* that discredited the Wise Men's influence and contributed to the diminishing prestige of great-power forums like the UN, "East Side Story" and *North by Northwest* anticipated this argument by a decade. Presaging this erosion, both narratives engage in what Hutcheon would term parodic inversion and trans-contextualization,[35] by recasting the UN as a site of amoral gang warfare rather than a dignified impartial arbiter and a beacon of peace committed to preventing war.

For young Americans reading "East Side Story" in 1963, particularly readers who had also seen *North by Northwest*, the starkest of these contradictions pitted their school-sanctioned celebration of what the UN promised against the realization that peace isn't always attainable, that violence sometimes proves unavoidable, and that conflict may turn uncontainable. Though Frank Jacobs tried to sidestep this realization at the end of "East Side Story" with the so-called free world's declaration of victory in the Cold War, many young *Mad* readers learned in both fighting and in resisting America's next undeclared Asian war as the decade unfolded that no wars, even Cold Wars, are ever decisively forestalled, let alone definitively won.

Notes

1. Harry S. Truman, annual message to Congress on the State of the Union, January 9, 1952, *Public Papers Harry S. Truman 1945–1953*, Harry S. Truman Presidential Library Museum, www.trumanlibrary.org/publicpapers/index.php.

2. Nathan Abrams, "From Madness to Dysentery: *Mad*'s Other New York Intellectuals," 446; James J. Kimble, "Mutually Assured Disparagement: Enmification and Enlightenment in Early 1950s *Mad*," chap. 15, 349; first published in *Studies in American Humor* n.s. 3, no. 30 (Fall 2014): 130.

3. Statistics from Kristin L. Matthews, "A *Mad* Proposition in Postwar America," 212.

4. Maud Lavin, "Neuman's Own."

5. Stephen E. Kercher, *Revel with a Cause: Liberal Satire in Postwar America*, 112.

6. David Samuels, "Q&A with Art Spiegelman."

7. Kercher, *Revel with a Cause*, 116, 118.

8. Jason Horowitz, "Senator Smiley: Al Franken Pulls no Punches, but Adds a Few Punch Lines."

9. Andrew Ross, *No Respect: Intellectuals and Popular Culture*, 11.

10. Abrams, "From Madness to Dysentery," 448.

11. Matthews, "A *Mad* Proposition in Postwar America," 212.

12. Linda Hutcheon, "The Politics of Postmodernism: Parody and History," 180.

13. Walter Isaacson and Evan Thomas, *The Wise Men: Six Friends and the World They Made*, 223, 323, 349.

14. "Trick or Treat for UNICEF."

15. Maria Reidelbach, *Completely Mad: A History of the Comic Book and Magazine*, 122.

16. Reidelbach, *Completely Mad*, 120–23.
17. Reidelbach, *Completely Mad*, 123.
18. Abrams, "From Madness to Dysentery," 246–47.
19. Tom Vallance, "Arthur Laurents: Playwright and Screenwriter Who Wrote the Books for *West Side Story* and *Gypsy*." For the complete text, see Leonard Bernstein, *West Side Story: A Musical*, based on a conception of Jerome Robbins, book by Arthur Laurents, lyrics by Stephen Sondheim.
20. On *West Side Story*, see Alan Nadel, *Demographic Angst: Cultural Narratives and American Films of the 1950s*, 222; on Jacobs as *Mad*'s poet laureate, see "Weird" Al Yankovic, foreword to *Mad's Greatest Writers: Frank Jacobs*, 5.
21. Quoted in Nick Meglin, "A Mad Look at Frank Jacobs," in *Mad's Greatest Writers: Frank Jacobs*, 8.
22. For assessments of Drucker's genius, see Mark Evanier, *Mad Art: A Visual Celebration of the Art of Mad Magazine and the Idiots Who Create It*, 74–76; Mark Voger, "Mad about Mort: Caricaturist Mort Drucker of Mad Magazine Talks about His Technique"; and Grant Geissman, introduction to 1960–1963, in *Mad About the Sixties: The Best of the Decade*, n.p.
23. Nadel, *Demographic Angst*, 216.
24. Owen Gleiberman, *Movie Freak: My Life Watching Movies*, 26.
25. Robert Bird, "Schematics and Models of Genre," in *Persistent Forms: Explorations in Historical Poetics*, edited by Ilya Kliger and Boris Maslov, 447.
26. For lyrics to Bernstein and Sondheim's "Gee, Officer Krupke," see https://lyrics.fandom.com/wiki/Leonard_Bernstein_%26_Stephen_Sondheim:Gee,_Officer_Krupke.
27. Andrew Glass, "Nikita Khrushchev barred from Disneyland, September 19, 1959."
28. Wilson Miscamble, *George F. Kennan and the Making of American Foreign Policy, 1947–1950*, xi–xii, 32.
29. Geissman, foreword to *Mad about the Sixties*, xiv.
30. "United Nations, New York City, New York."
31. Roger Ebert, introduction to *Mad About the Movies: Director's Cut*, n.p.
32. Nadel, *Demographic Angst*, 167–68.
33. David Halberstam, *The Coldest Winter: America and the Korean War*, 2.
34. Halberstam, *The Coldest Winter*, 1.
35. Linda Hutcheon, *A Theory of Parody: The Teachings of Twentieth-Century Art Forms*, 15.

17. Joining the Fray?

Mad on Richard Nixon and Spiro Agnew

Nicolas Labarre

MAD'S HUMOR BETWEEN the early 1960s and 1974, when the magazine experienced its peak in popularity, has often been described as broadly satirical rather than political. The magazine was famously characterized by Todd Gitlin in *The Sixties: Years of Hope, Days of Rage* (1987) as being "no friend of political action," while Theodore Roszak, in *The Making of a Counter Culture* (1969), compared its humor to that of the Katzenjammer Kids, a form of benign anarchy rather than an articulate social message.[1] The same point had been made more bluntly by rival magazine *Esquire* when it had lampooned *Mad* as "Bad" in 1964.[2] Al Feldstein, who edited the magazine during the whole period, concurred with this perception in many interviews throughout his career, stating, for example, in an interview for the *Comics Journal* in 2000: "Our job was to educate kids, not to tell them what to do. We're not revolutionists."[3]

While ample evidence supports these claims regarding the late 1950s to early 1960s issues of *Mad*, the tone was markedly different when it came to Richard Nixon and his vice president Spiro Agnew from 1968 to 1973 and in the immediate aftermath of the Watergate hearings. The most striking example of *Mad*'s virulence can be found on the back cover of issue #172 (Irving Schild [photog.], 1/75), which refers to President Ford's pardon of Nixon by asking " . . . So Why Not . . . Pardon Hitler!" above a full-page portrait of the Führer.

By late 1974 and early 1975, a majority of Americans had turned against Nixon, and for two years the press had been displaying a high level of hostility toward a president mired in scandals and outright lies. Still, the vehemence of this illustration stands out, especially in the context of a self-professed nonpolitical magazine. Moreover, *Mad* did not wait for the Watergate hearings of May–August 1973 to question the behavior of Nixon and his administration. In October 1973, a *New York Magazine* article even praised *Mad*'s "prescient" attacks on the president: "When you look back, *Mad* magazine's viewpoint on the passing parade . . . has often been clearer than *Time*'s or *Newsweek*'s."[4]

This essay examines this claim and the path that led to the back cover of issue #172 by following the way *Mad* portrayed Nixon throughout his career and contrasting it with the coverage he was receiving in the mainstream press, notably in political cartoons. It will seek to demonstrate that *Mad* paid constant attention to Nixon even before he was elected President—by the fiftieth anniversary of the magazine, no personality appeared more often than Nixon on the cover of the magazine ("The *Mad* 50th Anniversary Timeline 1952-2002" #423, 11/02: 16-18; 17)—even when his media footprint was reduced between 1964 and 1967, while he was out of office. It will also examine the increasing politicization of coverage that had initially been somewhat benevolent, notably under the influence of writer and caricaturist Max Brandel. Finally, it will describe *Mad*'s inability to cope with the Watergate scandal itself at a time when events accelerated far beyond the pace of publication of the magazine.

Nixon Before 1968: "A Poor Schnook"

Richard Nixon's ascent to the forefront of the American political scene closely parallels the history of *Mad*, first as a comic book and then as a magazine. Nixon's "Checkers" speech, in which he famously denied accusations regarding his campaign finances, was given on September 23, 1952. The first issue of *Mad* is cover-dated October–November 1952, and it was probably put on sale around August of the same year. The creation of the comic book thus coincided with an early apex of Nixon's career, as he became Eisenhower's vice president.

Although *Mad* as a comic book slowly moved from parodies of specific popular cultural objects to a broader form of satire,[5] Nixon was not mentioned in the twenty-three issues before *Mad* became a magazine. However, he was referenced as early as #28, in July 1956, Harvey Kurtzman's last issue as editor-in-chief before his replacement by Al Feldstein.[6] Nixon appeared in the footnote of an article entitled "Your Income Tax," which presented the U.S. tax system as a contest in which the aim is to win "BIG PRIZES—including up to five years free vacation at government expense!" (Shir-Cliff, #28, 7/56: 25-27; 25). The author suggests using interesting names to make sure a form will get noticed yet advises his reader against being too greedy: "Do not use names of important people like Richard Nixon and Mickey Mouse. Celebrities like these are probably already paying big taxes, and your ruse will be quickly spotted" (26).[7] At this point, the "Checkers" speech and Nixon campaign finance problems were four years old and hardly topical, though the text clearly echoed these issues. This first mention is noteworthy mostly because it positions Nixon not as a controversial political figure, which he was, but rather as a public celebrity, which he also was. This is a characterization *Mad* often used, both while Nixon served as Eisenhower's vice president and after he unsuccessfully attempted to succeed him. While part of the press maintained an adversarial relation to the vice president, described as a "partisan mud-slinger,"[8] his image in *Mad* was milder, mostly eschewing moral and political judgments.

On several occasions, Nixon was used as a generic celebrity (Jacobs and Clarke, "Custom-made Christmas Cards" #44, 1/59: 30-32; Jacobs and Clarke, "*Mad*'s Seed and Garden Catalog" #96, 7/65: 29-31). However, as one might expect, Nixon was cast most often as a politician, both before and after his presidential bid. Until the 1960 election, he was consistently represented as an aspiring figure: doodling a dismembered Eisenhower (Clarke, "Scratchpad Doodles" #39, 5/58: 10-12), as an anxious young senator (Belkin and Woodbridge, "Popular Politician" #55, 6/60: 31-34), as a young man listening to an uplifting graduation speech (Kogen and Orlando, "Graduation Speeches ... That Somebody Listened To" #48, 7/59: 40-41), as a youthful and smiling figure behind Eisenhower (Siegel and Orlando, "A Child's History of the Middle 1900's (1940-1960)" #58, 10/60: 21-25), or as a clone of the naïve Dagwood Bumstead, Blondie's husband in the eponymous comic strip, striving to make a career in Washington (Wood, "Comic Strip Heroes (Taken from Real Life)" #48, 7/59: 4-7). In the last two representations, Nixon is accompanied by a dog that must be Checkers, and while Nixon's earnestness is humorous to the extent that it can be contrasted with his public image in other media, it is not undermined in the articles themselves. *Mad* thus exaggerated the appeal of Nixon for the Republican Party, especially his youth and his seriousness[9] but did not appear to question it. A rare appearance of a scheming Nixon in Wally Wood's 1956 "Conventions Forecast" is a tongue-in-cheek one, part of an elaborate joke surrounding the summer political conventions: a headline screaming "Nixon will attempt a fix" is followed by an illustrated paragraph about Cosmo L. Nixon, "Convention Hall staff carpenter," attempting to fix the wooden structure of the podium (#29, 9/56: 41–42).

After 1960 and the election, however, Nixon's appearance of innocent candor was reframed to become a form of indictment. As early as April 1961, an ironic slant is inserted into his depiction: Pat and Checkers Nixon are among the nominees for a "Best Supporting Performance of 1960" award, in support of "plain, humble Richard Nixon" (Siegel and Drucker, "The United Nations Awards Show" #62, 4/61: 45-48). Prior to 1960, this plain humility was presented with a straight face, drawing not only from his self-portrayal in the Checkers speech but perhaps also playing into the stereotype of Nixon's upbringing as a Quaker. After the lost election, Nixon was cast as a fraud and a populist, already a crook. Siegel and Drucker emphasize this message later in the feature, in Nixon's lengthy acceptance speech upon finally receiving an award, albeit for "Best Costume Design for an Ensemble that was Made and Never Used":

> Thank you. As I sincerely said to Pat during our great Kitchen Debate this morning, I am sincerely grateful. What am I sincerely grateful for? I'll tell you what I'm sincerely grateful for. I am sincerely grateful for this honor, just as I am sure my opponent would have been sincerely grateful if he had received it instead of yours sincerely.
>
> What do I sincerely say now that the election campaign is over and my opponent has been inaugurated? I'll tell you what I sincerely say now that the election campaign is over and he has been inaugurated. I sincerely say that I am watching the trends carefully, that I have sincere faith in the American people, and that I sincerely believe in our ultimate victory. How do I sincerely mean that? I'll tell you how I sincerely mean that! I mean that with all my sincerest sincerity. (47–48)

While Mort Drucker drew a smiling and likable Nixon, the incremental repetition of sentence elements, the reference to the somewhat farcical 1959 "Kitchen Debate" with Khrushchev, and of course the overabundant "sincerely" all point toward the prefabricated nature of Nixon's "sincerest sincerity." This perceived hypocrisy, in line with *Mad*'s willingness to puncture self-promotional discourses, may explain why Nixon did not vanish from *Mad*'s pages, even after his defeat.

During the election, the magazine paid attention to all the candidates and seized on their most salient traits, with recurrent jokes about Kennedy's hair, for instance. Nixon's disastrous trip to South America and especially Venezuela, in April and May of 1958, was thus duly mocked (Belkin and Woodbridge, "Madison Avenue's Political Ad Campaigns" #56, 6/60: 4-9), as was his characteristic five o'clock shadow, described as a conscious campaign strategy in a Gillette pseudo-ad (Koch and Clarke, "Ad Testimonials from Politicians" #54, 4/60: 4-7), months before the televised debates and the popular perception that that same ungainly stubble may have cost him the election. Throughout this period, Nixon was mentioned on a regular basis, alongside the other candidates. After the election, however, most of the unsuccessful candidates (Hubert Humphrey, Adlai Stevenson, etc.) receded into the background for *Mad*, while Nixon did not: he was brought back to his unfortunate trip to Venezuela by Belkin and Drucker nearly three years after the incident ("If Countries Traded People Like Baseball Teams Do" #67, 12/61: 31-33), shown by Siegel and Drucker smashing a television set while moaning "That damn TV" ("*Mad* Magazine Presents a Day with JFK" #67, 12/61: 43-47; 46), and described by Jacobs and Orlando in a classified ad as having disgustedly "washed [his] hands" of politics ("When Newspaper Editors Go on Vacation and 'Summer Replacement' Editors Take Over" #74, 10/62: 24-25; 24). In "The Tenth Hour," published in 1963, Nixon is a delusional patient who thinks he is the president of the United States, comforted by an understanding psychiatrist. Again echoing the idea that Kennedy's looks and mastery of television won him the 1960 election, Nixon recounts his dream and simultaneously casts himself in the role of the born loser: "I see two men! One is rich and handsome—the other is a poor schnook! The rich handsome man is killing the poor schnook by beating him with a hairbrush" (Silverstone and Drucker, #80, 7/63: 43-47; 43).

This sequence occupies only two panels in a five-page parody of the then-popular TV doctor shows, but it was enough to warrant an angry letter, published in a subsequent issue, deploring the prejudice displayed by *Mad* in its handling of the former vice president. While praising the magazine's usual "wholesome satirical" tone, the author of the letter railed against the "slap in the face of all patriotic Americans" that he discerned in the parody ("Letters Dept." #82, 10/63: 2-3; 2). *Mad* was to receive and publish numerous such letters in the following years as the magazine took to publishing increasingly controversial and political pieces, but in 1963 such reactions were almost nonexistent. In fact, competitor *Esquire*'s parody of *Mad* in 1964 specifically mocked the lack of political coverage in the magazine.[10] While it is hard to draw any definitive conclusion from the letters published in the magazine—they were selected for publication and did not necessarily reflect a consensus among readers—this reaction of outrage is one of the first signs of the special status Nixon was to receive as a political figure in the magazine.

Almost a year earlier, on November 6, 1962, after losing the California gubernatorial race, he had famously declared to gathered journalists that they would no longer "have Nixon to kick around," as he was retiring from politics. The statement, which warranted a "political obituary" on ABC,[11] did not prevent him from maintaining a sizable presence in the press, nor did it prevent *Mad* from continuing to mock him. Throughout 1963, he was the punch line of Gerald Gardner's photo-cartoon series "Speaking from Pictures," which inserted humorous speech balloons into existing photographs. For instance, Jacqueline Kennedy is shown holding an ornamental knife while commenting, "It says: 'Regards from Pat Nixon'" (#77, 3/63: 16-17; 16); other installments appeared in #75 (12/62: 4-5), #76 (1/63: 14-15), and #79 (6/63: 13). In 1964, at a time when political news was dominated by the confrontation between Rockefeller and Goldwater for the Republican nomination, Nixon made an appearance as a contributor to Sam Hart's "Angry Magazine" (Hart and Woodbridge, #87, 6/64: 41-49), then as a countermodel for the aspiring presidential candidates imagined by Kogen and Rickard in "If Celebrities Ran for Political Office" (#90, 10/64: 4-5). Soon thereafter, Nixon's *Mad* persona again shifted to emphasize his lack of principles and his eagerness to come back to the political game. In 1965, in yet another ad mocking his five o'clock shadow, Nixon is made to state, "Hi there, Americans! You know, some things come naturally—like sacrificing principles!" (Axe, Weinstein, and Rickard, "When Politicians Do TV Commercials" #99, 12/65: 4-7; 4).

Other articles published in 1965 echoed this depiction of the former vice president as a politician apt to "change [his] colors to adapt to a new surrounding" (as Jacobs and Clarke put it in "*Mad*'s Seed" #96, 7/65: 30; see also Kogen and Clarke, "A Celebrity's Wallet" #99, 12/65: 33-34). The image aligned with frequent criticism of a politician whom Chief Justice Earl Warren described at the time as "completely unprincipled."[12]

However, this burst of interest, with three elaborate mentions in 1965, was followed by a nearly two-year gap during which Nixon was mentioned only in passing. The Nixon character had obviously exhausted its comic potential after having gone through a series of personas ranging from young enthusiast to sore loser to opportunist. This disappearance was not specific to *Mad*. A study of Nixon's exposure in the press from the early fifties to the late 1960s (see fig. 17-1) confirms that between 1965 and 1967 he returned to levels of anonymity he had not experienced since before his vice presidency. More broadly, the variations of Nixon's popularity in *Mad* can be said to mirror the trends observable in other publications over the same period, though of course the small number of occurrences makes this comparison imperfect. The only notable point of divergence occurred in 1965 and 1966, when *Mad* maintained its interest in the former vice president months after he had faded from public view. This lasting interest is one of the elements suggesting that there was a special and ingrained interest in Nixon from *Mad*'s staff.

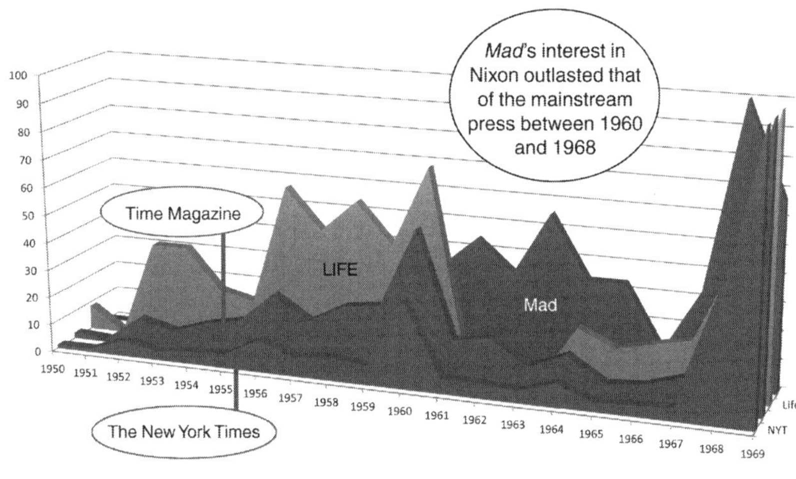

Fig. 17-1: The graph compares the annual number of articles mentioning Nixon to the number in the year when he was mentioned most often in that publication. For *Time*, *Life*, and the *New York Times*, the peak occurred in 1969. It occurred a year earlier, in 1968, for *Mad*. *Mad* paid attention to Nixon after 1961, at a time when he had largely disappeared from the public sphere. Data collection and graph by Nicolas Labarre.

The 1968 Election: "Best New Arrangement of the Same Old Song"

With the run-up to the 1968 election, Nixon returned to the public sphere as a matter of course, including *Mad*: he appeared in issue #113, on the cover of issue #114, and almost continuously afterwards. The representation of Nixon as a presidential candidate drew heavily from his previous characterization: willing to try anything to be elected, concerned about his looks, and worried especially about his beard. In a March 1968 feature, "Honest Comments on TV," he is presented as "desperate" and haunted by his reputation as a "born loser," though Jack Rickard, who was to draw him many times in the following years, portrayed him as pleasant and smiling (Koch and Rickard, #117: 20-23; 20–21). Similarly, in June 1968, Max Brandel made use of a very amiable photo of Nixon wearing an "Impeach Reagan" button, while Robert Kennedy and Ronald Reagan, for instance, were portrayed in much less flattering ways ("A *Mad* Portfolio of Some Famous 'Protest' Buttons We'd Like to See Worn by Some Famous People" #119: 35-39; 36).

Mad's attitude toward Nixon is aptly summed up by the Academy Award granted to the former vice president for the "Best New Arrangement of the Same Old Song" in "*Mad*'s Academy Awards for World Celebrities" by Max Brandel and Frank Jacobs (#123, 12/68: 26-28; 27), and to a lesser extent by his portrayal as the amiable comic strip caveman Alley Oop in the previous issue (Brandel and Clarke, "*Mad*'s Updated Comic Strip Heroes" #122, 10/68: 4-6; 6), at a time when the magazine was devoting acidic pages to President Lyndon Johnson. This caution can be explained both by the numerous surprises during an election year that made it difficult to identify Nixon as a major candidate before the Republican convention, and more generally by a publishing schedule that made *Mad* an awkward fit for close coverage of political news. These dual constraints explain the subdued treatment given to a candidate whom *Mad* had been mocking for a long time.

The name of satirist Max Brandel appears in connection with Nixon in most of these pre-election pieces. Brandel, who had started working for the magazine in 1966, was a political cartoonist in Europe before World War II. He switched mostly to photographic montages and arrangements when he came to the United States: with a few exceptions, this is the medium he used in *Mad*, where he brought a noticeably political sensibility in the late 1960s. He mounted virulent attacks on Johnson, the "Great

Society," and more generally on the state of the United States, with a focus on race relations and ecology. His most famous work before the Nixon presidency is probably "The Preamble Revisited" (#109, 3/67: 24–25), in which the words of the preamble to the American Constitution are used as captions for scenes of lynching, labor unrest, and a KKK march on the U.S. Capitol. Brandel, who also conceived lighter pieces, was to become the most active commentator on the Nixon administration in *Mad*, and this interest was already on display in the months leading to the presidential election.

Nixon as President: From Saint to Sickness

The same technical hurdles that hampered *Mad*'s timely treatment of the presidential campaign were also on display after the election. In early 1969, then in early 1973, several months elapsed without a mention of the president. In addition to the gap between the cover date and the actual publication, the time needed to conceive the contents made it impossible to mention or mock the newly elected president for months. Thus, Nixon as president did not appear until #125, in a Max Brandel's portrait of a pious man in prayer with the U.S. Seal as a saintly halo ("A Portfolio of Mad Portraits" 3/69: 14-16;16). The image is ironic, but also the closest thing in *Mad* to the "honeymoon" depiction granted the newly elected president by most of Nixon's antagonists in the press. When Nixon was elected in 1968, even *Washington Post* cartoonist Herblock (Herbert Block) stopped depicting him with a five o'clock shadow, symbolically giving him, in the artist's words, "a chance . . . to start afresh."[13] Three months later, Jack Rickard and Earle Doud provided an extended commentary on the election in "If the President Were Chosen Like 'Miss America,'" using the by then familiar formula conflating politics and show business. All the candidates are typecast, with Ronald Reagan as brash, upbeat, and ambitious, Hubert Humphrey as stolid understudy to Johnson, and so on. Nixon, who looks much older and grumpier than in Rickard's previous caricatures, in the bathing suit competition is for his part a sad, paranoid, and spiteful clown whose talent demonstration includes only the "crying parts," not the lyrics, of the aria from *Pagliacci* (#127, 6/69: 23-27; 24). The piece ends with Nixon wearing the crown while the master of ceremony sings "Can you believe that he's for real" and a brutish-looking cop hits a protester. For a few issues afterwards, Nixon was present, frequently mentioned, but mostly in passing. "If the President Were Chosen Like

'Miss America'" can be seen as the capstone to the 1956–1968 depiction of the man in *Mad*, from likable vice president to sore loser to president. Similarly, when Larry Siegel and John Johns depicted an unshaven Nixon in an undershirt trying to avoid a visit by the Agnews on a Sunday morning ("A *Mad* Look at Celebrities in Real-Life Situations" #133, 3/70: 38-40; 40), the joke was still a familiar one. During these months, *Mad* focused instead on Spiro Agnew—"A *Mad* Nature Study Guide" featured a creature called the "Agnu," who "until recently . . . was little known and rarely seen outside his small preserve" (Brandel and Jacobs, #128, 7/69: 12–14; 12)—and on Ronald Reagan, cast in the role of the crushed loser, a role previously held by Nixon himself.

According to Louis Liebovich, relations between Nixon and the press soured quickly throughout 1969 and became irreversibly damaged after Agnew's attacks on the media in November of that year.[14] This chronology applies to *Mad* to a certain extent, though the magazine was not a target of Agnew's condemnation. Before 1970, Nixon was faulted in *Mad* mostly for his character, and in every case he was presented alongside other politicians or popular performers. He was therefore used as a symptom of broader issues—the conflation of politics and show business or the inherent duplicity of politicians—but not as a subject in himself. That changed in the following five years, as Nixon became very much the subject and ended up being depicted as, among other things, a Nazi, a gangster, a violent cop, a traitor to his faith, the rallying cry for all discontents, and finally as "an illness lasting six years" in Jacobs's "Additions to the Dictionary" (#174, 4/75: 41).

The first example of this shift is a short piece written by Ronnie Nathan and again drawn by Jack Rickard, published in January 1970, in which Nixon is portrayed as sidestepping the issues of the day, seducing the public while accomplishing nothing: "If he won't lead us, we can't be misled!" ("Nixon's the One" #132: 15). The criticism is shallow (the same charge of inaction was leveled at Johnson in "If the President Were Chosen Like 'Miss America'"), focusing on rhetorical strategies rather than policies by mocking Nixon's overuse of the phrase "Let me make this perfectly clear," for instance, but this is the first piece dedicated solely to Nixon's presidency and agenda. The pile of files next to which he is shown idling is anything but humorous: from "conservation" to "Vietnam" to "riots and civil disorders," it encompasses all the major issues of the day, and in fact includes all the subjects that *Esquire* had mocked *Mad* for refusing to broach in 1964.

Five months and three issues later, Larry Siegel and Max Brandel published a piece with no equivalent for previous or following presidents: "The Richard M. Nixon Presidential Primer." The four-page satire is a first-person account of Nixon's trajectory, illustrated solely by photographic portraits and montages. Some of the attacks rely on the familiar characterization of Nixon as a dour man, now worried about his reelection. The description of Agnew as prankster and a fool—"You should see him at Official Functions with his funny lapel flower that squirts water!" (#135, 3/70: 45-48; 48)—similarly draws on the description of the vice president in other *Mad* articles at the time. However, "The Richard M. Nixon Presidential Primer" veers away from this formulaic approach, notably by asserting early on Nixon's conservatism in blunt terms, and by resurrecting and echoing all the past descriptions of the president at a time when opinion polls suggested that the general public had chosen to move beyond them:

> But there are some people who say,
> "Yes . . . but what about the OLD Nixon?
> You know the OLD Nixon we mean!
> You know, you know!
> The fiery Commie-baiter!
> The screamer!
> The mud-slinger!
> The character assassin!
> The guy with the heavy jowls
> And the Angry mouth
> And the narrow, shifty eyes!
> Tricky Dicky!
> What about THAT OLD Nixon?" (47)

This is an unusually detailed and virulent application of *Mad*'s stated goal, to "puncture the pomposity of politicians," as Feldstein put it in a 2000 interview.[15] In this passage, presented alongside a photograph of a weary-looking President at a press conference, the magazine positions itself as a counterdiscourse to Nixon's, and to his communication team's efforts to present him as a "new" Nixon. Siegel and Brandel's Nixon, far from being a unifying public figure, is aligned with specific political interests. He is a big-business Republican with a clear agenda:

> I don't just speak for myself.
> I speak for you millions of Americans out there.
> You millions of Americans who believe in me.
> You millions of bankers,
> And you millions of businessmen,
> And you millions of industrialists,
> And both of you Negroes. (45)

Their Nixon is also still a thug, using Agnew to do "the dirty jobs" (48) and punching his vice president in the mouth if he cannot be reasoned with.

The discontinuity that was so forcefully affirmed in public discourse is thus negated: as we have seen, the actual discontinuity in Nixon's role as a public figure had been exceptionally brief in *Mad*. The use of actual, mostly unedited photographs is crucial in creating a link to an apparently unmediated reality, as opposed to drawn caricature, in which the artist's hand is always visible; to quote Pascal Lefèvre, a drawing is always "signed."[16] Previously, Nixon had been drawn by various cartoonists, from Mort Drucker to Jack Rickard, or depicted in edited photographs. Both strategies drew attention to the satirical intervention or reinvention of the character. By contrast, Brandel and Siegel invite the reader to look at the "real" Nixon. The satirical intervention is to be found in the relatively invisible selection process, not in the pictures themselves. This indicial value of the photos is what allows the antiphrastic nature of the text to function, as the "testimony" of photographs puts the lie to the first-person narrative. Their presence thus anchors the satire by creating a contrast between the unworthiness of Nixon's self-account and readers' ability to come to their own conclusions by observing Nixon himself. The piece also relies on the cumulative effect afforded by its length to further emphasize its points. Finally, the context of the "Primer" works as a reinforcing factor; in this case, the article is followed by a back-cover photomontage, again conceived by Brandel. In the montage, a visibly angry Nixon is hiding behind a smiling Agnew mask under the caption "*Mad*'s Official Presidential Portrait." The image is only faintly humorous, and except for its unusual technique it has all the characteristics of a political cartoon, conforming to the formula established by *New York Times* cartoonist Ranan R. Lurie: 40 percent political analysis and 15 percent humor (the rest divided equally among art, talent, and caricaturization).[17] It bears mentioning that the vice president, whom *Mad* correctly described as an unknown figure a few months before—he is Vice President What's-his-name throughout Philip Roth's 1971 satire, *Our Gang*, for instance[18]—built a notable popularity on the strength of these attacks on the media. Satirizing Agnew may not have been a political risk, but it certainly went against majority opinion at the time.

The published reactions to "The Richard M. Nixon Presidential Primer" attest to its novelty. The piece elicited venomous reactions from the readers in the "Letters Dept." of #137 (09/70: 2-3)--"You've reached a new low . . . a low I did not think you were capable of" (3)--but also provoked one of the clearest expressions of *Mad*'s political stance during this period, in the form of a response to a chagrined reader:

> The latest Louis Harris poll, taken in March, 1970, shows that 72% of the people in the U.S. are satisfied with Richard M. Nixon as President. From the looks of your last issue (#135), you seem to have overlooked that fact.
>
> Winston C. Cavan
> Durham, N.C.
>
> The latest Alfred E. Neuman poll, taken in April 1970, shows that 28% of the people in the U.S. are satisfied with *Mad*. We know our audience—Ed. (3)

This answer explicitly positions *Mad* as a magazine for anyone *but* Nixon's Silent Majority, and therefore as willing to take political sides, if only in a plausibly deniable fashion. "The Nixon Primer" is one of the first concrete examples of that stance, but more would follow. From early 1970 to late 1972 and the post-presidential election break, Nixon was present in twenty of the twenty-three issues of the magazines, often with several pieces in one issue. These articles can be divided into two distinct categories.

The first category encompasses pieces covering the most salient events in American politics prior to Watergate. For instance, the magazine chronicled the rise in Spiro Agnew's popularity, Nixon's antagonism toward him, the long debate over whether Agnew should be replaced on the ticket for the 1972 election, as well as Nixon's fight with labor unions, his dithering on the Vietnam War, the concerns about the growing influence of Henry Kissinger, and Nixon's much-promoted trip to China in February 1972. In all these cases, *Mad* represented the events through its familiar mocking filter, deflating the politicians' self-aggrandizing communication. The most complete overview of the Nixon administration through this familiar satiric prism appears in "The White House Follies of 1972," written by Frank Jacobs and drawn by Mort Drucker (#150, 4/72: 4-11), which fits into a tradition of depicting life at the White House as a Gilbert and Sullivan comic opera. Over eight pages, Jacobs and Drucker cover most of the salient facts of Nixon's presidency—including a portentous aside about the excessive use of taping devices by the FBI—through established clichés regarding the various characters, mixed with comic opera conventions: Nixon is tricky, Agnew is dumb, Kissinger is manipulative, and men are dominated by their wives, who advise and guide them from backstage. Though more pointed comments appear in other pieces, most instances of *Mad*'s covering major news events parody a *mode of presentation* of political news and do not question the events themselves. They can no more be called political statements than what is probably still *Mad*'s most famous cover, Basil Wolverton's parody of *Life* in issue #11 (5/54).

The novelty then lies in the fact that these parodies cohabitated with a second category of articles, in which *Mad* published more vindictive indictments of Nixon and his messages, amplifying the trend started with the "Presidential Primer." A prime example is "That Sinking Feeling" (#145, 9/71: 24–25), created by Max Brandel with research assistance from Frank Jacobs, focused on the Vietnam War as a political matter. The two-page article is composed of six panels in which a photographed Nixon slowly sinks into the water while carefully dated speech bubbles quote from his speeches in chronological order (see fig. 17-2). The triumphant Nixon in the first picture is given a short line from a 1968 campaign speech: "I pledge to you the new leadership will end the war and win the peace," and as he slowly sinks, the excerpts get longer, exposing more unfulfilled promises. On the right side of the second page, Nixon is entirely underwater, and the last bubble ends with this admission, from a February 25, 1971, speech: "If winding down the war is my greatest satisfaction in foreign policy, the failure to end it is my deepest disappointment" (25).

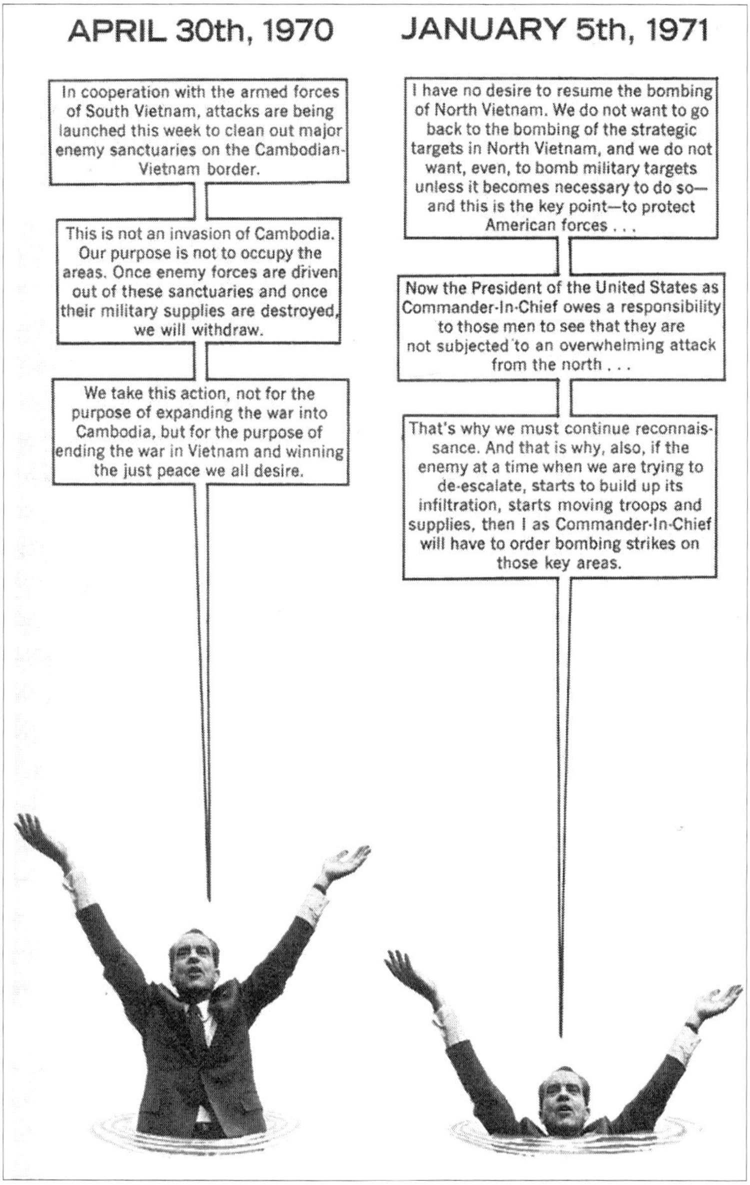

Fig. 17-2: "That Sinking Feeling" uses the mask of objectivity to attack Nixon: minimal editorial intervention suggests that Nixon's deceptions were self-evident (Brandel, Jacobs, and Nixon, *Mad* #145, 9/71: 24–25). MAD used with permission.

Brandel and Jacobs construct their piece as an exposé of Nixon's strategy, with as little mediation as possible. The President is even named as the writer, since the two creators (credited with the idea and research, respectively) limit their intervention to a careful selection of excerpts. What little humor is to be found in the piece lies in the proliferation of text, coupled with the gradual disappearance of the man, but juxtapositions of contradictory statements, such as the claim that bombing would stop in January 1971, hit directly at Nixon's inability or unwillingness to uphold his campaign promises. By removing every trace of personal intervention—there is no self-mocking caption, no marginal scribble, barely any graphic intervention—Brandel and Jacobs let the president stand on his own, again relying on the indicial value of photographs in addition to the authenticity of the excerpts. Two issues later, one reader pointed out in a published letter that repeating the Nixon speeches was not necessary since "[he] had got the jokes the first time [he] heard them" ("Letters Dept." #147, 12/71: 2-3; 2).

The president's approval rating had eroded at this point, reaching a first-term low of around 50 percent and providing a vindication of *Mad*'s oppositional stance. In April 1971, the magazine's front cover was a photograph of the White House with the placard "This Country Is Out of Order" (John Putnam [a] #142). In addition to the bluntness of its message, the cover is notable for introducing in *Mad* a visual strategy closely associated with political cartoons: the use of official buildings as a synecdoche for a whole branch of government. Garry Trudeau's comic strip *Doonesbury*, for instance, which rose to fame with his Watergate coverage, made systematic use of the device, starting in February 1973. The same motif is also frequent in Herblock cartoons about Nixon, as in the April 8, 1973, image of the White House caught in a tidal wave captioned "Watergate."[19] The cover of issue #142 is the first example in *Mad* of this motif, which was then abundantly used until the mid-'70s. It is significant that one of the most recognizable visual strategies of political cartoonists started being used only at this juncture, exemplifying the presence of a more journalistic strain of satire in the magazine.

In June of the same year, Max Brandel published a set of photomontages in which Nixon and Agnew are successively depicted from the imagined viewpoints of various groups. The ostensible purpose of the piece is to illustrate its title, "Nixon and Agnew as seen by . . . " (#143,

6/71: 12–14), and for that purpose the images are juxtaposed with depictions of the president and his vice president as knights in armor (as seen by " . . . Conservatives" [12]), cowboys (as seen by " . . . Six-Year-Olds" [14]), Nazis (as seen by ". . . The New Left" [12]), Klansmen (as seen by ". . . the N.A.A.C.P." [12]), clowns (as seen by " . . . Our Allies" [13]), or faces on Mount Rushmore (as seen by " . . . Themselves" [14]).

While *Mad* had an established tradition of using photocompositions for humorous purposes, the technique has also historically been used for political and propaganda purposes, a history that Brandel's article taps. Maria Reidelbach, who researched *Mad* extensively for her book *Completely Mad*, noted in her 1991 booklet on Kurtzman the resemblance between Brandel's and John Heartfield's work.[20] Heartfield was a satirist who created photomontages repurposing Nazi propaganda for oppositional purposes in the thirties, and it is entirely possible that Brandel, who was a Jew in Poland at the time, had discovered his work then.

In any case, it is hard to ascribe to a coincidence the fact that the photo of Hitler that Brandel used with Nixon's head was one that Heartfield himself had put on the cover of the anti-fascist *AIZ* in October 1934 to show Hitler gazing at his own reflection in Snow White's magic mirror (see fig. 17-3). While depicting Nixon as Hitler was a bold move in a widely circulated magazine, it must have had a peculiar resonance for Brandel, who was a concentration camp survivor. There is thus little doubt that the piece was *intended* as an attack on the president, and little doubt that it was read as one. Not only is the balance in the article entirely superficial, with negative images outnumbering positive depictions, but the existence of implicitly shared values among *Mad*'s readership—though the published correspondence suggests that the readership was not homogeneous—also means that even the openly flattering descriptions of the executive ticket were likely to be read ironically. This implication is especially true for the depiction of Nixon and Agnew in knightly attire, while Camelot imagery was still strongly associated with Nixon's 1960 opponent, John F. Kennedy.

In his account of the relationship between Nixon and the press, Louis Liebovich identifies two events that signaled the further deterioration of relations between the administration and the press after Agnew's attacks: the airing of the documentary *The Selling of the President* on CBS

John Heartfield
AIZ cover (August 1934)

Max Brandel, «Nixon and Agnew as seen by...» *Mad Magazine* #143 (June 1971)

Fig. 17-3: In "Nixon and Agnew as seen by . . ." (right), Max Brandel compares Nixon to Hitler, among others (*Mad* #143, 6/71: 12). The same photo of Hitler (left) had been famously used by John Heartfield in 1934 in the communist magazine *AIZ*, testifying to the fact that Brandel's joke was also meant as a virulent political statement. MAD used with permission.

in February 1971 and publication of the Pentagon Papers in the *New York Times* the following June.[21] Significantly, most of the critical pieces published in *Mad* which I have mentioned so far were conceived and even published before these incidents. In that respect, *Mad* can be said to have provided a form of political dissent that was not yet the dominant line in the mainstream press, vindicating the *New York Magazine* analysis from my introduction.

Mad's distrust of Nixon did not disappear as the president's popularity ascended again after the trip to China and until the 1972 election. When *Mad* presented "A *Mad* Guide to Political Types" in October 1972, the only commonality among the types was that they "distrust[ed] Nixon" (Jacobs and Woodbridge, #154, 10/72: 28–30). That may have been blatantly untrue on the verge of Nixon's landslide victory, but it reaffirmed *Mad*'s creed, just before another necessary hiatus on presidential coverage. The last pre-election image of Nixon was published on the back cover of issue #155, cover-dated December 1972: the Statue of Liberty crying, with photos of the two presidential tickets inserted in her headdress. Once more, Max Brandel was credited with the idea.

Thus, after a short period of indecisiveness in 1969, *Mad* presented a sternly critical portrait of the Nixon administration during its first term. Some of the pieces published were similar in tone to parodies and spoofs published during other administrations, with the Gilbert and Sullivan reprise serving as a prime example. Others, mostly connected with Max Brandel, shifted what had been general discontent with American society under Johnson toward open and at times violent criticism of the president himself. In his 1972 book on *Mad*, Frank Jacobs noted that Al Feldstein, the editor of the magazine, was concerned about the amount of Nixon material at one point—probably in 1970—and decided to restore a "balance."[22] By the time of the book's publication and the 1972 election, there was little evidence that this restoration had lasted for more than a few months.

Nixon in His Second Term: "Why Not Pardon Hitler!"

After the election, Nixon again disappeared from the magazine for two full issues. As in 1968, the lag between the conception of features and distribution of the magazine made it impossible for *Mad* to comment on immediate events. Max Brandel then welcomed him back to the magazine in early 1973 with two full pages featuring altered photographs. In one, a picture of the White House was topped by a gigantic "Nixxon" sign imitating the Exxon logo and captioned ". . . But It's Still the Same Old Gas" (#158, 4/73: 25). The other, an uncaptioned back-cover photograph by Irving Schild, showed a hand and forearm clad in the United States flag and making the V-for-victory sign with the fingers bloodily cut off (#158, 4/73). Though the picture ostensibly refers to the peace process in Vietnam, the close association between Nixon and the V-sign, as well as his role as commander-in-chief, makes it impossible to dissociate the comment from his presidency.

Watergate, which was becoming a national affair in the early months of 1973, proved more difficult to cover than the day-to-day workings of the Nixon administration in its first term, if only because the story evolved through sudden and unexpected revelations. Liebovich notes that as late as February 1973, a few weeks before he was forced to resign, H. R. Haldeman, Nixon's chief of staff and one of the key conspirators, did not appear overly worried in his personal diary.[23] Then in a few weeks between April and June, events spiraled out of control for the administration as the general public took interest in the long-simmering story. This pace, maybe coupled with Feldstein's decisions to reduce the space devoted to Nixon, explains *Mad*'s lateness in mentioning Watergate. The word *Watergate* did not appear until issue #162, cover-dated October 1973 and probably published in August, when a reader credited the magazine with "trying to prepare us for Watergate, way back in 1971!" ("Letters Dept." #162, 10/73: 2-3; 2). Similarly, when *Mad* published its own summary of Watergate by Silverstone and Clarke in December of the same year, as "Malice in Wonderland," juxtaposing quotes from *Alice's Adventures in Wonderland* with actual statements by the co-conspirators, the story extended only as far as June 1973 (#163, 12/73: 40-41). The Brandel back cover for the previous issue—another Irving Schild photo, this time headlined "If It Were Up to the Nixon Gang," of the White House with a tombstone bearing the inscription "In Memory of the Freedom of the Press" on the front lawn (#162, 10/73)—was several months late in expressing a widespread sentiment. With the administration having come to a "virtual halt" during the investigation, as Liebovich put it, and events moving too fast for the magazine's publishing schedule, *Mad*'s coverage of Nixon in 1973 and 1974 was constant but mostly unspecific.[24] For instance, several back covers in a row alluded to the situation in general terms: "Our Floundering Fathers," with Nixon as the anti-Washington (Jaffee and Rickard, #166, 4/74); "Nixon Slipped Here," with another photograph of the White House (Gore and Schild, #167, 6/74); then "Save the Eagle," in which the American eagle is strangled by magnetic tapes (Jacobs and Clarke #169, 9/74). In all three cases, contemporary editorial cartoons can be found with nearly the same composition or tagline,[25] with the crucial difference that these cartoons were published alongside more specific comments on the unfolding scandals, while *Mad* had to resort to generic representations and national symbols, eschewing specific references.

Ironically, by the time *Mad* finally devoted a cover to Watergate, Nixon had already resigned. The cover for the December 1974 issue pointed to the crisis with a pastiche of the poster of the movie *The Sting*, in which a grinning Nixon, next to an equally grinning Agnew, is burning up a subpoena from the House of Representatives (Mingo, #171). The issue probably went on sale in October, but the painting must have been commissioned several weeks before that, around the time of Nixon's resignation on August 8, 1974. Nixon dismissed the House subpoena late in May, and the only other article dealing with Watergate in the same issue makes reference to *The White House Transcripts* (published June 28, 1974), a book of redacted transcriptions of Nixon's Oval Office conversations, which the administration submitted to the House Judiciary Committee in April of the same year, while withholding the tapes themselves.

Mad did cover the aftermath of Watergate with a few farcical articles. The first was a gallery of dysfunctional Nixon commemorative items, such as "The Nixon Swamp," published in the same issue as the Hitler back cover (DeBartolo and Clarke, "Commemoratives to President Nixon" #172, 1/75: 30-31). Shortly afterwards, "A White House 'Garage Sale'" symbolically liquidated the Nixon-Agnew heritage through a series of items ranging from antiperspirant cans for TV appearances to a copy of *The Complete Dictionary of American Slang and Expletives* (Silverstone and Clarke, #174, 4/75: 32-33). Watergate also became a source of gags for in-house ads, running next to the readers' correspondence between 1973 and mid-1975 (#163 to #174). For instance, a bold headline screams "Nixon Cover-Up" above a paragraph advertising posters that you can use to "cover up any picture of Nixon you happen to have hanging around" (#169, 09/74: 2). Finally, in "Additions to the Dictionary," Frank Jacobs provided the aforementioned capstone to intense coverage of Nixon by describing the former president as "an illness lasting six years" (#174, 4/75: 41). The entry is strongly reminiscent of Ford's admission, upon taking office on August 10, 1974, that the "long national nightmare" was over, and of Herblock's 1974 assessment of Nixon as "an infection."[26] Ford, of course, was referring to the scandals collectively known as Watergate, while for *Mad* and Herblock, the problem lay in the President himself. In the explanatory quote, Jacobs added: "'You must let the Nixon run its course,' the doctor said." *Mad* certainly did a lot more to fight this perceived illness than let it run its course.

Although Jimmy Carter did receive some attention during his presidency, *Mad*'s interest in the new administration, and then in Ronald Reagan's, was noticeably less than what the magazine had shown to Nixon's. Max Brandel's sudden death of a heart attack in September 1975 may partly explain this. While he was not responsible for all the magazine's output regarding Nixon, Brandel was associated with the most salient pieces published about Nixon and might have continued publishing pieces on his successors.

Conclusion

To answer the initial question, *Mad* does not appear to have joined the fray regarding Richard Nixon. Quite the contrary, *Mad* anticipated the criticism regarding the president at a very early stage during his first term, siding with the minority of the country rather than with the majority who approved of his actions before 1971. *Mad* had also noticeably maintained an interest in Nixon in the 1960s, at a time when his visibility in the press had fallen back to the level he had known in the early 1950s. By contrast, *Mad* proved unable to keep up with the pace of the revelations during the Watergate era, toning down its coverage of the presidency at the precise moment when it was capturing the attention of the whole country.

Nixon would even continue to appear on a regular basis in the pages of *Mad* after his resignation, not as a reconciliatory presence but as a constant reminder of possible dishonesty and abuses of power by politicians. During the 1990s, for instance, he was used on several occasions in association with Bill Clinton to suggest the latter's lack of integrity. While Nixon did not receive sustained attention from *Mad* after Watergate, he remained something of a recurring feature long after the 1970s in a way that no other former president did, conclusively proving that he played and continues to play a special role in the magazine's history, a symbol of a brief period at the height of its popularity during which the magazine sought to take a political stand.

Notes

1. Todd Gitlin, *The Sixties: Years of Hope, Days of Rage*, 36; Theodore Roszak, *The Making of a Counter Culture: Reflections on the Technocratic Society and Its Youthful Opposition*, 24.

2. "Bad," 52–56.

3. Quoted in Daniel Gluckson and Al Feldstein, "Man Behind the Curtain Department: Al Feldstein Interview," 75.

4. Richard Reeves, "*Mad* Magazine—Witness for the People," 40.

5. Nicolas Labarre, "Du Kitsch Au Camp. Théorie de la culture de masse aux Etats-Unis, 1944–1964," 279–304.

6. All the dates given are the cover dates. However, magazines were post-dated to be able to remain longer on newsstands. Throughout the 1960s and 1970s, the gap between the actual publication date and the cover date appears to have been two to three months.

7. This rather minor occurrence of Nixon's name was found using the digital archive of *Mad* (available first as a CD-ROM and then a DVD-ROM entitled

Absolutely Mad Magazine: 50+ Years), which allows full-text search in the magazine. The articles are not tagged, however, and purely visual appearances are not identified. This article thus relies on extensive and manual reading of the magazine, focused on the period ranging from 1956 to 1980.

8. Joseph A. Palermo, "Politics, Public Opinion, and Popular Culture." In *Watergate and the Resignation of Richard Nixon: Impact of a Constitutional Crisis*, edited by Harry P. Jeffrey and Thomas Maxwell-Long, 18.

9. "Running Mate."

10. "Bad," 56.

11. Harry P. Jeffrey, "The Life, Presidency, and Resignation of Richard Nixon," in *Watergate and the Resignation of Richard Nixon: Impact of a Constitutional Crisis*, edited by Harry P. Jeffrey and Thomas Maxwell-Long, 6.

12. Edgar G. White, *Earl Warren: A Public Life*, 142.

13. Herbert Block, *Herblock Special Report*, 83–85.

14. Louis W. Liebovich, *Richard Nixon, Watergate, and the Press: A Historical Retrospective*, 1–10.

15. Quoted in Gluckson and Feldstein, "Man Behind the Curtain Department," 75.

16. Pascal Lefèvre, "Some Medium-Specific Qualities of Graphic Sequences," 16.

17. Ranan R. Lurie, *Nixon Rated Cartoons*, 15.

18. Philip Roth, *Our Gang (Starring Tricky and His Friends)*, 17.

19. Block, *Herblock Special Report*, 138.

20. Maria Reidelbach, *Harvey Kurtzman's Mad Lithograph Booklet—A History of the MADmen*, 4.

21. Liebovich, *Richard Nixon, Watergate, and the Press*, 116, 35–39.

22. Frank Jacobs, *The Mad World of William M. Gaines*, 42–43.

23. Liebovich, *Richard Nixon, Watergate, and the Press*, 75.

24. Liebovich, *Richard Nixon, Watergate, and the Press*, 79. In between these specific attacks on Nixon came the more generic criticism by Frank Jacobs and Irving Schild, "A *Mad* Medical Report," on the back cover of issue #168 (7/74): a photo of a battered Uncle Sam with descriptions of injuries and ailments head to toe.

25. See, for example, Block, *Herblock Special Report*, 130, 170, 218, 228.

26. Block, *Herblock Special Report*, 252.

PART IV.
THEORIES

18. "Comedy before Country":

Engaged Levity and Absurdist Critique in *Mad* Magazine

Jeffrey St. Onge

WHEN *Mad* MAGAZINE turned sixty years old, many commentators used the occasion to honor the magazine as a trailblazer of absurdist political satire. John Wenzel of the *Denver Post*, for example, noted that "for generations, *Mad* magazine has given us the silly, the gross and the absurd, poking fun at celebrities and politicians, all the while gleefully warping countless young minds."[1] Wenzel notes especially *Mad*'s "vicious political satire that has no allegiance to the right or left," pointing to the recent cover of "Alfred E. Neuman with a tiny President Obama on one shoulder and a tiny Mitt Romney on the other—both dressed as pitchfork-toting devils above the fiery headline "Welcome to Election Hell" (Fredrickson, #517, 10/12).[2] This cover exemplifies the magazine's style of political humor, which has consistently blended trenchant critique with hyperbolic exaggerations of political culture. *Mad*'s humor is one important part of its larger contribution to popular culture as a consistent source of absurdist satire aimed at everything from the deeply sacred to the profoundly stupid.

Upon inception, *Mad* was unique for its ability to blend multiple modes of comedy and critique into a magazine essentially intended for young adults, but with something to offer anybody with political opinions and a sense of humor. As Eric Drysdale describes the magazine's multilayered approach in the introduction to *Totally Mad: 60 Years of Humor, Satire, Stupidity, and Stupidity*, "No matter the level of sophistication you brought to *Mad*, there was always something dumb enough to keep your attention—if only the glorious weirdness of the pictures. And with any material that required deeper understanding, there was always a sense that you would get it eventually." Noting that *Mad* provided a sometimes challenging, yet joyful reading experience, Drysdale continues, "It felt like being guided into a new, dangerous place—but in the good hands of fun-loving friends eager to share new and hilarious truths about the world."[3] For *Mad*, life is a little bit ridiculous, and the ability to laugh at everything is an important one. In this essay, I explore how *Mad*'s satires of American politics provide a perspective on democracy that may be especially useful in the contemporary political climate, which is marked by division and antagonism. The magazine encourages what I will describe as *engaged levity*; it requires political knowledge and engagement, while simultaneously treating important subjects in a flippant and humorous way. My analysis focuses particularly on the send-ups of Presidents George W. Bush and Barack Obama to advance an argument as to how, with absurdist political humor, *Mad* operates as a key form of democratic dissent. As two of the nation's most visible recent political figures, these presidents provide a useful lens through which to assess *Mad*'s satire of political culture overall. *Mad*'s presidential satire is thus taken here to illustrate the magazine's general attitude toward politics, as its presidential critiques reflect its wider opinions on American culture.

This essay thus functions as an appreciation of both *Mad*'s humor and its role in contemporary American democracy. By holding up a fractured mirror to the commonplaces of political discussion, *Mad* interrupts the partisan nature of U.S. politics and frames it as essentially an exercise in absurdity. However, the sophistication of *Mad*'s multilayered satire encourages engagement rather than disengagement. In what follows, I discuss *Mad* in the context of scholarly work that addresses the role of satire in democracy. I then briefly discuss democratic deliberation, particularly what it may mean to shift from an antagonistic to an agonistic society, where politics are more cooperative than combative. I argue that *Mad*'s humor exemplifies Kenneth Burke's comic frame of acceptance, as it encourages reflection through humility.[4] To do this, I analyze *Mad*'s representations of Presidents Bush and Obama, focusing particularly on examples that reflect an engaged levity through its nonpartisan targeting of politicians. I conclude with a brief discussion of the importance of humor in democracy, specifically in the context of a deeply divided public.

Absurdist Political Satire and Agonistic Pluralism

While satire as a concept can be complex and difficult to define, it does have certain characteristics that make it unique as an art form. As George A. Test explains, satire generally has four definitional elements:

aggression, judgment, play, and laughter.[5] That is, satire must be *aggressive* toward some aspect of society, and it must advocate a point of view that runs counter to the status quo. In its aggression, it must make a *judgment*. *Mad* often judges politics as absurd in some way, a view that also satisfies the criterion of *play*. As Test explains about play, “In short, life is a game; some know it and some don’t. Those who don’t have lost the ability to be like a child, caught up in the world of work, science, progress, and utility.”[6] *Mad*’s message is consistently geared toward facilitating this revelation in readers, and it does so in part through a consistently humorous approach, thus bringing in the fourth element of satire: *laughter*. Altogether, *Mad* fulfills Test’s idea of the satirist as someone who “melds the roles of judge, castigator, jester, and trickster.” Together these roles give satire its force as a valuable mode of public critique—what Sophia A. McClennen describes as “a comedic and pedagogic form uniquely suited to provoking critical reflection [through] its ability to underscore the absurdity, ignorance, and prejudice of commonly accepted behavior by means of comedic critical reflection.”[7] *Mad* offers such a persistent comic and pedagogic stance on national politics: it pokes fun and consistently reminds us to laugh at American cultural life and thus has tremendous value in the current, divided political moment. Through its political satire, *Mad* has the potential to bring citizens together at least temporarily to see the inanity of *othering* political adversaries. That is, *Mad*’s humor can provide a moment of unity through ridicule of the entire political system. It may thus help bridge political divides, if only for a fleeting moment, which could encourage more cooperative and productive democratic deliberation.

Mad’s February 2014 issue provides one example of the magazine’s presidential satire. The cover story featured “The 20 Dumbest People, Events, and Things 2013” (Fredrickson, #525). Four of the twenty moments are dedicated to Obama (these include “White House Website Down,” on the failure of the Affordable Care Act website [Santopadre and McQuade 37]; *The Drone Ranger*, on his use of military drones [Lowe 33]; “Red Linings Playbook,” on his “bluff on Syria’s chemical weapons” [uncredited 41]; and “Blurred Laws,” on his NSA spying scandal, critiqued through a parody of Robin Thicke’s popular song “Blurred Lines” [Morse and Mejía 44-45]). The top spot on the list, however, went to the Republican Tea Party, which is portrayed as an out-of-control fraternity through a parody of the film *Animal House* (“National Buffoon’s

Abysmal House"). The tagline reads, "It was the Tea Party against the rules . . . the rules lost!" This faux-film was ostensibly written by Ayn Rand, directed by Ted Cruz, and starred President Obama as Dean Wormer (Rath and Richmond, #525, 2/14: 24–25). This list reflects *Mad*'s consistent approach of attacking all politicians with equal vigor. Indeed, its annual "Dumbest Moments" issue routinely criticizes both the president and the opposing party. (See chapter 7, 147–176, for a full discussion of the "*Mad* 20," including examples of several covers.[8])

"The 20 Dumbest People, Events & Things of 2006" issue, for example, offered a cover illustration of Vice President Dick Cheney holding a shotgun and standing next to a bullet-riddled Alfred E. Neuman, referencing the infamous hunting incident in which Cheney shot his friend Harry Whittington in the face (Fredrickson, #473, 1/07). Five years later, the cover for the "The 20 Dumbest People, Events and Things 2011" issue featured President Obama as a baby, swimming naked in a pool and chasing a dollar bill hung from a fishhook in a parody of Nirvana's *Nevermind* album cover (Fredrickson, #513, 2/12). The designation of "dumb" provides a useful way to summarize the magazine's attitude: politics in general is a practice in absurdity, regardless of political affiliation. *Mad* exists in part to point out the "dumbness" in U.S. politics, while at the same time demonstrating an engagement through persistent critique.

In this way, *Mad*'s humor is best described as *absurdist* political satire. Absurdism, explained Albert Camus in *The Myth of Sisyphus* (1942), constitutes the essential nature of the relationship between humans and the world. As he argues, "the Absurd is not in man (if such a metaphor could have a meaning) nor in the world, but in their presence together. For the moment it is the only bond uniting them."[9] Camus examines the myth of Sisyphus, who is condemned to the "hopeless labor" of repeatedly pushing a boulder up a hill for the entirety of his existence, and compares him to the "workman of today," who spends "every day in his life at the same tasks" and whose "fate is no less absurd."[10] The punishment for Sisyphus is condemnation to a life with no meaning or progress, but Camus argues that the myth should be read differently. Rather than focusing on the toil of carrying the stone up the mountain, attention should be paid to Sisyphus's thoughts on the way down, as he follows the rolling boulder, aware that he must once again push it to the top. As Camus writes:

> At that subtle moment when man glances backward over his life . . . in that slight pivoting he contemplates that series of unrelated actions which becomes his fate, created by him, combined under his memory's eye and soon sealed by his death. Thus, convinced of the wholly human origin of all that is human . . . he is still on the go. The rock is still rolling.[11]

Ultimately, Camus concludes that "the struggle itself toward the heights is enough to fill a man's heart. One must imagine Sisyphus happy."[12] Absurdism, then, is a moment of reflection in which we recognize the relative futility of our pursuits through an understanding of our routinized nature. It is the revelation that what we believe to be held sacred is essentially a trick of the mind, and that a recognition of this futility can allow for greater freedom to live life with enjoyment.

Camus's theory of the absurd is relevant to a discussion of *Mad* magazine and its satire, which functions as a persistent reminder that everyday life is an exercise in faith in a constructed political system. When held up to scrutiny, many of society's entrenched practices—judging a president by what occurs in the first one hundred days, for instance—seem to be rather inane. Camus offers a useful reminder that a practice need not be discontinued simply because it is absurd. Rather, we must learn to find joy in living in a world constructed in large part through arbitrary practices. *Mad* magazine—which essentially asks its readers to laugh at anything and everything—is one source for finding this joy.

A key aspect of *Mad*'s humor is its wide array of targets. As longtime editor Al Feldstein remarked in 2007, one of *Mad*'s most important contributions is its "bipartisan approach to all subjects." Feldstein continues:

> *Mad* was wide open. Bill [Gaines, publisher] loved it, and he was a capitalist Republican. I loved it, and I was a liberal Democrat. That went for the writers, too; they all had their own political leanings, and everybody had a voice. But the voices were mostly critical. It was social commentary, after all.[13]

For Feldstein, then, effective social commentary must blend a multiplicity of voices for the sake of critiquing the totality of political culture. Then-editor John Ficarra echoed Feldstein in the introduction to *Mad*'s special collection on George W. Bush: "Since its inception during the

Eisenhower Administration, *Mad*'s policy has always been to mock the man in office. We begin each new administration with a clean slate and we wait for them to do something really stupid before pouncing on them. (Usually that happens around day two)."[14] *Mad*'s absurdity is enacted in part through this mockery of the president; it is a foregone conclusion that each new president will almost immediately do something "really stupid." The wide range of perspectives and targets described by both editors reflects the variety in *Mad*'s approach. The political world is already understood as absurd, and *Mad* is always waiting with a small army of artists and writers ready to point that out. The magazine shows no concern for party politics and treats people of all political stripes equally.

One example of *Mad*'s political ambivalence is the cover of the May 2010 issue, which features mascot Alfred E. Neuman wearing an "I ♥ Obama" shirt, altered with a marker to read "♥'ed," in the past tense (Fredrickson, #503: 5/10). The right-wing political website *Newsbusters* interpreted this as an example of "former Obama-loving media members" turning on the president.[15] However, this image can also be read as a satire of those on the left who put faith in Obama to instigate massive structural changes—perhaps even structural changes not possible with the office of the presidency—and who had professed to lose that faith only fifteen months into his term. In 2008 *Mad* did, after all, feature a cover with Neuman, made to look like Obama, holding a bumper sticker that read, "YES WE CAN'T" (Fredrickson, #493, 9/08). That same issue included an unsigned parody movie poster for "The 46-Year-Old Political Virgin" (11) (based on the 2005 film *The 40-Year-Old Virgin*), which referenced the oft-repeated charge that Obama was too inexperienced for the office. Taken together, these examples demonstrate *Mad*'s ambivalence toward Obama, which reflects the magazine's orientation toward each president before him. That is, *Mad* cannot be characterized as a left- or right-wing magazine, as it offers wide-ranging social commentary not aligned with any political party.

Mad is, of course, not unique in its objective to attack political figures of all stripes. Russell Peterson, in his book *Strange Bedfellows: How Late-Night Comedy Turns Democracy into a Joke*, discusses in great detail political comedians who purport to be what he calls "equal opportunity offenders."[16] Peterson describes this humor, typified by late-night talk show monologues, "shock" humor shows such as *Family Guy* (Fox, 1999--)

and *South Park* (Comedy Central, 1997--), and sketch comedy programs such as *Saturday Night Live* (NBC, 1975--), as pseudo-satire because its chief characteristic is not political engagement, but rather nihilism. "[M]ost of the 'edgy' comedy sold and celebrated as such is . . . nihilistically 'neutral,'" he notes; "If the subtext of Jay Leno's topical punch lines is 'all politics is a joke,' the subtext of [shock humor] is 'nothing is sacred.' Well, if nothing is sacred, nothing is at stake."[17] Peterson argues that these forms of humor, while dealing with political subjects, use politics and politicians as subject matter only because they are in the news; no meaningful critique is actually advanced. Further, the jokes are often generic, simply using famous figures as easy punchlines and thereby contributing to a culture where "all politics is a joke."[18] He concludes that this type of humor is a negative contribution to political culture—an "easy nihilism" that combines generic humor with a sentiment that political engagement is not worth the effort.[19]

While nihilistic comedians share a stated commitment to skewering anything and everything, that characteristic alone is not problematic. Peterson contrasts pseudo-satirists with Jon Stewart and Stephen Colbert, two comedians with clear, if complex, political agendas. He explains the difference as follows: "For Stewart, as with the Equal Opportunity Offender mainstream, all things political are fair game; the difference is that he does not therefore pretend that they are *only* a game."[20] While Peterson does not explore *Mad* in detail, he does point out that, alongside Mort Sahl, Lenny Bruce, and Second City, the magazine was a key mid-twentieth century voice in "questioning authority, long before the sixties' long-haired kids made it the new national pastime."[21] Peterson's inclusion of *Mad* alongside Bruce and Sahl, two individuals he considers to be true satirists, suggests that the magazine is not easily placed in the category of pseudo-satire like other "equal opportunity offenders." As I have been arguing thus far, *Mad* certainly turns all things into a joke, but its position is not nihilism; it is, on the contrary, absurdity. Where nihilism leads to disengagement, absurdity promotes a different, valuable perspective on engagement. Indeed, *Mad* requires a level of political knowledge for its humor to make sense, and the more knowledge one has, the more one will glean from the jokes.

Politics in the United States is marked by antagonism; the U.S. has a deeply divided political culture where the primary tendency is for political debate to take the form of an "us vs. them" contest. *Mad*'s style of absurdist critique provides a useful contribution to this political culture, countering it by encouraging a certain type of democratic praxis best described as engaged levity. *Engaged levity* is used here to mean a continued appreciation for and entanglement in the political world (engagement), tempered by a comic distance that promotes reflexivity (levity). *Mad*'s multilayered satire requires and promotes some level of engagement—you must have some knowledge to get the jokes—and it encourages its readers to laugh at serious issues. Humor is a way of dissipating tension, and laughter can promote a momentary kinship among political opponents.[22] As such, engaged levity may be especially useful in the current climate, where increased division, noncooperation, government shutdowns, and political *othering* (e.g., "you're a socialist!") are the norm.

According to democratic theorist Chantal Mouffe, this shift away from the regular *othering* of political opponents is key to the maintenance of democracy. Mouffe's argument focuses on transforming a culture of antagonism into one of *agonism*, rooted in the Greek concept of the *agon*, which describes debate among opponents who see each other not as mortal enemies but as worthy opponents. She notes the importance of distinguishing between "two types of political relations: one of *antagonism* between enemies, and one of *agonism* between adversaries," and argues that "an adversary is a legitimate enemy, an enemy with whom we have in common a shared adhesion to the ethico-political principles of democracy."[23] In other words, Mouffe warns against viewing opponents as enemies who must be defeated, expelled from the nation, or otherwise eliminated from public discourse. In agonistic democracy, contestation would remain the norm, but it would be productive rather than reductive. Pluralistic politics, then, in the words of rhetorical critic Robert L. Ivie, "is foremost a matter of figuring out how a necessarily conflicted polity can bridge its divisions sufficiently for people to live together without sacrificing a healthy degree of diversity."[24] For Ivie, this analysis begets a key question: how can citizens in a pluralistic society not only coexist, but productively manage division so that democracy can thrive?[25] One approach to this question is to find sources of invention—ways of thinking and talking about democracy—that might temporarily bridge political divides and provide opportunities for citizens to view themselves as partners in democracy rather than mortal enemies.

Mad is one such source of invention in that it operates as a consistent and persistent rhetorical critique that helps expand what Kenneth Burke referred to as the comic "frame of acceptance." Burke defines frames as "the more or less organized system of meanings by which a thinking man gauges the historical situation and adopts a role with relation to it."[26] Humans are not inherently oriented to the larger society of which they are part; rather, individuals learn how to orient themselves through frames that define certain people, things, or situations as either "friendly or unfriendly."[27] Frames of acceptance encourage a worldview based in humility and understanding; they are in contrast to frames of rejection, which encourage hostility and othering. For Burke, enlargement of the comic frame is a necessary component in the progress of "humane enlightenment."[28] As he states, "the comic frame should enable people *to be observers of themselves, while acting*. Its ultimate would not be *passiveness*, but *maximum consciousness*."[29] Cultural artifacts that could enlarge frames of acceptance in a democracy suffering from deep division should thus be highlighted and mined to help instantiate a shift toward a more productive, agonistic politics.

Mad contributes to the expansion of comic frames of acceptance as its continual and varied critique of political culture promotes engaged levity through absurdism. Don J. Waisanen, who similarly described Jon Stewart and Stephen Colbert as examples of "pedagogical rhetorical criticism [that] provide us with ways to learn about and deal meaningfully with our environments," explains that these figures work within Burke's comic frame in part because of their ability to "draw attention to and debunk social absurdities and contradictions, while often providing incipient alternatives to myopic orientations."[30] Key to Burke's comic frame, according to Beth E. Bonstetter, is that critique "lampoons as much as it denigrates, and it *laughs* rather than condemns."[31] *Mad* provides a way to see "*all* members of a society as fools, as people who make mistakes," which, as Bonstetter notes, is the apotheosis of human enlightenment.[32] Because *Mad*'s satire extends to virtually any and every aspect of culture (including itself), it works as a continual rhetorical critique, consistently pointing out the absurdities of the political world. This generalizing of absurdity can bring readers together for a moment of clarity in an otherwise contentious political environment.[33] In other words, humor and laughter can help to alleviate tension and promote agonistic debate among individuals with seemingly incompatible values.[34]

My argument about *Mad*'s absurdist political humor is premised on the fact that the magazine satirizes politicians of every stripe, as this willingness to see everything (at least partially) as absurd—even for a moment—is of great value to democratic practice. The magazine acts as a key site of democratic dissent in promoting an engaged levity that both requires and encourages political literacy while taking comic aim at venerated political targets. In what follows, I examine a few different examples of *Mad*'s presidential satire, highlighting especially how they function in this way.

What, Me Worry?

In 2007, *Mad* published a movie poster for *Pirates of the Constitution: Head Man's Mess,* a film about "wiretapping, search & seizure, imprisonment, and torture" (Kovaleski and Fredrickson, #473, 01/07: 36). The parody, based on the hit film *Pirates of the Caribbean: Dead Man's Chest* (2006), featured George W. Bush, Dick Cheney, and Condoleezza Rice staring menacingly at the viewer as a flood engulfs the White House. A flaming skull with an American flag bandana floats among octopus tentacles; a pirate flag tops the White House. The tagline reads: "Now subverting a government near you." Years later, as part of *Mad*'s "20 Dumbest People, Events, and Things 2013," the magazine offered another parody poster, this time for *The Drone Ranger* (Loew, #525, 2/14: 33). This poster presented Obama as the Lone Ranger and Joe Biden as Tonto. Obama bears a wicked smile, while Biden has a shocked look on his face. Above and behind the two men are several unmanned military drones. The punning tagline—"now bombing everywhere"—is augmented by a paragraph that begins, "In 2009, President Obama received the Nobel Peace Prize. Apparently none of the Peace Prize judges live in a country where unmanned U.S. drones drop bombs on innocent people while killing or attempting to kill terrorists, would-be terrorists or Facebook friends of either" (33). This tagline highlights the contradiction inherent in a wartime president winning perhaps the most prestigious international peace award. Further, it questions the wisdom of those who chose Obama for the award so early in his term as president; the award was given with no knowledge of how he would eventually handle the two wars of the Bush administration.

Virtually every issue of *Mad* contains a parody movie poster, so it is not surprising that this comic vehicle is used to lampoon both Presidents

Bush and Obama. What is significant about this set of posters, though, is the continuity of the critique. Above the title on *The Drone Ranger* poster, a blurb reads "From the producer of *Pirates of the Constitution*," the title of the earlier parody Bush poster by Kovaleski. Aside from identifying the artist, the blurb implies that both Bush and Obama were working from the same playbook, perhaps one drawn up by the same individuals. These posters reflect a persistent argument from the magazine regarding both presidents and their actions in the name of fighting terror. In Desmond Devlin and Paul Coker's "*Mad*'s Handy Glossary to the War on Terror," the magazine accused Bush of defining "democracy" as "a hypothetical form of government promised to the people of Kabul, Baghdad, and Afghanistan"; further, the entry for "Hearts and minds of the Iraqi people" reads: "that stuff CNN and FOX don't show you, splattered all over the Iraqi rubble" (#438, 2/04: 6-17; 16–17). The harshness of this message is offset by the absurdity of the accompanying cartoon, which features images of exploding limbs, organs, and clothes exaggerated just enough to register as humor.

Mad also critiqued the handling of civil liberties in the War on Terror. On the cover of *Mad*'s "Special War on Privacy Issue," which was devoted to the National Security Agency wiretapping scandal, Obama is shown huddled with *Mad*'s iconic "Spy vs. Spy" figures, dressed in a similar hat and trench coat (Fredrickson, #523, 8/13). The spies hold binoculars and high-tech listening devices, and Obama displays a massive, toothy grin. Obama, drawn larger than the spies, is apparently in command; the implicit argument here regards his ostensible willingness to trade protection of civil liberties for information that could help in the War on Terror. These jokes about war are sophisticated, and they work on multiple levels. As such, they require some political literacy and engagement from the reader. They are perhaps inherently funny due to the exaggerated features in the drawings and the fact that they are caricaturing the president of the United States, but the humor also works because they make trenchant, and even audacious, points about war and surveillance.

In addition to being sophisticated, these jokes are patently absurd. The images of the presidents superimposed over posters for major motion pictures show no respect for the office of the presidency, which is the intended point. The act of spying and possibly violating both the U.S. Constitution and international law is translated through *Mad*'s iconic Cold War spoof of spies. Further, the death and destruction brought by war—perhaps the most serious topic of all—are handled in such a way as to condemn them through laughter and a sense that the very existence of war is irrational. These jokes are prime examples of *Mad*'s engaged levity: the critiques are packaged in an absurd form, almost suggesting that nothing can be done, so laughter is the best alternative.

Mad's humor usually skewers several targets at once, and its commentary on presidents frequently doubles as commentary on the media. A representative example is "*Mad*'s All-Inclusive Do-It-Yourself George W. Bush Press Conference" from May 2006, which demonstrated both Bush's lack of candor and his (perceived) tenuous grasp on language and politics (Jacobs and Drucker, #463: 20–21). The layout shows Bush involved in a press conference, flanked by a *Mad Libs*-style paragraph (i.e., a paragraph with several words blanked out) and lists of terms or phrases for the reader to use to both construct and answer reporters' questions. Some possible choices include "a slobbering mass of," "Cialis popping," "bleeding-heart," "Democrats," and "Bo Bice look-alikes" (20–21). The reader can insert these phrases to create a "typical" Bush press conference. The article paints an image of the president as an incompetent liar and the press conference as a circus with no real value, thus indicting media coverage of the president overall as ineffectual.

Obama's relationship with the press has also been a key aspect of *Mad*. A prime example of the magazine's approach here is its February 2009 issue, which features a cover and layout titled "The First 100 Minutes of the Obama Presidency" (Fibbers, Santopadre, and Friedman, #498, 2/09: 46–47). On the cover, Obama appears to be in hysterics, hands gripping his head, eyes wide and bloodshot, sweat on his face and arms. His mouth is open, and four cigarettes are clenched in his teeth. Papers and cigarette butts litter his desk (Obama's smoking would be a recurring theme in *Mad*), along with bottles of Pepto-Bismol, Excedrin, and a coffee cup with the "Change" logo on the front. Obama, frazzled, seems to regret running for president in the first place, and the totality of the image suggests that he was not at all ready for the job. The cover resonates with the widespread criticisms that Obama was too inexperienced or unqualified for the office.

The absurdity continues in the accompanying two-page layout, where each of the 100 minutes is listed with Obama's actions for that time period. Some of these actions refer to Obama's character: "Organize pick-up basketball game with Supreme Court"; "Just to be different, appoint staff members based on intellect and incompetence." Others critique Bush through the lens of Obama: "Rescind order that all White House TVs be set to FOX News"; "Scrape eight years' worth of chewing gum off the bottom of the Oval Office desk"; "Rescind Bush order to drill for oil in Arlington National Cemetery." Some play on Obama's perceived radical political inclinations: "Pressure Harry Reid to appoint Jeremiah Wright new Chaplain of the Senate"; "Go on Facebook; put out a friend request to Ahmadinejad." And some are just plain silly: "Fill out change of address forms"; "Pardon Mike Myers for *The Love Guru*" (46–47). In general, the article distills much of the media discourse surrounding Obama during his campaign and first three months in office. This piece offers an astounding amount of information for a two-page spread; some requires no political knowledge whatsoever. It is easy to imagine a twelve-year-old laughing at the gum-under-the-desk joke or the reference to Mike Myers's failed *Love Guru* project, for instance. Other aspects, such as the reference to Iran's president Mahmoud Ahmadinejad, however, require some political knowledge to make sense. While most adults certainly would have heard of the Iranian leader at the time, a reader would have to know that he was positioned as an enemy of the U.S., and that Obama was criticized heavily for saying that he would sit down with Ahmadinejad for the sake of diplomacy. Further, the jokes reference Obama's perceived radicalism; William Ayers, the anti-Vietnam protestor who co-founded the radical Weather Underground, was *not* a household name. Thus, we see again *Mad* promoting an engaged levity that encourages laughter through farce, along with a recognition that the entirety of the discourse surrounding Obama is at least somewhat ridiculous.

The piece also functions as a broad critique on the media spectacle surrounding Obama and the office of the presidency in general. For instance, at minute three, Obama "remove[s] that stupid flag pin from [his] lapel," a clear reference to the news coverage surrounding candidate Obama's statement about flag pins acting as substitutes for true patriotism. The media watchdog website *Fairness and Accuracy in Reporting* summed up the controversy by stating that the media, during a long presidential campaign, could "focus on the candidates' policies pertaining to the issues that Americans are most concerned about.... Or they can choose to direct their attention elsewhere—namely, to Barack Obama's lapel."[35] *Mad*'s references to William Ayers, Jeremiah Wright, Mahmoud

Ahmadinejad, and Hugo Chavez similarly speak to the countless articles, books, news specials, and websites devoted to exploring Obama's perceived radicalism and alien status, as well as his alleged communist sympathies.

The piece's most obvious commentary concerns the concept of the "first one hundred days" as a benchmark for judging a new president. Journalist Roland S. Martin points out the problem with this narrative, highlighting the abundance of media figures "speaking in breathless tones about the need for President Barack Obama to get off to a fast start and show all kinds of accomplishments in his first 100 days in office."[36] As Martin points out, though, the "problem with so much emphasis being placed on the first 100 days is that a premium is placed on speed, as opposed to thoughtfulness."[37] Without critical thought, it *seems* like a president should have some accomplishments by that time; however, the machinations of federal government are so slow and grinding that meaningful change rarely occurs quickly. Through exaggeration, *Mad* reminds readers of the constructedness of this framing device and promotes reflection on the burdens and expectations placed on the presidency by the news media and the citizenry.

As Kristin L. Matthews points out, "*Mad* used the comic magazine medium to challenge totalizing rhetoric within the American cultural, intellectual, and political establishment, and to call for readerly autonomy."[38] This totalizing rhetoric—the logic of bipartisanship in the United States—is attacked head-on by *Mad*. The magazine demonstrates the absurdity of deep political division, essentially framing it as akin to pushing a boulder up a hill ad infinitum. However, the existence and persistence of *Mad* suggest that we should not stop pushing this metaphorical boulder up the hill, but rather we should temper our expectations for the outcome. *Mad* teaches readers to approach politics with some levity, which, as I have argued, can be instructive to a culture marked by division and antagonism.

Mad's absurdist lens exaggerates the whole of political culture, including officeholders' personal features, the media, citizenship, policy, and policy's resultant effects. The magazine's primary opponent is seriousness, yet *Mad* is deeply engaged with politics. *Mad* takes aim at topics of great importance, including the fate of the nation and issues of life and death, approaching them with a humor and levity that might allow room for more productive debate. Numerous writers have considered the role of humor in relation to obstinacy and division. Mark Twain, for instance, argued that "humor is that great thing, the saving thing, after all. The minute it crops up, all our hardnesses yield, all our irritations and resentments flit away and a sunny spirit takes their place."[39] As Twain observes, when two individuals share a laugh, they also share a moment of catharsis and identification. Karin Fry, writing about existentialism in *South Park*, makes a similar point: "When the absurdity of life is acknowledged . . . a person achieves lucidity and clarity."[40] Humor is a way of dissipating tensions, and this dissipation can then clear room for productive debate that takes an agonistic, rather than antagonistic, form. This is why public speakers addressing hostile audiences often begin with a joke; the act of laughing together can soften the tensions that keep political opponents apart. Catharsis through humor can be an equalizing event, as laughter is fundamentally a nonpartisan activity. As George A. Test asserts, by "mocking behavior that is detrimental to social cohesion or which deviate[s] from group standards . . . [satire] can promote social communion through laughter."[41] From these standpoints, *Mad* functions as a valuable contribution to political culture by encouraging laughter rather than disengagement.

Kenneth Burke argues that positive human relations require the framing of political opponents "not as vicious, but as mistaken:" it requires a sense that "people are necessarily mistaken, [and] all people are exposed to situations in which they must act as fool."[42] As I have argued, *Mad*'s contribution to political culture comes through the self-knowledge it promotes; in the *Mad* universe, everybody is a potential fool who could perhaps be mistaken. While most readers will never be caricatured by *Mad*, their values certainly will be, as will the political figures they respect, the films and TV shows they like, and countless other cherished aspects of the world. *Mad* encourages its audience to approach life with engaged levity, which is conducive to democratic cooperation. The ideal of democratic practice is not perfect harmony, but rather productive agonism that allows citizens to debate issues passionately, ultimately seeing one another as fellow humans and not as enemies or *others*. I do not mean with this essay to minimize the importance of political struggle, or to suggest that politics itself should not be taken seriously. Rather, I hope for more engagement and greater democratic participation. One of the key problems in the contemporary political climate, though, is the divisive and counterproductive way in which people often talk about politics. *Mad* magazine is an example of how we might move political discourse in a more productive direction by approaching it with humility and a bit of absurdity. Simply put, if citizens can laugh together, they can work together.

Notes

1. John Wenzel, "*Mad* Magazine's Legacy of Humor and Subversion, Writ Large," paragraph 1.
2. Wenzel, "*Mad* Magazine's Legacy," paragraph 19.
3. Stephen Colbert and Eric Drysdale, introduction to *Totally* Mad*: 60 Years of Humor, Satire, Stupidity and Stupidity*, 6.
4. Kenneth Burke, *Attitudes Toward History*, 3rd ed., 5.
5. George A. Test, *Satire: Spirit and Art*, 15–30.
6. Test, *Satire*, 20.
7. Test, *Satire*, 30; Sophia A. McClennen, *Colbert's America: Satire and Democracy*, 1–2.
8. First published as Christopher J. Gilbert, "*Mad* About Stupidity, or Judging by Covers with Alfred E. Neuman," *Studies in American Humor*, n.s. 3, no. 30 (Fall 2014): 57–76.
9. Albert Camus, *The Myth of Sisyphus and Other Essays*, 30.
10. Camus, *The Myth of Sisyphus*, 119, 121.
11. Camus, *The Myth of Sisyphus*, 123.
12. Camus, *The Myth of Sisyphus*, 123.
13. Al Feldstein, "An Interview with Al Feldstein," interview by Jason Heller, paragraph 21.
14. John Ficarra, preface to *The Mad War on Bush*, 6.
15. Noel Sheppard, "Shocking *Mad* Magazine Cover: I 'Loved' Obama," paragraph 4.
16. Russell Peterson, *Strange Bedfellows: How Late-Night Comedy Turns Democracy into a Joke*, 10.
17. Peterson, *Strange Bedfellows*, 149.
18. Peterson, *Strange Bedfellows*, 149.
19. Peterson, *Strange Bedfellows*, 168.
20. Peterson, *Strange Bedfellows*, 10, 120.
21. Peterson, *Strange Bedfellows*, 31.
22. Hans Speier, "Wit and Politics: An Essay on Power and Laughter," 1357–58.
23. Chantal Mouffe, "Deliberative Democracy or Agonistic Pluralism?," 755.
24. Robert L. Ivie, "Rhetorical Deliberation and Democratic Politics in the Here and Now," 277.
25. Ivie, "Rhetorical Deliberation and Democratic Politics," 278.
26. Burke, *Attitudes Toward History*, 5.
27. Burke, *Attitudes Toward History*, 4.
28. Burke, *Attitudes Toward History*, 41.

29. Burke, *Attitudes Toward History*, 171.
30. Don J. Waisanen, "A Citizen's Guide to Democracy Inaction: Jon Stewart and Stephen Colbert's Comic Rhetorical Criticism," 121.
31. Beth E. Bonstetter, "Mel Brooks Meets Kenneth Burke (and Mikhail Bakhtin): Comedy and Burlesque in Satiric Film," 24.
32. Bonstetter, "Mel Brooks Meets Kenneth Burke," 27.
33. Karin Fry, "Oh My God! They Killed Kenny . . . Again: Kenny and Existentialism," 86.
34. Brett Biebel, "Standing Up for Comedy: Kenneth Burke and *The Office*," paragraph 2.
35. "Obama's Missing Flag Pin," paragraph 1.
36. Roland S. Martin, "To Focus on the First 100 Days is Absurd," paragraph 3.
37. Martin, "To Focus on the First 100 Days is Absurd," paragraph 8.
38. Kristin L. Matthews, "A *Mad* Proposition in Postwar America," 212.
39. Mark Twain, "What Paul Bourget Thinks of Us," 61.
40. Fry, "Oh My God!," 86.
41. Test, *Satire*, 65–66.
42. Burke, *Attitudes Toward History*, 41.

19. Genre Studies and *Mad* Magazine:

Changing and Challenging Genres, 1953–1966

Kathleen Mollick

THE BANE OF many adults for decades, *Mad* magazine remains a powerful cultural artifact of humor from the mid-1950s through the 1960s. As Grant Geissman observed in his foreword to *Mad About the Sixties: The Best of the Decade*, "Students of history who might want to get a feel for the mores, attitudes, pop culture, and politics of the sixties could do far worse than to study the material herein, because the tenor of the times is all there."[1] In its parodies of the popular culture of its time, *Mad* stands out for its ability to serve both as a lens through which certain teen-oriented aspects of American culture can be viewed, and as a snapshot of its less sophisticated attitudes. Indeed, as David Noonan claimed in his retrospective on *Mad*, the magazine's jokes about "what seemed . . . the very real possibility of nuclear annihilation" during the Cold War years profoundly affected what he identified as "Boomer humor."[2] *Mad*'s ridicule of authority figures and cultural icons makes it ripe for study through the genre theory of Mikhail Bakhtin, with its ability to expose the varied cultural meanings of a text. By applying this genre theory to the "Bat Boy and Rubin!" comic-book parody (Kurtzman and Wood, #8, 01/53: 1–7) and to the "Bats-Man" parody, when *Mad* had become a magazine (Silverstone and Drucker, #105, 9/66: 7–12), I will show how "Bat Boy and Rubin!" parodies then-current concerns about juvenile delinquency and horror comics in a more limited way than the "Bats-Man" parody, which addresses teens' challenging established authority, teenage sexual rebellion, and the celebrity culture that drove the television series. I will also discuss how parodies that were identified as the first of their kind also exemplify this trend: how *Mad*'s first parody of a television show, "Lone Stranger!" (Kurtzman and Davis, #3, 2–3/53: 1-7) is limited in its ability to address significant cultural issues compared to the first parody of a Broadway musical, "My Fair Ad Man" (Megliola [Meglin] and Drucker, #54, 4/60: 31–37), twenty issues into *Mad*'s life as a magazine. Ultimately, the change in genre from comic book to magazine provided a more open platform for *Mad*'s creators to explore the culture of their time through their use of parody.

Genre Theory and Parody

Elements of genre theory and parody illustrate how they can work together to highlight specific cultural elements, especially cultural commentary, in *Mad* as a comic and as a magazine. In "The Problem of Speech Genres," Mikhail Bakhtin argued that "[l]anguage is realized in the form of individual concrete utterances (oral and written) by participants in the various areas of human activity" and that these utterances can be found in daily conversation as well as textual forms.[3] Individual utterances vary in size and complexity from the one-word response to a question (itself a distinct utterance) to a multivolume novel of great length and scope: each is a single, complete act of communication understood as the speaker or writer's turn in a conversation—actual or abstract—with one or more other communicators.[4] The conversational context imposes certain constraints and practices on individual utterances—language, syntax, style rhetorical formulas, narrative forms all follow generic patterns—with the result that "even in the most free, the most unconstrained conversation, we cast our speech in definite generic forms."[5] Utterances therefore incorporate communal—and thus cultural—references to others in their respective genre, because each responds to previous acts of communication in speech or writing. As Bakhtin famously put it, "Any concrete utterance is a link in the chain of speech communication of a particular sphere":

> "Each utterance is filled with echoes and reverberations of other utterances to which it is related by the communality of the speech communication [. . .] Each utterance refutes, affirms, supplements, and relies on the others, presupposes them to be known, and somehow takes them into account."[6]

With context so broadly defined, genres encompass great depths of meaning. In particular, the words of a genre can carry its meanings through time. This capacity may partly explain *Mad*'s popularity, as it grew from the 1950s through the 1960s, as well as its longevity past its prime.

Analyzing the utterances found in different genres reveals that genre recognition, as manifest in creation and appreciation of parody, was a key element in the popularity of the magazine. And at its most successful, parody captures the cultural material within individual examples of its speech genre. Bakhtin emphasized this point in his later work, "From Notes Made in 1970–71," stating that "there can be neither a first nor a last meaning; it always exists among other meanings as a link in the chain of meaning. . . . this chain continues infinitely, and therefore each individual link in it is renewed again and again, as though it were being reborn."[7] One reason that meanings proliferate in parody, as Margaret Rose interprets Bakhtin, is that he treats parody as "a special type of double-voiced discourse. It serves two speakers at the same time. . . . And all the while these two voices are dialogically interrelated, they—as it were—know about each other [. . .] as if they hold a conversation with each other."[8] In short, by defining speech genres as the study of perpetual conversation—the language of everyday interaction—Bakhtin and Rose demonstrate that meanings preserved within genres can address not just what two or more characters discuss in a story, but also the cultural attitudes of their time.

The conversations between characters in "Bat Boy and Rubin!" (Kurtzman and Wood, #8, 01/53: 1-7) and "Bats-Man" (Silverstone and Drucker, #105, 09/66: 7–12) convey each parody's themes. In "Bat Boy and Rubin!," those themes are primarily the problems faced by teens in the 1950s, such as delinquency and comic books, particularly the crime- and horror-based comics that would become the topic of Senator Estes Kefauver's infamous 1954 hearings. Teen-based themes are also evident in "Bats-Man," but by 1966 the issues have changed. Challenges to authority, the sexual revolution, and the fascination with celebrity in popular culture now occupy the focus of the *Batman* parody.

Conversations between characters in the first-time parodies of television and Broadway, "Lone Stranger!" in 1953 and "My Fair Ad-Man" in 1960, respectively, also reveal cultural concerns of their times. Although the conversations in "Lone Stranger!" seem primarily focused on ridiculing authority, that same theme, along with a disdain of consumerism and pretentious intellectualism, is evident in "My Fair Ad-Man." Here we can see the role of speech genres in shaping *Mad*'s parodies as responses to the challenges of their own time. As Kathleen Hall Jamieson and Karlyn Kohrs Campbell point out, "Genres are not only dynamic responses to circumstances; each is a *dynamis*—a potential fusion of elements that may be energized or actualized as a strategic response to a situation."[9] Other genre scholars have also noted the connections between speech and cultural moment and the effectiveness of a genre for mining the richness of meaning in speech. Linda Hutcheon states that "doubled structures" within parody serve as "very much an inscription of the past in the present, and it is for that reason that it can be said to embody and bring to life actual historical tensions."[10] John M. Swales asserts further that "genres are important for integrating past and present."[11] The energy of the interactions within a genre can explain *Mad*'s ability to adapt and change to societal demands throughout the 1950s and into the 1960s, contributing to its continued relevance during that era. In this way, genre theory's emphasis on the ability of language to contain meaning for a variety of audiences over time makes it a viable lens for discerning how *Mad*'s parodies—as illustrated by differences between "Bat Boy and Rubin!" and "Bats-Man," on the one hand, and "Lone Stranger!" and "My Fair Ad-Man" on the other—demonstrate the role speech genres play in representing American culture of the 1950s and 1960s.

The *Mad* Comic and Genre Analysis: "Lone Stranger!" and "Bat-Boy and Rubin!" (1953)

After its debut in 1953, *Mad* quickly established a reputation for irreverent send-ups of popular culture, such as comics, films, and television shows. "Lone Stranger!" holds the honor of being the first television show parodied in *Mad* in early 1953.[12] At the end of the year, following its successful parody of *Superman*, *Mad* featured Harvey Kurtzman and Wallace "Wally" Wood's "Bat Boy and Rubin!" (#8, 12/53–1/54: 1-7). What a genre analysis of both "Lone Stranger!" and "Bat Boy and Rubin!" will demonstrate is that limitations shaping the utterances in these two parodies parallel the limitations faced by *Mad*'s creators in producing a deeper commentary on American culture.

Appearing in *Mad*'s third issue as a comic book parodying other comic books, "Lone Stranger!" (#3, 2–3/53: 1-7) is extremely limited in its parodic treatment of the television show. The basic plotline, written by Harvey Kurtzman with art by Jack Davis, follows the Lone Stranger from his attempts to mount his horse, Golden ("I never could jump on a hoss like they do in the movin' pitchers!"), eat a meal with his sidekick Pronto ("Where's that ol' rascal, Pronto? He promised he'd have brunch ready when I got back!" [2]), foil a stagecoach robbery, and ride off on Golden after afterwards ("Drat! Missed again! Come back here, Golden!" [7]).

"Lone Stranger!" contains comic elements of language use that characterize many *Mad* parodies; in this one, the Lone Stranger's code-switching refuses to follow a single generic pattern. At first, he speaks like a stereotypical figure from a Western, with his references to "hoss" and "movin' pitchers" early on. Then he moves into a German or Yiddish vernacular, asking Pronto, "Vas ist los?" Pronto responds telling the Lone Stranger that he's too thin and, mimicking the pidgin of the 1950s TV Indian, adding, "mebbe so you need take vacation for week in Catskills" (3). And when the Lone Stranger needs to clear up his identity with the townspeople trying to prevent him from robbing the stagecoach, he selects a British accent as a means of persuading the men that he is not the thief they think he is: "I say, fellows! You're making a teddible mistake!" (3) These changes appear to be played for humor alone; no character development or plot development explains when and why the Lone Stranger changes his accents. But they show the power of genre to create humor and parody by playing with readers' expectations.

The botched robbery of the stagecoach seems limited in its potential for humor as well. The humor here rests on depictions of the Lone Stranger being dropped from a cliff and then popping out of the cash box, and the visual humor intended in the unveiling of the Lone Stranger's admirer—the genre convention's grateful woman from the stage coach, who runs up to kiss him after he foils the robbery—as a man. When he wards off her efforts to express her gratitude with a kiss, she knocks him out with a gun, reveals that she is a man, and says with disdain, "You didn't figger on an inside man on this job!" (5). The language in these exchanges is limited in what they're conveying; the reference to "an inside man on this job" lands, but that's the extent of the dialogue in this scene. The concluding scenes are also mildly amusing because the humor is drawn from the Lone Stranger's desire for attention from his imagined TV audience; his audience reading the parody is also part of that viewership, waiting to see how he will exit. He holds off leaving until he has the attention of everyone, and then, as he makes his dramatic exit, he fails to get back up on his horse Golden and staggers off muttering into the sunset.

Genre theory exposes the limited cultural significance in the *Mad* comic book's foray into television parody, because the utterances do not reflect substantial relationships between the Stranger and others or develop meaningful interactions among them over time. The humor in the exchanges among the characters in the "Lone Stranger" parody is muted. The narrative lacks richness of language. The partnership between the Lone Stranger and Pronto is limited, in part because they rarely interact with each other in the parody. The Lone Stranger is not very cognizant of the world around him as he lurches from one mishap to another and Pronto serves as a Greek chorus, offering sarcastic asides about the Lone Stranger's behavior. Cultural commentary is also limited. When a drunken Pronto mistakes a hat rack for the Stranger because he "lookum mighty skinny" and suggests that he needs a vacation (3), the reference to the Catskills invokes the area's reputation for (Jewish) resorts and entertainment. That incident and the way Kurtzman and Davis play to the adolescent male audience by presenting a large woman who ends up being a large man are about the extent of the parody's cultural commentary.

"Bat Boy and Rubin!" is likewise limited in its ability to provide a deeper understanding of the culture at that time, yet details within this parody show the potential for generic complexity. One such example is its exploration of the dark side of power. After fighting with a gang they're investigating because of a series of murders in the fictional Cosmopolis, Rubin says to Bat Boy, "Sometimes I wonder, since you are a wealthy young socialite in real life, why you keep knocking yourself out on this 'Bat Boy' kick! It don't pay, you know!" (Kurtzman and Wood 7). Bat Boy's response is, "There are other things in life besides money . . . finer things! [. . .] Things like . . . like . . . like power! Rrow! Wurf! Grr!!" (7). Bat Boy's observation plays on the secrecy regarding Batman's identity as millionaire Bruce Wayne in the *Batman* comics, but it also identifies power as a theme at the heart of why someone like Bruce Wayne would don a costume and fight crime. Bakhtin's view of speech genres as having the power to communicate with an audience over time is evident in this exchange between Bat Boy and Rubin. Rubin wants to get paid for his work, but Bat Boy wants power, a desire that is further emphasized by the animal noises that he makes following this assertion. James J. Kimble has argued that this kind of portrayal of a superhero is part of what made *Mad* notable, because "while the publication's critique of the Cold

War era might have been funny, looking back [today] . . . makes it easier to see that critique was in many ways no laughing matter."[13] Yet Bat Boy's quest for power and wealth sets the stage for a conclusion in which he is revealed as a malevolent force, rather than a force for good, in his treatment of Rubin; the end thereby casts doubt on Bat Boy's behavior throughout the story. Bat Boy's secrecy also hints at larger faults within American society, as noted by Roland Vegso, who observed that the atomic bomb "marks an internal limit of democracy [. . .] The very same instance that is supposed to guarantee the security of democracy might actually lead to its destruction."[14] Bat Boy's ability to elude detection of his own criminal behavior is finally resolved by the end of the parody in a twist that offers an homage to the popular genre of horror comics.

Several grisly crimes mark the presence of the horror comics genre in "Bat Boy and Rubin!" After defeating three different crime gangs, Rubin hopes that he and Bat Boy have put an end to the murders that have been plaguing Cosmopolis. When Rubin starts shrieking about a pair of gloves in the glove compartment of the "secret Bat-O-Mobile" after getting rid of the Floogle gang, Bat Boy responds, "So what? Didn't you ever see gloves in a glove compartment?," and Rubin cries out, " . . . With hands in 'em?" (26). Another gruesome discovery occurs when Bat Boy and Rubin move on to round up the Flurgle gang. As they try to climb a building with the Bat-O-Lariet [sic], they find at the end of their rope a noose wrapped around the neck of a headless corpse (27). The discovery of the severed hands and the headless corpse creates an awkward juxtaposition with the comic exchanges between Bat Boy and Rubin. These clashing sensibilities highlight the concerns at the time about the impact of horror comics on teenagers. The audience wants to laugh rather than feel outrage at the body count.

The conflict between the horror comics genre and more standard comic book fare is further illustrated when Rubin hangs up Bat Boy's cape in his closet and a body falls out. As Rubin processes how this corpse was "killed in the same way as . . . the Floogle gang[,] Fleagle gang[, and] . . . the Flurgle gang" and begins to realize that "the murderer can only be one other person . . . one crazy mixed up kid and that is . . . IS . . . ," Bat Boy knocks Rubin unconscious, uses a hole punch to make a hole in two of Rubin's toes, and then announces, while drinking Rubin's blood through two straws (one for each toe, presumably), "Two tiny holes punched by the murderer . . . two tiny holes punched by me with my conductor's puncher . . . I . . . am a vampire Bat Boy!" (31). Bat Boy's clumsy method of drinking Rubin's blood and his self-revelation as a vampire provide an unsettling end to the conflict between Bat Boy and Rubin, as well as the conflict between the two genres. Carol Tilley states that critics targeted postwar superhero comics "because of their perceived violent and fascist elements."[15] Bat Boy's response to Rubin that being a secret crime fighter brings him the power he seeks illustrates Tilley's observation. Although there is an underlying humor in Bat Boy's use of a conductor's hole punch to get blood from his victims, the conclusion of the story is upsetting in the contrast between Bat Boy's jocular language and the revelation that he's killed his partner.

American society's fear in the 1950s that juvenile delinquency was an urgent problem is lightly touched on in this parody. The Fleagle gang, whom Bat Boy calls "dead-end kids" (Wood and Kurtzman 4), could be seen as representing the concern over teen crime in the 1950s. The reference probably comes from the Dead End Kids films of the late 1930s and early 1940s.[16] Bat Boy and Rubin try several times to stop the Fleagle gang, but all their methods fail. They finally resort to spanking them with hairbrushes, Bat Boy punningly observing that "If these kids weren't dead-end kids before . . . they'll be dead-end kids now! . . . Boy! Will their ends be dead!" (4). The kids, who engage in unnamed criminal activity, are suspected of playing a role in the murders around Cosmopolis, but the spankings they get from Bat Boy and Rubin indicate they need disciplinary punishment for their bratty behavior more than serious punishment for committing a capital offense. Although the Dead End Kids are not well-known today, the parody illustrates Swales's view that genre can show us the past within the present. The parody's reference to the Dead End Kids in relation to the Fleagle gang kids gives voice to contemporary concerns about juvenile delinquency—concerns that served as the catalyst for *Mad* to change genres itself the year after "Bat Boy and Rubin!" appeared. In much the same way that genre theory can bring out multiple readings of an artifact, the political and then economic pressures that came to bear on *Mad* required publisher William "Bill" Gaines to rethink how he was going to preserve his stake in the comics industry. Those pressures brought about the transition of *Mad* from comic book to magazine. That change, in turn, expanded the ways in which genre parody within *Mad* could be fulfilled.

Mad the Comic Becomes *Mad* the Magazine

Gaines had made a profitable business out of comic books, yet parents protested their contents as more teens bought comics in the years after World War II. Kristin L. Matthews pinpointed 1949 as the year that Gaines's problems began, observing that "Norbert Muhlen's infamous 1949 *Commentary* article ... claimed comic books primed American youth for totalitarianism."[17] Carol Tilley traced the popularity of Fredric Wertham's 1954 attack on comic books, *Seduction of the Innocent,* to its assertion that they had a provable link to juvenile delinquency and the weakening of teens' morality.[18] According to Yuri Shakouchi, the public responded favorably to these critiques and their assertions that "comic books ... led youth in unhealthy directions such as juvenile delinquency and homosexuality."[19] As more press attention focused on rising teen crime and with Senate hearings scheduled to take place in the spring of 1954, it was clear that sanctions of some kind would be leveled against comic books.

Among those who testified was William Gaines. He appeared in front of the Senate Subcommittee to Investigate Juvenile Delinquency on April 21 and defended his horror comic books as guided by "good taste . . . for a horror comic."[20] By September, Gaines and other comic book publishers created the Comics Magazine Association of America (CMAA) to deal with the threats to the industry.[21] But when the CMAA then created the Comics Code of America, committed to banning violent content, and created a certification system requiring "a stamp [to] be put on all comic books guaranteeing the contents were both educational and nonviolent," Gaines decided to sell off his entire horror comic book business and simply focus on *Mad*.[22] Gaines had tried an end run around the Code by refusing to seek a stamp, but then found difficulty getting distributors to carry his comics.[23] If he couldn't sell his publications, EC Comics wouldn't be able to stay in business, so Gaines and *Mad*'s editor Harvey Kurtzman devised a solution that allowed *Mad* to survive without a seal of approval.

Their solution to the problem was simple: they changed *Mad*'s category, or genre. *Mad* simply "transformed itself [. . .] into a magazine."[24] Maria Reidelbach described Kurtzman's plan to make the transition from comic to magazine as one that would shift to better paper, set type rather than hand lettering, and bimonthly publication.[25] Timothy Jones concludes that this transition from comic to magazine was critical: "Had

Gaines not managed to lead the fledgling *Mad* magazine to success, he probably would have been ruined."[26] As Jean-Paul Gabilliet put it, the change "freed Gaines and Kurtzman from the Comics Code's constraints and gave the magazine a broader scope than in its earlier comic book incarnation."[27] *Mad* could now explore other areas of parody and satire, moving from comics and ads to films and television, as well as to more freewheeling social commentary.

Mad Magazine and Genre Analysis: "My Fair Ad-Man" (1960) and "Bats-Man" (1966)

In comparison with "Bats-Man," Nick Megliola [Meglin] and Mort Drucker's "My Fair Ad-Man" (#54, 4/60: 31–37) demonstrates how expanding beyond cartoon parody freed the magazine to engage in wider political and social commentary. "My Fair Ad-Man" is, like "Bats-Man," a "first of its kind" parody, but displays a depth of content beyond that of "Lone Stranger!" Applying genre theory to this parody helps the audience see that it is not just a parody of the 1956 Broadway musical *My Fair Lady* (Alan Jay Lerner and Frederick Loewe's adaption of George Bernard Shaw's 1913 *Pygmalion*). It also satirizes the conflict in the late 1950s and early 1960s between the more traditional role of men in the workplace and the role of the beatnik, who questioned his place in American society. Its first panel credits the book "'You're a Pig, Mallion' by George Bernard Schwartz" (31) as the source of the *Mad* musical. The interplay between "you're a pig" and *Pygmalion* is in line with the play on words noticeable in other *Mad* parodies, such as "Lone Stranger!" and "Bat Boy and Rubin!" The comic significance in changing the name of Bernard Shaw to Bernard Schwartz extends beyond giving the English playwright a Jewish-sounding name: Bernard Schwartz was the birth name of actor Tony Curtis, who was famous for being able to imitate Cary Grant, the actor whose face artist Mort Drucker gave the Henry Higgins character in this parody.[28]

The panels that follow introduce other characters into the plot of the parody. Not only is Henry Higgins transformed into Henry Higgenbottom and Colonel Pickering into Charles Pickerwick, but the Eliza Doolittle character has been changed completely; a character who looks like Frank Sinatra takes on the Julie Andrews role as a beatnik named Irving Mallion. When Pickerwick challenges Higgenbottom to take the beatnik-speaking Mallion in hand to become an ad copywriter, Mallion agrees based on Higgenbottom's promise to get Mallion's novel published if he succeeds. By the end of the parody, Mallion succeeds in advertising to the point that he tells Higgenbottom and Pickerwick to burn his novel, prompting Higgenbottom to comment, "Then, I guess this musical is just about over!" and Pickerwick to respond, "Not quite! We've still got our reprise!" Joined by an audience, the three characters close the spoof by singing to the tune of "Get Me to the Church on Time": "'Cause we are the guys who make commercials; Here is our stirring battle song: 'We do the lying; You do the buying!'" (Megliola and Drucker 37).

Genre analysis of this parody is more complex because of the multiple layers of reference in its utterances, which resonated for both the audience of its time and more modern readers. Two instances illustrate the durability of speech genres within utterances, as Bakhtin observed: when Higgenbottom tells Mallion that looking like an adman is easier than thinking like one and when Higgenbottom insists that Mallion repeat (to the tune of "The Rain in Spain"), "An ad that's bad will end up spoofed in MAD!" (35). Humor arises not only within the panel as characters speak and react at these moments, but also between the writer and artist among themselves and with their audience; other jokes echo across time for modern audiences who may not completely understand how ads and *Mad* magazine are being mocked here, but would likely understand the idea that looking like a professional in any field is easier than actually being such a professional. Linda Hutcheon's view of genre theory as a way to show Bakhtin's concept of double-voiced interaction, and John M. Swales's view of genre as a means of preserving understanding across time both stand out in this exchange.

Lou Silverstone and Mort Drucker's "Bats-Man" (#105, 9/66: 7–12) demonstrates how the move from a comics genre to a magazine genre provided a better platform for cultural commentary. "Bats-Man" lampoons male authority figures and the young men out to challenge them, as evidenced by the conflict between Bats-Man and his young crime-fighting partner, Sparrow. In addition to the generational conflict about sexual mores that takes place within the parody, "Bats-Man" sends up the ABC television show *Batman* (1966-1968). The change to a magazine format provided *Mad*'s writers and artists with more room to explore the satiric potential in their targets.

The way in which speech utterances are used within this parody demonstrates how Drucker and Silverstone were able to elegantly lampoon authority. Bats-Man is the uptight, establishment "square" and is consistently portrayed as a buffoon. His initial conflict in "Bats-Man" is not with a crime gang, but with Finster Cleaners. Bats-Man chews them out for bringing him Superman's suit (7). Bats-Man is outraged when he learns that the cleaners sent *his* suit to the local ballet school. Neuman, Bats-Man's butler, comments as he holds the Superman suit, "You'd sure look ridiculous fighting crime in this outfit, Mr. Swain!" (7). The Superman suit Bats-Man has received in place of his cape is completely useless to him, but it slyly highlights the rivalry between comic book fans of Superman and Batman. For longtime fans of *Mad*, the suit also serves as a reminder of its previous popular parody, "Superduperman!" Bats-Man later tells Sparrow that the phone in his room is available for calling young women for dates, and Sparrow points out that the phone only goes to the Commissioner's office. Bats-Man retorts, "It just happens that the Commissioner is a very witty conversationalist!" (9). These examples show how Bats-Man is set up as an authority figure worthy of ridicule. Sent his rival's crimefighting outfit by mistake, laughed at by his butler, and hounded by Sparrow for not providing him with a proper phone line, Bats-Man is the hapless protagonist of this parody. Inept at presenting himself as the suave and strong crimefighting hero he is supposed to be, Bats-Man provides Sparrow with plenty of ammunition for the grudges he holds against his boss, grudges that eventually erupt into full-fledged conflict.

The conflict between Bats-Man and Sparrow is the generational conflict of the 1960s writ large. Unlike the more sinister Bat Boy and the less fortunate Rubin, Bats-Man and Sparrow take on roles with elements of a father-son conflict, or that of a complacent company executive and the ambitious junior partner. When Sparrow complains about the phone line, Bats-Man shouts, "What's wrong with you kids today? Your date will have to wait until evil and injustice have been erased from Gotham City! And after that, we've got problems in Asia! If you really feel the need for feminine companionship, there's always Aunt Hattie!" (9). A narrator's commentary then appears in the following panel, reading, "Leapin' Lizards! It's Sparrow Versus Bats-Man!" (9). The double-voiced quality that Bakhtin attributed to speech genres brings greater depth to understanding the language in this tirade. The problem of solving crime in Gotham, followed by the euphemistic "problems in Asia" (referring to Vietnam) exaggerates but encapsulates the domestic and international conflicts facing the country in 1966. Proposing Aunt Hattie as a substitute for young women closer to Sparrow's age also reflects the conflict between adults and teens. Sparrow has already lost out on one potential girlfriend who saw him running off with what appeared to be an older woman (but was actually Bats-Man). Sparrow's frustration after the phone argument illustrates Howard Brick's observation that in the 1960s, young people were looking for means of freeing themselves "from the grip of mortifying convention."[29] When Sparrow tries unsuccessfully to escape from the conventional life that Bats-Man represents, the conflict highlights how much meaning their argument carries because genre can preserve the past for a present audience. Even the "leapin' lizards" call back to the *Little Orphan Annie* comic strip emphasizes that Sparrow is viewed as a kid and not a threat, which, much like Bat Boy before him, he soon will be.

Sparrow's plan to resolve his conflict with Bats-Man provides another example of the depth of the parody in this *Mad* version. Sparrow decides that the only way to be his own man is to kill Bats-Man. Sparrow gives Bats-Man an electric razor with a laser in it, but Neuman uses it instead and decapitates himself, causing Sparrow to shout, "Holy Ichabod Crane!" (10). (Changing the name of Alfred from the *Batman* comic to "Neuman" here plays on the name of *Mad*'s icon, Alfred E. Neuman, while the headless butler evokes the many "headless horseman" folk tales and the rivalry between Ichabod Crane and Brom Bones for the attentions of Katrina Van Tassel in Washington Irving's retelling in "The Legend of Sleepy Hollow," a high school classic.) After failing to kill off Bats-Man, Sparrow decides, "There's only one way left to destroy Bats-Man—expose him!," with the narrator responding, "Holy Perversion, Sparrow! That Would Be Indecent!" (11). Although Sparrow undoubtedly has decided to unveil Bats-Man's identity, the narrator's comment refers to a socially embarrassing outcome. As much as Sparrow tries, however, he cannot catch Bats-Man until the end of the parody.

The only way in which the conflict between the two is resolved is through the vehicle of the television show. When Bats-Man is captured by Sparrow, he argues that keeping the show alive means that Sparrow can continue to earn "fringe benefits! Like, why do you think we have these gorgeous-doll guest stars?" (12). Unlike Bat Boy, Bats-Man doesn't physically overpower Sparrow in order to demonstrate his leadership; Bats-Man uses the influence of celebrity and the promise of getting the attention of many women to persuade Sparrow instead. What resolves the conflict between them is a shared view of the world and the rewards it can bring. In this instance, the utterances within the genre preserve not only the more sexist attitudes of the mid-1960s, but also the era's fascination with celebrity culture.

The more permissive views of teen sexual activity in the 1960s are also highlighted in "Bats-Man." Sparrow is unsuccessful in dating young women because of interference from his job as Bats-Man's crime-fighting partner. When he is turned down for a date by one classmate for his lack of athletic prowess and by another for running off with "a middle-aged lady" on a previous date, Sparrow seethes, "That was no lady—that was Bats-Man!" (7). When Sparrow decides to view Jill St. John in her dressing room through the Bat Scope, Bats-Man scolds him for doing so (8). When Sparrow complains that he has trouble getting dates because of Bats-Man's interference, Bats-Man announces it's time for a "man-to-bird talk!" (8). Sparrow just wants to engage in teen activities "like making out and sniffing glue and talking for hours on the phone" (8). Sparrow's subversive streak is evident in "Bats-Man," but unlike Rubin, Sparrow is in command of his world. Rather than being motivated to solve a series of unsettling events as Rubin does in "Bat Boy and Rubin!," Sparrow is trying (and failing) to build his own social life. Like other teens during the mid-1960s, he feels frustration with an authority figure for not allowing him to do what he wants to do. During that era, Howard Brick observes, "present in the experience of non-conforming youth . . . were both new, emergent social and cultural forms and signs of social distress marking the obsolescence of old social norms."[30] In an equally stereotypical view, Sparrow decides to symbolically kill his father by revealing who Bats-Man really is, an act that would give Sparrow free rein to use his power to pursue his romantic interests. But when he captures Bats-Man, Sparrow is impressed by Bats-Man's statement that Sparrow is now old enough to date the glamorous women who appear on the show. However indirectly, Sparrow believes that his dating life will get better, thanks in part to his guardian.

Examining the parody of the television show within the superhero parody of "Bats-Man" enables us to delve into the cultural resonance of the piece. Bats-Man reveals to Sparrow that the Commissioner is worried that "we've been on the air 15 minutes and we haven't had one fight, seen one weird villain, or scaled one wall!" (9). After Sparrow traps him,

Bats-Man struggles to identify his captor, noting, "I thought tonight's guest villain was supposed to be Laurence Olivier!" (12) The panel ends with a shout-out to the Beatles from Sparrow: "I dig, Bats-Man, I dig! Yeah! Yeah! YEAH!" (12). The *Mad* parody of Batman provides a means of comparing how the magazine format allows for greater genre flexibility than the 1966–68 television show, itself a parody of the comic book. Sparrow uses the same construct that Robin uses in the television show for creating exclamations (the word "holy" followed by a word or phrase relating to something that's just happened). Bats-Man's disappointment that his nemesis is Sparrow, rather than Laurence Olivier, acknowledges the show's reliance on famous actors, such as Cesar Romero or Burgess Meredith, as an important component of the program. Sparrow's interest in Jill St. John appears to be no random choice; she was a guest star in the first season of *Batman*, in the same year that this issue of *Mad* was published.[31] The Commissioner's call to Bats-Man asking why so little action was taking place in the first few minutes of the show also serves the same purpose: highlighting elements of the genre that *Mad* is parodying.

Conclusion

Mad's value as a cultural artifact is enhanced by reading it through genre theory, whose application to its parodies from the 1950s and 1960s highlights the strengths and weaknesses of *Mad*'s cultural commentary. In the 1950s, as *Mad* got off the ground, limitations in its development of parody mark the television and comic-book parodies in "Lone Stranger!" and "Bat Boy and Rubin!" In both cases, the protagonists are blustery and incompetent, but whereas the Lone Stranger remains a fairly one-dimensional figure at the close of his story, Bat Boy ends with his exposure at the end of "Bat Boy and Rubin!" as a corrupt, dark figure who feeds his bloodlust as a vampire by murdering his sidekick. This rather strange development is more in line with horror comics and comes unexpectedly as a denouement for the plot, but despite the juvenile nature of his interactions with other characters, his behavior shows more complexity than that of the Lone Stranger. These two artifacts from *Mad*'s comic book era demonstrate how genres act as repositories of cultural history, preserved through the language in the parodic interactions among characters, and to different audiences at different times, even when the parodies lack the full development they would acquire later.

By contrast, "My Fair Ad-Man" and "Bats-Man" represent the more robust parodies of the 1960s in *Mad* due to their deeply evocative generic language. The parody of "My Fair Ad-Man" is especially striking for its depth of reference from its very beginning. In lampooning the stage musical (which opened in 1956 but was still a hit in 1960, when the film was still four years off), creators Megliola [Meglin] and Drucker could expect their audience to know the hugely popular Broadway cast album and to appreciate the show's theme of social fakery as the foundation for their satiric critiques of the period's advertising and Beat cultures. One prevalent theme in this piece is resisting group thought of any kind. The men of Madison Avenue are open to criticism for their devotion to selling products to consumers using any means necessary, yet Irving Mallion and his Beat friends are not the heroes of this piece. They, too, are following a group mentality. Mallion is willing to give up his friends to move into commercial society, get his novel published, and position himself for financial success as a writer. This action demonstrates that he's not just a "fair ad-man," but a fair-weather friend for his original circle. When Mallion easily morphs into an ad man, he does so because the philosophy of the Beats is as easy to drop as the Madison Avenue philosophy is to pick up. The *dynamis* here—distrust of the men behind advertising, and scorn for the literary pretensions of the Beats—is fully developed within the utterances among the characters. "My Fair Ad-Man" preserves for a post-*Mad Men* generation the view that *Mad* magazine distrusted the worldview of these cool men, both in advertising and in literature.

Part of the success of the "Bats-Man" parody is that it more deeply probes the culture on which it comments. Bats-Man, no longer the bloodthirsty figure from "Bat Boy and Rubin!," is now a harried male authority figure challenged by his younger lieutenant, Sparrow. Unlike Rubin, Sparrow is now the aggressor, unhappy that Bats-Man is keeping him from enjoying himself as other teenagers do. And unlike the conclusion of the 1950s parody, one of the pair doesn't die at the hand of the other because Sparrow is ultimately persuaded by Bats-Man's argument that his dating life will be much better if he just continues to help fight crime. Fueled by the *dynamis* of the 1960s regarding the Vietnam War, generational conflict, and the success of the Batman television show, their dialogue highlights the value of genre theory for accessing the cultural commentary embedded in the parody.

Future readers of *Mad* will also be able to apply genre theory to different genres within the magazine to assess the effectiveness of its ability to offer cultural critiques over the many decades that it was published. Through genre theory, readers can appreciate the growth of *Mad*'s ability to crudely mock the adults in charge and to offer its uniquely weird perspective on popular culture, government, history, advertising, and its teen audience. Readers of the twenty-first century may not be able to fully appreciate the depth of the joy and hilarity that reading these comics and magazines inspired when they were first published, but because *Mad*'s talented creators so powerfully commanded the genres with which they worked, future readers can still find the humor and value of its cultural commentary as time goes by.

Notes

1. Grant Geissman, foreword to *Mad About the Sixties: The Best of the* Decade, xvi.
2. David Noonan, "The Way We Laughed," 1.
3. Mikhail Bakhtin, "The Problem of Speech Genres," in *Speech Genres and Other Late Essays*, edited by Caryl Emerson and Michael Holquist, 60.
4. Bakhtin, "The Problem of Speech Genres," 90–91.
5. Bakhtin, "The Problem of Speech Genres," 78.
6. Bakhtin, "The Problem of Speech Genres," 91.
7. Bakhtin, "From Notes Made in 1970–71," in *Speech Genres and Other Late Essays*, 146.
8. Margaret A. Rose, *Parody: Ancient, Modern, and Post-Modern*, 133–34.
9. Kathleen Hall Jamieson and Karlyn Kohrs Campbell, "Rhetorical Hybrids: Fusions of Generic Elements," 146.
10. Linda Hutcheon, *A Theory of Parody: The Teachings of Twentieth-Century Art Forms*, xii.
11. John M. Swales, *Genre Analysis: English in Academic and Research Settings*, 44.
12. Geissman, foreword to *Mad About the Fifties*, xvii.
13. James J. Kimble, "Mutually Assured Disparagement: Enmification and Enlightenment in Early 1950s *Mad*," chap. 15, 131; first published in *Studies in American Humor* n.s. 3, no. 30 (Fall 2014): 131.
14. Roland Vegso, *The Naked Communist: Cold War Modernism and the Politics of Popular Culture*, 70.
15. Carol Tilley, "Seducing the Innocent: Fredric Wertham and the Falsifications That Helped Condemn Comics," 384.
16. Cliff Larimer, "Gorcey Bigger Than Life."
17. Kristin L. Matthews, "A *Mad* Proposition in Postwar America," 212; Norbert Muhlen, "The Study of Man: Comic Books and Other Horrors," 80–87.
18. Tilley, "Seducing the Innocent," 383.

19. Yuri Shakouchi, "The Stereotypes of the Beatniks and Hip Consumerism: A Study of *Mad* Magazine in the Late 1950s and 1960s," 1272.

20. Peter Kihss, "No Harm in Horror, Comics Issuer Says," 34; Timothy Jones, "'Hello Again, You Little Monsters!'-Hosted Horrors of the 1950s and 1960s," 123.

21. Jones, "'Hello Again, You Little Monsters!'" 124.

22. Shakouchi, "The Stereotypes of the Beatniks and Hip Consumerism," 1272; Maria Reidelbach, *Completely Mad*, 30.

23. Shakouchi, "The Stereotypes of the Beatniks and Hip Consumerism," 1272. See also Amy Kiste Nyberg, *Seal of Approval: The History of the Comics Code.*

24. Shakouchi, "The Stereotypes of the Beatniks and Hip Consumerism," 1272.

25. Reidelbach, *Completely Mad*, 32–33.

26. Jones, "'Hello Again, You Little Monsters!'" 124.

27. Jean-Paul Gabilliet, *Of Comics and Man: A Cultural History of American Comic Books*, 62.

28. On Curtis's name, see Dave Kehr, "Tony Curtis, Hollywood Leading Man, Dies at 85"; on Curtis's Cary Grant imitation, see A. O. Scott, "Marvelous Invention of Movie Make-Believe."

29. Howard Brick, *Age of Contradiction: American Thought and Culture in the 1960s*, 66.

30. Brick, *Age of Contradiction*, 119.

31. "*Batman* (1966–1968): Full Cast and Crew," *IMBD*.

PART V.
LEGACIES

20. Sons of *Mad*:

Harvey Kurtzman and the Rise of Underground Comix (An Alternate-Universe Analysis)

Nicholas Sammond

THE STANDARD HISTORY of the emergence of alternative comix in the late 1960s and early 1970s—of bands of daring young men in San Francisco, Chicago, and New York sticking a collective thumb in the eye of a repressive status quo—is accurate in a narrow, genealogical sense. Those young men, many of whom got their start working with or learning from *Mad* creator and one-time editor Harvey Kurtzman, did alter the landscape of comics (converting them to comix), and radically challenged the mores of their day. Yet they were not alone, and that narrative has been maintained only by bracketing off the efforts of contemporary feminist, queer, and nonwhite artists to articulate *other* alternative visions of non-mainstream life and politics. For instance, a few years after R. Crumb began *Zap Comix* in 1968, and at roughly the same moment that Crumb, Spain Rodriguez, Gilbert Shelton, Robert Wilson, and their friends were forming what came to be seen as the epicenter of the San Francisco underground comix scene, a changing crew of women artists—Michelle Brand, Lee Marrs, Lora Fountain, Patti Moodian, Sharon Rudahl, Shelby Sampson, Aline Kominsky, Trina Robbins, Marie Haskell, and Janet Wolf Stanley—known as the *Wimmen's Comix* collective began a run of underground comix. That series would never achieve the recognition that work by their male counterparts received, but it ran for twenty years.[1] Likewise, a few blocks from where Crumb first peddled *Zap* #1 in a shopping cart, Emory Douglas, the Culture Minister for the Black Panthers, was producing, with Tarika Lewis, powerful graphic imagery for *The Black Panther Black Community Newsletter* (1969–1982). Drawing on iconography derived from newspaper circulars, Chinese propaganda posters, and South American woodcuts,

Lewis and Douglas forged a truly international graphic style that was not simply countercultural but ideologically specific and revolutionary. In a less revolutionary vein, Richard "Grass" Green, whose work has been compared to Kurtzman's, was penning underground comix, some of which, such as his *Super-Soul* series, were black-themed. Fellow African American cartoonist Larry Fuller created the black superhero Ebon, then went on to form Ful-Horne productions, which released a range of underground titles, including *Gay Heart Throbs* (1976–1981) and *White Whore Funnies* (1975–1979).[2] And a range of queer artists—including the iconic Tom of Finland (Touko Laaksonen), Mary Wings, Roberta Gregory, Howard Cruse, Burton Clarke, and the filmmakers/cartoonists Mike and George Kuchar—created work that generally has not been viewed as central to the received history of the birth and growth of alternative comix.

Yet even many of those artists and writers, while consigned to the margins of many accounts of the creation of comix, also count Harvey Kurtzman and *Mad* as formative influences in their lives. So, it is a bit of a truism in histories of the rise of underground comix, and in the memoirs of key players in those histories, that Harvey Kurtzman was the Godfather of the Underground. Perhaps nowhere is this better summed up than in Art Spiegelman's profile/obituary of Kurtzman in the March 29, 1993, issue of the *New Yorker*. Running alongside Adam Gopnik's one-page, two-column remembrance, and continuing as a stand-alone comic for two more pages, Spiegelman's loving graphic eulogy captures *Mad*'s apolitical irreverence, Kurtzman's influence on the first generation of underground cartoonists, and his difficult choices during his later years. Spiegelman's encomium praises Kurtzman as the man who "made me wanna be a cartoonist!"; Alfred E. Neuman has a cameo appearance next to the *New Yorker*'s Eustace Tilly. Spiegelman went on to say that "Harvey's *Mad* was more important than pot and LSD in shaping the generation that protested the Vietnam War."[3] Spiegelman was, of course, referring to EC Comics' *Mad*, which Kurtzman and publisher Bill Gaines converted from comic to magazine format in 1955 as a middle-finger response to the Comics Code and to the postwar repressiveness it represented. In his epic 2015 biography of Kurtzman, Bill Schelly echoed that sentiment:

> Many of [the 1950s readers of *Mad* later] participated in the antiwar demonstrations that became larger and more frequent as the US

> escalated its military involvement in Vietnam. R. C. Harvey wrote, "Through all the years of *Mad*, Kurtzman's influence on the American public was incalculable. Who can say but what the Vietnam War protest among American youth was not in some way inspired by the satire in *Mad*?"[4]

In that same biography, R. Crumb would say of Kurtzman, "The covers of *Mad* #11 and [the later Kurtzman publication] *Humbug* #2 changed the way I saw the world forever . . . !," and he and his brother published several issues of their homemade comic, *Foo*, in imitation of Kurtzman's post-*Mad* magazine *Humbug*. (The *Mad* cover was a brilliant Basil Wolverton parody of a *Life* magazine cover; the *Humbug* homage featured a visual pun on the danger of radiation involving a steam radiator. See fig. 20-1.) Other luminaries in the formative years of the underground scene, such as Denis Kitchen, Jay Lynch, and Gilbert Shelton, have been equally effusive in their praise and gratitude. As Gopnik put it in his obituary for Kurtzman, "There has scarcely been a single cartoonist or animator of note in the last forty years—from R. Crumb and Art Spiegelman to Monty Python's Terry Gilliam and the French cartoonist Goscinny, the co-inventor of 'Astérix'—who did not come under his direct influence and encouragement."[5]

So: *Mad* magazine was a major influence on the cartoonists who created many of the first underground comix, and its creator, Harvey Kurtzman, was mentor and friend to many of those men, and an inspiration to others. This is hardly news. This praise and celebration of the man, his work, and his influence have been inscribed and reinscribed so many times that there seems little point in revisiting those formative years one more time. Except that those repetitive acts of inscription and re-inscription may have an unintended effect of blotting out other strands of influence and other histories that pass in and through the creation of underground comix. They may obscure, for instance, the formative role of an emergent psychedelic rock and roll scene in San Francisco's Haight Ashbury and in New York City's Lower East Side and the influence of LSD and other drugs that fueled the phantasms of early underground comix. And a focus on Kurtzman and *Mad* as the necessary precursors to underground comix creates a tale of primogeniture in which one man hands down the scepter to the next man, and in which other voices—of women, queer men and women, cartoonists of color—become as a result

Fig. 20-1: R. Crumb identified two covers of magazines edited by Kurtzman as major inspirations. One was Will Elder and Jack Davis's cover for *Humbug* #2 (9/57), above, which mocked the horrors of radiation through a visual pun comparing the danger of radiation to a steam radiator. Not shown is the other, Basil Wolverton's famous cover for *Mad* #11 (5/54), "Beautiful Girl of the Month Reads 'Mad,'" which parodied a May 1953 *Life* magazine cover.

necessarily lesser, background noise, or supporting details to that main narrative.

This is not to suggest for a moment, however, that Kurtzman and *Mad* weren't incredibly influential, or that they aren't the primary focus of this essay. Nor will this essay attempt to gainsay that well-established history, to replace it with a better, supposedly truer story. It offers no corrections to an imagined historical record. Rather, it will try to investigate in greater detail *Mad*'s and Kurtzman's iconoclasm, asking what structured that irreverence, and how it influenced successive generations of cartoonists. When its descendants have referred to *Mad* as "revolutionary," do they have a real and specific revolutionary politics in mind, such as those of the Panthers, or are they using the word the way that most people misuse the term *surreal* today?—that is, not as something expressing in purposely illogical and fantasmatic ways the workings of the unconscious, but just as being really, really unusual. Generations of comics scholars and cultural historians have rightly praised *Mad* for its irreverent parodies and its iconoclastic resistance to the status quo, yet few of us have attempted to move beyond those vague praises and to consider in detail the relationship between the politics of the time and what Kurtzman and *Mad* did with them.

Compelling arguments have been made, for instance, for why the Comics Code appeared when it did and what it was supposed to correct or counteract.[6] Likewise, those accounts have detailed Gaines's eventual refusal to comply (totally) with the code and his economic and political reasons for doing so. Yet less has been said about how or what Kurtzman (and later Al Feldstein) articulated in *Mad*'s mockery of that moment—and in every subsequent moment since. *Mad* has been oppositional for over sixty years now—but oppositional to what, and how? The face of *Mad* has for all these decades been the idiot grin of Alfred E. Neuman, and his motto "What, Me Worry?" seems to refuse sustained analysis and beg its own parody. But that very refusal, that repetitive indifference, in that it fueled a comix movement *and* the political ambitions of leftists such as Students for a Democratic Society (SDS) founder Tom Hayden, begs at least a poke or two in its gap-toothed grin. For if there is one thing that has been consistent in *Mad* over all of its generations, it is a refusal to have a *specific* politics, because to do so would risk its satirical and parodic high ground, its seeming disinterest in anything other than mocking American pretensions, to meaning something, to being *significant*. The problem, and it is one worth discussing, is that a choice to not have a politics *is* a politics in itself.

If potential alternative histories are somewhat obscured by the oft-told tale of how Harvey Kurtzman and *Mad* spawned the 1960s in general and underground comix in particular, that may be because—between comics' ardent fan base and a growing consensus about the medium's cultural and artistic legitimacy—this sort of narrative of influence and connection has the advantage of being simple and legible. Such accounts create a sense of continuity and community, and of the practical and aesthetic working through of a relationship between biography, form, and content. Yet how might focusing on generation, the passage of knowledge and skill from one set of geniuses to the next, with an emphasis on aesthetics and style rather than content or message, inflect or obscure the ideological, discursive, and political forces at play in the development of underground comix?

Were it not for claims that first *Mad*, and then underground comix, were responsible for a social, political, and cultural revolution that radically changed life in the United States (if not the world), this might be a moot point. But those claims, and those of a sort of generational succession, have been made. Historian Elizabeth Freeman, discussing the challenges of writing histories of feminist and queer ephemera and performance, has noted that a generational model of history has advantages and disadvantages:

> the concept of generations linked by political work or even mass entertainment also acknowledges the ability of various technologies and culture industries to produce shared subjectivities that go beyond the family.... It may be crucial, then, to complicate the idea of horizontal political generations or waves succeeding each other in progressive time with a notion of "temporal drag" thought less in the psychic time of the individual than in the movement time of collective political philosophy.[7]

There is no doubt that *Mad* and its descendants contain moments of artistic and comic genius, and that each served as inspiration for sustained cultural and political critique. But most extant histories, built on the tried-and-true model of influence and succession, may overlook how those histories themselves are rich in confirmation bias and self-justification, retrospectively affirming an end point that obscures competing histories and contingent moments in favor of a tale that congratulates its protagonists for their wit and bravery. Writing specifically about the history of women's and queer comix, Margaret Galvan has noted, for instance, that accepted generational histories may unwittingly reproduce the structural inequalities that had initially favored some comix creators as discursive founders and marginalized the work of others. *Mad* and its purported inheritors in the underground scene undoubtedly were historically important participants in changes to American social and political life in the 1960s and 1970s. Yet by opting for a parodic form that eschewed any specific politics, they beg the question of *how* they had that effect, and whither it has taken us today. (Queer and women's comix creators such as Trina Robbins or Robert Triptow also count Kurtzman and *Mad* as influential, and they have felt no need to avoid a more explicit politics in their comix work.[8])

For the sake of argument, let's call *Mad*'s politics of refusing to have a politics an inchoate libertarianism—as opposed to the explicitly articulated libertarian ideology of someone like Ayn Rand—one that many underground cartoonists gladly adopted. Underground comix are usually described as graphic expressions of something called "the counterculture" of the late 1960s and 1970s, which formed in major metropolitan areas in the United States, especially in San Francisco and New York. That counterculture is usually tacitly understood as opposed to a dominant Cold War conservatism, as being inherently leftist, and as having been naturally aligned with the liberatory movements of that moment, such as the SDS, the Black Panthers, gay and women's liberation, free love and the (so-called) sexual revolution, and as expressing a general drive to, in the words of LSD guru Timothy Leary (1920–1996), "tune in, turn on, and drop out." (Leary, a Harvard psychology professor who advocated for the nonclinical use of LSD, influenced the Beats and the hippies, including the first generation of underground comix creators. "Tuning in" involved paying attention to current cultural trends; "turning on" meant taking LSD or "dropping acid"; and "dropping out" meant refusing to participate in mainstream culture and politics.) That is a great story, but it is only partly true, and in some ways not true at all. A counterfactual history begins in an alternate universe, in which the postwar conservativism that *Mad* was reacting against was as much the patronizing liberalism of the Cold War state as it was the rabid anti-communism of Joe McCarthy (and the hippie lifestyle was as suspect as the suburban existence that comix would critique). Likewise, the send-ups of popular cultural phenomena that Kurtzman and Gaines created weren't anti-elitist: they targeted not so much the abstract art that Clement Greenberg championed in the postwar moment as the kitsch against which he and Dwight Macdonald raged—the "middlebrow" culture of a rapidly expanding American middle class that had a hunger for distinction through consumption and an apparent lack of discernment or self-awareness. The quasi-libertarian critique that Kurtzman and other folks at *Mad* mounted reflected developments that David Riesman in 1950 saw in the "lonely crowd" and William Whyte in 1956 attributed to the culture of the Organization Man: the postwar consolidation of American social and cultural life, the anxiety and conformity spawned by that consolidation, and the too-easy accounts of that conformity by an equally anxious intellectual elite. Perhaps most importantly, countercultural critique, whether by *Mad* or its successors, was concerned less with articulating cultural and political alternatives than it was with skewering the foibles of what existed, dropping out rather than digging in or building barricades.

Amy Nyberg and Bart Beaty have each detailed how, in the 1950s and 1960s, the psychiatrist Fredric Wertham prosecuted his case against mass culture in general and specifically comics as being harmful for children, especially young boys. In *Fredric Wertham and the Critique of Mass Culture*, Beaty in particular paid close attention to how Wertham's jeremiad against comics, *Seduction of the Innocent* (1954), participated in a larger postwar project of applying psychoanalytic and neo-Freudian approaches to regulate social and cultural life in the United States. Wertham, along with other prominent social thinkers of the day—such as Margaret Mead, Benjamin Spock, and Erik Erikson—argued that the best way to avoid the horrors of a recently defeated fascism and the rising menace of Soviet totalitarianism was to model proper psychosexual relations for children, including through their media, which would thus provide them a natural model of home and family life under democratic capitalism.[9] (At its peak popularity, neo-Freudianism was also imagined as a tool to help adults to retroactively confront their own childhood traumas, which were presumed to be at the root of their adult social and behavioral problems.)

Beyond Wertham's attack on comics—including EC's horror and war titles, the latter of which were Kurtzman's forte—and in addition to neo-Freudian fantasies of better living through adjustment, an emergent cybernetics movement also imagined a harmonious and happy society through applying carefully regulated complex social and psychological feedback systems. Building on wartime research in weapons guidance, some members of the cybernetics movement of the 1950s and 1960s—best represented by the Macy Conferences on applied cybernetics—believed that it was possible to use a wide range of computational and behavioral tools to combat social ills such as crime, resource inequality, and discrimination to create a more orderly and just society.[10] Psychoanalysis was one tool in the cybernetics kit, as were a modified behaviorism, functional anthropology, and computer modeling of social problems. Both popular neo-Freudianism and the more elaborate imaginings of the Macy Conferences shared an optimistic belief in the benign uses of social control, a number of which had been beta-tested during World War II and now, some thought, needed to be adapted to the realities of the Cold War. What each expressed was a faith and confidence in regimes of regulation and control. And it was against this seemingly blind faith that self-marginalized groups such as the Beats and later the hippies, and involuntarily abjected groups such as people of color, women, queer folk, and anti-capitalist revolutionaries (and there was, of course, overlap and intersection among these groups) waged a struggle under the banners of nonconformity and noncompliance.

It would be somewhat accurate to describe, then, as many have, *Mad* magazine's irreverence as a response to the Comics Code, which was meant to limit the depiction of sex and violence in much the same way that the Motion Picture Production Code (MPPC) had done for the previous generation. (Although the MPPC remained officially in place until 1968, it was already eroding in the 1950s, especially following the *Miracle Decision* [*Burstyn v. Wilson*] of 1952, which prohibited religious rationales for film censorship as violations of the First Amendment.) The Comics Code took effect in the fall of 1954 and was itself a symptom of a larger set of social forces being brought to bear on social and cultural life in the United States. (Indeed, as Beaty points out in his book on Wertham, the Comics Code was not the first code of conduct for comics producers, only the most widely publicized and thoroughly applied). And, of course,

Mad had existed as a comic book since 1952, well before the institution of the Code. EC Comics may have converted it to magazine format, in part, to evade the Code, but its insouciant and disrespectful tone expressed a larger love/hate relationship with an emergent mass culture.

Yet even that partial explanation doesn't entirely get at why *Mad* developed a decidedly apolitical, yet highly critical, stance, especially given Kurtzman's efforts to confront social issues such as racism and economic inequality in his war and horror titles. He did lampoon Joseph McCarthy in #17 (Kurtzman and Davis, "What's My Shine!" 11/54: 7-1 [issue printed backwards]) and #23 (Kurtzman and Wood, "Gopo Gossum!" 5/55: 1-6), but each of those narratives seemed more a critique of engaging in politics *at all* than of the political issues and power over which McCarthy and his liberal opponents were struggling at that time. The 1954 parody began with a photograph of the Army-McCarthy Senate hearings, which it then mocked in comics form, drawn by Jack Davis, as "What's My Shine!" a send-up of the TV game show *What's My Line?* (CBS, 1950–1975) in which McCarthy tries to smear the mystery guest. The caption on the photograph begins, "Now you kiddies and grown-ups who just even glanced at [the televised hearings] were no doubt struck by the monotony of the show! . . . The lack of plot . . . The repetitious dialogue . . ." and goes on to critique the hearings in purely aesthetic terms (1). The 1955 item is a Wally Wood parody of Walt Kelly's *Pogo*, a newspaper strip with a decidedly liberal bent, in which the Pogo character (now "Gopo") tries to make the strip more popular by engaging in politics. Doing so attracts a wildcat named McCarthy (drawn as a hybrid of the ventriloquist's dummy Charlie McCarthy and senator Joseph McCarthy), who stirs the swamp dwellers into a frenzy of nonsensical political machinations. The story plays on Walt Kelly's 1953 story line featuring the character Simple J. Malarkey, a caricature of Joseph McCarthy. (The art for "Gopo Gossum" is signed *Walt Wood*, as an homage to Kelly.) One panel in the *Mad* story features a debate about the McCarthy character's name in which Gopo, asked if he's talking about Simple J. Baloney, replies, "That Simple J. Baloney is jes' a lot o' Malarkey! . . . He ain't no Baloney! . . . He real name is McCarthy!" (3). Neither article, though, opts for a coherent political or ideological critique of either the Red Scare or its liberal opposition. Instead, the lampoons proceed on aesthetic terms, criticizing the hearings for their lack of entertainment value and implicitly questioning their relevance.

This critique was and is not insubstantial: the McCarthy hearings, like the many United States congressional investigations that followed it, were often more a performance than a substantive legal proceeding, a somewhat neutered version of Stalin's show trials of the 1930s. (Still, the McCarthy Red Scare hearings of the 1950s were not completely lacking in consequence, in that they destroyed the careers and lives of some government employees, and their companion HUAC hearings in the House ruined the careers of many people in the private sector. Yet their value for those persecuting them lay in political performances of seeming diligence and patriotic fervor, which made the careers of red-baiters such as Richard Nixon.) The choice by Kurtzman, Gaines, and other *Mad* artists and writers to self-abject, to decline to join in shared performances of competing patriotisms, either on the left or the right, formed a politics of abstention, a willful refusal to cede the seemingly neutral higher ground from which their parodies could operate with a vernacular, quasi-Kantian disinterest in anything but the failing *form* of a political performance. By the 1950s, on the left, the Communist Party of the U.S.A. had suffered the consequences of internal strife and of its slowness to condemn Stalinism's brutal excesses. Likewise, socialism had largely been neutered by the broad brush of a hysteria that saw anything other than democratic capitalism as synonymous with communism, and the successes of the union movement during and after the war had blunted working-class desire for radical change. The Democratic Party was slowly splintering around civil rights and support for those same unions, which FDR had only recently brought into the Democratic fold. On the right, the Republican Party was also divided, between its moderate and rabid anti-communist wings. Into this mix add a generation of new, formerly working class, members of the middle class (then called by marketers the "Mass Class") and a younger generation of increasingly, if relatively mildly disaffected, working-class and lower-middle-class white youth (identified as "juvenile delinquents"), and a seemingly outsider critique becomes more attractive and sensible.

It is tempting to resort to biography here, to invoke Kurtzman's and Gaines's outsider status as working-class Jewish men growing up in a decidedly anti-Semitic and elitist American society before and after World War II. Kurtzman's parents emigrated to the United States to escape anti-Semitism in the Soviet Union, yet he eventually worked for a company that supplied cartoons to, among others, the *Daily Worker*, despite its pro-Soviet stance. Bill Gaines (the last name changed from *Ginzberg* by his father, Max) had an equally hardscrabble and politically complicated existence. Yet often biographies yield to a narrative that personalizes the historical and leads inevitably back to the tried and true tales of personal psychology and generational influence that this essay is trying to amend. Better, it seems, to delve into how *Mad*'s determined apolitical, unaligned stance could inspire a generation of socially and culturally rebellious and critical people, from those who subscribed to more coherent political programs—be they SDS founder Tom Hayden or democratic socialist underground comix publisher Denis Kitchen—to those, such as Spiegelman, Crumb, and Shelton, whose rebellion was more aesthetic and cultural than it was ideological. And, since Kurtzman left *Mad* in 1956, this inquiry involves examining what followed, for him and for other EC artists and writers, in the 1960s and 1970s.

In his careful and well-grounded history of underground comix, Charles Hatfield posits a number of interrelated causes for the relative lack of a clearly defined politics in their early days in North America. The U.S. Supreme Court decision *Miller v. California* enshrined "community standards" as the test for obscenity, allowing local jurisdictions more leeway in regulating the sale of materials they deemed offensive. At the same time, anti-drug laws that also targeted the paraphernalia used to consume them closed many of the head shops where comix had often been sold. Art Spiegelman said as much in a conversation with Hillary L. Chute, describing how and why he and Bill Griffith created *Arcade, The Comics Revue* in 1975:

> the comix ship seemed to be sinking in San Francisco, because of the closing down of head shops that provided a lot of the distribution. It was because of paraphernalia laws. Places that sell hash pipes are not allowed to exist.[11]

Hatfield also notes that the "shift among underground cartoonists [in the early 1970s] toward comic books (as opposed to the humor magazines and radical papers in which many had first gained notice) paralleled the shift [a generation earlier] in mainstream comics history away from newspaper strips, toward comics magazines as independent commodities."[12] So, a successful shift in format allowed for creative independence, but at a cost: "comix books urged the underground away from engagement in the radical press, thus in larger political issues, and toward a more reflexive involvement with 'comix' as such."[13] This move inward also involved a look backward. As Mike Kelly recounted in the *International Journal of Comic Art*, Spiegelman and Griffith designed *Arcade* on the model of *Mad* in order that the book would appear more a humor magazine than a comic book:

> As both Griffith and Spiegelman have said, the idea was to get *Arcade* onto the magazine rack next to titles such as *National Lampoon*. *Arcade* was engineered to make the same leap that *Mad* did in 1955 when it changed formats from a comic book to a humor magazine. Upon opening the cover, the reader is greeted with a carefully designed table of contents page. . . . The mere presence of a table of contents sets this publication in a new class, the clarity of design elevates it even further from the world of the undergrounds.[14]

As insightful as they are, Hatfield's and Kelly's overlapping narratives bear closer scrutiny. First, Kelly is right that from a design perspective, the short-lived *Arcade* (1975–1976) signaled a departure from its underground predecessors, yet as some have noted, the magazine's contents remained quite consistent with the comix from which it was distancing itself.[15] And it is important that many of the men and women who fueled the underground scene published in radical and alternative publications such as the *East Village Other*, *Ramparts*, the *Sunday Paper*, the *Berkeley Barb*, the *L.A. Free Press*, and *The Bugle*—although this was not necessarily their first foray into underground cartooning. Still, this story is well sedimented in the biographical retelling of many underground cartoonists. Of that time, for instance, Spiegelman says

> Jeez, well it started with me working in underground newspapers. Yes. And then through something called the Alternative Press Syndicate, those comics would spread around. I worked for some other papers as well. I did things directly for the *Rat*, which was a more political underground newspaper out of New York. And then in Chicago I think I did some things for the *Seed*. It's all a blur. Probably the first comics I did was when Jay Lynch started *Bijou Comix* [*Funnies*], which was the second or third underground comic title to come into existence.[16]

In this way, recollection gradually accumulates as history: A survey of the work of early underground artists in alternative publications suggests that much of it did not share the same pointedly political and often radical sentiments of many of the articles and editorials in those papers. Instead, it was countercultural in much the same way that comix books would be, breaking taboos around the depiction of sex and sexuality, drug use, and public decorum more generally. Also, because relatively few of those publications lasted beyond the early 1970s, they weren't reliable venues for comix. The *East Village Other* ran only from 1965 to 1972; *Ramparts* ran from 1962 to 1975; the *Sunday Paper* opened and closed with just seven issues in 1972; the *Berkeley Barb* published from 1965 until 1980; the *Free Press* ran from 1964 to 1978; the *Bugle* opened in 1970 and closed in 1978. Also, even those papers that lasted slightly longer than others could only offer so much space (or pay) to cartoonists, and as the alternative news market consolidated (especially under the Village Voice Media conglomerate in the 1980s), acceptance of radical points of view, or of the self-reflexive style of comix, dwindled. Lynda Barry, for instance, has reported that although she owed her start to the alternative press, the more she experimented with issues that were important to her—around girlhood and emotional life, for example—the less exposure she got in those venues.[17] This increasingly left comix books, anthologies, and collections as the primary outlets for cartoonists outside of the mainstream, even the underground mainstream. And that underground mainstream was dominated by straight, white men who imagined that their transgressive approach to cartooning equaled a radical politics. So, even though some cartoonists who produced for queer and women's comix also drew inspiration from Kurtzman and *Mad*, the networks of affiliation produced through his mentorship and his post-*Mad* publications tended to favor the young men who had shared his inchoate libertarianism.

This appends another caveat to Hatfield's otherwise meticulous and insightful structural read on the depoliticization of comix, that it is somewhat selective. While Spain Rodriguez's *Trashman* was (more or less) a Marxist avatar, few other creations from the early days of the underground had an explicit politics, other than that of breaking normative, mainstream taboos. Nor does it *necessarily* follow that the shift to book format, having removed the immediate political context, led to apolitical comix. (Consider, for instance, Lyvely and Sutton's *Abortion*

Eve or Rifas's *Corporate Crime Comics*, which both articulated an explicit politics.) Several women also got their start in the alternative press in the 1960s, such as Lee Marrs, Nancy Kalish, Willie Mendes, and Trina Robbins. When many of these women moved to book format, they did not evacuate their politics, perhaps because as feminists they didn't feel they could afford the luxury of more "universal" topics—they felt compelled to draw and write their experience as women in a world hostile to their politics. The founding collective of *Wimmen's Comix* (1972–1992), for example, remained committed to representing, debating, and exploring issues around feminism and women's experience in every single issue. (Trina Robbins told an interviewer in 2017 that the series suffered a serious setback in terms of distribution and sales after the 1973 *Miller v. California* decision redefined obscenity, yet *Wimmen's Comix* continued to publish and find a market for almost twenty years after that decision.[18]) Likewise, many histories of this period point to Justin Green's *Binky Brown Meets the Holy Virgin Mary* (1972) as heralding the autobiographical turn that Hatfield finds depoliticizing. Yet women's comix, and later gay comix, freely used autobiography without sacrificing any sense of liberatory politics.

Finally, there is a certain tidiness to the notion that the shift to book form undermined the radical nature of underground comix, a certain sense of historical continuity that elides part of that history. Some of the founding figures of the underground movement published in humor and "gentlemen's" magazines before or during their stints at alternative newspapers, and not all of that work was particularly radical. Given how large Kurtzman's influence looms in the history of underground comix, it isn't surprising that the titles he produced after leaving *Mad* in 1956 are among the best known in this regard. Erstwhile cartoonist turned soft-core pornographer Hugh Hefner—who would later furnish Kurtzman and Will Elder with regular employment producing the nudie strip *Little Annie Fanny* (1962–1988) for *Playboy*—provided the funding for a couple of Kurtzman's post-EC ventures. The first of these was *Trump*, a glossy satire magazine in the style of *Mad*. It opened and closed in 1957, the victim of cutbacks at *Playboy*.[19] Kurtzman followed this with the satire mag *Humbug* (1957–1958), which featured the work of many EC alumni, including Wally Wood, Jack Davis, Will Elder, and Al Jaffee. Kurtzman's next outing after *Humbug* lasted a bit longer. *Help!* (1960–1965) also featured many of the *Mad* crowd, as well as Woody Allen, Gloria Steinem, and future Monty Python members Terry Gilliam and John Cleese. *Help!* also carried early work by Robert Crumb, Jay Lynch, and Gilbert Shelton—all prior to their work for the *East Village Other*. Like much of Kurtzman's output, *Help!* was risqué and a bit naughty (cf. *Little Annie Fanny*) without venturing into territory as explicit as underground comix's depictions of depraved and anti-social behavior. Like its precursors, *Help!* eschewed a specific political critique in favor of more generic social and cultural satires. Art Spiegelman did not appear in *Help!*, though he would soon join Crumb, Lynch, and many other underground cartoonists in the *East Village Other* and its comix supplement, *Gothic Blimp Works*. Instead, in 1965, Spiegelman went to work for Topps, drawing insert cards for chewing gum packs, and soon after did some spec work for so-called gentlemen's magazines such as *Cavalier*, *Gent*, and *Dude*. (Spiegelman, Crumb, Lynch and others also contributed to Paul Krassner's *The Realist* [1958–2001]). In all these instances, the work that the founding members of underground comix produced, while irreverently mocking cultural and social mores, was generally no more or less political than their work for alternative news services.

How and why this distinction between political and "apolitical" (or implicitly libertarian) satire is significant for understanding the influence of Kurtzman and *Mad* on radical cartooning in the late twentieth century is aptly illustrated by the example of *witzend* (1965–1985). Initially produced by EC veteran Wally Wood, *witzend* was a comics anthology that featured non-Code work by a wide range of cartoonists, including Kurtzman and Elder, Will Eisner, Jack Kirby, Frank Frazetta, Steve Ditko, Art Spiegelman, Vaughn Bode, and Richard "Grass" Green. A debate in comic form that broke out between Ditko and the cartoonists Tim Brent and Bill Pearson (who took over the book from Wood in 1968) captures the tension between political and apolitical satire well (see fig. 20-2). In issue #3 of *witzend* (1967), Ditko began a limited series that featured the character "Mr. A" and anthropomorphized "The Avenging World." Ditko, who was sympathetic to Ayn Rand's Objectivism (effectively an extreme version of libertarianism) set out, in a series that spanned the next four issues of *witzend*, to in effect create a condensed comics version of Rand's novel *Atlas Shrugged* (1957), arguing for Objectivism and against what he saw as the moral relativism of 1960s counterculture.

Fig. 20-2: In *witzend* #3 (1967), Steve Ditko introduced his Objectivist superhero, Mr. A. © Ditko Estate, used courtesy of Ditko Estate.

Fig. 20-3. Editor Bill Pearson and cartoonist Tim Brent created Mr. E. to parody Ditko's libertarianism in *witzend* #7 (1970). Mr. E. © witzend, used courtesy of Bill Pearson.

By issue #7 (1970), after the series ended, there was pushback. In the letters section, one reader complained that "Ditko's atrocity in #6 was just unbelievable in its small-minded, arrogant ignorance. Sure comics are right-wing—it's an old tradition. But this kind of agit-prop has no place in a mag supposedly devoted to comic 'ART'. . . . If you want to run stuff promoting police actions at a time when cops are shooting unarmed demonstrators in the back with buckshot . . . it's your conscience. But to apply this simplistic individualism to entire nations is too much!" In that same issue, a few pages after part two of "The Avenging World," came a visual rebuttal titled "Paranoid Productions Presents. . . . Mr. E: Master of Mayhem," ostensibly by "Steve Diktato," but actually by Pearson and Brent (see fig. 20-3). Their parodic version of *Mr. A* begins with him beating a litterbug to death. He then returns to his lair, a dilapidated apartment with a George Wallace bumper sticker and crumpled copy of "Avenging World" on the wall, and works by Mickey Spillane, Hitler, Ayn Rand, Nietzsche, and bound copies of *Spiderman* on the table. Setting out later, he roams the city delivering Objectivist lectures to his victims before beating them to death. At the end of story, Mr. E. infiltrates a charity organization (which creates indolence and moral turpitude through handouts) and, discovering it is run by Shirley Temple and Bill "Bojangles" Robinson, begins to lecture and beat them—before finally taking his own life after Robinson convinces him that, by trespassing on private property and cursing in public, he, too, has broken the law and should be punished. The parody of Ditko's Objectivism uses a *reductio ad absurdum* to point out that, taken to its logical extreme, libertarianism is an inherently antisocial philosophy, and its principle of enlightened self-interest is in practice morally bankrupt. But Brent and Pearson were content to mock Ditko and leave it at that, rather than to offer a programmatic alternative.

On its face, pairing in a single issue Ditko's Objectivist screed with a parody of his work that foregrounded the inane cruelty of his philosophy would seem the picture of rectitude. Yet beyond the relative rarity of explicit political debate in any comic book, underground or otherwise, is another detail, which demonstrates the old dictum that the exception proves the rule. *Mad* veteran Wood created *witzend* and ran it for its first three years, then turned it over to Pearson. In issue #3, effectively Wood's last, he details his philosophy on the inside front cover, opposite the first installment of Ditko's "Mr. A." In a short editorial titled "BOMB PEKING! GIVE INDIANS THE VOTE! STATEHOOD FOR ARKANSAS!" Wood declares:

> Sure, we could have opinions. We could manufacture a point of view. But the Saturday Review and the Times have all the writers we wanted. And second rate words just take up space. . . . Besides which, we're not in the opinion business. WITZEND's function is to serve as a forum for innovators of popular art, for the benefit of the limited but ardent audience who appreciate their efforts. If our potential contributors have something to say, we're delighted to offer them the place to say it. And if they just want to show how well they can handle a brush, that's okay, too. Our only criterion is quality, in either case.[20]

Soon after this, Wood sold *witzend* to Pearson for $1.00. No reason was given, although some speculate that it had to do with projects Wood was undertaking with Marvel and DC. Yet in this editorial, Wood clearly outlines the libertarian-by-default, quasi-Kantian disinterest that he saw as inherent in the magazine, and which was later echoed in the letter complaining about Ditko in issue #7. It was a given: cartoons were popular art, and form always trumped content. Given the much more interested nature of the Marvel and DC titles that Ditko, Kirby, and Kane sometimes worked for—action comics being always invested in patriotism and (to put it in Superman's terms) "truth, justice, and the American way"—this marks not so much a general rule about comics and comic books as a belief that ideological disinterest was a necessary prerequisite for parody. It is the philosophy of *Mad* and its successors. The doctrinal tussle that marks *witzend* #7 is decidedly not in the mode that Kurtzman and his cohort imagined: taking sides was serious business, and never the business of parody or satire.

This little spat, as isolated as it was, illustrates the difference between the programmatic libertarianism imagined by Rand and her followers and the politics of refusal and self-abjection that defined the post-*Mad* alternative comix landscape. To put it in today's terms, it is the difference between the nearly logical libertarianism of a politician like Rand Paul (or his nuttier father, Ron) and the opt-out prairie-fire libertarianism of the (seditious, yet strangely unincarcerated) Cliven Bundy clan. The self-abjection practiced by Kurtzman and *Mad*, and by the (straight, male) cartoonists influenced by him, was not so much politically radical as formally and culturally transgressive. For example, in the summer of 1970, Kurtzman, Shelton, and Spiegelman attended a symposium at Goddard College in Vermont sponsored by the Alternative Media Project. According to Bill Schelly, the purpose of the symposium was to chart the future of underground media and to increase their influence on social and political life. Kurtzman and Shelton appeared on a panel titled "Comics and Mass Consciousness," and Kurtzman was quickly called out for the sexism of *Little Annie Fanny*, and of working for *Playboy*. Kurtzman replied, "It's sexist all right, sure. And it intends to be. . . . [Feminists and *Playboy*], they're both extreme, and I like to feel I can tolerate them both." Shelton chimed in, "What about the idea of the [*Fabulous Furry Freak Brothers*] in *Playboy*? Is there anything wrong with that? Does that mean I'm supporting *Playboy*'s policies, or does that mean I'm slipping a revolutionary message into *Playboy*?" (His stance presumes, of course, that a comix book primarily about doing drugs and having straight sex out of wedlock was inherently revolutionary.) Asked about how he drew a cartoon, Kurtzman responded by claiming that "one couldn't create a humorous comic strip if one had to conform to some political agenda."[21] The term *conform* is telling: it supposes that any political stance that is clearly and specifically articulated is imposed, rather than merely felt.

Although the founding lights of the underground comix movement like to credit Kurtzman for this stance, it was not his alone. Publisher William Gaines claimed that "we like to say that *Mad* has no politics and that we take no point of view."[22] Al Feldstein, Kurtzman's successor, confirmed this position, saying

> When the magazine went to press, [Gaines] would get the dummy, the mechanicals, and he would read it for the first time. He had no idea what was going to be in it or anything like that. He rarely instituted any kind of censorship except where I might have overstepped the legal bounds, or he thought he might get sued for copyright or something like that. But aside from that, he never said a word. We were at different poles politically, and some of the things he didn't agree with politically, but he still let it go because it was a cultural, social comment magazine and he knew it had to cover all bases.[23]

This had been *Mad*'s ethos from the beginning, then, and Kurtzman merely its first and most public face. And it was a stance that followed Kurtzman, Wood, and others into other publications after *Mad*.

Yet for Marrs, Crumb, Spiegelman, Skip Williamson, Shelton, and others, it was Kurtzman who was the godfather of underground comix. As Jay Lynch put it (in three different sources, blended by Schelly), discussing the importance of Kurtzman as a mentor, and *Help!* as a venue for young cartoonists:

> The core of what I like in comic art is *Mad* comics.... When we were kids, we thought we'd grow up to work for Kurtzman's *Mad*. Underground comix was just kind of an extension of *Mad*, or what *Mad* would have been if Kurtzman came around initially in 1968 rather than 1952.... In that sense, *Help!* was the first underground comic.[24]

This is the same sentiment that Spiegelman brought to Kurtzman's obituary in the *New Yorker*, a mixture of sincere gratitude, fondness, and protectiveness for a man whose heyday had passed, but who remained an active participant in a vital artistic mass medium, and who was a mentor devoted to developing young talent.[25] As Crumb put it in 2004, "[Kurtzman] really helped me and taught me a lot. I'd say he was the closest thing I had to a teacher and mentor in my life. In the middle '60s when I was in New York he was very helpful. He recognized my talent and gave me a lot of advice that was valuable about the business as well as artistic techniques, and even about life and love."[26] Comix artist and publisher Denis Kitchen recalled the incredible influence Kurtzman and *Mad* had on him as a child and young man, and later on the work he chose to draw, support, and publish:

> I remember instantly loving the fact that other comics were being parodied. I'm not sure that I knew the word "parody" or knew the word "satire" at that age. I just thought it was the coolest thing in the world that somebody was dissecting other comics in such a clever way. "Superduperman" [Kurtzman and Wood #4, 4–5/53: 1-8] was a mind-blower. It was inconceivable back then that Superman could actually fight Captain Marvel. Or show the ridiculousness of the Clark Kent disguise.... It made you look at iconic characters like Donald Duck and Superman in an entirely different light. And there was something so

> liberating in seeing them punctured so brilliantly. . . . Kurtzman wasn't signing those stories and I don't think I knew for a while to what degree he was really involved on every level of the work. . . . I just remember that the *Mad*s and the *Humbug*s were different than anything else and embodied some kind of zany energy and fearlessness. A handful of friends shared that feeling too.[27]

Yet there is more than simple protective fondness at play in the repeated praise of Kurtzman and of *Mad*. If one of the key elements that Hatfield locates in underground comix is self-reflexivity, that turning backward and inward requires—actually demands—an internalized historicity.

Cartoonists and cartoon fans alike tell and retell the history of comics because it affirms, nostalgically, a sense of comics being meaningful when so many others have derided the form as worthless, hackneyed, and infantile. And for the founding members of underground comix, that nostalgia feeds into and out of a larger sense of their own historical importance. Speaking to and reading interviews with these artists, writers, producers, and distributors provides a sense that many of them firmly believed that they were not only part of a revolutionary change in American culture and society, but were also in the vanguard of that change.

To be more explicit, in the years following World War II, given the anxious and repressive tenor of American social and cultural life, parody may have seemed by its very nature radical and progressive, and it inspired a segment of the baby boom generation primed to reject the genteel middlebrow offerings aimed at their parents. Bill Schelly, when asked about Kurtzman in 2015, reiterated and elaborated upon the claim he had made in his biography:

> In *MAD*, Kurtzman challenged the repressive status quo in the early 1950s by satirizing cultural figures, politicians, and rampant consumerism. . . . That kind of self-referential satire became the primary mode of humor in American culture, from *Saturday Night Live* to *The Simpsons*. I believe the questioning of authority in *MAD* led in some way to the counterculture moment of the 1960s and the anti-Vietnam war protests.[28]

In the 1950s, the status quo was such that even most self-professed liberals were by today's standards conservative. (Although by progressive or radical standards, today's liberals are conservative, too.) The parody that Kurtzman, Gaines, and *Mad* mounted introduced new forms of vernacular irreverence into the cultural lexicon and taught some baby boomers that they were not alone in their sense that much of the mainstream, mass-market, middlebrow cultural and social landscape was laughable—and that it *needed* to be laughed at, loudly. In rock and roll, the Beats, hard bop (for some), and, later, flower power, that generation found increasingly commodified forms of rebellion that seemed to have a critical effect, and which fueled what Horkheimer and Adorno named the culture industries. (Cultural critic Thomas Frank has detailed the process of commodifying rebellion during this period in *The Conquest of Cool* [1998]).[29]

All of which is to say that Harvey Kurtzman and *Mad* did play a significant role in tectonic shifts in social, political, and cultural life in the United States—but, contrary to the received history, not all those shifts were necessarily or automatically salutary. The same may be said of the influence of the first underground comix artists on the generations that followed them. Artists such as R. Crumb, Spiegelman (in his early years), Shelton, Williamson, and Lynch (to name a few), slighted parody in favor of satire, and intentionally pushed the boundaries of taste and taboo in an effort, they believed, to bare the demons of racism, sexism, and classism that lurked in the collective unconscious of the United States—and through that process to exorcise them. (Spiegelman would shift rapidly in the 1970s from stories about incest and necrophilia to formal experiments with comix form and narrative, which would lead to the works for which he is now most known, such as *Maus* [1980–1991] and *In the Shadow of No Towers* [2004]). Yet like Kurtzman, Gaines, and Wood, these underground artists did not prefer satire to parody in the service of a specific ideology or cause, but rather in a continuation of *Mad*'s stance of refusal. To be clear: there is no requirement that art, vernacular or elite, be political or ideological (although some have argued effectively that it cannot be otherwise), so the absence of those qualities is not necessarily a problem. There is no problem, except that so many—including many of the artists themselves—have claimed that underground comix, like *Mad* before them, *did* cause important shifts in the social and political landscape of the United States. Parody and satire are themselves now normative responses to the outrage of the day and mobilized on both the right and the left, an unintended result of these artists' rebellion that might tarnish the celebration of that accomplishment a bit.

Yet there is consensus that, without exception, everyone who crossed paths with Harvey Kurtzman found him a good and decent man—*Little Annie Fanny* aside. Even there, Denis Kitchen, in his heartfelt encomium to Kurtzman in *Harvey Kurtzman's Jungle Book* (1959/2014), paints a picture of Kurtzman after *Mad* and after the failures of *Trump* and *Humbug* as a hardworking family man with "a wife, a mortgage, and three young children (one with profound autism) and no immediate prospects for revenue."[30] What Hugh Hefner supplied to Kurtzman and Will Elder was a steady paycheck and work that sometimes embarrassed Kurtzman and the young artists he was mentoring.[31] According to Schelly, Crumb in particular was disappointed that Kurtzman debased himself by working for *Playboy*, complaining that "to me, Hefner was far below Kurtzman.... I considered *Playboy* a cornball, ridiculous, asinine publication, successful as it was."[32] This remark seems in some ways a description of distinction without a difference: although *Mad* parodied popular culture and social norms while *Playboy* blended soft-core pornography and lifestyle promotion, both celebrated an irreverent rejection of then-current standards of social respectability and normativity—as did comix creators such as Crumb.

If there is a legacy of Kurtzman's that isn't open to question, it is his commitment to mentorship. He was unfailing in his support of young cartoonists, and not only did he encourage and inspire underground artists to create and hone their craft, he also moved many of them to become mentors and community organizers in their own right. Denis Kitchen has even taken struggling cartoonists into his own home and has gone out of his way to support the artists whose work he has produced and distributed. Kitchen, who is straight, began *Gay Comix* in 1980 with Howard Cruse after he saw in *Wimmen's Comix* (1973–1992) an effort to give voice to a community and felt there was room (and a market) to do the same for an emergent gay community. Kitchen also devoted significant resources to publishing works by Kurtzman and his contemporary Will Eisner (e.g., Kurtzman, *My Life as a Cartoonist*; Kurtzman and Elder, *Executive's Comic Book*; Eisner, *Will Eisner's The Spirit*; Eisner, *Family Matter*). Lee Marrs, who saw in Kurtzman the essence of comix, founded Alternative Features Service (AFS) in 1971 in order to help journalists and cartoonists find outlets for their work in alternative and college newspapers.[33] In 1973, Marrs and a number of other women cartoonists in the San Francisco Bay area created *Wimmen's Comix*. This long-running anthology series not only gave space and voice to women cartoonists, but its editorial collective also encouraged and mentored new artists and writers, sharing knowledge and experience with those entering the business. And Art Spiegelman—whose graphic *New Yorker* obituary of Kurtzman, "A Furshlugginer Genius!," is set in Kurtzman's cartooning class at New York's School of Visual Arts—created *RAW* magazine with his partner Françoise Mouly (after he finished the sex-drugs-rock-and-roll phase of his underground work), and this publication not only challenged many of the formal conventions of comix and comic book publishing, but also provided space and a voice to a wide range of formal innovators in vernacular graphic arts such as Gary Panter, Lynda Barry, Julie Doucet, and Sue Coe. That is to say, while Kurtzman may not have espoused an explicit politics in his art and storytelling—indeed, even though he actively avoided them—he practiced a communitarian impulse that inspired those who followed after him. *Mad* set the tone with its irreverence and iconoclasm, and Harvey Kurtzman himself demonstrated a commitment to encouraging younger artists to perpetuate that ideal.

Still, it's important to distinguish between Kurtzman the man and Kurtzman the legend. What this gentle correction is meant to suggest is a genealogical and historical approach on the order of Greil Marcus's *Lipstick Traces: A Secret History of the Twentieth Century* (1989), which rewrote the received history of modern art by making the case for an artistic lineage stretching from Dada in the early part of the century to punk at its end.[34] More recently, Todd Haynes's film *Velvet Goldmine* (1998) updated Marcus's argument and corrected his genealogy by including queer performers and artists in the glam and punk movement.[35] To make this sort of correction is not to gainsay an accepted history, then, but to flesh it out. Art Spiegelman, Robert Crumb, Skip Williamson, Spain Rodriguez, Gilbert Shelton, Bill Griffith, Kim Deitch, and others were talented artists, entrepreneurs, and deft cultural critics (and those who still live still are). (Even artists and critics who can't stand Crumb's misogyny and racism, for instance, still grant him his immense talent and influence.) But so were the women and queer folk and people of color who were drawing, producing, and distributing comix in the 1970s and 1980s, and their inclusion in that history requires more than a footnote.

Likewise, even a history reconsidered would still acknowledge the enormous impact that Harvey Kurtzman and *Mad* had on social, political, and cultural life in the United States, and the immense debt that subsequent generations of vernacular artists owe to Kurtzman (and to Will Eisner) in terms of pathbreaking and mentorship. Yet if the purpose or even the unintended consequence of that acknowledgment is to further a romantic and outsized view of the importance of vernacular media such as comics and comix in the rise of the counterculture in the mid-twentieth-century United States, then it will have failed. For ideally, revisiting and revising an historical narrative needn't be about balancing truth against falsehood. It can also open access to other facets of a narrative, or even abandon the notion of a singular narrative in favor of modeling the meaning of a set of ephemeral objects and the events associated with them as in flux, dependent upon historical and historiographic processes and not simply a record of fact.[36] More to the point, a critical look at the influence of Harvey Kurtzman and *Mad* on the counterculture generally, and on underground comix specifically, would begin by asking, simply, what was the nature—and what were the limits—of that influence?

Ending this essay with a catalogue of those marginalized by the standard received history of the underground is, again, not simply an act of tardy amendment. Harvey Kurtzman and *Mad* specialized in forms of disinterested, seemingly apolitical, parody and satire that many have described as informing their political and social outlook. Likewise, the nominal discursive founders of the underground comix movement have claimed Kurtzman as a patron saint and in the early days of the underground practiced similarly disinterested forms of satire and parody. In essence, *Mad* and the core of underground comix in the 1960s and 1970s self-abjected, creating a margin that they did not have to occupy, but from which they could offer social commentary. But many of those excluded from that historical narrative, or relegated to its footnotes, also managed to engage in incisive social commentary without recourse to disinterested, apolitical humor. In Marxian terms, theirs was a standpoint epistemology in which involuntary marginalization produced both structural disadvantage *and* the critical advantage of being able to see clearly and comment incisively on the practices and conditions that produced that marginalization. This difference between those who self-marginalized and those who created comix from imposed margins begs further consideration, as does the near ubiquity of parody and satire today as a sort of normative non-normative discourse. And it may be, on further analysis, that the very interested comix of the margin may yield insight into how we arrived at the trollery of today.

Notes

1. Trina Robbins, *Pretty in Ink: North American Women Cartoonists, 1896–2013*, 129–38.

2. See Rebecca Wanzo, *The Content of Our Caricature: African American Comic Art and Political Belonging*, chap. 5.

3. Art Spiegelman, "A Furshlugginer Genius!" 76.

4. Bill Schelly, *Harvey Kurtzman: The Man Who Created Mad and Revolutionized Humor in America: A Biography*, 461.

5. Adam Gopnik, "Postscript: Kurtzman's Mad World," 75.

6. See Amy Kiste Nyberg, *Seal of Approval: The History of the Comics Code*; and Bart Beaty, *Fredric Wertham and the Critique of Mass Culture*.

7. Elizabeth Freeman, *Time Binds: Queer Temporalities, Queer Histories*, 64–65.

8. Trina Robbins, interview by Nicholas Sammond, San Francisco, CA, November 21, 2017; Robert Triptow, telephone interview by Nicholas Sammond, Hawaii and San Francisco, CA, September 21, 2017. On Wimmen's Comix, see, Margaret Galvan, "Archiving Wimmen: Collectives, Networks, and Comix."

9. See Nicholas Sammond, *Babes in Tomorrowland: Walt Disney and the Making of the American Child, 1930–1960*; and Ellen Herman, *The Romance of American Psychology: Political Culture in the Age of Experts*.

10. Claus Pias, ed., *Cybernetics: The Macy Conferences 1946–1953: The Complete Transactions*.

11. Hillary L. Chute, "Art Spiegelman."

12. Charles Hatfield, *Alternative Comics: An Emerging Literature*, 19.

13. Hatfield, *Alternative Comics*, 19.

14. Mike Kelly, "Art Spiegelman and His Circle: New York City Comix and the Downtown Scene," 320.

15. See, for example, M. Steven Fox, "Arcade."

16. Quoted in Chute, "Art Spiegelman."

17. Hillary L. Chute, *Outside the Box: Conversations with Contemporary Cartoonists*, 57–81.

18. Robbins, interview by Sammond.

19. Space does not permit a more detailed discussion of Kurtzman and *Trump*. See, for example, Schelly, *Harvey Kurtzman*, 343–68; or Michael Dooley, "*Trump*: A Smart, Sophisticated, Satirical Graphic Humor Magazine."

20. Wallace Wood, "BOMB PEKING!" *witzend* 3 (1967): 1.

21. Schelly, *Harvey Kurtzman*, 473–74.

22. Quoted in Nathan Abrams, "From Madness to Dysentery: *Mad*'s Other New York Intellectuals," 441.

23. Quoted in Abrams, "From Madness to Dysentery," 440*n*25.
24. Schelly, *Harvey Kurtzman*, 462.
25. Spiegelman, "A Furshlugginer Genius!," 76–77.
26. Quoted in Schelly, *Harvey Kurtzman*, 445–46.
27. Quoted in Jon B. Cooke, *Everything Including the Kitchen Sink: The Definitive Interview with Denis Kitchen*, 40.
28. Quoted in Stephen Heller, "The Man Who Changed Humor in America Forever."
29. Thomas Frank, *The Conquest of Cool: Business, Counterculture, and the Rise of Hip Consumerism*.
30. Denis Kitchen, "It's a Jungle Out There!," in *Harvey Kurtzman's Jungle Book*, by Harvey Kurtzman, 12.
31. Schelly, *Harvey Kurtzman*, 486–87.
32. Schelly, *Harvey Kurtzman*, 487. Crumb's disapproval was neither universally shared nor consistent. For instance, in 1969, Kurtzman sat in on a comix jam at the *East Village Other*—which resulted in the collaborative piece "Come the Revolution"—with the express purpose of gathering information for an alternative comix-themed episode of *Little Annie Fanny*; see Schelly, *Harvey Kurtzman*, 468. Likewise, collaborator and friend Skip Williamson, in whose *Bijou Funnies* (1968–1973) Crumb appeared, worked as the art director for the men's magazines *Gallery*, *Hustler*, and *Playboy*; see Patrick Rosenkranz, "Skip Williamson, 1944–2017."
33. Schelly, *Harvey Kurtzman*, 462.
34. Greil Marcus, *Lipstick Traces: A Secret History of the Twentieth Century*.
35. Todd Haynes, dir., *Velvet Goldmine*, film, 123 min.
36. Hayden White, *The Content of the Form: Narrative Discourse and Historical Representation*.

21. Quotations from the Future:

Harvey Kurtzman's "Superduperman!," Nostalgia, and Alan Moore's *Miracleman*

Brian Cremins

IN AN ESSAY included in the second issue of *Miracleman*, published by Eclipse Comics in 1985, Alan Moore describes the origins of his fascination with Mick Anglo's Marvelman, the British comics character first introduced in the 1950s as a replacement for Fawcett Publications' defunct Captain Marvel.[1] After several years of reading the Marvel and DC comics of the 1960s, Moore rediscovered Marvelman and decided to create a parody of the hero in the style of Harvey Kurtzman and Wally Wood's "Superduperman!," a story Moore discovered in one of the *Mad* paperback collections published by Ballantine Books.[2] In his essay, Moore recalls a moment in 1968 when he happened upon a collection of *Marvelman* comics:

> Turning the coarse black-and-white pages, filled with stories and illustrations that seemed crude and amateurish after exposure to the work of Kirby, Ditko and Lee, I was nonetheless overcome by that warm glow of nostalgia which is probably the single biggest factor keeping us interested in this medium, whatever amount of intellectual satisfaction we manage to glean on the side.[3]

Moore's remarks on the relationship between costumed heroes and nostalgia inform my reading of *Miracleman* and its debt to Kurtzman and Wood. As Moore has explained in his essay and in subsequent interviews, his work on *Miracleman* draws inspiration from both "Superduperman!" and Brian Eno's ambient music of the late 1970s and early 1980s.[4] Moore's revision of Anglo's Marvelman as filtered through the tragicomic vision of Kurtzman and Wood is an exercise in nostalgia, what Svetlana Boym describes as a "longing for a home that no longer exists or has never existed." As she observes, "Nostalgia is a sentiment of loss and displacement, but it is also a romance with one's own fantasy."[5] For Kurtzman, this fondness for and sentimentality over the past can obscure history and transform the present into a series of repetitions. As a result, when Moore returns to Superduperman! and Marvelman, and explores his affection for these heroes, he must confront the tragic rootlessness of Clark Bent, Kurtzman's caricature of Jerry Siegel and Joe Shuster's Clark Kent. However, like Brian Eno, Moore seeks to locate a possible future in the psychological wreckage of postwar America and Britain. Moore explores his fond memories for these relics of his childhood in order to understand a world built on the fantasies of 1950s consumer culture.

In the last installment of *Olympus*, Moore's third and final volume of his 16-issue *Miracleman* saga, the hero, more divine than human, points out that his comic book adventures function as the "mystery plays" of the utopian world in which he now exists. "Men read allegories into these childish tales, read revelations into every line," he reflects.[6] What might read like a celebration of these tales is in fact a warning: what Boym calls a "romance with one's own fantasy" is filled with dangers, ones first described in the pages of "Superduperman!" in 1953. This obsession with the past can leave one with no escape from the endless cycle of repetition that lies at the heart of serial narratives. However, as Moore has pointed out, his final volume of *Miracleman* is also a story about "joy" and the possibility of transformation.[7] After all, who wouldn't want to discover a magic word that would reveal one's secret, other self?[8]

In December 2004, Moore had the opportunity to interview Eno for BBC Radio 4's *Chain Reaction*. Early in the conversation, Moore, uncharacteristically reverential as he speaks with one of his musical heroes, asks a question regarding England's glam rock era of the early 1970s, a period in which Eno's band Roxy Music—along with David Bowie, Marc Bolan's T. Rex, and U.S. artists including Lou Reed and Jobriath—brought a Queer futurism to Western pop music.[9] What was the relationship, Moore wonders, between glam and the rock and roll of the late 1950s and 1960s? Eno argues that by the early 1970s "pop music . . . had become self-conscious." As an art form with "fifteen years" of history, he adds, pop music

> was just old enough for people to look back on people like Little Richard and Elvis and so on as sort of historical figures and to start to look at

> them as stylistic ideas. So there was quotation from the past like that and there was also quotation from a kind of imaginary future based on science fiction and *Star Trek* and various other things like that.[10]

Eno's comments suggest the impact that the aesthetic and ideological concerns of glam rock had on Moore's work as a comic book writer. *Miracleman,* filled with "quotation[s] from the past," also sets out to quote the future. But what is a "quotation from a kind of imaginary future"? How does one quote a text that does not yet exist, or that may never exist? By exploring his affectionate childhood memories of Anglo's character, Moore ultimately frees himself from his nostalgia for these superhero narratives. "Quoting from the future" is another means of *imagining* that future, not as a place that must be invented, but as a world that already exists, waiting to reveal itself once the past has been put to rest.[11] I understand *Miracleman,* then, as a kind of sequel to Kurtzman and Wood's "Superduperman!," one in which Moore explores his relationship with these characters in order to bid them farewell.

"Superduperman!," one of the most popular stories published during Harvey Kurtzman's run as *Mad*'s chief writer and editor, first appeared in issue #4, dated Apr.–May, 1953.[12] The plot is simple: Superduperman battles a menace called the Unknown Monster, only to discover that the villain, in reality, is none other than Captain Marbles, the alter ego of Billy Spafon. Marbles and Spafon are caricatures of Captain Marvel and Billy Batson, characters created by Bill Parker and C. C. Beck. Captain Marvel, who first appeared in *Whiz Comics* no. 2, published by Fawcett Publications in 1940, was, along with Superman, Batman, Wonder Woman, and Captain America, one of the most popular comic book characters in the U.S. in the 1940s. After a series of legal disputes with National Comics Publications, Inc. (later DC Comics) over claims of copyright infringement, Fawcett canceled all its Captain Marvel and Marvel Family comics in 1953.[13]

While Denis Kitchen and Paul Buhle argue that Kurtzman's "Superduperman!" is in part a satire of what came to be known as the Superman vs. Captain Marvel lawsuit,[14] Kurtzman himself tended to discuss the story in more general terms. The cartoonist explained,

> "Superduperman!" and "Mickey Rodent" are, of all the *Mad* stories, the ones that are engraved on my memory, perhaps because they sum up

> what *Mad* was all about: trying to make the truth visible. I think that the "Superduperman!" story states truths about the whole super-hero phenomenon that could not be stated as effectively any other way.[15]

According to Kitchen and Buhle, the cartoonist was "notorious for his hostility toward comic strip and comic book violence" and wanted "to bare the clichés and falsehoods of derring-do adventure."[16] While Kurtzman and Wood spend most of "Superduperman!" deconstructing and slyly ridiculing the storytelling conventions of an average Superman or Captain Marvel comic, the true focus of the narrative is the hero's pathetic alter ego Clark Bent. Brought to life by Wally Wood from Kurtzman's thumbnail sketches, Bent is a creature like the one Herbert Marcuse will describe a decade later in the first chapter of *One-Dimensional Man*, a being who exists in an "advanced industrial society" that celebrates "stupefying work where it is no longer a real necessity" in a landscape filled with "such deceptive liberties as free competition at administered prices, a free press which censors itself, [and the] free choice between brands and gadgets."[17] If "Superduperman!" embodies the anxieties of a nation still coming to terms with the trauma of World War II, it is also a study of loss—of what happens when heroic ideals and fantasies have crumbled, leaving behind those, like Clark Bent, who no longer believe in those values or in themselves.[18]

Kurtzman and Wood begin revealing the "truths about the whole super-hero phenomenon" in the image that opens the comic. At the center of the first panel, we see the title character, a brute who has earned a "Good Housebreaking" seal of approval (see fig. 21-1). He plunges his left fist into the chest of an old man. The old man's false teeth tumble from his mouth. As readers, we, too, are spectators, members of the crowd that surrounds the hero and applauds. Advertisements and scraps of paper urge us to "Post No Bills" but to drink, eat, smoke, buy, and chew all sorts of super products, from candy to "New Super Soap." Wood also fills the page's fourth panel with broadsides that read like epigrams from Ben Franklin's *Autobiography* or notes from Jay Gatsby's copy of *Hopalong Cassidy*: "Do It Now!"; "Think!"; "Virtue Is Its Own Reward." With his threadbare suit and his disheveled hair, Clark Bent is a grotesque figure, the "creep" whom Lois Pain will reject at the end of the story (Kurtzman and Wood, #4, 4–5/53: 1-8; 1).

Fig. 21-1: The opening page of Kurtzman and Wood's "Superduperman!" presents the hero as a brutal, violent creature and his alter ego Clark Bent as a lonely and tattered office boy (*Mad* #4, 4–5/53: 1). MAD used with permission.

Our hero is a violent product of the advertising world. In chapter four of *From Aargh! to Zap!*, Kurtzman and his cowriter Michael Barrier identify the truths that *Mad* hoped to reveal to its readers. To do so, Kurtzman compares his work on the magazine with the other stories he produced for EC Comics: "Just as there was a treatment of reality in the war books, there was a treatment of reality running through *Mad*; the satirist/parodist tries not just to entertain his audience but to remind it of what the real world is like."[19] In the hands of Wally Wood, the "real world" is a shadowy, desperate place, in which human interaction has been replaced by relationships based on exchange. In this landscape, everything—from the brick walls of tenement buildings to Superduperman's emblem—is up for sale. While these "brands and gadgets," to recall Marcuse's phrase, promise stability and comfort, even a superhero can't buy his way out of shame, isolation, and loss. These products, and the power fantasies used to sell them, are mere distractions, curiosities worthy only of scorn and ridicule. Wood's mastery of light and shadow brings Kurtzman's cynical but ultimately optimistic vision to life. Escape is possible, but only through laughter.

In an interview with John Benson, Kurtzman explained the collaborative process that produced "Superduperman!" An accomplished and distinctive cartoonist himself, Kurtzman provided Wood with pencil breakdowns of the action and pacing of the story. While Benson describes that first panel as an example of Wood "parodying the stiffness of the drawing on most superhero characters," Kurtzman points out that "[t]he action was essentially mine." After a brief discussion of some of the figure drawings in the story, Kurtzman adds, "Wally filtered them [Kurtzman's characters and layouts] through the Wally Wood brain and combined what I did with what he did, and essentially what he did was stiff. It's very hard to separate where I left off and Wally picked up."[20] As Benson suggests, Wood's style also highlights for readers the "stiffness" of Kurtzman's absurd but conventional superhero plot.

The premise of "Superduperman!" would have been familiar to readers of Superman and of Captain Marvel: the city is in danger, threatened by the Unknown Monster. W. Twitchell, the editor of the *Daily Dirt*, calls a meeting with his best reporters, including the voluptuous Lois Pain. From behind his cluttered desk, the editor in chief urges them "to go out there, gang! I want you to fight, I want you to die, for good ol' *Daily Dirt*, gang! Now get that story, gang!" (4–5). The other reporters, all men, stare wide-eyed at Lois Pain, who sits cross-legged on Twitchell's desk. Meanwhile, Clark Bent hopes to win Pain's affection with a pearl necklace he bought for her with his savings. Pain rejects him, but Bent has other work ahead of him. On the story's fourth page, he remarks, "The 'Unknown Monster,' eh! This is a job for *Superduperman!*" before ducking into a crowded phone booth.[21]

Kurtzman and Wood fill the next three pages with fight scenes. First, however, Superduperman encounters Billy Spafon. Like Billy Batson, and like Miracleman's alter ego Mike Moran, Spafon has a magic word that transforms him into a mighty, godlike being. However, unlike Captain Marvel, whose word *Shazam* calls on the power of Solomon, Hercules, Atlas, Zeus, Achilles, and Mercury, Billy Spafon's word *Shazoom* stands for "Strength/Health/Aptitude/Zeal/ Ox, Power of/Ox, Power of Another/ Money!"[22] While he might be a monster, Captain Marbles turns out to be more honest than the self-deluded Superduperman. Marbles has set clear goals for himself. He's not in the hero business for love or justice. The fame and the glory are okay, but mostly he's in it for the money. To prove it, he proudly wears a dollar sign on his chest.[23]

On the next page, Kurztman and Wood include a six-panel sequence in which Superduperman tosses a large safe and an entire building at Captain Marbles. The page's final panel is as messy as the story's opening: here, sitting on a pile of rubble, a kitchen sink perched on his blond head, Captain Marbles counts the money from the demolished safe (see fig. 21-2). Wreckage surrounds them. Behind Superduperman is the window of another tenement building. In the distance, we see more ruins, vacant windows, and a clear, empty sky. White light frames the right side of Superduperman's body. The two characters stand (or, in Captain Marbles's case, sit) revealed: Billy Spafon's greed, Superduperman's stupidity (6).

There's little time for reflection here as, on the next page, the battle continues. Finally, Superduperman tricks Captain Marbles, and the villain punches himself in the head with a loud "Ba-Roompf!" (7). This last panel, with Superduperman proclaiming victory while beating his chest, should bring the story to a close. Kurtzman and Wood, however, include a final page that imagines the bleak world that awaits Clark Bent after this display of heroism and self-sacrifice.

Writing a good story, Kurtzman explains in his autobiography, is like telling a joke. "The ending," Kurtzman writes, "must be like puncturing

Fig. 21-2: Captain Marbles, Kurtzman and Wood's caricature of Bill Parker and C. C. Beck's Captain Marvel, admits his love for "good ol' do re mi" ("Superduperman!," *Mad* #4, 4–5/53: 6). MAD used with permission.

a balloon—it should release the energy you've put in the story and set the reader up for a surprise. It should be sharp and short, like a balloon exploding. The main thing is to give the reader the excitement of the BANG!"[24] In the case of "Superduperman!," he explains, the joke ends when our hero, in the closing panels, reveals his double identity to Lois Pain: "But she *still* thinks Clark is a creep, because once a creep, always a creep! And that would be my punchline, my BANG!"[25] For a moment, we believe there might be a happy ending. Will Superduperman get the girl at last? In a conventional superhero comic, he would, but Kurtzman and Wood have a different fate in mind for the hapless office boy.

Now that Captain Marbles has been sealed in a "carbon steel block," Superduperman stands erect, as Lois Pain, transfixed, stares at him (see fig. 21-3). A group of young boys encircles the pair. One of them points at Superduperman while the others stare in admiration. Superduperman reminds Lois Pain of her conduct toward Clark Bent: "And as for you, *hah*, Lois Pain, girl reporter . . . [it] just so happens *my* true identity is *Clark Bent* . . . man assistant to the copy boy! Whata burner on you, huh?" (Kurtzman and Wood 8). Wood again fills this panel—like the one that opens the comic—with small, seemingly insignificant details: Lois Pain, the little boys, the carbon steel block, a crane, a man in a bow tie and tuxedo, two more tenement buildings.

The story's explosive ending—the "BANG!" that Kurtzman describes in his autobiography—takes place between the third and fourth panels of the story's eighth and final page. This is a moment like the one Scott McCloud describes in *Understanding Comics* when he discusses a two-panel sequence in which one character attacks another with an ax: "Every act committed to paper by the comics artist is *aided* and *abetted* by a *silent accomplice*," explains McCloud's avatar, "an *equal partner in crime* known as *the reader*."[26] Superduperman's moment of glory fades quickly as he leans towards Lois Pain and, laughing, takes hold of her arm: "*Hah*! And I supposen't now you'd give your bottom dollar for me to sniff your perfume I supposen't! Where'zat ol' bottom dollar?" Pain responds to the lewd comment, and to Superduperman's smarmy expression, with a blunt "*Hands off!*" before she clobbers him (8). This moment of rejection and humiliation takes place in the gutter that separates the panels. "To kill a man between panels is to condemn him to a thousand deaths," argues McCloud.[27] If this is true, the reader acts as the "silent accomplice" here, the one who, along with Lois Pain, "condemns" Superduperman/

Fig. 21-3: A defeated Clark Bent returns to his job as the assistant copy boy on the last page of Kurtzman and Wood's "Superduperman!" (*Mad* #4, 4–5/53: 8). MAD used with permission.

Clark Bent to this endless cycle of humiliation and frustration. We must imagine the force with which Lois struck him, the look of shock on his face, his collapse. In the next panel, Superduperman, a halo of cartoon stars circling his head, lies on his back as the little boys laugh at his misfortune. "Yer *still* a creep!" shouts Lois Pain (8). The boys invite us to laugh along with them as Kurtzman and Wood drive home their point: like Captain Marbles, Superduperman got just what he deserved.[28]

Kurtzman and Wood then include three panels that mirror the story's first page. On page 1, Wood slowly zooms in on the offices of the *Daily Dirt*, the skyscraper shrouded by thick, white clouds. We then see an open window, a "Post No Bills" sign just above the ledge, a figure inside a cramped office. Finally, we see Clark Bent himself. Kurtzman and Wood repeat this image of Clark Bent in the first of the final three panels on page 8. This time, however, Wood includes fewer of the self-help broadsides that appeared on page 1. The shadows are now deeper, the walls more textured. The white light that illuminated Superduperman has faded. In the next panel, which features a block of text that recalls the words that open the story, we read about this "incredibly wretched and miserable looking creep," not the "man assistant to the copy boy," as Superduperman described himself at the top of the page, but merely the "assistant copy boy," a figure wearing a heavy, brown suit covered in patches of red, yellow, and green (8).

In the story's last panel, we look upwards at the skyscraper as Clark Bent's final words—"Chugachugga chugga chug"—emanate from the office window. These sounds echo the violent, mechanical, onomatopoeic soundtrack of Walter Mitty's daydreams in James Thurber's 1939 short story: "ta-pocketa-pocketa-pocketa-*pocketa-pocketa*."[29] But while Thurber's hero ends a shopping trip with his wife to Waterbury, Connecticut, "erect and motionless, proud and disdainful,"[30] Clark Bent, no longer Superduperman, disappears, hidden by the gray and white clouds that obscure the building. All his disappointment and failure will return, haunting him again and again, just as comic book heroes with miraculous powers fight the same battles over and over, one issue after the next.

These fantasies, Kurtzman reminds his reader, fail in their promise to offer a means of escape from this cycle of despair and anxiety. In 1973, Arthur Asa Berger reflected on the limits of the Superman myth in a passage that anticipates Moore's conflicted heroes of the 1980s, noting that "by the time the average man reaches his middle thirties, life seems to close in on him and he begins to realize that not much is likely to change, that he isn't a superman, and that heroic will power is not enough to help him realize his dreams."[31] Kurtzman and Wood had reached that conclusion two decades earlier, but, despite the gloomy, definitive ending of Clark Bent's adventures, *Mad*'s mastermind wasn't done with the Last Son of Krypton just yet. In *Help* #15 (1962), Kurtzman and Will Elder's Goodman Beaver met the semi-retired hero in "Goodman Meets S*perm*an." In the early 1980s, cartoonist Don Simpson would also build on Kurtzman's example with Megaton Man, a grotesque hero whose adventures lampooned the worst excesses and absurdities of the Marvel and DC comics of the 1960s. While Kurtzman and Elder's S*perm*n and Simpson's Kitchen Sink series emphasized the slapstick absurdity of these superheroes and their dim-witted alter egos, Alan Moore explored more fully in *Miracleman* the silence and the tragedy that permeate the last three panels of "Superduperman!"

Another 1950s hero, the original Marvelman would never have sported a pound sterling symbol on his chest or harassed the innocent citizens as Captain Marbles does. His adventures also lacked the spirited inventiveness of artist C. C. Beck and writer Otto Binder's best Captain Marvel stories of the late 1940s and early 1950s. After Fawcett ceased publication of comics featuring Parker and Beck's beloved hero and the other members of the Marvel Family, Mick Anglo created a replacement for British readers.[32] Moore and artist Garry Leach revived the character for Dez Skinn's magazine *Warrior* in 1982. Three years later, cat yronwode and Dean Mullaney's Eclipse Comics, based at the time in Guerneville, California, began reprinting those stories for U.S. readers. Due to a concern about possible legal action from Marvel Comics, Eclipse used the name *Miracleman* for the character and for the series. The first Eclipse issue appeared in the summer of 1985.[33]

For Moore, writing Marvelman proved to be the realization of a childhood dream. In his interview with George Khoury, Moore explains that as an 11-year-old, he first read Kurtzman's work and felt inspired to write his own stories. "I wanted to do a super-hero parody story that was as funny as 'Superduperman' but I thought it would be better if I did it about an English super-hero," he explained; that "idea started to resurface again" after he had "started working in comics" as an adult.[34] In the essay that appears in *Miracleman* #2 (October 1985), Moore elaborates further: "I was struck," he writes, "by the image of the eternally youthful and exuberant hero as a middle-aged man, trudging the streets and trying fruitlessly to remember his magic word."[35] There are two levels of nostalgia at work here: in Moore's first installment of the series, Miracleman's alter ego Mike Moran hopes to return to a life of innocent adventure while Moore himself takes pleasure in remembering these relics from the popular culture of a different era.[36] Comics writer Grant Morrison suggests that Moran, who "[longs] with wistful, bittersweet nostalgia for the surging vitality and confidence of his youth,"[37] serves as a proxy for Moore's readers. Those readers, Morrison writes, are members of "comics' aging demographic, its shrinking fan market composed of people in their late teens, twenties, and even thirties who'd grown up with these heroes and still found it hard or unreasonable to let go."[38] Morrison's argument, while compelling, ignores the more personal dimensions of the series, in which Moore grapples with both his love for and his reservations about the superhero genre and the comics medium itself.[39]

To borrow a phrase from the first track of Roxy Music's 1972 debut album, Moore does indeed set out to "re-make" and "re-model" these fragments from his childhood. However, in the proposal he submitted to Dez Skinn, he makes clear his cautious relationship to nostalgia: "In my opinion," he writes, "the central appeal of nostalgia is that all this stuff in the past has gone. It's finished."[40] Moran, then, is not so much a stand-in for Marvelman's readers as he is for Moore himself, who wanted to contrast "the naïve and simplistic Marvelman concept of the Fifties" with "a cruel and cynical Eighties"; Moore was convinced that "[t]he resultant tension [would] hopefully provide a real charge and poignance."[41] What Moore failed to recognize, at least early in the series, was that Kurtzman had already applied this "cynicism" to characters like Superman and Captain Marvel. In "Superduperman!," he and Wood revealed the brutal emptiness of U.S. mass culture in the 1950s. While Kurtzman and Wood ignored the "poignance" of Clark Bent's failure, Moore placed that sense of loss—one only made worse by the pull of nostalgia—at the heart of his project. In *Miracleman*, Kurtzman's "Superduperman!" collides with Moore's sensibility, one shaped by postwar Britain, rock and roll, the Marvel and DC Comics of the 1960s, underground comix, glam rock, and the science fiction of Michael Moorcock and J. G. Ballard. In Kurtzman's narrative, Moore sensed a possible future even for the lonely, the isolated, and the forgotten.[42]

In his conversation with Khoury, Moore explains how "Superduperman!" inspired his work on other superhero comics:

> The way that Harvey Kurtzman used to make his super-hero parodies so funny was to take a super-hero and then kind of apply sort of real world logic to a kind of inherently absurd super-hero situation, and that was what made his stuff so funny. It struck me that if you just turn the dial to the same degree in the other direction by applying real life logic to a super-hero, you could make something that was very funny, but you could also, with a turn of the screw, make something that was quite startling, sort of dramatic and powerful. . . . [43]

In keeping with these themes of memory and nostalgia, the Eclipse version of *Miracleman* #1 begins with a 1950s flashback sequence. After Miracleman and the rest of the Miracleman Family defeat an army of time travelers, a page with five panels introduces the prologue of "A Dream of Flying" (see fig. 21-4).

Moore and artist Garry Leach begin the story not with one of Kurtzman and Wood's explosive opening panels but with a series of wide-angle rectangles. Leach closely followed Moore's directions for this opening sequence.[44] In his script, Moore explains his vision: "I see this as maybe a wide horizontal frame . . . in fact maybe it would look nice if all these first four prologue frames were horizontal ones arranged in tiers. See what you think."[45] We see two men in a truck on a motorway in "the sodium-lit hour before dawn."[46] These images, which were printed in black and white when they first appeared in *Warrior*, establish a pattern for the rest of this first installment: just as Superduperman's world is one of skyscrapers, tenements, and advertisements, Mike Moran's England is a world of machines, including the delivery trucks on the first page and the enormous spacecraft on the one that follows.

This is not a traditional splash page. The first time we clearly see our hero, he is fighting to escape a nightmare in which he and the other members of the Miracleman Family are destroyed by a nuclear bomb hidden in what appears to be an alien ship. The density of Moore's prose, and the heaviness of Leach's linework—which itself owes a debt to the realism of Wally Wood's other EC work—conveys the terror of what it

Fig. 21-4: Alan Moore and Garry Leach provide a shadowy, evocative opening to Mike Moran's story (*Miracleman* #1, Eclipse Comics [Marvel], 8/85: 12). Used with permission of Marvel Comics.

is to be Mike Moran: a man haunted by dreams, plagued by migraines, tethered to the earth and to its sodium lights and motorways.[47]

Assigned to cover the protests at a nuclear power plant, Moran moves ever closer to his destiny. "If only I could remember that damn word," he reflects as he rides the train. "Kimono? No. Komodo? No. Krakatoa? No. Jesus, this headache."[48] At the end of this first installment, Moran finally recalls his magic word, *Kimota* (*atomic* spelled with a *k* and reversed), which stares back at him on a sign that reads "Atomic Power Station." He speaks the word, regains his powers, and defeats the terrorists threatening the plant. In the final two panels of this first part of the narrative, Moore and Leach include an image that expresses the pleasure and excitement of Moran's sudden victory. The hero shouts, "I'm Miracleman . . . I'm back!!" With the earth beneath him and the moon at his back, he raises a fist in triumph (see fig. 21-5). "His face," Moore notes in his script, "is totally suffused with the most incredible smile of freedom, joy and exaltation."[49]

Moore's use of the word *joy* is significant. He will use the word again in his conversation with George Khoury when they discuss the third book of *Miracleman*, illustrated by John Totleben with colors by Sam Parsons. In a discussion of those later narratives in the series, Moore describes the visual complexity of Totleben's art: "I think we were closing in on something, an intensity. An intensity of vision and an intensity of language. I remember when I was writing the last book of *Miracleman*, I actually wrote with music. I don't very often do that."[50] Moore listened to Brian Eno's ambient works, including *Thursday Afternoon* (1985) and *Apollo: Atmospheres and Soundtracks* (1983, a collaboration with Daniel Lanois and Roger Eno). The music, Moore explains, had "an effect upon the prose" in *Swamp Thing* and in these final sequences of *Miracleman*: "It became a bit more cerebral, reflective, beautiful, well thought [out], more elaborate if you like. I was trying to actually get some of the same joyous quality into the language as John was getting into the artwork. To sort of come up with a prose style that lived up to John's extraordinary pictures."[51] By writing about these characters, by transforming them—by quoting from the past, in other words—Moore, like Mike Moran, sets out to free himself from the burden of that past, one obscured by the relics of the 1950s. At the same time, with Eno as his guide, Moore arranged the fragments of his childhood, those quotations, into a meaningful present, one shaped by the deceptively static nature of these ambient

Fig. 21-5: Mike Moran remembers his magic word and experiences the power it brings with it (*Miracleman* #1, Eclipse Comics [Marvel], 8/85: 19). Used with permission of Marvel Comics.

soundscapes.[52] While perhaps best known as a producer for bands including Devo, Talking Heads, and U2, Eno and painter Peter Schmidt also collaborated on a deck of cards called *Oblique Strategies*, a collection of often gnomic statements designed to assist when "a dilemma occurs in a working situation."[53] The most famous of these cards is the one that reminds us that "Repetition is a form of change." While Clark Bent is incapable of grasping that lesson, Mike Moran, if only briefly, discovers that repetition might be a source of joy, but only when practiced in silence. Some magic words, Moore suggests, are best remembered then left unspoken.

It may seem strange to speak of the "joy" of *Miracleman* given Mike Moran's fate on pages 10 and 11 of issue #14.[54] The issue includes two parallel narratives. In one, Miracleman dances and, as he does so, remembers the events leading up to the destruction of London, which readers experience in grisly detail in issue #15 (November 1988). On the left side of page 10, Miracleman, naked to the waist, covers his face as he recalls Moran's trip to the Scottish Highlands. Now alone, the hero's alter ego finds life unbearable without his wife Liz and their daughter Winter. To emphasize the character's pain, Totleben has designed these two pages as a series of fragments. Once Moran begins his climb, standing like Petrarch at the foot of Mont Ventoux, Miracleman's "dance grows weary, echoing his solitary ascent. It is the dance of crippled birds, of Bergman films and brown-skinned children holding sugar skulls." After this caption, there is a space, and then one final piece of text before Moran completes his last journey: "It is the dance of death."[55] Totleben frames this sequence with two panels that resemble a continent split in two. The two sides of Mike Moran/Miracleman have at last become separate entities. The orderly panels that Totleben includes between these two fractured, diagonal images suggest Moran's determination. He has no intention of ever returning to the foot of the mountain.

Moran appears determined as he climbs from one rock to the next. He then looks at one of the other hills in the distance, just before he unbuttons his shirt. Three panels later he is naked. He writes something on a sheet of paper. In the next panel, he places that sheet of paper beneath a stone, and then says his magic word—the one he struggled so long to remember—one last time. In the lower, right-hand corner of page 11, we see his note, a message to his alter ego: "Michael Joseph Moran 1942–1983." At the bottom of the sheet he has added the phrase

Fig. 21-6: Miracleman recalls his alter ego Mike Moran's final request (*Miracleman* #14, Eclipse Comics [Marvel], 4/88: 10-11). Scan courtesy of Dr. Gene Kannenberg, Jr. Used with permission of Marvel Comics.

"Rest in Peace." On the following page, Miracleman reflects on Moran's self-destruction: "The curious suicide was understandable: he'd tired of marvels; of their cost in human warmth. His wish was for oblivion. Respecting it, I've not pronounced my word of transformation since that night."[56] Here, Moore at last reveals the office boy's true fate, the grim "punchline" of "Superduperman!" Clark Bent is a suicide. Arthur Asa Berger argued in 1973 that Superman "symbolizes a basic split within the American psyche," one that represents a "disparity between [our] dreams and [our] achievements,"[57] a division especially evident in Kurtzman's parodies of the Man of Steel and of the World's Mightiest Mortal. In 1961, just three years before Marcuse's *One-Dimensional Man* and less than a decade after *Mad*'s fourth issue, Edward Robb Ellis and George N. Allen published *Traitor Within: Our Suicide Problem*, a study that sounded the alarm on the crisis while at the same time calling into question the nation's rosy assessment of its postwar achievements. How could it be that, in "the richest and technologically most advanced civilization in history," suicide remained such a problem, with 18,519 people having taken their lives in 1958?[58] While Mike Moran is a British character, his decision to end his life is the logical narrative conclusion of Kurtzman's "Superduperman!" Only a fan who loved and studied these old comics as much as Moore had could recognize in them the sadness that lies at the heart of these seemingly innocent childhood fantasies, ones that too often mask real-life tragedies.

It would be too easy, however, to argue that Moran's suicide is merely another of Moore's attempts to apply "real world logic" to these fictions.[59] With Kurtzman's parody as his model, he dispensed with slapstick humor and, as he noted to Khoury, sought to create the kind of emotional intensity not found in the pages of *Mad*. Clark Bent, like a shadow in the seventh circle of Dante's hell, is doomed to destroy himself for eternity. Just as Dante's suicides will harm themselves again and again, their wounds healing each time, so Clark Bent will, as Lois Pain remarks, always be a creep, always fail, always find himself lonely and consumptive in the offices of the *Daily Dirt*. At first glance, Bent might appear to be a not-so-distant relative of Arthur Miller's Willy Loman, a fatalistic variation on Thurber's Walter Mitty who ends his life and leaves his wife and sons to make sense of the world that destroyed him (Miller, perhaps unconsciously, suggests a link to Mitty by including Loman's fond memories of Waterbury's clock industry in the opening of the play). While Moore, like Kurtzman, is searching for the "truth" concealed by Miracleman's original adventures, what the British writer finds there is a space filled by the "waste" that surrounded Marcuse's one-dimensional man of the 1950s and early 1960s.[60] Kurtzman and Wood's "Superduperman!" demands that we, like Moore, grapple with the void that Clark Bent represents, but Moore's portrait of Miracleman's alter ego is more compassionate, more nuanced, and—to borrow one of Moore's own phrases—less "cruel" than Kurtzman and Wood's parody. Rather than condemning Miracleman's other self, casting him as one of Dante's hopeless shadows, Moore creates a full and even loving portrait of Moran, a working man who bravely struggles against the fate that pursues him.

In November 2013, Stuart Kelly asked Alan Moore a few questions about superhero comic books. Had the writer, for example, heard about Geoff Johns's Moore-inspired work on *Green Lantern*? Moore replied:

> I hate superheroes. I think they're abominations. They don't mean what they used to mean. They were originally in the hands of writers who would actively expand the imagination of their nine- to 13-year-old audience. That was completely what they were meant to do and they were doing it excellently.[61]

After a few remarks on Hollywood's successful comic book franchises, Moore adds, "I don't think the superhero stands for anything good. I think it's a rather alarming sign if we've got audiences of adults going to see the *Avengers* movie and delighting in concepts and characters meant to entertain the 12-year-old boys of the 1950s."[62] To quote again and again from the past is to admit a kind of failure, a capitulation to the repetition and drudgery of Marcuse's—and Clark Bent's—landscape of junk.[63]

In this grim assessment of the superhero genre, Moore sounds like a man trying one last time to protect the memories of that 11-year old kid who delighted in the comics of Mort Weisinger, Edmond Hamilton, Otto Binder, Curt Swan, Wayne Boring, Kurt Schaffenberger, and the other men and women who crafted Superman's adventures in the first place over half a century ago.[64] Moore understands what Moran recognized too late: some aspects of childhood are best left in the past. On the last page of *Miracleman* #16, our hero remembers his wife Liz. As he looks down upon London, he asks "why anyone should not wish to be perfect in a perfect world."[65] Miracleman finds himself speechless when he ponders the human need for change. In another caption, he admits, "Sometimes, I wonder why that bothers me, and sometimes. . . . " There is a pause. Moran's alter ego, his hand on his chin, looks regal in a costume that resembles the one worn by C. C. Beck's original Captain Marvel: ". . . sometimes," he concludes, bringing Moore's childhood dream to an end, "I just wonder." In his silence, Miracleman offers one last piece of advice. Even if you manage to remember your magic word, maybe it's better to keep it, and all the nostalgic wonders that it represents, to yourself.

Notes

1. For details on the demise of the original Captain Marvel and the National vs. Fawcett lawsuit, see the "Shazam" chapter of Jim Steranko's *The Steranko History of Comics 2*, 20–21; and Brian Cremins, *Captain Marvel and the Art of Nostalgia*, 3–8. Perhaps the best and most concise overview of these legal battles is Bob Ingersoll, "The Cheese Stands Accused! A Look at the Superman/Captain Marvel Litigation," 20–23.

2. George Khoury, "Revival and Revelation," 11. Now out of print, *Kimota!* is an essential resource on *Miracleman*, including an interview with Moore, his proposal and script for his first *Marvelman* story (57–65), and other features on the history of the character and the Eclipse series.

In this essay, I cite the Eclipse issues of *Miracleman* published in the mid-to-late 1980s. I therefore refer to the character as Miracleman and not as Marvelman unless I am specifically referring to Mick Anglo's work or to the installments that appeared in *Warrior* in the early 1980s.

In the section of the essay devoted to "Superduperman!," my close readings are based on the reprint in Harvey Kurtzman with Michael Barrier, *From Aargh! to Zap!: Harvey Kurtzman's Visual History of Comics*, 48–49.

3. Alan Moore, "M*****man: Full Story and Pics," 31.

4. See Khoury, "Revival and Revelation," 11–12, 17–18.

5. Svetlana Boym, *The Future of Nostalgia*, xiii. Among the many recent scholarly studies of nostalgia in the humanities and in the social sciences, Boym's is a good starting point. For older studies offering valuable insights on the history of nostalgia as both a medical term and as a philosophical idea, see Fred Davis, *Yearning for Yesterday: A Sociology of Nostalgia*; and Edward S. Casey, "The World of Nostalgia," 361–84, which points out that Johannes Hofer's 1688 definition of the term "goes so far as to claim that nostalgia is 'symptomatic of an afflicted imagination,' *not* of a disturbed memory" (366–67). Recent psychological studies of nostalgia and its effects on the human body, include Clay Routledge et al., "Finding Meaning in One's Past: Nostalgia as Existential Resource," 297–316. For a discussion of comic book collectors and nostalgia, see Bart Beaty's *Comics Versus Art*, chap. 7, esp. 152–82; and Cremins, *Captain Marvel*, chap. 5.

6. Alan Moore, John Totleben, Sam Parsons, Wayne Truman, and Letitia Gomez, "Olympus," 3.

7. Khoury, "Revival and Revelation," 17–18.

8. Regarding comic books, childhood, and nostalgia, Thierry Groensteen argues that we cannot "avoid seeing that so many of our paper heroes prolong the little boy's fantasies of freedom and omnipotence, and offer us a chance to act them out . . . vicariously." See Groensteen, "Why Are Comics Still in Search of Cultural Legitimization?," 11.

9. For a discussion of the interview with Eno, see Alan Moore, "Indoor Thunder: Landscaping the Future with Brian Eno," 29, 34.

10. Alan Moore, interview with Brian Eno, BBC Radio 4, Chain Reaction Series, December 14, 2004; reissued on MP3 as *Chain Reaction: Alan Moore Interviews Brian Eno*, series 5, episode 6, 2011.

11. Brian Eno anticipates these reflections on the relationship between past and future in his liner notes to *Ambient 4: On Land*, CD 1982, rev. February 1986: "This often happens: you imagine a territory rich in possibilities and try to think of how you might get to it, and then suddenly one day you look around and realise that you have been there for quite a long time."

12. Maria Reidelbach, *Completely Mad: A History of the Comic Book and Magazine*, 18–41, discusses "Superduperman!" in her history of *Mad* under Kurtzman. Denis Kitchen and Paul Buhle, *The Art of Harvey Kurtzman: The Mad Genius of Comics*, publish Kurtzman's pencil breakdowns of "Superduperman!" (96–97) and reprint the story itself (98–105). For Kurtzman's own views of the story and *Mad*, see Harvey Kurtzman, interview with Kim Thompson and Gary Groth, in *The New Comics: Interviews from the Pages of The Comics Journal*, ed. Gary Groth and Robert Fiore, 24–38; Kurtzman, *My Life as a Cartoonist*, with Howard Zimmerman; and Kurtzman with Barrier, *From Aargh! to Zap!*, 28–51. Kurtzman also briefly discusses *Mad* in the 1987 video documentary *The Masters of Comic Book Art*, directed by Ken Viola, 60 min., which features introductions to each segment by science fiction writer and essayist Harlan Ellison.

13. National almost sued EC over "Superduperman!," but Kurtzman saved the day, as detailed in Reidelbach, *Completely Mad*, 23: publisher Bill Gaines "considered submitting" before National took any further action, but "Kurtzman knew that the future of *Mad* lay in doing satires and parodies, and he was not about to let the success of his new comic be threatened." After Kurtzman intervened, National ultimately decided not to pursue the lawsuit. For more details on Kurtzman's forward-thinking action, see Kitchen and Buhle, *The Art of Harvey Kurtzman*, 86.

14. Kitchen and Buhle, *The Art of Harvey Kurtzman*, 86–87.

15. Kurtzman, commentary on "Superduperman!," in Kurtzman with Barrier, *From Aargh! To Zap!*, 48.

16. Kitchen and Buhle, *The Art of Harvey Kurtzman*, 86. On the role that truth plays in his parodies and satires—"I like to think that I pursued moral truths, but I don't like to think that I was telling anybody what's wrong and right"—see Kurtzman, interview with Thompson and Groth, in *The New Comics*, 32. For the impact of Kurtzman's satires on the underground comix artists of the 1960s and early 1970s in the U.S., see Art Spiegelman, "A Furshlugginer Genius!," 76–77; also reprinted in his *MetaMaus*, 191–92. For Spiegelman, "*Mad* was an urban junk collage that said 'Pay attention! The mass media are *lying* to you ... including this comic book!'" (76).

17. Herbert Marcuse, *One-Dimensional Man: Studies in the Ideology of Advanced Industrial Society*, 7.

18. For more on Superman and American notions of masculinity during World War II, see Michael Kimmel, *Manhood in America: A Cultural History*, 212; and Cremins, *Captain Marvel*, chap. 3.

19. Kurtzman with Barrier, *From Aargh! to Zap!*, 41.

20. Harvey Kurtzman, interview with John Benson, in *The Complete First Six Issues of Mad*, n.p. Kurtzman talks in more detail about Wood and other *Mad* artists in *My Life as a Cartoonist*: "Wally Wood would labor over a story," Kurtzman writes. "He was a very creative person, and he didn't like being forced to follow my layouts. So he would spend time trying to do the story in different ways. But most of the time, he would come back to my layouts" (68).

21. Kurtzman, *My Life as a Cartoonist*, 3–4.

22. Kurtzman, *My Life as a Cartoonist*, 5.

23. Readers familiar with Captain Marvel will know that the hero's emblem is a lightning bolt. See Gershon Legman, *Love & Death: A Study in Censorship*, 42, for his controversial discussion of Superman's *S* and Captain Marvel's symbol. Responses to Legman's analysis include Bradford Wright, *Comic Book Nation: The Transformation of Youth Culture in America*, 91–92; and Brannon Costello, "Fascism and Mass Culture in Howard Chaykin's *Blackhawk*," paragraph 2.

24. Kurtzman, *My Life as a Cartoonist*, 64.

25. Kurtzman, *My Life as a Cartoonist*, 64.

26. Scott McCloud, *Understanding Comics: The Invisible Art*, 68.

27. McCloud, *Understanding Comics*, 69.

28. The formula of the trick ending in which one character gets revenge on another would have been familiar to readers of EC's other comics, especially its horror titles; see Qiana Whitted, *EC Comics: Race, Shock & Social Protest*.

29. James Thurber, *The Thurber Carnival*, 47.

30. Thurber, *The Thurber Carnival*, 51.

31. Arthur Asa Berger, *The Comic-Stripped American*, 157.

32. For the complex history of Marvelman and *Miracleman*, see Pádraig Ó Méalóid, "Poisoned Chalice: The Extremely Long and Incredibly Complex Story of *Marvelman*." Ó Méalóid's series of articles began with the February 2, 2013, post at www.comicsbeat.com and includes an interview with Moore. Roy Thomas's fanzine *Alter Ego*, no. 87 (July 2009), includes several articles on Marvelman/Miracleman. Julian Darius provides links to other installments in "Why Miracleman Matters." For a critical overview of Moore's work, see Annalisa Di Liddo, *Alan Moore: Comics as Performance, Fiction as Scalpel*. When Marvel Comics brought the series *Miracleman* back into print in March 2014, Moore requested that his name not be used on the reprints, so he is listed instead as "The Original Writer."

33. Moore, "M*****man," 31, discusses "a certain major American comic company (not DC)" and the change from Marvelman to Miracleman.

34. Quoted in Khoury, "Revival and Revelation," 11.

35. Moore, "M*****man," 31.

36. Ben Saunders argues in *Do the Gods Wear Capes? Spirituality, Fantasy, and Superheroes*, 2, that *Miracleman* raises questions about love and "desire," contending that Mike Moran "wants to feel a love that is 'like poetry,' unsullied by either his own human imperfections or those of his no less human partner." For additional readings of Moore's *Miracleman* and its relationship to his other, better known work, see Paul Atkinson, "The Time of Heroes: Narrative, Progress, and Eternity in *Miracleman*," 44–63; and Cremins, *Captain Marvel*, chap. 4, which focuses on Moore's critique of racial stereotypes in the series.

37. Grant Morrison, *Supergods: What Masked Vigilantes, Miraculous Mutants, and a Sun God from Smallville Can Teach Us About Being Human*, 184.

38. Morrison, *Supergods*, 184.

39. Morrison, *Supergods*, 183–86, offers additional commentary on Moran's suicide.

40. Alan Moore, "Alan Moore's Original Proposal," in *Kimota!*, edited by George Khoury, 24.

41. Moore, "Alan Moore's Original Proposal," in *Kimota!*, edited by Khoury, 24.

42. In his 2011 interview with Chris Richards, Moore discusses his affection for Moorcock's work as both writer and editor: "I picked up *New Worlds* and realized at the age of 14 that it wasn't like any science fiction stories I had previously read. This was proper speculative fiction; it was people like J. G. Ballard and M. John Harrison, John Sladek, wonderful writers, and Moorcock himself of course." See Moore, interview with Chris Richards, in *The Art of Dismantling: A Radical Artisan Collective and Ongoing Interview Series*, audio and transcript.

43. Khoury, "Revival and Revelation," 11–12.

44. Moore, "Alan Moore's Original Proposal," in *Kimota!*, edited by Khoury, 24–29.

45. Alan Moore, "Alan Moore Script for *Miracleman* #1" in *Kimota!*, edited by George Khoury, 57.

46. Alan Moore, Garry Leach, and G. George, "A Dream of Flying," 12.

47. Moore, Leach, and George, "A Dream of Flying," 14.

48. Moore, Leach, and George, "A Dream of Flying," 14.

49. Moore, "Alan Moore's Script for *Miracleman* #1," 65.

50. Quoted in Khoury, "Revival and Revelation," 17.

51. Quoted in Khoury, "Revival and Revelation," 18. For detail on Eno's ambient records, see Eric Tamm's *Brian Eno: His Music and the Vertical Color of Sound*; Mark Prendergast, *The Ambient Century: From Mahler to Trance—The Evolution of Sound in the Electronic Age*; and David Sheppard, *On Some Faraway Beach: The Life and Times of Brian Eno*.

52. By the time Eno finished the album *On Land*, he found himself exploring the relationship between place and nostalgia, reporting, "One of the inspirations for this record was Fellini's 'Amarcord' ('I Remember'), a presumably unfaithful reconstruction of childhood memories"; see Eno, liner notes to *Ambient 4*.

53. Brian Eno and Peter Schmidt, *Oblique Strategies: Over One Hundred Worthwhile Dilemmas*, 5th ed., 2001, deck of 7 x 9 cm. printed cards in a black container.

54. Alan Moore, John Totleben, Sam Parsons, Wayne Truman, and Letitia Glozer, "Pantheon," 10-11.

55. Moore et al., "Pantheon," 10.

56. Moore et al., "Pantheon," 12. As Jules Feiffer remarks in his essay on Billy Batson and Captain Marvel in *The Great Comic Book Heroes*, 25, "How easy it became to hate 'Shazam! Shazam! Shazam!' That taunting cry worked fine for Captain Marvel but didn't do a damn thing for the rest of us."

57. Berger, *The Comic-Stripped American*, 157.

58. Edward Robb Ellis and George N. Allen, *Traitor Within: Our Suicide Problem*, 3.

59. Quoted in Khoury, "Revival and Revelation," 11–12.

60. Marcuse, *One-Dimensional Man*, 7.

61. Quoted in Stuart Kelly, "Alan Moore: 'Why Shouldn't You Have a Bit of Fun While Dealing With the Deepest Issues of the Mind?': Alan Moore Talks about *Fashion Beast*, Jacques Derrida and Modern Superheroes."

62. Kelly, "Alan Moore." Moore's comments provoked a range of responses from comic book fans and writers on the web; see, for example, Hannah Means Shannon, "Are We 'Emotionally Subnormal'? Pondering Alan Moore's Assessment of Superhero Readers;" and Chris Gavaler, "I Hate Superheroes."

63. In a discussion of Lawrence Kasdan's 1981 film *Body Heat*, Fredric Jameson offers a warning about this cultural inability to contend with the present: "It seems to me exceedingly symptomatic to find the very style of nostalgia films invading and colonizing even those movies today which have contemporary settings, as though, for some reason, we were unable today to focus our own present, as though we had become incapable of achieving aesthetic representations of our own current experience." See Jameson, "Postmodernism and Consumer Society" in *The Cultural Turn: Selected Writings on the Postmodern 1983–1998*, 9–10.

64. In 1986, Moore paid tribute to these writers in a two-part story: Alan Moore, Curt Swan, and George Perez, "Whatever Happened to the Man of Tomorrow? [Part I]" and Alan Moore, Curt Swan, and Kurt Schaffenberger, "Whatever Happened to the Man of Tomorrow? [Part II]."

65. Moore et al., "Olympus," 33.

PART VI.
RESOURCES

Mad's "Usual Gang of Idiots":

Selected Capsule Biographies

Joe Otto and *Judith Yaross Lee*

THE BRIEF BIOGRAPHIES below aim to historicize prominent members of "The Usual Gang of Idiots," especially those whose contributions to *Mad* receive attention in this volume. For a comprehensive list of every identifiable member of the Gang keyed to each issue's contents, see Doug Gilford's *Mad Covers Site*, www.madcoversite.com/ugoi-master.html, which supplied many details here on items published after the 2006 *Absolutely Mad* archive on DVD. Mike Slaubaugh's *MAD Magazine Lists*, http://users.pfw.edu/slaubau/mad.htm, also contains contributors' information. The noticeable lack of women listed below reflects the masculine culture that dominates commercial comics publishing. Contributions by women noticeably increased in the new series (#1, 6/18), when Suzy Hutchinson became art director.

Sergio Aragonés debuted in *Mad* with contributions across the January 1963 issue (#76): writing the cover (painted by Norman Mingo), creating "A MAD Look at the U.S. Space Effort" (20–21), and drawing "Drawn-Out Drama" pantomime narratives squeezed into the margins and gutters of other features. (*Totally Mad* credits Aragonés with art for "Mad's Bonus: Window Stickers" in the 1962 annual, but his first appearance in a regular issue undoubtedly comes in #76). Aragonés sustained this auspicious start with art, writing, or ideas in nearly every issue of *Mad* through the end of 2019 and into 2020.

Dave Berg first contributed to *Mad* magazine in 1957 with "Modern Furniture" under the byline David Berg (#34, 8/57: 20–23). His best known work is the feature "The Lighter Side of . . . ," which began as a continuing department with " . . . the Television Set" in issue #66 (10/61: 16–19) after he contributed five variations on the "A MAD Look at . . ." series, starting with ". . . the Telephone" (#64, 7/61: 8–11). A classmate of John Severin and other Gang members at the High School of Music and Art, Berg also attended Cooper Union Art School and worked at Will Eisner's comics studio with Al Jaffee. Berg's work continued to appear in the magazine after his death in 2002, often with new dialogue as "The Darker Side of *The Lighter Side*," through #544 (4/17): 34-36.

Max Brandel contributed comic ideas, including design concepts, and writing with a strong political edge from 1966 to 1974, beginning with "MAD Photos that Prove That West Is West and East Is East" (#105, 9/66: 4–6), his first comically juxtaposed, repurposed, or edited photographs and other ready-made images that anticipated the ironic humor of photoshopped images and internet memes. Born in Poland and held during WWII in a German POW camp at Tittmoning Castle, Bavaria, Brandel moved to New York after the war; New York's Museum of Jewish Heritage exhibited his wartime drawings in 2016. Brandel died in 1975 at the age of 64.

John Caldwell first appeared in *Mad* with "A MAD Look at Some Unfinished Sentences," a collaboration with artist Bob Clarke (#202, 10/78: 20–21). Four years later Caldwell returned to write and illustrate "Urologist," a five-panel gag strip in color on the back cover of issue #230 (4/82), and four years after that began to hit his stride with the melodramatic three-panel narrative generically titled "Drama on Page 19" in issue #262 (4/86: 19). His "Drama on . . ." strips returned intermittently through #418 (6/02) along with a variety of other solo contributions over the three decades following his first "Drama" to #538 (4/16), including gags for most of the "Fundalini Pages" after its start in #438 (2/04).

Bob Clarke was a long-time utility artist for *Mad*, first contributing "Motorist Beware!" to issue #30 (12/56: 16–17) and appearing at least once—typically two or three times, and occasionally four—in nearly every issue through 1994. Across his four decades with the magazine, Clarke collaborated with most of its regular writers, including Frank Jacobs, Al Jaffee, Tom Koch, Arnie Kogen, and Duck Edwing. Editors Meglin and Ficarra honored him with an "Artist Spotlight" in *Mad XL* 28, "MAD's Idiot of the Month" (7/04: 34–35). His last appearance before his death in 2013 was on the "Fundalini Pages" of #500 (6/09).

Paul Coker, Jr. first contributed to *Mad* magazine in 1961 with art for "A MAD Peek Behind the Scenes," written by Phil Hahn (#60, 1/61: 22–23). Coker's art appeared regularly, often multiple times per issue, through the end of the original series, when he contributed a self-portrait misnamed "Jason Justin Dustin" to the rogues' gallery of *Mad* artists "Gotcha! Mug Shots of Common (But Despicable) Criminals" (#550, 4/18): 33-35; 33). For example, Coker has five separate credits in the 96-page jumbo Special #109 (12/98) and drew the distressed cook and chaotic kitchen for the spread "Recipe Directions You Hope You Never Read," by writer Jeff Kruse (#547, 8/17: 48–49). Slaubaugh ranks Coker fifth among all contributors for the number of issues in which he has appeared: 372.

Jack Davis debuted at the same time as *Mad*, with "Hoohah!," a send-up of horror stories from the "Terror Dept.," in issue #1 (10–11/52: 1–8). Davis contributed art consistently through *Mad*'s height in popularity, regularly collaborating with other Usual Gang members on film and TV satires that exploited his talent for rendering comic action. Davis published in *Mad* only twice between June 1957 and December 1965, when he worked with Kurtzman on *Humbug* and *Help!*, but appeared in most issues for the next three decades, through #354 (2/97).

Dick DeBartolo first contributed to *Mad* in 1962, its tenth year, as co-author with Al Jaffee of "Some TV Ads We Never Got to See" (#69, 3/62: 36–39), with Jack Rickard's art depicting several scenes of how the random tests of a product (in this case margarine) might actually happen. DeBartolo continued to write for *Mad* across the next five decades, contributing major movie parodies and satires for the "*Mad* 20 Dumbest" issues as well as "Fundalini" and one-off items, often in a single issue. He remained active with the magazine through 2020, in its new California series, and ranks third among all contributors in the number of issues including his work.

Jerry DeFuccio debuted as a *Mad* contributor in 1953, authoring "The Parole," a short story featured in between comics (#4, 4–5/53: 1–2). DeFuccio received only five credits between 1952 and 1998, although as an editorial staffer he had his hand in many *Mad* features between 1956 and 1980.

Desmond Devlin began writing for *Mad* with "The MAD 1984 Quiz" (#253, 3/85: 34–35), and ranks among *Mad*'s top contributors despite a late start.

His talent for one-off topics—"MAD's Parental Guide for Safe TV Viewing" (#333, 1/95: 46–47), "MAD Salutes Baseball Then and Now" (#351, 11/96: 9), "MAD's Handy Glossary to the War on Terror" (#438, 2/04: 16–17)—made him particularly valuable for filling pages between departments, but he also wrote book, TV, and film parodies, including "Star Bores: Half-Assed Jedi" for the debut issue of the new California series (#1, 6/18: 2–7) and most, though not all, of the scripts for the "Melvin & Jenkins" mock etiquette series.

Mort Drucker first contributed to *Mad* in "TV Advertising Award" in issue #32 (4/57: 23), and over the next half century became one of *Mad*'s most important artists. His masterful caricatures of politicians, film and television stars, and other celebrities fostered the development of satire in *Mad*'s film and TV parodies, beginning with "The Night *The Price Is All Right* Has an Unexcited Guest," written by Larry Siegel in #51 (12/59: 9-12), and continuing through "The Chronic-Ills of Yawnia—Prince Thespian," written by Dick DeBartolo in #493 (9/08: 44-47). Drucker remained a *Mad* contributor through January 2010 (#502), when he lampooned Glenn Beck for the 2009 "*Mad* 20 Dumbest" list as if he'd authored a book entitled *Act Like a Lunatic, Think Like a Maniac*. The National Cartoonists Society honored Drucker in 1987 with its Ruben Award and again in 2015 with its first Medal of Honor for lifetime achievement. His death at age 91 on April 9, 2020, drew expressions of appreciation and grief from colleagues and fans alike.

Don "Duck" Edwing began contributing to *Mad* in 1962 with "Scenes We'd Like to See (The Abominable Snowman)" (#70, 4/62: 40). Edwing appeared in the magazine periodically in the 1960s, picking up his pace of contribution in the 1970s and 1980s. Only a few issues appeared without his byline on multiple items during these two decades. Edwing's scripts for "Spy vs. Spy," drawn by Bob Clarke and others, ran from January 1987 (#268) to December 1994 (#332), sustaining the feature between Antonio Prohías's retirement and Peter Kuper's arrival.

William "Will" Elder, who signed his work variably, contributed to *Mad* from its inception, drawing Kurtzman's comic "Ganefs!" in the debut issue (#1, 10–11/52: 1–6). He continued as a *Mad* artist throughout the 1950s, then not again until the 1980s. His few credits in the 1970s consist of reprints of his past work in bonus issues of *Mad*. Elder did contribute new art again in the '80s, often collaborating with Harvey Kurtzman for either the cover or a large, image-heavy inside feature. The "Special Art Issue" (#22, 4/55) presents a mock-biography of the 34-year-old Elder from "The Young Child!" (1–3) to "Senility!" (28), with the same set of his drawings.

Albert "Al" Feldstein was the editor of *Mad* from 1956 to 1984, steering the magazine through its peak years of popularity and influence. After working in other comics studios, Feldstein joined the staff of EC Comics as an artist in 1948, but rose to edit a wide range of genres and titles for EC by 1954, when he inaugurated *Panic* as an in-house imitation of *Mad*. That assignment recognized his success at editing *Mad* #5 (6–7/53) when Kurtzman was on medical leave, and paved the way for Feldstein's appointment after Kurtzman's 1956 departure. As a contributor, Feldstein has eight credits spread out from issue #2 in 1952 until issue #130 in 1969, but his editorial leadership remains his chief legacy. Under Feldstein, *Mad* hired many of "The Usual Gang of Idiots" (a phrase he coined), including Mort Drucker, Don Martin, and Dave Berg, fostered its consistent departments, and promoted a leading role for the mascot to whom he gave one of his own pseudonyms, Alfred E. Neuman.

John Ficarra was associate editor of *Mad* from 1981 to 1985, co-editor with Nick Meglin from 1985 until 2004, and editor from 2005 to 2018, when he retired and *Mad* left New York City for Burbank, California. He earned several writer credits beginning with "Mad's Table of Little-Known and Very Useless Weights, Measures & Distances" (#210, 10/79: 32–33) and contributed consistently between 1981 and 1983. Ficarra had the longest editorial tenure at *Mad*, thirty-three years.

Mark Fredrickson has created cover and inside art for *Mad* since Special #93, *Unplugged*, in May 1994, and became the primary cover artist setting Alfred E. Neuman in new political, social, and media contexts with #431 (7/03). His December 2004 cover (#448) in which Alfred replaced baby Jack-Jack of the *Incredibles* animated movie reappeared on the October 2018 issue of German *Mad* (#184), while Fredrickson's portrait of Alfred playing Whack-a-Mole with the heads of American celebrities felled by scandals graced the cover of n.s. #3.

William M. "Bill" Gaines was the publisher of *Mad*, the last surviving title of EC Comics, until his death in 1992, although he sold the company in 1961. He gave Harvey Kurtzman the go-ahead to start the parody comic in 1952 and oversaw the production of the publication through both the comic book form and the magazine incarnation, when his efforts to defend the comics industry and skirt censorship by the Comics Code killed the rest of EC's business. He likewise defended *Mad* against lawsuits threatening its reliance on parody. A hands-on publisher, Gaines took members of "The Usual Gang of Idiots" on trips to exotic locations and supported the editors' development of contributors' talents.

Stan Hart first contributed to *Mad* in 1962 as the writer of "Future TV Medical Shows" (#74, 10/62: 10–11), with art by Jack Rickard. A regular author of movie and TV parodies throughout his nearly five decades with *Mad*, Hart also wrote many one-off pieces poking fun at other aspects of popular culture; he appeared in more than 200 issues across his *Mad* career. His last movie satire was "The Yellow Mile," drawn by Mort Drucker, in #393 (5/2000: 6–9).

Suzanne "Suzy" Hutchinson joined *Mad* in October 2017 as art director for the California relaunch following stints with Dreamworks Animation and Disney Consumer Products. She assumed editorial leadership of the magazine after Executive Editor Bill Morrison's departure at the end of January 2019 and became managing editor with the April 2020 issue (n. s. #12).

Frank Jacobs began his career writing for *Mad* with a bang, having five credits in his first issue, #33 (6/57): the editors introduced his three-page "Why I Left the Army and Became a Civilian" (17–19), with art by George Woodbridge, by stating that it "immediately convinced us that he is a 'MAD' writer." Jacobs would go on to collaborate with most of *Mad*'s artists over his next five decades with the magazine. As the author of many inspired poetry and song parodies, Jacobs became known as "the poet laureate of *Mad*," and his talents remained vital and up to date as late as "A Google Glass-Wearer's Photo Album" (John Kershenbaum [a], #529, 10/14: 34–35). Jacobs published a biography of Bill Gaines, *The Mad World of William M. Gaines* (1972).

Abraham "Al" Jaffee first appeared in *Mad* as a writer for issue #25 (Aug.–Sept 1955), its second in the new magazine format, with "Baseball . . . Science or Skill?," drawn by Jack Davis (#25, 8–9/55: 13–17). Jaffee remained a contributor almost sixty years later, when n. s. #10 (12/19) carried his "Events That Inspired Al Jaffee's Signature, Part Two" (4); Mike Slaubaugh ranks him first among all artists and writers in the number of issues containing his work: 508 as of April 2020. The first "Fold-In," a feature that Jaffee devised and that has become his signature innovation, appeared in black-and-white on the inside back cover of issue #86 (4/64), showing Elizabeth Taylor kissing a random fan when the page is folded correctly. Along with other writing and art contributions, the Fold-In has run there ever since with brief exceptions (six issues lacking the feature ran another Jaffee page instead: #121, #190, #212, #219, #353, and #360)—and in color since #119 (6/68). The Fold-In briefly moved from the inside back cover in February 2019 to run as the 20th entry in the "Mad 20" of 2018, where Jaffee asked, "What Prominent Racist Fixture Was Taken Down This Year?" as a satiric image evoked the KKK, the 2017 Charlottesville "Unite the Right" march protesting removal of a Robert E. Lee monument, and (when folded), pizza magnate John Schnatter's 2018 racist remark (n. s. #5: 35). Jaffee holds the Guinness World Record, awarded on March 30, 2016, his 95th birthday (named "Al Jaffee Day" by New York Mayor Bill DeBlasio), for the longest career as a comic artist. Jaffee retired in January 2019, having contributed to more issues of *Mad* than any other artist or writer.

Jenette Kahn took over as the president and editor-in-chief of *Mad* magazine after founder Bill Gaines's death in 1992. She is first listed as "President & Editor-in-Chief" on the contents page of issue #322 (10/93). Kahn was an executive at DC Comics when Gaines died, and her involvement in the magazine signaled a shift toward its greater integration into DC's corporate structure.

Tom Koch began his career with *Mad* as the ghostwriter for comedians Bob [Elliott] and Ray [Goulding] (#34, 8/57 to #44, 1/59) in pages with art by Mort Drucker, but soon also appeared under his own name in #38 with "*Blood, Guts, A Roscoe and You* by Mickey Spitoon," drawn by George Woodbridge (3/58: 14). His writing was dramatized by those artists and most of the others in the Usual Gang—Jack Davis, Jack Rickard, Angelo Torres, Harry North, Esq., Bob Clarke, Bob Coker, and Rick Tulka; with Torres, Koch also collaborated on *History Gone Mad* (1977). Among the more than 300 pieces that Koch wrote for *Mad* across thirty-seven years, until 1995, perhaps best known is "*Mad* Magazine Introduces 43-Man Squamish" (#95, 6/65: 21–23), about a convoluted sport of his own comic invention that became a craze on college campuses as students formed their own 43-man squamish teams.

Arnie Kogen wrote for *Mad* occasionally after his debut, "Graduation Speeches . . . That Somebody Listened To" with artist Joe Orlando, in July 1959 (#48: 40–41), but became a regular member of the Usual Gang after collaborating with Wally Wood on "Comedy Albums by Musical Artists" (#66, 10/61: 4–8). Across five decades in which he contributed myriad one-off ideas to 159 issues of *Mad*, Kogen also wrote some of its most beloved movie and TV satires, teaming up with Mort Drucker, Angelo Torres, and Tom Richmond, for instance, to create "For the Birds" (#82, 10/63: 43-48), "Babewatch" (#328, 6/94: 43–47), and "The Dork Knight Reprises" (#519, 2/13: 48–54), respectively. His last contribution, "Decimated Survivor," drawn by Tom Bunk, ran in #545 (6/17): 48-52.

Peter Kuper took over drawing "Spy vs. Spy" in April 1997 based on a script by Michael Gallagher (#356: 12–13), collaborating with him, Duck Edwing, and a few others for most installments up to #419 (7/02). He has written and drawn most subsequent installments on his own, while teaming up with writers and editors for the occasional cover or inside feature, including "The Kuper Market" for the "Fundalini Pages" in #546–49 (10/17–2/18) and "Shorts and Briefs" for #1–5 of the new series (6/18–2/19).

Harvey Kurtzman created *Mad* as a parody of the comic book form and its most popular genres. Working for Bill Gaines at EC Comics, which published educational and dramatic titles, he received permission to create a funny comic book and enlisted EC artists Jack Davis, Wally Wood, Will Elder, and Jack Severin to realize his scripts and layouts. Kurtzman devised the shift from comic book to magazine not only to protect *Mad* from the Comics Code but also to fulfill his goal of editing a magazine. Indeed, he left EC in 1956 to do so, prompted in part by a conflict with Gaines over profit-sharing. Al Feldstein is credited as the editor of issue #29 (9/56), with Kurtzman's last editorial credit in issue #28 (7/56). Ideas and scripts that Kurtzman left behind on his departure appeared in print until 1958. For conceiving *Mad* and superintending the early realization of its parodic and satiric impulses, Kurtzman changed the course of American culture.

Paul Levitz never appeared in *Mad* as a contributor, but as executive vice president and publisher of DC Comics from 1990 to 2002 and its president from 2002 to 2009, he oversaw the activities of EC Comics for Warner Communications following EC publisher Bill Gaines's death in 1992.

Barry Liebmann wrote for *Mad* for thirty-eight years on a variety of subjects, but often on American politics. His first appearance was "If Children Treated Their Parents the Way Their Parents Treat Them," with art by Paul Coker, Jr. (#208, 7/79: 40–41); his last, with art by Rick Geary and Justin Peterson, was "America's Civil War vs. Captain America" (#540, 8/16: 32–34).

Don Martin first appeared in *Mad* soon after Harvey Kurtzman's departure as the artist for Al Feldstein's "Alfred E. Neuman Answers Your Questions" (#29, 9/56: 23, 45; #30, 12/56: 10, 31, 48), but quickly developed and drew his own zany characters and plots for pages and spreads that ran in every issue thereafter—247 issues in all—until March 1988 (#277). After a seven-year hiatus, during which he worked for the competing *Cracked* magazine, Martin received credit for a January 1995 publication related to a contribution to *MADtv*. His manic style embodied the magazine's comic sensibility, making him a particularly valuable contributor to *Mad*.

Nick Meglin, who came to EC Comics as a contributor to Feldstein's *Panic*, first received credit in *Mad* for "Bowling" (#30, 12/56: 20–23), Feldstein's second issue as editor. Meglin freelanced for the magazine in 1956 and appeared in the table of contents as Nick Megliola for the first time in issue #31 (Feb. 1957), for contributing ideas. He debuted as a member of the editorial staff in #59 (12/60), listed alongside Jerry DeFuccio as "AFTER THE EDITOR'S JOB." Meglin succeeded 25 years later, leading *Mad* from 1985 until his retirement in 2004 with co-editor John Ficarra. Notable contribution as a writer: "My Fair Ad-Man," a parody published as Megliola with art by Mort Drucker, in #54 (4/60: 31–37).

Hermann Mejía arrived at *Mad* in 1997 as the artist for Chris Hart's politically incorrect "PETArd's Animal Rights Newsletter" (#356, 4/97: 19–23) and within a few months picked up the assignment to draw Mike Snider's feature, "MAD's Celebrity Cause-of-Death Betting Odds," beginning with #366, on David Letterman (2/98: 48). As that feature lost steam, Mejía moved into movie and TV satires, collaborating with Arnie Kogen on "The Faketrix Retarded" (#433, 9/03: 8–13) and with Desmond Devlin on "Game of Groans" (#521, 6/13: 12–18), along with regular contributions to the "Mad 20 Dumbest."

Norman Mingo painted the original portrait of Alfred E. Neuman that standardized *Mad*'s characterization of the gap-toothed kid as the personification of the magazine's comic sensibility. After this debut on the cover of issue #30 (12/56), Mingo's renderings of Alfred appeared on nearly 100 covers of *Mad* as well as on specials and spin-off books.

Bill Morrison became vice president of *Mad* in June 2017 in anticipation of the June 2018 launch of the new series published in Burbank, California. A graphic artist who worked for Disney and *The Simpsons* before co-founding Bongo Comics with Matt Groening, Morrison earned an Eisner Award for his work on *The Simpsons Comic* #1 and served as president of the National Cartoonists Society when appointed to *Mad*. His experience as art director of the animated *Futurama* may have drawn some young, hip readers to *Mad*, but he quickly diversified its contributors' list and editorial staff with women and people of color (now also populating the art) while retaining stalwarts Sergio Aragonés and Al Jaffee and rebooting "The Lighter Side" with writer Tammy Golden (art by Jon Adams, n.s. 5, 2/19: 36–37). Under his leadership, *Mad* received a 2018 Eisner nomination for Best Humor Magazine. Morrison left the magazine at the end of January 2019, as n.s. #6 (4/19) appeared.

Harry North, Esq., worked for British comics publishers before he debuted in *Mad*'s U.S. and U.K. editions with #187 (12/76) as the artist for a *Mad* subscription ad (inside cover) and a spread featuring Frank Jacobs's bicentennial parody, "The Bauble Hymn of The Republic" (22–23). North's collaborations in eighty-plus issues over the next three decades ranged from one-off pieces with Tom Koch and Dick DeBartolo to film and TV satires with them and others, ending with art for Jacobs's political parody nodding to the Great Recession, "Bailout Hymn of the Republic" in #500 (6/09).

Teresa Burns Parkhurst began her *Mad* career with "The Jerry Springer Spaniel Show," imagining dogs whose lives matched those of Springer's human guests, for issue #430 (6/03: 26–27) and has since continued to draw her own comic ideas several times a year across some seventy issues, including two pages for the 2018 "Mad 20 Dumbest" (n.s. #5, 2/19): a commemorative plate for Trump's meeting with Vladimir Putin in Helsinki (25) and samples from Brett Kavanaugh's "Alibi-a-Day Desk Calendar" (32). The sole woman on Slaubaugh's list of the top seventy-five *Mad* contributors, where she ranked 48 in April 2020, Burns Parkhurst has taken on political and general social topics in the new series, in contrast to the adolescent-focused themes of her work under Meglin and Ficarra.

Kevin Pope debuted in *Mad* with his art for the "Melvin & Jenkins" mock-etiquette series featuring African American characters written by Desmond Devlin. A take-off on "Goofus and Gallant" from *Highlights for Children*, "Melvin & Jenkins" ran in most issues from #356 (4/97) to #397 (9/00), then irregularly as a stand-alone feature before moving to the "Fundalini Pages" from #438 (2/04) to #505 (10/10).

Antonio Prohías is known for creating the popular feature "Spy vs. Spy." Prohías debuted in *Mad* with this "Cloak and Dagger Department" feature in January 1961 (#60: 9, 14, 24) and continued to create it, for a total of 241 installments, until March 1987 (#269: 44). Bob Clarke and others, including Duck Edwing and George Woodbridge, sustained the strip until Peter Kuper took it up with #356 (3/97: 12–13).

Tom Richmond has become one of *Mad*'s top artists, with credits in more than 130 issues since he drew "Gadgets to Really Make Home Theater Like Going to the Movies!," written by Dick DeBartolo, for #399 (11/00: 30–31). More than fifty *Mad* film and movie parodies (most in collaboration with Desmond Devlin, Arnie Kogen, and Dick DeBartolo) have showcased his talent for caricature since "Malcontent in the Muddle," written by Devlin, in #403 (3/01: 7–12), including the pair's "A Listless Story" n.s. #5 (2/19: 2–7). Richmond served as president of the National Cartoonists Society from 2011 to 2015.

Jack Rickard first contributed art to *Mad* in 1961 with "Sneaky Camera" (#64, 7/61: 37–40), written by Larry Siegel, with whom he would continue to collaborate until 1984. That year he drew for pieces by Lou Silverstone, Frank Jacobs, and Siegel in *Mad 84*, a special issue of new material, as well as a final collaboration with Siegel in #245, "*Mad*'s Helpful Hints on Breaking Up with a Girl" (3/84: 30–33). Rickard appeared in more than 150 issues of *Mad* across his twenty-three years with the magazine.

Irving Schild is a Belgian photographer who contributed to 162 issues of *Mad* across half a century. The first of his many back covers, "Let's Kill-off Ridiculous Ad Campaigns," appeared in July 1965 (#96: back cover), and his photo contributions continued through June 2017 with a parody ad for "Glass Ceiling Plus," written by Alison Grambs, hawked a product to "wipe out gender inequality in the workplace" (#545: back cover).

John Severin reported starting his career by selling gag cartoons at $1 apiece to the weekly *Hobo News* while a student at New York's High School of Music and Art, and became Harvey Kurtzman's drawing partner for war comics at EC. That history made him a natural choice for early issues of *Mad*. Severin drew "Varmint!" for issue #1 (10–11/52: 25–31) and, except for #8 (12/53–1/54), continued through #10, when he withdrew from *Mad* to edit *Two-Fisted Tales* for EC. He bowed out with a Western movie parody, "Sane!" in #10 (4/54: 1–7).

Marie Severin worked as a researcher and staff colorist at EC Comics, lured there by her brother Jack, from 1949 to 1955; she left when Gaines's resistance to the Comics Code destroyed the firm's horror, war, and fantasy lines and *Mad* became a black-and-white glossy magazine. Her excellence as a colorist gave EC's publications a distinction much valued by Kurtzman and Gaines both inside and on covers, which needed to stand out on newsstands. Her final *Mad*-related credits at EC were *Mad* #23 (5/55) and its in-house imitation, *Panic* #12 (12/55–1/56). Issue #22, *Mad*'s special Art Issue, credits her as color editor.

Larry Siegel contributed writing to *Mad* for more than three decades, starting in 1958 with "Mad's M.T.V.B.A. Awards" (#43, 12/58: 2–3). From "The Night Peter Gone Cracked," drawn by Bob Clarke (#50, 10/59: 39–42), to "The Moron Downer Jr. Show," drawn by Jack Davis (#286, 4/89: 23-26), Siegel's parodies of TV shows, movies, and other genres of popular culture—magazines, songs, awards, advice columns—so perfectly fit the *Mad* formula that his byline often appeared three or more times per number through #293 (3/90). The editors honored him as *Mad* "Idiot of the Issue" in XL #33 (6/05).

Lou Silverstone debuted in *Mad* by co-authoring the first of the many TV parodies that became his chief contribution: "Bananaz (The 'Family Togetherness' Western)," written with Earle Doud and drawn by Mort Drucker (#73, 9/62: 5–9). Across the next three decades, he wrote dozens more, with twenty in the 1970s alone, tying Tom Richmond's record at 32nd place for appearing in 132 issues. His last TV spoof, a parody of the distinguished news magazine *60 Minutes*, "Six Minutes Looks at Smoking," drawn by Angelo Torres (#292, 1/90: 21–24), may have inspired his final contribution, with Mort Drucker, "A MAD Peek Behind the Scenes . . . The TV News Business" (#301, 3/91: 46–47).

Mike Snider began at *Mad* by contributing the idea for "Horror Movies Based on Everyday Disasters," written by Frank Jacobs and drawn by Jack Rickard (#217, 9/80: 19–21), but thereafter did his own writing. His "Celebrity Cause-of-Death Betting Odds," drawn by Hermann Mejía and others, ran in most issues from #358 (6/97) to #458 (10/05), moving to the "Fundalini Pages" with #438 (2/04). But most of his ideas across the 179 issues in which he appeared set aside formula for novelty, as in the punningly titled "*Mad* Sucker-Punches *The Contender*—A Knockout Collection of Outtakes," which offered new dialogue for film screen shots (#455, 7/05: 58–59).

Angelo Torres first contributed art to *Mad* magazine in 1969 with "Where Vultures Fare" in collaboration with Larry Siegel (#130, 10/69: 43–47). Torres drew for most issues of *Mad* thereafter well into the twenty-first century, specializing in TV and movie satires that exploited his talent for caricature beginning with a trifecta in issues #135–137: "Then Came Bombsome" with Dick DeBartolo (6/70: 35–39), "Room 222ZZZZZZZzzzzzzzz" with Stan Hart (7/70: 43–47), and "Makeus Sickby, M.D." with DeBartolo (9/70: 43–48). His final movie satire, "Repeat the Fock-Ups," with DeBartolo, ran in #452 (4/05: 29–32), though his art occasionally ran in the "Fundalini Pages" through 2009.

Rick Tulka contributed art for writer Russ Cooper's anachronistically titled "Hot Albums of the 1990s . . . A Look Back" in #282 (10/88: 14–15) and has collaborated ever since on one-off, rather than series, pieces with *Mad*'s best recent writers, including Tom Koch, Mike Snider, Desmond Devlin, as well as Frank Jacobs and Arnie Kogen. He continued as a member of the Gang in the new series, with drawings in the "Shorts & Briefs" department in issues n.s. #2 (8/18: 49) and n.s. #5 (2/19: 52), through his memoir, "The Wisenheim Museum: Becoming One of the Usual Gang of Idiots," for n.s. #9 (10/19): 27.

Sam Viviano served as *Mad*'s art director from 1999 to 2018, when the magazine ended its New York run. He stepped in to create the cover for #223 (6/81) after the death of Norman Mingo, a caricature of Larry Hagman as J. R. Ewing shooting himself in the head, with a flag of Alfred E. Neuman appearing out of the other ear. When the issue was the worst-selling to date, Feldstein refused to hire Viviano again. After Feldstein retired, however, editors Nick Meglin and John Ficarra assigned Viviano to writer Arnie Kogen's "Roger Ebore and Gene Sissy Review Three Films" (#253, 3/85: 4–12); Viviano drew the splash page, the spoof of *Ghostbusters*, and transitional panels between the spoofs drawn by Angelo Torres and Harry North. Thereafter Viviano alternated TV and film parodies with other work that utilized his talent for caricature, including the satire on Fox News CEO Roger Ailes for the "Mad 20 Dumbest" of 2016 (#543, 2/17: 27). His art for TV satire "The Monotonous Mrs. Mazel," written by Charlie Kadau, appeared in n.s. #9 (10/19): 30-34.

Wallace "Wally" Wood contributed the art for "Blobs!," by Harvey Kurtzman, for the first *Mad* comic book (#1, 10–11/52: 1–7)—and drew for every subsequent issue during Kurtzman's editorship. Probably best known for his work on the iconic "Superduperman!" (#4, 4-5/53: 1-8), a comic critique of superhero comics, Wood continued drawing for *Mad* for a decade after Kurtzman left, often with multiple credits per issue. Until 1964 Wood regularly brought his irreverent comic sensibility to writing not only by cherished *Mad* writers Frank Jacobs, Tom Koch, Duck Edwing, and Larry Siegel, but also by guest contributors such as Ernie Kovacs and Danny Kaye. Art for "Altar Ego" by Marilyn Ippolito in #143 (6/71: 29–30), with its elaborately detailed conclusion, closed Wood's distinguished career with *Mad*.

George Woodbridge joined The Usual Gang early in Al Feldstein's editorship with drawings illustrating the parodic lyrics of "The Wild West Is Where I Want To Be" for "Tom Lehrer Sings" in #32 (4/57: 36–37). In art for 248 issues across forty-five years with *Mad*, Woodbridge drew just four movie and TV parodies, and filled in on two 1993 "Spy vs. Spy" installments—a record that testifies to his versatility and skill in bringing novel comic ideas to life. He partnered with *Mad*'s most distinguished writers across its history—from Frank Jacobs, Larry Siegel, and Lou Silverstone to Dick DeBartolo and Mike Snider. In his final appearance in *Mad*, a year before his death, Woodbridge joined fellow artists in paying tribute to Dave Berg's "Lighter Side" feature in #427 (3/03: 29).

A *Mad* Timeline, 1952–2020

Leah Szalai and *Judith Yaross Lee*

INFORMATION ON *Mad* publication rates comes from the *Absolutely Mad* DVD archive and Gilford, circulation data mainly but not exclusively from Slaubaugh.

1952 Oct.–Nov., #1: EC Publications writer Harvey Kurtzman (1924–1993) collaborates with artists Wallace "Wally" Wood (1927–1981), Jack Davis (1924–), John Severin (1921–2012), and William "Will" Elder (1921–2008) to publish the first issue of *Mad*, along with EC's staff colorist Marie Severin (1929–2018). The venture is a result of Kurtzman's demand for pay equal to that of his coworkers. Publisher William Gaines (1922–1992) encourages Kurtzman to create a new humor title, thereby increasing Kurtzman's income by 50 percent.

1953 Jan.–Feb., #3: Kurtzman, who began parodying other comics and movie genres only indirectly, delivers *Mad*'s first real television show parodies, opening the issue with "Dragged Net!" (*Dragnet*; drawn by Elder, 1-8) and closing it with "Lone Stranger!" (*The Lone Ranger*; drawn by Jack Davis, 1-7).

Apr.–May, #4: Kurtzman and Wood's "Superduperman!" (1-8) is published in *Mad*, marking the first instance *Mad* parodied a comic not owned by EC. National Periodicals, the owner of *Superman*, responds with threat of a lawsuit. Although Gaines is tempted to give in, Kurtzman knows that parody and satire are to be the cornerstone of *Mad*; folding now would be giving up on the entire publication. *Mad*'s lawyer advises them to ignore the threat, and the conflict dissipates.

June–July, #5: Issue published under direction of Al Feldstein, who has moved over from EC's other titles to help Gaines with *Mad* while Kurtzman is ill with hepatitis.[1]

Dec. 18: Satiric illustrations by Will Elder of Clement Moore's "The Night Before Christmas" leads the Governor's Council of Massachusetts to ban the inaugural issue of *Panic*, *Mad*'s sister publication. Copies are pulled from newsstands by Dec. 21.[2]

Dec. 29: EC business manager Lyle Stuart and receptionist Shirley Norris are arrested in the company offices for selling *Panic* to a police officer. Charges are dropped immediately against Stuart, dismissed against Norris in January.[3]

1954 April, #10: *Mad* increases its frequency from bimonthly to 10 issues per year. The change is brought on by the dissolution of Kurtzman's war comic, *Frontline Combat*, sales of which plummeted when an armistice between North and South Korea ended the three-year-long Korean War on July 27, 1953.

Apr. 19: Psychiatrist Fredric Wertham publishes *Seduction of the Innocent*, a book that denounces comics—particularly horror and crime comics—as the root of juvenile delinquency and homosexuality. This publication is one of many contemporary attacks on comic books and their publishers.

Apr. 21: The United States Senate commences the Hearings Before the Subcommittee to Investigate Juvenile Delinquency to debate the influence of comic books on juvenile delinquency. Gaines volunteers to speak in defense of comics, and although no formal decision is made by the committee, unfavorable press coverage sours the public's opinion of comic books—and of Gaines.

Sept. 16: In response to the uproar in the comics industry, the Comics Magazine Association of America forms the Comics Code Authority (CCA). The CCA is responsible for censorship of comic publications.

Nov., #17: In an issue printed upside down and backwards, "What's My Shine" (7-1) explicitly satirizes the televised Army-McCarthy hearings while also alluding to the spectacle of the televised Kefauver hearings on comics.

The Mad Reader, a paperback volume consisting primarily of reprints, initiates *Mad*'s business model of marketing its brand by repackaging and reselling its copyrighted material. The model becomes more important over the years as new content fails to inspire readers at the same level as the old; the *Mad Reader* will have many reprintings and new editions itself.

1955: Amid the Code's challenges to EC's business model, *Mad* drops to eight issues this year.

Mar., #21: The gap-toothed kid, later named Alfred E. Neuman, makes his debut in a black-and-white sketched image on the cover of *Mad* in a fake advertisement as an "Idiot" rubber face mask being sold for $1.29. Kurtzman adopted the boy's image after seeing it on a postcard.

July, #24: The *Mad* comic book is remade into a bimonthly black-and-white magazine and the price increases from 10 to 25 cents. As *Mad* moves to magazine format, Kurtzman considers leaving *Mad* for a job at *Pageant*.

Stand-up comedian Ernie Kovacs (1919–1962) makes his first contribution to *Mad* with a send-up titled "Tom Swiffft and the Electric Ping Pong Ball," with art by Will Elder (47-48). Kovacs will make fifteen more appearances over the next three years.

Sept., #25: Al Jaffee (1921–) makes his first appearance in *Mad* with "Baseball . . . Science or Skill?" (13-17). Over the next sixty years, Jaffee will contribute to over 400 issues of *Mad*.

1956: *Mad* appears only four times this year.

Apr., #27: *Mad* appears on the stands after a four-month hiatus due to $100,000 in outstanding printing bills. Later this month Kurtzman demands ownership of 51 percent of the magazine's stock; Gaines declines and hires Al Feldstein to take his place.

July, #28: Kurtzman's last issue as editor.

Sept., #29: Feldstein debuts as editor. His first task is to hire an all new staff, as everyone except *Mad* art director John Putnam has left with Kurtzman.

Sept., #29: Don Martin (1931–2000), frequently labeled "*Mad*'s Maddest Artist," first appears in the magazine with his article, "Alfred E. Neuman Answers Your Questions" (23, 45).

Dec., #30: The full-color portrait of Alfred E. Neuman by Norman Mingo (1896–1980), commissioned by Feldstein as the personification of *Mad*, debuts on the cover. Mingo will continue to draw over 200 covers for *Mad* over the next 23 years. Also debuting are Bob Clarke with "Motorist Beware!," written by Herb Goldstein (16-17), and Nick Meglin with "Bowling," with art by Jack Davis (21-23).

1957: *Mad* publishes six bimonthly issues this year, February to December.

Jan.: Wood, Elder, and Davis again join Kurtzman in the creation of a new humor magazine, *Trump*. The magazine, funded by Hugh Hefner of *Playboy*, is cancelled after two issues. In August of 1957 they will create another magazine, *Humbug*, which runs for a year.

Apr., #32: Artist Mort Drucker (1929–2020) makes his *Mad* debut with "*Mad*'s TV Advertising Award Goes to the Most Nauseating T.V. Commercial of 1956: The Rolly Cigarette Ad" (23). Drucker will make over 400 contributions to *Mad* by 2010. Also debuting is George Woodbridge, with art to dramatize "Tom Lehrer Sings," Lehrer's 1953 song "The Wild West Is Where I Want to Be" (36-38, including a score with the melody and chords).

Mad runs its last paid ad until 2001.

June #33: Writer Frank Jacobs (1929–) debuts in *Mad* with "Baseball's Hall of Shame," with art by Joe Orlando (2-3). Jacobs will contribute to over 300 issues of *Mad*.

Aug. #34: Cartoonist Dave Berg (1920–2002) first appears in *Mad* with "Modern Furniture" (20-23). Berg will contribute to *Mad* over 300 times. Also in this issue, Tom Koch ghostwrites "Mr. Science" (Drucker [a], 12-14), the first of the Bob and Ray contributions that will run through #44, 1/59. His writing will eventually appear in more than 300 issues of *Mad*.

1958: *Mad* publishes seven issues this year. It also produces the first reprint magazine-format issue, *More Trash from Mad*, with a bonus color insert from the *Mad* comic.

Jan., #37: *Mad* publishes the Draft Dodgers Xmas Game. Readers who win the board game and successfully dodge the draft are encouraged to write to FBI director J. Edgar Hoover for an official draft dodger card. Many do, leading two unimpressed FBI officials to visit *Mad* to deliver a warning.

Mar., #38: Tom Koch publishes his first signed writing, "*Blood, Guts, A Roscoe and You* by Mickey Spitoon," with art by George Woodbridge (12-14).

Mar.: *Cracked*, the first non-EC imitation of *Mad* magazine, is produced. *Cracked* has similar layouts to *Mad*, and even features an Alfred E. Neuman-like character, Sylvester P. Smith.

1959: *Mad* establishes a stable eight-issue annual publication rate, which it maintains until 1994.

Feb. 5: Commanding General Edwin A. Walker grows suspicious of *Mad*'s political intentions and files a complaint with the FBI. He alleges that there is a secret message in each article. No actions are taken against *Mad*.

1960 Apr., #54: "My Fair Ad-Man" (31-37), written by associate editor Nick Meglin as Megliola (1935–2018), appears as *Mad*'s first musical parody. The feature sends up both the 1956 musical *My Fair Lady*, whose original cast recording topped sales charts that year, and the people who create advertisements.

1961: *Sing Along with Mad*, featuring song parodies by Frank Jacobs and Larry Siegel, is published as a supplement to the annual *More Trash from Mad* #4. Irving Berlin and other songwriters file suit, claiming infringement of their copyrighted lyrics.

Jan., #60: *Mad* celebrates the recent election with a double-sided cover: one side congratulates John F. Kennedy and the other side congratulates Richard Nixon. The day after Kennedy wins the 44th presidential election, the January issue of *Mad* hits the newsstands with the exclamation, "We were with you all the way, Jack!"

Antonio Prohías (1921–1998) debuts with "Spy vs. Spy" (9, 14, 24). Cuban-born Prohías had pitched the feature to *Mad* in July of 1960, just five months after Cold War tensions were heightened by Cuba's newly formed alliance with the Soviet Union, a serious threat to the U.S. considering Cuba's proximity. Prohías continues to publish "Spy vs. Spy" until his health declines in 1987. His successors include Don "Duck" Edwing (1934–2016), Robert J. "Bob" Clarke (1926–2013), George Woodbridge (1930–2004), and Peter Kuper (1958–).

Artist Paul Coker, Jr. (1929–), makes his first *Mad* appearance with "A *Mad* Peek Behind the Scenes" (22-23). His work will appear in *Mad* more than 350 times over the next sixty years.

Jan. 11: *The New York Times* reports that Gaines has sold EC Comics to Premier Industries for an undisclosed price estimated in the millions ("E. C. Publications"). He was unable to pay the taxes on *Mad*'s revenue. Gaines remains active as publisher until his death in 1992, despite subsequent sales to National Periodical Publications, owner of DC Comics, in 1964, which merged in 1967 with Kinney National Service. In July 1969 Kinney acquired film studio Warner Bros.-Seven Arts ("Warner") and renamed the conglomerate Warner Communications in February 1972.[4]

Oct., #66: Dave Berg publishes the first "The Lighter Side," with a strip about the experiences of owning a television set (16-19).

1962: *Mad*'s first musical endeavor, "Mad 'Twists' Rock 'n' Roll," is released on vinyl. Produced by Mike Russo, Jeanne Hayes, and The Dellwoods, the recording parodies popular songs.

Mar., #69: Writer Dick DeBartolo (1945–), later labeled "*Mad*'s Maddest Writer," debuts with "Some TV Ads We Never Got to See," drawn by Jack Rickard (36-39). DeBartolo will make over 400 contributions to *Mad*.

Apr., #70: Writer Don "Duck" Edwing first appears in *Mad* with "The Abominable Snowman," drawn by Joe Orlando (40), in the irregular feature "Scenes We'd Like to See." Edwing will contribute to over 250 issues of *Mad*.

July: Charles Winick of Columbia University publishes the first academic study of *Mad*, "Teenagers, Satire, and *Mad*," a content analysis augmented by interviews with teenage readers, in the *Merrill-Palmer Quarterly of Behavior and Development*. The article notes similarities between the 1930s magazine *Ballyhoo* and *Mad* and explores *Mad*'s surprising success in light of the relative scarcity of satire in other mass media of the day.

Oct., #74: Writer Stan Hart debuts with "Future TV Medical Shows," drawn by Jack Rickard (10-11).

1963 Jan., #76: Sergio Aragonés (1937–) appears in *Mad* with his soon-to-be regular feature, "A *Mad* Look At. . . . ," focused on ". . . the U.S. Space Effort" (20-21). Aragonés will make over 450 contributions to *Mad* during the next sixty years.

1964 Mar. 23: The US Court of Appeals for the Second Circuit sets a precedent for fair use of copyrighted materials in its decision on *Berlin v. EC Publications, Inc.* The court finds that most of *Mad*'s parodic lyrics in *Sing Along with Mad* (1961), a supplement to *More Trash from Mad #4*, do not constitute copyright infringement. This decision paved the way for future parodying artists, such as "Weird Al" Yankovic.

Apr., #86: Jaffee publishes his first *Mad* "Fold-In," featuring actors Elizabeth Taylor and Richard Burton on the inside back cover.

June 10: *The New York Times* reports that National Periodicals Publications, Inc., publishers of *Superman*, acquired *Mad* from Premier Corporation of America on June 9.

1965 Mar. 2: The U.S. Court of Appeals for the Second Circuit decides in the case of *Stuff v. EC Publications, Inc.*, that *Mad*'s use of the Alfred E.

Neuman image is not copyright infringement. The court finds that the image existed in American culture prior to the 1914 copyright of plaintiff Helen Pratt Stuff's husband.

1966 Jan. 9: *The Mad Show*, an off-Broadway musical, opens and reaches nearly 900 performances over the course of two years.

1967 Jan., #108: Writer Larry Siegel (1925–2019), a Jewish World War II veteran, publishes "Hokum's Heroes" (4-8), parodying the controversial sitcom *Hogan's Heroes* (CBS, 1965–1971), about a German prisoner-of-war camp in World War II.

July 21: *The New York Times* reports July 20 merger agreement, pending regulatory approval, between Kinney National Service and National Periodicals Publications, owner of *Mad.*

1968 June, #119: Jaffee's Fold-In now runs in color.

Oct.: Influenced by *Mad* magazine, Robert "R." Crumb publishes "Keep on Truckin'," a play on the Blind Boy Fuller song, "Truckin' My Blues Away." The graphic narrative appeared in the landmark first issue of *Zap Comix*.

1969 Jan., #124: *Mad* satirizes discrimination against the gay community with a back cover by Irving Schild titled "America's Going Drag." The issue comes just five months before Greenwich Village police raid the Stonewall Inn, a local gay bar, leading to riots that launch the gay liberation movement.

Oct., #130: Artist Angelo Torres publishes in *Mad* for the first time with the movie parody "Where Vultures Fare," written by Larry Siegel (43-47).

1970 Feb.: Betty Sanders reports in "*Mad* Magazine in the Remedial English Class" how students turned from uninterested to motivated when she replaced the previous reading material with copies of *Mad*.

Apr., #134: Jacobs and Aragonés publish "I Remember, I Remember the Wondrous Woodstock Music Fair" (24-26). The feature captures the essence of the Woodstock Music Festival—held in Bethel, New York, August 15–18, 1969—through renderings of grinning, fun-loving festivalgoers engaged in various activities.

Fall: *Mad Special #1* combines "a portfolio" of new material with reprints organized as portfolios of Don Martin and Dave Berg, TV and movie satires. The *Special* tests a way to expand the publication rate beyond eight issues without proportionately raising expenses with new material.

Nov.: Largely inspired by *Mad*, Henry Beard, Douglas Kenney, and Rob Hoffman create the humor magazine *National Lampoon*. It begins as a monthly publication and circulates until November 1998, ending with issue #249.

1971: *Mad* adds *Specials* #2–5 to its eight regular issues, effectively producing a monthly publication.

Sept., #145: Jacobs and Clarke publish "Greeting Cards for the Sexual Revolution" (30-32). The sexual liberation movement, which largely began with FDA approval of the Enovid brand oral contraceptive on May 9, 1960, pushed for acceptance of many nontraditional sexual behaviors such as having relations with multiple partners. *Mad* captures this new era in the greeting card "To A Very Special Girl" signed "Marvin, Danny, Harold, Bill, Sylvester, Fred, and Roy!"

Jacobs and Max Brandel publish "That Sinking Feeling" (24-25), a feature that lampoons Nixon's stance on the Vietnam War. In a 1968 presidential campaign speech, Nixon promised that the war—which began in 1955—would end under his leadership. Nixon's future speeches from 1969 to 1971 would reveal, however, that ending the war was not an option. U.S. involvement in the Vietnam war continues until 1973.

1972, Jan.: Inspired by Kurtzman and Will Elder's "Mickey Rodent" in *Mad* #19 (1/55), cartoonist Art Spiegelman publishes "Maus," a three-page narrative about his father's experience during the Holocaust, in the comics magazine *Funny Animals*; R. Crumb's "What A World" also appears in this issue. "Maus" is Spiegelman's first experiment in an eleven-year project that will be serialized in *Raw* (1980–91) and finally assembled as the full-length graphic narrative *Maus*, awarded a special Pulitzer Prize in 1992.

Feb.: *Mad*'s owner, National Kinney Corp., which had acquired the Warner Bros. film studio in 1969, changes its name to Warner Communications.[5]

Nov.: Jacobs publishes *The Mad World of William M. Gaines*, a biography of *Mad*'s founding publisher.

1974 Dec., #171: Arnie Kogen and Drucker publish "The Zing" (4-11), building a satire of the recent Watergate scandal atop a parody of the 1973 film *The Sting*. The issue hits newsstands four months after Nixon resigns the presidency.

1975 Mar., #173: In accordance with federal law, this issue of *Mad* publishes its circulation data for 1974, reporting an all-time high paid circulation of 2.4 million.

Oct. 11: *Saturday Night Live* (NBC), a sketch comedy show in the same vein of humor as *Mad*, airs for the first time.

1978 Oct., #202: John Caldwell debuts as a writer with "A MAD Look at Some Unfinished Sentences," a collaboration with artist Bob Clarke (20-21).

1981 Jan., #220: Jerry DeFuccio (1925–2001) contributes to his last issue of *Mad* as associate editor.

April, #222: John Ficcara (1984–) debuts as associate editor.

June, #223: Artist Sam Viviano draws his first *Mad* cover, which parodies the TV show *Dallas*. Mike Snider begins a 25-year career as a *Mad* writer with "A 'Let the Punishment Fit the Crime' Update" (art by Jack Davis, 31–33).

1983: Annual average circulation falls below 1 million per issue for the first time since reporting began.

1984 Mar.: Vincent P. Norris publishes an economic analysis of *Mad*'s ad-less and low cover-price business model in the *Journal of Communication*. Gaines, always defensive about his refusal to run ads, proudly shares the article with *Mad*'s board members.

Dec.: Al Feldstein retires as editor of *Mad* after twenty-eight years.

1985 Mar., #253: Desmond Devlin debuts with "The MAD 1984 Quiz" (34-35).

June, #255: Dick DeBartolo becomes *Mad*'s creative consultant, remaining in this role until 2009.

Sept., #256: Nick Meglin (1935–2018) and John Ficarra debut as co-editors following Feldstein's retirement. Sara Friedman, Charlie Kadua, and Joe Raiola step in as associate editors.

1986 April, #262: The first of many satiric references to Donald Trump appears on the back cover in a mock-ad for the Integrity Record Club, which offered an audio cassette of Trump's "Eve of Construction."

1988 Oct., #282: Rick Tulka begins three decades of drawing for *Mad* with "Hot Albums of the 1990s . . . A Look Back," written by Russ Cooper (14-15).

1991 Oct. 1: Artist, author, and longtime *Mad* devotee Maria Reidelbach publishes *Completely Mad*, a detailed authorized history of *Mad*.

Fall: *Super Special* #76 is published as Collector's Series #1, a limited edition with each copy identified by serial number; all contents except the bonus stickers insert are reprints.

1994: *Mad*'s annual publication rate increases from eight to nine issues.

May: Mark Fredrickson's cover for *Special* #93, *Unplugged*, marks the start of a long career as a *Mad* cover artist.

June, #330: Jenette Kahn becomes president and editor-in-chief of *Mad* magazine following Gaines's death. Paul Levitz rises to executive vice president and publisher, and Joe Orlando is the new vice president and associate publisher.

1996: *Mad* publishes 11 original issues this year, a combined Jan.–Feb. number followed by monthly issues. Circulation dips to an average of 309,911 copies per issue.

Summer: A new reprint series from the *Mad* comic book era, *Tales Calculated to Drive You Mad*, debuts. The eight issues, which will run through winter 1999, serialize *An Incomplete History of Mad Comics* by Frank Jacobs.

1997: *Mad* publishes 12 monthly issues of new material this year and will maintain this frequency through 2008.

April, #356: "Melvin & Jenkins' Guide to Personal Fitness" (39-41), written by Desmond Devlin and drawn by Kevin Pope, inaugurates a new mock-etiquette feature starring a pair of young African American men.

June 30: In an article by Constance Hays, the *New York Times* covers *Mad*'s plans to refresh its publication formula.

1999 Jan., #377: The first "*Mad* 20" is published as a color insert (17–32). Ginger Spice of the Spice Girls and TV shows *Ally McBeal* and *Jerry Springer* are among those satirized.

Aug. 3: *Totally Mad*, the first CD-ROM archive of *Mad* magazine, is released. The interactive, seven-disc set has every issue of *Mad* from 1952 to December 1998.

2000 June: *Mad*'s website, mad.com (now madmagazine.com), goes live.

2001 Feb., #402: *Mad* hits newsstands as a full-color glossy magazine.

Mar., #403: *Mad* resumes publishing paid, non-parody advertisements.

Following his debut in #399 (11/00), master caricaturist Tom Richmond contributes the first of some fifty film and TV parodies, "Malcontent in the Muddle," written by Devlin (7-12).

2002 July, #419: Greg Leitman and Hermann Mejía publish "Startling Similarities between Star Wars and the War on Terrorism" (20-21). The feature compares events of the War on Terrorism—which began after the September 11, 2001, terrorist attacks—with scenes from the *Star Wars* movie series.

Nov., #423: *Mad* publishes its 50th anniversary issue, including a timeline of key events in its history with comic commentary on them (16–18).

2003 Jan., #425: Kahn produces her last issue of *Mad* as president and publisher before leaving to pursue other opportunities. Paul Levitz debuts as president of DC Comics with issue #426.

June, #430: Artist Teresa Burns Parkhurst debuts with a feature page, "The Jerry Springer Spaniel Show" (26–27), She continues as a contributor under Ficarra and the new series edited by Bill Morrison.

2004 Jan., #437: Meglin publishes his last issue as editor. Ficarra continues to edit *Mad.*

Feb., #438: A new regular feature, "The Fundalini Pages," presents a collection of short gags.

2005 Aug.: *Mad* publishes *Mad Classics #1*, inaugurating a 25-issue series offering a few new pieces, including two installments of "Spy vs. Spy" (46, 74) amid the reprinted material.

2007 Jan. 24: *Absolutely Mad*, the first DVD archive of *Mad* magazine, replaces its predecessor, *Totally Mad*. The DVD archive has over 600 issues of *Mad* from 1952 to 2006, including specials.

2009 Apr., #500: After skipping the March issue, *Mad* shrinks its publication schedule to five issues per year, ending the monthly publication schedule in place since 1997.

Sept. 9: Paul Levitz announces that he will step down as president of DC Comics and become a contributing editor for DC Entertainment. Diane Nelson succeeds Levitz as president.

2013 Oct., #523: Artist Mark Fredrickson draws the "War on Privacy" cover depicting President Obama with his arms draped around the Black and White Spies; all three are smiling suspiciously. The art is in response to President Obama's defense of the National Security Administration's surveillance of citizens' telephone calls from June of this year.

2015 June: DC Comics, *Mad*'s parent, completes its relocation from New York City to Burbank, California, to enhance its synergy with Warner Bros. film studios.

Oct., #535: Mark Fredrickson's cover announces "Hillary's Furious Road to the White House" and "Our Collection of Ridiculous Political Movie Posters!," marking *Mad*'s intensified commitment to political satire in the run-up to the 2016 elections and after Donald Trump becomes the 45th President.

2017 March 6: Comics blog *BleedingCool.com* reports that *Mad* will join DC Comics in Burbank.

April, #544: Mark Fredrickson's cover announces "Believe Us—We Really Wish There Was . . . No Trump in This Issue"; a spread written by Jeff Kruse for the "Rank and Vile Department" (18–19) presents invidious comparisons with every other U.S. president.

June, #545: On the back cover, a parody ad for "Glass Ceiling Plus," written by Alison Grambs with a photo by Irving Schild, hawks a product to "wipe out gender inequality in the workplace" in an unusually strong feminist feature for *Mad*.

June 26: Diane Nelson, president of DC Entertainment, *Mad*'s parent within Warner Communications, announces the appointment of cartoonist Bill Morrison to replace John Ficarra as *Mad*'s executive editor. Morrison will assemble a new team in Burbank as Ficarra phases out operations in New York and then retires from *Mad*.

Oct., #547: *Mad* presents elaborate parodies of famous paintings that satirize President Donald Trump in "The Trump Collection 2017," billed as a special exhibition in "The MADropolitan Museum of Art" (27–36). Its lead painting, a two-page takeoff of *Washington*

	Crossing the Delaware depicting Trump boldly directing his boat toward a cliff, receives broad media attention.
2018 April, #550:	John Ficarra publishes his last issue, the finale of *Mad*'s original series, and retires after nearly forty years with the magazine, thirty-three of them as editor.
June, n.s. #1:	The first issue of *Mad*'s new series is published, listing women in key leadership positions—editor Allie Goertz, associate editor Paula Sevenbergen, art director Susy Hutchinson—and others inside. Al Jaffee's Fold-In runs in its usual place on the inside back cover.
Dec., n.s. #4:	In "The Ghastlygun Tinies" (18–21), a take-off on Edward Gorey's *Gashlycrumb Tinies* (1963), writer Matt Cohen and artist Marc Palm satirize inaction on mass shootings in American schools. The feature receives wide attention from the *New York Times* and other media.
2019 Jan.:	Vice-President and Executive Editor Bill Morrison leaves *Mad* at the end of the month. His name remains on the masthead through n.s. #7 (6/19)
Feb., n.s. #5:	Al Jaffee's Fold-In appears as #20 of "The Mad 20" (35).
April, n.s. #6:	The last of Al Jaffee's contemporary Fold-Ins as an ongoing feature runs on the inside back cover.
June, n.s. #7:	A fold-in by Al Jaffee deemed too controversial to run when created for #521 (6/13) satirizes American gun violence with a scene of moviegoers escaping a massacre.
July 4:	News circulates that DC has suspended new content for *Mad*, planning to fulfill current subscriptions with existing backlog and recycled content and concentrate on reprinting classic material.
August, n.s. #8:	The masthead lists the leadership as Senior Editor Dan Telfer, Editor Allie Goertz, and Art Director Suzy Hutchinson. Telfer and Goertz will remain on the masthead through n.s. #10 (12/19).

Dec., n.s. #10: An issue filled with original contents, including an elaborate, six-page fold-out parody of Dante's *Inferno*, "MAD's Tom Bunk Goes to Hell" (insert following p. 28), raises questions about plans for future issues.

2020 Feb., n.s. #11: Art Director Suzy Hutchinson takes *Mad*'s helm, with staff now reduced to three women and one man in a reversal of its longstanding gender ratio. The "Mad 20" for 2019 includes a recycled fold-in by Al Jaffee along with a new one by Johnny Sampson, "What 'Sparked Joy' for Millions of People This Year?" (35); the entry for #20, by writer Dick DeBartolo and artist Mark Fredrickson, "A MAD 'Ending' Target of Speculation" invites readers to determine *Mad*'s future by throwing of a dart at their target of options (40). The "Snappy Impeachments for Stupid Presidents" promised on p. 9 by the table of contents was MIA.

April, n.s. #12: Hutchinson adds Managing Editor to her title.

Bibliography

Compiled by *Kelley Macek*

Abbreviations:
(a) artist
(i) inks
(p) pencils
(l) lettering
(w) writer

Individual works from *Mad* are listed individually by writer and artist, and occasionally also by title, in the index, which refers readers to full in-text citations as well as chapter discussions in the body of this book.

In issues #1 to #23 (October–November 1952–May 1955), pagination starts over with number *1* for each feature; we have retained that pagination in the notes and bibliography rather than renumber the issues more conventionally.

Archives

Absolutely Mad Magazine: 50+ Years. Git Corporation, 2006. 1 DVD. Reprints #1 (October–November 1952) through #460 (December 2005).

The Mad Archives. 4 vols. New York: DC Comics, 2002–2012. Reprints #1 (October–November 1952) through #24 (July 1955).

Totally Mad: *Every Issue of Mad Magazine on CD-ROM*. Novato, CA: Broderbund, 1999. 7 CD-ROMs. Reprints #1 (October–November 1952) through #376 (December 1998). N.B. The title was reused for a 2012 anthology of selected reprints, cited below, edited by John Ficarra and with an introduction by Stephen Colbert and Eric Drysdale.

Mad Collections Cited

The Complete First Six Issues of MAD. West Plains, MO: Russ Cochran, 1985.

Inside Mad. Edited by John Ficarra. Introduction by Judd Apatow. Brief essays by contemporary comedians, film makers, writers, and *Mad* contributors. New York: Time Home Entertainment Inc., 2013.

Mad About Comic Strips. Edited by Nick Meglin and John Ficarra. Introduction by Ted Rall. New York: Mad Books, 2003.

Mad About the Fifties. Compiled by Grant Geissman. Foreword by Grant Geissman and Nick Meglin. Boston: Little, Brown, and Co., 1997.

Mad About the Movies: Director's Cut. Introduction by Roger Ebert. New York: Metro Books, 2008.

Mad About the Sixties: The Best of the Decade. Compiled and foreword by Grant Geissman. Boston: Little, Brown: 1995.

The Mad Archives. 4 vols. New York: DC Comics, 2002–2012.

MAD Cover to Cover: 48 Years, 6 Months, & 3 Days of Mad Magazine Covers. Edited with running commentary by Frank Jacobs. New York: Watson Guptill, 2000.

The Mad Fold-In Collection. By Al Jaffee. Vols. 1–4. San Francisco: Chronicle Books, 2011.

Mad's Greatest Artists: Dave Berg: Five Decades of "The Lighter Side of . . ." By Dave Berg. Foreword by Drew Friedman. Philadelphia: Running Press, 2013.

Mad's Greatest Writers: Frank Jacobs: Five Decades of His Greatest Works. By Frank Jacobs. Foreword by "Weird" Al Yankovic. Philadelphia: Running Press, 2015.

Mad's Greatest Artists: Mort Drucker: Five Decades of His Finest Works. By Mort Drucker. Edited by Greg Jones. Introduction by John Ficarra. Philadelphia: Running Press, 2012.

Mad Spy vs. Spy: The Complete Casebook. By Antonio Prohías. Edited by Charles Kochman. Introduction by Grant Geissman. Brief essays by Fabiola Santiago and Marta Rosa [Prohías] Pizarro. New York: Watson-Guptill Publications, 2001.

The Mad War on Bush. Edited and preface by John Ficarra. Introduction by Jimmy Kimmel. New York: EC Publications, 2007.

More Trash from Mad #4. New York: EC Publications, 1961.

Spy vs. Spy 2: The Joke and Dagger Files. By Peter Kuper with Duck Edwing, Bob Clarke, and Dave Manak. Edited by David Shayne. Foreword by J. J. Abrams. Brief essays by Peter Kuper; David Shayne; Duck Edwing and Dave Manak; and Sam Viviano. New York: Watson-Guptill, 2007.

Totally Mad: 60 Years of Humor, Satire, Stupidity and Stupidity. Edited by John Ficarra. Introduction by Stephen Colbert and Eric Drysdale. New York: Time Home Entertainment, 2012.

Sources Other Than *Mad*

Abrams, Nathan. "From Madness to Dysentery: *Mad*'s Other New York Intellectuals." *Journal of American Studies* 37, no. 3 (2003): 435–51.

Absurd Drama. Four plays by Eugene Ionesco, Arthur Adamov, Fernando Arabel, and Edward Albee. Introduction by Martin Esslin. London: Penguin, 1965.

Adcock, John. "Mysteries of Melvin." *Yesterday's Papers*, February 17, 2010. www.john-adcock.blogspot.com/2010/02/mysteries-of-melvin_17.html.

Bibliography

Aldama, Frederick L. *Your Brain on Latino Comics: From Gus Arriola to Los Bros Hernandez*. Austin: University of Texas Press, 2009.

"Alfred E. Neuman Joining Superman." *New York Times*, June 10, 1964, 61.

Alfred Hitchcock's "The Birds." Advertising poster, 28" x 22". 1963.

Alter Ego #87 (July 2009): 1-100.

Angell, Katharine S. Letter to Stephen Vincent Benet. November 3, 1928. Box 135. New Yorker Records. New York Public Library, New York, NY.

[Anthony, Norman.] "Why Not Make the Newspapers ALL Comics?" *Ballyhoo* 6, no. 3 (April 1934): 10.

Aragonés, Sergio. "Mi Hermano, Antonio." In *Mad Spy vs. Spy: The Complete Casebook*, by Antonio Prohías and edited by Charles Kochman, 246–48. New York: Watson-Guptill Publications, 2001.

Aristotle. *The Nicomachean Ethics*. Translated by Terence Irwin. 2nd ed. Indianapolis: Hackett, 1999.

———. *On Rhetoric: A Theory of Civic Discourse*. Translated by George A. Kennedy. New York: Oxford University Press, 2006.

Arnold, David. *The Handbook of Brand Management*. International Management Series. Reading, MA: Addison-Wesley, The Economist Books, 1992.

Atkinson, Paul. "The Time of Heroes: Narrative, Progress, and Eternity in *Miracleman*." In *The Contemporary Comic Book Superhero*, edited by Angela Ndalianis, 44–63. New York: Routledge, 2009.

"Bad." Illustrated by Blake Hampton. *Esquire*, August 1964, 52–56.

Bagdikian, Ben H. "The Wrong Kind of Readers: The Fall and Rise of *The New Yorker*." *Progressive* 47, no. 5 (May 1983): 52–54.

Bailey, Jason. "Who Said It: Presidential Hopeful Donald Trump or 'Idiocracy' President Camacho?" *Flavorwire*. September 16, 2015. https://www.flavorwire.com/537887/who-said-it-presidential-hopeful-donald-trump-or-idiocracy-president-camacho.

Bakhtin, Mikhail. "Discourse in the Novel." In *The Dialogic Imagination: Four Essays*, translated by Michael Holquist and Caryl Emerson, 259–422. Austin: University of Texas Press, 1981.

———. *Rabelais and His World*. Translated by Helene Iswolsky. Bloomington: Indiana University Press, 1984.

———. *Speech Genres and Other Late Essays*. Edited by Caryl Emerson and Michael Holquist. Translated by Vern W. McGee. Austin: University of Texas Press, 1986.

Banta, Martha. *Barbaric Intercourse: Caricature and the Culture of Conduct, 1841–1936*. Chicago: University of Chicago Press, 2003.

Barnosky, Jason. "The Violent Years: Responses to Juvenile Crime in the 1950s." *Polity* 38, no. 3 (July 2006): 314–44.

Barton, Edwin J., and Glenda A. Hudson. *A Contemporary Guide to Literary Terms*. Boston: Houghton Mifflin, 1997.

Bateson, Gregory. *Steps to an Ecology of Mind*. 1969. Reprint, Chicago: University of Chicago Press, 1972.

Bathrick, Serafina. "The *Mary Tyler Moore Show*: Women at Home and at Work." In *MTM: Quality Television*, edited by Jane Feuer, Paul Kerr, and Tise Vahimagi, 99–131. London: BFI, 1984.

"*Batman* (1966–1968): Full Cast and Crew." *IMBD*. www.imdb.com/title/tt0059968/fullcredits?ref_=tt_cl_sm#cast.

Baudrillard, Jean. *The System of Objects*. Translated by James Benedict. 1968. Reprint, London: Verso, 1996.

Beaty, Bart. *Comics Versus Art*. Toronto: University of Toronto Press, 2012.

———. *Fredric Wertham and the Critique of Mass Culture*. Jackson: University Press of Mississippi, 2005.

Becker, Ernest. *The Denial of Death*. New York: Free Press, 1973.

Becker, Leon Dische, and Art Spiegelman. "Art Spiegelman: My Life in Cartoons [Interview]." https://www.foldmagazine.com/art-spiegelman

Beckert, Clare M. "'Batman' Being Sold." *New York Times*, July 21, 1967: 39, 48.

Becket, Stefan. "The Origins of Derp." *New York*, June 4, 2013. https://nymag.com/intelligencer/2013/06/derp-meaning-origin.html.

Ben-Porat, Ziva. "Method in Madness: Notes on the Structure of Parody, Based on MAD TV Satires." *Poetics Today* 1, no. 1–2 (Fall 1979): 245–72.

Benson, John, ed. *The Sincerest Form of Parody: The Best 1950s* Mad-*Inspired Satirical Comics*. Seattle: Fantagraphics, 2006.

Berger, Arthur Asa. *The Comic-Stripped American*. Baltimore: Penguin, 1973.

Berger, John. *Ways of Seeing*. London: Penguin Books, 1972.

Bergson, Henri. *Laughter: An Essay on the Meaning of the Comic*. Translated by Cloudesley Brereton and Fred Rothwell. New York: Macmillan, 1911.

Bernstein, Leonard, composer. *West Side Story: A Musical*. Based on a conception of Jerome Robbins. Book by Arthur Laurents. Lyrics by Stephen Sondheim. New York: Random House, 1958.

Bernstein, Leonard, composer, and Stephen Sondheim (lyrics). "Gee, Officer Krupke!" LyricWiki, *Hey Fandom!* https://lyrics.fandom.com/wiki/Leonard_Bernstein_%26_Stephen_Sondheim:Gee,_Officer_Krupke

Berry, Mary Frances. Foreword to *There is No Such Thing as a Natural Disaster: Race, Class, and Hurricane Katrina*, edited by Chester Hartman and Gregory D. Squires, vii–viii. New York: Routledge, 2006.

Biebel, Brett. "Standing Up for Comedy: Kenneth Burke and *The Office*." *KB Journal* 7, no. 1 (2010). www.kbjournal.org/biebel.

Bird, Robert. "Schematics and Models of Genre." In *Persistent Forms: Explorations in Historical Poetics*, edited by Ilya Kliger and Boris Maslov, 429–58. Oxford: Oxford University Press, 2015.

Black, James Eric (Jay). "Amoozin' but Confoozin': Comic Strips as a Voice of Dissent in the 1950s." *ETC* 66, no. 4 (2009): 460–77.

Block, Herbert. *Herblock Special Report*. New York: Norton, 1974.

Boddy, William. *Fifties Television: The Industry and Its Critics*. Chicago: University of Illinois Press, 1993.

Bodroghkozy, Aniko. *Groove Tube: Sixties Television and the Youth Rebellion*. Durham: Duke University Press, 2001.

Bonstetter, Beth E. "Mel Brooks Meets Kenneth Burke (and Mikhail Bakhtin): Comedy and Burlesque in Satiric Film." *Journal of Film and Video* 63, no. 1 (2011): 18–31.

Booker, M. Keith. *Monsters, Mushroom Clouds, and the Cold War: American Science Fiction and the Roots of Postmodernism, 1946–1964*. Westport, CT: Greenwood Press, 2001.

Boorstin, Daniel J. *The Image: A Guide to Pseudo-Events in America*. 1962. Reprint, Kindle ed. New York: Vintage Books, 1992.

Botzakis, Stergios. "*Mad*." In *Icons of the American Comic Book: From Captain America to Wonder Woman*, 2 vols., edited by Randy Duncan and Matthew J. Smith, 1:464–71. Santa Barbara: Greenwood, 2013.

Bourdieu, Pierre. *Distinction*. Cambridge: Harvard University Press, 1984.

Boyd, Brian. "Laughter and Literature: A Play Theory of Humor." *Philosophy and Literature* 28, no. 1 (2004): 1–22.

Boym, Svetlana. *The Future of Nostalgia*. New York: Basic, 2001.

Bray, Glenn. *The Illustrated Harvey Kurtzman Index*. Sylmar, CA: G. Bray, 1976.

"Breck Shampoo." *Wikipedia*. en.wikipedia.org/w/k/Breck-Shampoo.

Brick, Howard. *Age of Contradiction: American Thought and Culture in the 1960s*. Woodbridge, CT: Twayne Publishers, 1998.

Brown, Peter Jensen. "The Real Alfred E. Revealed." *The Real Alfred E.* March 10, 2013. www.therealalfrede.blogspot.com/2013/03/the-real-alfred-e.html.

Brownmiller, Susan. *In Our Time: Memoir of a Revolution*. New York: Dell, 1999.

Brunsdon, Charlotte, Julie D'Acci, and Lynn Spigel, eds. *Feminist Television Criticism: A Reader*. Oxford: Oxford University Press, 1997.

Burke, Kenneth. *Attitudes Toward History*. 3rd ed. Berkeley: University of California Press, 1984.

———. *The Rhetoric of Religion: Studies in Logology*. Berkeley: University of California Press, 1970.

Buss, David M. *The Evolution of Desire: Strategies of Human Mating*. New York: Basic, 2003.

Camus, Albert. *The Myth of Sisyphus and Other Essays*. Translated by Justin O'Brien. New York: Knopf Doubleday, 2012.

Carabas, Teodora. "'Tales Calculated to Drive You MAD': The Debunking of Spies, Superheroes, and Cold War Rhetoric in *Mad* Magazine's 'Spy vs. Spy.'" *Journal of Popular Culture* 40, no. 1 (February 2007): 4–24.

Carlson, Peter. "What, Me 50? *Mad*'s Half-Century of Poking Society in the Eye." *Washington Post*, October 22, 2002, C2.

Carmody, Deirdre. "Her First Issue at the Ready, Tina Brown Talks About The New Yorker." *New York Times*, September 24, 1992, C18.

Carrasco, Jorge L. Catalá. "From Suspicion to Recognition? 50 Years of Comics in Cuba." *Journal of Latin American Cultural Studies* 20, no. 2 (June 2011): 139–60.

Carter, E. Graydon. "The Cosmos According to Mel Brooks." *Vogue* 177, no. 6 (June 1987): 220–21, 271–72.
Casey, Edward S. "The World of Nostalgia." *Man and World* 20 (1987): 361–84.
Cavna, Michael. "Mad Magazine, A Pioneer of Modern Satire, Will Soon Cease Publishing New Content." *Washington Post*, July 5, 2019, C1.
———. "MAD Magazine Inspired Weird Al Yankovic. Today, as Its First Guest Editor, He Exacts Revenge." *Washington Post*. April 21, 2015.
Cawelti, John. "The Sanity of *MAD*." In *American Humor: Essays Presented to John C. Gerber*, edited by John C. Gerber and O. M. Brack, 171–88. Scottsdale, AZ: Arete, 1977.
Chambers, Robert. *Parody: The Art That Plays with Art*. New York: Peter Lang, 2010.
Chandler, Doug. "Standpunkt: MAD als politische Zeitschrift." *Aufbau: Das Jüdische Magazin* 85 no. 5 (October–November 2019): 6–9.
Christen, Arden G., and Joan A. Christen. "'It didn't hurt a bit' Kid: Dental Precursor to *Mad Magazine*'s Alfred E. Neuman." *Journal of the History of Dentistry* 48, no. 2 (2000): 53–55.
Christie, Ian, ed., and Terry Gilliam. *Gilliam on Gilliam*. London: Faber and Faber, 1999.
Chute, Hillary L. "Art Spiegelman." *Print Magazine*, June 19, 2008. www.printmag.com/article/art_spiegelman_interview_part2/.
———. *Outside the Box: Conversations with Contemporary Cartoonists*. Chicago: University of Chicago Press, 2014.
Ciasullo, Ann M. "The Lighter—and Weightier—Side of *Mad*, Or: Everything I Needed to Know About Gender and Sexuality I Learned from Dave Berg." *Studies in American Humor* n.s. 3, no. 30 (Fall 2014): 77–94.
Clark, Michael. "Humor and Incongruity." In *The Philosophy of Laughter and Humor*, edited by John Morreall, 139–55. Albany: SUNY Press, 1986.
Clash, Jim. "Johnny Rivers Chats About His Big Hit, Secret Agent Man." *Forbes*. Forbes Media. May 14, 2015.
Cline, Austin. "The 1957 Supreme Court Decision: *Roth v. United States*." *Thought co*. www.thoughtco.com/roth-v-united-states-1957-supreme-court-decision-250052.
Cocksworth, Ashley. "*The Dark Knight* and the Evilness of Evil." *Expository Times* 120, no. 11 (2009): 541–43.
Colbert, Stephen, and Eric Drysdale. Introduction to *Totally Mad: 60 Years of Humor, Satire, Stupidity and Stupidity*, 5–6.
Conley, Thomas. *Toward a Rhetoric of Insult*. Chicago: University of Chicago Press, 2010.
Cooke, Jon B. *Everything Including the Kitchen Sink: The Definitive Interview with Denis Kitchen*. Amherst: DKP, 2016.
Costello, Brannon. "Fascism and Mass Culture in Howard Chaykin's *Blackhawk*." *ImageText* 7, no. 2 (2013).
Couch, N. C. Christopher, and Stephen Weiner. *The Will Eisner Companion: The Pioneering Spirit of the Father of the Graphic Novel*. New York: DC Comics, 2004.

Cremins, Brian. *Captain Marvel and the Art of Nostalgia*. Jackson: University Press of Mississippi, 2016.

———. "'What Manner of Man Is He?': Humor and Masculine Identity in Captain Marvel's World War II Adventures." *Studies in American Humor* n.s. 3, no. 27 (Winter 2013): 33–62.

Critchley, Simon. *On Humour*. London: New York: Routledge, 2002.

Czitrom, Daniel. *Media and the American Mind: From Morse to McLuhan*. Chapel Hill: University of North Carolina Press, 1982.

Darius, Julian. "Why *Miracleman* Matters." *Sequart Organization*, January 2, 2012. sequart.org/magazine/6473/why-miracleman-matters.

Dauber, Jeremy. *Jewish Comedy: A Serious History*. London: W. W. Norton, 2017.

Davies, Christie. *Jokes and Targets*. Bloomington: Indiana University Press, 2011.

Davis, Fred. *Yearning for Yesterday: A Sociology of Nostalgia*. New York: Free Press, 1979.

Davoren, Al. *R. Crumb: Conversations*. Jackson: University Press of Mississippi, 2004.

Dean, Michael, ed. *The Comics Journal Library Volume Eight: The EC Artists*. Seattle: Fantagraphics, 2013.

Decker, Dwight R., Gary Groth, and William Gaines. "The Man Behind EC: Interview with William Gaines" *Comics Journal* 81 (May 1983): 53–85.

"A Democratic Party of Youth and Unity." *Life*, August 27, 1956, 20–35.

Dentith, Simon. *Parody*. London: Routledge, 2000.

Desser, David, and Lester D. Friedman. *American-Jewish Filmmakers: Traditions and Trends*. Urbana: University of Illinois Press, 1993.

Di Liddo, Annalisa. *Alan Moore: Comics as Performance, Fiction as Scalpel*. Jackson: University Press of Mississippi, 2009.

Djerassi, Carl. "The Quest for Alfred E. Neuman." *Grand Street* 8, no. 1 (1988): 167–74. Reprinted in *Creativity, Delayed Recognition, and Other Essays*. Vol. 12 of *Essays of an Information Scientist*, edited by Eugene Garfield, 161–65. Philadelphia: ISI Press, 1989.

Dodds, Klaus. "Screening Geopolitics: James Bond and the Early Cold War Films (1962–1967)." *Geopolitics* 10, no. 2 (Summer 2005): 266–89.

Dooley, Michael. "*Trump*: A Smart, Sophisticated, Satirical Graphic Humor Magazine." *PrintMag*, July 22, 2015. www.printmag.com/publication-design/trump-graphic-humor-kurtzman/.

Doug Gilford's Mad Cover Site. Edited by Doug Gilford. www.madcoversite.com/.

Douglas, Susan. *Where the Girls Are: Growing Up Female with the Mass Media*. New York: Random House, 1994.

Dowding, Keith. *Encyclopedia of Power*. Thousand Oaks, CA: Sage, 2011.

Duncan, Randy, and Matthew J. Smith, eds. *Icons of the American Comic Book*. 2 vols. Santa Barbara, CA: Greenwood/ABC Clio, 2013.

"E.C. Publications Bought by Premier." *New York Times*, January 11, 1961, 34.

Ebert, Roger. Introduction to *Mad About the Movies: Director's Cut*, [i]. New York: Metro Books, 2008.

Eddings, Dennis W. "MAD about 'The Raven.'" *Edgar Allan Poe Review* 14, no. 2 (2013): 144–62.

"Edgar Allan Poe and Rufus Wilmot Griswold." *The Edgar Allan Poe Society of Baltimore*, January 22, 2009. eapoe.org/geninfo/poegrisw.htm.

Eisner, Will A. *A Family Matter*. Amherst: Kitchen Sink, 1988.

———. *Will Eisner's The Spirit: A Celebration of 75 Years*. Burbank: DC Comics, 2015.

Elder, Will. *The Million Year Picnic and Other Stories*. Illustrated by Will Elder with John Severin; written by Al Feldstein and Jack Mendelson with Nick Meglin and Ray Bradbury. Seattle: Fantagraphics, 2017.

Eliot, Marc. *Walt Disney: Hollywood's Dark Prince*. New York: Birch Lane Press, 1993.

Ellis, Edward Robb, and George N. Allen. *Traitor Within: Our Suicide Problem*. New York: Doubleday, 1961.

Engel, Bernd. *MADtrash.Com: The MAD Magazine Internet Database*. www.madtrash.com.

Engelhardt, Tom. *The End of Victory Culture*. New York: Basic, 1995.

Eno, Brian. Liner notes. *Ambient 4: On Land*, CD. 1982, revised February 1986. Virgin Records, 2004.

Eno, Brian, and Peter Schmidt. *Oblique Strategies: Over One Hundred Worthwhile Dilemmas*. 5th ed. 2001. Deck of 7 x 9 cm. printed cards in a black container.

Epstein, Lawrence J. *The Haunted Smile: The Story of Jewish Comedians in America*. New York: Public Affairs, 2001.

Estren, Mark James. *A History of Underground Comics*. Berkeley: Ronin, 1993. Reprint, *The History of Underground Comics: 20th Anniversary Edition*. Berkeley: Ronin, 2012.

Evanier, Mark. Introduction to *The Mad Archives*, vol. 4: 7–11. New York: DC Comics, 2002–2012.

———. *Mad Art: A Visual Celebration of the Art of Mad Magazine and the Idiots Who Create It*. New York: Watson-Guptill, 2002.

Feiffer, Jules. *The Great Comic Book Heroes*. New York: Bonanza, 1965.

Feldstein, Al. "The Al Feldstein Interview." Interview by S. C. Ringgenberg. Reprint of "Jolting Words with Al Feldstein in the EC Tradition." www.tcj.com/the-al-feldstein-interview/.

———. Interview by Margaret Cavin Hambrick. Deer Haven Ranch, Livingston, MT. July 15, 2000.

———. "An Interview with Al Feldstein." Interview by Jason Heller. *A.V. Club*, March 29, 2007. tv.avclub.com/al-feldstein-1798211079.

———. "Jolting Words with Al Feldstein in the EC Tradition." Interview by S. C. Ringgenberg. *Comics Journal* 177 (May 1995): 77–99.

Feldstein, Al (w), and Jack Davis (a). "My Gun Is the Jury!" *Panic* #1 (February–March 1954): 1–8.

Feuer, Jane. "MTM Enterprises: An Overview." In *MTM: Quality Television*, edited by Jane Feuer, Paul Kerr, and Tise Vahimagi, 1–31. London: BFI, 1984.

Ficarra, John. Introduction to *Mad's Greatest Artists: Mort Drucker: Five Decades of His Finest Works*, by Mort Drucker. Philadelphia: Running Press, 2012.

——— . Preface to *The Mad War on Bush*. New York: EC Publications, 2007.
Filkins, Dexter. "Rex Tillerson at the Breaking Point." *The New Yorker*, October 16, 2017.
Flanagan, Caitlin. "What Girls Want." *The Atlantic*, December 2008, 108–20.
Foucault, Michel. *Madness and Civilization: A History of Insanity in the Age of Reason*. Translated by Richard Joseph Howard. New York: Vintage, 1988.
Fox, M. Steven. "Arcade." *Underground Comixjoint*. comixjoint.com/arcade.html.
Foxe, Steve. "*MAD* Magazine Makes America Dumb Again with *MAD Dumps on Trump*." *Paste*. July 21, 2016. //www.pastemagazine.com/articles/2016/07/mad-magazine-makes-america-dumb-again-with-mad-dum.html.
"Frank Jacobs." *Wikipedia*. en.wikipedia.org/wiki/Frank_Jacobs.
Frank, Thomas. *The Conquest of Cool: Business, Counterculture, and the Rise of Hip Consumerism*. Chicago: University of Chicago Press, 1998.
Freeman, Elizabeth. *Time Binds: Queer Temporalities, Queer Histories*. Durham: Duke University Press, 2010.
Freud, Sigmund. *The Basic Writings of Sigmund Freud*. Translated by A. A. Brill. New York: Modern Library, 1938.
——— . *Jokes and Their Relation to the Unconscious*. Translated by James Strachey. New York: Norton, 1960.
Frickel, Scott, and M. Bess Vincent. "Hurricane Katrina, Contamination, and the Unintended Organization of Ignorance." *Technology in Society* 29, no. 2 (2007): 181–88.
Fried, Richard M. *The Russians Are Coming! The Russians Are Coming! Pageantry and Patriotism in Cold-War America*. New York: Oxford University Press, 1998.
Friedman, Barbara. "Nick Meglin: A Mad Perspective." Interview.
Friedman, Bruce Jay, ed. *Black Humor*. New York: Bantam, 1965.
Friedman, Drew. Foreword to *Mad's Greatest Artists: Dave Berg: Five Decades of "The Lighter Side of . . . "* by Dave Berg, 7–8. Philadelphia: Running Press Book Publishers, 2013.
Front-Line Combat. (*The EC Archives*). York, PA: Gemstone, 2008.
Fry, Karin. "Oh My God! They Killed Kenny . . . Again: Kenny and Existentialism." In *"South Park" and Philosophy: You Know, I Learned Something Today*, edited by Robert Arp, 77–86. Malden, MA: Blackwell, 2007.
Fry, William. "Fear of Laughter." Annual Conference, International Society for Humor Studies, April 1987, Arizona State University, Tempe, Arizona.
Frye, Northrop. "The Nature of Satire." In *The Educated Imagination and Other Writings on Critical Theory 1933–1963*, edited by Germaine Warkentin, 39–57. Ontario: University of Toronto Press, 2006.
Gabilliet, Jean-Paul. *Of Comics and Man: A Cultural History of American Comic Books*. Translated by Bart Beaty and Nick Nguyen. Jackson: University Press of Mississippi, 2010.
Gabler, Neal. *Walt Disney: The Triumph of the American Imagination*. New York Vintage, 2007.

Gaines, William. Testimony of William M. Gaines, Publisher, Entertaining Comics Group, New York, N. Y., Day 1, Wednesday, April 21, 1954. United States Senate, *Hearings Before the Subcommittee of the Committee on the Judiciary to Investigate Juvenile Delinquency*, 83rd Congress, Second Session Pursuant to s. 190, 1954. www.thecomicbooks.com/gaines.html.

Gaines, William, and Al Feldstein. "Disclaimer I." In *The Mad Morality; Or, The Ten Commandments Revisited*, by Vernard Eller with cover art by H. Hughey. Nashville: Abingdon Press, 1970.

Galloway, Alexander R. "The Unworkable Interface." *New Literary History* 39, no. 4 (Autumn 2008): 931–55.

Galvan, Margaret. "Archiving Wimmen: Collectives, Networks, and Comix." *Australian Feminist Studies* 32 (2017): 22–40, 91–92.

Garrett, Leah. "'Shazoom. Vas Ist Das Shazoom?' *Mad* Magazine and Postwar Jewish America." *Journal of Modern Jewish Studies* 16, no. 1 (2017): 57–79.

Gavaler, Chris. "I Hate Superheroes." *The Hooded Utilitarian: A Pundit in Every Panopticon*, March 5, 2014. www.hoodedutilitarian.com/2014/03/i-hate-superheroes.

Gehman, Richard. "It's Just Plain MAD." *Coronet Magazine*, May 1960: 96–103.

Geissman, Grant. *Feldstein: The Mad Life and Fantastic Art of Al Feldstein!* San Diego: IDW, 2013.

———. Foreword to *Mad About the Sixties: The Best of the Decade*, vii–xvi. Boston: Little, Brown, 1995.

———. Introduction to *Mad Spy vs. Spy: The Complete Casebook*, by Antonio Prohías and edited by Charles Kochman, 6–11. New York: Watson-Guptill Publications, 2001.

Geissman, Grant, and Nick Meglin. Foreword to *Mad About the Fifties*, vii-xvi. Boston: Little, Brown, and Co., 1997

Gilbert, Christopher J. "*Mad* About Stupidity, or Judging by Covers with Alfred E. Neuman." *Studies in American Humor* n.s. 3, no. 30 (Fall 2014): 57–76.

———. "Toward the Satyric." *Philosophy and Rhetoric* 46, no. 3 (2013): 280–305.

Gilbert, Michael T. "Total Control: A Brief Biography of Wally Wood." www.twomorrows.com/alterego/articles/08wood.html.

Giroux, Henry A. "Reading Hurricane Katrina: Race, Class, and the Biopolitics of Disposability." *College Literature* 33, no. 3 (2006): 171–96.

Gitlin, Todd. *The Sixties: Years of Hope, Days of Rage*. New York: Bantam, 1987.

Glass, Andrew. "Nikita Khrushchev barred from Disneyland, September 19, 1959." *Politico*, September 19, 2012. www.politico.com/story/2012/09/this-day-in-politics-081359.

Gleiberman, Owen. *Movie Freak: My Life Watching Movies*. New York: Hachette, 2016.

Gluckson, Daniel, and Al Feldstein. "Man Behind the Curtain Department: Al Feldstein Interview." *Comics Journal* 225 (July 2000): 64–85.

Glynn, Lenny. "Trump's Taj—Open at Last, with a Scary Appetite." *New York Times*, April 8, 1990, F5.

Goldberg, Michelle. "Everyone in Trumpworld Knows He's an Idiot." *New York Times*, January 4, 2018.

Gombrich, E. H. "The Mask and the Face: The Perception of Physiognomic Likeness in Life and in Art." In *Art, Perception, and Reality*, edited by Ernst H. Gombrich, Julian Hochberg, and Max Black, 1–46. Baltimore: Johns Hopkins University Press, 1973.

Gopnik, Adam. "Postscript: Kurtzman's Mad World." *New Yorker*, March 29, 1993, 74–77.

Gould, Jack. "Television in Review: McCarthy-Army Inquiry, Like Veteran Video Favorites, Has Its Own Hooper." *New York Times*, April 26, 1954, 32.

"Greatest of All Time Billboard 200 Albums." *Billboard*. n.d. www.billboard.com/charts/greatest-billboard-200-albums.

Green, Daniel. "A World Worth Laughing At: *Catch-22* and the Humor of Black Humor." *Studies in the Novel* 27, no. 2 (1995): 186–96.

Greenberg, Clement. "Avant-Garde and Kitsch." In *Art and Culture: Critical Essays*, 3–21. Boston: Beacon Press, 1961.

Griffin, Dustin. *Satire: A Critical Reintroduction*. Lexington: University Press of Kentucky, 1994.

Grimes, William. "Antonio Prohías, 77: Drew 'Spy vs. Spy' Cartoon." *New York Times*, March 2, 1998, A14.

Groensteen, Thierry. "Why Are Comics Still in Search of Cultural Legitimization?" In *A Comics Studies Reader*, edited by Jeet Heer and Kent Worcester, 3–11. Jackson: University Press of Mississippi, 2009.

Groth, Gary, and Kim Thompson, eds. *The Comics Journal Library Volume Seven: Harvey Kurtzman*. Seattle: Fantagraphics, 2006.

Gunn, Joshua. *Modern Occult Rhetoric: Mass Media and the Drama of Secrecy in the Twentieth Century*. Tuscaloosa: University of Alabama Press, 2005.

Gustines, George Gene. "From Trash to Auction, Faster Than a Speeding . . . Well, You Know." *New York Times*, June 30, 2008, E5.

Hajdu, David. "The Parody Racket: From Ridicule to the Ridiculous." *The New Republic*, October 13, 2014, 52–55.

———. *The Ten-Cent Plague: The Great Comic-Book Scare and How It Changed America*. New York: Farrar, Straus, and Giroux, 2008.

Halberstam, David. *The Coldest Winter: America and the Korean War*. New York: Hyperion-Hachette, 2007.

Hamill, Pete. "Milton Caniff." In *Masters of American Comics*, edited by John Carlin, Paul Karasik, and Brian Walker, 229–37. Los Angeles: Hammer Museum; Museum of Contemporary Art, 2005.

Hannay, James. "Political Satire and Squibs.—Burns." In *Satire and Satirists: Six Lectures* by James Hannay. London: Bogue, 1854.

Hariman, Robert. "Public Culture and Public Stupidity Post-9/11." In *Rhetorical Democracy: Discursive Practices of Civic Engagement*, edited by Gerard A. Hauser and Amy Grim, 95–98. Mahwah, NJ: Erlbaum, 2008.

Harvey Kurtzman: Retrospective of a MAD Genius. San Francisco: Cartoon Art Museum, 1995. Exhibition Catalog.

"Harvey Kurtzman Tribute." *Comics Journal* 157 (March 1993): 4–17.

Harvey, Robert C. "News & Notes." *Cartoonist Profiles* 134 (June 2002): 64–71.

Hatfield, Charles. *Alternative Comics: An Emerging Literature.* Jackson: University Press of Mississippi, 2005.

Hays, Constance L. "Tradition on Trial as Editor Rethinks Cartooning Style at *The New Yorker.*" *New York Times*, June 9, 1997, D1, 26.

———. "'What? Me Worry?': *MAD*'s Humor is Racier, Its Readers Elusive." *New York Times*, June 30, 1997, D10.

Hedges, Chris. "For Mad, a Reason to Worry: Struggling for Relevance in Sarcastic World." *New York Times*, March 28, 2001, B1.

Heller, Stephen. "The Man Who Changed Humor in America Forever." *The Atlantic*, April 30, 2015.

Hendershot, Cynthia. *I Was a Cold War Monster: Horror Films, Eroticism, and the Cold War Imagination.* Bowling Green, OH: Bowling Green University Popular Press, 2001.

Hendrix, Grady. "Cahiers du CinéMAD." *Film Comment.* Film Society of Lincoln Center. March–April 2013. www.filmcomment.com/article/mad-magazine-movie-parodies.

Herman, Ellen. *The Romance of American Psychology: Political Culture in the Age of Experts.* Berkeley: University of California Press, 1995.

Hilmes, Michele. "Where Everybody Knows Your Name: *Cheers* and the Mediation of Cultures." *Wide Angle* 12, no. 2 (April 1990): 64–73.

Hitchens, Christopher. "Why Women Aren't Funny." *Vanity Fair*, January 2007, 54–59.

Hoberman, J. "Vulgar Modernism." *Artforum* 20, no. 6 (February 1982): 71–76.

Hoey, Edmund A., and Al Feldstein. "READ Goes MAD—Interview with Al Feldstein 1966." Reprint, *MADtrash.Com: The MAD Magazine Internet Database*, November 18, 2013. madtrash.com/read-goes-mad-interview-al-feldstein-1966.

Holt, Jennifer. "*N.Y.P.D. Blue*: Content Regulation." In *How to Watch Television*, edited by Ethan Thompson and Jason Mittell, 271–80. New York: NYU Press, 2013.

Horn, Maurice. *Sex in the Comics.* New York: Chelsea, 1985.

Horowitz, Jason. "Senator Smiley: Al Franken Pulls no Punches, but Adds a Few Punch Lines." *Washington Post*, March 18, 2010. www.washingtonpost.com/wp-dyn/content/article/2010/03/17/AR2010031703618.html.

"Hot 100—1964 Archive." *Billboard*, n.d. www.billboard.com/archive/charts/1964/hot-100.

Humbug. Seattle: Fantagraphics, 2009.

Hutcheon, Linda. "The Politics of Postmodernism: Parody and History." *Cultural Critique* 5 (Winter 1986-1987): 179–207.

———. *A Theory of Parody: The Teachings of Twentieth-Century Art Forms.* New York: Methuen, 1985.

Hutchisson, James M. *Poe*. Jackson: University Press of Mississippi, 2005.

Hylton, Richard D. "More Details Released in Trump Refinancing." *New York Times*, June 18, 1991, D2.

Ingersoll, Bob. "The Cheese Stands Accused! A Look at the Superman/Captain Marvel Litigation." *Alter Ego* 3 (2000): 20–23.

"Intersections: Of 'Maus' and Spiegelman: 'Mad' Inspired Comic Book Look at the Holocaust." Narrated by Susan Stamberg. *Morning Edition*. NPR. January 26, 2004. Audio file, 7:05 min., and transcript. www.npr.org/templates/story/story.php?storyId=1611731.

Isaacson, Walter, and Evan Thomas. *The Wise Men: Six Friends and the World They Made*. New York: Touchstone, 1986.

"It Happened One Day in Mosinee." *American Legion Magazine*, June 1950, 32, 34.

Ivie, Robert L. "Rhetorical Deliberation and Democratic Politics in the Here and Now." *Rhetoric and Public Affairs* 5, no. 2 (2002): 277–85.

Jacobs, Frank. "Frankly Mad: The Frank Jacobs Interview." Interview by Scott Gosar. *The Mad Store*, November 12, 2006. www.themadstore.com/franklymad.htm.

———. Introduction to *The Mad Archives*, vol. 3: 7–11. New York: DC Comics, 2002–2012.

———. *The Mad World of William M. Gaines*. Secaucus, NJ: Lyle Stuart, 1972.

Jaffee, Al. *The Official Al Jaffee Website: Creator of the Mad Magazine Fold-In & Guinness World-Record Holder for the Longest Career in Comics*. www.originalaljaffee.com/splash.

Jameson, Fredric. *The Political Unconscious: Narrative as a Socially Symbolic Act*. Ithaca: Cornell University Press, 1982.

———. "Postmodernism and Consumer Society." In *The Cultural Turn: Selected Writings on the Postmodern 1983–1998*, 1–20. New York: Verso, 1998.

Jamieson, Kathleen Hall, and Karlyn Kohrs Campbell. "Rhetorical Hybrids: Fusions of Generic Elements." *Quarterly Journal of Speech* 68, no. 2 (May 1982): 146–57.

Jaramillo, Deborah. "The Family Racket: AOL Time Warner, HBO, *The Sopranos*, and the Construction of a Quality Brand." *Journal of Communication Inquiry* 26, no. 1 (January 2002): 59–75.

Jeffrey, Harry P. "The Life, Presidency, and Resignation of Richard Nixon." In *Watergate and the Resignation of Richard Nixon: Impact of a Constitutional Crisis*, edited by Harry P. Jeffrey and Thomas Maxwell-Long, 1–16. Washington, DC: CQ, 2004.

Jones, Timothy. "'Hello Again, You Little Monsters!'—Hosted Horrors of the 1950s and 1960s." In *The Gothic and Carnivalesque in American Culture*, by Timothy Jones, 123–50. Cardiff, Wales: University of Wales Press, 2015.

Jonsson, Patrik. "General Honoré, Katrina and the Army behind Him, Retains Civic Aims." *The Christian Science Monitor*, January 14, 2008. https://www.csmonitor.com/USA/Society/2008/0114/p02s01-ussc.html.

Kaminer, Michael. “Learning To Be Jewish From *Mad* Magazine.” *Forward*, November 3, 2013. https://forward.com/schmooze/186234/learning-to-be-jewish-from-mad-magazine.

Kaplan, Arie. *From Krakow to Krypton: Jews and Comic Books*. Philadelphia: Jewish Publication Society, 2008.

Karlin, Susan. “The Ascent of ‘Mad’: See 60 Years of Comic Subversion.” *Fast Company*, October 12, 2012. www.fastcompany.com/1681754/the-ascent-of-mad-see-60-years-of-comic-subversion.

Kauffmann, Stanley. *A World on Film: Criticism and Comment*. New York: Harper & Row, 1966.

Kaufman, David E. *Jewhooing the Sixties: American Celebrity and Jewish Identity—Sandy Koufax, Lenny Bruce, Bob Dylan, and Barbra Streisand*. Waltham, MA: Brandeis University Press, 2012.

Kehr, Dave. “Tony Curtis, Hollywood Leading Man, Dies at 85.” *New York Times*, September 30, 2010, www.nytimes.com/2010/10/01/movies/01curtis.html.

Kelly, Mike. “Art Spiegelman and His Circle: New York City Comix and the Downtown Scene.” *International Journal of Comic Art* 10, no. 1 (Spring 2008): 313–39.

Kelly, Stuart. “Alan Moore: ‘Why Shouldn’t You Have a Bit of Fun While Dealing With the Deepest Issues of the Mind?’ Alan Moore Talks about *Fashion Beast*, Jacques Derrida and Modern Superheroes.” *The Guardian*, November 22, 2013. www.theguardian.com/books/2013/nov/22/alan-moore-comic-books-interview.

Kennedy, John F. “Inaugural Address, January 20, 1961.” USG-17. John F. Kennedy Presidential Library and Museum, U.S. National Archives. Video digitized from historical footage, 4 reels, 35 mm. film, 16 min. www.jfklibrary.org/Research/Research-Aids/Ready-Reference/JFK-Quotations/Inaugural-Address.aspx.

Kercher, Stephen E. *Revel with a Cause: Liberal Satire in Postwar America*. Chicago: University of Chicago Press, 2006.

Khoury, George, ed. *Kimota! The Miracleman Companion*. Raleigh: TwoMorrows, 2001.

———. “Revival and Revelation.” In *Kimota!*, edited by George Khoury, 11-23. Raleigh: TwoMorrows, 2001.

Kierkegaard, Soren. *Concluding Unscientific Postscript*. Translated by David F. Swenson and Walter Lowrie. Princeton: Princeton University Press, 1968.

Kihss, Peter. “No Harm in Horror, Comics Issuer Says.” *New York Times*, April 22, 1954, 1, 34.

Kimble, James J. “Mutually Assured Disparagement: Enmification and Enlightenment in Early 1950s *Mad*.” *Studies in American Humor* n.s. 3, no. 30 (Fall 2014): 123–34.

Kimmel, Michael. *Manhood in America: A Cultural History*. New York: Free Press, 1996.

“Kinney Seeks Name Change.” *New York Times*, December 15, 1971, 103.

Kitchen, Denis. "It's a Jungle Out There!" In *Harvey Kurtzman's Jungle Book*, by Harvey Kurtzman, 11–24. Milwaukie, OR: Kitchen Sink-Dark Horse, 2014.
Kitchen, Denis, and Paul Buhle. *The Art of Harvey Kurtzman: The Mad Genius of Comics*. New York: Abrams ComicArts, 2009.
Koch, Tom, and Angelo Torres. *History Gone Mad*. New York: Warner Books, 1977.
Koestler, Arthur. *The Act of Creation: A Study of the Conscious and Unconscious in Science and Art*. New York: Macmillan, 1964.
Kompare, Derek. *Rerun Nation: How Repeats Invented American Television*. New York: Routledge, 2005.
Kramer, Chris A. "An Existential Account of the Role of Humor Against Oppression." *Humor* 26, no. 4 (2013): 629–51.
Kuper, Peter. Email to Judith Yaross Lee, April 18, 2020, 4:41 p.m.
Kurtzman, Harvey. "The Face Is Familiar, Have We Met?" *New York Times*, January 10, 1975, 37.
———. *The Grasshopper and the Ant*. Northampton, MA: Denis Kitchen Publishing Co., 2001.
———. *Harvey Kurtzman's Jungle Book*. 1959. Milwaukie, OR: Kitchen Sink-Dark Horse, 2014.
———. *Harvey Kurtzman's Strange Adventures*. New York: Epic Comics; Byron Preiss, 1990.
———. *Hey Look!* Princeton, WI: Kitchen Sink, 1992.
———. Interview with John Benson. In *The Complete First Six Issues of Mad*. West Plains, MO: Russ Cochran, 1985.
———. Interview with Kim Thompson and Gary Groth. In *The New Comics: Interviews from the Pages of the Comics Journal*, edited by Gary Groth and Robert Fiore, 24–38. New York: Berkley Books, 1988.
———. *My Life as a Cartoonist*. With Howard Zimmerman. New York: Minstrel/Pocket Books, 1988.
Kurtzman, Harvey, with Michael Barrier. *From Aargh! to Zap!: Harvey Kurtzman's Visual History of the Comics*. New York: Prentice Hall, 1991.
Kurtzman, Harvey, and Will Elder. *Executive's Comic Book*. New York: Macfadden, 1962.
———. *Goodman Beaver*. Princeton: Kitchen Sink, 1984.
———. *Playboy's Little Annie Fanny*. Chicago: Playboy, 1972.
———. *Playboy's Little Annie Fanny: 1962-1970, 1970-1988.* Edited by Hugh Hefner. 2 vols. Milwaukie, OR: Dark Horse Comics, 2001.
Labarre, Nicolas. "Du Kitsch Au Camp. Théorie de la culture de masse aux Etats-Unis, 1944–1964." PhD diss., Université Rennes 2, France, 2006.
Lambert, Josh. *Unclean Lips: Obscenity, Jews, and American Literature*. New York: NYU Press, 2014.
Landa, Robin. *Designing Brand Experiences*. Clifton Park, NY: Thomson Delmar Learning, 2006.
Lane, Tahree. "Mad for Alfred." *Toledo Blade*, January 20, 2008.

Lanters, José. "Irish Satire." In *A Companion to Satire: Ancient and Modern*, edited by Ruben Quintero, 476–92. Malden: Blackwell, 2007.

Larimer, Cliff. "Gorcey Bigger Than Life." *Red Bluff (California) Daily News*, November 11, 2006, updated May 16, 2018. www.redbluffdailynews.com/2006/11/11/gorcey-bigger-than-life/.

Lavin, Maud. "Neuman's Own." *New York Times*, September 14, 2003.

Lawrence, W. H. "Army Charges a 'Doctored' Picture Was Submitted by M'Carthy's Side; Cohn, in Wrangle, Admits It Was Cut." *New York Times*, April 28, 1954, 1, 18.

Lee, Judith Yaross. *Defining* New Yorker *Humor*. Jackson: University Press of Mississippi, 2000.

———. *Twain's Brand: Humor in Contemporary American Culture*. Jackson: University Press of Mississippi, 2012.

Lee, Judith Yaross, and John Bird, eds. *"Mad" Magazine and Its Legacies*. Special issue, *Studies in American Humor* n.s. 3, no. 30 (Fall 2014): 1–216.

Lefèvre, Pascal. "Some Medium-Specific Qualities of Graphic Sequences." *SubStance* 40, no. 124 (2011): 14–33.

Legman, Gershon. *Love & Death: A Study in Censorship*. 1949. Reprint, New York: Hacker Art, 1963.

———. "The Psychopathology of the Comics." *Neurotica* 1, no. 3 (Autumn 1948): 3-30.

Lent, John A. "Cuba's Comic Art Tradition." *Studies in Latin American Popular Culture* 14 (January 1995): 225–44.

———. "Cuban Cartoonists: Masters of Coping." In *Redrawing the Nation: National Identity in Latin/o American Comics*, edited by Héctor Fernández L'Hoeste and Juan Poblete, 81–95. New York: Palgrave Macmillan, 2009.

Levin, Bob. *The Pirates and the Mouse: Disney's War Against the Counterculture*. Seattle: Fantagraphics, 2003.

Levitz, Paul. "'Farewell to a Friend': Paul Levitz on MAD Magazine's Nick Meglin." *CBLDF: Comic Book Legal Defense Fund*, June 4, 2018. cbldf.org/2018/06/farewell-to-a-friend-paul-levitz-on-mad-magazines-nick-meglin.

———. "Inside the Editorial Process: *Mad* Veterans Jaffee and Meglin Look at Their Editors." Interviews with Al Jaffe and Nick Meglin. *Studies in American Humor* n.s. 3, no. 30 (Fall 2014): 7–24.

Lieber, Keir A., and Daryl G. Press. "The End of MAD? The Nuclear Dimension of U.S. Primacy." *International Security* 30, no. 4 (Spring 2006): 7–44.

Liebovich, Louis W. *Richard Nixon, Watergate, and the Press: A Historical Retrospective*. Westport, CT: Praeger, 2003.

Littleton, Cynthia. "FX Networks Chief John Landgraf: 'There Is Simply Too Much Television'." *Variety*, August 7, 2015. variety.com/2015/tv/news/tca-fx-networks-john-landgraf-wall-street-1201559191/.

"LOOK for the DATE on the CANDIDATE." *Ballyhoo* 2, no. 6 (July 1932): 2–3.

Lurie, Ranan R. *Nixon Rated Cartoons*. New York: Quadrangle-New York Times, 1973.

Lyons, Bonnie K. "American-Jewish Fiction Since 1945." In *Handbook of American-Jewish Literature*, edited by Lewis Field, 63–64. Westport, CT: Greenwood, 1988.

Lyvely, Chin, and Joyce Sutton. *Abortion Eve*. [1–33.] www.ep.tc/eve/index.html.

Macdonald, Dwight. "A Theory of Mass Culture." In *Mass Culture: The Popular Arts in America*, edited by Bernard Rosenberg and David Manning White, 59–73. 1953. Glencoe, IL: Free Press, 1965.

Mackay, Ellin. "Why We Go to Cabarets: A Post-Debutante Explains." *New Yorker*, November 28, 1925, 7–8.

Marcoci, Roxana. "Comic Abstraction: Image-Breaking, Image-Making." In *Comic Abstraction: Image-Breaking, Image-Making*, 9–39. New York: The Museum of Modern Art, 2007.

Marcus, Greil. *Lipstick Traces: A Secret History of the Twentieth Century*. Cambridge, MA: Belknap Press of Harvard University Press, 1989.

Marcuse, Herbert. *One-Dimensional Man: Studies in the Ideology of Advanced Industrial Society*. Boston: Beacon, 1964.

Martin, Mike W. "Humor and Aesthetic Enjoyment of Incongruities." In *The Philosophy of Laughter and Humor*, edited by John Morreall, 172–86. Albany: SUNY Press, 1986.

Martin, Roland S. "To Focus on the First 100 Days is Absurd." *CNN: Politics*. January 28, 2009. www.cnn.com/2009/POLITICS/01/28/martin.hundred.days/index.html.

The Masters of Comic Book Art. Directed by Ken Viola. Ken Viola Productions, 1987. Video, 60 min. www.youtube.com/watch?v=_kkzrs1HUsk.

Matthews, Kristin L. "The ABCs of *Mad* Magazine: Reading, Citizenship, and Cold War America." *International Journal of Comic Art* 8, no. 2 (Fall 2006): 248–68.

———. "A *Mad* Proposition in Postwar America." *Journal of American Culture* 30, no. 2 (2007): 212–21.

McClennen, Sophia A. *Colbert's America: Satire and Democracy*. New York: Palgrave MacMillan, 2011.

McCloud, Scott. *Understanding Comics: The Invisible Art*. Northampton, MA: Tundra, 1993.

McDaniel, James P. "Liberal Irony: A Program for Rhetoric." *Philosophy and Rhetoric* 35, no. 4 (2002): 297–327.

McGrath, Charles. "The Triumph of the Prime-Time Novel." *New York Times Magazine*, October 22, 1995. www.nytimes.com/1995/10/22/magazine/the-prime-time-novel-the-triumph-of-the-prime-time-novel.html.

McLuhan, Marshall. *The Mechanical Bride: Folklore of Industrial Man*. New York: Vanguard, 1951.

———. *Understanding Media: The Extensions of Man*. New York: McGraw-Hill, 1964.
Means Shannon, Hannah. "Are We 'Emotionally Subnormal'? Pondering Alan Moore's Assessment of Superhero Readers." *Bleeding Cool*, November 29, 2013. bleedingcool.com/2013/11/29/are-we-emotionally-subnormal-pondering-alan-moores-recent-statement-about-superhero-readers.
Meglin, Nick. E-mail message to Judith Yaross Lee. October 11, 2013.
———. Introduction to *The Mad Archives*, vol. 1: 7–12. New York: DC Comics, 2002–2012.
———. "A Mad Look at Frank Jacobs." In Jacobs, *Mad's Greatest Writers: Frank Jacobs*, 7–9. Philadelphia: Running Press, 2015.
———. "The Old Pro." In *Mad Spy vs. Spy: The Complete Casebook*, by Antonio Prohías and edited by Charles Kochman, 134–37. New York: Watson-Guptill Publications, 2001.
Meredith, George. "An Essay on Comedy." In *Comedy*, edited by Wylie Sypher, 48–49. Baltimore: Johns Hopkins University Press, 1956.
Mertes, Micah. "*Mad* Magazine Veterans Will Discuss Movie Parodies." *Omaha World-Herald*, August 10, 2016.
Miller, John Jackson. "*Mad* Sales Figures." In *Comichron: A Resource for Comics Research*. comichron.com/titlespotlights/mad.html.
Mink, Andreas. "Leitartikel: Die Welt von MAD." *Aufbau: Das Jüdische Magazin* 85, no. 5 (October–November 2019): 3.
Minow, Newton. "Television and the Public Interest." Speech to the National Association of Broadcasters. May 9, 1961. www.americanrhetoric.com/speeches/newtonminow.htm.
Miscamble, Wilson. *George F. Kennan and the Making of American Foreign Policy, 1947–1950*. Princeton: Princeton University Press, 1993.
Mitchell, W. J. T. *Picture Theory: Essays on Verbal and Visual Representation*. Chicago: University of Chicago Press, 1994.
———. *What Do Pictures Want? The Lives and Loves of Images*. Chicago: University of Chicago Press, 2005.
Moore, Alan. "Alan Moore's Script for *Miracleman* #1." In *Kimota! The Miracleman Companion*, edited by George Khoury, 57–65. Raleigh: TwoMorrows, 2001.
———. "Indoor Thunder: Landscaping the Future with Brian Eno." *Arthur* 17 (July 2005), 29, 34.
———. Interview with Brian Eno. BBC Radio 4, Chain Reaction Series, December 14, 2004. Reissued on MP3 as *Chain Reaction: Alan Moore Interviews Brian Eno*, series 5, episode 6. 2011.
———. Interview with Chris Richards. In *The Art of Dismantling: A Radical Artisan Collective and Ongoing Interview Series*. March 17, 2011. www.theartofdismantling.com/2011/03/17/alan-moore-2/. Audio and transcript.
———. "M*****man: Full Story and Pics." *Miracleman* #2 (October 1985). Eclipse Comics: 15, 31.
Moore, Alan (w), Garry Leach (p, i), G. George (l), "A Dream of Flying." *Miracleman* #1 (August 1985). Eclipse Comics.

Moore, Alan (w), Curt Swan (p), George Pérez (i). "Whatever Happened to the Man of Tomorrow? [Part I]." *Superman*, no. 423 (September 1986).

Moore, Alan (w), Curt Swan (p), Kurt Schaffenberger (p, i). "Whatever Happened to the Man of Tomorrow? [Part II]." *Action Comics*, no. 583 (September 1986).

Moore, Alan (w), John Totleben (p, i), Sam Parsons (c), Wayne Truman (l), Letitia Glozer (ed.). "Olympus." *Miracleman* #16 (December 1989). Eclipse Comics.

———. "Pantheon." *Miracleman* #14 (April 1988). Eclipse Comics. 1–15.

[Moore, Clement Clarke (w),] and Will Elder (a). "The Night Before Christmas." *Panic* #1 (February–March 1954). Reprinted in *The Million Year Picnic* by Will Elder, 88–94. Seattle: Fantagraphics, 2017. [N.B. Writer not credited in magazine.]

Morreall, John, ed. *The Philosophy of Laughter and Humor*. Albany: SUNY Press, 1986.

———. "Funny Ha-Ha, Funny Strange, and Other Reactions to Incongruity." In *The Philosophy of Laughter and Humor*, edited by John Morreall, 188–207. Albany: SUNY Press, 1986.

———. "A New Theory of Laughter." In *The Philosophy of Laughter and Humor*, edited by John Morreall, 128–38. Albany: SUNY Press, 1986.

Morrison, Grant. *Supergods: What Masked Vigilantes, Miraculous Mutants, and a Sun God from Smallville Can Teach Us about Being Human*. New York: Spiegel & Grau, 2012.

Mouffe, Chantal. "Deliberative Democracy or Agonistic Pluralism?" *Social Research* 66, no. 3 (1999): 745–58.

Muhlen, Norbert. "The Study of Man: Comic Books and Other Horrors." *Commentary*, January 1949, 80–87.

Mulkay, Michael. *On Humor: Its Nature and Its Place in Modern Society*. Cambridge: Basil Blackwell, 1988.

Mulvey, Laura. "Visual Pleasure and Narrative Cinema." *Screen* 16, no. 3 (October 1975): 6–18.

Mulvihill, Jason. "The Golden Age of Bond: Creation of a Cold War Popular Hero (1962–1965), Part II." *International Journal of Instructional Media* 28, no. 4 (December 2001): 337–53.

———. "James Bond's Cold War, Part I." *International Journal of Instructional Media* 28, no. 3 (September 2001): 225–36.

Müller, Mario. "Deutsche Ausgabe: Mut zur Zahnlücke." *Aufbau: Das Jüdische Magazin* 85, no. 5 (October–November 2019): 24–27.

Nachman, Gerald. *Seriously Funny: The Rebel Comedians of the 1950s and 1960s*. New York: Pantheon, 2003.

Nadel, Alan. *Demographic Angst: Cultural Narratives and American Films of the 1950s*. New Brunswick, NJ: Rutgers University Press, 2017.

Neal, Jim, and Don Thompson. "Harvey Kurtzman Dies, Creator of 'Mad.'" *Comics Buyer's Guide* 1009 (March 19, 1993): 6.

Neale, Steve, and Frank Krutnik. *Popular Film and Television Comedy*. London: Routledge, 1990.

Nelson, T. G. A. *Comedy: An Introduction to Comedy in Literature, Drama, and Cinema*. Oxford and New York: Oxford University Press, 1990.
Neuendorffer, Art. "Who Is Alfred E. Neuman?" *What Me Worry?*, n.d. www.lecon-combre.com/concpost/us/postcard4/alfred_e_neuman_documents.html.
Newcomb, Horace, and Paul Hirsch. "Television as a Cultural Forum." In *Television: The Critical View*, edited by Horace Newcomb, 561–73. 6th ed.New York: Oxford University Press, 2000.
Newman, Michael Z., and Elana Levine. *Legitimating Television: Media Convergence and Cultural Status*. New York: Routledge, 2012.
Nguyen, Tina. "An 'Idiot' and a 'Dope': McMaster Reportedly Unloads on Trump During a Private Dinner." *Vanity Fair*, November 20, 2017.
Nietzsche, Friedrich. *Beyond Good and Evil: Prelude to a Philosophy of the Future*. Translated by Walter Kaufmann. New York: Vintage, 1966.
———. *The Gay Science*. Translated by Thomas Common. Mineola: Dover, 2006.
———. *Twilight of the Idols*. Translated by Richard Polt. Indianapolis: Hackett, 1997.
Noonan, David. "The Way We Laughed." *Newsweek*, February 19, 2007, 1–4.
Norris, Vincent P. "*Mad* Economics: An Analysis of an Adless Magazine." *Journal of Communication* 34, no. 1 (March 1984): 44–61.
Novick, Peter. *The Holocaust in American Life*. New York: Houghton Mifflin, 1999.
"Now Comics Have Gone Mad." *Pageant*, June 1954, 88–93.
"Number of TV Households in America, 1950-1978." americancentury.omeka.wlu.edu/items/show/136.
Nyberg, Amy Kiste. *Seal of Approval: The History of the Comics Code*. Jackson: University Press of Mississippi, 1998.
"Obama's 'Missing' Flag Pin." *FAIR: Fairness & Accuracy in Reporting*, October 10, 2007. fair.org/take-action/media-advisories/obamas-missing-flag-pin.
Oliensis, Ellen. *Horace and the Rhetoric of Authority*. New York: Cambridge University Press, 1998.
Olson, Elder. "The Poetics of Comedy." In *The Theory of Comedy*, 25–44. Bloomington: Indiana University Press, 1968.
Ó Méalóid, Pádraig. "Poisoned Chalice: The Extremely Long and Incredibly Complex Story of *Marvelman*." *The Beat: The News Blog of Comics Culture*. WordPress. February 10, 2013. www.comicsbeat.com/poisoned-chalice-the-extremely-long-and-incredibly-complex-story-of-marvelman-introduction.
Opdycke, Kelly. "A Comic Revolution: Comedian Bassem Youssef as a Voice for Oppressed Egyptians." *Colloquy* 9 (Fall 2013): 1–20.
O'Sullivan, Sean. "*The Sopranos*: Episodic Storytelling." In *How to Watch Television*, edited by Ethan Thompson and Jason Mittell, 65–73. New York: NYU Press, 2013.
Palermo, Joseph A. "Politics, Public Opinion, and Popular Culture." In *Watergate and the Resignation of Richard Nixon: Impact of a Constitutional Crisis*, edited by Harry P. Jeffrey and Thomas Maxwell-Long, 17–30. Washington, DC: CQ, 2004.

Panic. Edited by Al Feldstein. New York: E.C. Comics, 1954-1956.
Park, David. "The Kefauver Comic Book Hearings as Show Trial: Decency, Authority and the Dominated Expert." *Cultural Studies* 16, no. 2 (March 2002): 259–88.
Parker, Dorothy. "Reading and Writing: Far from Well." *New Yorker*, October 20, 1928, 98–99.
Parton, James. *Caricature and Other Comic Art in All Times and Many Lands*. New York: Harper and Brothers, 1877.
Peterson, Russell L. *Strange Bedfellows: How Late-Night Comedy Turns Democracy into a Joke*. New Brunswick, NJ: Rutgers University Press, 2008.
Pew Internet and American Life Project. *Cable and Internet Loom Large in Fragmented Political News Universe: Perceptions of Partisan Bias Seen as Growing, Especially by Democrats*. Pew Research Center, January 11, 2004. people-press.org/reports/display.php3?ReportID=200.
"Philosophy of Humor." *Encyclopedia of Philosophy*. Stanford: Stanford Center for the Study of Language and Information, November 20, 2012. plato.stanford.edu/entries/humor.
Pias, Claus, ed. *Cybernetics: The Macy Conferences 1946–1953: The Complete Transactions*. Chicago: University of Chicago Press, 2016.
Pilcher, Tim, with Gene Kannenberg, Jr. *Erotic Comics: A Graphic History from Tijuana Bibles to Underground Comix*. New York: Abrams, 2008.
Pitt, William Rivers. "The Mad Genius of Donald Trump." *Truthout*, April 21, 2011. truthout.org/articles/the-mad-genius-of-donald-trump/.
Pizarro, Marta Rosa. "Snapshots of My Father." In *Mad Spy vs. Spy: The Complete Casebook*, by Antonio Prohías and edited by Charles Kochman, 17–18. New York: Watson-Guptill Publications, 2001.
Poe, Edgar Allan. *The Works of the Late Edgar Allan Poe*. Vol. 3. Edited by R. W. Griswold. New York: J. S. Redfield, 1850. www.eapoe.org/works/editions/grvoliii.htm.
Popkin, Henry. "The Vanishing Jew of Our Popular Culture." *Commentary* 14 (July 1952): 46–55.
Portnoy, Eddy. "Review of Mary-Lou Weisman's *Al Jaffee's Mad Life*, 'It's a Mad Mad MAD World.'" *Forward*, October 1, 2010. forward.com/culture/131480/it-s-a-mad-mad-mad-world.
Preminger, Alex, O. B. Hardison Jr., and Frank J. Warnke, eds. *The Princeton Handbook of Poetic Terms*. Princeton: Princeton University Press, 1986.
Prendergast, Mark. *The Ambient Century: From Mahler to Trance—The Evolution of Sound in the Electronic Age*. New York: Bloomsbury USA, 2001.
"The Press: Sassy Newcomer." *Time*, September 24, 1956, 73.
Pringle, Henry. "The Anatomy of *Ballyhoo*." *Outlook and Independent* 160, no. 1 (January 6, 1932): 13–14.
Prohías, Antonio (a). "El Hombre Siniestro." Reprinted in *Mad Spy vs. Spy: The Complete Casebook*, by Antonio Prohías and edited by Charles Kochman, 22–25. New York: Watson-Guptill Publications, 2001.

——. "La Mujer Siniestra." Reprinted in *Mad Spy vs. Spy: The Complete Casebook*, by Antonio Prohías and edited by Charles Kochman, 26–27. New York: Watson-Guptill Publications, 2001.

Quiroga, José. *Cuban Palimpsests*. Minneapolis: University of Minnesota Press, 2005.

Rall, Ted. Introduction to *Mad About Comic Strips*, edited by Nick Meglin and John Ficarra, n.p. New York: Mad Books, 2003.

Rauser, Amelia Faye. *Caricature Unmasked: Irony, Authenticity, and Individualism in Eighteenth-Century English Prints*. Newark, DE: University of Delaware Press, 2008.

Reeves, Richard. "*Mad* Magazine—Witness for the People." *New York Magazine*, October 1, 1973, 40–45.

Regan, Robert. "Hawthorne's 'Plagiary'; Poe's Duplicity." *Nineteenth Century Fiction* 25 (December 1970): 281–98. Reprinted in *The Naiad Voice: Essays on Poe's Satiric Hoaxing*, edited by Dennis W. Eddings, 73–87. Port Washington, NY: Associated Faculty Press, 1983.

Reidelbach, Maria. *Completely Mad: A History of the Comic Book and Magazine*. Boston: Little Brown, 1991. Reprint ed., New York: MJF Books, 1997.

——. *Harvey Kurtzman's Mad Lithograph Booklet—A History of the MADmen*. Prescott, AZ: Another Rainbow, 1992.

——. Introduction to *Against the Grain: Mad Artist Wally Wood*, edited by Bhob Stewart, 1. Raleigh: TwoMorrows, 2003.

Rhodes, Gillian. *Superportraits: Caricatures and Recognition*. East Sussex, UK: Psychology Press, 1996.

Richardson, Mike, and Steve Duin. *Comics: Between the Panels*. Milwaukie, OR: Dark Horse, 1998.

Richmond, Tom. "The End of the MADness." *Richmond Illustration, Inc! Caricature and Cartoon Art Studios*, July 4, 2019. www.tomrichmond.com/the-end-of-the-madness.

——. "Sunday Mailbag: Who Is Alfred E. Neuman?" *Tom's Mad Blog*, September 25, 2011. www.tomrichmond.com/2011/09/25/sunday-mailbag-268.

Riesman, David, Reuel Denney, and Nathan Glazer. *The Lonely Crowd: A Study of the Changing American Character*. New Haven: Yale University Press, 1950.

Rifas, Leonard. *Corporate Crime Comics*. [Princeton, WI]: Kitchen Sink, 1977–1980.

Ringgenberg, S. C. "Jolting Words with Al Feldstein in the EC Tradition!" *Comics Journal* 177 (May 1995): 77–99.

Ringgenberg, Steven. "Features: Al Feldstein: 1925–2014." *The Comics Journal Online*, May 2, 2014. www.tcj.com/al-feldstein-obituary/.

Robbins, Trina. Interview by Nicholas Sammond. San Francisco, CA, November 21, 2017.

——. *Pretty in Ink: North American Women Cartoonists, 1896–2013*. Seattle: Fantagraphics, 2013.

Rocher, Sofia. "MAD Magazine Comic Artist Honored for Career Spanning 73 Years." *Guinness World Records*, April 18, 2016.

Rodman, Lawrence. "*Mad*'s Guest Writers." In *Comic Books and the Cold War, 1946–1962: Essays on Graphic Treatment of Communism, the Code and Social Concerns*, edited by Chris York and Rafiel York, 169–78. Jefferson, NC: McFarland, 2012.

Ronell, Avital. *Stupidity*. Champaign: University of Illinois Press, 2002.

Rose, Margaret A. *Parody: Ancient, Modern, and Post-Modern*. Cambridge: Cambridge University Press, 1993.

Rosen, Ronald S. *Music and Copyright*. Oxford: Oxford University Press, 2008.

Rosenkranz, Patrick. *Rebel Visions: The Underground Comix Revolution 1963–1975*. Seattle: Fantagraphics, 2003.

———. "Skip Williamson, 1944–2017." *Comics Journal*, March 17, 2017. www.tcj.com/skip-williamson-1944-2017/.

Rosenthal, Irving, and Stewart Kampel. "Cartoonists." In *Encyclopaedia Judaica*, edited by Michael Berenbaum and Fred Skolnik, 4:499–501. 2nd ed. Detroit: Macmillan Reference USA, 2007.

Ross, Andrew. *No Respect: Intellectuals and Popular Culture*. New York: Routledge, 1989.

Ross, Harold W. Letter to Hugh Wiley. October 15, 1925. Box 2. New Yorker Records. New York Public Library, New York, NY.

Roszak, Theodore. *The Making of a Counter Culture: Reflections on the Technocratic Society and Its Youthful Opposition*. 1969. Reprint, London: Faber & Faber, 1972; Berkeley: University of California Press, 1995.

Roth, Philip. *Our Gang (Starring Tricky and His Friends)*. New York: Random House, 1971.

Rothkopf, David. "America's Golden Age of Stupidity." *Washington Post*, July 25, 2017.

Rothman, Stanley, and S. Robert Lichter. *Roots of Radicalism: Jews, Christians, and the New Left*. New York: Oxford University Press, 1982.

Rothstein, Edward. "Connections; Is It Still a Mad, Mad, Mad, Mad World?" *New York Times*, September 18, 1999, B11.

Routledge, Clay, Constantine Sedikides, Tim Wildschut, and Jacob Juhl. "Finding Meaning in One's Past: Nostalgia as Existential Resource." In *The Psychology of Meaning*, edited by Keith D. Markman, Travis Proulx, and Matthew J. Lindberg, 297–316. Washington, DC: American Psychological Association, 2013.

Rowen, Bob. "Right vs. Left Politics in the Cold War and the Improbable Saga of Major General Edwin Walker." Paper presented at the New York Military Affairs Symposium, CUNY Graduate Center, New York, NY, May 29, 2009. www.bobrowen.com/walkermedia.

"Running Mate." *New York Times*, July 12, 1952, 12.

Rycroft, Eleanor. "The Vice and the Fool." *Staging the Henrician Court: Bringing Early Modern Drama to Life*. stagingthehenriciancourt.brookes.ac.uk/research/the_vice_and_the_fool.html.

Sammond, Nicholas. *Babes in Tomorrowland: Walt Disney and the Making of the American Child, 1930–1960*. Durham: Duke University Press, 2005.

Samuels, David. "Q&A with Art Spiegelman." *Tablet*, November 13, 2013. www.tabletmag.com/jewish-arts-and-culture/152310/art-spiegelman-jewish-museum.

Sanders, Betty. "*MAD* Magazine in the Remedial English Class." *The English Journal* 59, no. 2 (1970): 266-72.

Santiago, Fabiola. "A Cartoonist in Times of Revolution and Censorship." In *Mad Spy vs. Spy: The Complete Casebook*, by Antonio Prohías and edited by Charles Kochman, 14–16. New York: Watson-Guptill Publications, 2001.

Saunders, Ben. *Do the Gods Wear Capes? Spirituality, Fantasy, and Superheroes*. New York: Continuum International Publishing Group, 2011.

Schelly, Bill. *American Comic Book Chronicles: The 1950s.* Raleigh: TwoMorrows, 2013.

———. *Harvey Kurtzman: The Man Who Created Mad and Revolutionized Humor in America: A Biography*. Seattle: Fantagraphics, 2015.

Schleiner, Winfried. "Imaginative Sources of Shakespeare's Puck." *Shakespeare Quarterly* 36 (1985): 65–68.

Schumacher, Michael. *Will Eisner: A Dreamer's Life in Comics*. New York: Bloomsbury, 2010.

Scorza, Jason A. *Strong Liberalism: Habits of Mind for Democratic Citizenship*. Lebanon, NH: Tufts University Press, 2008.

Scott, A. O. "Marvelous Invention of Movie Make-Believe." *New York Times*, October 1, 2010.

Scott, Cord A. "Cold War Politics, Cuba, and Spy vs. Spy." *Journal of Graphic Novels and Comics* 10 (2019): 1–10.

Scott, Nathan A. "The Bias of Comedy and the Narrow Escape into Faith." *The Christian Scholar* 44, no. 1 (Spring 1961): 9–39.

Shakespeare, William. *Hamlet*. Edited by Harold Jenkins. Arden Edition of The Works of William Shakespeare. New York: Routledge, 1982.

Shakouchi, Yuri. "The Stereotypes of the Beatniks and Hip Consumerism: A Study of *Mad Magazine* in the Late 1950s and 1960s." *Journal of Popular Culture* 48, no. 6 (December 2015): 1270–86.

Shayne, David. *"Feel Like Reading a Spy Story?"* In *Spy vs. Spy 2: The Joke and Dagger Files*, by Peter Kuper with Duck Edwing, Bob Clarke, and Dave Manak. Edited by David Shayne. Foreword by J. J. Abrams. Brief Essays by Peter Kuper; David Shayne; Duck Edwing and Dave Manak; and Sam Viviano, 13-17. New York: Watson-Guptill, 2007.

Sheppard, David. *On Some Faraway Beach: The Life and Times of Brian Eno*. Chicago: Chicago Review Press, 2009.

Sheppard, Noel. "Shocking *Mad* Magazine Cover: I 'Loved' Obama." *Newsbusters*. Media Research Center. March 24, 2010. www.newsbusters.org/blogs/nb/noel-sheppard/2010/03/24/shocking-mad-magazine-cover-i-loved-obama.

Sherman, Nancy. "*Hamartia* and Virtue." In *Essays on Aristotle's* Poetics, edited by Amélie Oksenberg Rorty, 177–96. Princeton: Princeton University Press, 1992.

Silow-Carroll, Andrew. "From the 'Usual Gang of Idiots,' a Lifelong Education in Irony." *Forward*, November 1, 2002.

Silverman, Kenneth. *Edgar A. Poe, Mournful and Never-Ending Remembrance*. New York: Harper Collins, 1991.

Silverman, Rachel E. "Comedy as Correction: Humor as Perspective by Incongruity on *Will & Grace* and *Queer as Folk*." *Sexuality & Culture* 17 (2013): 260–74.

Skinn, Dez. *Comix: The Underground Revolution*. New York: Thunder's Mouth, 2004.

Skow, Jack. "Mad: Wild Oracle of the Teenage Underground." *Saturday Evening Post*, December 21, 1963, 62–65.

Slade, Joseph W. "Wally Wood: Picturing Adolescent Sexuality in *Mad*'s Early Parodies." *Studies in American Humor* n.s. 3, no. 30 (Fall 2014): 41-56.

Slaubaugh, Mike. *Mad Magazine Lists*. users.pfw.edu/slaubau/mad.htm.

Sloane, David E. E. *American Humor Magazines and Comic Periodicals*. New York: Greenwood Press, 1987.

Sloane, Leonard. "Mergers Set in Show Business." *New York Times*, March 19, 1969, 68.

Smith, Adam. "On the Waterfront: Hoboken's Last Drop." *Jersey Digs*, January 28, 2016. https://jerseydigs.com/on-the-waterfront-hobokens-last-drop/.

Smith, C. Alphonso. *Edgar Allan Poe: How to Know Him*. Garden City, NY: Garden City Publishing, 1921.

Smothers, Dick. Conversation with M. Thomas Inge. American Film Institute Theatre, Silver Spring, MD. June 18, 2003.

Socolow, Michael J. "In Its Heyday, *Mad* Magazine Was A Lot More Than Silly Jokes." *Smithsonian Magazine* [online], May 11, 2018. www.smithsonianmag.com/history/heyday-mad-magazine-lot-more-than-silly-jokes-180969055. First published in *The Conversation*, May 11, 2018; updated 2019. theconversation.com/mad-magazine-is-finished-but-its-ethos-matters-more-than-ever-before-95708.

Soper, Kerry. "Folding Against the Establishment: Satiric Distance and Difference in Al Jaffee's Back Cover Feature in *Mad* Magazine." *Studies in American Humor* n.s. 3, no. 30 (Fall 2014): 95–110.

Speier, Hans. "Wit and Politics: An Essay on Power and Laughter." *American Journal of Sociology* 103, no. 5 (March 1998): 1352–1401.

Spiegelman, Art. *Breakdowns: Portrait of the Artist as a Young %@&*!*. London: Viking-Penguin Books, 2008.

———. "A Furshlugginer Genius!" *The New Yorker*, March 29, 1993, 76–77. Reprinted in *MetaMaus*, 191–92.

———. "H.K. (R.I.P.)." *The New Yorker*, March 29, 1993, 75.

———. *In the Shadow of No Towers*. New York: Knopf Doubleday, 2004.

———. "The Lives They Lived: Antonio Prohías, Yin and Yang, Cold War Style (cover story)." *New York Times Magazine*, January 3, 1999, 32.

———. *Maus: A Survivor's Tale*. 1986. Reprint, New York: Pantheon Books, 1992.

———. *MetaMaus*. New York: Pantheon, 2011.

Spiegelman, Art, and Phillip Johnston. "*WORDLESS!*" Lecture and performance of still images with musical accompaniment. Logan Center Performance Hall, University of Chicago, January 25, 2014, Chicago, IL. art-spiegelmans-wordless.tumblr.com.

Spiegelman, Art, and W. J. T. Mitchell. "Public Conversation: What the %$#! Happened to Comics?" *Critical Inquiry* 40, no. 3 (Spring 2014): 20–35.

Spotnitz, Frank. "Tracing the Worrisome Origin of Alfred E. Neuman," *Chicago Tribune*, October 8, 1985.

Steranko, Jim. *The Steranko History of Comics 2*. Reading, PA: Supergraphics, 1972.

Sterling, Christopher H., and John M. Kittross. *Stay Tuned: A Concise History of American Broadcasting*. 2nd ed. Belmont, CA: Wadsworth Publishing Company, 1990.

Steves, Rick. "The Sound of Music: Fact and Fiction." In *Rick Steves' Vienna, Salzburg and Tirol*, 274–75. 6th ed. Berkeley: Avalon Travel, 2019.

Stewart, Bhob, ed. *Against the Grain: Mad Artist Wally Wood*. Raleigh: TwoMorrows, 2003.

"Such Goings on About Town!" *Ballyhoo* 1 (September 1931): 2.

Sutton, Dana Ferrin. *The Greek Satyr Play*. Meisenheim am Glan: Hain, 1980.

Swales, John M. *Genre Analysis: English in Academic and Research Settings*. Cambridge: Cambridge University Press, 1990.

Sweet, Sam. "A Boy with No Birthday Turns Sixty." *Paris Review*, March 3, 2016.

Tamm, Eric. *Brian Eno: His Music and the Vertical Color of Sound*. Cambridge, MA: Da Capo Press, 1995.

Taussig, Michael. *Defacement: Public Secrecy and the Labor of the Negative*. Stanford: Stanford University Press, 1999.

Test, George A. *Satire: Spirit and Art*. Gainesville: University of Florida Press, 1991.

Thompson, Ethan. "What, Me Subversive? *Mad* Magazine and the Textual Strategies and Cultural Politics of Parody." In *Parody and Taste in Postwar American Television Culture*, edited by Ethan Thompson, 45–75. New York: Routledge, 2011.

Thompson, Timothy, and Anthony J. Palmeri. "Attitudes toward Counternature (with Notes on Nurturing a Poetic Psychosis)." In *Extensions of the Burkeian System*, edited by James W. Chesebro, 269–83. Tuscaloosa: University of Alabama Press, 1993.

Thurber, James. *The Thurber Carnival*. New York: Modern Library, 1957.

Tilley, Carol. "Seducing the Innocent: Fredric Wertham and the Falsifications That Helped Condemn Comics." *Information and Culture* 47, no. 4 (2012): 383–413.

"Time'ly News." *Ballyhoo* 1, no. 2 (September 1931): 11.

Tong, Ng Suat. "EC Comics and the Chimera of Memory." *Comics Journal* 250 (February 2003: 115-22.

"The Town that Saw Red." *Catholic Digest*, July 1950, 65–68.

Tracy, Marc. "Mad Magazine, Irreverent Baby Boomer Humor Bible, Is All but Dead." *New York Times*, July 5, 2019, B1.

"Trick or Treat for UNICEF." UnicefUSA.org. www.unicefusa.org/trick-or-treat/learn-more.

Triptow, Robert. Telephone interview by Nicholas Sammond. Hawaii and San Francisco, CA, September 21, 2017.

Truman, Harry S. Annual Message to Congress on the State of the Union, January 9, 1952. *Public Papers Harry S. Truman 1945–1953*. Harry S. Truman Presidential Library Museum. www.trumanlibrary.org/publicpapers/index.php.

——— . Remarks in New York City at the Dedication of Idlewild International Airport, July 31, 1948. *Public Papers Harry S. Truman 1945–1953*. Harry S. Truman Presidential Library Museum. www.trumanlibrary.gov/library/public-papers/168/remarks-new-york-city-dedication-idlewild-international-airport.

Trump. Edited by Harvey Kurtzman. 1957. Reprint ed., Milwaukie, OR: Dark Horse Comics, 2009.

"Trump: 'I Am a Very Stupid Human Being.'" News in Brief. *The Onion*, May 16, 2017, 11:39 a.m. politics.theonion.com/trump-i-am-a-very-stupid-human-being-1819579927.

Twain, Mark. *Adventures of Huckleberry Finn*. Illustrated by E. W. Kemble. New York: Charles L. Webster, 1885.

——— . "What Paul Bourget Thinks of Us." *The North American Review* 160 (1895): 48–62.

Two-Fisted Tales (The EC Archives). 2 vols. York, PA: Gemstone, 2007.

"United Nations, New York City, New York." *The Hitchcock Zone*. http://the.hitchcock.zone/wiki/United_Nations,_New_York_City,_New_York.

"The United Nations in Films." *France Diplomatie*. www.diplomatie.gouv.fr/en/french-foreign-policy/united-nations/colonne-droite-2518/annexes/article/the-united-nations-in films.

United States District Court, Southern District of New York. *Berlin v. EC Publications, Inc.*, 219 F. Supp. 911, June 27, 1963. *Justia*. law.justia.com/cases/federal/district-courts/FSupp/219/911/1438356.

United States Second Circuit, Court of Appeals. *Berlin v. EC Publications, Inc.*, 329 F. 2d 541, March 23, 1964. *Justia*. law.justia.com/cases/federal/appellate-courts/F2/329/541/146502/.

——— . *Stuff v. E. C. Publications, Inc.* 342 F.2d 143. March 2, 1965. *Leagle*. www.leagle.com/decision/1965485342f2d1431456.

United States Supreme Court. *Miller v. California*, 413 U.S. 15, June 21, 1973. *Justia*. supreme.justia.com/cases/federal/us/413/15.

Vallance, Tom. "Arthur Laurents: Playwright and Screenwriter Who Wrote the Books for *West Side Story* and *Gypsy*." *Independent*, May 16, 2011.

Vegso, Roland. *The Naked Communist: Cold War Modernism and the Politics of Popular Culture*. Bronx: Fordham University Press, 2013.

Velasquez-Manoff, Moises. "Trump Ruins Irony, Too." *New York Times*, March 20, 2017.

Vidmar, Neil, and Milton Rokeach. "Archie Bunker's Bigotry: A Study in Selective Perception and Exposure." *Journal of Communication* 24, no. 1 (Winter 1974): 36–47.

Vinciguerra, Thomas. "MAD Magazine Taught Us to Laugh but Now We Laugh At It." *The Daily Beast*, February 9, 2018.

Voger, Mark. "Mad about Mort: Caricaturist Mort Drucker of Mad Magazine Talks about His Technique." *NJ.com*. Advance Local Media. December 28, 2012. nj.com/entertainment/index.ssf/2012/12/mort_drucker_mad.html.

Voloj, Julian. "Geschichte: Von MAD zu 'MINO.'" *Aufbau: Das Jüdische Magazin* 85, no. 5 (October–November 2019): 10–13.

———. "Hintergrund: Wer war Alfred E. Neuman?" *Aufbau: Das Jüdische Magazin* 85, no. 5 (October–November 2019): 14–19.

———. "Kreative Stimmen: Die Köpfe hinter den Figuren." *Aufbau: Das Jüdische Magazin* 85, no. 5 (October–November 2019): 20–23.

Waisanen, Don J. "A Citizen's Guide to Democracy Inaction: Jon Stewart and Stephen Colbert's Comic Rhetorical Criticism." *Southern Communication Journal* 74, no. 2 (2009): 119–40.

Wanzo, Rebecca. *The Content of Our Caricature: African American Comic Art and Political Belonging*. New York: NYU Press, 2020.

"Warner Bros. Picks New Chief Officer and Head of Board." *New York Times*, August 5, 1969, 41.

Warshow, Robert. "Paul, the Horror Comics, and Dr. Wertham." In *The Immediate Experience: Movies, Comics, Theatre and Other Aspects of Popular Culture*, by Robert Warshow, 44–62. Garden City, NJ: Doubleday-Anchor, 1964.

"We Nominate for Oblivion." *Ballyhoo* 1, no. 1 (August 1931): 15.

Weber, Bruce. "Al Feldstein, the Soul of *Mad* Magazine, Dies at 88." *New York Times*, May 1, 2014.

Weiman, Robert. *Shakespeare and the Popular Tradition in the Theater: Studies in the Social Dimension of Dramatic Form and Function*. Edited by Robert Schwartz. Baltimore: Johns Hopkins University Press, 1978.

Weisman, Mary-Lou. *Al Jaffee's Mad Life: A Biography*. New York: Harper, 2010.

Wenzel, John. "*Mad* Magazine's Legacy of Humor and Subversion, Writ Large." *Denver Post*, November 4, 2012.

Wertham, Fredric. *Seduction of the Innocent*. New York: Rinehart and Winston, 1954.

"What the 'Well-Dressed Men' at Harvard Are Wearing." *Ballyhoo* 2, no. 1 (January 1932): inside cover.

White, Edgar G. *Earl Warren: A Public Life*. New York: Oxford University Press, 1982.

White, Hayden. *The Content of the Form: Narrative Discourse and Historical Representation*. Baltimore: Johns Hopkins University Press, 1987.

Whitted, Qiana. *EC Comics: Race, Shock, and Social Protest*. New Brunswick, NJ: Rutgers University Press, 2019.

Wilder, Billy. Interview by Johnny Carson. *The Tonight Show Starring Johnny Carson.* NBC, January 3, 1973.

Williams, Betsy. "North to the Future: *Northern Exposure* and Quality Television." In *Television: The Critical View,* edited by Horace Newcomb, 141–54. 5th ed. New York: Oxford University Press, 1994.

Williams, David R. "Health Effects of Dramatic Social Events: Ramifications of the Recent Presidential Election." *New England Journal of Medicine,* June 8, 2017.

Williams, Robert I. *Comic Practice/Comic Response.* Newark, DE: University of Delaware Press, 1993.

Wilson, Derek. "From SHAZAM! to KIMOTA! The Sensational Story of England's Marvelman—the Hero Who Would Become Miracleman." *Alter Ego* 87 (July 2009): 4–15.

Winick, Charles. "Teenagers, Satire, and *Mad.*" *Merrill-Palmer Quarterly of Behavior and Development* 8, no. 3 (July 1962): 183–203.

Winston, George. "Why the Rosenbergs Were Executed." *War History Online.* www.warhistoryonline.com/featured/why-the-rosenbergs-were-executed.html.

Witschonke, Christopher. "A 'Curtain of Ignorance': An Analysis of Holocaust Portrayal in Textbooks from 1943 through 1959." *Social Studies* 104, no. 4 (2013): 146–54.

Wood, Wallace. "BOMB PEKING!" *witzend* 3 (1967): 1.

———. "The Children." *Weird Science-Fantasy* 23 (March 1954): 1–8. Reprinted in Wood, *Woodwork,* 115–22.

———. *The Compleat Sally Forth.* Seattle: Fantagraphics/Eros Comix, 1998.

———. "The Disneyland Memorial Orgy." *The Realist* 74 (May 1967): 12–13.

———. *Gang Bang.* 3 vols. Van Nuys: Nuance, 1981–1983.

———. "My Word." *Big Apple Comix* 1 (1975): 8–10.

———. "The Pipsqueak Papers." *witzend* #3, #4, #5, 1967–1968. Reprinted in *Wallace Wood's Pipsqueak Papers.* Seattle: Fantagraphics/Eros Comix, 1993. Reprinted in *witzend.* 2 vols. Seattle: Fantagraphics, 2013.

———. Wallace Wood Estate. www.wallacewoodestate.com.

———. *Woodwork: Wallace Wood 1927–1981.* Palma, Mallorca: Casa Solleric, 2010.

Wood, Wallace, and Ray Bradbury. "There Will Come Soft Rains." *Weird Fantasy* 17 (January–February 1953: 25–31). In *Woodwork by Wallace Wood,* 103–09. Palma Mallorca: Casa Solleric, 2010.

Wright, Bradford W. *Comic Book Nation: The Transformation of Youth Culture in America.* Baltimore: Johns Hopkins University Press, 2001.

Yankovic, "Weird" Al. Foreword to *Mad's Greatest Writers: Frank Jacobs,* edited by Frank Jacobs, 5–6. Philadelphia: Running Press, 2015.

Yoe, Craig, and Joe Shuster. *Secret Identity: The Fetish Art of Superman's Co-Creator Joe Shuster.* New York: Abrams ComicArts, 2009.

Young, Dannagal G. "Laughter, Learning, or Enlightenment? Viewing and Avoidance Motivations Behind *The Daily Show* and *The Colbert Report*." *Journal of Broadcasting & Electronic Media* 57, no. 2 (2013): 153–69.

Young, William H., and Nancy K. Young. *The 1950s*. Westport, CT: Greenwood Press, 2004.

Contributors

Nathan Abrams is a professor of Film Studies at Bangor University in Wales. He is founding co-editor of *Jewish Film and New Media: An International Journal*. His most recent book is *The New Jew in Film: Exploring Jewishness and Judaism in Contemporary Cinema* (Rutgers University Press, 2012). He is currently working on two projects: ethics and ethnics in the work of Stanley Kubrick and *Hidden in Plain Sight: Jews and Jewishness in British Film, Television, Popular Culture* (Northwestern University Press).

Don Baird has presented at international conferences of the International Society for Humor Studies on topics ranging from "The Humor of Muhammad Ali" to "Humor and Social Protest." He annually offers a memorial to humorists who have died the previous year at conferences of the Association for Applied Therapeutic Humor. He contributed entries on Ring Lardner and Johnny Carson to *American Political Humor: Masters of Satire and Their Impact on U.S. Policy and Culture*, edited by Jody Baumgartner (ABC-Clio, 2019). Don holds a Master's degree in Counseling Psychology from Northwestern University.

John Bird is Emeritus Professor of English at Winthrop University. He is the author of *Mark Twain and Metaphor* (University of Missouri Press, 2007), editor of *Mark Twain in Context* (Cambridge University Press, 2020), as well as a number of articles on Mark Twain and on American humor. He is a past president of the Mark Twain Circle of America and the American Humor Studies Association. He discovered *Mad* at age ten in his cousin's basement in 1964; when his parents told him and his brother it was a magazine they should not read, he and Jimmy pooled their allowance and sent off for a subscription. And so the madness began.

James D. Bloom is Professor of English and American Studies at Muhlenberg College. He has published five books: *Hollywood Intellect* (2009), *Gravity Fails* (2003), *The Literary Bent* (1997), *Left Letters* (1992) and *The Stock of Available Reality (1984).* For the past five years he has been working on a book tentatively titled *The Male Gaze Reader.*

Ann M. Ciasullo is Professor of English and Women's and Gender Studies at Gonzaga University. She has presented and published essays on topics as wide-ranging as Hollywood bromance films, 1970s lesbian feminism, and the television series *Mad Men*. In a Polaroid picture from her ninth birthday in 1978, she can be seen striking a confident pose while holding *Mad* Super Special #27 in front of her face, thereby creating a strange amalgam of herself and Alfred E. Neuman (yeech!).

Brian Cremins is an Associate Professor of English at Harper College in Palatine, Illinois. He is the author of *Captain Marvel and the Art of Nostalgia* (University Press of Mississippi, 2016) and, with Brannon Costello, the co-editor of *The Other 1980s: Reframing Comics' Crucial Decade*, forthcoming from Louisiana State University Press. On a family trip to New York State in 1983, he bought his first *Mad* paperback, *Greasy Mad Stuff*, and read it cover to cover while listening to his mom's cassette copy of Culture Club's *Kissing to Be Clever*.

Dennis W. Eddings is Emeritus Professor of English at Western Oregon University. A noted Edgar Allan Poe scholar, he has published and presented on Poe and Mark Twain, as well as on Poe's influence on Twain. He is an Honorary Member of the Poe Studies Association, a life member of the American Humor Studies Association, and has been a member of the Mark Twain Circle since its inception. His acquaintance with *Mad* commenced in the summer of 1953 and he has been a reader since then, which undoubtedly explains a great deal.

Christopher J. Gilbert is Assistant Professor of English at Assumption College, where he teaches in the media and communication programs. His work on the role of humor in cultural politics and on comic responses to controversy and conflict has appeared in such leading journals as *Communication, Culture, and Critique,* and he is the author, most recently, of *The Good, The Bad, and The Ugly: Caricature and National Character in U.S. War Cultures.* Naming his childhood memories of *Mad* would overflow this space.

Margaret Cavin Hambrick is Chair and Professor in the Department of Communication and Philosophy at Florida Gulf Coast University. She has published articles in *Peace & Change* and book essays in which she examined the dissent rhetoric of various activists, such as William Sloane Coffin, Helen Caldicott, Sis Levin, and Glenn Smiley.

M. Thomas Inge, Blackwell Professor of Humanities at Randolph-Macon College, is one of the founders of the American Humor Studies Association, co-edited its newsletter and journal, and has served as editor of *Studies in American Humor*. He has published books on Mark Twain, William Faulkner, George Washington Harris, humor of the Old Southwest, and the comics, including *My Life with Charlie Brown* and *Charles M. Schulz: Conversations*, both in collaboration with Charles Schulz. He is general editor of two book series with the University Press of Mississippi: "Great Comic Artists" and "Conversations with Comic Artists." *Mad* comic books largely shaped his education and love of humor.

Peter Kaminsky worked at *National Lampoon* from 1974 to 1978. He is one of the creators and head writer of the Kennedy Center Mark Twain Prize for American Humor. He is also a creator of the Gershwin Prize for Popular Song, presented by President Obama at the White House. His "Outdoors" column has appeared in the *New York Times* for 25 years. He is the author of twenty-three books, mostly on food and flyfishing. His father, Lucian, wrote for Jackie Gleason's *American Scene* magazine.

James J. Kimble is Professor of Communication & the Arts at Seton Hall University. His research on domestic propaganda, war rhetoric, and visual imagery has reached a worldwide media audience of over 1.2 billion people in more than a dozen languages. His most recent book, co-edited with Trischa Goodnow, is *The Ten-Cent War: Comic Books, Propaganda, and World War II*. He has vivid memories of growing up during the Cold War and concluding that "Spy vs. Spy" was on to something.

Nicolas Labarre teaches American society and culture at University Bordeaux Montaigne. He started thinking and writing about *Mad* a long time ago, during his PhD thesis on American theories of mass culture. He is the author of *Heavy Metal, l'autre Métal Hurlant* (Bordeaux University Press, 2017) a cultural study of *Heavy Metal* magazine and of numerous articles regarding adaptation and genre in comics.

Judith Yaross Lee is Distinguished Professor Emerita of Communication Studies at Ohio University, Athens, Ohio. Her many publications on American humor and periodical culture—interests that she should probably credit to her childhood passion for *Mad*—include *Garrison Keillor: A Voice of America* (1991), *Defining "New Yorker" Humor* (2000), and *Twain's Brand: Humor in Contemporary American Culture* (2012), all published by the University Press of Mississippi, along with two other volumes and six dozen essays. A vivid *Mad* memory: leading a neighborhood delegation of kids, quarters in hand, across busy streets to the newsstand for the newest 25-cent (cheap!) issue.

Paul Levitz was the Publisher of *Mad* from 1992–2009. He is a comic fan (*The Comic Reader*), writer (*Legion of Super-Heroes*), editor (*BATMAN*), and executive (decades at DC Comics, ending as President and Publisher). He has written books about popular culture (*Will Eisner: Champion of The Graphic Novel*) and teaches at several universities, including Columbia and Pace.

Kelley Macek is a doctoral student and Graduate Teaching Associate in the School of Communication Studies at Ohio University studying rhetoric and public culture. She uses humor as an instructional approach and finds having a sense of humor to be an excellent survival technique. As a combat veteran, now retired from the Army, she credits *Mad*'s satiric pokes at politicians and the military with the preservation of that sense of humor through wartime.

Kathleen Mollick is a professor of English in the Department of English and Languages at Tarleton State University in Stephenville, TX, where she serves as the Director of Composition and the Writing Intensive Program, and co-edits *The Popken Writer*, a collection of research-based papers written by first-year writing students. With Michele Lockhart, Dr. Mollick has co-edited *Political Women: Leaders and Language* (2013), *Global Women: Studies in Feminist Political Rhetoric* (2014) and *Hillary Rodham Clinton and the 2016 Presidential Election* (2015).

Joseph Otto received a B.A. in Music from Ohio University's Honors Tutorial College in 2016. At an early age he developed an interest in comic strips, with *Calvin & Hobbes* among his favorites. The opportunity to be involved with a book on *Mad* was a natural fit with Joe's dry sense of humor.

Alan Rankin is a writer and comics creator with an abiding interest in the unexplored corners of history, including *Mad*. His work has appeared in *Poopsheet*, *Comic Effect*, *Not My Small Diary*, and all over the Internet. Find his latest obsession at alanrankin.com.

Nicholas Sammond is Professor of English and the Cinema Studies Institute at the University of Toronto. His books include *Birth of An Industry: Blackface Minstrelsy and the Rise of American Animation* (Duke University Press, 2015), *Babes in Tomorrowland: Walt Disney and the Making of the American Child, 1930–1960* (Duke University Press, 2005), and the edited volume *Steel Chair to the Head: Essays on Professional Wrestling* (Duke University Press, 2005).

Joseph W. Slade is Emeritus Professor of Media Arts and Studies and co-director of the Central Region Humanities Center at Ohio University. The founding editor of the *Markham Review: An Interdisciplinary Journal of American Literature and Culture* (1968–1990), he is also the author of dozens of articles and book chapters. Professor Slade's books include *Thomas Pynchon* (Warner, 1974; Lang, 1990), *Pornography and Sexual Representation: A Reference Guide* (3 vols., Greenwood, 2001), *Pornography in America: A Reference Handbook* (ABC-Clio, 2000), *Beyond the Two Cultures: Essays on Science, Technology, and Literature* (co-editor, Iowa State University Press, 1990), and *The Midwest* (Encyclopedia of American Regional Cultures, co-editor, Greenwood, 2004).

Michael J. Socolow is Associate Professor of Communication and Journalism at the University of Maine. He is a media historian whose research centers upon America's original radio networks in the 1920s and 1930s. His scholarship on media history has appeared in *Journalism & Mass Communication Quarterly*, *The Journal of Broadcasting and Electronic Media*, *Technology & Culture*, and other scholarly journals. He is the author of *Six Minutes in Berlin: Broadcast Spectacle and Rowing Gold at the Nazi Olympics* (University of Illinois Press, 2016). He was awarded the 2018 Broadcast Historian Award by the Library of American Broadcasting Foundation and the Broadcast Education Association for *Six Minutes in Berlin*.

Kerry Soper teaches in the American Studies and Interdisciplinary Humanities programs at Brigham Young University. His research focuses on the history of comedy and satire in U.S. culture, with a special emphasis on comic strips and other graphic media. His work has appeared in the *Journal of American Studies*, *Studies in American Humor*, *Journal of Popular Culture*, *Columbia Journal of American Studies*, *Journal of the Gilded Age and Progressive Era*, and *International Journal of Comic Art*. He has published two books with the University Press of Mississippi: *Garry Trudeau: Doonesbury and the Aesthetics of Satire* (2008), and *We Go Pogo: Walt Kelly, Politics, and American Satire* (2012).

Jeffrey St. Onge is an Assistant Professor of Communication Studies at Ohio Northern University. His research focuses on rhetoric and media, with a particular interest in how rhetorical criticism can help shape political culture toward more productive ends. His work has appeared in *Rhetoric and Public Affairs*, *Rhetoric Society Quarterly*, and *Rhetoric Review*, among other venues. He credits *Mad* magazine for the development of his offbeat sense of humor and love of the absurd.

Leah Szalai completed her PhD in communication studies at Ohio University and served as the managing editor of *Studies in American Humor* from January 2013 to December 2014. The journal's special triple issue on *Mad*—which led to this book—was her introduction to the magazine. This experience gave her the privilege of discovering *Mad* alongside rich analyses of its cultural impact. Leah currently works in the corporate sector as an editor. She has written several novellas and manages a blog that caters to indie authors.

Ethan Thompson is Professor of Media Arts at Texas A&M University–Corpus Christi. He is the author of *Parody and Taste in Postwar American Television Culture* (2011), co-editor of books including *Television History, The Peabody Archive, and Cultural Memory* (2019); *How to Watch Television* (2013); and director of the documentary, *TV Family* (2016). He grew up reading *Mad*, then reconnected in graduate school after happening upon the collection *Mad About the Fifties*, which led to a dissertation on parody and early television.

Index

Contents of *Mad* are indexed by title and under their creators' names, where they are listed as Works. To avoid duplication of page numbers for items that receive substantial discussion, the notation *q.v.* directs readers to the title entry. Italics denote pages with full citations to *Mad* features; boldface denotes illustrations in the text.